MORAL THEOLOGY

A Complete Course Based on St. Thomas Aquinas and the Best Modern Authorities

VOLUME I

BY JOHN A. MCHUGH, O.P. AND CHARLES J. CALLAN, O.P.

REVISED AND ENLARGED BY EDWARD P. FARRELL, O.P.

MORAL THEOLOGY

A Complete Course Based on St. Thomas Aquinas and the Best Modern Authorities

VOLUME I

BY JOHN A. MCHUGH, O.P. AND CHARLES J. CALLAN, O.P.

REVISED AND ENLARGED BY EDWARD P. FARRELL, O.P.

Edited and Re-Typeset by Paul A. Böer, Sr.

VERITATIS SPLENDOR PUBLICATIONS

et cognoscetis veritatem et veritas liberabit vos (Jn 8:32)

MMXIV

The text of this book is excerpted from:

Moral Theology: A Complete Course Based on St. Thomas Aquinas and the Best Modern Authorities. John A. McHugh, O.P. and Charles J. Callan, O.P. (New York: Jospeh F. Wagner, Inc., 1929).

The text of this work is in the public domain.

Retypeset and republished in 2014 by Veritatis Splendor Publications.

Veritatis.splendor.publication@gmail.com

AD MAJOREM DEI GLORIAM

CONTENTS

PREFACE 17

INTRODUCTION 21

Definition of Moral Theology (1-3).—The Objects of Moral Theology (4-5).—The Sources of Moral Theology (6-12).—The Methods of Moral Theology (13-14).—The History of Moral Theology (15-16).—The Division of Moral Theology (17-18).

PART I GENERAL MORAL THEOLOGY 29

Question I THE LAST END OF MAN AND THE MEANS TO THAT END 29

Art. 1: THE LAST END OF MAN 29

The Existence of the Last End (19).—The Nature of the Last End (20).—The Attainment of the Last End (21).

Art. 2: ACTS AS HUMAN 30

Introduction (22).—Definition (23).—Knowledge Requisite for a Human Act (24-33).—Consent Requisite for a Human Act (34-39).—Obstacles to Consent (40-55).—Two Kinds of Voluntary Acts (56-62).

Art. 3: ACTS AS MORAL 42

Introduction (63).—Definition (64-69).—The Sources of Morality (70-75).—Good Acts (76-78).—Bad Acts (79-81).—Indifferent Acts (82-86).—Perfect and Essential Goodness (87-88).—Morality of the External Act (89-93).—Morality of the Act Indirectly Willed (94-95).—Morality of the Consequences of an Act (96).—Imputability (97-105).

Art. 4: ACTS AS MERITORIOUS 56

Introduction (106).—Definition (107).—Divisions of Merit (108-115).

Art. 5: THE PASSIONS 58

Introduction (116).—Definition (117).—Division
(118-120).—Moral
Value of the Passions (121-131).

Question II GOOD AND BAD HABITS 65

Art. 1: HABITS IN GENERAL 66

Definition (133).—Division (134-136).—
Strengthening and Weakening of Habits (137-
139).—Habits and Morality (140-141).

Art. 2: GOOD HABITS OR VIRTUES 68

Definition (142).—Division (143-152).—Properties
of the Virtues (153-158).—Complements of the
Virtues (159-166).

Art. 3: BAD HABITS OR VICES) 75

Definition (167).—Divisions (168).—Mortal Sin
(169-179).—Venial Sin (180-184).—Imperfections
(185).—Change in the Gravity of Moral Defects
(186-196).—The Distinctions of Sins (197-219).—
Comparison of Sins (220-229).—The Subjects of
Sins (230-245).—The Causes of Sin (246-267).—The
Motives of Sin (268-271).—The Results of Sin (272-
283).

Question III LAW 106

Art. 1: LAW IN GENERAL 106

Definition (285).—Division (286-287).—Collision of
Laws (288-292).—The Basis of All Laws (293-294).

Art. 2: THE NATURAL LAW 111

Meaning (295-296).—Division (297-304).—
Properties (305-327).

Art. 3: THE POSITIVE DIVINE LAW 126

Meaning (328-330).—Division (331).—The Mosaic Law (332-345).—The Law of the New Testament (346-369).

Art. 4: HUMAN LAW 142

Definition (370).—Division (371).—Qualities (372-374).—Obligation of Human Laws (375-384).—Interpretation of Law (385-386).—Those Subject to Law (387-388).—Change of Law (389-390).—The Law of Custom (391-400).—Dispensation (401-410).—Epieikeia (411-417).

Art. 5: ECCLESIASTICAL LAW..158

Introduction (418-419).—General Law of the Church (420-422).—Lawgivers in the Church (423-424).—Subject-Matter of Church Law (425-426).—Those Bound by General Laws (427-434).—Those Bound by Particular Laws (435-446).—Promulgation (447-449).—Irritant Laws (450-458).—Laws Based on Presumption (459-461).—Fulfillment of Law (462-482).—Interpretation (433-486).—Cessation of Obligation (487-499).—Cessation of Law (500-505).—Custom (506-513).—Laws in a Wide Sense (514-541).

Art. 6: CIVIL LAW..196

Meaning (542).—Origin (543-545).—Subject-Matter (546-549).—Those Subject to Civil Law (550).—The Obligation of Civil Law (551-556).— Special Kinds of Laws (557-572).—Other Questions (573).

Question IV CONSCIENCE...208

Art. 1: THE LAW OF CONSCIENCE 208

Definition (575).—Division (576-579).—Obligation of Conscience (580-587).—Results of Conscience (588-592).

Art. 2: A GOOD CONSCIENCE 217

Introduction (593).—Definitions (594).—Divisions
(595-596).—The Lax Conscience (597-606).—The
Scrupulous Conscience (607-613).— Scrupulosity
(614-635).—Practical Conclusions (636-639).

Art. 3: A CERTAIN CONSCIENCE..237

Introduction (640).—Necessity of Certitude (641-
642).—Kinds of Certitude (643-653).—An Uncertain
Conscience (654-655).—Doubt and Suspicion (656-
661).—Opinion (662-671).—The Moral Systems
(672-675).—Tutiorism (676-679).—Laxism (680-
681).—The Other Systems (682).-Probabiliorism
(683-687).—Equiprobabilism (688-700).—
Probabilism (701-730).—Compensationism (731-
738).—Practical Conclusions (739-742).

PART II SPECIAL MORAL THEOLOGY 283

Question I THE DUTIES OF ALL CLASSES OF MEN.............283

THE INFUSED VIRTURES...284

Art. 1: THE VIRTUE OF FAITH...284

Introduction (746-749).—The Meaning of Faith
(750-753).—The Object of Faith (754-781).—The
Acts of Faith (782-796).—The Habit of Faith (797-
807).—The Gifts of Understanding and Knowledge
(808-811).

Art. 2: THE SINS AGAINST FAITH 313

Introduction (812).—The Sin of Unbelief (813-
825).—Heresy (826-834).—Apostasy (835-839).—
The Sin of Doubt (840-846).—Credulity and
Rationalism (847).—Dangers to Faith (848).—
Dangerous Reading (849-866).—Dangerous Schools
(867-874).—Dangerous Marriages (875-881).—
Dangerous Communication (882-888).—The Sin of

Blasphemy (887-903).—Sins of Ignorance, Blindness, Dullness (904-912).

Art. 3: THE COMMANDMENTS OF FAITH..........................360

Introduction (913).—The Commandment of Knowledge of Faith (914-924).—The Commandment of Internal Acts of Faith (925-937).—The Negative Commandment of External Profession of Faith (938-943).—Dangers of Profession of Unbelief (944).—Forbidden Societies (945-955).—Communication in Worship (956-975).-Coöperation in Religious Activities (976-986).—The Affirmative Commandment of External Profession of Faith (987-1008).

Art. 4: THE VIRTUE OF HOPE...411

Definition (1009-1017).—The Object of Hope (1018-1026).—The Excellence of Hope (1027-1035).—The Subject of Hope (1030-1040).—The Gift of Fear of the Lord (1041-1058).—The Sins against Hope (1059-1091).—The Commandments of Hope and of Fear (1092-1104).

Art. 5: THE VIRTUE OF CHARITY...450

Definition (1105-1114).—The Excellence of Charity (1115-1120).—Production of Charity (1121-1132).—The Object of Charity (1133-1157).—The Order of Charity (1158-1182).—The Acts of Charity (1183-1192).

Art. 6: THE EFFECTS OF CHARITY 481

Internal Effects of Charity (1193).—Joy (1194).—Peace (1195-1197).— Reconciliation (1198-1204).—Mercy (1205-1209).—External Effects of Charity (1210).—Beneficence (1211-1215).—Almsgiving (1216-1257).— Fraternal Correction (1258-1294).

Art. 7: THE SINS AGAINST LOVE AND JOY.......................518

Introduction (1295).—Hate (1296).—Hatred of God
(1297-1303).—Hatred of Creatures (1304-1311).—
Gravity of the Sin of Hatred (1312-1316).—Species
of the Sin of Hatred (1317-1319).—The Sin of Sloth
(1320-1325).—Laziness (1326).—Lukewarmness
(1327).—The Sin of Envy (1328-1331).—Emulation
(1332).—Jealousy (1333).—Fear (1334).—
Indignation (1335-1336).—Gravity of the Sin of
Envy (1337-1344).—Means of Overcoming Envy
(1345-1346).

Art. 8: THE SINS AGAINST PEACE 539

Introduction (1347).—Discord (1348-1354).—
Contention (1355-1362).—Acts of Sin against Peace
(1363).—Schism (1364-1375).—War (1376-1427).—
Fighting (1428-1434).—Duelling (1435-1439).—
Sedition (1440-1443).

Art. 9: THE SINS AGAINST BENEFICENCE 574

Introduction (1444).—Scandal (1445-1446).—
Definition of Scandal (1447).—Causes of Scandal
(1448-1458).—Results of Scandal (1459-1464).—
Sinfulness of Scandal (1465-1474).—Persons
Scandalized (1475-1476).—Duty of Avoiding
Scandal (1477-1487).—Duty of Repairing Scandal
(1488-1492).—Denial of Sacraments in Case of
Scandal (1493-1494).—Seduction (1495-1505).—
Coöperation in Sin (1506-1508).—Kinds of
Coöperation (1508-1512).—Sinfulness of
Coöperation (1513-1514).—Lawfulness of Material
Coöperation (1515-1525).—Lawfulness of
Immediate Coöperation (1526-1527).—Special Cases
of Coöperation (1528).-Coöperation in Reading
Matter (1529-1530).—In Dances and Plays (1531-
1532).—In Selling (1533-1536).—In Providing Food
and Drink (1537-1539).—In Renting (1540-1541).—
In Service (1542-1544).—Duties of the Confessor as
Regards Coöperation (1545-1546).

Art. 10: THE COMMANDMENTS OF CHARITY 629

Introduction (1547-1552).—The Commandment of
Love of God (1553-1560).—The Commandment of
Love of Self (1561-1578).—The Commandment of
Love of Neighbor (1579-1584).—Fulfillment of the
Commandments of Charity (1585-1608).

Art. 11: THE GIFT OF WISDOM..660

Introduction (1609).—The Nature of the Gift of
Wisdom (1610-1614).— The Persons who Possess
Wisdom (1615-1618).—The Beatitude and the Fruits
that Correspond to Wisdom (1619-1620).—The Sins
Opposed to Wisdom (1621-1625).

MORAL THEOLOGY

A Complete Course Based on St. Thomas Aquinas and the Best
Modern Authorities

BY JOHN A. MCHUGH, O.P. AND CHARLES J. CALLAN, O.P.

REVISED AND ENLARGED BY EDWARD P. FARRELL, O.P.

NEW YORK CITY JOSEPH F. WAGNER, INC.
LONDON: B. HERDER

Nihil Obstat
ELWOOD FERRER SMITH, O.P., S.T.M.
BENJAMIN URBAN FAY, O.P., S.T.LR.

Imprimi Potest
VERY REV. WILLIAM D. MARRIN, O.P., P.G.,
S.T.M.
Provincial

Nihil Obstat
JOHN A. GOODWINE, J.C.D.
Censor Librorum

Imprimatur
+ FRANCIS CARDINAL SPELLMAN
Archbishop of New York

New York, May 24, 1958

The nihil obstat and imprimatur are official declarations that a book or
pamphlet is free of doctrinal or moral error. No implication is
contained therein that those who have granted the nihil obstat and
imprimatur agree with the contents, opinions or statements expressed.

PREFACE

The purpose of the present work is to give a complete and comprehensive treatise on Catholic Moral Theology, that is, on that branch of sacred learning which treats of the regulation of human conduct in the light of reason and revealed truth. This new work strives to deal with the subject as a systematic and orderly whole, and is based throughout on the principles, teaching and method of St. Thomas Aquinas, while supplementing that great Doctor of the Church from the best modern authorities. Needless to say, there are many questions and problems connected with modern life that did not exist when the great classic works on Moral Theology were written, and to these naturally special attention has been given in the treatment that follows.

Nowadays, since the appearance of the New Code and of many special works on Canon Law, it would be a mistake to encumber the pages of a work like the present one with canonical questions of interest only to the specialist, and which are ably and abundantly treated in fine commentaries on the Code that are already available. Likewise, it would be an error to treat here matter pertinent only to Dogmatic Theology or History. All digressions, therefore, into alien fields have been avoided in this work, with the result that a greater number of useful moral questions have been herein considered.

But not only is it necessary to avoid irrelevant subjects, but it is also needful not to sacrifice essentials for accidentals in any work of this kind. It is the fault of too many textbooks on Moral Theology to stress controversies, cite authors, and quote opinions, at the expense of the principles and reasons that govern and explain the teaching given. This work eschews that method, and is at pains everywhere, first of all, to lay the foundations on which the superstructure is to be built, namely, the definitions and rules that are presupposed to moral judgments and conclusions. Obviously, this is a more logical way of proceeding, and it consequently enables the student much more easily to understand and retain the matter studied, since he can thus reason questions out for himself. Moreover, such a method makes for brevity and renders it possible, as said above, to treat more subjects than could otherwise be treated; it makes it possible to condense the matter of many pages of larger and less accessible works into brief and terse paragraphs. But from this it should not be gathered that the work which follows aims to present Moral Theology in a dryly scientific fashion. On the contrary, it has been our endeavor to treat the matter in a way that is at once clear, solid, comprehensive and interesting. Since the general and the abstract do not make the same strong impression as the particular and the concrete, laws and axioms are copiously illustrated throughout with pertinent and practical examples that often amount to brief *casus conscientiæ*, thus combining the theory and the practice of Moral Theology.

It would be a mistake to think that, while Moral Theology is a technical and scientific treatise on human conduct, it deals exclusively or primarily with vice and sin, and that it is intended only to enable the priest rightly to administer the Sacrament of Penance, distinguishing between the various classes of sins and their consequences. Of course, it does all this, but it should do much more; for it has also a much higher purpose, which is to enable man, not only to know what is forbidden and how he may escape from moral disease and death, but also to understand what are his duties and how he may live the life of grace and virtue. The subject is indeed more positive than negative, and it should be discussed accordingly. Thus, far from being useful merely to confessors as a guide by which they may detect and distinguish mortal and venial sins and the higher and lower degrees of culpability, Moral Theology in its broader aspect should be of the greatest service likewise to the individual in forming his own habits and character, and in particular to those who have the guidance of others, whether in or out of the confessional, such as pastors, preachers, teachers, and the like. Consequently, the present work has been written with a view to the homiletic and pastoral functions of the priest, as well as those that pertain strictly to the administration of the Sacraments.

Heretofore works on Moral Theology in English have been altogether too few or too fragmentary, whereas they have been abundant in the vernaculars of Continental Europe—German, French, Spanish, Italian, etc. This does not mean that the present work is intended to replace the Latin text-books used in our seminaries, but rather that it should enable students and priests to get a more thorough and ready knowledge of an all-important subject, and to adapt it more easily to the varying needs of the ministry.

The section of this work on Law has been carefully read by two eminent civil lawyers.

THE AUTHORS.
May 10, 1929.

REVISOR'S NOTE

This is a revision, not a rewriting. Various deletions and additions have been made with the intent of bringing the work up to date within the scope of the original plan and methods of the authors. In this way it has been possible to preserve the features that have made this manual a standard guide for the past thirty years.

EDWARD P. FARRELL, O.P., S.T.LR., S.T.D. Washington, D.C., June 8, 1958

John A. McHugh, O.P. and Charles J. Callan, O.P.

MORAL THEOLOGY
A Complete Course

INTRODUCTION

1. Definition.—Moral Theology is defined: (a) etymologically, as the study of God, considered as the beginning and the end of man's moral life, i.e., of those acts that proceed from reason and will; (b) scientifically, as that part of Sacred Theology which treats of God as our Last End, and of the means by which we may tend to Him.

2. Hence, Moral Theology differs from various related sciences or habits. Thus: (a) it differs from Ethics, which is the science of human conduct as directed by reason to man's natural end, for Moral Theology uses faith as well as reason, and is concerned with man's supernatural end; (b) it differs from faith, since it includes not only principles revealed by God, but also conclusions derived from them; (c) it differs from synderesis, or the habit that perceives the natural principles of morality that are self-evident to the mind, for Moral Theology deals also with supernatural truths and with truths that are not self-evident; (d) it differs from conscience, which draws conclusions for individual cases, since Moral Theology is concerned with general conclusions.

3. Relation of Moral Theology to Dogmatic Theology.—(a) They do not differ as two distinct sciences, for the main object, in the light of which all else is studied, is the same in both—viz., God. (b) They do differ as two quasi-integral parts or branches of the same science, Dogma being concerned more with the speculative, and Moral with the practical aspects of theology. Dogmatic Theology is the more important of the two, as treating more directly on divine things and as being the basis of Moral Theology.

In Dogma, God Himself is considered in His own nature and creatures as they proceed from Him as from an exemplary and efficient cause, or Creator. Moral Theology continues the pursuit of knowledge of God, concentrating upon Him as He is the Final Cause of things. Creatures emanate from God by way of creation, and this is part of the subject-matter of Dogma; but creatures return to Him, each in its own proper way by virtue of its nature created by God and directed by His Providence and Government, and this return of creatures to God constitutes the general subject-matter of Moral Theology. As Divine Providence and Government are continuations of His Creation, Moral Theology continues to study and to unfold the implications of Dogma's consideration of God as Creator. God is known to have created as an Intelligent Being ordering His handiwork to Himself as end. His special masterpiece, man, special because he is made to the Image of God, returns to God in a special way proper to him as an Image, i.e., by way of acts of his intellect and will guided and moved by Divine Providence and Predestination. It is of this special way of returning to God by man, His image, that Moral Theology treats. Thus it adds to and perfects Dogmatic Theology, enriching our knowledge of God by way of making explicit the implications of Divine Creation and Providence to His image, man.

4. The Objects of Moral Theology.—(a) The central theme or object of Moral Theology, which is considered for its own sake and to which all else is secondary (*objectum formale quod*), is God as the supernatural End or Destiny of man.

(b) The secondary object (*objectum materiale*) is the means by which one is advanced towards one's Last End (such as human acts, virtue, grace, the Sacraments), or the obstacles which hinder one from attaining that End (such as vice, temptation, etc.).

(c) The medium through which the above objects are known (*objectum formale quo*) is the light of natural reason illuminated by faith studying the sources of divine revelation and deducing conclusions from doctrines revealed by God.

5. Hence Moral Theology includes: (a) the revealed doctrines concerning man's destiny and duty that are contained in the written and oral Word of God and as interpreted by their custodian, the Catholic Church; (b) the conclusions that are contained in revelation; (c) the duties of man to human laws that are based on the divine natural or positive law; (d) the opinions of theologians on matters that are disputed, as in the controversy about the systems of conscience.

6. The Sources of Moral Theology, therefore, are: (a) Holy scripture; (b) tradition; (c) the decisions of Popes, Councils, and Congregations,

Laws, etc.; (d) the authority of Doctors and theologians; (e) natural reason.

7. Holy scripture.—"All scripture, inspired by God, is profitable to teach, to reprove, to correct, to instruct in justice" (II Tim., iii. 16). (a) Thus, the deeds narrated in scripture contain lessons for our instruction; but not all of them, even though they be concerned with holy men, are offered for our imitation. (b) The laws of the Old Testament known as ceremonial (such as the rite of circumcision), and those called judicial (such as the prohibition against the taking of interest), are no longer obligatory; but the moral precepts, such as those found in the Decalogue, always remain in force. (c) The ordinances of the New Testament are of three kinds: the Gospel counsels, which are not laws, but invitations to a higher practice of virtue than is necessary for salvation (e.g., the advice of our Lord that one sell all and give to the poor); the laws of the New Testament, which are the commands that it imposes for all times (such as the precepts that one believe the Gospel message, receive Baptism, hear the Church, etc.); temporary regulations, which are those dispositions that were made only for passing circumstances (such as the prohibition issued by the Apostles against the eating of animals that had been suffocated).

8. Tradition.—Tradition contains those doctrines concerning faith and morals, not found in scripture, that were given orally by Christ or inspired by the Holy Spirit, and that have been handed down from one generation to another in the Catholic Church.

Tradition becomes known to us: (a) through the teaching of the Church expressed by her solemn or ordinary magisterium; (b) through the writings of the Fathers of the Church; (c) through the practice of the Church expressed in her universal customs and laws; (d) through the worship of the Church expressed in her universal forms of prayer and liturgical observance.

9. Decisions.—In addition to divine tradition just spoken of, Moral Theology uses: (a) Apostolic tradition, which comes down from the Apostles, but whose subject-matter is not a teaching revealed to them, but an ordinance which they themselves made as rulers of the Church (e.g., the law that Sunday be sanctified as the Lord's day); (b)

ecclesiastical tradition, which contains regulations made by the authorities in the Church and handed down to succeeding times (e.g., the introduction of certain days of feast or fast).

10. Authority of Doctors and Theologians.—(a) St. Thomas Aquinas has been recognized by the Church as her highest theological authority, and the Code of Canon Law (Canons 589, § 1, and 1366, § 2) orders that in all seminaries and religious houses of study the courses of theology shall be made according to his method, teaching and principles.

(b) When the theologians agree with unanimity that a certain doctrine pertaining to faith or morals is divinely revealed, it would be next to heresy to hold the opposite; if they agree only that it is certain, it would be rash to contradict them, unless new and serious objections unknown to them can be offered; if they are divided between schools and systems (even though great claims for opinions are made by their partisans), it is lawful for competent theologians to use their own judgment and decide for the side that seems to have the better arguments in its favor.

11. Reason.—The uses of natural reason in Moral Theology are: (a) it demonstrates certain preambles to the teachings of Moral Theology, such as the existence of God, His omniscience and veracity; (b) it corroborates from philosophy many of the revealed teachings, viz., that man's end is not in things finite, that he has duties to God, to society, to himself, etc.; (e) it affords analogies in the natural order by which we may illustrate the end and duties of man in the supernatural order; (d) it supplies the means by which the teachings on morals may be developed into the conclusions that are contained in them, by which those teachings may be defended against the fallacious objections of adversaries, and by which the whole may be arranged scientifically into a body of doctrine.

12. Moral Theology is served not only by the various branches of philosophy (such as Ethics, Theodicy, Psychology, Logic), but also by many of the natural sciences. Thus: (a) Medicine and Physiology are useful for understanding the morality and imputability of acts; (b) Sociology and Economics may throw light on problems concerning justice; (c) Jurisprudence is, of course, closely related to questions

concerning duties that arise from human laws; (d) History confirms the teachings of Christian morality by the lessons of experience.

13. The Method to Be Followed in Moral Theology.-(a) The positive method is a simple statement of moral principles and doctrines, with little attention to argument, except such as is found in the positive sources (e.g., scripture, tradition, the decisions of the Church).

(b) The Scholastic method is a scientific statement of moral teaching through accurate definition of terms, systematic coordination of parts, strict argumentation and defense, attention to controversies, and recourse to philosophy and other natural knowledge.

(c) The casuistic method, or case-system, is the application of moral principles to the solution of concrete problems of lawfulness or unlawfulness.

14. The Scholastic method is the one best suited for the study of Moral Theology, because it is more scientific, and fits one better to understand, retain, and apply what one learns. But it is not exclusive of the other methods, since it perfects the positive method, and is the groundwork for the case method. Each method has a special suitability for certain ends. Thus: (a) the positive method is well adapted to preaching, and hence was much in favor with the Fathers of the Church, as can be seen from their moral homilies and treatises; (b) the Scholastic method is the best for study, teaching, apologetic, and was followed by the great classical works of theology in the Middle Ages and later; (c) the case method is very helpful to the seminarian and the priest in the exercise of the ministry of the confessional.

15. The History of Moral Theology.—There are three periods in the history of Moral Theology: the Patristic, the Medieval, and the Modern.

(a) The Patristic Period (1st to 12th century).—The moral writings of the-Fathers are popular, exhortatory, and occasional; and it is not till the Middle Ages that we meet with works of systematic Moral Theology. The following are among the most notable moral works of the Fathers: the *Pædagoga* of Clement of Alexandria (d. about 217), which explains what the everyday life of the Christian should be; the*Catecheses* of St. Cyril of Jerusalem (d. 386); the *De Officiis Ministrorum* of St. Ambrose (d. 397), a Christian counterpart of Cicero's work *De Officiis*; the *De Civitate Dei* of St. Augustine (d. 430), which contrasts love of God and love of self; the *Expositio in Job seu Moralium libri XXV* of St. Gregory the Great (d. 604), which consists of moral instructions based on the Book of Job.

Celebrated among the ascetical and mystical writings are: the *Ladder of Paradise* of St. John Climacus (6th century), the Conferences of Cassian (about 416), the *Libri V de Consideratione* of St. Bernard (d. 1153). St. Gregory the Great's *De Cura Pastorali* is a systematic work of pastoral theology, and is regarded as a classic.

(b) The Medieval Period (12th to 16th century).—The method of the moralists of this period differs from that of the Fathers in that the former is systematic and philosophical, and more proximately adapted to the use of confessors. The masterpiece of scientific Moral Theology is of course found in the *Summa Theologica* of St. Thomas Aquinas (d. 1274). Works of casuistry were composed by St. Raymond of Pennafort (about 1235), by John of Freiburg (d. 1314), by John of Asti (about 1317), by Angelus of Chiavasso (about 1476), by Sylvester Prierias (d. 1523). The *Summa Theologica* of St. Antoninus of Florence (d. 1459) has been called an inexhaustible storehouse for manuals of casuistry.

Among the ascetical writers are: St. Bonaventure, the Seraphic Doctor (d. 1274), John Gerson (d. 1429), John Tauler (d. 1361), Bl. Henry Suso (d. 1366), and Denis the Carthusian (d. 1471).

(c) The Modern Period (16th century to the present).—Characteristic of this period are the commentaries written on St. Thomas, the controversies over the systems of conscience, the appearance of numerous manuals and special treatises, and the attention given to changed conditions of society and ecclesiastical discipline. Noteworthy among modern works are: the Commentary on St. Thomas by Cajetan (d. 1534); the writings of Bartholomew de Medina (d. 1581), called the father of moderate Probabilism; the *De Pænitentia* of Lugo (d. 1660), a handbook that combines speculative and casuistical theology; the *Roman Catechism*, which was issued by the authority of the Council of Trent in 1566; the *Theologia Moralis* of St. Alphonsus Liguori (d. 1787), a work whose authority is universally recognized; the celebrated treatise on the virtues by Lessius (d. 1623); the classic work of Suarez (d. 1617), *De Religione*; the *Summa Casuum Conscientiæ* of Toletus (d. 1596); the commentaries of Francis de Victoria (d. 1546), which are writings of extraordinary merit. More recent works are so numerous that it is impossible to mention them here.

18. Among the many modern works on Moral Theology which have been published abroad, not a few are in the vernacular—in German, French, Italian, Spanish, etc. While they are not intended to replace the Latin text-books used in seminaries, these are nevertheless a very great help to a fuller knowledge of the matter treated and to a more ready use of it in the work of the ministry.

So far there has been a dearth of works on Moral Theology in English; and it is this want that has occasioned the present work, which aims at presenting Moral Theology, not only in its essentials, but even more in detail and with greater fullness than is done by most of the text-books commonly in use. And yet, while pursuing this larger and more comprehensive plan, the authors of this new work have tried to be as brief and compact as possible. It has been their endeavor especially to avoid digressions into other fields and to sum up pertinent matter in as clear and simple a manner as the subjects treated will permit.

17. The Division and Order of Parts in Moral Theology.—The arrangement of his matter made by St. Thomas Aquinas in the *Summa Theologica* is admittedly unsurpassed and unsurpassable in the qualities that good distribution should have, viz., clearness, connection between parts, completeness. Hence, we cannot do better than follow the order he has used in his treatment of moral subjects. His general division is as follows:

(1) The Last End of Man.—From the Last End acts derive their morality, those being good that advance man towards its attainment, and those evil that turn him away from its possession. The Last End is considered; (a) as to its existence; (b) as to its nature (i.e., the constituents of supreme beatitude).

(2) The General Means Tending to the Last End.—God is approached, not by the steps of the body, but by the operations of the soul, and thus it is human acts that lead one to one's Last End. These acts are

considered: (a) as they are in themselves or absolutely, and according to the twofold division of acts proper to man (human acts) and acts common to man and beast (passions); (b) as to the internal principles from which they proceed, i.e., habits, whether good (virtues) or bad (vices); (c) as to the external principles by which they are influenced. The external principle of evil is the demon, who tempts man to sin. The external principle of good is God, who instructs us by His law and the voice of conscience, and assists us by His grace.

(3) The Special Means Tending to the Last End.—These are our own good works; hence, here are considered the virtues incumbent on all classes of men, i.e., the theological and moral virtues.

18. Some of the topics just mentioned (e.g., divine grace) are discussed fully in works on Dogmatic Theology, and hence may be omitted here. Again, since the Last End of man is considered at great length in dogmatic works on Eschatology, little need be said about it here. Hence, it will be convenient to divide this work into two parts as follows: General Moral Theology, in which are treated the more remote principles on duty, such as the Last End, human acts, good and bad habits, laws and conscience, grace; (b) Special Moral Theology, in which are treated the more immediate rules concerning duty, i.e., man's obligations as regards the virtues and the Commandments.

PART I
GENERAL MORAL THEOLOGY

Question I
THE LAST END OF MAN AND THE MEANS TO THAT END

Art. 1: THE LAST END OF MAN

(*Summa Theologica*, I-II, qq. 1-5; *Contra Gentes*, IV, cc. 1-63.)

19. Existence of the Last End.—Every deliberate act proceeds from the will, and, since the will pursues good as its goal, it follows that every deliberate act is done for some good or end. But, if this end is an imperfect good, it is desired not for itself but as leading up to a perfect good, that is, to one which will leave nothing beyond it to be desired; in other words, the intermediate end is willed on account of a last end. Hence, all that a man wills, he wills directly or indirectly on account of a last end. All men desire their own happiness and perfection; but not all understand in what beatitude consists, since some aim ultimately at finite goods.

20. Nature of the Last End.—As man's Last End is that object which will make him perfectly happy, it cannot consist: (a) in external goods, such as wealth, honors, fame, glory and power, since one might have all these and yet be very unhappy; (b) in goods of the body, such as health, beauty, pleasure and strength, since all these things are passing, and moreover satisfy only a part, and that the lower part, of man; (c) in goods of the soul, such as wisdom or virtue, since man's intellect is never content with particular truth, nor his will with particular good, the former always reaching out for the highest truth, the latter for the highest good. Hence, the Last End of man is the Infinite Good, or God "who satisfieth thy desire" (Psalm cii. 5).

21. Attainment of the Last End.—God being supersensible, the act by which He is attained cannot be any operation of the senses, but must be an act of the higher powers. Man possesses his Last End through the vision of God, from which result beatific love and every good that is compatible with the glorified state. For "we see now through a glass in a dark manner, but then face to face" (I Cor., xiii. 12); and there shall

be "glory and honor and peace to everyone that worketh good" (Rom, ii. 10).

Art. 2: ACTS AS HUMAN

(*Summa Theologica*, I-II, qq. 6-17.)

22. Human acts are a means to man's Last End, inasmuch as they are meritorious—i.e., labors that deserve a recompense (I Cor., iii. 8), struggles that deserve a crown (II Tim., ii. 5). But works are not meritorious unless they are one's own (human) and good (moral); and, since the reward is supernatural, they must also be the fruit of grace. Hence, we shall speak of acts in the following order: (a) acts as human and free (Art. 2); (b) acts as morally good (Art. 3); (c) acts as supernaturally meritorious (Art. 4).

23. Definition.—Those acts are called human of which a man is the master, and he is master of his actions in virtue of his reason and his will, which faculties make him superior to non-human agents that act without reason and freedom. Hence, the following kinds of acts done by a human being are not called human: (a) those that are not under the control of the mind, because one is permanently or temporarily without the use of reason or without knowledge (e.g., the acts done by the insane; by those who are unconscious or delirious, under the influence of hypnotism or drugs, distracted or carried away by vehement fear, anger, etc.; by infants and uninstructed persons); (b) those that are not under the control of the will, even though they are known (e.g., automatic acts, such as the acts of the vegetative powers, growth, circulation of the blood; pathological acts, such as convulsions; acts done under external violence).

24. Knowledge Requisite for a Human Act.—An act is human, or voluntary, when it is deliberately desired; and, since nothing can be deliberately desired unless it is known, an act done without knowledge is not human or voluntary. Thus, a delirious patient does not will the language he uses, for his mind is confused and he does not understand what he is saying.

25. The condition of a person without knowledge is ignorance, which is defined as the absence of knowledge in one who is capable of knowing.

Ignorance is of various kinds. From the viewpoint of that which is not known (i.e., of the object of the ignorance), there is ignorance of the substance of an act and ignorance of the quality of an act. For example, Titus driving rapidly in the dark runs over and kills a pet animal of his neighbor, but knows nothing of this happening (ignorance of the substance of the act); Balbus, a child, fires a pistol at his playmate, not knowing that this causes death (ignorance of the physical quality of an act), and that it is the sin of murder (ignorance of the moral quality of an act).

26. With reference to the will of the person who is ignorant, three kinds of ignorance may be distinguished.

(a) Ignorance is concomitant (simultaneous with the act of the will), when it is not voluntary, and yet is not therefore the reason of the act that follows it, since that act would have been done, even had there been knowledge. This may be illustrated by the example of a hunter who intended to kill an enemy, and killed him only accidentally while shooting at an animal.

(b) Ignorance is consequent (after the act of the will), when it is voluntary, which may happen in different ways: first, when ignorance is affected, as when a person expressly desires to remain ignorant about his duties, so that he may have an excuse for his sins, or that he may not be disturbed in his evil life; secondly, when he neglects to acquire the knowledge he ought to possess, as when a hunter kills a man, thinking him an animal, because he took no pains to be sure before firing.

(c) Ignorance is antecedent (before the act of the will), when it is not voluntary, and is the cause of the act that follows since the act would not have been done, if there had been knowledge. For example, a hunter who has used reasonable diligence to avoid accidents, kills a man whom he mistook for a deer.

27. With reference to the responsibility of the person who is ignorant, there are two kinds of ignorance. (a) Ignorance is invincible when it cannot be removed, even by the use of all the care that ordinarily prudent and conscientious persons would use in the circumstances. Thus, a person who has no suspicions of his ignorance, or who has

tried in vain to acquire instruction about his duties, is invincibly ignorant. (b) Ignorance is vincible when it can be removed by the exercise of ordinary care. There are various degrees of this species of ignorance: first, it is merely vincible, when some diligence has been exercised, but not enough; secondly, it is crass or supine, when hardly any diligence has been used; thirdly, it is affected, when a person deliberately aims to continue in ignorance.

28. Influence of the Various Kinds of Ignorance on the Voluntariness of Acts.—(a) Ignorance of an act, whether as to its substance or quality, makes an act involuntary, when the ignorance itself is involuntary, as will be explained in paragraph 29. Hence, if we refer to ignorance that is not blameworthy and to the guilt of violating the law of God, we may say: "Ignorance excuses."

(b) Ignorance does not make an act involuntary before human law, unless the law itself presumes the ignorance or the ignorance is proved, as will be explained in the Question on Law (see 489 sqq.). For, when law is sufficiently promulgated or a fact pertains to one's own self, the presumption is that ignorance does not exist, or that it is culpable. Hence, the general rule of law common to all forms of jurisprudence: "Ignorance does not excuse" (cfr. Canon 16 of the Code of Canon Law).

29. Effects of Concomitant, Consequent, and Antecedent Ignorance.— (a) Concomitant ignorance does not make an act involuntary, because it does not cause anything that is contrary to the will; but it does make the act that is performed non-voluntary, since what is unknown cannot be actually desired.

(b) Consequent ignorance cannot make an act entirely involuntary, since such ignorance is itself voluntary; but it does in a certain respect make an act involuntary, i.e., inasmuch as the act would not have been done save for the ignorance. (c) Antecedent ignorance makes an act entirely involuntary.

30. Effects of Invincible and Vincible Ignorance.—(a) Invincible ignorance, even of what pertains to the natural law, makes an act involuntary, since nothing is willed except what is understood. Hence,

no matter how wrong an act is in itself, the agent is not guilty of formal sin (see 249), if he is invincibly ignorant of the malice involved.

(b) Vincible ignorance does not make an act involuntary, since the ignorance itself is voluntary; hence, it does not excuse from sin. It does not even make an act less voluntary and less sinful, if the ignorance is affected in order that one may have an excuse; for such a state of mind shows that the person would act the same way, even though he had knowledge.

31. Vincible ignorance makes an act less voluntary and less sinful: (a) when the ignorance is not affected, for the voluntariness is measured by the knowledge, and knowledge here is lacking; (b) when the ignorance, though affected, was fostered only through fear that knowledge might compel a stricter way of life; for such a state of mind seems to show that one would not act the same way if one had knowledge.

32. Like to ignorance are the following: (a) error, which is a judgment not in agreement with the facts (e.g., Balbus, a young child, thinks stealing is lawful, because older persons are represented as stealing in the moving pictures); (b) forgetfulness, which is ignorance of what was once known (e.g., Titus made a study of his duties as a Catholic when he was young, but at present what he does not know about those duties is not inconsiderable); (c) inadvertence, which is a lack of attention to what is being done (e.g., Caius, who is absent-minded, sometimes gets his hair cut and goes away without paying, or takes money that does not belong to him).

33. The principles and conclusions given above with regard to ignorance will apply also to error, forgetfulness and inadvertence; for in all these cases the lack of actual knowledge at the moment an act is done, is either willed or not willed, and accordingly the act itself is either voluntary or not voluntary. In the examples mentioned above, Balbus does not will the guilt of theft, since he does not know it; but his elders do will that guilt, because they should know it. Titus is responsible for neglecting his duties, if he has forgotten them through his own neglect of them or other fault; otherwise, he is not responsible. Caius' inattention is involuntary, if due to mental concentration or distraction, and if it is not desired by him; it is voluntary, if he is aware

of it and cultivates it, or if he does not try to be more attentive to his duties.

34. Consent Requisite for a Human Act.—To be human, an act must proceed not only from knowledge, but also from inclination; that is, it must be voluntary. Three things are necessary in order that an act be voluntary: (a) it must be agreeable to an internal principle, i.e., in most moral matters to the will. Hence, an act that is done against one's will on account of external violence is not voluntary; (b) it must be caused by the will. Hence, a shower of rain is said to be agreeable to the gardener, but not voluntary since his will is not its cause; (c) it must be performed with a conscious purpose. Hence, natural acts (such as sleeping) and spontaneous acts (such as stroking one's beard absent-mindedly) are not voluntary acts.

35. Kinds of Voluntary Acts.-(a) A voluntary act is free or necessary, according as one can or cannot abstain from it. The vision of God in heaven is voluntary to the blessed, since they look at Him knowingly and gladly; but it is not free, since they cannot avert their gaze from that which makes them blessed. The love of God on earth is voluntary, since chosen; but it is also free, since man is able to turn away from God.

(b) An act is perfectly or imperfectly voluntary, according as the deliberation and consent that precede it are full or only partial.

(c) An act is said to be simply—that is, absolutely—voluntary, when it is wished under circumstances that exist here and now, although in itself, apart from those circumstances, it is not wished. It is said to be voluntary under a certain aspect, when it is desired for itself, but not under existing conditions. Thus, if an arm needs to be amputated to save life, the amputation is absolutely voluntary, while the preservation of the arm is voluntary only in a certain respect. Hence, an act is voluntary simply or absolutely when one chooses it, all things considered; it remains involuntary under a certain respect, inasmuch as the choice is made with reluctance.

(d) An act is voluntary in itself or directly, when it is desired in itself for its own sake (i.e., as an end), or for the sake of something else (i.e., as a means). It is voluntary in its cause or indirectly, when it is not desired in itself, either as a means or an end, but is foreseen as the result of something else that is intended. Examples: Titus quarrels with his neighbors, at times because he likes to quarrel, and at other times because he wishes to make them fear him; hence, his quarrels are directly voluntary. Caius is a peaceful man who dislikes quarreling; but he likes to drink too much occasionally, although he knows that he always quarrels when he is under the influence of liquor. Thus, his quarrels are indirectly voluntary.

36. An act is voluntary in its cause in two ways: (a) approvingly (physically and morally voluntary in cause), when one is able and obliged not to perform the act that is its cause (e.g., the quarrels of Caius mentioned above are approved implicitly by him, since he could and should prevent the intoxication which is their cause); (b) permissively (physically voluntary in cause), when one is not able or not obliged to omit the act that is its cause (see 94 sqq.). Examples: Balbus, in order to make a living, has to associate with persons of quarrelsome character, and as a result often hears shocking disputes. Titus, a military commander, orders an enemy fortification to be bombarded, although he knows that this will involve the destruction of other property and the unavoidable killing of some non-combatants or neutrals. Caius writes a book whose purpose and natural result is edification, but he foresees that evil-minded persons will misunderstand it and take scandal.

37. Omissions, as well as acts, may be voluntary. (a) Thus, they are directly voluntary, when they are willed as an end or as a means to an end. Example: Titus fails to reprove the disorders of those in his charge because he likes disorder, or because it illustrates his theory that everyone should go through an evolution from roughness to refinement. (b) They are indirectly voluntary, when their cause is willed with approval or permitted with disapproval. Example: Balbus does not like to miss Mass, but he fails to rise from bed when he hears the church bell ringing, and as a result does not get to church. If his failure to get up was due to laziness, the omission of Mass was approved by Balbus; if it was due to illness, the omission was only permitted.

38. The effect that follows upon an omission may also be voluntary. (a) Thus, it is directly voluntary, if the omission is chosen as a means to the

effect. Example: Caius hears Titus say that he is going to make a certain business deal, and he knows that Titus will suffer a great loss thereby; but he wishes Titus to lose his money, and therefore says nothing about the danger. (b) It is indirectly voluntary, if one foresees the effect, and approves or permits it. Examples: Balbus sees Titus attacked by a hoodlum and realizes that, unless assisted, Titus will be badly beaten up; but he is such an admirer of pugilism that, in spite of his sorrow for Titus, he decides not to stop the fight. Caius sees his friend Sempronius drowning, and fails to go to his assistance, because to his regret he is not an expert swimmer.

39. The effect of an omission is indirectly voluntary and approved by the will when one is able and bound to do what one omits. Example: Balbus receives some confidential documents with the understanding that he will guard them sacredly; but fearing to lose the good graces of Titus, who is curious and loquacious, he omits to put the papers away as promised, with the result that Titus finds them and reads them.

40. Obstacles to Consent.—The obstacles to consent are all those factors that take away or lessen the voluntariness of an act. (a) Thus, the actual obstacles that affect the intellect are reduced to ignorance, spoken of above; those that affect the will are passion and fear, and that which affects the external powers is coercion. (b) The habitual obstacles are habits and abnormal mental states.

41. Fear is a disturbance of mind caused by the thought that a future danger is impending. It is an obstacle to consent in various ways: (a) it lessens or takes away freedom of judgment, inasmuch as it hinders or suspends the reasoning processes; (b) it lessens the voluntariness of choice, inasmuch as it makes one decide for what is not of itself agreeable.

42. An act done under fear that impeded the use of judgment is: (a) involuntary, if the fear was so great that one was temporarily out of one's mind. Example: Titus is so panic-stricken at the thought that a wild animal is pursuing him that he fires a revolver in every direction; (b) less voluntary, if the fear prevents one from thinking with calmness and deliberation. Example: Caius is being questioned by a stern

examiner who demands an immediate reply. Fearing to hesitate, Caius gives what he knows is a "bluffing" answer.

43. The acts of one who is under fear are of various kinds.

(a) Acts are done with fear, when the fear is concomitant—i.e., when it is not willed and does not cause the act, but is merely its occasion or would rather prevent it. Examples: Julius is ordered under pain of death to drink a glass of wine, a thing he was intending to do and which he would have done even without any threats. Balbus walks along a lonely road, because he must get home, but he trembles at the thought of robbers. Caius, a highwayman, at the point of the revolver, forces Balbus to hand over his purse, but he fears that the police may arrive before he has secured the money. Titus, a business man, makes a trip by air, because he must reach another city without delay, but he has some apprehensions about his safety. All these men act, not because of, but apart from or in spite of their fears.

(b) Acts are done through fear, when fear causes an act that would not otherwise be performed. The fear may be antecedent (i.e., unwilled) or consequent (i.e., willed). Examples: Balbus, in the case mentioned above, surrendered his purse because of involuntary fear which was caused by the revolver of the robber. Claudius makes an act of sorrow for sin because of voluntary fear which he produces by thinking of the punishment of hell.

44. The effects of fear, which do not take away the use of reason, on the voluntariness of acts are as follows.

(a) Acts done with fear are not made really involuntary on account of the fear that accompanies them, for they are done for their own sake, not out of fear or as a consequence of fear. They may be called relatively involuntary in the sense that, by reason of fear, they are comparatively unpleasant, unless one enjoys the thrill of danger. Examples: Balbus, Caius and Titus, in the cases mentioned above, acted with perfect willingness. Whether they enjoyed their experiences or not, depends on their attitudes towards adventure and excitement.

(b) Acts done through fear are voluntary simply and absolutely, for the act done under the impulse of fear is what the agent considers here and now as most desirable. Examples: Balbus' surrender of his purse and Claudius' act of contrition are just what these two men wish to do as best suited to the circumstances.

(c) Acts done through fear are involuntary in a certain respect, if the agent can retain his inclination towards the opposite of the act and still avoid what he fears; otherwise, they are in no way involuntary. Examples: Balbus retains his liking for the money taken from him by force, and hence the surrender of it to the highwayman, although voluntary, if all things are considered, is not voluntary, if only the money itself is considered. Claudius, on the contrary, retains no liking for his sins, for he knows that, if he does, he will defeat the purpose of his act of sorrow, which is to escape the pains of hell; hence, his contrition, although the result of fear, is in no respect involuntary.

45. Passion is a movement of the sensitive appetite towards its object through love, desire, hope, or its repose therein through delight. It tends towards good, as fear tends away from evil (see 117 sqq.). Passion is an obstacle to consent in the following ways: (a) it takes away voluntariness (i.e., the quality of proceeding from an internal principle with knowledge of the end of the act), whenever it is so intense as to prevent knowledge; (b) it diminishes liberty (i.e., the quality of being perfectly voluntary, or indifferent as between many acts), even when it does not prevent knowledge.

46. Spiritual appetites fortify the reason, but the opposite is true of sensible appetites; for these latter draw all the attention to things that are lower and away from those that are higher, and impede the exercise of imagination and other senses that serve the reason. In extreme and rare cases passion may be so intense as to distract from or prevent altogether the exercise of reason, or to produce insanity. Thus, we sometimes hear of persons losing their minds through affection for money, or of performing irrational deeds under the excitement of joy.

47. With reference to the will, passion is twofold. (a) It is antecedent, when it precedes the act of the will and causes it. In this case the passion arises not from the will, but from some other cause (e.g., the bodily state, as when a sick man longs for food that is forbidden). (b) Passion is consequent when it follows the act of the will and results

from it. This may happen either without the will choosing the passion (as when the very vehemence with which the will desires some object causes a corresponding sensitive emotion to awaken), or because the will has deliberately aroused the emotion in order to be able the better to act through its coöperation.

48. Antecedent passion makes an act more voluntary, since it makes the will tend with greater inclination to its object; but it likewise makes an act less free, since it impedes deliberation and disturbs the power of choice. Example: A man who takes extreme delight in sports, plays voluntarily, but is less free than if he were not so immoderately inclined that way.

49. Consequent passion which results naturally from an intense act of the will does not increase the voluntariness of the act, since it is not its cause; but it does show that the act of the will is intense, for it is only that which is willed vehemently that overflows from the will and affects the emotions.

50. Consequent passion which results from the deliberate choice of the will increases the voluntariness of the act that follows, since the act is performed with greater intensity on account of the passion that has been deliberately excited.

51. What has been said about the passions that tend to sensible good can be applied also to the passions that are concerned with sensible evils, such as hatred, sadness, aversion, boldness, anger. If they are antecedent, they increase the voluntariness of an act, but diminish its freedom; and, if they cause a passing frenzy or insanity, they take away all responsibility. If they are consequent, they either increase the willingness of the act, or indicate that it is willed with great intensity.

52. Violence, or coercion, is the use of force by an external agent to compel one to do what one does not want to do. Its effects on voluntariness are: (a) it cannot affect the internal act of the will, else we should have the contradiction that the act of the will was both voluntary, as proceeding from the will, and involuntary, as proceeding from external coercion; (b) it can affect external acts, such as walking, and so make them involuntary. If a boy is driven to school, the violence

makes his going involuntary, but it does not make his will not to go to school involuntary.

53. Habits.—Characteristic of habits is a constant inclination, resulting from repeated acts, to perform similar acts (see 133 for definition of habit). Its effect[s] on the voluntariness of acts are:

(a) if the habit is in a sense involuntary, i.e., caused by free acts but retracted by a sincere act of contrition, it diminishes or even takes away voluntariness. If the actual advertence to the act is imperfect, the voluntariety is diminished; if advertence is totally absent, all voluntariety is taken away. Thus a drunkard who retracts his habit and makes an act of true contrition may again fall into sin because of the acquired dispositions to drink. Then the sins are less voluntary or at times, owing to total lack of advertence, may be regarded solely as material sins.

(b) if the habit is voluntary, i.e., acquired by free acts and not retracted, it increases the voluntariness in respect to the inclination to act. Should all advertence and deliberation be taken away, a rare occurrence, it diminishes the liberty of the act and consequently its morality as good or bad. Voluntariety, however, is not taken away entirely, since the habit itself was freely willed and hence acts flowing from it are voluntary in cause (see 35.). If sufficient advertence remains, the habit diminishes the freedom of the act owing to the impeding of reason; but this diminution of liberty is in accord with the will of the individual who freely contracted and conserves the habit to have facility in acting. Accordingly, absolutely speaking, a voluntary habit increases the voluntariety of acts caused by that habit and consequently increases their goodness or evil. Thus St. Thomas asserts that one who sins from habit sins from certain malice, i.e., not from ignorance or passion, but from the will's own choice.

54. Natural propensities are inclinations that arise from bodily constitution or physical condition (e.g., a strong native attraction to temperance or to intemperance not acquired by frequent acts). Natural propensities have the same kind of influence on the willingness of an act as involuntary habits (see 53.).

55. Pathological states are diseases of the brain or nerves that react upon the intellect and the will, such as various kinds of neuroses and

psychoses, hysteria and epilepsy. The influence of pathological states on the voluntariness of acts seems similar in kind to that ascribed to antecedent passion (see 48.). Caution must be observed in applying these principles to particular kinds of mental diseases.[1]

[1] In doubt whether an act associated with a pathological state is free or not, the rule of moralists is lenient. When the act is sinful, it is not imputed as gravely sinful, for man is innocent until proven guilty. If the act is good, it is presumed voluntary and free and, consequently, meritorious. See Prummer, D.M., O.P., *Manuale Theologiae Moralis* (Barcelona: Herder, 1946), I. n.93.

56. Two Kinds of Voluntary Acts.—Having discussed human or voluntary acts in general, we shall now indicate in particular the acts that are of this kind. There are two classes of voluntary acts: (a) those elicited by the will; (b) those commanded by the will.

57. Acts Elicited by the Will.—The first class of acts under the control of the will are those that are performed by the will itself—i.e., that are begun and completed in that power of the soul.

58. There are three acts of the will that are directed to the end the will has in view, viz., wish, intention and fruition. Wish is the love or inclination of the will towards the end without any reference to the means by which it is to be obtained: this is the first act of the will. Intention is the direction of the will to the gaining of the end through certain means. Fruition is the enjoyment of the end after it has been gained: this is the last act of the will.

59. There are three acts of the will that are directed to the means and that follow after intention, viz., consent, election, and use. Consent follows upon the counsel of the intellect, and is an act of the will agreeing to several means as suitable for the intended end. Election follows after a practical judgment of the intellect about the means consented to, and is an act of the will which chooses one of the means in preference to the others, as being most suitable for gaining the intended end. Use is the act by which the will directs and moves the other powers to employ the particular means that has been chosen.

60. Acts Commanded by the Will.—The second class of acts that are under the control of the will are those that proceed, not from the will itself, but from the other powers under the direction of the will.

61. Acts commanded by the will are of various kinds: (a) intellectual acts, such as judgment, reasoning, etc., performed under the direction of the will, (b) sensible acts such as sight, hearing, imagination, the passions of love, hate, etc.; (c) external corporal acts, such as walking, writing, etc. None of the foregoing acts need be commanded by the will, as they may be indeliberate (see 23).

62. The following kinds of acts are not subject to the control of the will: (a) intellectual acts, such as the assent of the reason to self-evident truths, as regards the specification of the act; (b) sensible acts, such as the passions considered as arising from bodily dispositions before they are adverted to; (c) acts of the vegetative life, such as digestion and growth; (d) bodily movements, such as the circulation of the blood and the beating of the heart.

Art. 3: ACTS AS MORAL

(*Summa Theologica*, I-II, qq. 18-20.)

63. In order that an act be a means by which man may tend to his Last End, it is not sufficient that it be human (proceeding from knowledge and will); it must also be morally good.

64. Definition.—Morality is the agreement or disagreement, of a human act with the norms that regulate human conduct with reference to man's Last End. The act which is in agreement with those norms is morally good; the act which is in disagreement with them is morally bad. An act that neither agrees nor disagrees with the norms of morality, is called morally indifferent.

65. The constitutive norm of morality is that which gives an act its moral quality. (a) Proximately, this is the relation of agreement or disagreement of the act to the rational nature of man considered in its entirety and with reference to its true happiness; (b) remotely, this norm is the relation of the act to God, the Last End of man.

66. Hence, that which makes an act morally good is its agreement with the nature of man as a rational being destined for heaven, and its promotion of the glory of God, which is the purpose of all creation.

67. The manifestative norm of morality is that through which the moral quality of acts is known. (a) Proximately, this is right reason, which is the superior faculty and guide of the will; (b) remotely, it is the divine intellect, from which reason receives its light.

68. The preceptive norm of morality is that which points out duty with respect to good and evil. (a) Proximately, it is conscience; (b) remotely, it is the law of God.

69. The species of morality are three: (a) an act is morally good when it is in harmony with the norms of morality mentioned above (e.g., prayer, works of charity); (b) an act is morally bad when it is out of harmony with those norms (e.g., blasphemy, injustice); (c) an act is morally indifferent when, if considered in the abstract, it neither agrees nor disagrees with moral norms (e.g., walking, riding, etc.).

70. The Sources of Morality.—The sources from which the morality of an act is derived are its own tendencies and modes, in so far as they have a relation of agreement or disagreement to the standards of morals. These sources are: (a) the object of the act, from which it derives its essence (e.g., God is the object of charity); (b) the circumstances of the act, by which it is modified accidentally (e.g., fervor is a circumstance of the act of charity); (c) the purpose or end of the agent, which is the chief circumstance (e.g., to please God, as the purpose of a work of charity).

71. The object of an action is that to which it primarily and naturally tends as to its term and end, and from which it is named. Thus, an alms is directed immediately and of its own nature to the relief of the poor (end of the act); it is only secondarily and from the direction given it by the agent that it tends to generosity and edification, since the agent may give stingily, or from a bad motive (end of the agent).

72. The circumstances are all those conditions, different from the object, that affect the morality of the act. The chief moral circumstances are: (a) the time (i.e., the duration, the character of the

day, as a holyday, fast-day, etc.); (b) the place (i.e., in public or in private, in church or elsewhere, etc.); (c) the manner (i.e., the advertence or inadvertence, the cruelty, etc.); (d) the quantity or quality of the thing done (e.g., that an alms is large or small, that the person who is helped is more or less deserving, etc.); (e) the purpose of the agent (e.g., that an alms is given to honor God); (f) the quality or condition of the agent (e.g., that the giver of an alms is poor himself); (g) the means used (e.g., that a benefactor's own money is used against himself).

73. With reference to their influence on the moral character of acts, circumstances are divided as follows: (a) circumstances that change the kind of morality, by making what was good to be bad, what was indifferent to be good or bad, what was venial to be mortal, what belonged to one class of mortal sins to take on another character, etc.; (b) circumstances that change the degree of morality, by making a good act more or less good, or by making a bad act more or less bad.

74. The purpose or end of an action is the reason which induces the agent to act. It is the chief circumstance of an act, and hence is treated as a separate source of morality.

75. The end or purpose is twofold. (a) It is the total end when it alone is intended, so that the action is done with no other aim in mind. Thus, if one helps the poor only to practise charity, the total motive is charity. (b) The end is partial when it is intended along with another motive of equal or unequal force. Thus, if a person helps the poor in order to relieve them and also to benefit temporarily by his charity, the assistance of others is only a partial motive of his act; and if he would not give alms except in view of the personal advantage he expects, charity becomes the secondary motive.

76. Good Acts.-An act is said to be entirely good when all its elements—its object, circumstances and purpose—are in conformity with the standards of morality. Thus, an alms given to one in need, in a considerate manner, and purely out of love for God, is good in every respect. Furthermore, the fact that the circumstances and purpose of the act are good increases the goodness derived from the object of the act.

77. An act is likewise entirely good when at least one of its elements is good, the others being indifferent, and none evil; for it is the good alone that is intended (see 85), and this gives the moral color to the whole act. This happens as follows: (a) when the object is indifferent and the purpose good, as when one takes a walk for the purpose of performing a work of mercy; (b) when the object is indifferent and a circumstance good, as when one eats a meal with intentional moderation; (c) when the object is good and a circumstance indifferent, as when one prays with unintentional stammering.

78. An act is partly good when, while its object is good, there is some evil in the circumstances that does not neutralize or transform the object. This happens in the following cases: (a) when the object is good and some minor circumstance, not intended as affecting the substance of the act, is evil, as when a person prays with distractions; (b) when the object is good and a partial, but not predominant motive is slightly evil, as when a person prays in public in order to give edification and also incidentally to help his reputation. In both these cases the good—i.e., the worship of God—is desired for itself as good, and the evil that is simultaneously desired does not change this good object.

79. Bad Acts.-An act is called entirely evil when all its elements—its object, circumstances and purpose-are contrary to the moral norms. Thus, to steal, on a large scale, in order to drive the victim to desperation is an act that is entirely wrong. The wickedness of the circumstance and of the motive increases the wickedness of the object of the act.

80. An act is likewise called entirely bad, when one or more of its elements are of themselves good or indifferent, but when there is an element which is evil and which neutralizes or transforms the good. This happens in various ways:

(a) when the object is evil, and the purpose is good, as when one steals in order to pay one's debts. The good end is wished only as obtainable through a wicked means, and thus ceases to be good;

(b) when the object is good or indifferent, and the total purpose is evil, as when one talks or prays with no other motive than to annoy another person. The good is willed, not as good, but only as a means to evil;

(c) when the object is good or indifferent, and a partial but ulterior purpose is evil. For example, if a person extinguishes a fire in order to save a neighbor's house and thus be enabled to rob him; if a person takes physical exercises to develop his strength so as to be enabled to bully a neighbor. The good act and the immediate end in these cases are intended not for the sake of their goodness, but as instruments to the accomplishment of the evil ulterior end;

(d) when the object is good or indifferent, and an evil circumstance is intended, not as a circumstance, but as forming a unit with the object and as affecting the substance of the act—for example, when a person intends prayer precisely as distracted, thus converting prayer into a sin. The good object is willed in such cases, not as good, but as vitiated by an evil circumstance.

81. Although an act is totally evil when the good in it is absorbed by the evil, the presence of what is good in itself can diminish, though it cannot take away, the evil. Thus, to lie in order to help a neighbor is totally evil; yet, it is not as great an evil as to lie to hurt that neighbor.

82. Indifferent Acts.—An act is entirely indifferent if all the elements in it—its object, circumstances and purpose—are neither harmonious nor discordant with the standards of morality. Such an act would be walking home rapidly in order to eat a meal, if besides these factors, which bear no relation to good morals, there was nothing else in the act that did bear such a relation.

83. As to the actual existence of a human or voluntary act that is morally indifferent, we conclude: (a) Considered in the abstract and universally, some human acts are morally indifferent; for if acts be considered with reference to their objects alone and apart from the circumstances that accompany them, and as they are classified in the mind, it is clear that many of them have no determinate relations to moral norms—e.g., reading, writing, walking, etc. (one can read either good or bad literature); (b) considered in the concrete, and as they happen in individual cases, no human acts are morally indifferent, since the purpose of the agent is either according to right reason or against it, so that, in spite of the indifferent object, the act becomes either good or bad by reason of the presence or absence of the good purpose.

84. Considered even in the concrete and in individual cases, all acts that are not human, but indeliberate or involuntary (see 23 sqq.), are morally indifferent—or, more correctly, unmoral, as being outside the genus of moral acts on account of the absence in them of will, which is the prerequisite of morality. Thus, absent-minded acts are neither good nor bad morally.

85. As to the kind of intention required to make an indifferent act morally good, or which should be had when the act is objectively good, we conclude: (a) The good intended must not be solely a sensible good (i.e., the pleasure that the act gives), but also and chiefly a rational good (i.e., its conformity to moral standards), since man, unlike the animals, was made, not for sensible, but for rational good. Hence, to eat deliberately with no other end than that of gratifying the palate, is to eat without a moral purpose worthy of a human being, and is a bad act.

(b) The moral good of virtue which is intended in acts must not be regarded as the supreme good, but should be referred to God, since He alone is the Last End (see 20). Hence, to eat and drink with moderation solely because that is reasonable and suitable to human nature, if one excludes the Last End, is to slight the necessary purpose and is morally bad. (c) The intention of moral good or virtue in human acts need not be actual or reflex. Thus, a person who has a previously formed intention of living reasonably, or who at the time of eating intends to eat moderately for the sake of health, sufficiently intends a moral end. Likewise, it is not necessary that the reference of an act to the Last End be made actually or explicitly. Hence, every person in the friendship of God, in all his deliberate acts that are not evil, has a sufficient reference of them to God contained in the fact that he has chosen God for his Last End, or in that here and now he intends some motive that becomes a rational being.

86. An actual and explicit intention of the moral goodness of an act, and an actual and explicit reference of the act to the Last End, though not necessary, increase the moral value of what is done.

87. Axiom of Pseudo-Dionysius: "That act is good whose causes are complete; that act is evil in which a single cause is lacking."

(a) This axiom can be understood as referring to perfect good, and the meaning then is that an act is not perfectly good in the moral sense unless all its elements—its object, purpose and circumstances—are good; just as an oration is not called perfect, unless all its elements—the speaker, the matter, the style and the delivery—are what they should be. Hence, a single defect is enough to make an act fall short of perfection.

(b) The axiom can be understood of essential goodness, and the meaning then is that an act is not essentially good unless all the causes that contribute to essential goodness—the object of the act and any circumstances that may through the intention of the agent take on the character of object—are good; just as a man is not said to be healthy, unless his heart, lungs, and all the other chief parts of the body are sound. Hence, an act is substantially bad, if either its own end (the object of the act) or the special purpose had in mind by the agent (the end of the agent) is bad, as explained above in 79-81.

88. The axiom of Dionysius does not mean: (a) that an act cannot be essentially or substantially good and at the same time accidentally bad (see 78), for, if even one circumstance not properly attended to could change an act from good into bad, how few good acts would be done even by the most saintly persons! Example: Caius who sacrifices himself for the service of God and his neighbor, now and then feels some slight vanity over his work. His acts remain substantially good. (b) The axiom does not mean that an act cannot be substantially bad and yet have good circumstances that diminish its badness (see 81).

89. Morality of the External Act.—Having considered the morality of the internal act, we shall now turn to the external act (such as giving an alms, stealing, and the like), and inquire whether it has a morality of its own distinct from that of the internal act (see 56 Sqq.).

90. If the external act be considered precisely as it is the object, or effect, of the internal act of the will, it does not add any essential morality to the internal act, since, having no freedom of its own, it is moral only in so far as it proceeds from the will. In this sense, then, he who gives an alms to the poor, and he who would give it if he could, are equal in goodness of will; and he who wishes to defraud, and he who actually defrauds, are equal in malice of will.

91. If the external act be considered precisely as it is the term towards which the internal act tends, it completes the essential morality of the internal act by extending and communicating it without. For, though this external act cannot add a distinct morality of its own, it does carry the internal morality to its natural conclusion and diffuses its good or evil. In this sense, he who actually gives an alms is more deserving than he who really desires to give but is unable; and he who really defrauds is more reprehensible than he who wishes to defraud but cannot.

92. If the external act be considered precisely as something added to the internal act, it can increase the accidental morality of the internal act by the reaction of the external circumstances on the will. This can happen in such ways as the following: (a) the performance of the external act, being pleasurable or difficult, increases or decreases the intensity of the will to act; (b) the performance of the external act, since it requires more time than the internal act, prolongs the latter; (c) the external act by reason of repetition may also increase the strength of the internal act.

93. Furthermore, it is through the external act that edification or scandal is given, that penalties or rewards for overt action are deserved, etc. Examples: Titus bears murderous hatred towards Balbus, but keeps it concealed. Caius also hates Balbus, and first calumniates him, thus giving scandal, and then kills him, thus making himself liable before the law.

94. The Morality of the Act That Is Indirectly Willed.—An act is said to be willed indirectly, or in its cause, when it is foreseen as the result of another act which alone is directly intended (see 35 sqq.). According to the different moral character of the acts, there are four cases in which the act is willed indirectly:

(a) when both the act directly willed and the resultant act are bad. Examples: Titus is heartily opposed to quarreling and blasphemy; but he makes himself drunk to forget his troubles, foreseeing that he will quarrel and blaspheme while in that state. Balbus has a real dislike for uncharitable thoughts; but he chooses the company of a notorious scandalmonger in order to be amused, knowing that thoughts against charity will be caused by listening to him;

(b) when the act directly willed is bad and the resultant act is good. Example: Caius is very miserly when sober, but liberal when intoxicated; to vary the monotony of his life, he decides to become intoxicated, but grieves at the thought of the money he may give away to some deserving charity before he returns to his senses. Sempronius decides on an act of injustice with sorrow over the unbidden thoughts of remorse or repentance that will follow his act;

(c) when both acts are good. Example: Out of charity Titus makes up his mind to visit a pious relative who is ill; and he foresees that thoughts of improving his own conduct—a thing not pleasing to him—will be occasioned by this visit;

(d) when the act directly willed is good and the resultant act is bad. Examples: Balbus takes a drug prescribed for his health, although he foresees it will make him unable to go to church. Caius gives alms to the poor, intending only an act of charity, but he knows that thoughts of vainglory will arise.

95. The act indirectly willed sometimes gives, sometimes does not give, a new morality. (a) Thus, if it is good, it adds no internal goodness, since the will only permits, without intending the good act. Example: Caius, who does not intend, but regretfully permits his act of charity which he foresees, does not desire the act of charity. (b) If it is bad, the act indirectly willed adds a bad act of the will, if the will desires evil by permitting what it has no right to permit. Example: Titus who does not prevent, when he should, what will lead to blasphemy on his part, implicitly desires the act of blasphemy.

96. The Morality of the Consequences of an Act.—Man's life receives its moral character, not only from his internal and external acts which are done in the present and from those which he knows will result from them in the future, but also from the influence his acts exercise now and afterwards upon his fellowman. It is this influence upon others that we now speak of as the consequences of an act. According to the case, the consequences sometimes add, sometimes do not add, to the morality of an act. The good men do lives after them, and also the evil. There are various kinds of consequences:

(a) foreseen consequences, which, if intended, add to the morality of an act, since it is clear that one who wishes the many good or evil results of his act is better or worse in intention than another who has no such wish. Thus, one who knows that many will be edified or scandalized by his conduct, and wills the result, is better or worse than if he had no such will about those consequences;

(b) unforeseen consequences, which, if they follow naturally and usually from an act, make the act in itself better or Worse according to their character. Thus, the teaching of Christian doctrine is good as conveying a knowledge of truth, but it is made better on account of the spiritual benefit of others that naturally results from it. Similarly, the teaching of evil is made worse on account of the evil consequences it usually produces;

(c) unforeseen consequences, which, if they follow only accidentally and rarely from an act, do not affect its morality, since an act must be judged by what belongs to its nature, not by what is merely occasioned by it. Thus, the fact that an alms is used by the recipient as a means to intemperance does not detract from the goodness of the almsgiving done for the sake of charity. Likewise, the fact that an injury is used by the sufferer as an occasion for spiritual profit does not lessen the wickedness of the injurious act.

97. Imputability.—Just as an act may be an act done by man (i.e., higher than the operations of brutes) and yet not be human (i.e., not performed in the manner that is proper to man as man; e.g., an act of reasoning or of decision during a dream, see 23 sqq.), so an act may be moral (i.e., in conformity or disagreement with the standards of right) and yet not imputable as good or bad to the agent (e.g., a prayer or imprecation said by an infant, or the drunkenness of one who did not realize the power of a liquor).

98. Imputability is that property of an act by which it belongs to its agent, not only in its physical nature as something of himself or as an effect produced by him or in its human quality of subjection to his will, but in its moral character of goodness or badness. From contact with the moral object, the agent takes as his own something of the

brightness or defilement of that object, and so becomes chargeable himself with goodness or badness.

99. The conditions for the imputability of an act are:

(a) the act must be human—i.e., it must be performed knowingly and willingly (see 23 sqq.). One is not chargeable with the quality of the act, if not responsible for its very substance. Example: Titus suffers such intense pain that he does not know what he is saying, and he blasphemes. The morality of blasphemy is not unknown to him, but his present act is not voluntary, and hence is not imputable;

(b) the morality of the act must be known, or be something that should be known, at least in a general way, to the agent; for no one is responsible for what he is wholly ignorant of through no fault of his own. Example: Titus, Caius, Balbus and Sempronius rob the orchard of their neighbor. Titus in good faith thinks he is doing an act of virtue, because the owner owes money to his companions. Caius thinks that some kind of sin is being committed, but he does not know whether it is theft, or gluttony, or what. Balbus thinks that only a venial sin of stealing is being perpetrated. Sempronius, the youngest of the crowd, looks on the whole affair as a part of the day's sport. All committed theft, and the act is wrong; but Titus and Sempronius were not guilty of sin, since they were in good faith. Caius and Balbus committed sin, the species and degree depending on the knowledge they had or should have had (see 588 sqq.);

(c) the morality of the act must be willed. If the act is good, the goodness must be intended, since a person should not get credit for what he does not wish. Example: Titus does not believe in virtue, and Caius is opposed to helping the poor; but both give an alms to a beggar, the former in order to get rid of the beggar, the latter in order to get rid of some old clothes. Hence, neither wishes or receives credit for the charity done. If the act is bad, the badness is sufficiently intended by the performance of what one knows is forbidden and wrong. The will chooses contact with the evil object, and thus implicitly with the evil of the object. Example: Balbus protests that he does not wish to harm anyone, and then proceeds to calumniate his neighbors. His disavowal of sinful intent does not make him any the less responsible for his calumny.

100. Imputability may be conceived as making one responsible for the moral quality of an act in three ways: (a) generically, if one should get the credit or discredit of goodness or badness only; (b) specifically as to kind, if one gets the credit or discredit of a particular category of goodness or badness; (c) specifically as to degree, if one gets the credit or discredit of higher or lower grades of the same virtue or vice, or if one is made guilty of mortal or venial sin. These points will be discussed in the articles on the virtues and vices (see 186 sqq.).

101. Goodness is imputable as follows:

(a) As regards internal acts, a person is credited with all the goodness of the object, end, and circumstances, in so far as it is known and willed by him. Example: Titus purposes to pray in a penitential posture, in order to obtain the virtue of humility. Hence, he has the credit of worship, mortification and humility through his holy desire. If he thought of the penitential posture, not as a moral circumstance, or if he regretted it, he would have the act, but not the credit of mortification;

(b) As regards external acts, a person is credited with the greater readiness or intensity or duration which, through it, his will gives to what is good. Example: If Titus prays in the manner above described, his good will is intensified, and he has the credit of this increase in the accidental goodness of his act;

(c) As regards acts indirectly willed, one is not credited with their goodness, if this is merely permitted. Example: Sempronius, who is sorry that thoughts of a better life will go through his mind as a consequence of going to church, has not the credit of those good thoughts;

(d) As regards consequences that were foreseen, or that naturally result from an act, one is not credited with their goodness, unless it was wished. Example: Balbus teaches religion to children because he is paid to do so; Caius does so because it is a good act. The consequence that these children afterwards live virtuously is not morally creditable to Balbus, since he thought nothing about it; but it is a circumstance that increases the goodness of Caius' act, since he intended his teaching precisely as it is a good work;

(e) As regards consequences that are not natural results of an act, if they were not foreseen or intended, they are not credited to the agent. Example: Titus speaks a simple and ordinary word of good advice to Sempronius, but the impression is so great that Sempronius undertakes and accomplishes extraordinary things, which Titus would not have deemed possible or advisable.

102. Evil is imputable as follows:

(a) As regards the internal act, a person is guilty of all the evil of the object, end and circumstances, as far as it is known and willed by him. Example: Balbus wishes he could steal all the possessions of Caius, and thereby drive the latter to suicide. Balbus has committed theft and murder in his heart;

(b) As regards the external act, one is guilty of all the circumstances of greater willingness, etc., which it adds to the internal act. Example: If Balbus actually steals from Caius and causes his death, his malice is shown to be very strong and to extend to the evil consequences of his external acts;

(c) As regards acts indirectly willed, one is guilty of the evil they entail, if one could and should have prevented it. Example: Balbus is guilty of the blasphemies he foresees will take place when he has taken too much drink, for he could and should have kept sober.

(d) As regards the evil consequences of acts, foreseen or natural, one is responsible for the evil, if one could and should have prevented it. Examples: Titus knows that a beggar will use profane language if denied an alms, but Titus cannot spare the money and is not responsible for what happens. Sempronius blasphemes in the company of many, and is therefore guilty of the sin of scandal, since he has no right to blaspheme;

(e) As regards the evil consequences of acts that could not have been foreseen, they are not imputable. Example: Balbus steals fifty cents from Caius, and the latter is so heartbroken that he commits suicide.

Balbus is not responsible for the suicide, since such a thing was far from his thoughts when he stole.

103. It was just said (102, d) that when two results, one good and one evil, follow an act, the evil is imputable if it could and should have been prevented. It is not always easy, however, to determine at once when the evil result should be prevented, and, as cases of double effect are many, it will be useful to give rules that are more particularized, and that enable one to decide when it is lawful to do that from which will follow an act indirectly willed, or a consequence that is evil.

104. It is lawful to perform an action from which an evil effect is foreseen when the following conditions are present:

(a) the action willed itself must be good or at least indifferent; for clearly, if the action is bad, it is also unlawful;

(b) a good effect must also follow from the act, and it must not be caused by the evil effect; for the end does not justify the means. Thus, it is not lawful to take what belongs to others in order to give alms, for the evil effect (stealing) results from the act (taking) immediately; whereas the good effect (almsgiving) results only mediately through the theft;

(c) the agent must intend only the good effect, since it is unlawful to wish evil. Thus, if one foresees that one's virtuous life will cause the sin of envy in a neighbor, this evil result of one's virtue must not be entertained by one as something pleasing;

(d) the agent must have a reason sufficiently weighty for permitting the evil result that follows his act. Evil should not even be permitted, unless there is adequate compensation in the good that is intended.

105. To judge whether a reason for permitting an evil effect is proportionately grave, the following rules should be kept in mind:

(a) the greater the evil that results, the greater must be the good that is intended. Thus, it is not lawful to kill a robber in order to save a small amount of money: but it is lawful to kill an aggressor, if this is necessary in order to save one's life;

(b) the greater the dependence of the evil effect on one's act, the greater must be the reason for performing the act. Example: Titus gives permission to his class to play a game against another class, foreseeing quarrels and disputes between the teams. Less reason is required for granting the permission, if Titus knows that higher authority will grant it, should he refuse it;

(c) the more nearly the evil effect follows upon the act, the greater must be the reason for the act, Thus, less reason is required to direct a person who looks like a heavy drinker to the city than to direct him to a bottle of strong drink;

(d) the more certain it is that the evil effect will follow, the greater is the reason required for placing its cause. For example, one who speeds in an automobile on an unfrequented road, does not require the same excusing cause as one who speeds on a thoroughfare where many other cars are passing;

(e) the more obligation one has to prevent the evil effect, the graver is the reason required for placing its cause. Thus, since parish-priests, lawgivers, superiors and policemen are bound by their office to prevent moral disorders, a far greater cause is required in them, than in persons who have no such charge, for doing what will have an evil consequence.

Art. 4: ACTS AS MERITORIOUS

(*Summa Theologica*, I-II, q. 21.)

106. When the morality of an act is attributable to one as one's own, one becomes worthy of praise and reward, if the act is good, but deserving of censure and punishment, if the act is evil.

107. Definitions.—Merit is the right to a reward arising from works done for God. Demerit is the debt of punishment incurred on account of works done against God.

108. Divisions.—According to the difference of the person who confers the reward, there are two kinds of merit: (a) human merit, or the claim which a person has to a reward from his neighbor, or from

society, for the benefits he has conferred upon his neighbor or society; (b) divine merit, or the right a person has to receive a reward from God for the fidelity wherewith he has exercised stewardship over his acts, of which God is the Last End, or wherewith he has served society, of which God is the Supreme Ruler. Only divine merit is here considered.

109. According to the difference of the object of the reward, there are two kinds of merit: (a) natural merit, which makes one worthy of a reward that does not exceed the native powers or exigencies of a created being, such as success, prosperity, or other goods that do not constitute the Last End of man (see 20). Thus, we read in scripture of pagans or sinners who were blest with temporal happiness on account of their natural virtues; (b) supernatural merit, which makes one worthy of the beatitude surpassing mere created power that God has prepared for those who serve Him (see 20). It is only this kind of merit that is being considered here; for, since the Last End of man is a supernatural reward (viz, the Beatific Vision of God), it follows that the acts by which he tends to that End must be not only human and moral, but supernaturally meritorious.

110. There are four kinds of supernatural merit: (a) condign merit in the stricter sense, that is merit which arises from justice, and which presupposes no favor on the part of the rewarder. In this sense Christ merited, since even the grace which made His merits supernatural was due to Him as the God-Man; (b) condign merit in the less strict sense, that is merit which arises indeed from justice, but presupposes a favor on the part of the rewarder. In this way the righteous merit before God, since their works confer a right to their own reward, while the grace which enables them to perform their works is a divine favor; (c) congruous merit in the stricter sense, that is merit which arises not from justice (since there is no equality between the work and the reward), but from the fitness of things, because the person who merits is a friend of God. In this way all who are in the state of grace can merit spiritual goods for others; (d) congruous merit in the wide sense, that is merit which arises from the liberality of God, who answers a good work as if it were a prayer. In this way the good works done by sinners can be said to merit conversion for them.

111. The second kind of merit mentioned above—i.e., condign merit in the less strict sense—is that with which we are chiefly concerned here, since it is the kind of merit that must be found in human acts in order that they may lead man to a supernatural reward. A fuller treatment of merit is found in Dogmatic Theology in the Question on Grace.

112. The conditions requisite for the kind of merit now in question are: (a) that the work done be human, that is, free, morally good, and supernatural (i.e., proceeding from sanctifying grace and divine charity); (b) that the one who merits be in the wayfaring state (i.e., that he have not already passed to final reward or punishment), and that he be in the state of grace; (c) that God has promised a reward for the work done. From the statements made above, it follows that all the human and morally good works of those who are in the state of grace possess condign merit.

113. The objects of condign merit—i.e., the rewards promised by God for the good works done for Him in this life—are: (a) an increase of sanctifying grace; (b) the right to eternal life; (c) the attainment of eternal life, if the one who merits dies in grace; (d) an increase of glory.

114. The conditions for the merit of strict congruity are the same as those given above (112), except the promise made by God, which is not required. Examples of this kind of merit are the sanctity of the Blessed Virgin, which made her deserve more than others to be the Mother of God, and the conversion of St. Paul through the merits of St. Stephen.

115. For the merit of wide congruity it is necessary that the work done be morally good. Examples of this kind of merit are the sighs of the ancient Patriarchs, as obtaining the coming of the Messiah. The just man can merit with the merit of wide congruity the following: (a) his own conversion after a future fall; (b) his final perseverance; (c) temporal goods.

Art. 5: THE PASSIONS

(*Summa Theologica*, I-II, qq. 22-48.)

116. Having discussed the acts proper to man, we shall now speak of the passions, which are common to both man and beast.

117. Definition.—The passions—also called the emotions, affections, or sentiments—are acts of desire; but, unlike the acts of the will, they are directed, not to good apprehended by the higher knowing power of the intellect, but to good apprehended by the lower knowing power of sense and imagination. They are defined as: acts or movements of the sensitive appetite which arise from the representation of some good in the sense faculties, and which produce some transformation in the body, such as palpitation of the heart, increased circulation of the blood, paleness, blushing, etc.

118. Division.—There are two classes of passions; (a) the concupiscible, which have as their object sensible good considered as delightful, or sensible evil considered as unpleasant, and which are love and hatred, desire and flight, delight and sadness; (b) the irascible, which have as their object sensible good or sensible evil considered as difficult to attain or to avoid, and which are hope and despair, boldness and fear, anger.

119. The concupiscible passions are defined as follows: (a) love, the first of the passions and the cause of all the others, tends to sensible good considered as desirable, abstracting from its presence or absence; while hatred is the aversion from sensible evil considered precisely as unsuitable and abstracting from its presence or absence; (b) desire tends to sensible good that is absent, and flight turns away from sensible evil apprehended as future; (c) delight is the affection produced in the sensitive appetite by the presence and possession of the object desired; (d) sadness is the passion which dejects the soul on account of the presence of an evil.

120. The irascible passions are explained as follows: (a) hope reaches out towards a future good whose attainment is difficult, but not impossible; despair turns away from a good that seems impossible of attainment; (b) bravery goes out to attack an evil that seems difficult and imminent, but not unconquerable; fear falls back before a future difficulty that seems irresistible; (e) anger is the desire of vengeance for an injury received.

121. Moral Value of the Passions.—The Stoics held that all the passions are diseases of the soul, and that one is perfect when one arrives at the

condition of being passionless or apathetic. Lucretius, on the contrary, taught that all the impulses of passion are good. The truth is that the passions are good or evil according to the way they are considered. (a) Physically, the passions are good, since they are the acts of natural powers, or the perfection and complement of something good in itself. (b) Morally, they are indifferent, if they are viewed in themselves, as the product of the sensitive appetite. For this appetite is an irrational power of the soul, similar to that of the beasts, and acts are not moral unless rational—i.e., an act is good or evil only from its relation to reason. (c) Morally, the passions are good or bad, if commanded by reason and will, for thus they partake of the good or evil that is in the acts from which they proceed, just as the acts of the external members of the body are moral in so far as they execute the commands of the will. The passions are voluntary if commanded by the will, or not forbidden by it. Examples: Our Lord looked about Him with anger, being grieved at the blindness of His enemies who watched Him in the synagogue (Mark, iii. 5); He wept over the destruction of Jerusalem (Luke, xix. 41); He was sad at the approach of His passion (Mark, xiv. 34).

122. The passions are morally good: (a) if they are directed by the will to a morally good object; for example, shame is a praiseworthy passion, because it is fear of what is dishonorable, and pity is also good, because it is according to right reason, being sorrow for the misfortune of another; (b) if they are chosen by the reason for a good purpose; for example, it is good to excite the emotion of joy that one may pray with greater fervor, or to arouse the feelings of pity, fear, or hope, in order that one may be more earnestly moved to acts of mercy, repentance, courage; (c) if the circumstances are moderated according to right reason; for example, to grieve over the death of a friend excessively, so that one is unfitted for duty and suffers in health, is unreasonable; but to grieve even unto tears, as Christ did at the tomb of Lazarus, is an act of piety. Similarly, the slight anger of Heli was blamable and the great anger of Moses was laudable, because the evils in both instances called for severity (I Kings, ii, iii; Exod., iii).

123. The passions can either diminish or increase the goodness of an act. (a) They diminish its goodness, if they are antecedent—i.e., prior to the judgment of the reason—for they thus obscure the mind and make the act that follows less voluntary. For example, there is less goodness

in an alms given under an impulse of sentimentality than in one given after serious consideration of the matter and from a motive of charity. (b) They increase its goodness if they are consequent—i.e., subsequent to the judgment and the result of the vehemence of the will, or of deliberate encouragement by the will (see 47 sqq.)—for, just as the external act increases the goodness of the internal act, so is it better that man should tend towards good, not only with the will, but also with the emotions. Examples: The spiritual gladness of the Psalmist is seen to have been more than ordinarily great from the fact that it acted upon his feelings, and both heart and flesh rejoiced (Ps, lxxxii. 3); to sing a hymn in order to encourage oneself to greater fervor or devotion adds to the goodness of what is done, through the greater promptness or ease it causes in the act that follows.

124. The passions are morally evil: (a) when they are commanded by the will and directed to an object, a purpose, or circumstances that are evil, Thus, envy is an ignoble passion, since it is unreasonable, being sorrow at another's success. Examples; Titus drinks to excess for the delight of intoxication (bad object); Balbus purposely excites his imagination, that he may hate more bitterly and act more cruelly (bad end); Sempronius loves his children so immoderately that he grows morose and jealous (bad circumstance). (b) The passions are also morally evil when they should be forbidden and are not forbidden by the will. Example; Caius is surprised by a sudden burst of anger, which, though he judges to be unreasonable, he does nothing to check.

125. The passions can remove, diminish or increase the evil of an act. (a) Thus, antecedent passions take away all evil, if (a thing that is rare) they prevent entirely the use of reason; they diminish malice if they obscure the judgment. Examples: Balbus, fearing that he is about to drown, becomes panic-stricken, seizes Titus and almost drowns him. Caius, threatened with a black eye if he refuses, calumniates: his calumny would be worse if he acted coldbloodedly. (b) Consequent passions increase the evil, for then they manifest a strong intention, or are the result of direct purpose. Examples: Sempronius attacks the conduct of an opponent, not with dispassionate argument and from a love of truth, but with bitter personal feeling and from a desire of revenge. Titia works herself into a rage that she may be the more ready for an encounter with a person of whom she is unjustly jealous.

126. Though the passions are physically good and in their nature morally indifferent, they may have physical reactions or moral consequences that are harmful or evil. These dangers may be physical, mental or moral.

(a) Physical Dangers of the Passions.—It is a well-known fact that there is a close connection between the passions and the nerves, heart, and bodily organism in general, and that strong or persistent emotion can work great detriment to the health, producing disease, unconsciousness, or even death.

(b) Mental Dangers of the Passions.—It is admitted by all that the passions disturb the judgment, and can even take away the use of reason. For they act upon the body or the senses, and these in turn affect the mind in a way similar to what happens in sleep or intoxication. Thus, love makes one blind to the defects of the objectof one's love; fear makes one magnify the evil of what is dreaded; melancholy unbalances the mind, etc.

(c) Moral Dangers of the Passions.—It is likewise a matter of common experience that the passions are a source of many temptations and sins. Often they are antecedent (i.e., not premeditated or willed), as when they arise from bodily states over which one has no control or from imaginations strongly fixed in the mind, and at the same time tend to that which is not according to right reason, rebelling against the law of the mind. Thus, a person whose health is bad is easily dispirited, and this feeling occasions temptations to despair; one whose memory is haunted with the image of a lost parent becomes a prey to sadness, which makes it difficult to perform duties with zest and diligence.

127. A passion may become morally bad on account of the physical or mental evils connected with it. (a) Thus, a person has duties to his own well-being, and he indirectly wills (see 35 sqq., 94 sqq.) to neglect these duties, if he indulges harmful passions. Example: Sempronia grieves immoderately over the death of her mother, with the result that her health and mental vigor are impaired. (b) A person also has duties with respect to the life, health, and happiness of his neighbor, and he chooses to neglect these duties if he unjustly provokes emotions in others, foreseeing injurious consequences (see 96 sqq.). Examples: Titus

so vexes Balbus by petty annoyances that the latter loses appetite and sleep, and becomes an invalid. Sempronia so exasperates her father by long-continued unfilial conduct that the latter becomes insane. Caius appeals to prejudices in order to have injustice done to a rival.

128. As to passions that incite to evil or deter from good, we must observe the following: (a) if the passion is consequent, one is placing oneself or others in danger of sin, and one's conduct must be judged according to the principles given in 258 sqq. (Examples: Titus likes to brood over his troubles, although this causes temptations to neglect duty; Sempronia makes remarks to a hot-headed acquaintance which are a provocation to great uncharitableness); (b) if the passion is antecedent, it constitutes a temptation which one is bound to resist (see 252 sqq.). Example: Balbus has a natural dislike for Caius, and often feels impelled to judge him rashly or treat him unjustly.

129. Antecedent or involuntary passions, as well as other involuntary acts of imagination, thought and will, tending to evil, are sometimes called "first motions of the soul," as distinguished from consequent or voluntary passions and acts, which are known as "second motions of the soul." The first motions are of two kinds: (a) those that precede all deliberation and consent, actual or virtual (*motus primo-primi*), and these are free from all sin; (b) those that precede full deliberation and consent, but follow on partial deliberation (*motus secundo-primi*). These latter are venial sins.

Most theologians since the Council of Trent maintain that the inordinate movements of passion which precede the advertence of reason, such as lust, envy, sloth, etc., are not sins. The Council of Trent defined that the *fomes peccati* has never been understood by the Church to be truly a sin in the baptized, but has been called sin by St. Paul in the sense that it is from sin and inclines to sin (Council of Trent, fifth session). On the basis of this text some authors argue that it is of faith that the inordinate motions called *primo-primi* are not sins for the baptized. The condemnation of both the fiftieth proposition of Baius: _The evil desires to which reason does not consent, and which man endures unwillingly (*invitus*), are prohibited by precept_; and his fifty-first: *Lust, or the law of the members, and evil desires of it, which men suffer unwillingly, are true disobedience of the law*, is interpreted as establishing as certain the non-sinfulness of such movements in infidels. (See Merklebach, O.P.,*Summa Theol.* Mor., Vol. I, n. 448).

St. Thomas taught otherwise that such inordinate movements of passion are venial sins (*Summa. Theol.* I-II, q. 74, a. 3, ad 2um; *de Malo*q. 7, a. 6. ad 4m; *de Veritate*, q. 25, a. 5). Although they precede the deliberation of reason, they attain to the order of moral acts, however imperfectly, insofar as sensuality in man by its nature is made to be subject to reason. Reason can and ought to control these motions, but fails to do so owing to the great number of them possible to occur. Hence they are not involuntary, but indirectly voluntary as sins of omission (*II Dist.* 24, q. 3, a. 2; *de Veritate*, q. 25, a. 5;*Quodlib.* IV, q. 11, a. 1). Since these movements are indirectly voluntary, St. Thomas' teaching does not conflict with the Council of Trent which speaks of the *fomes* as habitual dispositions and not of its acts which St. Thomas considers. Clearly, too, his teaching does not fall under the condemnation of the propositions of Baius; with Baius the motions are involuntary, but for St. Thomas indirectly voluntary.

St. Thomas distinguishes the motions of sensuality differently from modern manualists. For him the motions-*primo-primi* arise from corporal dispositions which are not under the control of reason and hence can not be sins. Motions-*secundo-primi* arise from some apprehension of the internal senses proper to the passions and can, at least if taken singly, and ought to be ruled by reason. Thus, they are moral acts (*de Malo*, q. VII, a. 6, ad 8um; *II Dist.* 24, q. 3, a. 2).

130. Bodily suffering or sickness is sometimes called a passion of the body, but, unlike the passions of the soul, it is a physical evil. Morally considered, it is indifferent in itself, but it has contacts with morality in various ways. (a) Thus, it may receive morality from the will. Examples: Sufferings endured with resignation are acts of virtue; sickness or pain inflicted upon others is imputable to the unjust cause. (b) It may affect the morality of the act of the will. Examples: Severe toothache or other exquisite pain is an extenuating circumstance in sins of grumbling, for the suffering draws so much attention to itself that deliberation on other things is much diminished; weakness of stomach may be a moral advantage in freeing one from temptations to over-eating.

131. Though the passions are good in themselves, they are often morally dangerous. The regulation of the passions through the virtues of fortitude and temperance will be treated later on, but we shall indicate here some natural means by which, God helping, their first motions may be controlled. (a) Thus, if a passion is not strong, it may be repressed directly by command of the will. Example: The impulse to anger may sometimes be checked by the command of silence. (b) If a passion is strong, it may be combated through other activities which are its opposites or which, through the amount of energy they call for, will diminish proportionately the force of the passion. Examples: In time of fear one can fall back on thoughts of confidence; in time of mourning one can seek joy or alleviation in the society of friends or in the repose of sleep. Study or other strenuous occupation is an excellent means to overcome impetuous passion.

(c) If a passion is persistent, it may be diverted to some lawful object vividly represented and held in the imagination and thoughts. Examples. Those who are inclined to love immoderately the world or the things that are in the world should direct their love to divine goodness. Those who are inclined to be too fearful of men should think how much more God is to be feared.

Question II
GOOD AND BAD HABITS

132. Having considered human acts and the passions, we now pass to a consideration of the principles from which acts proceed proximately. These principles are, first, the faculties, powers or forces of the soul (such as the intellect, will, sense, appetite, and vegetative powers); and, secondly, the habits which permanently modify the faculties. For some faculties may be turned in various directions, either favorably or unfavorably, as regards their ends, and it is the stable bent given to a faculty that is called a habit. Thus, the intellect may be directed towards its end, which is truth, by the habit of knowledge; or away from that end by the habit of ignorance. Likewise, the will may be directed towards or away from its end, which is good, by virtue or vice. The faculties are treated in Psychology, but the habits, since they turn the faculties towards good or evil, must be considered in Moral Theology, as well as in philosophy.

Art. 1: HABITS IN GENERAL

(*Summa Theologica*, I-II, qq. 49-54.)

133. Definition.—A habit is a perfect and stable quality by which a being is well- or ill-affected in itself, or with regard to its motions. It differs from mere disposition or tendency, which is an imperfect and transitory quality. Thus, a sallow complexion is a habit; a blush, a disposition.

134. Division.—Habits are variously divided, as follows:

(a) From the viewpoint of their subject, they are either entitative or operative, according as they affect directly the nature or the powers of a being. Thus, in the soul there are the entitative habit of sanctifying grace and operative habits like science and virtue; while in the body are entitative habits of health, beauty, etc.

(b) From the viewpoint of their object, habits are good (i.e., virtues) or evil (i.e., vices);

(c) From the viewpoint of their cause, habits are infused or acquired, according as they are supernaturally produced by God, or are naturally obtained by man through repeated acts, or result from nature without repeated acts. Faith in a baptized infant is an infused habit; knowledge obtained through study is an acquired habit; the perception that the first principles of truth are to be granted is natural.

135. Operative acquired habits are defined as qualities not easily changed, by which a faculty that is able to act in various ways is disposed to act in one way with ease, readiness and pleasure. Thus, by training a man acquires a correct carriage, and is able to walk straight without difficulty.

136. Operative infused habits are enduring qualities that give to a faculty the power to perform acts that are supernatural. Thus, the infused virtues of faith, hope and charity give to the intellect and the will the ability to elicit acts with reference to supernatural truth and good. Facility and promptitude with respect to these acts come through the use of the infused power.

137. Strengthening and Weakening of Habits.—Habits are increased: (a) extensively when they are applied to more objects—thus the habit of science grows as it is applied to more truths; (b) intensively, when they are rooted more firmly in their subject and become easier to exercise. This last comes about when intense acts of a habit are frequently repeated. Thus, a habit of virtue or vice becomes a second nature, and it is exercised with ever greater delight and resisted with ever-increasing difficulty.

138. The infused habits cannot be diminished, but they can be destroyed (see 745). As to the acquired habits, they are weakened and destroyed chiefly in two ways: (a) by acts opposed to them, especially if these acts are earnest and frequent—thus, evil custom is overcome by good custom, and vice-versa; (b) by long discontinuance or disuse. Thus, a person who has learned a foreign language will forget it, if he fails to speak, read or hear it. The knowledge of first principles, speculative or moral, is not lost, however, through forgetfulness, as experience shows.

139. Accidentally, a habit may be corrupted through injury of an organ that is necessary for the exercise of the habit. Thus, right moral judgment may be lost if certain areas of the brain are affected.

140. Habits and Morality.—The importance of habits in man's moral life is very great. (a) Habits are an index to a man's past career, for the ease and facility he now possesses through them is the result of many struggles and efforts and difficulties overcome, or of defeats and surrenders and neglected opportunities. (b) Habits constitute a man's moral character. Morally, a person is the sum of his moral habits and dispositions grouped around the central interest or idea of his life. He who would know himself, therefore, cannot do better than to examine what are his habits, and which is the predominant one among them. (e) Habits are a prophecy of the future. Habits are not irresistible and do not destroy freedom, but they produce such ease and readiness for acting in one particular way that the probabilities are, when habits are strong, that a person will continue to follow them in the future as he has done in the past, thus progressing or deteriorating, as the case may be.

141. Duties as regards Habits.—(a) Bad habits should be avoided and those that have been formed should be destroyed (see 138). The means to accomplish these victories are divine help obtained through prayer and the other instrumentalities of grace, watchfulness through self-examination, and the cultivation of a spirit of self-denial, as well as attack made on the habit that is forming or already formed (see 255 sqq.)

(b) Good habits should be acquired, and those already possessed should be exercised and put to the best advantage. The means to this end, in addition to those that are supernatural, are especially a realization of the importance of good habits, a great desire to have them, and constant and regular effort to practise them (see 137).

Art. 2: GOOD HABITS OR VIRTUES

(*Summa Theologica*, I-II, qq. 55-70.)

142. Definition.—A virtue is a good habit of the free powers of the soul, that is a principle of good conduct, and never of conduct that is evil. Hence, the following are not virtues: (a) an occasional inclination to good, for this is not a fixed habit; (b) good habits of the body or of the vegetative powers, etc. (such as beauty and health), for these are not free; (c) knowledge of the right or affection for it without any reference to practice, for virtue is a principle of right living; (d) habits that can be applied indifferently to good or bad conduct, such as human opinion.

143. Division.—The virtues are divided: (a) according to their different causes, into infused and acquired virtues (cfr. 134 sqq.);(b) according to their different objects, into intellectual, moral and theological virtues.

144. The intellectual virtues are those habits that perfect the intellect with reference to its good—i.e., truth, speculative or practical.

145. The speculative virtues are three: understanding, knowledge and wisdom.

(a) Understanding or intelligence is the habit of perceiving truths that are not in need of proof, as being self-evident. Axiomatic truths or first principles are the object of this virtue.

(b) Knowledge or science is the habit of perceiving truths that are learned from other truths by argumentation, and that are ultimate in some category of being. The object of this virtue embraces the various sciences (like astronomy) which are conclusions from principles.

(c) Wisdom is the habit of learning through reasoning the truth that is absolutely ultimate; it is the knowledge of things in their supreme cause, God. Examples are theology and philosophy in their highest sense.

146. The practical intellectual virtues are two: prudence and art.

(a) Prudence is an intellectual virtue which indicates in individualcases what is to be done or what is to be omitted, in order that one may act according to the requirements of good morals.

(b) Art is an intellectual virtue which indicates in individual cases how one must act in order to produce things that are useful or beautiful (e.g., music, painting, building, etc.).

147. The intellectual virtues, except prudence, are not perfect virtues, since, While they make an act good, they do not necessarily make the agent good. A man may have great knowledge about morality, or be able to produce excellent works of art, and at the same time be not virtuous, or have no love for his work.

148. Prudence is an intellectual virtue, since it resides in the intellect; but it is also classed among the moral virtues, since its object is the direction of human acts to their right end.

149. The moral virtues are those habits that perfect the will and the sensitive appetite with reference to their immediate and respective objects; that is, they are habits concerned with acts as means to the Last End. They make the act good, and make good also him who performs it; and they are thus superior as virtues to the intellectual habits.

150. There are four principal moral virtues: (a) in the intellect there is prudence, which guides all the actions and passions by directing the other moral virtues to what is good according to reason; (b) in the will there is justice, which inclines a person to make his actions accord with what he owes to others; (c) in the irascible appetite is fortitude, which

subjects to reason the passions that might withdraw from good, such as fear of dangers and labors; (d) in the concupiscible appetite is temperance, which represses the motions of passions that would impel one to some sensible good opposed to reason.

These four virtues are also called cardinal virtues, because all the other moral virtues hinge on them.

151. The theological virtues are those that perfect the intellect and the will with reference to God, their ultimate, supernatural object. They are three: (a) faith, which is a virtue infused into the intellect, giving man supernatural truths that are perceived by a divine light; (b) hope, which is a virtue infused into the will, enabling man to tend towards the supernatural destiny disclosed by faith as towards an end possible of attainment; (c) charity, which is a virtue infused into the will, uniting man's affections to the object of his hope and transforming him into its likeness.

152. Causes of Virtues.—The causes of virtue are three: (a) nature, which is the cause of the inchoative intellectual and moral virtues, that is, of the theoretical and practical principles that are naturally known, and of the inclinations to virtue that arise from an individual's bodily constitution; (b) practice, which is the cause of perfected intellectual and moral virtues, that is, of the good habits that are formed by repeated acts (e.g., knowledge obtained through study, temperance fixed in the character through continued effort); (c) infusion from on high, which is the cause of the virtues that surpass nature (i.e., of the theological virtues and of the moral virtues that are concerned with our acts as ordered to the supernatural). ·

153. Properties of the Virtues.—From the definition of virtue given above certain properties result.

(a) Since a virtue makes conduct agree with a certain fixed standard, it does not allow of excess or defect. Hence, virtue follows the golden mean.

(b) Since the other moral virtues would go to extremes without the guidance of prudence, and since prudence would not judge aright without the right dispositions of the other virtues, it follows that the four moral virtues, at least in their perfect state, must always be together. And because charity is the fulfillment of the whole law, he who has charity has also all the other infused virtues.

(c) Since the virtues are directed towards objects of varying degrees of excellence, and since they are habits, and are capable of increase and decrease (137 sqq.), it follows that both virtues of different species, and those of the same species, are or may be unequal.

(d) Since some of the virtues imply conditions that will not exist in the life to come, it follows that these virtues will be somewhat changed in the blessed. Thus, temperance, which subdues the rebellion of the passions, will not be exercised in heaven, where the passions do not rebel.

154. The golden mean is found differently in different virtues.

(a) In the case of justice, the mean is determined by an external object that is invariable, since justice gives what is due to others, neither more nor less; in the case of fortitude and temperance the mean is determined by prudent judgment and is not invariable, since these two virtues are concerned with the regulation of the internal passions according to conditions of individuals and circumstances. Thus, a debt of ten dollars remains the same whether the debtor is rich or poor, whether the creditor needs it or not. But a glass of liquor, which would be just enough for one who was well, might be far too much for him when he was sick; and a danger which a man might be expected to encounter, might be too much for a woman or a boy.

(b) The mean of the intellectual and speculative virtues is the agreement with objective truth, as lying between the extremes of false affirmation and false negation. The mean of the practical virtue of prudence, as regulating the moral virtues, is right reason, considered as directive of the desires and conduct so as to avoid excess and defect.

(c) The theological virtues have no mean, as far as their object is concerned, since God, being infinite in truth, power and goodness, cannot be believed in, hoped in, or loved too much. By reason of their subject, however, these virtues have a mean, since it is possible for one to exceed, for example, in hope by presumptuously expecting what is not due to one's condition.

155. Without charity one may possess certain other virtues. (a) Thus, one may have the natural or acquired moral virtues, as is the case with many pagans, but such virtues are imperfect, since they do not direct their subject to the Supernatural End of man; (b) one may have the supernatural or infused virtues of faith and hope, as is the case with Christians who are not in the state of grace. Even such faith and hope are imperfect virtues, and are not meritorious.

156. Considered precisely as virtues (cfr. Article on Hope), the three groups rank as follows: (a) the theological virtues are the most excellent, since they deal directly with man's supernatural end; (b) By reason of their object, universal truth, the intellectual virtues are superior to the moral virtues, which are concerned with particular goods; (c) the moral virtues, nevertheless, are more perfect as virtues, for, so considered in the order of action, in perfecting the appetites, they are more properly principles of action.

157. The highest of the virtues within each group are the following:

(a) Charity is greater than faith and hope, since it implies union with its objects, while the other two imply a certain distance from their object;

(b) Justice is superior to fortitude and temperance, since it deals with actions by which man is rightly ordered, both as to himself and as to others, while the others deal with the passions and the right disposition of man as to himself. The order of the moral virtues is: prudence, which is the guide of the others; justice, which deals with man's actions and orders him rightly, both as to himself and as to others; fortitude, which governs the passions, even when life and death are the issues; temperance, which governs the passions in affairs of less importance;

(c) The chief of the intellectual virtues is wisdom, which considers the supreme cause of things, and therefore judges the other virtues of the intellect.

158. In the blessed the virtues will remain, but changed in some respects. (a) Thus, the rectitude of soul contained in the moral virtues

will endure, but there will be no rebellious passions to overcome, no dangers to oppose, no debts of justice to be discharged, as in this life; (b) the intellectual virtues acquired in this life will remain, but the soul separated from the body will not employ sense images as in its earthly existence; (c) faith and hope will give place to vision and realization, but charity will never fall away.

159. The Complements of the Virtues.—The virtues are habits that supply the soul with an internal guide (prudence), and with inclinations to follow its direction (moral virtues). But there is also a higher Guide who speaks to the soul, and it is necessary that the inclinations of virtue be carried out in a suprahuman mode. Hence, the virtues are completed by certain adjuncts. These are: (a) the Gifts of the Holy Ghost, which are habits infused into the soul, making it sensitive to the guidance of the Holy Spirit and docile under His direction; (b) the Fruits of the Holy Ghost, which are acts that grow out of the virtues and have a special spiritual sweetness attached to them; (c) the Beatitudes, which are activities of special excellence having a corresponding special reward attached to them, The acts are produced by the infused virtues and the Gifts, especially by the Gifts.

160. There are seven Gifts of the Holy Ghost, which are divided as follows:

(a) There are the Intellectual Gifts, which make the soul more responsive to the light which the Holy Spirit sheds upon truths held by faith. These Gifts assist the intellect, first, in its apprehension of the mysteries of faith, that it may be made to grasp more clearly what it believes (Gift of Understanding); secondly, in its judgments, that it may be illuminated so as to adhere to the principles of faith and depart from their opposites, whether there be question of judgments about divine things (Gift of Wisdom), or created things (Gift of Knowledge), or human actions (Gift of Counsel);

(b) There are the Appetitive Gifts, which make the soul more ready to follow divine motions and inspirations. These Gifts aid the irascible affections by giving them a confidence of victory over every peril and by assuring safe arrival at the term of life (Gift of Fortitude); they aid the will in its social relations by leading to a filial love and devotion toward God (Gift of Piety); they assist the concupiscible affections by filling them with a reverence of God's majesty and a horror of offending Him (Gift of Fear of the Lord).

161. The Gifts of the Holy Ghost are superior to the moral and intellectual virtues, for these virtues perfect the powers of the soul that they may be always ready to follow the guidance of reason, while the Gifts make the powers of the soul docile to the guidance of the Holy Ghost.

162. The Gifts of the Holy Ghost are inferior to the theological virtues, for these virtues unite the soul to the Holy Ghost, while the Gifts only make the soul ready to receive His illuminations and inspirations.

163. There are twelve Fruits of the Holy Ghost enumerated by St. Paul (Gal. v, 22-23). (a) Some of these acts grow out of the indwelling Spirit, and are delightful to the spiritual taste because they perfect the agent in himself. Charity, joy, and peace indicate that the soul is rightly disposed as to what is good; patience and longsuffering, that it is not disturbed by evils. (b) Others of these Fruits give spiritual delight because they perfect the agent in his relations to his fellows. Good will and kindness show that one is well-disposed towards others; meekness and fidelity, that injury does not overcome him, or make him deceitful. (c) Still other Fruits are delightful because they order a man's life rightly as to external actions or internal passions, such as modesty, continency, chastity.

164. There are eight Beatitudes enumerated by our Lord. (a) Some of these are acts that surpass the virtues as regards the use of external goods and the government of the passions. Thus, it is lawful to have possessions, but the poor in spirit despise them; it is lawful to exercise the irascible passions according to reason, but the meek under divine guidance keep themselves in tranquillity; it is lawful to rejoice according to moderation, but the mourners, when this is better, refrain from all rejoicing. (b) Other Beatitudes are acts that surpass the virtues of justice or liberality to one's neighbor. Thus, those who hunger and thirst after justice not only discharge their obligations, but they do so with the greatest willingness; the merciful bestow their bounty, not only on their friends and relatives, but on those who are most in need. (c) Still other Beatitudes are concerned with the acts that most fit one for the

contemplation of divine things, namely, that in oneself one be pure or heart or free from the defilements of passion, and that one be peaceful with reference to others. (d) The final Beatitude is the crown of the others; for one is perfectly attached to poverty of spirit, meekness, etc., when he is prepared for their sake to suffer persecution.

165. The rewards promised to the Beatitudes are conferred, not only in the life to come, but also in the present life. But they are not necessarily temporal or corporal rewards (such as riches, pleasure, ete.), but spiritual beatitude, which is a foretaste and figure of the eternal joy to come.

166. All the Beatitudes may be called Fruits of the Holy Ghost, since they are the outgrowth of the indwelling Spirit and are filled with spiritual sweetness. But the Beatitudes are really more excellent than the Fruits, since they are works of more than ordinary excellence; whereas every work of virtue that gives delight may be called a Fruit of the Holy Spirit.

Art. 3: BAD HABITS OR VICES

(*Summa Theologica*, I-II, qq. 71-89.)

167. Definition.—A vice is a habit inclining to moral evil. A sin is an act resulting from a vice, or tending to the formation of a vice; or it is any thought, word, deed or omission against the law of God.

168. Divisions.—There are various divisions of sins. Thus:

(a) according to the kind of delight that is taken in evil, sins are either spiritual (e.g., vainglory) or carnal (e.g., intemperance);

(b) according to the person who is more directly offended by evil, sins are either against God (e.g., heresy, despair, blasphemy), or against one's neighbor (e.g., theft, calumny), or against oneself (e.g., intemperance, suicide);

(c) according to the greater or less gravity of the evil, sins are either mortal (e.g., blasphemy) or venial (e.g., idle thoughts);

(d) according as the evil is done by acting or not acting, sins are either of commission (e.g., theft) or of omission (e.g., failure to pay debts);

(e) according to the progress of a sin, there are three stages: first, it is a sin of the heart when it exists only in the mind, as when one entertains a wish for revenge; secondly, it is a sin of the mouth, when it is manifested in words, as when one uses contumelious language; thirdly, it is a sin of work when it is carried out in act, as when one strikes another in the face;

(f) according to the manner in which they deviate from the golden mean, sins are either of excess (e.g., extravagance) or of defect (e.g., miserliness);

(g) according to the manner in which its guilt is contracted, sin is either original (i.e., the loss of grace inherited from Adam) or actual (i.e., the stain derived from one's own wrongdoing; sec 272 sqq.).

169. Mortal Sin.—A sin is mortal or deadly, when by it a person turns away from God, his Last End, and prefers to Him some created good, thereby incurring the debt of eternal punishment.

170. The first condition necessary in order that a sin may be judged mortal is that the matter of the sin be grave, either in itself or in the opinion of him who commits it; it must include turning away from God and the substitution of some created good as the Last End.

171. The matter of a sin is known to be grave: (a) when the law of God or of the Church declares that it is seriously displeasing to God, or that it will separate one from His favor or rewards; (b) when right reason shows that it does great injury to the rights of God, of society, of one's neighbor, or of oneself.

172. The matter of a sin is grave in two ways. (a) It is grave from the character of the act and without exception, when the good which is injured is infinite, or is a finite good of greatest importance and indivisible, Thus, heresy, despair, and simony against divine law are always serious, because they offend against an infinite good; while murder, though it injures only a finite good, is nevertheless always grave matter because earthly life is of highest importance among finite goods,

and if taken away is taken entirely. (b) The matter of a sin is grave from the character of the act but with exceptions, when the good that is injured is of grave importance, but finite and divisible. Thus, the worship we give to God is finite and admits of more and less; and hence a sin against worship, though serious from the nature of the offence, may be slight on account of the smallness of the irreverence. Similarly, though theft injures a grave right, it is not grave matter when the amount stolen is small.

173. The second condition required that a sin be mortal is that there be full advertence to the grave malice of the act, for one cannot be said to separate oneself from God unless one has made the same amount of deliberation that is required for any temporal affair of great moment.

174. Advertence is the act by which the mind gives attention to something. It is of two kinds: (a) full advertence, when there is nothing to impede perfect attention, as when a person is wide awake, in full possession of his faculties, and not distracted; (b) partial advertence, when there is something that, prevents entire attention, as when a person is only partly awake; or not entirely conscious, or distracted with many things.

175. Hence in the following cases, even though there be serious matter, a sin is not mortal, on account of lack of full advertence. (a) When without one's will there is no full advertence to the act itself, as happens with those who are half-asleep, or who are under the influence of drugs, or who are mentally confined by anxiety or physical pain, etc. (see on Human Acts, 24 sqq.). (b) A sin is not mortal when there is no full advertence to the sinfulness or to the gravity of the act. Those who through no fault of their own are unaware that an act is sinful, or that it is a mortal sin (e.g., children, the half-witted, or the uninstructed), have no full advertence to the malice of the act; likewise, those who, without being responsible for their inadvertence, do not think at the moment of the sinfulness or seriousness of what they do (e.g., those who think out plans for revenge before they have taken second thought on its immorality).

176. Signs that indicate that there was no full advertence are: (a) if afterwards one can scarcely recall what happened; (b) if shortly afterwards one cannot be sure what was one's state of mind at the time.

177. Though full advertence is required for a mortal sin, it is not required that this advertence be the most perfect. (a) It is not necessary that the advertence be preceded by long deliberation, for advertence can be full even when the consideration is only momentary, (b) It is not necessary that advertence be continued during the commission of a sin, for what follows is foreseen if adverted to at the beginning. (c) It is not necessary that advertence to the malice of the sin be clear or exact. One who perceives that there is some special malice in robbing a church, even though he does not understand just what the malice is, has sufficient advertence to become guilty of sacrilege. Likewise, one who has doubts as to whether a certain sin is mortal, or who suspects that it is mortal, has sufficient advertence for grave guilt if he commits that sin. (d) It is not necessary that advertence to the malice of the sin be reflex (i.e., that one advert to the fact that one is conscious of the gravity of the sin); for to will the malice, it suffices that one be conscious of the malice. (e) It is not necessary that advertence to the malice of the sin be explicit (i.e., that one have in mind the precise nature of sin as an offense against God, which produces a stain on the soul and incurs the debt of punishment); for to will evil and its gravity, it suffices that one perceive the evil and its gravity, even though one does not analyze the meaning or seek out the ultimate reasons.

178. The third condition required that a sin be mortal is that full consent of the will be given it, for no one separates him self from God except through his own free choice. (a) Consent is not full, when there has not been full advertence, or when an act has been done under violent compulsion; (b) consent is full when there has been full advertence and no forceful compulsion (see above on Violence, 52).

179. Indications that consent was not full are: (a) if before the sin the person was of tender conscience and had habitually a horror of grave sin; (b) if at the time of the sin the person recoiled from thesinful suggestion—e.g., if he had a hatred for it as soon as it was fully perceived, or if he was saddened at the temptation, or if he kept from an external act that could have been easily performed; (c) if after the sin

the person was conscientious, and yet had doubts as to whether consent was given.

180. Venial Sin.—A sin is venial, or more easily pardonable, when by it one turns inordinately towards some created good, not so, however, as to forsake God as one's Last End or to prefer self-will to the divine friendship.

181. The first condition required that a sin be called venial is that its matter be light, either in reality, or in the invincible belief of him who commits it. The criteria by which we may know what matter is light are authority and right reason (see above, 171).

182. The matter of a sin is light in two ways. (a) From the character of the act, the matter is light when the good which is injured is finite and of minor importance. Thus, truth about trivial things is of less importance among finite goods, and consequently a small lie about some unimportant matter, which helps and does not harm the neighbor, is light matter. (b) From the quantity of the matter, the matter is light when the good injured is of major importance but divisible. An example here is a theft that works only small harm (see above, 172).

183. The second condition for a venial sin is that there be some advertence to the malice of the act. (a) The advertence is not full when the matter is grave, and the act done without compulsion, for else the sin would not be venial but mortal. (b) The advertence may be full or partial when the matter is light.

184. The third condition for a venial sin is that there be some consent of the will to the malice of the act. (a) The consent is not full when the matter is grave, for else the sin would be mortal. (b) The consent may be either full or partial when the matter is light.

185. Imperfections.—The description of venial sin just given indicates that it is a voluntary transgression of the law of God in matters of lighter importance, and is thus distinguished from the various classes of moral imperfections. These latter imperfections are:

(a) natural imperfections, which are the falling short on the part of good acts of the higher degree of goodness they might have possessed.

Since man is finite by nature, it is inevitable that he be limited in the good he does; and hence this kind of imperfection is not a transgression or a sin;

(b) personal imperfections which are voluntary but not transgressions, are acts or omissions whose motive is reasonable, but which are contrary to that which is of counsel. Example: to omit hearing a Mass that is not obligatory, when one is able to assist at it, but has a good reason for staying away;

(c) personal imperfections which are transgressions but not voluntary, are acts or omissions done without deliberation, but which are opposed to some law of less importance. Example: To pray with involuntary distractions.

186. Change in the Gravity of Moral Defects.-An imperfection becomes a sin: (a) if the motive for omitting what is of counsel only is sinful (e.g., to neglect a Mass that is not of obligation out of contempt); (b) if a slight indeliberate transgression has a cause that was voluntary (e.g., involuntary distractions caused by previous neglect).

187. Venial sins become mortal when that which in itself is a slight offense, becomes in the individual agent a grave offense by reason of some change in the object or of some grave malice in the purpose, circumstances, or the foreseen results (see above 97 sqq.).

188. A change in the object makes venial sin mortal: (a) when that which is light matter objectively is apprehended subjectively as grave matter (e.g., a person tells a small lie or commits a trifling theft, thinking these to be mortal sins); (b) when that which is light matter by itself becomes knowingly grave matter through the additions that are made to it (e.g., a thief steals small amounts frequently with the intention of having a great amount of ill-gotten money after a time).

189. It should be noted that, while the matter of venial sins may coalesce so as to form grave matter and constitute a mortal sin, as just explained, venial sins themselves do not, from mere multiplication, ever become mortal, since the difference between mortaland venial sin is not one of quantity, but of kind. Hence, when acts are slightly sinful but do

not coalesce, they multiply venial sins, but do not form mortal sin. Example: Coming a few minutes late for Mass every Sunday.

190. The multiplication of venial sins, especially when they are held as of no importance, disposes for the commission of mortal sin: (a) directly, by forming a habit that calls for ever greater indulgence (e.g., petty thefts lead to dishonesty on a large scale); (b) indirectly, by familiarizing one with wrongdoing and chilling the love for virtue.

191. The wrong purpose of the agent makes an act that is only venially sinful (as far as the object is concerned) to become mortally sinful, when the purpose contains a grave malice in itself, for the act is then intended only as a means to what is seriously wrong (see above 80). Example: To tell a small lie in order to break up friendships and sow hatreds.

192. The circumstances of an act that is only venially sinful in itself also make the act mortally sinful, when there is grave malice in such circumstances. Cases of this kind are the following:

(a) The circumstance of the person committing the sin sometimes changes the malice from light to grave. Example: Unbecoming levity in one in authority may cause serious disrespect for his office and thus be gravely sinful;

(b) The circumstance of the manner in which an act is performed may change it from a venial to a mortal sin, as when the sin is committed out of contempt, or is so coveted that it would be preferred to a grave obligation. Examples: One who violates a law of lesser moment, not because he regards it as bad, but because he wishes to show his disregard of all law and authority; or one who is so attached to games of chance that he is prepared to steal a large sum rather than give them up.

193. The serious harm that is foreseen as a result of venial sin also changes the malice from slight to serious. Examples: One who jokingly annoys another, knowing that this will provoke grave dissensions; or one who tells small lies to persons who are known for their uncharitable distortions and exaggerations; or one who agrees to take too much strong drink knowing from experience that this invariably leads to serious excess.

194. Mortal sins become venial when that which in itself is a grave offense, becomes light by reason of some change in he object or lack of full consent in the subject.

195. A change in the object makes a mortal sin venial: (a) when that which is grave matter objectively, is apprehended through inculpable, or only venially culpable ignorance as light matter (e.g., when an uninstructed child thinks that a serious calumny is only a venial sin); (b) when a sin whose character is serious but whose matter is divisible is small as to matter (e.g,, to be absent from a small part of the Mass on Sunday); (e) when a law whose obligation is grave will cause more than slight inconvenience in a particular case, and thus becomes of light obligation for that case (e.g., to miss Mass on Sunday because of a difficulty that was not unsurmountable, but yet considerable).

196. Lack of sufficient advertence or of full consent makes a mortal sin venial; (a) when without serious fault one does not advert to a gravely sinful act (e.g., a desire of revenge); (b) when without serious fault one does not know or does not think about the grave malice of what one is doing (e.g., to repeat a story, not knowing or not remembering at the time that it is a serious calumny); (c) when on account of considerable excitement, fear or other disturbance, one gives only partial consent to an act that is mortally sinful (e.g., when one, on being suddenly insulted, replies with a serious imprecation).

197. The Distinction of Sins.—There are three kinds of distinction of sins: (a) sins that differ according to theological species, that is, according as they turn or do not turn the sinner away from God as his Last End. There are only two theological species of sin, viz., mortal and venial; (b) sins that differ according to moral species, that is, according to their essences, or the various kinds of finite good to which they turn the sinner. There are many moral species of sins, for example, infidelity, uncharitableness, etc.; (c) sins that differ according to number, but agree according to moral species (e.g., two distinct acts of uncharitable hatred).

198. The criteria for the specific distinction of sins are two:

(a) that which makes sins to differ specifically is the difference of the objects to which they tend, inasmuch as these created goods are out of harmony in specifically different ways with the standards of morality (e.g., pride and gluttony); (b) that by which we recognize the specific difference of sins is the opposition they have to virtues or laws that are specifically different. Thus, pride is opposed to humility, gluttony to temperance—two different virtues.

199. The following rules assist us in recognizing specific distinctions of sins. (a) Those sins are specifically different which are opposed to virtues that are specifically distinct. Thus, infidelity and despair are different in species, because opposed to faith and hope, which are two distinct species of virtue. (b) Those sins are specifically different that are opposed to specifically different objects of one and the same virtue—that is, to functions of the virtue, or to laws concerning it that have intrinsically different motives. Thus, sins of murder, theft, and false testimony, though opposed to the same virtue of justice, are specifically distinct, since they contravene obligations of that virtue whose purposes are morally distinct. (c) Those sins are specifically different that are opposed in specifically different ways to the same object of the same virtue, one opposing that object by way of excess and the other by way of defect. Thus, miserliness and extravagance are specifically distinct sins, because one falls short of, while the other goes beyond, the golden mean that is found in liberality.

200. Sins are not specifically distinct: (a) when they are opposed to the same virtue in ways that are physically, but not morally, contrary. Thus, sins of omission and sins of commission are physically opposites, but they are not morally so, unless they offend against different moral objects in the ways explained in the preceding paragraph. Hence, to steal and to refuse to pay debts, to take and to keep what belongs to another, are not specifically different sins; whereas to violate two distinct precepts about the same virtue, one a command and the other a prohibition, is to commit two species of sin, one by omission, and the other by commission;

(b) when they are opposed to the same virtue with reference to commands that differ in their lawgivers, but not in their motives. Thus, God, the Church, and the State all forbid theft; but he who steals is not therefore guilty of three sins, for each lawgiver forbids theft from the same intrinsic motive, viz., because it is an injury.

201. One and the same act contains in itself many sins, when it has many malices specifically different. Thus, he who kills his parents violates two commandments relative to the virtue of justice; he who steals from a church is guilty of theft and of sacrilege.

202. Sins that are multiplied numerically within the same species are committed in three ways: (a) by purely internal acts, that is, acts that are completed within the powers of the soul and do not tend to execution in some external act (e.g., unbelief, envy, pride, delight in the thought of sin, etc.); (b) by internal acts that are not completed in the will, but tend to execution in some external act (e.g., the purpose or desire to injure another, to lie, etc.); (c) by external acts that are performed or neglected by the bodily faculties under command of the will (e.g., theft, quarrels, lies, omissions of duty, etc.).

203. Acts may be numerically one or many in two ways.

(a) Physically, there is one act when the agent moves or puts into action a power of the soul or body only once (e.g., to steal from a church). Physically, there are many acts when the agent exercises different operative faculties, or the same one different times (e.g., to put one's hand many times into a money box in order to steal the entire contents).

(b) Morally, there is one act when a single physical act does not contain more than one species of morality, or when several physical acts are united as parts of one whole by reason of the intention of the agent, or the nature of the acts themselves. For example, the wish to steal is morally one act. The intention to steal, the decision to use certain means to accomplish this intention, the various attempts made, and finally the carrying out of the plan—all these form morally but one act, since the acts that follow are only the development of the original intention. Similarly, several curses hurled at another form morally one act, if all are uttered under the influence of the same passion of anger. Finally, acts of spying on another, of entering his house without permission, and of taking his property unlawfully, are morally one act, because the first acts are naturally the preparation for what follows.

204. Morally, there are several acts when a single physical act contains several species of malice (as when one steals from a church), or when

John A. McHugh, O.P. and Charles J. Callan, O.P.

there are several physical acts not united by any bond of common purpose or natural subordination (as when one steals on different occasions because an opportunity suddenly presented itself, or as when one misses Mass on different Sundays).

205. Objects of acts may also be numerically one or many in two ways.

(a) Physically, an object is one when it has its own proper individuality different from that of others. Thus, each coin in a pocket-book is physically one thing, each member of a family is physically one person. Objects are physically many, when they include more than one distinct thing or person. Thus, physically a pocket-book contains many objects, as does also a family.

(b) Morally, objects that are physically many become one, if they are not such as to require morally distinct acts in their regard, and if they form according to prudent judgment parts of an integral or collective whole. Otherwise, these objects are morally many. Example: Missing Mass for a whole year constitutes, morally speaking, many objects, since it implies many independent external omissions, or morally distinct acts. A box of ordinary coins, though it contains many individual pieces of money, is commonly regarded as one integral object; and likewise religious, civil, domestic, and financial bodies, though each is made up of many members, are each, morally speaking, but one person. The possessions of different proprietors, however, are not one moral object; neither do the individual, personal rights of the members of one group constitute a single object.

206. It is clear that two sins specifically different in malice are also numerically different (e.g., a sin of theft and a sin of calumny). The rules that follow will pertain only to sins that are of the same species, but that differ numerically within the species (e.g., two distinct sins of theft, two distinct sins of calumny).

207. The rules for the numerical distinction of sins within the same species suppose: (a) that the distinction be not taken from the object, which gives the specific difference, but from the repetition of acts with regard to one object, made either actually (by different acts) or equivalently (by what is equal to different acts); (b) that the distinction

be not taken from a physical but from a moral consideration of the acts.

208. Three rules of numerical distinction will be given, one for each of the three following hypotheses: (a) many distinct acts are concerned with morally distinct objects of the same species; (b) many distinct acts are concerned with what is morally one object; (c) one act is concerned with what are physically many, but morally one object.

209. First Rule of Numerical Distinction.—Many sinful acts, each of which is concerned with an object that is distinct in number (morally speaking) from the objects of the other acts, make as many numerically distinct sins as there are acts and objects numerically distinct. Example: He who fires distinct shots and unjustly kills three persons is guilty of three murders.

210. Second Rule of Numerical Distinction.—Many sinful acts, all of which are concerned with an object that is (morally speaking) one and the same in number, make as many numerically distinct sins as there are acts numerically distinct according to moral estimation.

211. When the acts concerned with the same object are purely internal, they are multiplied numerically, according to moral estimation, in the following cases:

(a) when they are repeated after having been renounced by an act of the will. Example: He who hates in the morning, repents at noon, and returns to his hate in the afternoon, commits two sins of hatred;

(b) when they are repeated after having been voluntarily discontinued, if the interval between the two acts is so considerable that the second act is not a mere continuation of the first. Example: He who in his mind reviles an enemy passing by, then turns his attention to his work and thinks no more about his anger, and later, seeing his enemy again, reviles him mentally a second time, commits two sins;

(c) when they are repeated after having been involuntarily discontinued, if a notable period (say, three hours) intervenes between the two acts. Example: He who thinks thoughts of hatred until he falls asleep, or until he is distracted from them by something unusual going on about him, or by the entrance of a visitor, commits a second sin of hatred, when he returns to the same thoughts, if the interruption was so long that there is no moral connection between the two acts.

212. When acts tending to the same object are internal, but directed towards completion in some external act, they are multiplied numerically, in moral estimation, in the following cases:

(a) when they are repeated after having been renounced. Example: He who decides to steal, but repents for his sin, and then again decides to steal, commits two sins;

(b) when they are repeated after voluntary discontinuance, if the interval is not merely momentary. Example: He who thinks over a plan to acquire money unjustly, and then deliberately turns his thought away and gives all his attention to lawful affairs, but later resumes the dishonest planning, commits a new sin;

(c) when they are repeated after involuntary discontinuance, if the interval is notable in view of the external act desired, and nothing external was done that could serve as a link to unify the two acts. Example: A burglar plans a robbery that could easily be carried out at once, but he takes no steps to execute his plan, and soon forgets about it. A month later, passing the house he had intended to rob, he remembers his plan and carries it out. Two distinct sins were here committed.

213. Involuntary discontinuance does not, however, separate the acts into two distinct sins: (a) if the interval was brief in view of the external act that was desired (e.g., if the burglar above mentioned had forgotten his plan for a few days only before he renewed it and carried it out); (b) if something had already been done by reason of the first act (e.g., if the burglar, after resolving to rob the house, had procured keys or tools for the purpose, and had kept them with this in mind, although he allowed months and years to pass without making any attempt to fulfill his design).

214. When the acts tending to the same object are external, they are multiplied numerically in moral estimation, and make distinct sins as follows: (a) if the internal acts from which they proceed are numerically

distinct sins (e.g., if a burglar attempts to rob a house, but leaves his work unfinished because he becomes conscience-stricken or is interrupted, and later makes another plan and another attempt, there are two sins); (b) if the external acts are of such a kind that no internal intention can make them morally one act, even when one follows directly upon the other (e.g., missing Mass on Sunday and again on the following day, a holyday, makes one guilty of two distinct violations of the law).

215. In the following cases, however, distinct external acts with reference to the same object do not multiply the number of sins: (a) when these acts form a part of one moral whole, and are intended as such by the agent (e.g., one who reads a forbidden book, but divides it into parts, reading only so many pages a day); (b) when these acts have to one another the relation of means to a common end, and they are intended as such by the agent (e.g., various preparations made for robbery).

216. Third Rule of Numerical Distinction.—One sinful act, internal or external, that is concerned with objects that are physically many, but morally one, makes but one sin in number. Example: He who steals a purse that contains ten bills commits one sin; he who calumniates a family of ten persons commits one sin; he who steals what is the common property of three proprietors commits one sin.

217. When the objects are not morally one of themselves, they may become so through the belief of the one who acts, since distinct malices are not incurred except as apprehended (see 588-592). Example: He who tells three different lies against a neighbor (e.g., that he is a thief, a drunkard and a liar), commits one sin of calumny, if he has in mind general injury to reputation, but does not think at the time of the special injuries contained in his calumny. Likewise, he who calumniates before ten persons commits but one sin of calumny, if, being in a passion, he thinks only of the harm he wishes to cause and not of the number of persons who are present.

218. When the objects are morally one, they may become many through the intention of the one who acts. Example: He who calumniates a family of three persons by saying they are all dishonest, commits three

sins, if he intends three distinct injuries (e.g., against the business of one, the religious reputation of another, and the friendship of the third). So also he who steals part of the money in a purse, and later on, having another opportunity, decides to steal the rest, commits two sins.

219. When the objects are not morally one in themselves and cannot be apprehended as such, distinct sins are committed. Example: He who intends to miss Mass all year, foresees at least in a confused way many distinct violations of the law; he who purposes to rob various proprietors foresees at least in a vague way many separate and complete external acts of robbery.

220. Comparison of Sins.—Sins that differ in species differ also in gravity, those being more serious that depart further from the norms of reason and the law of God.

221. Other things being equal, those sins are worse that offend against a more noble object or a more noble virtue. Hence, sins that are directly against God (such as infidelity, despair, and hatred of God) are the most serious of all; while sins against human personality (such as murder) are more serious than those against human rights (such as theft).

222. Of those sins that are opposed to the same virtue, that one is worse which is opposed to the principal inclination of the virtue. Thus, avarice is more foreign to the virtue of liberality than the opposite vice of prodigality; timidity is more contrary to bravery than its opposite rashness.

223. The gravity of a sin is increased in the following ways:

(a) by the circumstances, in so far as they give it a new species of malice (e.g., theft from a church) or increase its malice within the species (e.g., money given prodigally and to those who do not deserve it, or money stolen in a large quantity);

(b) by the greater willingness with which the sin is committed. Hence, those who sin through ignorance or under the excitement of passion are less guilty than those who sin in cold blood;

(c) by the condition of the person offended. Thus, a sin is made worse according as the person offended is nearer to God by reason of his personal holiness or the sacredness of his state or the dignity of his office, or is nearer to the offender himself. Hence, an injury is greater if done to a priest, a public official or one's own family, than if done to another who has not the same claim to honor or justice;

(d) by the condition of the person who sins. Those who are better instructed or otherwise better advantaged, or who are supposed to give good example to others, sin more grievously by reason of their greater ingratitude and of the greater scandal they give, whenever they sin deliberately;

(e) by the evil results that follow from the sin, when these are willed, even indirectly or implicitly, as when one spreads stories that are bound to cause enmities, strifes, and a lowering of ideals (see 96).

224. Spiritual and carnal sins, considered precisely as such, and other things being equal, may be compared from two viewpoints, viz., of malice and of reputation. (a) From the viewpoint of malice, spiritual sins are worse, since, while a carnal sinner is carried away by strong passion and offends directly only his own body, he who commits spiritual sins acts with greater freedom and offends directly against God and his neighbor. Hence, the Pharisees, though they despised the fallen woman, were worse than she, since in the eyes of God their pride, envy, detraction, hypocrisy, etc., were more hateful crimes.

(b) From the viewpoint of reputation, carnal sins are worse, since they liken man more to the beast, and are thus more infamous.

225. In actual experience, carnal sins are frequently more grave than non-carnal sins.

(a) Many carnal sins are not purely carnal, but also contain other malice, and cause directly more injury to God or the neighbor than a non-carnal sin of the same category. Example: Adultery combines both lust and injustice, and is a greater injustice than the non-carnal sin of theft. Rape combines lust and injury, and is more injurious than the non-carnal sin of anger resulting in bodily blows. Lascivious conversation combines impurity and spiritual damage to another, and is more harmful than the non-carnal sin of detracting that other and causing him some temporal injury.

(b) Many carnal sins are accompanied by greater malice or greater scandal, or are followed by greater evils than purely spiritual sins. Example: Sins of impurity or drunkenness, committed habitually and deliberately or by adults, are more malicious than sins of pride or anger committed rarely or without full deliberation, or by children. Drunkenness or licentious language and suspicious intimacies, committed by those from whom good example is expected, do more to undermine religion than sins of impatience or uncharitableness in the same persons. The results of a man's pride (such as ambition, arrogance, luxurious living and deceitfulness) are often less disastrous than the results of his intemperance (such as detraction, immodesty, fights, extravagance, disgrace of family, etc.).

226. Sins different in species rank in the order of gravity, as said above, according to their objects. For, just as diseases are considered more serious when they affect more important vital organs or functions, so sins are more grave when they affect more radical principles of human conduct. The greater the object or end of action that is injured, therefore, the greater is the harm done and the greater the sin committed. Hence: (a) sins committed directly against God are worse than sins committed against creatures, for God is the end of all creatures; (b) sins committed against persons are greater than sins committed against things, for persons are the end of things.

227. Of the sins committed against God, the rank according to gravity is: (a) sins against the personality of God—that is, against the divine nature—such as hatred of God (the greatest of all sins), infidelity, despair; (b) sins against the peculiar possessions of God—that is, His external honor and glory, and those things that belong to Him in a special way, such as the humanity of Christ hypostatically united to the Word, the Sacraments, and things consecrated to God. Such sins are idolatry, superstition, perjury, the sins of those who had Christ crucified, simony, sacrilege, unworthy reception of the Eucharist or other Sacrament, violation of vows, etc.

228. Sins committed against creatures, other things being equal, rank in gravity as follows: (a) Sins against personality are greater than sins against possessions. Example: The sin of murder, which is against personality, is worse than the sin of theft, which is against possessions. (b) Sins against being are greater than sins against wellbeing. Examples: Murder is worse than mutilation, and scandal that causes another to lose his soul is worse than scandal that only diminishes another's goodness; murder and the irreparable scandal take away life, mutilation and the lesser scandal only diminish the perfection of the life that is had. (c) Sins against those who have a greater claim are greater than sins against those who have a less claim. Examples: It is a greater sin to neglect one's own salvation than that of a neighbor; to murder a member of one's own family, a benefactor, or a person distinguished on account of his position or virtue, is a greater crime than to murder a stranger, an enemy, a private individual, or one of bad life. (d) Sins against possessions that are dearer are graver offenses. Examples: It is worse to steal away the peace of a household than to carry off its material treasures; it is worse to rob a man of his good name than to defraud him of his wages.

229. The above rating of sins is based on their natures considered in the abstract, that is, according to the essential relations they have to their own proper objects. It is impossible to consider any other factor when drawing up general rules of comparison; for the circumstances that enter into concrete cases of sin are innumerable, and hence have to be left out of consideration. By reason of these factors other than the object, however, the ranking of sins according to gravity given above may be changed or reversed.

(a) In the act of a greater sin there may be extenuating circumstances, or in the act of a lesser sin aggravating circumstances that change their respective order. Example: Detraction is from its nature worse than theft; but, if the detraction does only small harm and the theft great harm, the theft is worse on account of the circumstances.

(b) In the persons who commit the sins there may be circumstances that change the order of guilt, so that he who commits the greater sin is less guilty. Examples: By his careless handling of a revolver, Balbus unintentionally causes lasting injury to a bystander. Caius without malice aforethought, but enraged by an unexpected insult, strikes a blow that destroys the sight in one eye of his adversary. Titus, angry because he has been dismissed from his employment, revenges himself by defacing a precious work of art. The bodily injuries caused by the first two men are more harmful than the injury to property done by Titus; but they sinned, the one from ignorance and the other from passion, whereas Titus sinned from malice. Hence, while the sins of Balbus and Caius are objectively or materially greater, that of Titus is greater subjectively or formally (i.e., as to guilt).

230. The Subjects of Sin.—By the subjects of sin we understand the powers of the soul in which sin is found. These powers are sometimes called the material causes of sin, just as the objects to which the sins tend are called their formal causes.

231. Just as virtuous habits have their seats in the will (e.g., justice), in the reason (e.g., prudence), and in the sensitive appetites (e.g., fortitude and temperance), so also contrary habits of vice may be found in these same faculties. (a) From the sensitive appetites proceed impulses caused by sense apprehension or bodily states, which, when they are inordinate and voluntary, are sinful (e.g., lust, envy; see 129, on Second Motions). (b) From the reason proceed false judgments caused by vincible ignorance, wrong direction deliberately given to the passions, pleasurable dwelling on inordinate thoughts, etc. (c) From the will proceed consent given to sins of the other powers, desires to commit sin, joy over sin already committed, etc.

232. As was said above (89-93), the external acts of the members of the body have no morality of their own, since they are completely subject to the will. Consequently, there are only three classes of sins, if classification is made according to the faculties from which the sins proceed: (a) sins of sensuality, which were spoken of above when we treated of the passions (177 sqq.); (b) sins of thought; (c) sins of desire and reminiscent approval.

233. Pleasurable dwelling on inordinate thoughts occurs when one deliberately, even though it be only for a moment, turns over in his mind some sinful object, delighting in it as if it were actually present, but not desiring that it be actually done. Example; One who imagines

his neighbor's house burned down, and rejoices at the mental picture, though for interested reasons he does not wish any conflagration in the vicinity.

234. The sinful thoughts just described are not to be confused with thoughts in which the object of the delight is something else than a sinful picture represented in the mind.

Thoughts of this latter kind are: (a) those in which one takes delight in an external act of sin being committed, as when one destroys one's neighbor's property with great internal satisfaction; here the thought forms one sin with the outer act; (b) those in which one delights in the mental image, not as it represents something morally wrong, but as it contains some object of lawful delight. There is a distinction between bad thoughts and thoughts on things that are bad. Examples: A moralist may think with pleasure about theft, not because he approves of it, but because it is a subject he has to know. A person may read detective stories with great interest, not because crime appeals to him, but because the style of the author is good, the details of the plot exciting, the manner of the crime mysterious, etc. There is danger in thoughts of this kind, however, if one indulges in them from mere curiosity, or immoderately, or if sin itself may take an attraction through them.

235. The gravity and species of pleasurable dwelling on inordinate thoughts vary according to the thing thought on (see on Objects, etc., 70 sqq.). (a) If pleasure is taken only in the object represented, the sin has the moral character of that object. Example: He who delights at the thought of theft, is guilty of theft; and if he thinks of a great theft, he is guilty of mortal sin. (b) If pleasure is also taken in the circumstances imaged in the mind, the sin takes on the added malice contained in the circumstances. Example: He who delights over the thought of the robbery of a church, is guilty of mental theft and sacrilege.

236. The following are signs that delight taken in a thought about sinful things is about their sinfulness, and not about some other of their properties: (a) if one thinks about them without any lawful necessity (such as that of study), but through mere curiosity, or without any good reason; (b) if at the same time one loves to think on them frequently

and lingeringly, or shown great satisfaction whenever they are mentioned. Example: One who thinks about injustices for pastime and admires them as great exploits, who idolizes criminals as heroes or martyrs.

237. Sinful joy is an act of the will by which one takes delight in sins already committed by oneself or by others. We must distinguish between sinful joy and joy about things that are sinful.

(a) Sinful joy rejoices over the iniquity contained in past acts, either because it loves that iniquity in itself, or because it loves it as the cause of some gain. Examples: An unjust and revengeful man rejoices when he thinks of the oppression he exercised against some helpless person who had incurred his wrath. A criminal recalls with joy the perjuries by which his helpers secured his escape from justice.

(b) Joy about things that are sinful or consequent on sin rejoices, not that what was done was wicked, but over other circumstances that were good or indifferent. Examples: An employer admires in the conduct of a dishonest employee, not the injustice committed, but the shrewd manner in which the fraud was perpetrated. A bystander is very much amused to witness a fight, not because he likes discord, but because the acts and remarks of the fighters are comical. A man rejoices when he hears that a friend has committed suicide and made him his heir, if the joy is confined to the second part of the news.

238. The moral gravity and species of evil rejoicing has the same character as the past sins that are its object (see 70 sqq.). For to rejoice over sin is to approve of it, and therefore to be guilty of it in will. Example: A prisoner who, to overcome melancholy, thinks over the times he became intoxicated in the past, is guilty again of those sins, with their number and circumstances adverted to.

239. What has been said about evil rejoicing applies likewise: (a) to boasting over sin committed, because this implies complacency in the sin; (b) to sorrow over sin omitted, because this means that one approves of sin rather than virtue.

240. To be sorry because one performed good that was not obligatory is not sinful of itself, but it may become so by reason of the evil motive

of the sorrow, or of the danger of sin. Examples: If a person is sorry that he performed many unnecessary devotional exercises, because he injured his health thereby, his sorrow is not sinful. If he grieves over this because he now dislikes religion, his sorrow is made bad by his evil motive. If he regrets that he married, this is sinful if it leads him to neglect the duties of his state and commit injustice.

241. Evil desires are acts of the will by which one deliberately intends to commit sin in the future. They are of two kinds, viz., absolute and conditional: (a) absolute or efficacious desires are those in which the mind is fully made up to carry out the evil design, come what may; (b) conditional or inefficacious desires are those in which the purpose to commit sin hinges upon the fulfillment of some event or circumstance that is explicitly or implicitly willed.

242. Absolute evil desires have the same moral gravity and species as that to which they tend (i.e., they take their character from the object, end and circumstances). Example: He who plans to steal a large sum from a benefactor in order to be able to live in idleness and dissipation, sins gravely against justice, and is also guilty of ingratitude and intemperance, for he has committed all these sins in his heart.

243. Conditional evil desires, if they are indeliberate and express rather the propensity of nature than the considered will of him who makes them, are not formally sinful. Examples: A poor man who unthinkingly wishes that stealing were lawful; a sufferer who under the influence of pain wishes that the Almighty had not forbidden suicide.

244. Conditional desires, if made deliberately, are of two kinds. (a) There are some desires in which the condition willed (e.g., if this were not a sin, if this were lawful, if this were allowed by God, etc.) takes away the malice of the act desired, since some laws may be dispensed or changed. Examples: "Would that God had not pronounced against taking the property of others!" "I would stay away from church, if this were not Sunday." Desires of this kind are not sinful on account of their object, which is not really wished, but on account of their end, or their lack of useful purpose, and of the danger that the conditional may become absolute. (b) There are other desires in which the condition does not take away the malice of what is desired, either because the

condition is not at all concerned with the malice, or because it wishes something to become lawful which even God cannot make lawful. Examples: "I would steal, if this could be done safely." "I would blaspheme, if God permitted." These desires partake of the malice of the things that are wished.

245. Just as we distinguished above between bad thoughts and thoughts on things that are bad, so may we distinguish between bad desires and desires of what is bad. For bad desires that are not mere velleities are sinful, as we have just seen; whereas the desire of what is physically evil is good, if the evil is wished, not for its own sake, but for the sake of some greater good. Example: To desire out of hatred that a neighbor lose his arm is a bad desire and sinful; but if one wished this as a means to save the neighbor's life, while he still desires something evil, it is not the evil but the benefit that is intended, and hence the desire itself is not bad.

246. The Causes of Sin.—The causes of sin are partly internal (i.e., those which are in man himself) and partly external (i.e., those which are without).

247. The internal causes of sin are: (a) ignorance in the intellect; (b) passion in the sensitive appetites; (c) malice in the will.

248. Since ignorance and passion may render an act involuntary (see 40 sqq.), the sins that result from them are of two kinds, viz., material and formal. (a) Material or objective sins are transgressions of the law that are involuntary, and consequently not imputable as faults. Examples: Blasphemies uttered by one who is delirious or hypnotized; breaking of the fast by one who is inculpably ignorant of the law; imprecations pronounced by a person out of his mind through fear. (b) Formal or subjective sins are transgressions of the law that are voluntary, and hence imputable as faults. They are not only against the law, as is the case with material sins, but they are also against conscience.

249. Ignorance, passion and malice cause sin as follows:

(a) Every sin results from practical error (i.e., from a wrong decision as to what one should do here and now), for the will chooses wrong only after the intellect has decided on wrong. In this sense, then, it is said that all who sin are in error (Prov,, xiv. 22), and that every sinner is in ignorance (Aristotle, *Nich. Ethics*, Bk. III, c.1, 1110b 27). But not every sin results from speculative error (i.e., from a false notion or judgment about the lawfulness of an act in general). else we should have to hold that everyone who sins is in error against the faith;

(b) Speculative ignorance causes formal sin, when the ignorance is culpable and leads to wrongdoing, as when a person has never taken the pains to learn what the law of fast requires and in consequence violates the law, or when an automobilist through carelessness does not see a person crossing the street and runs him down. Speculative ignorance causes material sin, when the lack of knowledge is inculpable and leads one to do what one would not otherwise do, as when a child shoots a playmate, not knowing that this is a sin, or a soldier shoots a comrade whom, on account of darkness, he mistook for an enemy spy;

(c) Passion, by clouding the judgment and vehemently inciting the will, leads one to act against one's better knowledge and to choose inordinately the concupiscences of pleasure, or possessions, or glory (I John, ii. 16). If the passion is voluntary, the resulting sin is formal; but, if the passion is involuntary and takes away the use of reason, the sin caused is material;

(d) Malice is found in a sense in every formal sin, inasmuch as every sin is committed out of choice. But malice in the strict sense, as here understood, is a choice of sin made, not on account of preceding ignorance or passion, but on account of some corrupt disposition of the sinner which makes sin pleasing or acceptable to him, such as a vicious habit or inclination which he cultivates, or willful despair or presumption which he entertains.

250. Ignorance and passion do not always make an act involuntary (see 40 sqq.), and hence three kinds of formal sins may be distinguished according to the three kinds of causes from which they proceed:

(a) sins of weakness, which are those that result from antecedent concupiscence or other passion that lessens without taking away the voluntariness of an act. Since the First Person of the Trinity is especially described by the attribute of almighty power, sins of this kind are sometimes called sins against the Father;

(b) sins of ignorance, which are those that result from antecedent and vincible ignorance. Since wisdom is especially attributed to the Second Person of the Trinity, sins of this kind are called sins against the Son;

(c) sins of malice, which are those that proceed entirely from a free will that is undisturbed by ignorance or passion. Since love is especially ascribed to the Third Person of the Trinity, sins of this class are sometimes called sins against the Holy Ghost. Example: One whose heart is so set on wealth that he decides to sacrifice the friendship of God for new acquisitions; one who sees clearly the offense to God a sin entails, and deliberately chooses it; one who is so jealous of a neighbor that he schemes to ruin him; one who sins habitually without fear or remorse.

251. Other things being equal, sins of malice are graver than sins of weakness and sins of ignorance, since the former are more voluntary, more enduring, and more dangerous. But just as sins of ignorance and sins of weakness may be mortal, as when their object is seriously wrong, so sins of malice may be venial, as when their object is not seriously wrong. A fully deliberate lie that works no great harm is venially sinful, whereas a murder committed by one who was intoxicated or moved by rage is a mortal sin, if there was sufficient reflection.

252. The external causes of sin are: (a) the devil or other evil spirits, who by acting on the imagination or other sensitive powers of the soul attempt to draw mankind to destruction; (b) the world, that is, the persons and things about us, which by their seductiveness, or by their principles and examples, tend to draw away from the practice of virtue.

253. Since free consent is implied in the concept of formal sin, none of the internal or external causes of sin just mentioned, the choice of the will alone excepted, can actually effect sin. Hence the distinction between temptation and sin. The rebellion of the passions, the suggestions of evil spirits, the seductions of the world, are temptations; if the will does not yield to them, there is no sin, but rather virtue and merit.

254. In the presence of temptation fully adverted to, it is not lawful to remain indifferent (neither consenting nor dissenting), since this

without just cause exposes one to the danger (see 258 sqq.) of being overcome by sin.

255. Resistance to temptation is made by the act of the will which commands the other powers not to yield and withholds its own consent to the sin suggested. This resistance may be:

(a) implicit or explicit, according as the dissent is expressed in what contains it, or is expressed in itself. Examples: Contempt of a temptation or displeasure over its presence is implicit resistance, while the resolve never to yield to it is explicit resistance;

(b) internal or external, according as it remains in the will, or is also exercised by the other powers. Examples: Displeasure over an uncharitable thought is internal resistance, while the reading of a book to divert the mind from the thought is external resistance;

(c) indirect or direct, according as the means employed to drive away a temptation are flight or attack. Examples: One who is disturbed by thoughts of hatred, resists them indirectly if he goes to the opera in order to be calmed by music, while he resists them directly, if he reads prayerfully I Cor. xiii, in order to become more charitable;

(d) virtual or actual, according as the act of dissent made, and not retracted, is adverted to or not. Examples: If a man rejects a temptation of envy as soon as he notices it, and repeats this act of rejection until the temptation has disappeared, his resistance is actual; if he rejects the temptation once for all as soon as it appears, but is not able to think of this purpose at each instant, his resistance was actual at the beginning, but virtual afterwards.

256. General rules regarding resistance to temptation: (a) it is a grave sin not to resist temptation, when the sin suggested is grave, the danger of consent serious, and the negligence considerable; otherwise the sin is venial; (b) negligence is considerable when the resistance used is not at all in proportion to the temptation. Example: If a man were suddenly to advert to the fact that a shrewd plan he had decided on was gravely unjust, he would be seriously negligent if he put off recalling the decision till he had dwelt more fully on its appealing features.

257. The kind of resistance to be opposed to temptation depends on the character and urgency of the temptation and the disposition of the person tempted. (a) Generally speaking, the more serious the temptation, the stronger should be the resistance. Example: One who knows from experience that temptations to hatred overcome him, if he uses only internal resistance, should make use of external resistance also. (b) In those cases in which the violence of the temptation increases in proportion to the strength of the resistance, it is better that the resistance be internal, indirect, etc. Examples: Temptations against faith are often overcome more readily by turning the mind away from the doubts suggested to other matters. Temptations that last a long time may be conquered more easily by despising them than by worrying about them and renewing protest after protest. The same is true as regards temptations against purity.

258. Danger of sin is the likelihood that it will be committed in certain circumstances. It is of two kinds, proximate and remote. (a) Danger of sin is proximate, when there is moral certainty that in given circumstances sin will be committed, either because the generality of mankind falls in such cases (absolute danger), or because in them a particular individual has always fallen (relative danger). Examples: Associating with depraved persons is a proximate danger of sin for anyone, since it is a matter of universal experience that evil associations corrupt good morals. Taking strong drink is a proximate danger for one who has never imbibed moderately in the past. (b) Danger of sin is remote, when the likelihood that sin will be committed is not morally certain, and does not exclude a serious and well-founded probability or expectation to the contrary. Example: There is remote danger in an occasional drink, if a person who had several times relapsed into intemperance, has practised abstemiousness for years.

259. Possibility of sin is the conceivability but unlikelihood that it will result from a certain set of circumstances. Example: Attention to business sometimes makes a man avaricious, practices of piety may degenerate into hypocrisy, etc., but there is no natural connection between industry and devotion, on the one hand, and greed and insincerity, on the other hand. Sin follows naturally from its danger, but only accidentally from its possibility.

260. It is not lawful imprudently to expose oneself to the danger of sin, since it is manifestly against reason to risk spiritual loss without cause. The character of the sin of him who does this differs according to circumstances. (a) He who rashly exposes himself to the proximate danger of grave sin, or to what he foresees will become proximate danger, is guilty of grave sin and of the species of sin to which he exposes himself—and this even though the sin does not actually follow. For to love what is so closely related to the sin is to love the sin itself. (b) He who rashly exposes himself to the remote danger of grave sin or to the proximate danger of venial sin is venially guilty. For, while such action is unreasonable, it does not imply affection for grave sin.

261. It is lawful to expose oneself to the danger of sin, if this can be done according to the laws of prudence, for otherwise absurdities would follow (e.g., that urgent duties should not be performed, if one feared they contained the danger of sin). The requirements of prudence referred to are: (a) that the one who exposes himself to the danger of sin be sure that his motive is good (viz., that he firmly intends to avoid the sin to which he may be tempted and to accomplish only the good he desires); (b) that the action he performs and which involves the danger is necessary, and bears a correspondence in importance to the gravity of the sin and the proximity of the risk; (c) that means be employed (e.g., prayer, pious thoughts, spiritual reading, and the use of the Sacraments), which will so reduce the danger that one has confident assurance that the danger will be encountered safely.

262. It is lawful to expose oneself to the possibility of sin, for, since almost every action may be perverted, one who wished to avoid the possibility of sin would have to leave this world and become confirmed in grace.

263. The Occasions of Sin are external circumstances—persons, places or things—which tempt one to sin. Examples: Persons who invite others to defraud and show how it can be accomplished, theatres where irreligious plays are staged, books that aim to depreciate virtue, etc.

264. The occasions of sin are of various kinds. (a) They are proximate or remote, according as it is morally certain, or only likely that they will lead to sin. (b) Occasions are necessary or free, according as one is able

or not able to abandon them without difficulty. For example, one who chooses dishonest persons as his associates is in a free occasion of sin; one who is imprisoned with criminals is in a necessary occasion of sin. An occasion of sin is also necessary when the impossibility of leaving it is not physical, but moral. Examples: A wife who is bound to a provoking husband; a person who cannot give up an employment that offers many temptations, without suffering great temporal or spiritual injury, or without incurring a worse condition. (c) Occasions are present or absent, according as one has the occasion with him or must go to seek it. Examples; Intoxicants kept in his home are a present occasion of sin for a drunkard; atheistic lectures are an absent occasion of sin for one who has to go out to hear them.

265. It is not lawful to remain in a free occasion of sin,, whether it be present or absent; for to do so is to expose oneself rashly to the danger of sin (see 258 sqq.).

266. It is not lawful for one who is in a necessary occasion of sin to neglect means that are adapted to preserve him from the moral contagion by which he is surrounded; for to neglect spiritual safeguards and protections in such a case is to refuse to resist temptation (see 252 sqq.). The means that should be used depend on circumstances, but prayer and firm resolves to avoid sin should be employed in every case.

267. The gravity of the sin committed by one who freely remains in an occasion of sin, or who does not use the requisite spiritual helps in a necessary occasion, depends on various factors: (a) if the sin to which he is tempted is light, he does not sin gravely; (b) if the sin to which he is tempted is serious, and the occasion is proximate, he sins gravely; (c) if the occasion is remote, he sins venially.

268. The Motives of Sin.—The purposes that lead men to sin can be considered as follows: (a) according to the predominant vices of individual men, which are for them motives for committing their other sins (particular motives)—e.g., a man whose chief sin is unbelief and who is led by it to intolerance, blasphemy, despair, etc.; (b) according to the natural relation to error and sin, and the sensitive appetites tending inordinately towards delights or away from difficulties; (c) the body which had been in subjection to the soul and endowed with freedom

from suffering and mortality, became burdensome to the soul and subject to pain and death.

274. The consequences that are common to all sin, both original and actual, are: (a) the sinner loses the spiritual beauty to which sin is opposed, and this loss is called the stain of sin, since the soul defiles itself by inordinate contact with what it loves; (b) the sinner incurs the debt of punishment, since sin is an injustice against the internal law of reason and against the external law of God and man.

275. The stain of sin is not: (a) a mere privation or absence of grace, for otherwise all sins would be the same; nor (b) a mere passing shadow over the soul, since the bad state of the will can remain after the act of sin.

276. The stain of sin differs according to the sin. (a) The stain of original sin is the privation of original justice (i.e., of the subjection of reason and will to God), as being a voluntary privation through the will of the first parent Adam; (b) the stain of mortal sin is the privation of sanctifying grace, as connoting the act of the individual will through which it was incurred; (c) the stain of venial sin is the privation of the fervor of charity resulting from the sin, inasmuch as it, to some extent, hinders the beauty of interior grace from appearing in external acts.

277. The stain of grave sin is the disfigurement of death, for (a) it removes the principle of supernatural existence (i.e., grace); (b) it takes away the principles of supernatural activity (i.e., the infused habits), though faith and hope may remain; (c) it deprives the soul of the rights that belong to the spiritually living (i.e., of merits already acquired).

278. The stain of venial sin is the disfigurement of disease, for (a) it disposes one for spiritual death (i.e., for mortal sin); (b) it lessens spiritual vitality, by setting up habits that make the practice of the virtues more difficult.

279. The penalty of sin is threefold according to the threefold offense of sin. (a) Inasmuch as sin is against reason, it is punished by remorse of conscience; (b) inasmuch as it is against ecclesiastical, civil or other human law, it is punished by man; (c) inasmuch as it is against divine law, it is punished by God.

280. The punishment of sin is twofold according to its duration. (a) Grave sin, since it deprives of spiritual life and turns man away from his Last End, introduces a radical and, of itself, irreparable disorder, and thus incurs an eternal punishment; those who die in grave sin will be sentenced to eternal punishment. (b) Venial sin does not inflict spiritual death, but is a defect or excess, not as regards the Last End, but as regards the means to the Last End. Thus, it incurs, not an eternal, but a temporal punishment.

281. The punishment of sin is twofold according to its quality. (a) Sin by which man turns away from his Last End is punished by the pain of loss, the deprivation of eternal happiness which was despised. This pain may be called infinite, inasmuch as it is the loss of Infinite Good. (b) Sin, in so far as it is an inordinate turning towards created things, is punished by the pain of sense, which comes through creatures. This pain is finite.

282. Sin may be a punishment of sin: (a) if a later sin results from a former sin (e.g., God may permit those who refuse to serve Him, to become the servants of their passions); (b) if the commission of sin is accompanied by internal or external sufferings (e.g., the jealous indulge their vice at the expense of great mental torment).

283. Not all the afflictions that befall mankind are chastisements. In the strict sense, only those evils are punishments which are inflicted by the lawgiver against the will of the offender as a vindication of justice violated by the personal offense of the latter. Hence we must distinguish punishment from the following: (a) from satisfaction, which is compensation willingly endured for one's own sin, or freely offered for another's (e.g., David after his repentance performed penance for his sins; Christ on the cross offered His satisfaction for the human race); (b) from medicinal afflictions, which are intended, not as reparations to injured justice, but as remedies to preserve men against sin or relapse, or to afford them opportunities for progress (e.g., the calamities of Job, the condition of the man born blind, the dolors of the Blessed Virgin, the physical evils Which in this world sometimes happen to subjects as a punishment on their rulers, etc.); (c) from the natural defects of fallen human nature, such as hunger, thirst, disease, etc. These are only indirectly the consequences of original sin, the direct

punishment, from which they follow, being the infirmity and corruption of nature produced by original sin.

Question III
LAW

284. In the previous Question we considered the internal principles of human acts—that is, habits, good and bad, from which they proceed. Now we shall turn to the external principles, good and bad, that move one to one's acts. The external principle that moves to evil is the demon, who tempts us to sin; the external principle that moves to good is God, who instructs us by His law and helps us by His grace to fulfill it. Temptation has been discussed already, and grace belongs to Dogmatic Theology; the next Question to be considered, therefore, is Law.

Art. 1: LAW IN GENERAL

(*Summa Theologica*, I-II, qq. 90-92.)

285. Definition.—Law is an ordinance of the reason for the common good promulgated by him who has authority in the community.

(a) It is an ordinance, that is, a command or prohibition which has obligatory and lasting force. Hence, advice is not a law, because not obligatory; a rule that binds only during the lifetime of the lawgiver or of those who received it is not strictly a law, because not enduring.

(b) It is an ordinance of the reason, since the rule and standard of human acts is reason (see 64 sqq.). Hence, the arbitrary will of a ruler commanding what is against reason would not be law, but rather iniquity.

(c) It is made for the common good, that is, it must tend to promote, directly or indirectly, general happiness, which is the end of society. Hence, the commands of a tyrant which benefit a few at the expense of public peace and prosperity are not truly laws.

(d) It is made by him who has authority, that is, by the person or persons who have the lawmaking power according to the form of government. Hence, the decisions of an advisory body or the decrees of a usurper are not laws.

(e) It is made by the proper authority in a community, that is, as here understood, in a self-sufficing community, which has its own means for attaining its end and is independent in its own order of other societies. Hence, the regulations made by parents for their family are not called laws, since the family is not a self-sufficing society.

(f) It is an ordinance that has been promulgated, that is, brought to the notice of those whom it binds. Hence, a law that has been drawn up but not published as such, is not obligatory even for those who know of its existence. A law becomes obligatory, however, as soon as it has been promulgated, and the presumption then is that the law is known; but he who is inculpably ignorant is not guilty of formal sin if he breaks the law.

286. Division.—According as the immediate lawgiver is God or man, laws are divine or human. Divine laws are threefold: (a) the eternal law is the ordinance of the divine mind which from eternity has directed the motions and actions of all creatures for the common good of the universe; (b) the natural law is the light of man's reason as an impression and reflection of the eternal law; (c) the positive divine law is that which God of His free will has added to the natural law, viz., the Mosaic law under the Old Testament and the law of the Gospel under the New Testament.

287. Human laws are ecclesiastical or civil according to the authority from which they originate.

288. Collision of Laws.—Not infrequently it happens that opposite laws seem to call for fulfillment at the same time, as, when in case of unjust attack it seems that one is bound to defend oneself and bound not to injure the other party. Hence arises a conflict of obligations and rights. But the difficulty is only apparent; for, since God is a just and wise lawgiver, He does not intend either that one should be held to impossibilities, or that a superior obligation should yield to one that is inferior. Hence, the rule in such cases of apparent collision of laws is:

(a) if a person can recognize which of the two obligations is superior, he is bound to follow that one; (b) if he is unable to discover after careful examination which obligation has the greater claim, and must decide at once, he may decide for the law whose observance seems to him safer; or, if he sees no difference as regards safety, he may decide for either as he wishes. If the decision is wrong, the error is involuntary, and hence not imputable as sin.

289. When the contending precepts belong to different categories of law, the higher law must be followed. (a) The natural law has precedence over the positive law, divine or human. For example, the natural law of self-preservation allowed David to eat the loaves of proposition, a thing forbidden by the positive divine law. The same law of self-preservation allows a starving man to take what does not belong to him according to human laws, if it is necessary for his life. The same law of self-preservation excuses one from assisting at Mass, if one is very ill.

(b) The positive divine law has precedence over human law. Example: The command of Christ to his Apostles to preach His Name was to be obeyed rather than the command of the Sanhedrin to the contrary (Acts, v. 19). (c) The ecclesiastical law has precedence over civil law, for the end of the Church is higher than that of the State, and the Church's judgment about the means to her end should prevail.

290. The precedence of ecclesiastical over civil law does not mean that the Church has the right to interfere in matters that belong to the jurisdiction of the State, or that the Church should insist on settling every dispute by its own action alone.

(a) A law on matters purely civil and political made by the Church in opposition to a law of the State would not prevail over the latter, for, as the Church admits, "whatever is to be ranged under the civil and political order is rightly subject to the civil authority" (Leo XIII).

(b) A law on matters directly or indirectly spiritual, made by the Church but not necessary to her end, can be made the subject of negotiation or even of compromise by the Church in order to avoid a conflict of laws; in fact, the Church has shown her willingness to make concessions, where possible, for the common peace and happiness.

291. When contending laws belong to the same category of laws, the more important, or more urgent, or more necessary law prevails.

(a) The law that defends greater goods (those that are spiritual, internal, or common) has precedence over the law that defends lesser goods (the temporal, external, or private). Examples: The natural law that one must save oneself from persecution and death yields to the natural law that one must not blaspheme or deny God, and hence one must prefer to die rather than blaspheme. The law that one may not expose one's life to danger yields to the law that the common welfare must be defended; hence, citizens are obliged to go to war when the nation calls, pastors and physicians to remain at their posts in time of pestilence, disaster, etc.

(b) Obligations of justice have precedence over obligations of charity, for in the former case a stricter right is in question. Example: Titus is keeping $5.00 in order to pay a debt to Caius, who needs the money today; Balbus, who is very poor, asks Titus to give the money to him. Titus should pay Caius.

(c) Negative or prohibitory laws have precedence over affirmative or preceptive laws (see 371). Example: Titus is asked to write out a testimonial stating that he knows that Balbus is honest, competent, etc. Balbus has claims on the help of Titus on account of a promise made in the past; but Titus knows very well that Balbus is not competent, honest, etc. The law forbidding lies prevails here over the law that one keep a promise made.

292. Since rights and duties are correlative—there being a duty that corresponds to every right, and vice versa—and since both are regulated by law, the principles given for the apparent collision of laws can be applied to the apparent collision of rights.

(a) Rights of a higher kind have preference over rights of a lower kind. Therefore, the rights that arise from birth itself, or from the fact that one is a human being (e.g., the right to life), are superior to the rights that are acquired through some condition, such as inheritance or contract (e.g., the right to property, etc.). Example: Titus must get his child, who is in danger of death, to a hospital without delay. Balbus is getting ready for a pleasure ride, but Titus takes his car since there is no other ready means of getting to the hospital. Titus acts within his natural rights, if the car is returned safely and as soon as possible to the owner. According to civil law his act would be technical larceny, but in view of the necessity courts and juries would certainly not insist on the letter of the law.

(b) Inalienable rights (i.e., those which one may not renounce, because they are also duties), such as the right to serve God, the right to live, etc., are superior to alienable rights (i.e., those which one may renounce), such as the right to marry, the right to own property, etc. Example: One may surrender the right to drink intoxicants in order to serve God or preserve one's life.

293. The Basis of All Laws.—Prior to every other law and the ground and principle of all laws is the Eternal Law; for, since this is the plan of Divine Wisdom directing from eternity all acts and movements to their particular ends and to the end of the universe, it follows that all other laws are reflections of the eternal plan and realizations of the divine decree. The Eternal Law differs from other laws in various ways:

(a) as to duration. The Eternal Law existed before anything was made, whereas all other laws begin to exist when they are promulgated;

(b) as to breadth of application. The Eternal Law regulates, not only contingent things (such as actions) but also necessary things (such as that man should have a soul, hands and feet); for all things created, whether they be contingent or necessary, are subject to divine government. Human laws, as is evident, cannot regulate what is necessary (e.g., it would be foolish for them to decree that men must or must not have souls);

(c) as to subjects. The Eternal Law rules, not only rational creatures (i.e., angels and men), but also irrational creatures, such as matter, plants, and animals. The former are ruled through commands, which require that they direct themselves to their End; the latter are ruled through the inclinations given them by God, which move them to the ends He desires them to attain. Human laws cannot regulate the acts of irrational creatures, for these creatures cannot understand a command as such, and man cannot give them natural inclinations (e.g., it would be foolish to make a law for cats against the catching of birds).

294. The laws to be considered in the pages that follow are temporal and moral. Thus: (a) they are laws promulgated at some particular time, either from the beginning of humanity (as is the case with the Natural Law) or later (e.g., the Mosaic Law, the Christian Law, etc,); (b) they are laws regulating, not the necessary (as is the case with metaphysical or mathematical laws), but the contingent; (c) they are laws given, not to the irrational creature (as is the case with physical and biological laws), but to the rational, that it may attain its end through self-government in accordance with law.

Art. 2: THE NATURAL LAW

(*Summa Theologica*, I-II, qq. 93, 94.)

295. Meaning.—The Natural Law is so called for the following reasons: (a) it is received by man, not through special promulgation, but along with his rational nature. Hence, St. Paul says that the Gentiles, who had not received the laws specially promulgated, were a law unto themselves, that is, through their rational nature (Rom., ii. 14); (b) it includes only such precepts as can be known or deduced from the very nature of man, and thus some pagans fulfilled the Law of Moses naturally, i.e., as regards its natural precepts (Rom., ii. 14); (c) it can be known from the natural light of reason without instruction, being a law written on the heart of man (Rom, ii. 15).

The Natural Law is defined theologically as a participation of the Eternal Law in man. Three elements constitute its essence in its integrity: (a) a passive participation of the Eternal Law consisting in man's nature and faculties with their inclinations to their proper acts and ends. This man shares with all creatures. (b) an active participation in the Eternal Law proper to man. This consists in the activity of man's intellect through which he shares in God's providence and government in a special way as one who can rule himself and others. Reason, reflecting upon the natural inclinations and ordering them to their proper acts and ends, formulates (c) a dictate or command of the practical reason. This command constitutes the essence of Natural Law. "Hence the Psalmist after saying (Psalm, IV. 6): *Offer up the sacrifice of justice*, as though some one asked what the works of justice are, adds: *Many say, Who showeth us good things*, in answer to which he says: *The light of thy countenance, O Lord, is signed upon us.* Thus the Psalmist implies that the light of natural reason, whereby we discern what is good and bad, which is the function of the Natural Law, is nothing else than an imprint on us of the divine light. It is therefore evident that the Natural Law is nothing else than the rational creature's participation in the eternal law" (*Summa Theol.* I-II, q. 91, a.2).

296. Relation of the Natural Law to Other Laws.-(a) The Natural Law is inferior to the Eternal Law; for, while the Eternal Law exists in the mind of God, underived from any other law and is regulative of all created things, the Natural Law exists in the mind of man, as a derivation and image of the Eternal Law and a rule for man's acts only. (b) It is superior to Positive Law, for all Positive Law is a deduction from or a determination of Natural Law.

297. Division.—Since Natural Law is the reflection of the eternal plan of Divine Wisdom in the reason of man, we cannot distinguish different species of it according to difference of lawgivers or subjects. The objects regulated are, however, different; and hence we may distinguish various precepts of Natural Law.

(a) According to the difference of persons to whom natural duties are owed, there are natural laws concerning God (e.g., that God must be honored), natural laws concerning self (e.g., that one must not commit suicide), and natural laws concerning the neighbor (e.g., that injustice must not be done).

(b) According to the difference of natural inclinations in man, there are, first, natural laws common to him with all beings (e.g., the law of self-preservation, and hence it is a natural duty of man to take sleep, food, drink, remedies, etc., as necessary for life); secondly, natural laws common to him with all sentient beings or animals (e.g., the law of preservation of the species, and hence it is a natural duty of man to rear and provide for his children); thirdly, natural laws proper to man as a rational being (e.g., the laws that he should cultivate his powers of mind and will, and hence it is a natural duty of man to further religion and education, and to organize into societies and to respect the rights of others).

298. According to their necessity for the primary or the secondary end of a natural inclination, the laws of nature are divided into primary and secondary. (a) The primary end of a natural inclination is the conservation of a natural good; and so it is a primary law of nature that man should take the food, drink, sleep and exercise necessary for life, and that he should avoid poison or other things that cause death. (b) The secondary end of a natural inclination is the betterment of a natural good, or its easier conservation; thus, it is a secondary law of nature that man should use those kinds of food or drink that promote his health, that he should be careful about his diet, practise moderation, etc.

299. Primary and secondary laws of nature are also explained as follows: (a) a primary law is one that expresses the principal purpose of a natural inclination (e.g., social good, that is, the begetting and rearing of children, is the primary law of the married state); (b) the secondary law is one that expresses a less important purpose of a natural inclination. For example, individual good (i.e., companionship, mutual assistance, the practice of virtue and freedom from temptation) is the secondary purpose to be promoted in the married state.

300. Precepts of the Natural Law may be divided also on account of the different relations they have to one another or to our knowledge.

(a) According to the priority they have among themselves, the laws of nature are divided into the first principle and the secondary principles. The first principle, which is general, which depends on no other, and which is the root of all the others, is: "Good must be done, evil omitted." The secondary principles are particular, and they apply this general principle to the natural inclinations of man mentioned above, which reason indicates as ends of action—i.e., as goods to be sought.

(b) According to the priority they have with respect to our knowledge of them, the laws of nature are divided, first, into axiomatic precepts, which are evident and are granted by all (e.g., that good is to be done, that one should follow reason, that one should not do to others what one does not wish done to oneself etc.), and, secondly, into inferred precepts (e.g., that one should not steal from others, as one does not wish others to steal from oneself).

301. The inferred precepts are also of two kinds, namely, general and particular. (a) The general precepts are those that are deduced immediately from the axioms as universal conclusions (e.g., the commandments of the Decalogue, the principle that one should return what one borrowed). (b) The particular precepts are those that are deduced only remotely from the axioms as conclusions about cases in which many particular conditions and circumstances are involved (e.g., many conclusions about contracts, the conclusion that a loan is to be paid in some particular way, at this particular time, etc.).

302. According to the invariability or permanence of their subject-matter, the laws of nature are of two kinds, namely, necessary and contingent. (a) The necessary laws are those whose matter always bears the same relation of essential conformity to or difformity from reason. For example, the command, "Thou shalt not take the name of the Lord in vain," is necessary, because God remains always worthy of honor, and there is no conceivable or possible case in which it could become useful to speak of Him with dishonor. (b) The contingent laws of nature are those whose matter generally, but not always, bears the same essential relation to right reason. For example, the command, "Thou shalt not kill," is contingent, because, though man generally remains worthy of having his life respected by others, there are cases when it might be injurious to the common welfare, and hence to natural law, that an individual be permitted to live, as when he has committed and been convicted of a capital crime.

303. According to the manner in which they oblige, the laws of nature are twofold, namely, absolute and relative. (a) Absolute laws are those that oblige for every case and condition, because the matter with which they are concerned is intrinsically good or bad in every instance (e.g., the laws forbidding marriage between parent and child, the law against polyandry). (b) Relative laws of nature are those that oblige except in case of a most grave public necessity, because the matter with which they are concerned is generally and of its very nature becoming or unbecoming (e.g., the laws forbidding marriage between brother and sister, the law forbidding polygamy).

304. According to the manner in which the obligation is contracted, laws of nature are of two kinds, viz., those whose obligatory force

depends entirely on the nature of things (e.g., the law that God must be honored), and those whose obligatory force depends upon, an act of the will of man freely undertaking an obligation, which the nature of things then demands that he fulfill (e.g., the laws that those who have made vows, oaths, contracts, etc., should live up to that which they have freely promised).

305. Properties.—Since the Natural Law is the reflection of God's Eternal Law impressed on the rational nature of man, it has the following properties: (a) it is both declarative and imperative; being immanent in man, it declares to him his duty; being transcendent in its origin, it speaks with the voice of authority; (b) it is universal, or for all, for it declares the necessities of nature, which are the same in all men; (c) it is unchangeable, that is, it admits of neither abrogation, nor dispensation, nor emendatory interpretation, for the essences of things, on which it is based, do not change; (d) it is recognizable and indelible, that is, it cannot fail to be known and cannot be forgotten by mankind, for it is promulgated through the light of reason given to man.

306. The Natural Law is of universal obligation. It is in force in all places, at all times, and for all persons. (a) Thus, those who have not the use of reason, such as infants and the insane, are subject to the Natural Law on account of their human nature which is injured by any transgression of its inclinations. Their ignorance, of course, excuses them from formal sin (see 24 sqq., 97 sqq.). Example: It is sinful to induce or permit children to blaspheme or become intoxicated, not only because of scandal or of harm done to them, but also because such things are necessarily repugnant to their dignity as human beings. (b) those who have the use of reason are subject to the Natural Law, and their transgressions are imputable as formal sins and incur the debt of punishment.

307. The Natural Law is unchangeable, not as regards additions, but as regards subtractions. (a) Additions may be made to the Natural Law, for, in many points not determined by it, it is well that supplementary regulations be made to provide for particular situations. These additions, made by Positive Law, divine and human, are amplifications rather than changes, for they must not be out of harmony with Natural Law. (b) Subtractions may not be made from the Natural Law—that is,

there can be no exception when it declares that a certain thing must always be observed, and there can be no abrogation when it declares that a certain thing must be observed usually.

308. From the foregoing it follows that no precept of the Natural Law can be abrogated—that is, repealed and deprived of all force, so that what was today a precept of nature should no longer be such tomorrow; for the necessities of nature on which the Natural Law is based do not change.

309. As to the question whether any precepts of the Natural Law may be dispensed or not, distinction must be made between two kinds of dispensation.

(a) A dispensation in the strict sense is granted when a legislator relaxes for a particular case the obligation of a law, although the subject-matter of the law still remains. Example: Titus is in the class of those who are bound by the law of fast, but he is exempted by competent authority from the obligation of the law.

(b) A dispensation in the wide sense is granted when the subject-matter of the law is taken away by the legislator himself or by another, so that it ceases to be comprehended under the law, although the obligation of the law still remains. Example: Balbus owed money to Caius, but, as Caius forgave him the debt, he is no longer in the class of those who are bound by law as debtors to Caius; he is not exempted, however, from the obligation of the general law that one must pay one's debts.

310. There are various opinions as to the possibility of a dispensation from the Natural Law granted by God, but the following doctrine seems the most probable.

(a) God Himself cannot dispense in any way from those precepts whose matter is necessary (see 302), such as axiomatic precepts (viz., those that prohibit malice and those that command duties to be fulfilled at a proper time and place). For all the subject-matter of these precepts is intrinsically either consonant with or dissonant from right reason. Example: God could not by decree abolish the Ten Commandments, for, as long as God is God, He must remain worthy of worship, praise and love; and, as long as man is man, it must be against his rational nature to murder, steal, lie. etc.

(b) God cannot grant a dispensation in the strict sense from those precepts of the Natural Law whose matter is contingent, such as the precepts against the taking of human life, against taking possessions from others against their will, etc. For, as long as the subject-matter of these precepts remains what it is supposed to be by the law, transgression of them is necessarily opposed to reason. Example: God cannot command the killing of a person who has the right to life, nor the taking of property that rightly belongs to another.

(c) God can grant a dispensation in the wide sense from contingent precepts of the Natural Law—that is, He can make a change as regards the subject-matter, so that it no longer falls under the law. Thus, since God is the supreme Lord of life and property, He can without injury to human rights command that a person be put to death or deprived of his property by another. These acts would not constitute murder (i.e., unjust homicide) or stealing (i.e., unlawful taking); for God has a higher claim on life and possessions than the immediate owners have. Examples: The command to Abraham to kill his son was not a dispensation from the law against murder any more than the sending of death to the first-born of Egypt was the commission of murder by God. The command given the Israelites to carry away with them the goods of the Egyptians was not a dispensation from the law against theft, any more than the destruction of the fruits of the Egyptians by plagues was the commission of theft by God.

311. Is God able to make a decree which sets up a most grave public necessity opposed to the observance of a law of nature?

(a) If there is question of absolute laws (see 303), this cannot be done, for God cannot deny Himself by making a disposition contrary to His Eternal Law. Example: We do not read that God ever sanctioned polyandry or marriage between parent and child, and it seems that He could never permit such things as lawful.

(b) If there is question of relative laws (see 303), the decree in question can be made by God; for the unbecomingness of that which is forbidden by a relative law passes away in the face of a great need.

Example: Since God desired the propagation of the human race from one man and one woman, marriage between brothers and sisters was not against the Natural Law at the beginning. Since God desired the speedy multiplication of the chosen people after the patriarchal era, polygamy was not repugnant to nature among the Jews of that period.

312. Is God able to remove a natural obligation in a case of private necessity, that is, when the fulfillment would be harmful to an individual?

(a) Natural obligations that do not depend upon any free consent of the will given to them (see 304) cannot be removed except by a dispensation widely so-called and when their matter is contingent (as explained in 309-310). Examples: God could not dispense an individual from the duty of confessing Him in order to escape death, for the subject-matter of the law here is necessary. God, could dispense an individual from the obligation of not taking the property of another, for God is the principal owner of all things, including those possessed by others.

(b) Natural obligations that depend upon the act or deed of human beings consenting to obligation (see 304) can be removed. For since human beings cannot know all the circumstances existent, or all the conditions that will arise, it can happen that a thing agreed to or promised is only seemingly good, or will change from good to bad, so that while the promise or agreement made is in itself good and naturally obligatory, its fulfillment would work harm and evil, or be useless, or would prevent the accomplishment of a greater good. It is reasonable, therefore, that God should release from obligation here, thus changing the subject-matter of the law, so that it is no longer comprehended under the law (see 309-310). Example: Titus vows or swears that he will give a certain alms or make a certain pilgrimage; but, when the time for fulfillment arrives, his circumstances have so changed that it would not be advisable for him to keep the promise made. The Church, acting in the name of God, can declare that the subject-matter of this promise has become harmful and is not longer suitable, and hence that the obligation has ceased.

313. Human Authority and Modification of the Natural Law.

(a) Additions to the Natural Law may be made, not only by positive laws of God, but also by human laws of Church or State, through the introduction of that which Natural Law permits, or the determination or confirmation of that which Natural Law contains implicitly or explicitly. Examples: Division of property rights introduced by the law of nations; conditions for valid contracts determined by particular codes; the laws against theft and murder confirmed by definite penalties prescribed for those crimes.

(b) Subtractions from Natural Law cannot be made by any human authority, for God has not delegated His power of dispensing which He has as supreme owner of all things. Examples: No human authority could authorize a father to sacrifice his innocent son, nor permit a servant to carry away the effects that belong to his employer.

314. Apparent Cases of Dispensation from Natural Law made by Human Authority. (a) The Church frees from the obligation of vows, contracts and promissory oaths, from impediments to marriage, from espousals, etc. In so doing, however, she does not dispense from the Natural Law that vows, contracts, etc., should be fulfilled, but only declares in the name of God that the subject-matter of an obligation contracted by act of man's will has become unsuitable for vow, contract, etc., and hence is no longer comprehended under the law.

(b) Societies or private individuals can free from the obligation of paying or returning to them what they have a right to, as when a creditor forgives a debt, or an owner permits a thief to keep what he stole. In so doing, however, they do not dispense from the law of nature that one should pay one's debts and not keep ill-gotten goods; they only change the quality of the things in question so that they cease to be due another or ill-gotten, and hence no longer fall under the law. This differs, too, from the dispensation that God can grant; for He can transfer rights without the consent of the immediate owner (see 310).

315. Interpretation—that is, explanation of the law which indicates whether or not it obliges in a particular case—may be applied to the Natural Law as follows:

(a) Interpretation which explains the intention the lawgiver had in making the law and the sense he gave to the words of the law (verbal interpretation), may be made when either a law itself is not entirely clear, or some person is not clever enough to see its meaning. Example: The commandment, "Thou shalt not kill," needs to be interpreted, for it does not forbid every kind of killing.

(b) Interpretation which explains the intention a lawgiver would have had, had he foreseen a particular case in which his law would be harmful, and which therefore sets the will of the lawgiver against the words of the law (emendatory interpretation, *epieikeia*), may not be applied to the Natural Law; for God, unlike human legislators, foresees things not only in general, but also in particular, and hence there is no room for correction or benign interpretation of natural laws. Example: Titus, who was a chronic invalid, committed suicide in order that his family might be freed from distress. He argued that the Fifth Commandment did not foresee the difficulties of earning a living under modern conditions, and that his sacrifice would be pleasing to God. Titus did not reason well, for suicide is forbidden for motives that apply universally (e.g., that society, and especially one's family, are injured by the act of suicide).

316. Verbal interpretation of the Natural Law is made as follows: (a) by private authority—that is, by those who are competent, on account of learning and prudence, to understand the meaning of the law, such as moral theologians; (b) by public authority—that is, by those who are appointed to rule, with the prerogative of declaring the meaning of the Natural Law. The Pope, since he must feed the flock of Christ, is divinely constituted to interpret Natural Law, and does so authentically and infallibly. Thus, the Church declares that certain matrimonial impediments are natural, and therefore incapable of being dispensed.

On the competence of the Church to give authoritative interpretations of the natural law in the field of morals, Pius XII has spoken clearly and forcefully: ". . . it must openly and firmly be held that the power of the Church has never been limited to the boundaries of strictly religious matters' as they are called; but the whole content of the natural law, its institution, interpretation and application are within its power insofar as its moral element is concerned. For the observation of the natural law, by the ordination of God, is the way by which man must strive to attain his supernatural end. On the road to this supernatural end. it is the

Church that is his leader and guide. This is the way the Apostles acted, and from the earliest times the Church held to this way of acting as it does today—and not in the manner of a private leader and counselor, but from the command and authority of God" (AAS 46 [1954] 671-672).

317. From the foregoing it follows that the Natural Law is so unchangeable that it cannot be abrogated or properly dispensed, or given an emendatory interpretation. But, though the law itself remains, there are cases in which non-observance of it is excused from guilt. These cases can be reduced to physical and moral impossibility.

(a) In cases of physical impossibility (i.e., when the powers requisite for observance are wanting), one is manifestly excused; for law is reasonable, and it is not reasonable to require impossibilities. Examples: Infants are not guilty of sin against the Natural Law, when they do not pray; for they lack the use of reason, which is presupposed by the notion of prayer. He who is unable to work is not obliged to earn support for relatives.

(b) In cases of moral impossibility (i.e., when a law cannot be kept without the infringement of a higher law or the loss of a higher good), one is also excused; for it is unreasonable to prefer the less to the more important. Example: Titus lends a revolver to Balbus. Later he asks that it be returned to him, as he wishes to kill himself. Now, property is less valuable than life, and hence Balbus is unable in this case to observe the law which requires that things borrowed must be returned.

318. Moral impossibility is also defined as the inability to observe the law without serious injury or loss to oneself or a third party. Serious injuries are such as deprive some one of great goods, such as the use of reason, life, knowledge, friendship, health, reputation, property. Serious losses are such as prevent one from obtaining notable goods, The following rules indicate when grave inconvenience excuses, and when it does not excuse, from the guilt arising from the non-observance of Natural Law:

(a) when the law is negative (i.e., prohibitory), no inconvenience excuses from sin; for that which is forbidden by the Natural Law is always morally evil, and hence more to be shunned than even the greatest physical evil, or death. Example: One is obliged, under grave or light sin, as the case may be, to forfeit all temporal goods rather than blaspheme, murder, lie, etc.;

(b) when the law is affirmative (or mandatory), an inconvenience which, all things considered, is really and relatively grave, excuses from sin; for that which is commanded by the Natural Law is not always morally obligatory, but only at the right time and in the right circumstances (see 371), and hence its omission is not always morally evil. Examples: Sempronius vowed that he would go on foot to a place of pilgrimage, but when the day came he had a sprained ankle that would be badly injured if he walked. Caius received a jewel stolen from Balbus and promised that he would return it at once to the owner, but he finds that he cannot do so now without danger, either of the arrest of himself or of the one who took the jewel. Titus sees a person who has been seriously injured lying by the roadside, but he is tired, and neither gives help himself nor summons aid. In the first two cases the inconvenience is grave, and hence Sempronius may ride to the place of pilgrimage, and Caius may return the jewel to Balbus later; but the inconvenience of Titus is slight, and does not excuse him from sin.

319. Just as the Natural Law is unchangeable, because based on the unchangeable Eternal Law instituting the nature of man, so is it easily knowable, because it is promulgated by the light of reason. Hence: (a) invincible ignorance of the entire Natural Law is impossible in any person who has the use of reason; (b) complete forgetfulness of the Natural Law by mankind is impossible.

320. Those who have not the use of reason, either habitually (as children and the insane) or actually (as the intoxicated), may be invincibly ignorant of the Natural Law—for example, they may be unable to perceive even the difference between right and wrong. As to those who have the use of reason, they can be ignorant of the Natural Law only as follows:

(a) they cannot ever be invincibly ignorant of the most general precepts (such as "good is to be done," "evil is to be avoided"), for since they know the difference between right and wrong, they must also perceive that which is contained in the concepts of right and wrong, viz., that the former is something desirable and which ought to be done, the latter something undesirable which must not be done;

(b) one cannot, as a rule, be invincibly ignorant of those precepts that are immediately inferred as necessary conclusions from the most general precepts (such as "that which was borrowed must be returned"), for the conclusion follows so easily from the manifest principle that only in exceptional cases could one be excused for not knowing its truth;

(c) one can, even as a rule, be ignorant of precepts that are inferred as necessary but very remote conclusions from the most general precepts, (such as "that which was borrowed must be returned at such a time or place, or in such a manner or condition"), for this conclusion is so far removed from its premise, and there are so many factors to be considered, that considerable knowledge and skill in reasoning are required for a correct judgment—things in which many people are lacking.

321. The Commandments of the Decalogue follow directly from the most general precepts of the Natural Law, and so to them may be applied what was said in the previous paragraph. Hence: (a) generally speaking, no person who has the use of reason can be invincibly ignorant of the Commandments. St. Paul blames the pagans as inexcusable in various sins committed against the Decalogue; (b) in special cases, a person who has the use of reason can be invincibly ignorant of one or more Commandments; for while the Commandments may be easily inferred by most persons from the common principles of right and wrong, there are sometimes involuntary impediments that hinder the right employment of reason. Thus, children and older persons whose mentality is undeveloped, although they know the difference between right and wrong, are frequently unable to draw the conclusion that follows from it (e.g., that one should not tell lies).

322. The Commandments regarding which invincible ignorance may most easily exist are: (a) those that deal with merely internal acts, for the malice of violating them is less apparent. Hence, many theologians admit that even among Christians the wickedness of sinful thoughts

and desires may be inculpably unknown, at least when the wickedness of the corresponding external acts is also not known; (b) those that deal withthe control of sensuality, for the impulse to inordinate acts is at times most vehement. Unde theologi sunt qui affirmant malitiam peccatorum externorum contra sextum invincibiliter ignorari posse, non solum apud infideles, sed etiam apud Christianos, ita quod ab adolescentibus facile ad tempus ignorari possit malitia mollitiei.

323. If a Commandment be applied to some particular case in which there are many circumstances to be considered, or some reason that appears to change the subject-matter of the law, even adults who have the perfect use of reason may be invincibly ignorant; for in such instances we are considering, not an immediate, but a remote conclusion from the general principles of Natural Law.

(a) If the case is difficult relatively (i.e., in view of the training or lack of education of the person studying it), there can be invincible ignorance, at least for a time. Examples: Jepthe, according to St. Jerome, appears to have been invincibly ignorant that it was not lawful for him to slay his daughter. Being a soldier and living in a rude age, he perhaps did not appreciate the sacredness of human life. Unlettered persons might conceivably think in good faith that it is not wrong to commit perjury in order to help one in danger, to steal in order to pay debts, to think evil if there is no intention to fulfill it, to do what the majority do or what is tolerated, etc.

(b) If the case is difficult absolutely (i.e., in view of the matter itself, which is complicated and obscure), there can be invincible ignorance, even for a long time. Thus, it is so difficult to settle many problems pertaining to justice (i.e., to the application of the Seventh Commandment) that we find professional theologians who take opposite sides, or admit that, speculatively speaking, they do not know where the truth lies.

324. The Natural Law can never be erased from the hearts of men. (a) In abnormal circumstances only, as when the general power of reasoning has been weakened or lost, can the Natural Law be forgotten. Thus, to a degenerate who becomes violently insane murder and other crimes may appear as good acts. But no community could govern itself

by the standards of madmen and long survive. (b) In normal circumstances (i.e., as long as the general power of reasoning remains unimpaired), the Natural Law cannot be forgotten, as far as its general principles or immediate conclusions are concerned, although it may be overlooked or lost sight of when it is applied to particular cases, or when remote conclusions are deduced from it.

325. As long, therefore, as a body of men remain sane, even though they be uncivilized or addicted to crime, they cannot become oblivious of the Natural Law. (a) The general principles ("good is to be done," "evil is to be avoided") cannot vanish from the mind, although, in particular affairs, anger, pleasure, or some other passion may prevent men from thinking about them. Thus, when the mob spirit takes hold of a crowd, it becomes intent only on violence or revenge, and gives no thought to conscience. (b) The secondary precepts, such as those contained in the Decalogue, cannot be obliterated from the mind, although in applying them to concrete situations a people may go astray.

There are many examples of laws, both ancient and modern, which permitted or commanded, for particular cases, things contrary to the current application of natural precepts. Thus, the Spartans and the Romans ordered the murder of infants who were weakly and of slaves whose master had been killed. Some ancient races encouraged robberies committed beyond the boundaries of the states, and savage tribes have been found who had the practice of putting to death parents who were aged or infirm.

326. The causes of wrong applications of the Natural Law are the following:

(a) Some causes are involuntary. Thus, the correct application may be difficult, as when more than one moral principle has to be considered and applied; or, if the case is not difficult, the person who makes the application may be mentally undeveloped, or his mind may be blinded on account of his bad education or environment. Examples: The races who saw no infamy in robbery committed against their neighbors, lived in a wild age when such acts of violence seemed necessary as measures of self-protection. The savage killed his aged parents, because to his untutored mind this seemed an act of mercy.

(b) Some causes are voluntary, such as neglect of the truth, vicious habits, etc. Examples: St. Paul blames the pagans for their idolatry, because they had darkened their own minds about God. Pirates and bandits who came to regard violence as necessary for their own defense were responsible for their state of mind, inasmuch as they had chosen a life of crime.

327. Transgression of Natural Law, therefore, is not imputable as formal sin if it is not voluntary. Hence: (a) lack of knowledge excuses, when ignorance is involuntary (e.g., those who have not the use of reason, as infants and the unconscious; children and others mentally undeveloped who cannot grasp the meaning of some precept; educated persons who are unable to get a right solution of some knotty problem of morals, etc.); (b) lack of consent excuses in whole or in part (as when one acts through fear).

Art. 3: THE POSITIVE DIVINE LAW

(*Summa Theologica*, I-II, qq. 98-108.)

328. Meaning.—The Positive Divine Law is the law added by God to the Natural Law, in order to direct the actions of man to his supernatural End, to assist him to a better observance of the Natural Law, and to perfect that which is wanting in human law.

(a) The Last End of man is not natural, but supernatural (see 20), and hence it was necessary that, in addition to the precepts which guide man towards his natural beatitude, there should be added precepts that will guide him towards his supernatural beatitude: "The Law of the Lord gives wisdom to little ones" (Ps. xviii. 8).

(b) The light of natural reason was sufficient to instruct man in the Natural Law, but through sin that light had become obscured, with the result that evil customs set in, and very many were at a loss how to apply the Natural Law, or applied it wrongly. Hence, it was most suitable that the Natural Law should be summed up in brief commandments and given externally by the authority of God. This was done through the Decalogue, which is a part of the Positive Divine Law of both the Mosaic and the Christian dispensations: "The testimony of the Lord is faithful" (Ps. xviii. 8).

(c) Human laws are the product of fallible human judgment; they can direct only such acts as are external, and they are unable to forbid or punish many evil deeds. Hence, it was necessary that there should be positive divine laws to supply for what is wanting in human law: "The law of the Lord is unspotted, converting souls" (Ps. xviii. 8).

329. The Positive Divine Law differs from the Natural Law as to subject-matter, permanence, and manner of promulgation.

(a) The precepts of the Natural Law are necessary, since they follow as necessary consequences from the nature of man, the precepts of the Positive Law of God, excluding those that are external promulgations of the Natural Law, are not necessary, since they follow from the free decree of God raising man to that which is above his nature.

(b) The precepts of the Natural Law are unchangeable, since the nature of man always remains the same. Of the precepts of the Positive Law of God some were changed, because given only for a time (such as the ceremonial laws of Judaism); others, absolutely speaking, could be changed, because not necessarily connected with the end God has in view (e.g., the laws concerning Sacraments).

(c) The precepts of both kinds of law are immediately from God; but the Natural Law is promulgated only in a general way, through the light of reason given to man along with his nature, while the Positive Law of God is proclaimed by special commands (e.g., "thou shalt not steal").

330. The Positive Divine Law contains two kinds of precepts, viz.,natural and supernatural commandments. (a) The natural precepts were given in order to recall to the minds of men the laws knowable through reason which had become obscured through passion, custom or example. The Commandments given to Moses on the tablets of stone renewed the natural precepts which God had written through reason on the hearts of men. (b) The supernatural precepts were given in order to point out to men the duties their supernatural destiny imposed. Example: The precepts of faith, hope, charity.

331. Division.—There are four historical states of man with reference to his Last End, and to each of these correspond positive divine laws.

(a) The state of Original Innocence is that which existed in Paradise before the Fall. Man had been raised to the supernatural state, and hence he was obliged to the supernatural acts of faith, hope, charity, etc.; he was subject to God, both as to body and soul, and hence he was obliged to offer some kind of external sacrifice; he was sanctified immediately by God, and hence was not bound to the use of any sacraments; but he was still in a state of probation, and was subject to various special regulations, such as the commands to avoid the fruit of a certain tree, to labor in Eden, etc.

(b) The state of the Law of Nature is that which existed from the Fall to the giving of the written law through Moses. It is called the state of the Law of Nature, not in the sense that there were no supernatural precepts then in force, but in the sense that there were as yet no written precepts. In that period man knew the Natural Law, not from commandments written on tablets of stone, but from the law of reason inscribed in his heart; he knew the supernatural precepts, not from scriptures given him by God, but from tradition or special divine inspiration. In addition to the inner acts of supernatural worship and faith in the Messiah to come and the outer sacrifices, there were during this state certain rites of purification, or sacraments, by which fallen man was purified from sin. A special precept of the patriarchial times was the prohibition made to Noe against the eating of flesh with blood in it.

(c) The state of the Mosaic Law is that which existed from the giving of the law on Sinai until the giving of the New Testament law by Christ.

(d) The state of the Christian Law, or of the New Law, is that which began with Christ and the Apostles and will continue till the end of the world.

332. The Mosaic Law.—This was the special law of God to the Jews, the people chosen by God as the race from which the Saviour of the world was to come. It has two periods: the period of preparation and the period of the Law.

(a) The period of preparation for the Law began with the Promise or Covenant given to Abraham. A law is not given except to a people (see 285), and, as the peoples of the world at that time had returned to the general corruption that reigned before the Deluge, God chose Abraham to be the father of a new nation in which true religion should be preserved until the Redeemer of the world had come. The rite of circumcision was ordered as a mark of the covenant and a sacrament of remission.

(b) The period of the Law began with the promulgation of the Decalogue on Sinai. The descendants of Abraham had grown into a nation and had been freed from slavery, and they were thus ready to receive a special law. Their history thereafter shows how God trained them according to the pattern of the Mosaic Law and prepared them for the providential mission, which, through the Messiah, should be theirs, of giving to the world the perfect and universal Law of the Gospel.

333. The Excellence of the Mosaic Law.—(a) The Law was good (Rom, vii. 12): it commanded what was according to reason and forbade what was opposed to reason; it had God for its Author and prepared man for the Law of Christ. (b) The Law was imperfect (Heb., vii. 19); it was given for a time when men were spiritually but children and not ready as yet for the teaching and morality of the Gospel; it forbade sin and provided punishments, but the necessary helps for observing it came only from faith in Christ, the Author of the New Law.

334. The Subjects of the Mosaic Law.—(a) The Jewish people were bound by the Mosaic Law. God had chosen Abraham by gratuitous election to be the forefather of the Messiah, and it was by gratuitous election that He gave the Jews a Law which would lend them a special holiness befitting the promises made their race. The Jews, therefore, were bound to more things than other nations, as being the Chosen People; just as clerics are bound to more things than the laity, as being the ministers of God.

(b) The Gentiles were not bound by the laws peculiar to the Mosaic Code, but only by the common precepts, natural and supernatural, that were in force in the state of the Law of Nature. But it was permitted to

Gentiles to become proselytes, that by observing Mosaic rites they might more easily and more perfectly work out their salvation.

335. The Duration of the Mosaic Law.—(a) The Law began when experience had proved that knowledge is not sufficient to make man virtuous, that is, at a time when, in spite of the Natural Law, the peoples were turning to polytheism and vice: "The Law was given on account of transgression" (Gal, iii. 19).

(b) The Law ended when experience had shown that external observance is not sufficient for holiness, that is, at the time when Judaism was degenerating into formalism, putting the letter before the spirit of the Law: "What the Law could not do, God sending His own Son, hath condemned sin in the flesh, that the justification of the Law might be fulfilled in us" (Rom., viii. 3, 4).

336. Deuteronomy, vi. 1, describes the Mosaic Law as precepts, ceremonies and judgments; and the commandments of the Old Testament can be classified according to this threefold division. (a) The moral precepts defined the duties to God and man that arise from the dictates of reason and the Natural Law; (b) the ceremonial prescriptions were determinations of the religious duties to God contained in the moral law, and rules concerning the performance of worship based on the positive ordinance of God; (c) the judgments were determinations of social duties contained in the moral law; they were the civil or political code of the theocratic nation which had its force from the positive ordinance of God.

337. The moral precepts are contained in the Decalogue, which is a sum of the whole Natural Law, inasmuch as the general principles of the Natural Law are implicit therein in their immediate conclusions, while the remote conclusions are virtually found in the Commandments as in their principles (see 301).

338. The Decalogue expresses man's duties: (a) towards God, viz., loyalty (First Commandment), reverence (Second), service (Third)—all of which are Laws of the First Table; (b) towards parents (Fourth), and all fellow-men, viz., that no injustice be done them by sins of deed (Fifth, Sixth, Seventh), of mouth (Eighth), or of heart (Ninth, Tenth)—all of which are Laws of the Second Table.

339. The further moral precepts which were added after the giving of the Decalogue can all be reduced to one or the other of the Ten Commandments. Examples: The prohibition against fortune-telling belongs to the First; the prohibition against perjury and false teaching, to the Second; the commandment to honor the aged, to the Fourth; the prohibition against detraction, to the Eighth.

340. The ceremonial laws, which prescribed the manner of performing the divine worship or of acting as befitted the Chosen People, and which prefigured the worship and people of the New Testament, were numerous, in order that the Jews might be more easily preserved from pagan rites and customs. The ceremonies they regulated were of four kinds: (a) the sacrifices through which God was worshipped and through which the sacrifice of Christ was prefigured (e.g., the holocausts, peace-offerings, sin-offerings); (b) the sacred times and places, things and persons set apart in order to give more dignity to divine worship and to foreshadow more distinctly the good things to come; (c) the sacraments by which the people or sacred ministers were consecrated to the worship of God and were made to prefigure Christ (e.g., circumcision and the consecration of Levites); (d) the customs which regulated the details of life so that both priests and people might act as became their special calling, and might be types and figures of the Christian people (e.g., the laws about food, dress, etc.).

341. Unlike the moral laws, which had existed before Moses as the Natural Law and which continue under the Christian dispensation, the ceremonial laws were temporary. Thus: (a) before Moses other ceremonies were observed by the patriarchs (e.g., the sacrifice of Abel, the altars of Abraham and Jacob, the priesthood of Melchisedech, etc.); (b) after the coming of Christ, distinctions of food, new moons, sabbaths, and other Mosaic ceremonies were abrogated, since the figures of future things had been superseded by rites that commemorated benefits that were present.

342. We may distinguish four periods in the history of the Mosaic ceremonial law: (a) from Moses until Christ, it was the divinely ordained manner of worshipping God, and was obligatory for the Chosen People; (b) at the death of Christ, when the New Testament began, the Mosaic ceremonial ceased to be obligatory; (c) until the Gospel had

been sufficiently promulgated (i.e., until the destruction of the City and the Temple of Jerusalem), the ceremonial law was permitted to Jewish converts, not as prefiguring Christ, but as a form of divine worship; (d) after the Gospel had been sufficiently proclaimed, it was no longer lawful to conform to the Mosaic observances.

343. The judgments or judicial laws of the Old Testament were intended; (a) to regulate the relations of the people of God to one another and to strangers according to justice and equity, and thus to prepare them for the coming of the Messiah; (b) to be, consequently, in some sort a figure of the social constitution of the Christian people.

344. The judicial laws, like the ceremonial, expired with the New Testament. But since, unlike the ceremonial laws, they were not appointed directly as prefigurative of Christianity, their provisions, if not opposed to Christian law, could be used as part of the civil code of a Christian State.

345. There were four kinds of judicial precepts:

(a) those concerning rulers. The government was monarchical and aristocratic, as being administered by Moses and his successors with the assistance of a body of elders; but it was also democratic, inasmuch as the princes were chosen from the people and by the people;

(b) those concerning citizens. Excellent laws concerning sales, contracts, property, and the administration of justice, are laid down in the Pentateuch;

(c) those concerning foreigners. The relationship of the Jews to other nations, whether in peace or in war, was regulated by wise and humane laws;

(d) those concerning families. The rights and duties of husband and wife, parent and child, master and servant, were carefully and considerately provided for.

346. The Law of the New Testament.—This is the special law given by God through Christ to the whole world, and which endures till the end

of time. Its character will be understood most readily from a comparison of it with the Law of the Old Testament.

(a) In both Testaments grace and the Holy Spirit are given through faith in Christ (the internal law), and doctrines, commandments and ceremonies are prescribed (the external law). But, whereas the Old Testament is principally a law of works, the New Testament is principally a law of faith (Rom., iii, 27); the former is concerned mostly with the external conduct, the latter regulates, not only actions, but also the internal movements of the soul, of which faith is the first.

(b) In both Testaments men are justified and saved through faith and works (Heb, xi., 39; Rom., i. 16), and not through the external written law or the letter. But it is only through Christ, the author of the New Law, that men are enabled to perform what the law requires: "The law was given by Moses; grace and truth came by Jesus Christ" (John, i. 17).

347. Comparison of the Two Testaments from Other Viewpoints.—(a) The aim of both Laws is to secure obedience to God and holiness for man. But the New Testament, since given to those who were better prepared and more perfect, unveils more clearly the mysteries of faith, enjoins more perfect works, and supplements the Commandments with counsels of perfection (cfr. the Sermon on the Mount).

(b) Both Laws make use of threats, promises and persuasion in order to move men to obedience. But, as the Old Law was for those who were spiritually but children, it dwells especially on the punishments to be meted out to transgressors and the external rewards that will be given to the obedient (the law of fear); whereas the New Law, being for those who are spiritually mature, holds out as inducements chiefly the love of virtue and rewards that are internal and spiritual (the law of love).

(c) The author of both laws is God. But, while the Old Law was announced through God's servants as the preparatory dispensation, the New Law was proclaimed by the Son of God Himself as the final economy of human salvation: "God, who at sundry times spoke in times past to the fathers by the prophets, last of all in these days hath spoken to us by His Son, whom He hath appointed heir of all things" (Heb, ii. 1).

348. Differences in the Precepts of the Two Laws.—(a) There is no opposition between the commandments of the two Laws; for the ceremonial and judicial precepts of the Old Law, which contained figure and prophecy, are fulfilled in the precepts of Christ, while the moral laws of the Old Testament are confirmed and perfected by the moral laws of Christ: "I am not come to destroy, but to fulfill" (Matt., v. 17).

(b) There is no substantial difference between the faith and works of the two Testaments. For, that which is now believed explicitly and clearly, was believed implicitly and in figure in the Old Testament, and the greater things that now are commanded were contained germinally in the precepts of the Old Law.

349. The Old and the New Law Compared as to Difficulty.—(a) If we consider the difficulty that arises from the fulfillment of external works, the Old Law was much more difficult. For while the Law of Moses imposed numerous and complicated ceremonies and observances, the Law of Christ commands but few and simple rites. Of the Old Law St. Peter says that it was a yoke, "which neither our fathers nor we have been able to bear" (Acts, xv. 10)—that is, it was extremely burdensome; but of His own Law Christ says: "My yoke is sweet, and My burden light" (Matt, xi. 30). Even the additions made by Christ to the Old Law (e.g., the prohibition against divorce) really facilitate that which the Old Law itself intended—viz., the perfection of man. Hence, the Old Law is the law of servitude; the New Law, the law of liberty.

(b) If we consider the difficulty that arises from internal works, or the dispositions and motives with which precepts are to be fulfilled, the New Law is more difficult; for it inculcates a loftier piety and gives more attention to the spirit with which God is to be worshipped. But, since love is the all-inclusive commandment of Christ, and since gladness and fervor are easy to the lover, the commandments of Christ "are not heavy" (I John, v. 3).

350. The External Works Commended by Christ.—(a) Since the New Law is the law of grace, it commands only those things by which we are brought to grace, or by means of which we make use of grace already received. We receive grace only through Christ, and hence there are

commandments regarding the Sacraments; we make right use of grace by faith that worketh through charity, and hence there are the precepts of the Decalogue to be kept.

(b) Since the New Law is the law of liberty, it does not determine the details of the moral law, nor prescribe minutely how we must worship God and observe justice to others, as was done in the ceremonial and judicial laws of the Old Testament. Minor dispositions of this kind have no necessary relation to internal grace, being morally indifferent. Hence, Christ left many things free, to be determinedlater according to conditions, either by the individual (in personal matters) or by the spiritual or temporal authority (in matters of public concern). It is contrary to the spirit of the Gospel, however, that mankind should be oppressed with numerous and burdensome observances.

351. The Internal Works Commanded by Christ.—In the Sermon on the Mount were given the commandments of the New Law that summarize the entire duty of the Christian as to his internal acts: "Everyone that heareth these My words, and doeth them, shall be likened to a wise man that built his house upon a rock" (Matt., vii. 24). Thus, there are: (a) internal acts commanded as regards our own wills and purposes (we must avoid not only external, but also internal sins and the occasions of sin; we must not only do good, but we must have a good motive, not placing our end in human applause or riches); (b) internal acts commanded as regards our neighbor (we must not judge him rashly, unjustly, presumptuously; nor must we trust him imprudently); (c) interior dispositions with which we must perform our duties (we must avoid inordinate cares, imploring and expecting the divine assistance; but we must also avoid carelessness, having our minds set on the narrow way, and eschewing seductions).

352. The Teaching of Christ on the Three Classes of Precepts: Moral, Ceremonial and Judicial.—(a) As regards the moral precepts (i.e., the Decalogue or Natural Law), not one jot or tittle was to pass away. But so little was the soul of these precepts then recognized that Christ gave a new commandment of love, by which His followers were to be known; and He reduced the whole law to the two commandments of love of God and love of our neighbor.

(b) As regards the ceremonial precepts (i.e., the forms of Jewish worship), these were to be superseded. Christ declared the manner in which God was to be worshipped, namely, in spirit and in truth. He instituted the Sacrifice of the New Testament, appointed the ritual of the Sacraments (e.g., of Baptism and the Eucharist), and taught a form of prayer which was to be used by His disciples. Other things He left to be determined by the Church.

(c) As regards the judicial precepts (i.e., the civil laws of the theocratic nation), these ceased to be necessary with the coming of Christ, whose Kingdom is spiritual and with whom there is no distinction of Jew or Gentile, since His law is for all. In fact, with the destruction of Jerusalem in A.D. 70, foretold by Christ, both the Temple worship and the separate national life of Israel came to an end. In correcting the false interpretations which the Pharisees put upon various judicial precepts of their law (e.g., in showing them that the law of retaliation and the law that public enemies should be put to death did not authorize revenge and hatred), Christ indicated the spirit that should animate all civil laws, namely, love of justice. He left it to the wisdom of future lawgivers to apply the rule of justice to the relations between man and man, nation and nation, as circumstances would require.

353. The precepts by which Christ established the primacy of the Pope and the hierarchy may be called judicial. But the details of this constitution He left the Church to determine.

354. The Duration of the Law of Christ.—(a) The Beginning.—The New Law was given through the revelation made by Christ and the Holy Ghost to the Apostles; it was ratified at the Last Supper and in the death of Christ, when the New Testament was proclaimed and the Old Testament came to an end; it was promulgated, first at Jerusalem on the day of Pentecost, and later throughout the world by the preaching of the Apostles.

(b) The End.—The Law of Christ continues till the end of time; for this generation—that is, this last period of world history under the Christian dispensation—shall not end until Christ returns to judge mankind; "Behold, I am with you all days, even unto the consummation of the world" (Matt., xxviii. 20).

355. The Subjects of the Law of Christ.—(a) The Law of Christ is for all: "Going, therefore, teach ye all nations. teaching them to observe all things whatsoever I have commanded you" (Matt., xxviii. 19).

(b) The Law of Christ does not oblige all in the same way. Those outside Christianity are obliged directly by the commands to believe and to be baptized. Christians are obliged directly by the laws of faith and works accepted in Baptism.

356. Ignorance of the Law of Christ.-(a) Outsiders may be in invincible ignorance of the Law of Christ. For many persons through no fault of their own, in times past or even today, have not heard the Gospel message: "How shall they believe Him of whom they have not heard?" (Rom, x. 14).

(b) Christians may be in invincible ignorance of the Law of Christ. For, just as want of a preacher causes a pagan to be invincibly ignorant of the necessity of Baptism, so a lack of instruction in Christian doctrine might leave a baptized person inculpably ignorant (e.g., of the duty of receiving the Eucharist).

357. Dispensation from the Law of Christ.—(a) Its Possibility.—It cannot be denied that Christ could have dispensed from the positive precepts of His law, either directly or through His Church; for those precepts depend on His will, and, like every other legislator, He can relax His law or delegate others to do so.

(b) Its Reality.—Some believe that Christ granted dispensations from His Law (e.g., that He freed the Blessed Virgin and the Apostles from the duty of receiving Baptism, that he authorized the Apostles to give Baptism without mentioning the Trinity), but these opinions seem unlikely and are not well supported. Some also believe that the power of loosing granted the Church (Matt., xvi. 19) includes the power of dispensing from the Law of Christ. The contrary, however, seems more probable. For the power of loosing is certainly limited to such matters as the good of the Church and of souls requires, and it is more advantageous for the Church and its members that the laws given by Christ Himself should be absolutely unchangeable, in order that the unity of the Church and its dependence on its Founder may be more manifest.

On the other hand, the alternate opinion has solid grounds and arguments, and merits due consideration. Some authors distinguish a twofold law of Christ; (a) absolute, that which obliges immediately and of itself independently of any action of man; e.g., the law concerning the necessity of Baptism or determining bread and wine as the matter of the Eucharist; (b) hypothetic, which presupposes some human action; e.g., the law of the indissolubility of matrimony which urges after man has freely willed to be bound by the laws of matrimony. Similarly, the binding force of vows presupposes the taking of the vow.

As to the absolute law, no human authority may dispense from it. As already indicated, the good of the Church, its unity and stability, seem to demand an unchangeable law. In regard to the hypothetical law, many of the more modern authors assert that the Holy Pontiff can at times dispense. The power of loosing implies a power of dispensing in the Church which has been used in particular cases; e.g., *ratum et non consummatum* matrimony. Moreover, the power to dispense seems extremely useful and almost necessary for the prudent and wise governing of the Church. For, with a change of circumstances an individual might be impeded from doing a greater good because of a preceding act of will; e.g., one might be impeded from embracing the religious life because of a prior vow to remain in the world to assist in Catholic Action (see Fanfani, O.P., *Theol. Moral. Manuale*, Vol. I, n. 134).

358. Interpretation of the Law of Christ.-(a) Private interpretation (*epieikeia* or equity) is used in extraordinary cases, not foreseen by the lawgiver, and it declares that a particular case does not fall under the Law. This kind of interpretation applies only to human laws, since God foresees things not only universally, but also in particular (cfr. on Natural Law, 315). (b) Public interpretation of the Law of Christ is made by the Church, in virtue of the commission: "Teach all things whatsoever I have commanded" (Matt, xxviii. 20).

359. Public Interpretation of the Law of Christ—(a) The Church is able to give a declarative interpretation of the Positive Divine Law—that is, to explain its meaning, to show what cases are comprehended in the law, what cases are not, when one is obliged, when one is excused, etc. Example: The Church interprets the doctrine of Christ on the indissolubility of marriage, explaining when the bond is absolutely

indissoluble, the conditions under which it may sometimes be dissolved, etc.

(b) The Church is able to give determinative interpretation of the Positive Divine Law—that is, to settle in what manner a law must be fulfilled. Examples: Christ gave the command that the Eucharist should be received, but it was the Church that determined when and how often one must receive Communion to comply with the wishes of Christ. Christ instituted only generically the essential rite of some Sacraments, leaving it to the Church to determine the rite more specifically.

360. The Law of Christ and Impossibility.—(a) Impossibility does not excuse from a law, in which an act is necessary not because it is prescribed, but is prescribed because it is a necessary means without which, even if one be not guilty of negligence, salvation cannot be had (necessity of means). Example: Infants who die without Baptism are not held guilty of neglecting the Sacraments, but lack of it deprives them of the supernatural bliss promised by Christ. Only Baptism confers regeneration, and only the regenerated are capable of the vision of God.

(b) Impossibility can excuse from a law in which an act is necessary because it is prescribed, and which therefore makes one guilty of sin, if one willfully neglects it (necessity of precept). Example: An adult who dies without the Eucharist cannot be saved if he was guilty of grave negligence; but he can be saved, if it was not his own fault that he did not receive Holy Communion. The Eucharist increases supernatural life, but inculpable lack of it does not exclude from that life.

361. Impossibility—or what is called impossibility—does not always excuse even from those divine laws which have only the necessity of precept.

(a) Physical impossibility is the lack of power to perform an act; for example, it is physically impossible for a blind man to read. This kind of impossibility, of course, excuses from guilt and punishment. Example: Titus is dying and thinks of the command that he should receive Viaticum. But he is unable to receive Communion without vomiting. Hence, in his case the impossibility excuses from the divine command.

(b) Moral impossibility is the inability to perform an act without serious inconvenience; for example, it is morally impossible for one who has weak eyes to read small print. This kind of impossibility does not excuse, if a greater evil will result from the non-observance of the law than the evil of inconvenience that will result from its observance. Examples: Eleazer would not eat the meats forbidden by the law of Moses, preferring to die rather than give public scandal (II Mach., vii. 18). The command of Christ that pastors minister to their flocks obliges, even if it involves danger of death, when there is a great public necessity (as in time of pestilence) or an urgent private necessity (as when an infant is about to die without Baptism).

362. Moral impossibility excuses from divine laws that have only necessity of precept, if the inconvenience is serious, even when compared to the evil of violating the law; for God does not wish commands freely instituted by His will to oblige more rigorously than the commands of the Natural Law (see 289, 317). Examples: Christ excused David for eating the loaves of proposition (which was forbidden by the law of Moses) on account of urgent necessity. A most grave external inconvenience excuses from the law of integrity of confession (see Vol. II).

363. What is the nature of the Church's action in dissolving the bond of marriages that are not ratified, or not consummated after ratification (see Vol. II), with reference to Christ's law of indissolubility? (a) Some see in this an application of other divine laws that limit the law of indissolubility, and that were enunciated by Christ Himself in His teaching on the supremacy of faith over other bonds, the superiority of virginity to marriage, the power of the Church in loosing, etc. (b) Others see in this an interpretation, declarative or expansive, of the law of indissolubility. (c) Still others regard these dissolutions as a removal of the proper matter of the obligation contracted through the act of the human will (cfr. the Natural Law, 312). The power of loosing would apply here as in the case of vows. Some authors call this removal of matter "annulment of act," "remission of debt," "permission"; while others call it "dispensation" (see 314). Those who consider the dissolution of *ratum non consummatum* matrimony as "dispensation" list the law of indissolubility as hypothetical positive law (see 357).

364. Counsels.—In addition to its precepts (which are obligatory), the New Law contains counsels, which are optional, but which are expressly recommended.

365. A counsel is a moral direction by which one who is willing is advised to prefer a higher to a lower good, in order thereby to tend more efficaciously towards perfection and to merit a greater reward.

(a) A counsel is not something commanded. Example: Our Lord's direction to the disciples on their first mission that they should not carry their sustenance with them was required as a duty that they might learn to trust in Providence. Hence, it was not a counsel.

(b) A counsel is not everything good that is not commanded. Example: Marriage is not commanded to all, but it is not a counsel, since the opposite good, viz., celibacy, is better (I Cor., vii. 38).

366. That which is only counselled as to its actual performance, is commanded as to its acceptance by the will for a case of necessity. Example: Our Lord's direction that good be done to personal enemies does not command that one actually confer favors on them outside of the case of necessity (this is only counselled), but only that one be so charitably inclined that one is ready to help even a personal enemy who is in serious need.

367. The superiority of the counsels may be seen from the attitudes men take to the goods of this world.

(a) Some are taken up entirely with the things of earth, making temporal goods the end of life and the standard of action. These do not keep the Commandments and cannot be saved.

(b) Some use the goods of this world not as ends, but as subordinate to things that are higher. These keep the Commandments and will be saved; but their solicitude about temporal concerns lessens the attention they could give to things of the spirit.

(c) Some renounce entirely the goods of this life, in order to give themselves as completely as possible to the things of God. These observe the counsels, and can more readily attain to holiness and salvation; for, being freed from numerous cares about earthly things, they can devote themselves more easily and earnestly to things that are heavenly.

368. The Three Counsels.—There are many counsels given in the Gospels, but all can be reduced to three, according to the three chief earthly goods that may be surrendered, and the three kinds of temptation that come from those goods.

(a) The counsel of poverty requires that one give up entirely external goods or wealth, from which comes the concupiscence of the eyes: "If thou wilt be perfect, go sell what thou hast, and give to the poor, and thou shalt have treasure in heaven" (Matt, Xix. 21).

(b) The counsel of chastity requires that one renounce entirely carnal goods of pleasure, from which arise the concupiscence of the flesh: "He that giveth his virgin in marriage, doth well; and he that giveth her not, doth better" (I Cor., vii. 38).

(c) The counsel of obedience requires that one deny oneself the good of the soul which is one's own will, from which comes the pride of life: "Come follow Me" (Matt, xix. 21).

369. The counsels can be followed in two ways. (a) They are followed completely, when one accepts them as a rule for one's whole life, as is done by those who embrace the state of perfection in the religious life, taking by vow the three evangelical counsels of poverty, chastity and obedience. (b) They are followed partially when one practises them in particular instances. Examples: A wealthy man who gives to the poor when there is no obligation to do so, practises the counsel of poverty in that case. A person who renounces his own legitimate wishes in some matter, practises the counsel of obedience in that case, as when he confers some favor on one who has offended him, or pardons a debt. Married persons who practise conjugal abstinence for the sake of religion, follow a counsel of chastity (I Cor., vii. 5).

Art. 4: HUMAN LAW

(*Summa Theologica*, I-II, qq. 95-97.)

370. Definition.—Since human perversity often needs a check in regulations that are not expressly contained in the Natural or in the Divine Law, other laws must be made by society, drawn from those higher laws as conclusions or added to them as determinations, in order to meet special circumstances and necessities.

371. Division of Human Laws.-Human laws are variously divided.

(a) According to the difference of legislators, laws are either ecclesiastical or civil.

b) According to their mode of derivation from the Natural Law, laws belong either to the law of nations (*jus gentium*) or to civil law. To the *jus gentium* belong those laws which are derived from the Natural Law as conclusions from premises, e.g., the right to private property without which men cannot live peacefully in society. To civil law belongs whatever is derived from Natural Law by way of positive determination by a legislator; e.g., Natural Law dictates that the evil-doer be punished; but that the punishment take a particular form, imprisonment, exile, death, is a determination depending upon the will of the legislator.

The *jus gentium* is not international law which derives its force and sanction from the free will of the legislator. The law of nations is common to all men and derives its force from the conviction of men that such a law is demanded for the good of mankind. It is not a secondary precept of the Natural Law which is derived from the primary precepts necessarily. Rather it is based upon a contingent set of circumstances; it does not spring from man's nature absolutely considered, but from the way in which man acts and reacts in his society.

(c) According to the difference of their objects, laws are either affirmative (i.e., preceptive) or negative (i.e., prohibitive). An affirmative law obliges always, but not for every occasion; a negative law obliges always, and for every occasion. Example: The Third and Fourth Commandments are always in force, but it is not necessary to elicit a positive act of compliance at every instant. The other Commandments, which are negative, are not only in force always, but it is necessary at every instant to omit what they forbid.

(d) According to the obligation which they impose, laws are either moral, penal, or moral-penal. Moral laws oblige under pain of sin, penal laws under pain of punishment, moral-penal laws under pain of both.

(e) According to their inclusiveness, laws are either personal or territorial. The former affect the person for whom the law is made, and oblige him even when he is outside the territory of the lawgiver. The latter affect the territory, and hence do not oblige a subject when he is outside the territory affected by the law.

(f) According to their effect, prohibitive laws are either merely prohibitive or irritant. The former make what is forbidden illegal, the latter make it also void.

372. Qualities.—The objects or content of human law must be of such a character: (a) that they do not conflict with the Natural or the Divine Law; (b) that they be beneficial to the community for which they are made.

373. Laws fail to be of public benefit in such cases as the following: (a) if they are made without a broad view of the public good, which has regard for different classes of people and various interests, and which provides for the future as well as for the present; (b) if, losing sight of the fact that the majority are not perfect in virtue, the lawgivers require so much that the law falls into contempt, and graver evils result than would have happened otherwise. Hence, it is advisable that human laws confine their prohibitions to graver misdeeds, especially those that are harmful to others and to society, and restrict their commands to such good acts as promote the common weal. Multiplicity of laws, excessive penalties for minor offenses, cruel and unusual sanctions, lead to lawlessness.

374. Human laws should not prescribe what is too difficult.

(a) They should not prescribe heroic virtue, unless the common safety demands it, or a subject has voluntarily obliged himself to it. Example: Soldiers in war and pastors in time of pestilence must expose themselves to danger of death; but for ordinary occasions the law should not oblige one to risk one's life or other great good.

(b) They should not prescribe agreement with the mind of the legislator or a virtuous performance of what is prescribed, unless the thing ordered itself demands this. Examples: The law of annual Confession and of the Easter Communion requires, not only that these Sacraments be received, but that they be received worthily, for an unworthy Confession is no Sacrament, and an unworthy Communion does not satisfy the command of Christ, of which the Church command is but a determination. On the other hand, the Lenten fast observed by one who is not in the state of grace is an act good in itself and satisfies the law. He who hears Mass on a holyday, not knowing that it is a holyday, satisfies the obligation, though he had no intention of fulfilling it.

375. Obligation of Human Laws.—All human laws that are just, whether they be ecclesiastical or civil, made by believers in God or unbelievers, are obligatory in conscience, (a) From the beginning the Church has made laws and imposed them as obligatory (Acts, xv. 29; I Cor., vi. 4; I Cor., xi. 5; I Tim., v. 9-12), and has recognized as obligatory the laws of the State, without regard to the moral or religious qualifications of the rulers (I Peter, ii. 13-16; Rom., xiii. 1-7).

(b) Human laws are necessary. The Natural Law does not prescribe definite penalties, while the Positive Divine Law prescribes only such as are remote and invisible; and hence, if there were no human laws holding out the threat of determined and present punishments, the Divine laws would be contemned. Moreover, since the higher laws are sometimes unknown, or prescribe no time, place or manner of accomplishment, or do not command things that would be useful for their observance, it is necessary that there be laws made by man to secure the better knowledge and fulfillment of the laws given by God Himself.

376. A human law is unjust in two ways:

(a) if opposed to the rights of God. Examples: The command of Pharaoh that the Hebrew male children be murdered (Exod., i. 17), the command of Antiochus that his subjects sacrifice to idols (I Mach., ii. 16-20), the command of the Sanhedrin that the Apostles should cease to preach (Acts, v. 29);

(b) if opposed to the rights of man. This happens in three ways: First, when the purpose of the law is not the common good, as when the lawgiver seeks only his own profit or glory; secondly, when the maker of the law has not the requisite authority; thirdly, when the law itself, although for the common good and made by competent authority, does not distribute burdens equally or reasonably among the people. Examples: Achab and Jezabel, in the affair of the vineyard of Naboth, had in view not the public, but their own private benefit (III Kings,xvi). The sentence of death pronounced on our Lord by the Sanhedrin was illegal, because, among other reasons, the body was not assembled according to law, and hence had no authority to give sentence. The commands given the Israelites by Pharaoh (Exod., v. 18), and to their subjects by Oriental despots (I Kings, viii), were unjust, because the former discriminated against the Israelites, and the latter bore down too heavily on all the people. The former civil laws that prescribed the same penalty of hanging for a slight misdemeanor (such as the theft of a loaf of bread by a boy) as for the capital crimes of piracy or murder, the Stamp Act of George III, and some modern laws that sentence to life imprisonment those who have been four times convicted of slight offenses, are more recent examples of unjust laws.

377. Obedience to unjust laws is not obligatory in the following cases. (a) If a law is opposed to the rights of God, it is not lawful to do what that law commands or permits, nor to omit what it forbids. Examples: If a law permits one to practise polygamy, or commands one to blaspheme religion, one may not use the permission or obey. If a law forbids one to give or receive Baptism, it has no force. (b) If a law is certainly opposed to the rights of man in any of the three ways mentioned in the previous paragraph (376, b), it does not of itself oblige in conscience, since it lacks some essential condition of a true law, and even the consent of the majority or of all does not make it just. However, it may oblige accidentally, on account of the greater evils that would follow on disobedience, such as scandal, civil disturbances, etc. The duty of subjects is to remonstrate against such a law and to work for its repeal.

378. The obligation of all laws is not the same in kind, or degree. (a) Moral laws oblige one to do what is commanded or to omit what is forbidden, as a duty owed in conscience; hence, he who violates a law

of this kind is guilty of moral fault. Penal laws oblige one to follow what they prescribe, if one would be free from guilt before the law and not liable in conscience to the penalty prescribed; hence, he who violates a penal law is guilty of juridical fault, and, if he further illegally resists the penalty, he becomes guilty also of moral fault. (b) Moral laws are not all of the same obligatory force, some of them obliging under grave sin, others under venial sin.

379. The following human laws are recognized as moral laws: (a) ecclesiastical laws, with few exceptions; (b) civil laws that confirm the Eternal or Divine Law, or that pertain directly to the common welfare, such as the laws that determine the duties of public officials, the rights of inheritance, etc.

380. The following human laws are generally regarded as merely penal: (a) ecclesiastical laws which expressly state that their observance is not required under pain of sin (e.g., the statutes of many Religious Orders); (b) civil laws of minor importance, or which the legislator imposes as a purely civil duty (e.g., some traffic regulations).

381. Moral laws oblige under grave sin if the two following conditions are present: (a) if the thing prescribed by the law is of great importance, because of its nature or circumstances; (b) if the lawgiver intended to impose a grave obligation.

382. A matter of light moment cannot be made the object of a law that binds under grave sin, for this would impose an intolerable burden, and would thus be contrary to the common good. What is unimportant in itself, however, may become important on account of its purpose or other circumstance.

383. The intention of the legislator to impose a grave moral obligation is recognized either: (a) from his own declaration, as when a church law is commanded under threat of the divine judgment; or (b) from circumstances that indicate such an intention, such as the gravity of the subject-matter of the law or the kind of penalty it prescribes, the general opinion of authorities, or the common practice of the community.

384. By obliging to the observance of what they command and the avoidance of what they forbid, laws indirectly oblige to what is necessary for such obedience. (a) Hence, the law obliges one to make use of the ordinary means for its fulfillment. Examples: He who has not used ordinary diligence to know the law, sins against the law if he violates its prescriptions. He who eats meat on a day of abstinence, because he neglected to provide himself with other food, is guilty of sin. (b) The law obliges one to use sufficient diligence in removing impediments to its fulfillment or dangers of its violation. Examples: The law of hearing Mass on Sunday obliges one not to stay up so late on Saturday that fulfillment will be impossible. The law of fasting obliges one to avoid dangerous occasions of its violation.

385. Interpretation.—Though laws are carefully framed as to language, doubts about their meaning will often arise—in ordinary cases, because of lack of understanding or changes of conditions, and in extraordinary cases, because from the circumstances the law seems inapplicable. Hence the need of explaining the law, which is done in ordinary cases by interpretation, in extraordinary cases by *epieikeia* (see 411 sqq.).

386. Interpretation is a genuine explanation of the law, that is, one that states the meaning of the words of the law according to the intention the lawgiver had in mind when he chose them. It is of various kinds.

(a) According to the author from whom it proceeds, interpretation is authentic, if it comes from the lawgiver himself or from another authorized by him; it is usual, if it comes from common usage (i.e., from the manner in which the law is customarily observed); it is doctrinal, if it is made by learned men according to the rules of correct exegesis,

(b) According to the effect, interpretation is declarative, if it clears up what was obscure in the law; it is supplementary, if it extends or limits the law, by adding to or subtracting from the cases included under it.

(c) According to the manner in which it is made, interpretation is strict or wide, Strict interpretation gives to a word of law that least inclusive and most proper signification it bears (e.g., it understands "son" to stand for son by birth). Wide interpretation gives to a word a more inclusive and less proper signification (e.g., it understands "son" to stand for son by birth or by adoption).

387. Those Subject to Law.—Only those are morally obliged to observe human law who are subjects of the lawgiver and who have the use of reason. (a) Those who are not subjects in any sense are not bound, for to obligate by law is an act of authority and jurisdiction; (b) those who have not reached the age of reason, or who are habitually insane, are not themselves morally bound, since they are incapable of moral obligation. Of course, they may be restrained as to acts, and their rights may be determined.

388. The lawgiver himself, even though not subject, is held to observe the laws he makes. Thus: (a) if the lawmaking power resides in a legislative assembly, each legislator is subject to the body and hence to its laws; (b) if the lawmaking power is vested in an individual, he is not subject to the coactive force of his own laws, since he cannot punish himself; but he is subject to their directive force, inasmuch as the higher law of nature requires that the superior show good example by observing what he requires of others.

389. Change of Law.—The growth of knowledge and experience, or the change of social circumstances, requires now and then that human laws be improved or adapted to new conditions. But, since laws derive a great part of their influence from custom, they should not be changed unless the break with custom is compensated for by the urgent necessity of the new law, by its manifest advantage, or by the evident iniquity or harmfulness of the old law, In brief, the common good should be the norm by which to decide whether a law should be retained or changed.

390. Constitutional law, as being fundamental and organic, is more immutable than ordinary law. (a) If given to a society established according to the positive ordinance of a superior, it cannot be abrogated or modified by the legislative authority of that society, since this would be contrary to the will of the founder. Hence, the Church has no power to change the fundamental constitution given her by Christ, who prescribed the religious society as established by Him to be necessary. (b) If a constitutional law is given to a society which is

perfect and necessary from the law of nature, such constitution can be modified for extraordinary reasons and in the special ways provided (e.g., by amendments approved by the people).

391. The Law of Custom.—Custom (i.e., a long-continued practice that has acquired binding force) is able to establish a new law or to do away with an old law. For the will of the lawgiver is manifested not only by words, as happens in the written law, but also and more clearly by repeated and continued acts, as happens in the case of the unwritten law of custom. In a democracy it is the consent of the people who follow the custom as law that imposes the obligation; in a monarchy it is the consent of the ruler who permits the custom.

392. With reference to their legal effects, there are three kinds of customs: (a) customs according to the law, which are those that confirm by use an existing law; in this way custom interprets law (see 386); (b) customs beside the law, which are those that introduce a new obligation that is not prescribed by any written law; in this way custom establishes law; (c) customs contrary to law, which are those that remove the obligation of a previous law; in this way custom repeals, at least in part, the law to which it is opposed.

393. Custom has not the power to establish or repeal a law, unless it possesses the requisites of law itself (see 285). Hence arise the following conditions:

(a) Since the exercise of the legislative power requires freedom, customs do not possess legal force unless they have been practised freely. Hence, a custom that has been established by force does not suffice;

(b) Since laws can be made only for perfect societies, customs have not the force of law, unless they are practised by a perfect society, or by a majority of its members who are representative. Hence, a custom observed by a family or by a minority of the voters in a body that has its own jurisprudence has not the status of law;

(c) Since laws must proceed from competent authority, customs do not make or unmake law, unless they have the approval of the ruling power. In a society where the legislative function rests with the people (e.g., in the ancient democracy of Athens), the fact that they follow a custom with the purpose of enacting it into law or of using it against an existing law is sufficient approval. But if the supreme power is not with the multitude, their customs do not obtain the force of legislative acts, unless approved by the constituted authority;

(d) Since law needs to be promulgated, a custom, to have the effect of law, must be practised by public acts through which it becomes known to the people as a whole.

394. Customs that have the other requisite conditions begin to be obligatory or derogatory as soon as the approval of competent authority is had. (a) If the approval is given expressly, the custom has the force of law at once; (b) if it is given tacitly, inasmuch as the lawgiver, knowing the custom and being under no restraint, does not disapprove, the custom has the force of law as soon as tacit consent is recognized by the learned and prudent; (c) if it is given by the law itself, which explicitly accepts reasonable customs, the custom has the force of law when it has lasted for ten years, or other length of time prescribed.

395. If the superior disapproves of a custom or maintains diplomatic silence for fear of greater evils, his consent is withheld, and the custom cannot be deemed as of legal force.

396. There are other conditions necessary that a custom may acquire the force of law. (a) Since a law is an ordinance knowingly imposed by the will of the legislator, a custom does not constitute a law if it is followed through the erroneous conviction that it is already a law, or if there is nothing to indicate a will to make it obligatory. Signs of the intention to raise a custom to the dignity of a law are the punishment of transgressors of the custom, the observance of the custom even at the cost of great inconvenience, the opinion of the good that it should be followed, etc. (b) Since a law cannot prescribe except what is reasonable and for the common good, a practice opposed to the Natural or Divine Law, or expressly reprobated by written law as an abuse, or one that is injurious to the welfare of the community, cannot become unwritten law through custom.

397. There are special conditions in order that a custom may do away with an existing law. (a) A written law is not repealed unless the

legislator wills to take away its obligation, and hence desuetude or a custom contrary to law does not abrogate a law unless it manifests a purpose not to be obligated by what the law prescribes. This it does if the whole people regard a certain law as a dead letter, or feel that circumstances or the common welfare require the opposite of what the law requires, and have no scruple in acting uniformly according to this conviction.

(b) A written law is not repealed, if it is immutable, or if a change would be prejudicial to the common interest; similarly, therefore, a custom cannot abolish a law, unless this law is one that can be abrogated by human acts, and that is not essential to the public good. Hence, customs contrary to the Commandments or to the Law of Christ, customs that are expressly condemned in Canon Law as corruptions, customs that encourage lawlessness or afford occasions of sin, can never do away with a law, no matter how long or by how many they are practised.

398. Those who start a custom contrary to law are sometimes in good faith, and hence are not guilty of disobedience. (a) It may be that they are in ignorance of the law, but have the interpretative will not to be bound by it; (b) it may be that they know the law, but sincerely think that, on account of conditions, it has ceased of itself.

399. Even when a custom has been started in bad faith, it may continue through good faith, and so become not a violation, but an abrogation of the law. Changed conditions may make the law useless or harmful; or the very fact that it is no longer observed may make it too difficult to enforce.

400. Today customs do not so often attain the force of law. Moreover, so difficult is it to know whether any custom has all the qualities necessary for establishing, modifying, or abrogating a law that only an expert is competent to judge in this matter.

401. Dispensation.—Human law has not the immutability of the Divine Law. Hence, not only may it be changed, but it may also be dispensed. Dispensation is a relaxation of the positive law made for a particular case by him who has the competent authority.

(a) It is a relaxation of the law—that is, it takes away the obligation of the law. Thus, it differs from permission, which is fulfillment of what is conditionally allowed by the law.

(b) Dispensation is made for a particular case—that is, it is granted when the provisions of the law, though beneficial to the community as a whole, are not suitable for a particular person or case. Thus, it differs, first, from abrogation and derogation, which remove the obligation of the whole or a part of the law for the entire community; and, secondly, from privilege, which is granted permanently as a private law.

(c) Dispensation is given by competent authority—that is, by the legislator or others who have the lawful power. Thus, it differs from *epieikeia* and private interpretation, which are made by those who have no power to dispense.

(d) Dispensation is a relaxation of the positive law, for since the Natural Law is immutable (see 305), no dispensation can be given from its requirements. Thus, dispensation differs from the official declaration or interpretation of the Natural or Divine Law (see 315).

402. Those who have the power to dispense from a law are the lawgiver and others duly authorized. (a) The lawgiver himself can dispense as follows: in his own laws, since he was able to make them; in the laws of his predecessors, since his authority is equal to theirs; in the laws of his inferiors, since they are his subordinates. (b) Others can dispense who have received from the law, from their superior, or from custom the necessary authority to dispense.

403. Those Who May Be Dispensed from a Law.—(a) Since dispensation is an act of jurisdiction, only those can be dispensed who are in some way subject to the dispenser. Since, however, the jurisdiction used in dispensing does not impose an obligation but grants a favor, it is held that he who has the power to dispense others may also dispense himself, if his power is not restricted. (b) Since dispensation is an act of authority, it may be exercised even in favor of one who is absent, or ignorant of the dispensation or unwilling to accept it. But, since as a rule favors should not be forced, the validity of a dispensation generally depends upon the consent of the one dispensed.

404. The power of dispensing has for its end the common good, and therefore it must be exercised: (a) faith fully, that is, not for reasons of private interest or friendship; (b) prudently, that is with knowledge of the case and with judgment that there are sufficient reasons for dispensation.

405. In order that the reason for a dispensation be sufficient, it is not required that it be so grave as to constitute a physical or moral impossibility of keeping the law, since the obligation of the law ceases in the face of impossibility (see 317, 487), without the need of dispensation. Hence, lesser reasons suffice for dispensation.

406. A dispensation must be granted whenever the law itself or justice requires it. The following cases are usually given: (a) when there exists a reason that requires, according to law, that a dispensation be granted; (b) when the common good, or the spiritual good of an individual, or his protection from some considerable evil, demands the concession of a dispensation.

407. A dispensation may be either granted or denied, when the case does not demand it and the superior after careful investigation is not certain whether the reason is sufficient or insufficient; otherwise, a greater responsibility would rest on the superior than the law can be thought to impose—viz., that of attaining certainty where it cannot easily be had.

408. He who dispenses without a sufficient reason is guilty of the sin of favoritism, and is responsible for the discontent and quarrels that result. He is guilty of grave sin thus: (a) if serious scandal or other inconvenience is caused, even when the dispenser is the lawgiver himself; (b) if the law obliges under grave sin and the dispensation is not granted by the lawgiver, but by an inferior who usurps the right to dispense.

409. The subject of dispensation is guilty of sin: (a) if he asks a dispensation when he knows for certain that there is no sufficient reason for it; (b) if, having been denied a dispensation, even though unjustly, he acts against the law; or if he knowingly makes use of an invalid or expired dispensation.

410. Sufficient reasons for a dispensation can be reduced to two classes: (a) private welfare (e.g., the difficulty of the law for the petitioner, a notable benefit he will receive through the dispensation, etc.); (b) public welfare (e.g., the benefits that are secured to the community, or the evils that are avoided through the dispensation).

411. *Epieikeia.*—Since human laws regulate particular and contingent cases according to what usually happens, and since they must therefore be expressed in general terms, exceptional cases will occur that fall under the law, if we consider only the general wording of its text, but that do not fall under the law, if we consider the purpose of the lawgiver, who never foresaw the exceptional cases and would have made different provision for them, had he foreseen them. In such exceptional cases legalism insists on blind obedience to the law-books, but the higher justice of *epieikeia* or equity calls for obedience to the lawgiver himself as intending the common welfare and fair treatment of the rights of each person.

412. *Epieikeia* may be defined, therefore, as a moderation of the words of the law where in an extraordinary case, on account of their generality, they do not represent the mind of the lawgiver; which moderation must be made in the manner in which the lawgiver himself would have made it, had he thought of the case, or would make it now, were he consulted. Hence, *epieikeia* differs from the various causes that take away the obligation of a law, for it supposes the non-existence of obligation from the beginning and non-comprehension in the law.

Thus: (a) it is not revocation, desuetude, restrictive interpretation, or dispensation; (b) it is not cessation on account of impossibility; (c) it is not presumed permission or self-dispensation.

413. In its use *epieikeia* is at once lawful and dangerous.

(a) It is lawful, for it defends the common good, the judgment of conscience, the rights of individuals from subjection to a written document, and from oppression by the abuse of power;

(b) it is dangerous, for it rests on the judgment of the individual, which is prone to decide in his own favor to the detriment of the common good as well as of self.

414. *Epieikeia* by its very nature imposes certain limits on its use.

(a) It is based on the fact that a certain case is not comprehended in a law, because the legislator did not foresee it.

Hence, *epieikeia* is not applicable to the Divine Law; for the Divine Lawgiver foresaw all cases that could arise, and so excluded all exceptions (see 315). This is clear as regards the Ten Commandments and other precepts of the Natural Law, since they deal with what is intrinsically good or bad, and are unchangeable (see 307). But it applies also to the prescriptions of the Positive Law of God, and apparent cases of *epieikeia*, such as the eating of the loaves of proposition by David (I Kings, xxi. 6), can be explained by the cessation of law or divine dispensation. Examples: One may not excuse certain modern forms of cheating on the plea that they were not thought of when the Decalogue was given. One may not omit Baptism on the ground that Christ Himself would have excused from it, had He foreseen the circumstances.

(b) *Epieikeia* is based on the principle that the words of a law must be subordinated to the common good and justice. Hence, it is not applicable to those laws whose universal observance is demanded by the common good—that is, to irritant laws. Any hardship suffered by an individual through the effect of such laws is small in comparison with the injury that would be done to the common welfare if there were any cases not comprehended in such laws; for irritant laws are the norms for judging the validity of contracts and other acts, and public; security demands that they be uniform and certain. Example: One may not contract marriage with a diriment impediment, on the plea that the Church would not wish the impediments to oblige under the serious inconvenience that exists in one's case.

415. The dangers of *epieikeia* also place limitations on its use.

(a) There is the danger that one may be wrong in judging that the lawgiver did not wish to include a case under his law. If this is not certain, one should investigate to the best of one's ability, and have recourse, if possible, to the legislator or his representative for a declaration or dispensation. It is never lawful to use *epieikeia* without reasonable certainty that the legislator would not wish the law to apply here and now.

(b) There is the danger that one may be in bad faith in deciding that the common good or justice requires the use of *epieikeia*; the motive in reality may be self-interest or escape from obligation, Hence, a person should not use *epieikeia* except in necessity, when he is thrown on his own resources and must decide for himself; and, even then, he must be sure that he acts from sincerity and disinterestedness.

416. Cases in which the use of *epieikeia* is lawful are the following:

(a) Epieikeia in a wide sense—that is, a benign interpretation made by a private individual that a particular case is not comprehended in the intention of the lawgiver, because the latter had not the power to include it—may be used for all cases in which the opposite interpretation would set the law up in opposition to the common welfare or would work injustice to individuals. Example: The law that goods borrowed must be returned to their owners yields to *epieikeia*, if there is question of putting weapons into the hands of one who would use them against the public security or for the commission of murder;

(b) *Epieikeia* in a strict sense—that is, the judgment that a particular case is not included in the intention of the lawgiver, because the latter had not the wish to include it—may be used for all those cases in which the opposite interpretation would suppose in the lawgiver a severity that is not likely. "The rigor of the law may be extreme injustice" (Cicero, *De Officiis*, I, 10). Example: Titus has the opportunity to make a notable sum of money on a Sunday morning, but cannot make use of the opportunity without missing Mass that day. Caius on a fast day feels well, but is tired and will be not a little inconvenienced if he fasts. Both Titus and Caius may use *epieikeia*, for the Church does not wish to be unkind, nor, generally speaking, to have her laws oblige rigorously and for every case.

417. Though all human law is subject to *epieikeia*, the practice of the civil law does not always allow it. (a) Action on individual responsibility makes one guilty of technical violation. Example: Balbus, fearing that his house may be robbed or he himself assaulted, borrows a revolver and practises shooting. He had not time to get the necessary permit, but

argued that necessity knows no law. But, if he is arrested, the court may hold him guilty of violating the law. (b) Action in a court of equity, however, will give relief for cases not provided for in law. Example: One may obtain an order from the court restraining a neighbor from injury, when the law itself gives only the right to recover damages for injury done.

Art. 5: ECCLESIASTICAL LAW

418. The Church, being a perfect and independent society, has the power to make laws for its members in order to promote the common spiritual welfare. These laws are not an encroachment on the liberty of the Gospel, for Christ Himself bestowed on the Church legislative and other governmental powers suitable to her mission. The charter of the legislative authority of the Church is contained in the words of Christ to Peter: "I say to thee that thou art Peter, and upon this rock I will build My Church, and the gates of hell shall not prevail against it. And I will give to thee the keys of the kingdom of heaven. And whatsoever thou shalt bind upon earth, shall be bound also in heaven; and whatsoever thou shalt loose on earth, it shall be loosed also in heaven" (Matt., xvi. 18, 19; see also Matt., xviii. 17; Luke, x. 16).

419. The character of laws made by the Church is as follows:

(a) their purpose is to guide and assist the individual that he may more easily and perfectly fulfill the laws of Christ, and to protect and promote the welfare of the Church as a whole;

(b) their contents generally do not impose what is the height of perfection, but what is the minimum necessary for salvation (see 374);

(e) their number, unlike that of the laws of the Synagogue, is few. There are only six precepts of the Church that bind all the faithful; the other laws of the Church do not all oblige each individual, some being for prelates, some for priests, some for religious, some for judges, etc.;

(d) their obligation is not so strict as that of the laws of the Old Testament, for they are more easily changed or dispensed.

420. General Law of the Church.—The general law of the Church is found in the five books of the Code of Canon Law, promulgated by Benedict XV on May 27, 1917. It applies only to the Latin Church, except in those matters that of their nature affect the Oriental Church as well, and it has been in force from Pentecost Sunday, May 19, 1918.

421. The effects of the Code on the older legislation are as follows:

(a) it retains in their entirety liturgical laws that are not expressly corrected; agreements of the Holy See with various nations, even if they are opposed to the Code; favors, privileges and indults that are not revoked (Canons 2-4);

(b) disciplinary laws of ecclesiastical origin opposed to the Code are to be held as revoked, even if they are particular, unless the contrary is provided. Disciplinary laws of ecclesiastical origin omitted by the Code are retained in force, if they are particular; they are abrogated, if they are general and not contained at least implicitly in the Code; if a general law decreed a penalty, it must be expressly mentioned in the Code to retain force (Canon 6);

(c) customs, universal or particular, opposed to the Code, when expressly disapproved by it, must be corrected, even if immemorial; when they are not expressly disapproved by the Code, they may or may not be continued, as a rule, according as they are immemorial—or one century old—or not (Canon 5).

422. The rules laid down for the interpretation of the Code are as follows: (a) in those parts where the Code agrees with the older legislation, it is to be interpreted by means of the latter; (b) in those parts where it certainly disagrees with the older legislation, it is to be interpreted from its own phraseology (Canon 6).

423. Lawgivers in the Church.—The Pope, as Vicar of Christ and Visible Head of the Church, has supreme legislative power in the Church (Canon 218): "Thou art Peter, and upon this rock I will build My Church ....And I will give to thee the keys of the kingdom of heaven, etc." (Matt., xvi. 18, 19). Thus, the Pope can legislate: (a) for the whole Church, either alone or with the body of the Episcopate subject to him in an Ecumenical Council, either directly or through

Congregations; (b) for any part of the Church, either directly or through representatives. Thus also, by Papal concession, legates may legislate for a place to which they are sent, *Prælati nullius* for a territory over which they are placed, General Chapters for a Religious Order, and the like.

424. The Bishops, "placed by the Holy Ghost to rule the Church of God" (Acts, xx. 28), have legislative power within their own territory, dependently on the Pope (Canon 335). (a) They can make laws, each for his own diocese, either in or out of a synod; (b) when gathered together in council, provincial or plenary, they can legislate for ecclesiastical provinces, or for all the faithful of their country.

425. Subject-Matter of Church Law.—The end of the Church being the glory of God and the salvation of souls, she can legislate concerning all matters that are sacred or that refer, directly or indirectly, to the satisfaction of man or the worship of God (see Leo XIII, Const.*Immortale Dei*, d. 1 Nov. 1885).

(a) The Church can call to mind those things that are already prescribed by the Divine Law, Natural or Positive; and, although she cannot dispense in these laws (see 313-814 and exception as to hypothetical positive law in 357), she can interpret them authoritatively, and can decide when obligations of the Divine Law, that depend upon an act of the human will, cease (see 315-316).

(b) The Church can determine those things that were left undetermined in the Divine Law. Examples: The manner in which the Lord`s Day is to be sanctified, the times and frequency with which the Divine law of Communion is to be fulfilled, the way in which the obligation of fasting is to be complied with, etc.

(c) The Church can make laws in matters that were left free by our Lord whenever this will promote the better observance of His law (e.g., many church laws for the clergy and religious, for the conduct of worship, for administration, etc.).

426. The acts that may be commanded by the Church are of various kinds.

(a) The Church may command acts that are purely external (e.g., fasting) and acts that are partly external and partly internal, that is, those external acts to which, from the nature of things or from law, a special moral act of the intellect or will must be joined (e.g., a true oath, a worthy confession or Communion).

(b) The Church may command acts that are purely internal, that is, acts of the intellect or will that are not necessarily connected with any external act (such as meditation, the intention in applying Mass, ctc.), whenever she is explaining, applying, or determining the Divine Law, or acting in virtue of the power of Christ. Examples: The Pope may define a dogma to be accepted internally. A confessor may impose as penance a pious meditation. The Church prescribes the days when pastors must intend to offer Mass for their people. A religious superior may command a spiritual retreat.

(c) It is more probable that, apart from instances such as those just given, the Church cannot legislate regarding acts that are purely internal. For unlike the divine Legislator, who sees the internal acts of the soul and who can pass judgment on them, the Church cannot read the heart or judge the conscience. Hence, it would appear useless for the Church to give commandments about acts that elude her knowledge, all the more so since the Divine Law has given commands and prohibitions regarding internal acts and no one can escape the judgment of God.

427. Those Bound by General Laws.—The general laws of the Church oblige all and only such persons as are at once subjects of the Church and capable of receiving a law (Canon 12).

(a) By Baptism one becomes a member of the Church, and hence it is the baptized who are subject to ecclesiastical laws; (b) by her laws, the Church commands only human and deliberate acts or omissions, and hence it is only those who can reason that are subject to those laws. (c) Moreover, unless the law expressly rules otherwise, those who, although they have attained the use of reason, have not yet completed their seventh year are not bound by purely ecclesiastical law. Specific exceptions are stated in the law. Thus: (1) Canons 854, §2, and 940, §1, regarding the reception of the sacraments in danger of death, Canon

859, §1, stating the precepts of Easter Communion, and Canon 906, containing the precepts of annual confession, declare that the law in these matters is binding on persons having the use of reason, regardless of the actual completion of the seventh year, The law of fasting in Canon 1254, §2 binds after the completion of the twenty-first year. (2) Canon 1099 explicitly exempts non-Catholics, in their own marriages, from the ecclesiastical form of marriage; also Canon 1070 exempts them from the impediment of disparity of cult. (3) The habitually insane are considered as infants under seven (Canon 88, §3). Accordingly, although they are bound by the Divine Law during lucid moments, they are not usually bound by purely ecclesiastical laws during this period.

428. By the unbaptized are here understood, not only those who have never received Baptism (such as infidels, pagans, Mohammedans, Jews, catechumens), but also those who were baptized invalidly. The divine law of receiving Baptism and entering the Church applies to these persons, but, as long as they are unbaptized, they are not subjects of the Church. Thus: (a) directly they are not obliged by any ecclesiastical law, and hence it is not sinful in itself to ask them to do what is forbidden by such laws (e.g., work on a holyday); (b) indirectly they become subject to ecclesiastical law when they enter into law-governed relations with the baptized who are subject to church law. Example: An unbaptized person who marries a Catholic is married invalidly, unless the law on dispensation has been observed.

429. Baptized non-Catholics include heretics and schismatics. Thus: (a) objectively, these persons are obliged by ecclesiastical laws, unless they are excepted by the law itself, and hence it is not lawful directly to induce them to transgress a Church law (e.g., to eat meat on Friday); (b) subjectively, they are generally excused from formal sin in the non-observance of Church laws, and it is not a sin to co-operate materially in such non-observance (e.g., by giving meat on Friday to a Protestant in good faith who requests it or wishes it).

430. It is held that the Church is more lenient as regards those baptized as non-Catholics, that is, those who were born and brought up in some non-Catholic sect. Thus: (a) laws that have for their object the sanctification of the individual (such as fasting and abstinence, Sunday

Mass, etc.), are not insisted on for them, since this would hurt rather than help their spiritual interests; (b) laws that have for their object the protection of the public welfare (such as the laws regarding mixed marriage), apply also to baptized non-Catholics.

Other authors do not admit this distinction and hold that these non-Catholics are bound by the laws of the Church, since Canon 87 expressly states: By Baptism man is constituted a person in the Church of Christ with all the rights and duties of Christians.

Apostates and excommunicated persons are certainly bound by all ecclesiastical laws.

431. Oriental Catholics are not bound by pontifical laws (Canon 1) except in the following cases: (a) when the matter is dogmatic; (b) when the law implicitly extends to them, since it contains a declaration of natural or divine law; (c) when the law is explicitly extended to them. An example of (a) is Canon 218; of (b) Canon 228,2°; of (c) Canons 622, §4 and 1099, §1, 3°.

432. It is a general rule that all persons baptized, as just explained, are subject to ecclesiastical laws, if they are habitually able to reason; but that they are not subject to those laws, if they are not habitually able to reason.

First Rule.—Persons habitually able to reason are all those who in their normal state are able to understand the difference between right and wrong, that is, the majority of those who have completed seven years of age. Such persons are subject to ecclesiastical laws, even when actually they are unable to reason on account of temporary intoxication, delirium, derangement, unconsciousness, etc. Hence, one who would offer meat on Friday to a person momentarily unbalanced on the plea that his condition excused him from the law, would do wrong; for the state of passing irresponsibility excuses from formal sin (see 249), but not from the law.

Second Rule.—Persons habitually unable to reason are all those who have not yet learned the difference between right and wrong (e.g., infants and idiots), or who have permanently lost all knowledge of right and wrong (e.g., the hopelessly insane). These persons are not bound by ecclesiastical laws, at least not by those that are directive. Hence, in itself it is not wrong to give meat on days of abstinence to such persons, even when they are Catholics.

433. Exceptions to the first rule just given are as follows:

(a) According to Canon Law, the age of reason comes legally when one has completed seven years (Canon 12). If a boy or girl is able to reason before that age, he or she is not obliged by laws that are purely ecclesiastical, although it is advisable that parents accustom their children to the hearing of Mass, to abstinence, etc., as soon as this can be conveniently done. If a child has passed the seventh year and does not appear able to reason, he is not bound by ecclesiastical laws.

(b) According to Canon Law, the age of puberty is fixed for males at the completion of fourteen years of age, for females at the completion of twelve years of age (Canon 88, §2). These who have not attained this age are excused from all penal laws, unless a law expressly states the contrary; for on account of the want of mature judgment they deserve leniency (Canon 2230).

(c) The age of majority in Canon (as in Civil) Law is reached when one has completed twenty-one years (Canon 88, §1). Minors in the exercise of rights are subject to the power of parents or guardians, except where the contrary is declared by the law, as is the case for the reception of the Sacraments and the choice of a religious life (Canon 89). They are not obliged by the law of fast (Canon 1254, §2).

434. There are some exceptions to the second rule given in 432. Thus, those laws of the Church that grant favors or that invalidate acts can apply even to those who are habitually unable to reason (such as infants and the perpetually demented); for laws of this kind are not directive of the acts of subjects.

435. Those Bound by Particular Laws.—The particular laws of the Church oblige all those who are subject to her general laws, and who become subject to the laws of a locality by reason of domicile or personal presence (Canon 13, §2).

436. There are two kinds of domicile. (a) A true domicile or home is acquired in a place in two ways: immediately, when one takes up one's abode there, with the intention of remaining permanently or indefinitely; finally, after ten years, when one has lived there so long, even though there was no intention of remaining permanently (Canon 92, §1). (b) A quasi-domicile or residence is acquired in a place in two ways: immediately, when one takes up one's abode there with the intention of remaining there for at least the greater part of the year; finally, after the greater part of the year, when one has lived there so long (Canon 92, §2).

437. With regard to abode, four classes of persons are distinguished in Canon Law (Canon 91): (a) an inhabitant, who is one that has a domicile in a place and is present there; (b) a resident, who is one that has a quasi-domicile in a place and is present there; (c) a stranger, who is one that is outside the places of his domicile and quasi-domicile; (d) a *vagus* or homeless person, who is one that has no domicile or quasi-domicile anywhere.

438. The rules as regards those who are not strangers are: (a) inhabitants and residents are subject to the diocesan, provincial, and other particular laws of their territory (Canon 13, § 2); (b) the homeless are subject to the local laws of the territory where they are present (Canon 14, § 2).

439. The rules for strangers with reference to general laws (Canon 14, § 1, n. 3) are; (a) a stranger is obliged to follow these laws, if they are observed in the place where he is, even though they are not in force in the place of his domicile or quasi-domicile; (b) a stranger is not obliged to observe general laws, if they are not in force where he is, even though they are in force in the place of his domicile or quasi-domicile. Thus, the general law of abstinence on Friday does not oblige one who is travelling in a place where the law has been suspended, even though he would be obliged by it at home. The traveller would do better, however, to keep to the practice of his home.

440. The rules for strangers with regard to the particular laws of their own domicile or quasi-domicile (Canon 14, § 1, n. 1) are; (a) they are obliged in two cases—first, when those laws are not territorial but

personal and obligatory on them everywhere (as is the case with the statutes of religious superiors), and secondly, when the violation of a territorial law would be harmful in its own territory (as when by fiction of law one must be considered as present on account of the law of residence); (b) they are not obliged in other cases. Thus, if one is travelling on a feast-day that is a diocesan holyday in one's home diocese, but not in the diocese where one is, one is not obliged to hear Mass.

441. The following are the rules for strangers with regard to the particular laws of the place where they are: (a) they are obliged in two cases—first, when natural law itself requires that a territorial law be observed by all, and secondly, when the Church includes strangers among those who are subject to a territorial law; (b) they are not obliged in other cases. Thus, if a person is travelling on a feast-day that is observed as a holyday of obligation both in his home diocese and in the diocese where he is, but not as a general holyday of the Church, he is not obliged to hear Mass; for the law of his home diocese does not bind him, since he is out of its territory, and the law of the diocese where he is does not bind him, since he is not a subject of that law.

442. The natural law requires that strangers should conform themselves to local laws in the following cases:

(a) when non-observance would be a cause of scandal, which the natural law commands one to avoid. In this sense we understand the rule of St. Ambrose: "When you are at Rome, do as the Romans do." Hence, if a stranger would cause real scandal by eating meat on a local day of abstinence, he would be obliged to abstain from it;

(b) when a local law deals with the solemnities required for validity of contracts (Canon 14, § 1, n. 2). If strangers were not obliged by laws of this kind, they could take advantage of the inhabitants, a thing that is contrary to natural justice. Thus, "the place rules the act";

(c) when the local law has for its object the maintenance of public order (Canon 14, § 1, 11. 2); for the natural law demands that public safety be guarded. Hence, a stranger who commits a crime is subject to the penalties of the local law (Canon 1566).

443. Examples of territorial laws that oblige even strangers according to the precept of the Church are the laws that require all, even strangers, to follow the Calendar of the Church where they celebrate Mass, and to say the *collectæ imperatæ* prescribed by the bishop of the local diocese.

444. The rules given for strangers can be applied also to those who are in places exempt from local jurisdiction (e.g., in the monasteries of exempt regulars). The exempt are those who by fiction of law are held to be outside the territory of every diocese, and are subject, not to the local bishop, but directly to the Pope (Canon 515).

445. There are various cases, however, in which exempt religious aresubject to the territorial laws of the diocese where they are. Thus: (a) when they accept parishes in a diocese, they are subject to the Ordinary in those matters that pertain to the parishes; (b) when the common good or the avoidance of scandal requires it, they should conform to a diocesan law.

446. Those who have a personal privilege can use it anywhere, for a personal privilege, like a personal precept, follows the person, not the territory.

447. Promulgation.—Church laws are promulgated as follows: (a) the laws of the Holy See are promulgated by publication in the official periodical, *Acta Apostolicæ Sedis*. They become effective three months from the date of publication, unless from the nature of the case they oblige at once, or it is otherwise provided in the law itself (Canon 9); (b) the laws of a bishop are promulgated in the manner he decides, generally by publication in the official periodical of the diocese. They become effective as soon as published, unless it is otherwise provided in the law itself (Canon 335, § 2).

448. When a law has been promulgated and become known, if it begins to be observed, it is said to be accepted; if it is not observed, it is said to be not accepted. This acceptance is not essential to law. Hence: (a) the observance of a law by the people is not necessary for the obligatory force of the law, for otherwise the lawgiver would be without real authority; (b) the approval of ecclesiastical laws by the State is not necessary for their validity, since Church and State are distinct and independent societies within the proper sphere of each.

449. A law that has been promulgated may fail to obtain force in the following ways: (a) through contrary custom, already existing and not excluded by the law, or then arising to abrogate the law (see 391 Sqq.); (b) through appeal entered with the lawgiver. Thus, if a bishop deems a law of the Pope unsuited to his diocese, he explains the reasons to the Holy See, and pending the answer it is considered that the lawgiver does not wish the law to oblige.

450. Irritant Laws. Laws Based on Presumption.—There are two classes of human laws that deserve particular mention on account of special difficulties regarding them: (a) irritant laws, which would seem to be unjust, since they declare null what according to natural law would be valid; (b) laws based on presumption, which would seem to be of uncertain force, since presumptions are often contrary to fact.

451. An irritant or inhabilitating law is one that expressly or equivalently declares that certain defects make an act void or voidable, or a person incapable. Such laws are just, even when made by human authority, since it is the common good that makes them necessary, and the natural law itself requires that the common good be promoted.

452. Irritant laws are of various kinds.

(a) They are morally or juridically irritant, according as that which is taken from the irritated act is either the natural value it has in conscience, or the positive value it derives from the law. Hence, an act may be legally null (i.e., have no value that the law recognizes or protects) and at the same time morally valid (i.e., of just as much force in conscience as though no irritant law existed).

(b) Irritant laws are merely irritant or irritant and prohibitive, according as they make an act invalid but not illicit, or both invalid and illicit. Thus, a law that requires certain formalities for making a will invalidates the act of writing an informal will, but does not make it an offense; but the church law of diriment impediments makes a marriage contracted with one of these impediments both null and sinful.

(c) Irritant laws are merely irritant or irritant and penal, according as the legislator does not or does intend them as punishments. For example, the law of clandestinity is merely irritant; the law regarding the impediment of crime is probably both irritant and penal.

453. Laws that are merely irritant do not oblige one in conscience to omit the act, but only to suffer the effect of irritation; but laws that are both irritant and prohibitive oblige one in conscience to omit the act. Example: In itself, it is not unlawful to make an informal will, but it is unlawful to marry with a diriment impediment.

454. As to the time when irritant laws obtain their effect, the following points are important.

(a) Ecclesiastical voiding laws oblige at once in conscience, although like other laws of the Church they are not retroactive, unless the contrary is provided, and they do not oblige in case of a doubt concerning the law. Example: If espousals are made without the canonical formalities, there is no duty to live up to them as such, either in conscience or before the law.

(b) Civil voiding laws are generally only civilly irritant, for as a rule external means are sufficient for the purpose of those laws; thus, they produce civil irritation at once, but moral irritation only after pronouncement by the courts. Hence, after a judicial sentence the voided act becomes such morally, since the decision is founded on a presumption of common danger (see below, 459). Examples: One who has received money through a will which he knows to be informal (i.e., legally invalid), may retain possession until the civil authority declares that he has no rights to the money. But, on the other hand, one who has been disinherited through a will naturally good, but not made in due form, has the right to contest, if we except the case of pious bequests (see Vol. II).

455. Laws that make an act voidable or rescindable do not irritate before declaration of nullity by a judge. Hence, an act that is rescindable according to law retains its natural force until the court has decided against it. Example: Acts that were done under the influence of grave and unjust fear, or that were induced through deception, are held as valid until declared null by a judge.

456. As to the effects of ignorance on acts irritated by law, the Code
states that ignorance of irritating (invalidating) and inhabilitating
(disqualifying) laws does not excuse from their observance, unless the
law expressly states otherwise (Canon 16, § 1). Moralists discuss the
influence of ignorance (as well as force or fear) on such acts as follows:
(a) if the law is irritant and not penal, it has its effect, in spite of
ignorance, oversight, etc.; for this the common good requires. Example:
One who marries his cousin in good faith, being invincibly ignorant
that it is against the law, contracts invalidly; (b) if the law is irritant and
penal, the irritation being decreed solely as a punishment, ignorance,
oversight, etc., sufficient to excuse from fault, excuse also from the
penalty of irritation; for penalty presupposes fault. Before the law,
however, ignorance and error as to law or penalties are not presumed
but must be proved. (Nevertheless, it must be noted that according to
some authors no penalty is necessarily or primarily intended in
ecclesiastical irritating and inhabilitating laws. Though punishment
actually results from the matrimonial impediment of crime, for
example, the impediment as such primarily is a personal disqualification
intended to protect the dignity of the sacrament and good morals.
Ignorance, then, does not excuse from it. Some authors maintain that
this is true of all ecclesiastical disqualifying laws.)

457. Generally speaking, *epieikeia* may not be used in the interpretation
of irritating and inhabilitating laws. Since they transcend the individual
welfare, they demand uniform observance of all subject to them. Some
authors permit the use of *epieikeia*, however, in particular cases in which
the law itself aims to protect the individual, whereas its observance
would tend rather to harm the individual or at times even the interests
of the community. Accordingly, it seems probable that an irritant law
may cease in case of impossibility or of a most grave inconvenience that
is common. Example: If in a pagan country Christians were so few that
they could marry only infidels, and if distance or other circumstances
made it impossible to seek a dispensation, the diriment impediment of
disparity of worship would seem to cease for those Christians.

458. Some authors hold that an irritant law may also cease on account
of impossibility, or of a most grave inconvenience that is only private;
but this opinion cannot be deemed certain. An example of private
inconvenience is the case of an invalidly married person who is near to

death and unable to seek the dispensation from the impediment that has made the marriage null.

459. A law based on presumption is one in which the lawgiver rules for certain cases according to what experience shows in their regard—viz., that such cases are generally dangerous, or indicative of a particular fact. These laws are not of uncertain force, for the cases in which they cease to oblige are few and definite.

460. When a law is based on a presumption of common danger and that danger does not exist in a particular instance, the law nevertheless obliges (Canon 21); for the end of the law is the common good, and if it ceased for an individual whenever its presumption of danger was not true in his case, everyone could persuade himself that the law did not apply to him, and thus the common good would be defeated. Examples: The law against the reading of irreligious books is based on the presumption of common danger of sin, the law against clandestine marriages on the presumption of common danger of fraud; hence, they oblige even in the particular instances where these dangers are absent. Examples of laws based on the presumption of common danger can be found in Canons 199; 409, § 1; 420; 422; 1022; 1028; 1114; 1116; 1138; 1396; 1398.

461. When a law is based on the presumption of a particular fact that usually happens in the cases with which the law is concerned, and the fact in an individual instance did not happen, does the law oblige?

(a) In conscience the law does not oblige of itself, because presumptions must yield to the truth; but it may oblige accidentally, if non-observance would cause great public or private harm. Example: The law presumes that a person born and brought up among Catholics has been baptized, and is therefore subject to the church laws. But if, in fact, the person was never baptized, he is not subject to those laws, as long as he remains unbaptized, unless there be some accidental necessity of keeping them, such as the danger of scandal.

(b) Before the public authority the law in question does oblige until the non-existence of the fact presumed by the law has been proved in the manner required by law. Example: When parties contract marriage according to the form prescribed by the Church, the presumption is that the contract was valid, and, as long as that presumption is not overcome, the Church will not sanction a new marriage by either of the parties. But if it can be proved in court that threats or violence produced lack of consent, the obligation not to contract a new marriage will terminate before the law.

462. Fulfillment of Law.—With reference to the manner of fulfilling a law there are a number of questions to be considered: (a) as to the external acts, whether or not one can fulfill the law for another, whether or not the omission of some slight detail renders compliance insufficient, whether or not he who cannot fulfill the whole law is bound to fulfill a part of it, whether or not several obligations can be satisfied at the same time or by the same act, etc.; (b) as to the internal acts, whether or not one must have the intention of meeting the wishes of the lawgiver, whether or not one must be in the state of grace, etc.

463. Personal fulfillment is not always necessary; for an affirmative law requires either that some thing be given, or that some personal act be performed. (a) When the law requires that some thing be given (e.g., that taxes be paid), the obligation can be satisfied through another, since a thing can be transferred from one person to another, who agrees at least interpretatively; (b) when the law requires that a personal act be performed (e.g., that Mass be heard on Sunday), the obligation cannot be satisfied through another, for actions cannot be transferred from one to another.

464. Minute fulfillment is not always necessary; for sometimes the minor details of the fulfillment of a law are expressly prescribed, sometimes they are not.

(a) If these details are required by the law itself or by the nature of the case, the law is not satisfied if they are neglected. Example: Friday abstinence ends exactly at midnight, and hence to eat meat even one minute before midnight is to break that abstinence.

(b) If the law does not prescribe minute details, these are not required for the fulfillment of the obligation; for laws should not be unduly burdensome. Example: One who is a few minutes late for Mass does not miss Mass, if he is present for the essential parts of the Mass.

465. Partial fulfillment is required of him who cannot make complete fulfillment, only when the part is commanded for its own sake; for that which is commanded by a law is considered by the lawgiver as either an indivisible unit, or as a whole composed of parts that have singly an independent moral value and obligation.

(a) If the thing commanded is morally an indivisible unit (e.g., a pilgrimage to a shrine), he who is not able to fulfill the whole law is bound to nothing. Example: One who has made a vow to go on pilgrimage to a distant sanctuary, is not bound to go part of the way, if he is unable to make the entire journey.

(b) If the thing commanded has parts that contribute to the end of the law, he who is able to fulfill only one or more such parts is obliged according to his ability; if it is certain that he can perform even a part, he is bound to that; if it is not certain that he can perform even a part, it would seem that generally he is excused from all. Examples: A cleric who can say some but not all the Hours of his Office, is obliged to say what he can. A person who can certainly abstain, but who cannot fast, is bound during Lent to abstain.

466. Simultaneous fulfillment by one act of several obligations is lawful, if the obligations differ only materially. They are said to differ only materially, if the motive of the legislator in giving different commands about the same thing is the same in each instance; they differ formally, if the legislator has a different motive in each instance. The motive is recognized either from the express declaration of the lawgiver, or from interpretation given through authority or custom.

(a) When two commands differ only materially, it can be presumed that the legislator is not unwilling that they be fulfilled by one and the same act, unless it is clear that he wishes them to be fulfilled by distinct acts. Example: If one falls sick at Easter time and receives the Viaticum, it is not necessary for him to receive Communion again in order to make his Easter duty; for the divine law of Viaticum and the church law of Easter Communion have the same motive, and hence can be fulfilled by one and the same Communion.

(b) When two commands differ formally, it can be presumed, unless the opposite is manifest, that the legislator wishes them to be complied with by distinct acts. Example: If a confessor imposes a fast as a penance, this penance cannot be performed on a fast day; for the motive of the law of fast is general, that of the sacramental penance is particular.

467. Simultaneous fulfillment by several acts of several obligations is sometimes possible, sometimes impossible. For the acts prescribed by different laws are either capable or incapable of being done at the same time. Thus, it is possible to hear a Mass and to say a penance of some Hail Marys at the same time. But it does not seem easy for an ordinary person to give attention to four or more Masses at the same time.

(a) If the acts do not impede one another and the legislator is not unwilling, several laws can be fulfilled at the same time. Example: If two Masses are being said on adjoining altars, one can hear both—the one to satisfy the Sunday obligation, the other to perform a penance received.

(b) If the acts impede one another, or if the legislator wishes his laws to be fulfilled at distinct times, the different obligations cannot be satisfied simultaneously. Examples: If a distracted person has received a penance to hear six Masses, he cannot hear them all at once, on account of the division of attention necessary. If the confessor told a person to hear Mass "three times," the latter cannot satisfy by hearing three Masses at one time.

468. When a law prescribes not only what is to be done, but when it is to be done, the time must be observed. But the obligation does not always cease with the expiration of the time.

(a) If the time set by the law is a limit beyond which the obligation ceases, he who has not complied within that time has no further obligation. Examples: He who did not fast on Christmas Eve, would not be obliged to fast on Christmas Day. He who did not hear Mass on Sunday, would not be obliged to hear Mass on Monday.

(b) If the time set by the law is not a limit to terminate the obligation, but a date fixed in order to insist on the obligation, he who has not complied within the prescribed period, is nevertheless still obliged. Examples: He who has not made the Easter duty by Trinity Sunday, is obliged to receive Communion after Trinity. He who has not paid a debt on the day required by law, is bound to pay it after that day.

469. It depends on the intention of the lawgiver whether the time he prescribes for fulfillment is a limitation of the obligation or not. The intention of the lawgiver is known either from the words or purpose of the law, or from custom.

470. If the law declares that some duty must be performed within a determined period, allowing freedom for earlier or later performance within the period, the following points must be considered. (a) A person is not obliged to comply early, if he intends to comply before the period has ended. (b) He is obliged to comply early, if he foresees that later he will not be able to do what is required. Examples: If a person who has not made his Easter duty has the opportunity to receive Communion on Easter Sunday, and will not have another such opportunity till Christmas, he is obliged to receive on Easter Sunday. But, if he can communicate any Sunday during the Paschal time, he is not bound to do so on one of the early Sundays. If one can hear an early Mass, but not another Mass, on a holyday, one must hear the early Mass.

471. Just as one may not delay fulfillment until after the time set by law, so neither may one anticipate fulfillment before the time determined, unless the law may be considered to allow this. Examples: If a person has heard Mass on Saturday, he has no right to make this count for the following day. A rosary said before confession cannot be considered as performance of the penance, if in confession one is given the rosary to say.

472. It is held that a cleric who said the Breviary in the morning, just before he was ordained subdeacon and undertook the obligation of the Office, satisfied by that anticipated recitation; likewise, that a traveller who heard Mass in a place where a holyday of obligation of the general law was not in force, has satisfied by anticipation, if later in the morning he reaches as his destination a place where the holyday is observed. For in both these cases the law intends that the Office be said, or the Mass be heard within the day.

473. If a person who is now able to do what the law requires, foresees that he will not be able to do this when the time set by the law arrives, he is not obliged to anticipate fulfillment, even when he has the privilege of anticipation. Examples: A cleric who at 2 p.m. is able to anticipate Matins for tomorrow, and who knows that later, on account of an operation, he will not be able to say his Office, is not bound to anticipate; for no one is obliged to use a privilege. A person who is able to hear Mass on Saturday, and who knows that all of Sunday must be spent on the train, is not obliged to hear Mass on Saturday, though of course this is the better thing to do.

474. The internal acts concerned in the fulfillment of a law are: (a) those in the intellect, such as knowledge; (b) those in the will, such as consent, motive.

475. Knowledge of what one is doing is sometimes necessary, sometimes unnecessary for the fulfillment of a law.

(a) If the law is prohibitive, knowledge is not necessary, since nothing more is required by the law than the omission of what is forbidden. Example: He who ate no meat on a day of abstinence has fulfilled the law, even though he was unconscious all day.

(b) If the law is preceptive of a payment to be made, knowledge is not necessary, since the law requires nothing more than the effect of an external act. Example: He who pays his taxes while intoxicated fulfills his obligation, even though he does not know what he is doing.

(c) If the law is preceptive of an act to be performed, knowledge is required, for it is supposed that the act will be exercised in a human manner. Example: He who sleeps all during Mass on Sunday does not fulfill his duty, for the law intends that one assist at Mass in a human way (i.e., with consciousness of what is being done).

476. Fulfillment of a law is not morally good and meritorious, unless it is voluntary (see 97 sqq.); but the legal obligation is sometimes satisfied even by an unwilling fulfillment.

(a) When the law commands a payment to be made, one may will the contrary of what is commanded and yet fulfill one's obligation.

Example: He who pays his taxes unwillingly and under compulsion satisfies the law, which requires not an act, but its effect.

(b) When the law forbids something, it is possible that one does not will the omission commanded and yet fulfills one's obligation. Example: He who intends to eat meat on a day of abstinence which he thinks is a meat day, but, being unable to find what he wants, omits the meat, satisfies the law, which requires only that one omit what is forbidden and have no will to violate the law.

(c) When the law commands that an act be performed, one must perform the act willingly, since the law being for humans intends that fulfillment be made in a human manner. Examples: He who is dragged to church and forcibly detained there during Mass, does not satisfy the law of sanctifying the Sunday, since force makes his assistance at Mass involuntary (see 52). A child that goes to church only to escape punishment satisfies its duty, if, in spite of reluctance, it really intends to hear Mass, for fear does not necessarily make an act involuntary (see 41 sqq.).

477. As to the intention required in fulfilling a law, it is to be noted that one must have, at least implicitly, the intention of doing what the law prescribes, in the case given in the third section (c) of the preceding paragraph. Example: He who goes to church on Sunday while Mass is being said with no other purpose than that of hearing the music or of waiting for a friend, does not satisfy the Sunday duty, since he does not at all intend to hear Mass.

478. The following kinds of intention, though to be recommended, are not necessary for the fulfillment of a law.

(a) It is not necessary, as a rule, that one intend to satisfy one's obligation, for human lawgivers have not generally the power or the intention to command acts that are purely internal (see 374, 426). Examples: He who hears Mass on a holyday not intending to perform his duty, as he does not know that it is a holyday, has satisfied the law. He who says the rosary out of devotion and then remembers that he has an obligation of saying it because of a promise made or of a penance received, can regard the rosary said as a fulfillment of his obligation.

(b) It is not necessary that one intend that which the lawgiver had in mind as the purpose of the law; for "the end of the law is not a part of the law." Example: A person who takes only one full meal during Lent, observes the letter of the law; but he misses its spirit if he eats or drinks greedily, daintily or copiously, in order to avoid the mortification intended by the law.

479. If one intends to perform what a law prescribes, but at the same time expressly intends not to satisfy, by that performance, the obligation imposed, one's act is sufficient or insufficient for fulfillment according to the source from which the obligation arises.

(a) If the obligation arises from the will of the lawgiver, the act is a sufficient fulfillment, since the human lawgiver, as said in the previous paragraph, does not concern himself with what is purely internal. Example: If a person hears Mass on Sunday out of devotion, intending to hear another Mass in satisfaction of the Sunday duty, he is not bound to hear a second Mass, as he has already done all that the law requires.

(b) If the obligation arises from one's own will, as in the case of a promise or a vow, the act above described is not sufficient fulfillment; for, as the obligation arose from the will, so also the mode of fulfillment is to be determined by the will. Example: One who has vowed to hear Mass, and who now while hearing Mass expressly determines that not this but another Mass will be in satisfaction of his vow, is bound by his vow to hear another Mass.

480. As to virtuous dispositions in fulfilling a law, it is to be observed that, while a good lawgiver always wishes them, he does not always require them as a duty of obedience. The virtuous dispositions referred to are of two kinds: (a) habitual, that is, the permanent spiritual condition of the soul, such as the state of grace, the habit of charity, etc.; (b) actual, that is, the good manner in which the commanded act is done, such as devout attention in hearing Mass, heartfelt contrition in making confession, freedom from vain-glory in fasting, etc.

481. Virtuous dispositions are or are not commanded according as that which is prescribed is or is not a mixed, or a purely external act (see above, 426).

(a) When a mixed act is commanded by law, the virtuous disposition that the nature of the case calls for, but nothing further, is strictly prescribed. Hence, the law of Easter Communion requires that Communion be received in the state of grace, the law of yearly confession that the penitent be truly contrite, the law of Sunday Mass that there be sufficient attention to the Mass; but more perfect dispositions (such as freedom from venial sin in the communicant, perfect contrition in the penitent, the state of grace in him who hears Mass) are not required for the fulfillment of the laws we are considering.

(b) When a purely external thing is commanded, the law does not require internal dispositions, and hence one who performs what is required is not obliged to repeat it on account of the imperfect way he obeyed. Example: He who fasts while he is not in the state of grace is not obliged to fast again to make good what was lacking in his previous disposition.

482. Of course, what was said in the preceding paragraph has to do only with single laws, and with what is strictly needed for the fulfillment of the law. Hence: (a) he who sins because of the way in which he fulfills one law, violates another law (e.g., one who is willingly, though not entirely, distracted at Mass, obeys the church law of assistance at Mass on Sunday, but he disobeys the divine law that he worship God devoutly);

(b) he who has less devotion in obeying a law than he might have had, does not deserve reprehension as a transgressor, but his conduct is less praiseworthy.

483. Interpretation.—The meaning of interpretation and its various species were explained above in 315 sqq.

484. As to the force of interpretation of church laws, the following points must be noted:

(a) Authentic interpretation given in the form of law has the force of law; if it is merely declarative of words of the law certain in themselves, it does not need promulgation and is retroactive; if it is supplementary, it needs promulgation and is not retroactive, since it is a new law (Canon 17, § 2);

(b) Authentic interpretation given in the form of judicial sentence or of rescript in a particular matter has not the force of law; and it obliges only the persons and affects only the things concerned (Canon 17, § 3);

(c) Usual interpretation has the force of law when it is given through a legitimate custom (see above, 391 sqq.), for "custom is the best interpreter of law";

(d) Doctrinal interpretation has not the force of law, since it does not proceed from the lawgiver. Its value depends on the reasons and the authority by which it is supported. When all the doctors agree, their interpretation is morally certain; when they disagree, the various interpretations have more or less probability.

485. Rules for Doctrinal Interpretation.—(a) The words must be understood in their proper sense according to text and context, unless this be impossible; if doubtful, they must be judged according to parallel places in the Code, the circumstances, reason of the law, and the mind of the lawgiver (Canon 18).

(b) Things that are burdensome should be understood in their most restricted sense (Canon 19), things that are favorable in their widest sense. Thus, the censure pronounced against simony is understood in the narrow sense of simony against the divine law; a privilege granted to the clergy is understood in the wide sense as given to all the clergy.

(c) Things that remain obscure should be understood in the sense that is least burdensome to subjects.

(d) A particular law derogates from a general law; but a general law does not derogate from a previous particular law, unless derogation is expressly mentioned in the general law; for the particular law is considered an exception to the general law (Canon 22).

486. Authentic interpretations of ecclesiastical laws are given by the legislator, his successor, or one delegated by either (Canon 17, § 1). (a) The Pope is the authentic interpreter of all ecclesiastical laws. A special

commission appointed by the Pope interprets the general law of the Code. (b) The bishop is the authentic interpreter of diocesan laws made by himself or by his predecessors.

487. Cessation of Obligation.—The ordinary ways in which a law ceases to be obligatory for an individual are: (a) on the part of the subject, that he ceases to be subject to the law (exemption), or is unable to observe it (excuse); (b) on the part of the lawgiver, that he removes the obligation for the individual (dispensation).

488. As to exemption from Church laws note: (a) he who ceases to be subject to the law (e.g., one who has received a privilege of exemption, or who has departed from the place where the law is in force), is of course not obliged by the law; (b) neither is he guilty of any fault if he brought about his freedom only just before the law became effective and with the sole purpose of being exempt; for the law does not oblige that one remain subject to it.

489. Excuses from the law are reduced to two, namely, ignorance and impossibility.

(a) Ignorance excuses from the guilt of non-observance, if it is inculpable (see 24 sqq.). The question now is whether or not and when it excuses from legal consequences, such as invalidity, penalty, reservation of sin, etc.

(b) Impossibility excuses from both obligation and guilt.

490. Ignorance of ecclesiastical law or of a penalty attached to the law has the following effects determined in the law: (a) No kind of ignorance excuses from irritating or inhabilitating laws, unless the contrary is expressly provided for in the law itself (Canon 16, § 1). Thus a person who contracts marriage, while ignorant that he and the other person are first cousins, is invalidly married.

(b) Affected ignorance of ecclesiastical law or of the penalty alone does not excuse from any penalties *latae sententiae* (Canon 2229, §1).

(c) If the law contains the following words: *praesumpserit, ausus fuerit, scienter, studiose, temerarie, consulto egerit,* or others similar to them which require full knowledge and deliberation, any diminution of imputability on the part of either the intellect or the will exempts the delinquent from penalties *latae sententiae* (Canon 2229, §2). (d) If the law does not contain such words, crass or supine ignorance of the law or even of only the penalty does not exempt from any penalty *latae sententiae*; ignorance that is not crass or supine exempts from medicinal penalties, but not from vindicative penalties *latae sententiae* (Canon 2229, §3, 1°).

491. Other specific determinations of the law include: (a) Inculpable ignorance of the law itself excludes moral imputability (Canon 2202, §1); actual inculpable inadvertence or error in regard to the law has the same effect (Canon 2202, §3). (b) Culpable ignorance, or culpable inadvertence, or error concerning the law or concerning the fact diminish imputability more or less in proportion to the culpability of the ignorance (Canon 2202, §1). (c) If the ignorance, even inculpable, affects only the fact of the existence of the penalty, it does not exclude imputability of the delict, but it does diminish it (Canon 2202, §2).

492. Absolute or physical impossibility (i.e., the want of the power or of the means of complying with a law), of course, excuses from its observance; for no one is bound to what is impossible. This applies to divine law, and hence much more to human law. Example: He who is unable to leave the house is not obliged to go to Mass.

493. Moral impossibility—that is, the inability to comply with the law without extraordinary labor, or the imminent danger of losing a notable good or of incurring a great evil—does not excuse from the observance of ecclesiastical law when this law receives through circumstances the added force of the negative law of nature. This happens when the evil that will result through the observance of the law bears no proportion to the evil that will result from its violation, the former being private or temporal or human, the latter public or spiritual or divine; for the law of nature forbids that the common welfare, or the salvation of a soul, or the honor of God be sacrificed for the benefit of an individual, or for the life of the body, or for the welfare of a creature. Example: The command to abstain from meat on Friday obliges, if one has been ordered to violate it as a sign of contempt of God or of religion, even though death is threatened for refusal.

494. Moral impossibility excuses from the observance of a human law in the following cases:

(a) One is excused when a considerable loss in health, reputation, spiritual advantage, property, etc., or a grave inconvenience will result from observing a law which is not a prohibition of nature in the sense of the previous paragraph; for the legislator cannot impose obligations that are needlessly heavy, and hence positive law does not oblige in case of such moral impossibility. Example: Our Lord reproved the inhuman rigor of the Pharisees, who insisted that their regulations must be observed, whatever the difficulty or cost.

(b) One is excused when a lower or less urgent law is in conflict with a law that is higher or more urgent. In such a case the greater obligation prevails, and the lesser obligation disappears. Examples: The divine laws that one must preserve one's life or administer Baptismto a dying person prevail over the human law of attendance at church. The less urgent law of fasting yields to the more urgent law of devoting oneself to duties required by one's state of life, if there is a conflict between the two laws.

495. The loss, evil or inconvenience that constitutes moral impossibility with respect to a law, must bear a proportion to the law itself; and hence the higher or the more imperative the law, the greater must be the reason that suffices to excuse from it.

496. Only a learned and prudent man can determine whether moral impossibility exists with reference to a particular case, and hence it would be dangerous for those who are not theologians to decide, either for themselves or for others. The points that have to be considered in judging are: (a) whether or not the difficulty is of a gravity proportionate to the importance of the law (e.g., a graver reason is required to excuse from a law that obliges under mortal sin than to excuse from a law that binds under light sin); (b) whether or not the difficulty is grave in relation to the person concerned (e.g., an obligation that is easy for a healthy person may be very difficult for one who is infirm).

497. It is never lawful to bring about either physical or moral impossibility of observing a law, if this be done with the sole or

principal purpose of escaping one's duty. Example: To go away on Saturday in order to avoid Mass on Sunday.

498. It is lawful to cause impossibility of observing a law, if there be some sufficient reason for doing this; for it is lawful to do something from which two effects, one good and the other bad, result, if the good effect is the one intended, and there is a sufficient reason for permitting the evil effect (102 sqq.). Example: It is sometimes lawful to do some extra work that is very useful, even if the labor makes one unable to observe a fast.

499. The sufficient reason spoken of in the last paragraph is one that is proportionate to the urgency and importance of the command and to the frequency of the non-observance. Examples: A greater reason is required to take up some work which will make it impossible to keep the fast, if this be done on the fast day itself, than if it be done the day before. A far greater reason is required to take up some work that makes the observance of the fast impossible, if this happens frequently or habitually, than if it happens only once or twice.

500. Cessation of Law.—A law ceases in two ways.

(a) It ceases from without (i.e., from the act of the legislator), when he abolishes it, by total or partial revocation (abrogation, derogation), or by the institution of a new law directly contrary to it (obrogation). In the new Code of Canon Law there are many instances of revocation or obrogation of older legislation (see Canons 22, 23), as in the matter of censures and matrimonial impediments. Examples: In the diocese of X a minor feast was made a holyday of obligation. This law was abrogated, if later on it was decreed that neither the prohibition against servile works nor the precept of hearing Mass was obligatory for that feast; it was derogated from, if later it was decreed that servile works were permitted, but Mass was obligatory for that day; it was obrogated, if a later law included the minor feast in a list of special days of devotion for which the hearing of Mass was recommended.

(b) A law ceases from within (i.e., of itself), when through change of conditions the purpose for which it was made no longer exists, or is no longer served by the law.

501. The purpose for which a law was made ceases to be served by the law in two cases.

(a) A law no longer serves its purpose, if, from having been a benefit, it has become a detriment, inasmuch as its observance now would be wicked, or impossible, or too burdensome. In this case the law ceases, since it is now contrary to the supreme law that the common welfare be promoted. Example: A particular law forbade the use of fat or grease in the preparation of food on days of abstinence. Later, it became impossible to procure the substitutes previously used.

(b) A law no longer serves its purpose, if, from having been useful, it has become useless, inasmuch as it is no longer necessary for the end intended by the lawgiver. In this case the law ceases, for regulations should not be imposed needlessly. Example: The Council of Jerusalem made a law that the faithful should abstain from using as food animals that had been strangled (Acts, xv. 20). The purpose of the law was to avoid offense to the Jewish converts, who at that time formed a large part of the Christian community and who had a religious abhorrence for such food. But shortly afterwards, the Gentile element having become stronger in the Church, no attention was paid to ceremonial rules of Judaism.

502. A law ceases to serve its purpose also as follows:

(a) The law becomes harmful or useless with reference to the purpose of the lawgiver generally and permanently, if the changed conditions affect the whole community or the great majority, and are lasting. In this case the law ceases; for, since it is made for the community as a whole and as a lasting ordinance, it cannot endure, if it becomes permanently unserviceable to the community. Examples are given in the previous paragraph.

(b) The law becomes harmful or useless with reference to the lawgiver's purpose privately or temporarily, if the harm or uselessness affects only individuals, or is not lasting. In this case the law continues to be an instrument of public welfare, or is only momentarily deprived of its beneficial character. Hence it endures; but for temporary inconvenience to the public a remedy is had in suspension of the law, for inconvenience to individuals in dispensation. Example: If the use of fats or grease were forbidden on days of abstinence, and if for a time only it were impossible to obtain the substitutes for the preparation of the food, the law would not cease, but would be suspended until such time as substitutes could be obtained.

503. The inconvenience caused to individuals from the fact that a law does not serve its purpose in a case before them, does not always justify the use of *epieikeia*.

(a) If the observance of the law would be detrimental to the purpose intended by the lawgiver, *epieikeia* might be used; for the lawgiver does not intend that his law should be an obstacle to what he has in view as its end. Example: Caius needs to read a book placed on the Index in order to defend the Faith against attacks, but he is unable to request the general faculty to read forbidden works. Obedience to the law in this case would defeat the purpose of the law, which is the protection of faith, and hence Caius may use epieikeia.

(b) If the observance of the law would be unnecessary, but not detrimental as regards the purpose of the lawgiver, *epieikeia* may not be used; else the law would lose its force through the judgments of individuals in their own favor, and the common welfare would suffer. Examples: Titus has an opportunity to read a book placed on the Index, but has not the time to apply for permission. The work was condemned as dangerous to faith; but Titus is strong in faith, and wishes only to study the literary qualities of the writer. Sempronius, a parish priest, is requested to officiate at a marriage immediately, without proclaiming the banns or seeking a dispensation from proclamation. The purpose of the law of banns is that impediments may be detected and invalid marriages avoided, and Sempronius is absolutely certain that there is no impediment in the case before him. Titus and Sempronius must observe the law, and the same must be said as regards every actual case in which there is the possibility of self-deception and peril to the common good. The theoretical case, in which neither of these inconveniences would be present, need not be considered.

504. The purpose of the law ceases to exist as follows:

(a) adequately, when all the reasons on account of which it was made are no longer in existence; in such a case the law itself ceases, for the lawgiver is not considered as intending to oblige when the reason for obligation has ceased. Example: If the bishop orders prayers to be said for rain, the prayers cease to be obligatory when rain has come;

(b) inadequately, when the reason for the law has ceased partially, but not entirely. In such a case the law does not cease, for it still remains useful. Example: If the bishop orders prayers for peace and rain, the prayers are obligatory until both requests have been obtained.

505. A law ceases, therefore, in greater or less degree, according to circumstances. (a) It ceases entirely or partially, according as it is revoked or as it becomes useless as to all its provisions, or only as to one or more of them; (b) it ceases permanently or temporarily, according as the revocation or cessation is only for a time, or for good.

506. Custom.—In Canon Law custom can interpret, abrogate or introduce law, provided: (a) it has the qualities of legitimate custom, and (b) its existence is proved juridically, or is notorious.

507. According to their extension, customs are of various kinds. (a) Universal customs are those that prevail in the entire Church; (b) particular customs are those that are confined to a territorial portion of the Church (e.g., a province of the Church or of an Order); (c) special customs are those that are followed in societies that are smaller, but capable of having their own laws (e.g., independent monasteries); (d) most special customs are those observed by individuals, or by communities not capable of having their own legislation (e.g., parishes). At the most, customs of this last class have only the force of privilege (Canon 26).

508. Custom is formed as follows. (a) As to origin, it arises from the practice of the people, when this practice is followed with the purpose of making or unmaking a law. Hence, the habitual way of acting of an individual, even if he be the superior, does not give rise to a custom. By "people" here is meant a community capable of having its own law (Canon 26). (b) As to legal force, custom arises solely from the consent of the Pope or other prelate, when this consent is expressed by the law or lawgiver, or tacitly admitted by him. Hence, a custom not approved by the superior has no legal force (Canon 25).

509. A custom can introduce or abrogate any kind of ecclesiastical law or other custom—penal, prohibitive, irritant—if it is reasonable and has lasted the prescribed time (Canons 27, 28). Examples: A law that forbids contrary customs can be abrogated, according to the Code, by such customs when they are immemorial, or a century old (Canon 27, § 1). The impediment of disparity of worship became diriment through custom; it was custom that introduced the obligation of the Divine Office, and that mitigated the early law of fast.

510. A custom expressly disapproved of in law is not reasonable or legitimate, and cannot derogate from an existing law, nor establish a new law (Canons 27, 28).

511. The time prescribed by the Code of Canon Law for the acquisition of legal force by customs that have not the personal consent of the lawgiver is as follows: (a) forty continuous and complete years are required to unmake an ordinary law; one hundred years to unmake a law that forbids future contrary custom (Canon 27, § 1); (b) forty continuous and complete years are likewise required to make a new law (Canon 28).

512. The effect of the Code on customs previously existing was considered above under 421.

513. Like the written law, custom ceases: (a) from within, when its purpose has ceased entirely; (b) from without, when it is abrogated by desuetude, or by a contrary law or custom (Canon 30).

514. Laws in a Wide Sense.—In addition to laws strictly so-called, there are laws in a wide sense, commands or provisions made by ecclesiastical superiors that have not all the conditions given above (see 285) for law. Such are: (a) precepts, which differ from law, because they are given not to the community or permanently, but to individuals or temporarily; (b) rescripts, which are given with regard to particular cases and without the solemnity of law; (c) privileges, which are not obligatory; (d) dispensations, which are relaxations of law granted to individuals.

515. A precept is a command given to individuals, or for an individual case, by a competent superior.

(a) It is a command obliging in conscience, and so differs from counsel, desire, exhortation.

(b) It is given to individuals, and thus differs from law, which has the character of universality and stability. A precept may be imposed on a community, but even then it is particular, as being given only for an individual case or for a certain length of time—for a month or a year, or during the lifetime of the superior.

(c) It is given by a competent superior. Even here precept differs from law, since laws can be made only by one who has jurisdictional or public authority (see above, 285), while precepts may be given also by those who have only dominative or private authority (as parents, heads of families, husbands, employers, abbesses). In canonical matters precepts may be given by religious superiors, parish priests, rectors of seminaries, and for the court of conscience by the confessor.

516. Precept is similar to law: (a) as to its object, which must be just, good, and possible of observance; (b) as to its binding force, since it can be imposed even on those who are unwilling.

517. Precepts are personal (i.e., they affect the person to whom they are given wherever he may be), unless they are given as territorial (Canon 24). Hence: (a) a precept given by one who has no territorial authority (e.g., a religious superior) is personal; (b) a precept given by the Pope, whose authority includes every territory, is also personal; (c) a precept given by the bishop is personal, if given to an individual; it is personal or territorial if given to a community, according to the nature of the case or the wording of the precept. Example: The precept not to go to theatres during a journey, imposed by a bishop under pain of suspension, obliges everywhere, both as to fault and as to penalty.

518. As to the force of precepts: (a) morally or as to fault, they oblige, so that the violator is guilty of disobedience and of sin against any particular virtue the superior willed to impose under precept; (b) juridically or as to the penalty prescribed, they do not oblige, unless the precept was given legally—i.e., by a written document, or in the presence of two witnesses, etc. (Canon 24). Example: If a precept was given under the penalty of loss of office, but without the legal

formalities, the canonical process and sentence of deprivation could not be resorted to.

519. A precept expires of itself with the expiration of the authority that gave it (e.g., at the death or cessation of office of the superior), unless the precept was given by document or before witnesses (Canon 24).

520. A rescript is a written reply made by the Holy See or the Ordinary to a request, statement, or consultation. Replies of this kind are employed in reference to the concession of benefices and to dispositions to be made concerning litigation and judicial procedure. Usually they grant favors, either transitory—e.g., a dispensation—or permanent—e.g., a privilege (Canons 36-62).

521. A privilege is a special and permanent right granted by a ruler to an individual or community to act contrary to or beyond the law.

(a) It is a permanent right, and so resembles law, which is also stable and forbids interference with what it grants.

(b) It is a special right, and so it differs from law, which is general and imposes obligation. It is sometimes styled "private law." Moreover, law requires promulgation, privilege requires only acceptance.

(c) It is granted by the ruler (i.e., by the Pope, bishop, or other legislator), and thus it differs from permission granted by a simple superior.

(d) It is granted to a person, that is, to an individual (Titus, Caius, Balbus, etc.) or to a congregation or community; for, if granted to all, it would not be special.

(e) A privilege gives the right to act contrary to the general law (e.g., by exempting from a tax) or beyond the general law (e.g., by granting the power to dispense). Thus, a privilege differs also from prerogatives that are set down in the Code itself (e.g., the special rights and faculties of Cardinals, bishops, regulars, etc.), all of which are laws and not privileges in the strict sense.

522. The rules for interpretation of privileges are similar to those for the interpretation of law (see 483 sqq.). They should be neither

extended nor restricted, but should be understood according to the meaning of the words themselves (Canon 67), yet so that the party receiving the privilege will seem to have obtained a favor (Canon 68). If the meaning intended is doubtful, the following rules of the Code (Canons 50, 68) should be followed: (a) wide interpretation is to be given to the privileges that are beyond or outside of the law and that are not prejudicial to others, as well as to privileges that were given as a reward of merit; (b) strict interpretation is to be given to privileges that are contrary to law (saving the cases of privileges granted to pious causes or in favor of a community), to privileges granted because of an agreement made, and to privileges that are prejudicial to third parties.

523. A privilege is a favor, and hence does not as such impose the duty of acceptance or use; but obligations owed to others often make it necessary to avail oneself of a privilege (Canon 69).

(a) Prerogatives granted in the law cannot be renounced by individuals, since their preservation is required by the common good. Example: A cleric has no right to abandon an immunity which the law gives to his state.

(b) Privileges granted to a community can be renounced by the community, but not by its individual members. An individual member is not bound, however, to use the privilege, unless there be accidental reasons, such as the command of a superior, that require him to do so.

(c) Privileges granted to individuals need not be used by them, unless there be accidental reasons that call on one to use a privilege. Example: A priest who has the privilege of a private oratory is not bound to establish such an oratory; but a priest who has the privilege of absolving from reserved cases is bound in charity to use it, if a penitent would otherwise suffer.

524. Dispensation differs from privilege: (a) because the former from its nature is temporary, the latter permanent; (b) because the former is always contrary to the law, whereas the latter may be only beyond the law.

525. The Pope can dispense as follows: (a) in all ecclesiastical laws he can grant a dispensation strictly so-called (Canon 81); (b) in divine laws

in which the obligation depends on an act of the human will (such as the laws of oaths, vows, contracts, etc.), he can grant a dispensation improperly so-called (see above, 313 sqq., 357), In other divine laws, he can interpret or declare, but he cannot dispense.

526. The Ordinary can dispense as follows: (a) in the general law of the Church when he has an explicit or implicit faculty from the Pope or from the law (Canon 81); (b) in diocesan laws and, in particular cases, also in laws of provincial and plenary councils, when there is just reason (Canon 82); (c) in papal laws made for a particular territory, when faculty has been given explicitly or implicitly, or recourse to the Holy See is difficult (Canon 82); (d) in all ecclesiastical laws that are dispensable, when there is doubt of fact (Canon 15).

527. The pastor can dispense as follows: (a) from the general law concerning feasts of obligation and from the laws of fast and abstinence. The dispensation can be granted either to his own subjects or to strangers, but only for a just reason, in individual instances and for particular individuals or families. The bishop may dispense the whole diocese, but the pastor cannot dispense the whole parish (Canon 1245). (b) When there is danger of death, the pastor can dispense from matrimonial impediments as provided in Canon 1044.

528. Religious superiors, local superiors included, can dispense in the laws and statutes of their own institutes, except where this is forbidden. In clerical and exempt institutes the superiors can also dispense the subjects and all who live day and night in the religious house (such as students, guests and servants) from the general laws of the Church, as follows:

(a) The higher superiors, such as abbots, generals, provincials, have the same authority in this respect as the bishop has with reference to his own diocese. Hence, they can dispense in all ecclesiastical laws in which the Pope dispenses, when there is doubt of fact, or recourse to the Holy See is difficult (Canons 15, 81); in case of necessity, they can dispense from the laws of abstinence individuals, or an entire convent, or an entire province (Canon 1245, § 2); they can dispense in irregularities as provided in Canon 990, § 1.

(b) The other superiors, local superiors included, can dispense their subjects from the laws of fast and abstinence in the same manner as pastors are able to dispense their parishioners (Canon 1245, § 3), Religious superiors are also able to dispense the private non-reserved vows of their subjects (Canons 1313, § 2, 1314).

529. Confessors, when delegated, can dispense as follows: (a) with ordinary faculties, from impediments, irregularities and penalties, as provided in Canons 1044, 1045, 985, 990, 2290; (b) with privileged faculties, from simple vows not reserved to the Pope, if no injury is done to the rights of a third party; and from occult irregularity produced by delinquency, that from homicide excepted. (In the internal sacramental forum the confessor can dispense from the impediments indicated in Canons 1043-1045.)

530. Priests that assist at marriages can dispense from impediments as provided in Canons 1043-1045.

531. The manner of seeking dispensations is as follows: (a) for the usual dispensations (e.g., those from fast, abstinence, observance of feasts, and the vows that may be dispensed by confessors) no particular procedure is required; (b) for the dispensation that must be sought from the Holy See, if the matter belongs to the internal forum, the petition is sent to the Sacred Penitentiary through the Confessor or Ordinary; if it belongs to the external forum, it is sent to the competent Congregation through the parish priest or Ordinary. Dispensation from public marriage impediments must be sent through the Ordinary.

532. The manner of preparing a petition for dispensation is as follows: (a) the name of the penitent must not be given in petitions to the Sacred Penitentiary, but the name and address of the party to whom the reply is to be sent should be clearly given; (b) the petition should be sent by letter. It may be written in any language, and should state the case with its circumstances, the favor that is asked, and the true reason for asking it.

533. A dispensation is invalidated as follows: (a) through defect of the petition, if it contains a substantial error, and the dispensation is given on condition of substantial truth (Canon 40); (b) through defect of the petitioner, if he is incapable of receiving the favor asked (Canon 46); (c)

through defect of the dispensation, as when the requisite signature or seal is omitted; (d) through defect of the dispenser, as when he lacks jurisdiction, or grants without a just and proportionate reason a dispensation for which he has only delegated power (Canon 84).

534. If a dispensation is unjustly refused, note the following: (a) ordinarily, the subject has not the right to hold himself free from the law; (b) in extraordinary circumstances, when the law ceases, or no longer obliges (see 487 sqq.), the subject is free.

535. The faculty of dispensing should be interpreted as follows: (a) widely, when it was granted for cases in general (Canon 200, §1); (b) strictly, when it is granted for a particular case (Canon 85).

536. A dispensation itself should be interpreted strictly in the following cases: (a) when the dispensation has an odious side, as when it is contrary to law and advantageous to private interest or is detrimental to a third party; (b) when wide interpretation is dangerous, as favoring injustice, promoting ambition, etc. (Canons 50, 85).

537. A dispensation ceases intrinsically in the following ways: (a) by the lapse of the period of time for which it was granted; (b) by the entire and certain cessation of the motive of the dispensation, if the effect of the dispensation is divisible—that is, if the motive for dispensation has to be existent each time that the law calls for an act or omission (Canon 86). Example: If one is dispensed from the fast or Office on account of ill-health, and later recovers, the dispensation ceases.

538. A dispensation ceases extrinsically in the following ways: (a) by the act of the one who dispensed, if he validly recalls the dispensation, or by his cessation from office, if he limited the dispensation to his own term of authority (Canons 86, 73); (b) by the act of the one who was dispensed, if he renounces the dispensation without detriment to any third party, and with the consent of the superior (Canons 86, 72).

539. A dispensation does not cease in the following cases through the cessation of the motive for which it was given:

(a) If the motive ceases only partially or doubtfully, even though the effect of the dispensation be divisible—that is, requiring the existence of the motive for the grant each time the dispensation is used. For, if the dispensation ceased in such cases, its benefit would frequently be in great part lost on account of the worry and scruple to which the persons dispensed would be exposed. Example: Balbus has been dispensed from fast on account of poor health. Later on he improves, but has not recovered his strength entirely, or at least is not certain of his recovery. He may continue still to use the dispensation.

(b) A dispensation does not cease if the motive ceases entirely and certainly, but the effect of the dispensation is indivisible—that is,removing the entire obligation once for all.

Example: Titus is a widower with several young children. He wishes to marry in order to have a home for the children, and this wish is the motive of a dispensation given him from an impediment of affinity to the marriage he contemplates. But before the marriage takes place, the children die, The dispensation still holds good.

540. A dispensation does not cease by reason of the grantor in the following cases:

(a) It does not cease through the grantor's cessation from authority, if it was given independently of his term of office. Example: Sempronius received a dispensation "valid until recall," but never made use of it. Although now the grantor has died, the dispensation continues in force.

(b) It does not cease, if the grantor invalidly recalls the dispensation, as when he dispenses from delegated power and his authority ceases with the act of dispensation. Example: Balbus, a confessor, dispensed Caius from the law of abstinence, but now wishes to recall the dispensation. The dispensation remains.

541. A dispensation does not cease on account of the person dispensed in the following cases:

(a) It does not cease when he leaves the territory of the dispenser, if the dispensation was personal. Example: A person dispensed from the general law of fast by indult granted to his diocese cannot use that dispensation outside the diocese; but if he has a personal dispensation, he is dispensed everywhere.

(b) It does not cease when the grantee fails to use it, or acts contrary to it, if there is no renunciation on his part. Examples: Sempronius has been dispensed from the fast of Lent, but he fasts on some days. This non-use of the dispensation on some days does not renew the obligation. Balbus has received a dispensation to marry Sempronia, but he changes his mind and marries Claudia. This act contrary to the dispensation does not take away its force, and, if Claudia dies, he will be free to marry Sempronia.

Art. 6: CIVIL LAW

542. Meaning.—Just as the Church has the right and duty to make laws which will promote the spiritual welfare of her members, so has the State the power and obligation to legislate for the temporal happiness of its citizens: "There is no power but from God and those that are, are ordained of God. He (the ruler) is God's minister to thee for good" (Rom., xiii. 1, 4).

543. Origin.—The authority to make civil laws resides in that person or body to whom according to the constitution of the State the legislative function belongs. (a) In an absolute monarchy, the legislative authority is vested in the prince; (b) in a state that has an appointed or hereditary aristocracy, the legislative power may be entrusted, at least in part, to a body of nobles; (c) in a limited monarchy or republic the lawmaking function belongs to the people, who exercise it either directly or (as is the case in most modern states) indirectly through elected representatives.

544. The acceptance of civil law by the people is not necessary for its obligation, for obedience to higher powers is commanded (Rom., xiii, 5), and, if law has no authority, the common welfare is defeated. Several points must, however, be noted.

(a) The foregoing principle is to be understood of law in itself, for, if there is question of the form of government or of him who exercises the powers of sovereignty, acceptance by the people may be said to be necessary in the sense that the multitude may set up the particular system of rule which it prefers, and may designate the individuals who are to wield authority under the constitution adopted.

(b) The principle given above is to be accepted regularly speaking, for there may be cases in which the acceptance of the people is required by law itself. Example: Under former civil constitutions, if in a certain place a lawful custom was in force, a contrary law which did not expressly abolish the custom did not oblige unless accepted. But this example is theoretical, for modern civil codes do not recognize the derogatory force of custom. If the constitution of the state calls for a referendum or plebiscite (i.e., submission to the electors for ratification), then the bill passed by the legislature or a measure proposed by the initiative body lacks force until accepted. This illustrates acceptance of a proposed law, but the acceptance is supplemented by some ministerial act.

(c) The principle given above is to be understood of the taking effect of a law, for the continuance of a law may depend on the acceptance of the people in the sense that a contrary custom of the people is able to abrogate law, if the superior consents (see 500 sqq.). Few codes of modern states give legal force to popular custom; they suppose that, if a law is not satisfactory to the people, the way is open to its repeal through exercise of the suffrage. But, morally speaking, there is no obligation to obey a law that has fallen into desuetude.

545. As to laws made by one who has no lawful authority, we should note: (a) of themselves, they have no binding force, since law is an act of authority; (b) from the necessities of the case, they are obligatory, if, being otherwise just, they are accepted by the great body of the people; for to resist them then would be prejudicial to public order.

546. Subject-Matter.—The objects or classes of temporal goods that fall under the regulation of civil law are many:

(a) external goods, or goods of fortune, which should have the protection of the State; and the laws regarding them should promote agriculture, commerce, industry, the arts, etc.;

(b) the goods of the body, which are more important still, and hence the law should favor the family and the increase of its members, and should provide for the health and well-being of the citizens by sanitary regulations and measures of relief for the needy, the unemployed, the orphans, and the aged;

(c) the goods of the mind, which are necessary for progress and happiness, and hence the law should provide the means for instruction in the secular arts and sciences and for the general diffusion of useful knowledge;

(d) the goods of the will (i.e., virtue and morality), which are most important both to the individual and the community, and hence the law must safeguard public decency and sobriety, and restrain and punish the opposite crimes and vices;

(e) the social goods of the people, which are promoted by wise legislation concerning the form and administration of government, the mutual duties and rights of citizens, the protection of the State and of its members, etc.

547. The relation of civil law to natural law is as follows:

(a) The State has no power to make laws that are opposed to nature, for, since law is an ordinance according to reason, any human command that is contrary to nature and therefore to reason is not law, but the corruption of law. No sin, not even a venial sin, can be made obligatory by law. Example: The rule of Sparta that sickly infants were to be put to death was not law but legalized murder.

(b) The State has the power to declare and enforce by suitable sanctions the conclusions that are derived from the general principles of the law of nature; for many people might be ignorant of these conclusions or inclined to disregard them, unless they were promulgated and confirmed by human law. Example: The natural law requires that parents provide for their young children, and that children assist their needy parents; the civil law adopts these natural principles, compels their observance, and punishes transgressors.

(c) The State has the power to make concrete and to determine the provisions of the natural law that are abstract or general. Example: The natural law decrees that some form of government be set up, that the people contribute to the support of the government, that crimes be punished, that the general welfare be served, etc.; the civil law determines the special form of government, the manner in which the revenues are to be obtained, the specific penalties for each crime, the public measures that are best suited to the circumstances, etc.

548. The relation of the civil law to divine and ecclesiastical law is as follows:

(a) In matters purely spiritual the State has no power to legislate, since its end and authority are confined to things temporal; and hence the State has no right to interfere with the faith, worship and government of the Church. But, since morality promotes the prosperity of the State, and since the end of the individual is spiritual, the civil law should respect and favor religion.

(b) In matters that are partly spiritual, partly temporal, the State has the power to legislate on those aspects that are temporal, yet so as not to infringe on divine or ecclesiastical right. Example: Civil laws on education have the right to regulate non-religious subjects, courses, standards, etc.; but they have no right to proscribe religious training, or to prescribe the teaching of irreligion or immorality, State laws on marriage may require registration, settle the civil effects of marriage, etc., but they have no right to interfere with the unity of marriage or the sanctity of the marriage bond.

549. The State is for the individual, and not the individual for the State; hence, civil law should not interfere with human liberties, except where this is necessary for the common peace and safety or the lawful opportunity of the people as a whole. Hence:

(a) Human liberties that are not inalienable may be limited by the law, when the public good or the welfare of individuals requires this (see 292). Examples: The State has the right to regulate the acts of those who are unable to take care of themselves in matters of importance; to forbid what is detrimental to the common interest (such as hunting and fishing at certain seasons), to protect the public when it neglects to protect itself, etc. Uncalled-for interference by government with the personal and private affairs of individuals—paternalism in government—is of course to be avoided, for restriction of liberty is something disagreeable and should not be resorted to without necessity.

(b) Human rights that are fundamental (such as the rights to live, to marry, to rear a family, to be free, to pursue happiness) should not be trespassed on by civil law. Thus, the State has no right to forbid marriage to the poor, but on the contrary it has the duty to remove conditions that cause poverty. But, when the common welfare demands the sacrifice, the State has the right to call on citizens to expose even life and fortune in its defense.

550. Those Subject to Civil Law.—Civil laws oblige all those who are in any way subject to their authority.

(a) Citizens, when in the country, are bound by all the laws that pertain to them; when outside the country, they are bound by some laws, such as those that regulate their personal status and office, but not by others, in particular such as are of a territorial character.

(b) Aliens are bound by the laws of the country that include them, such as those that regulate public order and the making of contracts.

551. The Obligation of Civil Law.—Civil law, when it has all the conditions of valid law, even if the legislator is non-religious or anti-religious, is obligatory not only before the State, but also before God (i.e., in conscience). This is; (a) by reason of the natural law, of which it is a derivation (see above, 313); (b) by reason of divine positive law, for it is frequently declared in scripture and in the Church's teaching and practice that lawful authority represents God and must be obeyed for conscience' sake: "Render to Caesar the things that are Caesar's" (Matt, xxii 21), "Be subject of necessity, not only for wrath, but also for conscience' sake" (Rom, xiii. 5).

552. Are subjects obliged to offer themselves for punishment prescribed by law?

(a) If the fault committed was merely juridical (i.e., before the law), the penalty is certainly not obligatory before sentence. Example: Balbus through sheer accident, and without design or negligence, kills a man. If involuntary homicide is punished by imprisonment, Balbus is not bound to give himself up. English common law, it should be noted, presumes a man innocent until proved guilty, and a man cannot be convicted of any degree of homicide on his own confession alone. But he may plead guilty to minor offenses.

(b) If the fault committed was theological (i.e., before God) and the penalty is primitive (i.e., the loss of some right or privilege), the penalty is obligatory in conscience. In Canon Law such penalties are sometimes *ipso facto*, that is, before sentence (e.g., suspension of a cleric); but the civil law, it seems, imposes penalties only after judicial declaration. Example: Titus on account of bribery has forfeited the right to vote; but he has not been declared guilty by court, and hence may continue to use the right of suffrage.

(c) If the fault was theological and the penalty incurred is active (e.g., exile, imprisonment, fine), the penalty is not obligatory before sentence; for it would demand too much of human nature to require that one deliver oneself up to exile, accept confiscation, etc. The apprehension and detention of the guilty is imposed by law as a duty on the police and other officers, not on the guilty.

553. The kind of obligation imposed depends on the will of the lawgiver: (a) he can oblige under pain of sin, or under pain of nullity or punishment; (b) he can oblige under pain of grave sin, or under pain of venial sin.

554. Generally speaking, the legislator is held to oblige under pain of sin in the following cases: (a) when the law is a just determination of the natural law (e.g., the laws that determine ownership); (b) when the law is directly concerned with and necessary to the public good (e.g., laws on national defense in time of war, laws that impose necessary taxation, etc.; see above, 379).

555. The legislator is held not to oblige under sin in the following cases: (a) when the law is enacted as penal, or is prudently regarded as such—as is the case with laws that are of minor importance or that can be enforced without a moral obligation—laws useful rather than necessary; (b) when the law is merely irritant or inhabilitating, the subject is not obliged to omit the act invalidated, but only to suffer the consequence of nullity before the law.

556. In doubt as to the obligation of a law, what is the duty of the subject? (a) If there is doubt concerning its justice, the subject can always observe it with a safe conscience. One may obey an unjust law, until it is judicially declared unjust, if it is not manifestly opposed to divine or human rights. (b) If there is doubt whether a law obliges under sin or not, the subject does not sin directly by non-observance (see 375, 376, 377, 561).

557. Special Kinds of Laws.—Laws that determine ownership are those that define in distinct and explicit terms the rights of citizens as to property, in such matters as goods lost or found, prescription, inheritance, copyright, distribution of property of intestates, rights of wives, capacity of minors, contracts, etc. It is commonly held that these laws are obligatory under sin, even before judicial decision: (a) because they are determinations of the natural law made by the authority that represents God in matters temporal; (b) because they are necessary for the peaceful existence of society.

558. Irritant or voiding laws are those that deprive certain acts of legal value. The common welfare requires that certain acts, even if valid naturally, may be made invalid by the State (e.g., contracts entered into by minors, donations made under fear, wills devised irregularly), and hence there is no doubt that the effect of invalidation can be imposed under pain of sin.

(a) This holds even before judicial decision, if it is clear that the lawgiver ought to intend and does intend to deprive an act of its moral validity from the beginning. Example: If a lawsuit would put one party (e.g., a minor) under great disadvantage, the law can irritate a contract in conscience and before judgment is rendered.

(b) An irritant law does not oblige under sin before declaration of nullity, if it is not clear that the legislator intended this; for it can be presumed that the State is content with external means as long as these are sufficient for its ends; and, since invalidation of acts is odious, it calls for certain expression of his intention by the lawgiver. But after sentence has been given, that which is civilly null is also null morally. Hence, if the courts declare a will to be of no effect, because it was not drawn legally, the decision is binding under sin.

559. Civil lawgivers in modern times do not, as a rule, concern themselves with moral or natural obligation as such, but rather consider only what regulations will best promote the peaceful intercourse of society. Hence, the question whether a civil irritation obliges in conscience ipso facto (i.e., before judicial declaration of a case) has to be decided generally, not from the words, but from the purpose of the law.

(a) An irritant law should be regarded as obligatory *ipso facto*, when the general purpose of law (viz., the common good) or the specific purpose of this law requires that there should be obligation in conscience even before a court decision. Examples are laws irritating agreements to do what is illegal, laws whose purpose is to protect minors or others who would be at a disadvantage in case of litigation, or to lessen the number of cases before the courts.

(b) An irritant law should be regarded as not obligatory *ipso facto*, when the end of the law does not clearly demand obligation before judicial declaration; for, as remarked above, the invalidation of an act is something odious, and hence not to be taken for granted. Thus, laws that void an act, contract or instrument on account of lack of some legal form, do not affect the natural rights or obligations before sentence.

560. Though the civil lawgiver has the right to annul certain acts, and thus to extinguish moral rights or obligations that would otherwise exist, laws seemingly irritant frequently have a different intention.

(a) Laws that make a claim unenforceable in court do not destroy the natural right of the claimant. Example: The Statute of Limitations in modern states generally bars the right to pursue a debtor in court after six years; nevertheless, the moral obligation of the debtor remains.

(b) Laws that make an act or contract voidable do not nullify, but only grant to the person concerned the right to attack validity before the courts. Hence, if the conditions for valid contract required by natural law are present (knowledge, consent, etc.), moral rights and obligations are not voided. Example: Under the civil law some contracts made by minors may be retracted by them. But, as long as such a contract is not disavowed, the other party has a moral right to insist on its execution; if it has been ratified after majority, the former minor has no moral right to seek the benefit of the law by asking for rescindment.

561. With reference to penalty, four kinds of laws can be distinguished.

(a) Purely preceptive laws are such as oblige under pain of sin, but not under pain of punishment. There are church laws of this kind (such as the command to assist at Mass on Sunday), and there are also some civil laws that do not oblige under penalty (e.g., statutes governing the age for legal marriage, for, if a couple misrepresented their age, they might be prosecuted for the misrepresentation, but not for the act of marriage).

(b) Purely penal laws are such as oblige under pain of juridical fault and punishment, but not under pain of sin (e.g., a law that punishes negligence in driving as defined by itself, even though there be no moral culpability involved).

(c) Mixed laws disjunctively are such as oblige under sin either to obey the law or to suffer the penalty (e.g., a law that commands one either to get a license before fishing or hunting, or to pay a fine if caught doing these things without a license).

(d) Mixed laws conjunctively are such as oblige under pain of both sin and punishment (e.g., the laws that forbid injustice and command the punishment of transgressors).

562. There is no question about the existence of laws of the first and fourth classes just described, but some authorities argue against the existence of the other two classes, maintaining that a law that does not oblige in conscience is an impossibility. They argue: (a) the teaching of scripture and of the Church supposes that all just laws oblige in conscience; (b) the lawgiver holds the place of God, and hence one cannot offend against the law of man without offending God; (c) human law, being only a reaffirmation or determination of thehigher law, obliges in conscience like the law on which it is based; (d) directions of a superior that do not oblige under sin are counsels rather than laws.

563. To these and similar arguments the defenders of the existence of penal laws reply: (a) such laws do not oblige in conscience, under pain of sin and of offense to God, to do or to omit as the law prescribes, just as a vow which gives one the option of not playing cards, or else of giving each time an alms, does not bind one in conscience not to play cards; (b) but those laws do oblige one in conscience to respect their juridical value, not to resist their enforcement, and to pay the penalty of violation, just as the vow mentioned obliges one in conscience to give an alms each time one plays cards. The Church recognizes penal laws (see 450), and there is no reason why civil law may not be penal.

564. Even when the transgression of a purely penal law is not sinful by reason of the civil law, it will frequently, if not usually, be sinful by reason of repugnance to the law of God. Thus: (a) the transgression will be sinful, if there is a wrong intention (such as contempt for the law) or wrong circumstances (such as culpable neglect or some inordinate passion); (b) the transgression will be sinful, if one foresees or should foresee evil consequences, such as scandal (see 96).

565. It is generally admitted that some civil laws are purely penal, since they impose penalties for fault, negligence, or responsibility that is only juridical at times. Examples: A law that imposes a fine on all motorists caught driving over a certain speed limit, even though they be free of moral guilt; or that makes the owner of a car pay damages for injuries caused while it was used by his chauffeur.

566. Even these laws oblige under sin to some extent. (a) The transgressor is morally bound to the penalty prescribed by law, after sentence has been passed; and such penalties are just, for the common good requires them. Example: The speed violator is held to pay the lawful fine when it has been imposed. He may have been guiltless of sin, but the fine makes him more careful the next time. (b) The officers of the law are morally bound to apprehend and convict transgressors.

567. Many civil laws are commonly regarded nowadays as disjunctively preceptive or penal; and, since the custom of the prudent affords a good norm of interpretation (see above, 484 sqq., 506 sqq.), this common view is a safe guide, Example: Even conscientious persons do not feel that they have committed a sin if now and then they run a car

without a license, or fish in a government reservation without the permit required by law, when there is no danger or damage to anyone.

568. Whether most modern legislatures intend practically all or the great majority of their laws that are not declarations of natural law or provisions essential to public welfare to be purely penal or only disjunctively preceptive, is a disputed question. For the affirmative view it is argued:

(a) Moral obligation is not necessary, since the enforcement of the law is well taken care of by the judiciary and the police;

(b) Moral obligation would be harmful, for the laws that are put on the statute books every year, along with those already there, are so numerous that, if all these obliged in conscience, an intolerable burden would be placed on the people;

(c) Moral obligation is not intended, for legislatures as bodies either despise or disregard religious motives when framing laws; and so many jurists today believe that the danger of incurring the penalty prescribed by the law is the only obligation the lawgiver intends to impose, or that moral obligation must come from conscience (i.e., be self-imposed);

(d) Moral obligation is not admitted by custom, the best interpreter of law, for most citizens today regard civil legislation as not binding under sin.

569. Opponents of the view just explained answer:

(a) The prevalence of crime and the ineffectiveness of the courts in so many places prove the need of moral obligation of civil laws; and, even if the laws are well enforced, this will scarcely continue, if respect for them is lowered;

(b) Though there is an excess of legislation, it is not generally true that the individual citizen is burdened in his daily life by a multitude of laws;

(c) Lawmakers today are not more irreligious than the pagan rulers to whom the scriptures commanded obedience; and, even though they do not themselves believe in religion or the obligation of conscience, they do intend to give their laws every sanction that the common good requires, and thus implicitly they impose a moral obligation wherever the contrary is not manifest;

(d) The statement that the majority of the people in modern states regard the civil legislation as a whole as not obligatory in conscience may be passed over, as there is no proof for it. Moreover, the customary interpretation of the citizens does not make penal the laws which the elected representatives intended as preceptive, without the consent of the latter (see 394).

570. Signs that a law is merely penal are the following:

(a) The express declaration of the lawgiver that it obliges only under penalty. Examples: In the Dominican Constitutions it is declared that they oblige, not under fault, but only under penalty (No. 32). The same is true of the Franciscan, Redemptorist and most recent religious Constitutions. Some civil laws, it is said, are formulated thus: "Either do this, or pay the penalty on conviction." Other laws define punishable negligence in such a way that it does not ultimately suppose sin.

(b) Another sign of a penal law is the implicit declaration of the lawgiver. If a heavy penalty is prescribed for a transgression regarded by all as very slight proportionately, the government implicitly declares that it imposes no other obligation than that of penalty. Blackstone, in his "Commentary on the Laws of England" (1769), considers as purely penal all those laws in which the penalty inflicted is an adequate compensation for the civil inconvenience supposed to arise from the offense, such as the statutes for preserving game and those forbidding the exercise of trades without serving an apprenticeship thereto (Vol. I, Sect. 58).

(c) A third sign is the interpretation of competent authorities. Example: Practically all Catholic moralists, and the opinion of the people generally, consider as penal some laws that are merely useful, but not necessary (e.g., prohibitions against smoking or spitting in certain public places, laws on permits for fishing, hunting, etc.).

571. Whatever may be said about legislatures in general, it cannot be argued that in the United States they are indifferent or contemptuous as regards the moral obligation of law; the public acts and speeches of

Congress and of the State Assemblies show that the elected representatives of the people respect religion, and do not wish to deprive themselves of its help in their deliberations and decisions. Nevertheless, the opinion is very prevalent among lawyers that purely positive law in the United States is not intended to oblige under sin.

572. In practice, the attitude of the citizen to civil law should be one of respect and loyalty.

(a) If a law is good, even though the legislator did not impose a moral obligation, it should be obeyed; for reason and experience show that disregard for law is a source of scandal and of many public and private evils.

(b) If a law is not good, every lawful means should be used to have it repealed as soon as possible. But the principle that a bad law is always best overcome by being rigidly enforced, is not borne out by history, and sometimes the public good demands disregard for unreasonable ordinances. The so-called "Blue Laws" are a case in point.

573. Other questions pertaining to civil law that will be found elsewhere are: (a) the obligation of customs, taxation and military duty; (b) the power of the State to inflict capital punishment.

Question IV
CONSCIENCE

574. In order that man many tend to his Last End, it is not sufficient that the way be pointed out in a general manner (as is done by the natural and positive laws), but these laws must be applied to each act in particular by the practical reason or conscience, as it passes judgment on the right or wrong of an action in the light of all the circumstances.

Art. 1: THE LAW OF CONSCIENCE

(*Summa Theologica*, I, q. 79, aa. 11-13.)

575. Definition.—Conscience is an act of judgment on the part of the practical reason deciding by inference from general principles the moral goodness or malice of a particular act.

(a) It is an act, and as such it differs from moral knowledge and intellectual virtues, which are not transitory but enduring. Moral understanding (synderesis), by which everyone naturally perceives the truth of general and self-evident principles of morality; moral science, by which the theologian or ethician knows the body of conclusions drawn from moral principles; prudence, by which the virtuous man is able to make right applications of moral rules to individual cases—all these are permanent states and are preparatory to the act of conscience, in which one makes use of one's knowledge to judge of the lawfulness or unlawfulness of an action in the concrete, as attended by all its circumstances.

(b) Conscience is an act of judgment, and thus it differs from the other acts employed by prudence—from counsel about the right means or ways of action, and from command as to their use. Counsel inquires what is the right thing to do, conscience gives the dictate or decision, the moral command moves to action.

(c) Conscience is in the reason—that is, it is a subjective guide, and thus it differs from law, which is objective.

(d) Conscience is in the practical reason. Unlike other judgments, which are speculative and deal not with action or only with theoretical aspects of action (e.g., the judgment that God is perfect, that the active faculties are distinct from the soul, etc.), conscience is concerned with action from the view-point of its moral exercise.

(e) Conscience is the inference from general principles, and thus it differs from moral understanding (synderesis). This latter is a habit by which everyone who is mentally developed is able to perceive without argument that certain more general propositions of morality must be true, such as the axioms of the natural law (see above, 319 sqq.); conscience draws conclusions from those axioms.

(f) Conscience judges concerning the morality of an act. Here lies the difference between consciousness and conscience; consciousness is a psychological faculty whose function is to perceive one's own states and acts; conscience is a moral judgment concerning the lawfulness or unlawfulness of those states or acts. Thus, consciousness testifies that one is considering the performance of a certain act, conscience judges the morality, and permits or forbids; or consciousness testifies that a certain thing was done or not done in the past, conscience declares the morality—condemning, excusing, or approving what took place.

(g) Conscience judges concerning a particular act—that is, it considers an act that is to be done here and now (or was done), with all the attendant circumstances. Conscience, thus, differs from moral science, which, though it systematizes the body of conclusions drawn from the natural and positive laws, is not able to make the applications for the innumerable cases that arise. Even works containing moral cases, which give solutions for concrete instances, do not take the place of conscience in such instances, for it is still the individual who judges about those solutions or about their applicability to his particular circumstances.

576. Division.-Conscience is variously divided. (a) According as the act judged is in the future or in the past, conscience is antecedent or consequent. The antecedent conscience is a monitor which decides that a future act will be lawful or unlawful; the consequent conscience is a judge which causes peace or remorse for what has been done in the past. (b) According to the kind of direction or decision it gives, antecedent conscience is commanding, forbidding, permitting or counselling; while consequent conscience is excusing, approving, or condemning (Rom., ii. 15).

577. According as it agrees or disagrees with the external divine or human law, conscience is true or false. (a) A true conscience judges that to be good and commanded which is really good and commanded. Example: According to law, one may use money of which one has the disposal. A sum of money before Balbus is really at his disposal. Hence, his conscience is true if it decides that he may use this money.

(b) A false conscience judges the lawful to be unlawful, or vice versa: "The hour cometh that whosoever killeth you will think that he doth a service to God" (John, xvi. 2). Example: Balbus would have a false conscience, if he decided that he had no right to use the money before him. This would happen if he was mistaken about the general principle, or about the fact that the money was at his disposal, or if he drew a wrong inference from the premises.

578. According to its qualities and suitability as a guide of conduct, conscience may be viewed either with reference to the will or to the intellect. (a) With reference to the will, conscience is either good (right) or bad (wrong), according as it does or does not proceed from a well-meaning intention and a right disposition towards one's end and duties. Example: If the Balbus mentioned above decided that the money was at his disposal because he wished to know the truth and had investigated to the best of his ability, his conscience would be good. But, if he decided this without sufficient investigation and only because he was prejudiced in his own favor, his conscience would be bad.

(b) With reference to the intellect, conscience is either certain or uncertain, according as the mind assents to its judgment without or with fear of error. Examples: If Balbus decides that he has the right to use the money, and is so firmly convinced that his judgment is true that he has no fears or doubts, his conscience is certain. But, if there remain solid difficulties or objections against his judgment which he cannot satisfactorily answer so that he assents to his view only with the fear that he may be wrong, his conscience is uncertain.

579. A conscience may have some and lack others of the qualities just mentioned.

(a) The same conscience may be true and bad, or false and good—that is, the judgment of the intellect may be in agreement with objective facts, but at the same time it may be directed by a wrong will and intention, or vice versa. Examples: Caius, through no fault of his own, is convinced that he is bound to tell a lie to help Sempronius, because Sempronius once helped him by lying. His conscience is false, but good. Titus is really not bound to pay a sum of money demanded of him. But the arguments by which he persuades himself that he is not bound are not honest, since he has recourse to what he knows are hair-splitting distinctions, quibbles and sophistical reasonings. His conscience is true, but bad.

(b) The same conscience may be good and uncertain, or bad and certain. Examples: If the Caius above-mentioned believes he is bound to lie, but has some qualms or suspicions that such conduct might not be right after all, his conscience would be good, seeing that he meant to do what is right; but it would be uncertain, seeing that he is not sure he is right. If the Titus above-mentioned had so habituated himself to insincerity and illogical reasoning that he no longer had any fears about his own judgments, and gave firm and unhesitating assent to his decision that he was not bound to pay the money demanded, his conscience, though bad, would be certain subjectively.

580. Obligation of Conscience.—Man is bound to be guided by conscience, both negatively and positively—that is, he must neither disobey when it forbids, nor refuse to obey when it commands.

(a) It obliges by reason of divine command, since it acts as the voice or witness of God making known and promulgating. to us the moral law. Hence "all that is not from conscience is sin" (Rom, xiv. 23).

(b) Conscience obliges from the nature of things, for, since the will is a blind faculty, it must be guided by the judgment, of the intellect, and must follow the inner light given it about the law. Apart from revelation, there is no other way of learning what God wishes one to do here and now.

581. The authority of conscience is not, however, unlimited.

(a) Conscience is not independent of external law and authority. It is not autonomous morality of the reason or will, nor private inspiration or interpretation; for its function is not to establish law or pass judgment on it, but to apply the law as expounded by the Church to a present case. Hence, conscience must aim to be true—that is, to agree with and express the objective law.

(b) Conscience is not independent of the righteousness of the will. It is not a speculative judgment, whose value depends solely on agreement between the mind and the facts, as is the case with a conclusion of pure science. It is a practical judgment, which has to guide all man's conduct, and thus its value depends on the relation of the means it selects to the end towards which the means should be directed. Hence, conscience must be good—that is, a judgment dictated by a will well disposed towards the true end of life.

(c) Conscience is not independent of the certainty of the intellect. It is a judgment formed, not by sentiment, emotion, or one's own wishes, but by evidence and firm conviction; for its office is to guide man reliably in the most important of affairs. Hence, conscience must be certain—that is, a judgment to which the intellect yields its unhesitating assent.

582. In order, therefore, that conscience may be the proper rule and moderator of man's moral life, it must have the following qualities:

(a) It must be good, and practically true—that is, in agreement with the Last End of man and, as far as the efforts of the individual can attain to such agreement, with the objective law—for the standard of moral good is not each one's wish or opinion, but God as the Last End and the external natural and positive law as means to that End.

(b) It must be certain—that is, without fear that one is wrong; at least, it must have that degree of certainty which is possible in moral matters. For to act with the fear that one is committing sin, is to be willing to do what may be sin, and is thus consent to sin.

583. Since conscience that has the requisite conditions is our immediate guide in moral matters, it follows: (a) that a conscience which is true objectively, good, and certain must be followed, whenever it commands or forbids; (b) that a conscience which is in invincible error (see 30), but seems to him who has it to be not only true but certain, must also be followed when it forbids or commands. Examples: If a child were told and believed that he was obliged to tell a lie to prevent an evil, he would be bound to do this. If a person eats what he wrongly thinks to be forbidden food, he is guilty of the violation he apprehends.

584. Exception.—If invincible error results from lack of sufficient intelligence to be capable of sin (see above, 249, 387), then the failure to follow one's conscience in such error does not make one guilty. Example: If a person unable to walk were persuaded that he was bound nevertheless to walk to church for Mass, his conscience would not make his omission sinful. Conscience supposes sane judgment, but the judgment we are now considering is not sane.

585. A conscience that has not the requisite conditions is not a safe guide, and hence it cannot be followed.

(a) An erroneous conscience may not be followed, if the error is vincible and there is danger of sin; neither may one act against it if there be danger of sin. To follow such a conscience would be to do what is wrong and to act in bad faith (i.e., to have a bad and erroneous conscience); not to follow it, would be to act against one's judgment, wrongly formed though it was, and to do insincerely what is right (i.e., to have a bad, though true conscience). Example: A person who has made up his mind that dishonesty is necessary in his business, but who realizes that his reasons are not convincing, sins against sincerity if he follows his opinion; he sins against conviction, if he does not follow his opinion. But his predicament is due to his own sophistry or bad will, and the escape from it requires only that he be honest enough with himself to inquire about the matter.

(b) A doubtful conscience may not be followed, if the doubt is such that one is not reasonably sure that a certain act is lawful. Example: If a man does not know whether a certain remedy will be helpful or seriously harmful to another, his conscience is doubtful as to the lawfulness of administering the remedy, and it may not be followed. If in spite of this he makes use of the remedy, he is guilty of the harm he foresaw, even though it does not happen.

586. Exception.—It is lawful to follow a vincibly erroneous conscience, if there is no danger of sin in this. Example: If a person has neglected inquiry about holydays of obligation, and through his own neglect believes that Good Friday is a holyday, he does not sin by attending the services that day.

587. The signs of a vincibly erroneous conscience are: (a) that in the past one did not use the same diligence to inform oneself about one's religious duties as is employed by conscientious persons; (b) that in the present one has fears, doubts or suspicions as to one's own sincerity of judgment.

588. Results of Conscience.—The results of following an erroneous conscience are as follows:

(a) He who follows an erroneous conscience, commanding or forbidding or permitting, is not guilty of sin if his ignorance is invincible. Example: A child who thinks he is obliged to lie because he has been told to do this, is excused from sin on account of his ignorance.

(b) He who follows an erroneous conscience, commanding or permitting evil, is guilty if his ignorance is vincible. Example: A grown person who has persuaded himself that deception is lawful, obligatory or advisable, or that truthfulness is forbidden, but who ought to know better, is not excused by the conscience he has formed (see above, 97 sqq.).

589. The results of disobeying an erroneous conscience are as follows:

(a) He who disobeys an invincibly erroneous conscience, is guilty. Example: The child who refuses to tell a lie when he thinks he ought to do so because it has been commanded, is guilty of disobedience.

(b) He who disobeys a vincibly erroneous conscience, is also guilty. Example: Caius promises to tell a lie to help another party. The doubt occurs whether or not this is lawful, and he takes no pains to settle it correctly, but decides offhand that a promise must be kept. When the time comes, Caius becomes alarmed and does not keep his promise, lest he get into trouble. He is guilty.

590. If a conscience which was vincibly erroneous in its origin is here and now invincibly erroneous, the acts that result from following such a conscience are to be judged as follows:

(a) They are materially evil in themselves and formally evil in their cause. Example: Titus, who intends to take a position in which he will have to advise others, foresees that later on he may make mistakes costly to others, as a result of his present lack of sufficient study. He secures the position, and tries to make up for former neglect of study, but on one occasion injures a patron by wrong advice which he would not have given, had he worked more faithfully as a younger student. The wrong advice is objectively sinful in itself, as being an injury; it is subjectively sinful in its cause, as being the result of negligence which foresaw what might happen.

(b) The acts in question are not formally evil in themselves. Example: Titus was formally guilty of injury to others at the time he foresaw what would happen on account of his negligence; he was not formally guilty at the time he did the injury, because he had tried meanwhile to repair his negligence and was not conscious of his ignorance.

591. The kinds of sin committed in consequence of an erroneous conscience are as follows:

(a) Sin committed by following a vincibly erroneous conscience is of the same gravity and species as the act for which the conscience is responsible, but the ignorance is an extenuating circumstance. Example: He who blinds his conscience so that it decides in favor of grave calumny, is guilty of mortal sin against justice; but he is less guilty than if he had sinned without any permission from conscience.

(b) Sin committed by disobeying an invincibly erroneous conscience is of the gravity and species apprehended by the conscience. Example: A person who tells a small lie, thinking it a mortal sin against charity, is guilty of the malice he understands to be in his act.

(c) Sin committed by disobeying a vincibly erroneous conscience is of the species that was perceived. Example: Caius who did not live up to his promise of telling a lie, after he had decided that to keep his word was the right thing to do, was guilty of a breach of promise. As to the gravity of sin against a vincibly erroneous conscience, it is always the same as that apprehended by the conscience, unless what is seriously wrong is culpably mistaken for what is only slightly wrong. Examples: If Caius, just referred to, thought that his desertion of his friend inflicted a grave injury, he was guilty of grave sin. A person who persuades himself by vain reasonings that complete intoxication does not differ in gravity from incipient intoxication, is nevertheless guilty of the greater malice, if he puts himself in the former state; for his wrong opinion cannot change the fact, and his culpable ignorance cannot excuse him.

592. An erroneous conscience may apprehend something not wrong as wrong, but in an indeterminate manner.

(a) If the species of evil is not determinate before the conscience, but an indifferent act is thought to be sinful without any definite species of sin being thought of, he who acts against such a conscience seems to commit a sin of disobedience. Example: A person who thinks that smoking is a sin, of what kind he does not know, must have at least vaguely the opinion that it is forbidden by the divine law; and hence, if he smokes, he is guilty of disobedience.

(b) If the gravity of the putative sin is not determinate before the conscience, but an act is thought to be sinful without the degree of sinfulness being at all known or thought of, he who acts against such a conscience commits a mortal or a venial sin according to his own disposition with respect to sin. If he is so attached to the sin he apprehends that he intends to commit it, whether it be great or small, he is guilty of mortal sin, at least in so far as he exposes himself to it. But if he is habitually resolved not to commit grave sin, it can be presumed that he would not do that which he apprehends as sinful, if he thought it was a grave offense, Example: If a person erroneously thinks that it is a sin to read a certain book, and then reads it without adverting at all to the gravity of the sin he apprehends, his greater or less guilt will have to be judged by his character. If he is so conscientious that he would stop reading at once if he feared the book was seriously harmful, he sins only venially; but if he knows that he is lax and is yet resolved to read the book at all costs, it seems that he is guilty of grave sin.

Art. 2: A GOOD CONSCIENCE

(*Summa Theologica*, I-II, q. 19, aa. 5, 6.)

593. As was explained in the previous article, conscience is not a proper guide unless it is good. In this article we shall speak of the good conscience and of its opposite the various kinds of bad conscience.

594. Definition.—The distinction of good and bad conscience is applied both to consequent and antecedent conscience (see 576).

(a) The consequent conscience is good, and one is said to have a good conscience, if it testifies that past acts were rightly performed, that past sins were forgiven, that one is in the friendship of God, etc.; "The end of the commandment is charity from a good conscience" (I Tim., i. 5); "War a good warfare, having faith and a good conscience" (ibid., 19). The consequent conscience is bad if it testifies in a contrary way: "Let us draw near with a true heart, having our hearts sprinkled from an evil conscience" (Heb., x. 22).

(b) The antecedent conscience, with which we are now concerned, judges about the morality of an act to be performed here and now, or in the future. It is called good, if it is made by one who is in good faith—that is, one who sincerely loves goodness and who decides according to the truth as far as he is able to see it. It is called bad, if it is the judgment of one who is in bad faith—that is, one who is in error through his own fault, or who arrives at the truth by reasonings that are not honest or not understood by him. Example: Speaking of those who, though fearing that idol meats were forbidden, yet ate of them because they saw others do this, St. Paul says: "There is not knowledge in everyone. For some until this present, with conscience of the idol, eat as a thing sacrificed to an idol, and their conscience being weak is defiled" (I Cor., viii. 7).

595. Divisions.—By training and care a good conscience is developed and becomes better. (a) A vigilant conscience is one that asserts itself promptly and strongly under all circumstances. (b) A tender conscience is one that inclines to a careful observance of all the Commandments and to a purification of the inner workings of the soul. A possessor of this kind of conscience is called conscientious. (c) A timorous conscience moves one through filial fear to shun even the slightest sins and imperfections, and to use all prudent efforts to avoid occasions and dangers of sin. The possessor of this kind of conscience is called God-fearing.

596. A bad conscience that is in vincible error is divided according to its effects into the scrupulous and the lax conscience. (a) The lax conscience errs on the side of liberty. It is moved by trivial reasons to judge the unlawful to be lawful, the gravely sinful to be only slightly evil, that which is commanded to be only counselled, and so on.

(b) The scrupulous conscience errs on the side of obligation. It is moved by trivial reasons to judge that there is sin in something lawful, grave sin in something venially wrong, and obligation in something that is only counselled; it sees inhability or defect where these do not exist, and so on.

597. The Lax Conscience.—According to the more or less control it has over one, the lax conscience may be divided into the incipient and the habitual. (a) It is incipient when one is becoming familiar with careless decisions and less responsive to remorse about evil done. In this state the conscience is said to be sleeping. (b) It is habitual when through long-continued habit one has become enamored of a worldly, frivolous conception of life, and is rarely visited by compunction. In its worst state, when there is little hope of cure, a lax conscience is said to be seared or cauterized (I Tim., iv. 2).

598. According to the greater or less responsibility of the one in error, a lax conscience is either malicious or not malicious. (a) It is malicious when it results from one's own disregard for religious truth, as in the case of the pagans who did not care to know God, and were thus led into perverse conceptions of morality. St. Paul calls such a conscience a reprobate sense (Rom., i. 28). (b) It is not malicious when it results from some less blamable reason, as in the case of the Christians at Corinth who thought that the eating of idol meats was sinful, but that it was to be practised on account of the example of others. St. Paul calls this a weak conscience (I Cor., viii. 10).

599. Laxity of conscience is either partial or entire. (a) A conscience entirely lax takes an easy and indulgent view in all things. It is careless both in little and great matters, both in directing self and in directing others. (b) A conscience partially lax is too liberal in some things, but not in others. Examples: Titus is very exacting with his girls, and wishes to have them models of virtue; but he is too easy with himself and his boys. Balbus is very loyal to friends, but has no sense of justice as regards those who do not agree with him. Sempronius tries to serve both God and mammon, being very faithful to church duties, but at the same time dishonest in business matters.

600. A conscience partially lax may even combine scrupulosity and laxism (see 610), becoming like a mirror that reflects large objects as small and vice versa; or like a color-blind eye: "Woe to you that call evil good and good evil, that put darkness for light and light for darkness" (Is., V. 20). This kind of conscience is called pharisaical.

(a) One may be lax and scrupulous about the same kind of things. Examples: Caius regards great disobedience in himself as a mote which he doesn't need to worry about, but small disobedience in his children as a beam in the eye which he is seriously bound to extract (Matt, vii. 3-5). Titus is lax about almsgiving to those from whom he can expect nothing, but scrupulous about almsgiving to those from whom he expects a return later on.

(b) One may be scrupulous and lax about different things, straining at gnats and swallowing camels. Example: The Pharisees were scrupulous about external observances and minor things of the law, such as tithes; but they were lax about inward justice and the weightier things of the law, judgment, mercy and faith (Matt, xxiii. 13-31).

601. Causes of a Lax Conscience.—(a) If the laxity is inculpable but habitual, it is caused generally by lack of Christian training in childhood and the influence of evil principles and practices that are widespread. In particular cases a lax decision of conscience may be due to want of sufficient consideration or to a sudden storm of passion that obscures the reason, when one has no time for deliberation; and thus it is inculpable.

(b) If the laxity is culpable, its usual causes are an easy-going view of God's law and its obligation (Is, xliii. 24); or a self-love that sees in one's vices nothing but virtue or amiable weakness; or a long-continued indulgence of sin that has destroyed all refinement of conscience.

602. Special Dangers of a Lax Conscience.—(a) If the laxity is inculpable, it is an occasion of demoralization to others and a preparation for formal sin in him who has the conscience;

(b) if the laxity is culpable, it is the cause of formal sin; and if it is not corrected, it naturally leads to moral blindness, hardness of heart and impenitence: "There is a way that seemeth to man right, and the ends thereof lead to death" (Proverbs, xvi. 25).

603. Since a lax conscience is a species of erroneous conscience, the rules given above as to the kind of sins committed in consequence of an erroneous conscience, apply also to the lax conscience (see above, 588 Sqq.).

(a) When the laxity is concerned with the existence of sin, the conscience taking what is sinful for something lawful, he who follows such a conscience is guilty or not guilty according as his ignorance is culpable or inculpable (i.e., as he acts from a bad or a good conscience). Examples: The man who practises dishonesty, because he has cheated his conscience by sophistry into deciding that dishonesty is lawful; the child who uses profane language without realization of sin, because he hears his elders use it. But if the lax conscience takes what is sinful for a duty, he who disobeys it is guilty of sin. Example: The person who refuses to tell a lie when he thinks he ought to lie on account of a promise made.

(b) When the laxity is concerned with the gravity of sin, the conscience taking what is mortal for venial sin, he who disobeys such a conscience is guilty of mortal or venial sin, according as his ignorance is culpable or inculpable (i.e., as he acts from a bad or a good conscience). Examples: A child who thinks that calumny or missing Mass is only a venial sin, because he sees grown up persons treat these things lightly; a person that, to solace his conscience, advises with lax associates who always approve of what he wishes to do or has done.

604. He who knows, or who has good reason to think, that his conscience is lax, should guide himself by the following rules: (a) with reference to the past, if there is a doubt whether or not sin was consented to or was grave, the presumption is against him, for laxity willingly contracted makes one responsible for what ensues; (b) with reference to the future, a person must make use of the means prescribed for one who is in danger of sin (see above, 258 sqq.), for a lax conscience places one in danger of sin.

605. Remedies Recommended for a Lax Conscience.—(a) The defect of will or character should be corrected. Example: The presumptuous should reflect on the justice of God, and recall that the broad way leads to perdition. Those in whom the wish is father to the lax judgment should make war on the passion that leads them astray. Those who have become lax through bad habits, should set about acquiring good habits, like that of going to the Sacraments frequently. (b) The error of the intellect should be corrected. Example: If a person's religioustraining has been neglected, he should do what he can to get

correct information and advice as to his duties. If one has been influenced by lax ideas or conduct, one should change one's reading or associations.

606. Is a lax person held responsible, if he does not know that he is lax? (a) If his conscience is invincibly erroneous, he cannot know that it is lax, and hence he is not responsible; (b) if his conscience is vincibly erroneous, he ought to know that he is lax, and hence he is responsible. Examples: The boy Caius keeps whatever he finds, because he thinks he has a right to do this. The man Titus does not like cheating, but he cheats habitually, because he thinks he has as much right to do so as others. Both the boy and the man are lax, but neither considers himself lax; the difference is that Titus can and ought to know that he is lax.

607. The scrupulous Conscience.—This is a species of erroneous judgment that sees sin where there is no sin, or grave sin where there is only light sin, and whose reasons are trivial or absurd. (a) It differs, therefore, from a strict or tender conscience, which, while it does not exaggerate sin, judges that one should try to avoid even slight sin and imperfection. This is the golden mean between a lax and a scrupulous conscience. Persons with this sort of conscience are sometimes called scrupulous or singular, because they are more exact than the majority. More accurately they are to be called conscientious or God-fearing.

(b) The scrupulous conscience differs also from scrupulosity, which is a state of mind in which one whose judgment is not erroneous, is nevertheless tormented by fears or doubts about his moral condition.

608. The rules given above (588 sqq.) for the erroneous conscience apply also to the scrupulous conscience. (a) He who follows a scrupulous conscience does not sin by this, even though he is vincibly in error; for there is no danger of sin in doing more than is required. Example: Caius is too lazy to make inquiries about his religious duties, but he has the exaggerated notion that grace at meals obliges under pain of grave sin. He does not sin by following his conscience, for grace at meals is recommended to all. (b) He who disobeys a scrupulous conscience commits the sin his conscience apprehends. Example: If Caius omits grace, he is guilty of grave sin.

609. Special Dangers of a scrupulous Conscience.—(a) As to himself, the scrupulous person suffers from his conscience; it makes him guilty of sin where there should be no sin, and by its exaggerated strictness it often drives him to the other extreme of laxity. (b) As to others, the scrupulous person is an annoyance and a detriment; he tries to impose his conscience on them, or at least he makes virtue appear forbidding.

610. It is possible for a conscience to be scrupulous and lax at the same time, over-indulgent on some points, over-severe on others (see 600). (a) It may be scrupulous as regards others, and lax as regards self, or vice versa. Example; Parents sometimes are too lenient with themselves, but rule their children with extreme severity; in other cases they are meticulous as to their own conduct, but think they must allow their children every indulgence.

(b) A conscience may be scrupulous in minor matters and lax in major matters. Example: The Jewish leaders scrupled to take the money from Judas or to enter the house of Pilate, but they did not hesitate to condemn our Lord unjustly.

(c) A conscience may be scrupulous as to externals, lax as to internals. Example: The Pharisees made much of bodily purifications, but gave little thought to purity of mind and heart.

611. The Perplexed Conscience.—Like to the scrupulous conscience is the perplexed conscience, which judges that in a particular instance one cannot escape sin, whether one acts or does not act. Example: Titus fears that, if he goes to church, he will sin by endangering his health, which is feeble; that, if he does not go to church, he will sin by disobeying the law. This seems to have been the conscience of Herod, who thought he was confronted with the alternative of perjury or murder when the head of John the Baptist was asked of him (Matt, xiv. 9).

612. St. Alphonsus gives the following directions to assist one who is perplexed in conscience:

(a) If without serious inconvenience decision can be delayed, reliable advice should be obtained (e.g., from the confessor).

(b) If decision cannot be delayed, the alternative that seems the lesser evil should be chosen. Example: The natural law requires that Titus should not expose his life to danger unnecessarily. The positive law of the Church requires that he go to Mass on Sunday. It is a less evil to omit what is required by the law of the Church than to omit what is required by the law of God. Hence, Titus should decide that he is not obliged in his circumstances to go to church.

(c) If decision cannot be delayed and the party cannot decide where the lesser evil lies, he is free to choose either; for he is not bound to the impossible.

613. If, in the supposition last mentioned, the perplexed person acts with the feeling that he is committing sin through necessity, is he really guilty or not?

(a) If by the feeling of guilt is meant, not a judgment of the mind, but a scruple or doubt, he is not guilty, as we shall see below when we speak of scrupulosity.

(b) If by the feeling of guilt is meant a judgment of the mind that he has to sin and an intention to welcome the opportunity, he is guilty; but his guilt is considerably diminished by the error and his difficult circumstances. Example: Titus thinks that he sins whether he obeys or disobeys an order to take a good dose of whiskey. He decides to take the dose, and feels rather pleased at the thought that he will become intoxicated.

(c) If by the feeling of guilt is meant a judgment that one has to sin, accompanied by sorrow at the necessity, one is not guilty, if one thinks the matter over to the best of one's ability before acting; there is some guilt, if the perplexity arises from previous culpable negligence and no effort whatever is made to remedy this before acting. Example: Gaia asks her mother if she may go for a ride. The mother fears that, if she refuses, Gaia will become desperate; if she permits, Gaia will meet unsuitable companions. If the mother's perplexity is due to the fact that she has never taken any interest in Gaia, she is responsible if she carelessly makes a wrong decision; but if the perplexity arises only from the difficult character of Gaia, the mother is not responsible.

614. Scrupulosity.—Like to the scrupulous conscience is the state of scrupulosity, which manifests itself in moral matters especially as a vain fear or anxiety concerning the presence or magnitude of sin in one's act. A psychopathic state, scrupulosity is usually listed as a form of psychasthenia which is characterized by weakness of soul, inability to cope with problems, and a lack of psychic energy. Clinically examined, the psychasthenic presents the following characteristics: (1) physically, he is listless and always tired; (2) intellectually, his tiredness makes it impossible for him to concentrate for long periods of time; (c) psychologically, he is an introvert concerned with himself as the center of his interests and activities.

The more common manifestations of the psychasthenic's difficulties include: self-diffidence, uncertainty, hesitation, obsessions and scruples. A species of psychasthenia, scrupulosity may be described as an inordinate preoccupation with the moral and religious order, a special type of worry directed toward the morality of actions.

(a) scrupulosity must be distinguished, however, from the scrupulous conscience, inasmuch as scrupulosity is not a judgment, but a fear that accompanies one's judgment. Example: A scrupulous person knows very well that it is not a sin to omit grace, nor a grave sin to pray with some voluntary distraction; but he worries over these things as if they were sins, or grave sins.

(b) scrupulosity must be distinguished from the tender conscience, inasmuch as scrupulosity is an exaggerated and harmful solicitude. A person of tender conscience is careful even in smaller duties, but in a quiet and recollected way, whereas the scrupulous person is all excitement and distraction.

(c) scrupulosity must be distinguished from the anxious or doubtful or guilty conscience, inasmuch as scrupulosity is a baseless fear or phobia. Examples: A person who has practised injustice for many years, has good reason to be perturbed in conscience when he reflects that restitution or reparation is a prerequisite to pardon; but a mother who did all she could to train her children well, is scrupulous, if she is constantly reproaching herself that she should have done better. A person who makes a contract while fearing that it may be unlawful, because good authorities hold its unlawfulness, acts with a doubtful conscience; but if he fears that the contract is unlawful, in spite of the fact that others regard it as lawful and that his only reason for doubt is that they may be wrong, he is scrupulous. The Egyptians at the time of the plagues could reasonably forecast grievous chastisements on account of their wickedness (Wis., xvii. 10); but a good person who worries constantly over the possibility of being damned must be scrupulous.

615. Scruples may be divided in various ways, but the simplest division seems to be by virtue of object, extension and duration. By reason of object, scruples may center on only one or, at most, a few moral activities, e.g., duties of charity, or sins against chastity, or they may embrace the whole moral life of the individual. By reason of extension, some scruples are limited to interior actions, others extend to external manifestations. By reason of duration, scruples may be classified as intermittent, or temporary, and quasi-permanent which is characteristic of the constitutionally scrupulous person whose physical and psychical disposition incline him to scrupulosity.

616. The signs or external manifestations of scrupulosity have been variously divided, but a simplified division into intellectual, or cognitive, affective, or volitional, and compulsive suffices for our present purpose.

(a) Intellectual: habitual abulia, i.e., an inability to decide, coupled with and interacting with constant doubt.

(b) Affective: closely allied to the intellectual state is the feeling of insufficiency which extends to actions, to the individual's own personality, to his desire for higher goals, to his abilities, etc. This fosters and strengthens the inability to decide. Inordinate fears, anxieties and sadness contribute to the genesis and growth of the sense of inadequacy.

(c) Compulsive: numerous compulsion factors are present in more serious cases of scrupulosity, e.g., obsessions, phobias, and compulsions properly so called, which concern external actions or rituals.

Obsessions include irresistible, persistent and irrational ideas accompanied by feelings of tension and fear. These ideas which plague the individual are "discordant," that is, out of harmony with his habitual attitude, and "impulsive," tending to reduce themselves spontaneously to action. The scrupulous person is frightened and flustered by the thought of doing a thing for which he has a positive abhorrence and by his inability to get the thought out of his mind.

Phobias refer to habitual, irrational fears of a definite entity associated with a high degree of anxiety and unwarranted by objective reality. They are very intense fears, completely out of proportion to their causes or objects.

Finally, compulsions strictly so called may be defined as irresistible, unreasonable urges to perform actions to free the individual from an obsessing idea. Tension and anxiety are associated if the act or external ritual is not performed.

For the confessor, the recognition of a scrupulous person is not too difficult. The penitent's own difficulties present the first and most obvious sign, e.g., irrational doubts about consent to temptation, as to the gravity of a sin, etc., and undue concern about circumstances. Concomitant signs confirming the judgment that a person is scrupulous include:

(a) Obstinacy of judgment; Although the scrupulous person seeks advice, frequently from many confessors, he tends to follow his own judgment. He is inclined to think that the confessor has not understood him, that he has not given a complete picture of his state of soul, etc.

(b) Inconstancy in acting owing to inability to judge rightly and the consequent frequent changes of judgment for light reasons.

(c) Irrelevant accusations of multiple circumstances that tend to lose the sin in the maze of circumstances.

(d) External motions by which the individual tries to do away with the fear, sin, or other difficulty.

617. Causes of a scrupulous Conscience.—Although the signs of scrupulosity are easily recognizable, the causes are not clearly defined, and authors are not entirely agreed in this matter. A listing of probable causes would include internal causes:

(a) physical—the physical causes are virtually unknown. Most authors admit a constitutional disposition to scrupulosity, just as there is one to its quasi-genus, psychasthenia. Reductively this might involve disorders in the vago-sympathetic nervous system and the neuro-endocrine system. (b) psychical—the cause is attributed to too low a psychic tension. The inability to cope with obsessions and the attacks of phobias serve to exhaust the individual; (c) moral—perhaps a suspicious and melancholy character, a disposition that is overly impressionable and changeable, or a self-opinionated nature, overconfident of its own ability.

618. The external causes of scrupulosity are: (a) the devil, who excites vain fears in order to diminish devotion, to discourage the use of prayer and of the Sacraments, to drive to tepidity and despair; (b) the neighbor, who teaches scrupulosity by his words or example; association with persons who are scrupulous; the reading of spiritual books of a rigoristic character; assistance by persons of a timid character at terrifying sermons on the divine justice; overly protective and overly rigorous education.

619. Though God cannot be the cause of scrupulosity in the same way as the evil spirits (who use it for man's destruction), nor in the same way as human agencies (which are unable to bring good out of the evil they cause), He does in exceptional cases directly permit even saintly persons to be vexed by scrupulosity that they may thereby satisfy for sin, or exercise themselves in humility and patience, or shake off spiritual torpor.

Scrupulosity that is supernatural in origin is much rarer than that which has a natural source, and it can be usually recognized by certain signs, like the following; (a) when it cannot be accounted for by natural causes, and is generally short in duration; (b) if it is from the evil spirits, it leaves the soul shaken or dismayed, if from God, it is followed by light and peace.

620. Dangers of scrupulosity.—The evil results of indulged scrupulosity are as follows: (a) temporal evils—the constant fears and worries of the scrupulous affect the brain and nerves, break down the bodily vigor, and lead to neurasthenia, hysteria, insanity or monomania; (b) spiritual evils—time is wasted in useless regrets and anxieties, prayer becomes a torture, confidence in God decreases, and, seeing they do not find consolation in virtue, the scrupulous often end in vice and despair.

621. Rules to be observed by the scrupulous.—(a) They must not yield to their scruples. As was said above, scrupulosity is not a conscience, but only the counterfeit appearance of a conscience; not a help to the soul, but a grave drawback and danger. Hence, the scrupulous must learn to despise their foolish fears and imaginations. (b) They must follow blindly the commands of a prudent spiritual director. To attempt to make decisions for themselves is a harrowing experience for scrupulous persons, and one fraught with great peril. They must protect themselves, therefore, by following the decisions made for them by one who will guide them aright. Gradually, as their condition improves, however, they must learn to take the initiative and thus prepare themselves to act as responsible persons capable of forming a correct judgment.

622. Not to follow their scruples means: (a) that scrupulous persons should recognize their scruples for what they really are (i.e., for a spiritual disorder), and that they should firmly resolve to use the means to get rid of them; (b) that they will prevent scruples from arising by keeping themselves occupied with external things, or by interesting themselves with matters that will exclude the worrisome thoughts; (c) that they will banish scruples at once, as they would a temptation. The two key aims of the scrupulous individual is to counteract his introversion by greater social activity and to re-train his faculty so that he will be in control at all times.

623. Though the scrupulous are obliged not to heed their scruples, they rarely sin by heeding them, because their condition is such that they are not responsible. For, as was said above (40 sqq.), fear and other passions lessen or remove deliberation and the voluntariness of acts.

624. To give absolute obedience to the spiritual director means: (a) that scrupulous persons should recognize that it is wrong for them to depend on their own prudence, whereas they are absolutely safe in following the advice and precepts of the spiritual father who holds the place of God; (b) that they should avoid changing directors, and should adhere strictly to the rules prescribed for them.

625. Qualities required for a successful direction of the scrupulous are:

(a) Knowledge. The spiritual physician must be able to distinguish scrupulosity from spiritual diseases or conditions that are similar, lest he prescribe what is not suitable for the case. Example: A person of tender conscience should continue in that state, a person of scrupulous conscience needs instruction that he may put aside his erroneous views; a scrupulous person stands in need of special guidance. He must also recognize that scrupulosity is a mental illness that at times requires the expert treatment of a psychiatrist. Knowing his own limitations and the need of expert therapy, he should not hesitate to send the penitent to a competent doctor.

(b) Prudence. Some persons pretend scrupulosity in order to get a name for holiness, or to make a good impression; needless to say, they must be dealt with cautiously, as they often prove very unscrupulous. With a person who is really scrupulous, the spiritual director must carefully obtain all the knowledge necessary to ascertain the true state of soul, prudently bring the individual to recognize that he is a sick person, help to restore his confidence in himself, in his confessor, in God, etc.

(c) Patience. The scrupulous are almost as troublesome to their directors as they are to themselves; but they are heavily burdened and are unable to help themselves. The law of charity applies. They have the same right to charitable treatment as others who are physically suffering and needy.

(d) Firmness. Disobedience will defeat every effort of a director to help a scrupulous person. On this point, therefore, there must be no leniency: the rules laid down must be insisted on, the reasons should not be given, and no argument or discussion should be allowed. The director should speak with certainty and authority; he should be brief, and, if he must repeat, he will do well to use the same words.

(e) Good judgment. After deciding that a person is scrupulous, the director must discover what is the particular form of scrupulosity in the case, and must apply remedies that are suitable.

626. Rules Concerning Persons Scrupulous about Past Confessions.— (a) For the first time the confessor may permit a general confession of the past life, if the scrupulous penitent has fears about previous confessions and has not already made such a general confession. Let the individual relate his whole story at once, with all its details and complications. This might perhaps take more than one confession to complete, but the full recital is necessary if the scrupulous person is to have confidence in his director's knowledge of his exact state of soul. (b) After this general confession, no mention of past confession must be permitted, unless the scrupulous person is ready to swear without hesitation that he is sure that a sin certainly grave was committed by him and never rightly confessed.

627. Rules Concerning Persons scrupulous about Present Confessions.—(a) Before confession, the penitent must be content with a certain brief space of time appointed by the confessor for making his examination of conscience and act of contrition. A longer time spent in these preparations is useful to other penitents, but harmful to the scrupulous.

(b) During confession only those sins need be mentioned which are seen from a brief examen to be both certain and grave, and only those circumstances whose declaration is absolutely necessary. If the scrupulous penitent begins to speak of doubtful sins or irrelevant details, the confessor must forbid him to go on; for though confessions must be complete, whenever possible, doubts and details must not be permitted in the case of such scrupulous persons (see Vol. II).

(c) After confession, if the confessor judges that there is not sufficient matter for absolution, he must not yield to the penitent's fears, but must assure him that he does not need absolution and that he may go to the Sacraments Without it.

628. Rules Concerning Persons scrupulous about the Performance of Duties.—(a) The scrupulous person should be instructed that positive laws, divine as well as human, do not oblige in case of moral

impossibility (i.e., when their observance is too burdensome); that the matter about which he has scruples has become too difficult for him, and hence that he is not obliged to it as others are.

(b) The scrupulous person should be commanded to leave undone what his vain fear calls on him to do; and, if this does not suffice, he should be told that he is not bound by the duty which causes him such anxiety. Example: Titus is scrupulous about the performance of obligatory prayers, so much so that he is not satisfied until he has repeated them several times, lest some syllable may have been omitted or hurried over, or the intention or attention may have been lost sight of at some part of the prayer, or the devotional posture may not have been observed throughout. If Titus cannot learn to say these prayers without making senseless repetitions, he should be told that the obligation has ceased until such time as he is able to fulfill it without torture to himself or others.

629. Of course, if harm is done to another by the incomplete performance of a duty, even a scrupulous person cannot be dispensed from repetition. Example: If a priest has not pronounced a sacramental form correctly, the fact that he is scrupulous does not excuse him from repeating the form correctly.

630. Rules Concerning Persons Scrupulous about the Commission Of Sin.—(a) The scrupulous person should be told that he is scrupulous, that his scrupulosity is not a conscience that he is obliged to follow, but a vain fear which he is obliged to struggle against by observing the directions given him.

(b) He should be directed not to deliberate long before acting, but to do what seems right to him at first; not to conclude after acting that he has committed sin, unless this appears certain and evident. Since the scrupulous are over-careful, the presumption is in their favor, and they can act and judge prudently by disregarding their fears and doubts. If by deciding offhand they sometimes sin or fail to recognize sin in a past act, this will come from invincible ignorance, and they will be excused from responsibility.

631. Since a disease is best cured by removing its cause, the confessor, when he has diagnosed a case of scruples, should prescribe remedies that are opposed to the source of the trouble.

(a) If scrupulosity seems to come from God, the penitent should be encouraged to regard it as a means of satisfaction for past negligences or as an occasion of virtue and progress, to pray incessantly for light and assistance, and to follow the guidance which God has provided. (b) If scrupulosity appears to be the result of diabolical obsession, and exorcism seems to be called for, the sufferer should not be told this. (c) If scrupulosity comes from associations or reading, the sufferer should avoid these occasions, and cultivate the companionship of persons or books that are cheerful and that give a hopeful outlook on one's duty and destiny.

632. Remedies for Scruples That Are Mental in Origin.—(a) Those who suffer from fixed ideas, phobias, and delusions, should not be reproved harshly and told that their fears are insane, but should be treated with kindness and firmness. In ministering to these troubled minds, the best course seems to be kind assurance that they have nothing to fear, along with insistence that they imitate the example of the generality of good people, avoid singular practices of piety, discuss their anxieties only with their director, and give themselves to some occupation that will distract their attention from their manias.

(b) Those whose minds are over-active and given to doubts and objections must avoid introspection and the study of moral problems that are too difficult for them; they must take a proper amount of suitable recreation, think and plan how they may help others who are in need, and avoid idleness.

633. Remedies for Scruples Whose Origin is Moral.—(a) If scruples arise from a stubbornness of character, the penitent must be told that the confessor is better fitted to judge the case, and that it is the height of rashness and presumption for a scrupulous person to prefer his ideas to those of the priest.

(b) If a melancholy or timid nature accounts for the existence of scruples, confidence and cheerfulness should be inculcated, and the penitent should be encouraged to meditate frequently on the goodness of God, and to remember always that God is not a harsh taskmaster, but a kind Father.

(c) Those who are scrupulous because their character is fickle and easily moved by every suggestion or imagination, need to cultivate seriousness, and to hold strongly to their judgments and resolves deliberately formed. Obedience to their director will be of more lasting benefit to these and other psychical scrupulants than psychiatric treatments through hypnotism, mental suggestion, and psychoanalysis; observance of the rules prescribed is an excellent cultivation of will-power, and it is sustained and perfected by the motives and helps which religion alone can supply.

634. Remedies for scrupulosity Whose Cause Is Physical.—(a) The physician is the proper person to care for bodily ills; hence, a scrupulous person who is troubled with headaches, dizziness, sleeplessness, loss of appetite, nervousness, hallucinations, etc., should go to a competent and conscientious specialist in the healing art. Removal of the causes of hurry and worry, moderate but sufficient diet, fresh air and exercise, and especially congenial occupation and surroundings are by general consent included among the best natural cures.

(b) The confessor, if he perceives that illness is the cause of scruples, should forbid any spiritual practices that cause or aggravate the malady. Example: scrupulous penitents should not be permitted to practise mortification by depriving themselves of necessary sleep, food, exercise or fresh air, or to use devotions or austerities for which they are physically unfit.

635. Persons who are scrupulous and lax at the same time need to be directed so as to overcome both spiritual maladies.

(a) If they are more scrupulous than lax, the case is less difficult, as they incline rather to the safer side, and it will suffice to apply the remedies indicated above for laxity and scrupulosity, as they are needed. Example: Titus, on account of scrupulosity, spends too much time at his prayers, and thus neglects the exercise and recreation which are necessary for his health. He should be instructed to limit his devotions, to have a regular time for them each day, and to realize that he has an obligation to take proper care of his health.

(b) If persons are more lax than scrupulous, the case is difficult, as they incline more to evil; indeed, if the trouble is Pharisaism, it is well-nigh incurable, on account of the pride and blindness that oppose resistance to every effort to cure. These persons need to be treated with severity, since nothing else will make any impression; they should be told in plain language how they stand and what is in store for them, unless they repent. Examples: Caius is extremely careful not to be guilty of sins of commission, but he thinks nothing of sins of omission; he would not take a postage stamp without express permission of the owner, but he neglects from year to year to pay bills, and sees nothing wrong in this. Titus thinks himself a saint because he worships the letter of the law, when it is to be applied to others; but he cares nothing about its spirit, and, though indulgent to self, is a tyrant with others. Both these men need to be told that, far from being good, they are very bad; that, far from being secure, they are in great danger. If insensible to reproofs, they should be reminded of the woes that await the wilfully blind (Matt., xxiii. 13 sqq.).

636. Practical Conclusions.—An instrument is called good when it produces with sufficient exactness the effects for which it was intended; it is bad, if it fails to produce those effects. Thus, a timepiece, a compass, or a thermometer is good if it indicates accurately, and bad if it indicates inaccurately. But, as it would be harmful to guide oneself by an unreliable instrument (e.g., by a watch with a defective mainspring, or which runs fast or slow), one naturally corrects the defects and regulates the working of the mechanism. Now, from what has been said above in this article, we see that conscience can be a deceptive indicator, and that its accuracy can be improved. Hence, the need of correcting a bad conscience and of cultivating a good conscience.

637. Remedies for a bad conscience and means for cultivating a good conscience are as follows:

(a) The remote causes of a bad conscience are in the will itself. A person judges wrongly often because he is wrong in himself, wrong in his intentions and purposes with regard to life as a whole, wrong in his attitude towards a particular line of duty, wrong in his lack of sincerity with himself. Hence, the correctives needed are a sincere love of God and of virtue, courage to wish the truth, and an honest examination of motives and actions: "The sensual man perceiveth not the things that are of the Spirit of God, but the spiritual man judgeth all things" (I Cor., ii. 14, 15).

(b) The immediate causes of a bad conscience are in the intellect. One judges wrongly because one clings in time of doubt to erroneous ideas or principles. The remedy, therefore, is to seek diligently for light through prayer, to study the lives and conduct of those who are models, to consult with the prudent and the conscientious. The bad conscience says to God: "Depart from us, we desire not the knowledge of Thy ways" (Job, xxi. 14); but the good one says: "Teach me Thy justifications. Thy testimonies are my delight, and Thy justifications my counsel" (Ps. cxviii. 12, 24).

638. Signs of a Good Conscience.—(a) Extraordinary holiness is not necessary before one may consider one's conscience good, for there are degrees of goodness. If, therefore, a person's external life is directed by the duties of his state, and his internal life, as far as he can judge, is free from serious guilt and guided by love of God and hatred of sin, he may safely regard his will as good. If sometimes he sins venially, this is not because he lacks a good conscience, but because he does not always follow it.

(b) Extraordinary diligence in studying one's duties is not necessary before one may regard one's conscience as good, for otherwise a heavier burden would be imposed than we can suppose God to intend. A person who is using all the means for obtaining religious instruction that are used by others in his position and who are conscientious, may safely regard himself as free from voluntary error. If sometimes he judges wrongly, the mistake will be involuntary and not due to a bad conscience. Of course, one whose conscience is not in vincible error may sin even mortally, not because his conscience is bad, but because he does not follow it.

639. The following are means for preserving and maintaining a good conscience: (a) we should judge our motives frequently with the severity

with which we judge the motives of another (Rom., ii. 1), and as before God (I Cor., ii. 10); (b) we should measure our actions, not by the standards of the world, its maxims and examples, but by those of Christ (I John, ii. 15-17; III John, 11).

Art. 3: A CERTAIN CONSCIENCE

(*Summa Theologica*, I-II, q. 57, a. 5; II-II, q. 47, a. 9.)

640. As was said above, only that conscience is a safe guide which is not only good—that is, in agreement, as far as one's efforts can secure this, with the external law—but also certain. A certain conscience is one which, without any prudent fear of erring, judges that a particular act is obligatory or unlawful, and hence here and now to be done or omitted.

641. Necessity of Certitude.—We must be sure we are right before we act; otherwise, we expose ourselves to the danger of sinning, and therefore commit sin (see 582). Hence, it is necessary to act with a certain conscience, and unlawful to act with an uncertain conscience. "If the trumpet give an uncertain sound, who shall prepare himself to the battle?" (I Cor., xiv. 8) may be accommodated to conscience. In Rom., xiv. 22, 23, the Apostle declares that he who acts with conviction is blessed, whereas he who acts in uncertainty is condemned. Examples: Sempronia doubts whether it is sinful to sew on Sunday; she is not sure, but has grave suspicions that sewing is servile work; if she goes ahead, she will be guilty of violating the law, as being willing to take the risk, and therefore the responsibility. Titus offers another a drink, being uncertain whether it has poison in it or not; he is guilty of sin, since he has no right to expose himself to sin and his neighbor to the danger of death.

642. Those persons who act with a doubtful conscience, and later discover that what they feared might be wrong was not wrong, or not so bad as they suspected, must bear in mind: (a) that their past conduct is not to be judged by their newly acquired knowledge, for that conduct must be judged by the knowledge had at the time. Example: Sempronia does some work on Sunday, doubting whether she is committing a grave or a slight sin. Later she discovers that it was really only a venial sin, and she congratulates herself that she did not sin seriously. Her judgment is wrong, because she did not know at the time of the work

that it was not a grave sin; (b) that they must guide themselves in future acts by their newly acquired knowledge.

643. Kinds of Certitude.—Judgments may be certain in a greater or less degree.

(a) They are metaphysically certain, when error is absolutely impossible, the opposite of what is held by the mind being a contradiction in terms which omnipotence itself could not make true. Example: The judgments that the same, identical act cannot be both good and bad, that good is to be done and evil to be avoided, that God is to be honored, are metaphysically certain, since they result immediately from the very concepts of being, of goodness, and of God.

(b) Judgments are physically certain, when error is impossible according to the laws of nature, the opposite of what is held by the mind being unrealizable except through intervention of another cause. Example: The judgments that he who takes poison will destroy life, that he who applies fire to a house will destroy property, are physically certain. because natural agencies, like poison and fire, act infallibly when applied to suitable matters and under suitable conditions and left to their course, unless they are overruled by superior power.

(c) Judgments are morally certain, when error is impossible according to what is customary among mankind, the opposite of what is held by the mind being so unlikely that it would be imprudent to be moved by it. Examples: One is morally certain that what a reputedly truthful and competent person relates to one is true. A person is morally certain that a conclusion he has drawn about his duty in a particular instance is correct, if he believes that he has overlooked no means of reaching the truth. Testimony and inference, since they come from free and fallible agencies, may lead into error; but, when they appear to have the requisite qualities indicative of truth, they are for the most part reliable and in practical life have to be considered as such.

644. As to the certainty that is required in the judgment of conscience, the following points must be noted:

(a) Metaphysical certainty is not required, since conscience does not deal with primary propositions, but with deductions about particular acts. The first moral principles, which are the object of synderesis, and at least some of the general conclusions, which are the object of moral science, are metaphysically certain (see above 145, 300), as they are based on necessary relations; but the particular conclusions, which are the object of conscience, are concerned with the contingent and the individual.

(b) Physical certainty is not required for the judgment of conscience, since conscience is not concerned with the activities of natural agents, but with the activities of moral agents that act with freedom and responsibility.

(c) Moral certitude, therefore, is sufficient for the conclusions drawn by conscience. That a higher kind of certitude is not necessary should not surprise us, for it would be unreasonable to expect that the same degree of assent be given to judgments that are concerned with particular and contingent cases as to those that are concerned with universal and necessary principles.

645. Moral certitude is of two kinds: (a) certitude in the strict sense, which excludes not only the fear of error, but every doubt, prudent and imprudent, great and small, Example: Titus thinks of a way in which he could easily make money dishonestly; but his conscience sees that the thing is manifestly wrong and decides without the slightest fear or doubt that it must not be done; (b) certitude in the wide sense, which excludes all fear of error and every serious or prudent doubt, but not one or other slight and imprudent doubt. Example: Caius was baptized by an excellent priest, but the date was omitted in the register. The doubt occurs to Caius that perhaps something essential was also omitted, and that it may be his duty to seek another Baptism. His doubt is unreasonable.

646. Moral certitude in the wide sense is sufficient for a safe conscience, even in matters of great importance, since it is frequently the only kind of certitude one can have, and he who would strive to be free from every slight and baseless suspicion would be soon involved in a maze of scruples and perplexities. Example: If the Caius above referred to were to yield to his doubt and be rebaptized, a similar doubt about the

second Baptism might easily arise in his mind, and he would be no more contented than before.

647. From the point of view of its object, certitude is twofold. (a) Speculative certitude refers to a judgment considered as a general law, abstraction being made from particular circumstances. Example: It is speculatively certain that farm work on a holyday is a forbidden kind of work, and that clerics are obliged to say the Divine Office. (b) Practical certitude refers to a judgment which is an application of a general law to a particular case, consideration being given to all the pertinent circumstances. Example: It is practically certain that Titus may make hay on a holyday, if otherwise he will suffer great loss; and that a cleric is excused from the Divine Office, if his physician has warned him that he is physically or mentally unable to perform it.

648. Speculative certainty is not sufficient for conscience, but practical certitude is required, since conscience refers not to abstract laws but to concrete cases—not to what is right if only the object of the act is considered, but to what is right when one considers the object, the motive, and all the circumstances here and now present.

649. From the point of view of the arguments on which it is based, certitude is of two kinds. (a) Demonstrative certitude is the assent that rests on a conclusion logically drawn from certainly true premises. Example: Caius argues that he is obliged to go to Mass on Sunday, because the law is certain, and it is also certain that the law applies to him. (b) Probable certitude, which is the assent that rests on a conclusion, whose premises, though not certain, seem to be true, and against which there is no counter conclusion, or none that cannot be readily answered (see 703). Example: Caius is pretty sure that he is seriously ill, because he perceives a number of alarming symptoms; the possibility that these may be due to imagination is excluded by the fact that they are new and sudden. Caius, therefore, concludes that he may hold himself excused from attendance at Mass.

650. Probable certitude is sufficient for conscience, for in moral matters it is impossible to have at all times reasons that amount to a demonstration, and hence a person acts prudently in following a decision that is solidly probable and unopposed by any contrary serious

probability. What is called "probable certitude" here is very different from probable opinion, about which there will be question below (662 sqq.)

651. From the point of view of the manner in which it is obtained, certitude is again twofold. (a) Direct certitude is that which is obtained from principles that are intrinsic to the case by applying to the matter the law concerning it. Examples: A judge who decides according to the evidence and proofs given in court that an accused is guilty, and a son who concludes from the Fourth Commandment that he is bound to help his parents in necessity, have direct certainty in their judgments, because they argued from principles that deal with the question before them. (b) Indirect certitude is that which is obtained from principles that are extrinsic to the case by applying to the matter in hand reflex principles (i.e., rules that direct how one should act in doubt) or the principle of authority (i.e., the argument drawn from the opinion of those who are acknowledged as competent to decide). Examples; If a judge is not able to form a certain judgment from intrinsic reasons concerning an accused, because strong arguments have been given both for guilt and for innocence, he has recourse to principles that have reference to his own state of doubt, and which declare that he must acquit when he is not certain of guilt. If a man is not able to decide whether the Fourth Commandment obliges him to keep his grandparents or mother-in-law in his home, when they upset his family and are able to take care of themselves, he can have recourse to the external principle of authority by consulting his confessor.

652. Direct certitude is not necessary for the judgment of conscience, for often, as in the cases just mentioned, it is not possible. Moreover, indirect certitude suffices to give one who is in doubt such practical assurance that one's fears become unimportant and one is able to act prudently in spite of them.

(a) The principle of authority—that "in doubt we can safely follow the advice of those who are experts and truthful"—is reliable, as both the conditions required for authority (viz., knowledge and truthfulness) and also daily experience show.

(b) Reflex principles likewise, although they do not prove what is deduced from them, are well founded, and point so clearly the side to be taken when judgment is suspended between alternatives that they enable one to act with all the certitude that prudence demands. Example: The principle that "in doubt decision should be given in favor of the accused," is based on the fact that a man's right to his life and liberty is so certain that he does not forfeit that right unless it is proved convincingly that he is guilty.

653. Examples of uncertain and certain consciences are the following:

(a) Uncertain conscience: It is lawful to make a just contract (major premise certain); but this contract is just (minor premise a matter of doubt or opinion); therefore, this contract is lawful (conclusion a matter of doubt or opinion).

(b) Conscience directly certain: It is lawful to make a just contract (certain); but this contract is just (certain); therefore, I may make this contract (certain).

(c) Conscience indirectly certain: It is lawful to follow competent advice or a moral system approved by the Church (certain); but a competent spiritual adviser or an approved system of Moral Theology holds that this kind of contract is lawful (certain); therefore, it is lawful for me to make this contract (certain).

654. An Uncertain Conscience.—Uncertainty of conscience can be understood in two senses.

(a) Conscience is uncertain in a more strict sense, if the verdict of the moral judgment on a question of lawfulness or unlawfulness is that no decision can be given either way, either because there are no reasons of importance on either side (negative doubt), or because the opposing reasons balance so perfectly that it is impossible to choose between them (positive doubt). Examples: Titus, wishing to do some drawing on Sundays, asks himself whether drawing is servile work. Not knowing the definition of "servile," he can only reply to his doubt that he has no reasons either for affirmation or for negation. Caius reads moral authors on the same question, and the pros and cons seem to him so equally strong that he cannot pronounce for either side.

(b) Conscience is uncertain in a less strict sense, if the verdict of the moral judgment on a question of lawfulness or unlawfulness is that the mind inclines to one side more than the other, but cannot decide in its favor (suspicion), or that it decides for one side, while perceiving that the arguments for the contrary are not to be despised (opinion). Example: Titus decides to spend a good part of Sunday taking photographs. Caius argues that this is unlawful; Sempronius, that it is lawful. Titus thinks the arguments of both are strong, but is better pleased with those of Sempronius. If he feels he cannot act on either opinion, his state of mind is what we called suspicion; if he feels that the opinion of Sempronius has prevailed, his state of mind is one of opinion.

655. From what was said above concerning the certitude requisite for conscience (see 641 sqq.), it follows that: (a) when the state of mind is positive or negative doubt, one is not allowed to act; for a person who is ignorant of what he should do, or who is fluctuating between opposites, runs the risk of sin and its consequences, if he acts blindly; (b) when the state of mind is suspicion, one is not allowed to act, for conscience must be more than conjecture or inclination; (e) when the state of mind is opinion, one is or is not allowed to act, according as the opinion has or has not the qualities required for certitude that is moral and practical (as explained above in 643 sqq.).

656. Doubt and Suspicion.—The following are the duties of a person whose state of mind about his obligation is one of doubt or suspicion:

(a) If he has no time to resolve his hesitation but must decide at once, he should follow the rules given for a perplexed conscience (see above, 611 sqq.). Example; Sempronius is ordered by his father to go on an errand; by his mother, to remain at home. He does not know whom he should obey, but argues that there can be no harm in performing the errand, since he feels that he is forced anyway. Sempronius' impromptu decision proceeds from a sense of moral responsibility; it is good, and as certain as he is able to make it.

(b) If a person has time to resolve his hesitation, he should not trust to common sense, but should consult moral theology, if he is competent to understand and apply it, or should have recourse to his confessor, if he is not a theologian. The attention given to his problem should be proportionate to the gravity of the duty in question, its importance for third parties, etc. (see below, 667 Sqq.). Example: If a layman is uncertain whether a practice he follows in his business is dishonest, he should consult a priest; if the priest is uncertain, he should refer to his theology and study the matter until he is able to give a well-founded, morally certain judgment.

657. Reflex principles by the aid of which a negative doubt may be solved, when the question is about the existence or non-existence of some fact connected with obligation, are the following:

(a) If the fact at issue is one about which presumption may be had from general or personal experience, the doubt may be settled by the principle: "In uncertainty decide according to what usually happens." Examples: Titus is uncertain whether his boy of seven years has the use of reason and is bound to go to Mass. As a rule, children attain discretion at the age of seven; and hence Titus should take his boy to Mass. Fr. Caius is uncertain whether he has said Terce. His experience is that such uncertainties on his part have always been baseless in the past; hence, he may consider that he has said Terce as usual.

(b) If the fact at issue is one about which no presumption is afforded, either from general or personal experience, recourse may be had to the principle: "A fact should not be taken for granted, but must be proved." Examples: Sempronia doubts whether her practice of saying the Rosary daily was the result of a vow; but, as there is no proof or circumstantial evidence of a vow, it may be held that her practice originated in a resolution. Caius, a stranger, claims that Titus owes him for an unpaid debt of his father. Titus knows nothing of the alleged debt, and the only substantiation for its existence is the word of the stranger. Titus is not obliged to pay.

658. Presumption of a fact is of three kinds according to Weight:

(a) Violent presumption is based on indications so significant or numerous that it leaves only slight room for evasion. This kind of presumption suffices, but is not essential in solving doubts. Example: Caius has no direct proof or disproof that he paid Titus in a certain business transaction, because all the papers have been lost. But he remembers distinctly that he drew the money and went personally to the office of Titus on the day payment was to be made, and that the latter, up to the time of his death several months later, always acted as if full settlement had been made.

(b) Strong presumption is based on circumstances or signs so moving that they permit one to infer a fact as being their natural or usual accompaniment or result. This kind of presumption suffices in solving the doubts we are considering. Example: If Caius, spoken of above, has no individual recollection of any circumstances bearing on the payment of his debt to Titus, but knows that it was his invariable custom to pay all his debts promptly, the presumption that he paid this debt is strong.

(c) Light presumption occurs when the reasons are so slight, that they hardly ever suffice to permit us to infer a given fact from them. Example: If we suppose that Caius was dilatory in paying debts, and that he has no better indication of payment having been made than the fact that Titus gave him a cigar about the time of their business transaction, there is little presumption that the debt was paid.

659. Reflex principles that may be used to settle negative doubts about the quality of an act performed are the following:

(a) If there is an individual presumption, the quality of the act may be inferred from what usually happens. Example: Sempronius cannot remember whether a certain good work he undertook was prompted by zeal or ambition. But, as he usually tried to keep his motives pure, it may be concluded that the work in question proceeded from a right intention.

(b) If there is no individual presumption, the quality of an act may be settled from general presumptions or principles. When the act was according to law, and the doubt concerns its validity or sufficiency, one may take it that all was rightly done; for it usually happens that he who complies with the substance, also complies with what is accessory. Moreover, the welfare of the public and of individuals require that an act done outwardly according to law should be deemed as rightly performed unless the contrary can be proved. Hence the rules: "In doubt decide for the validity of what was done"; "What has been done is presumed to have been rightly done." Examples: Caia cannot remember whether she really consented when she married Titus. Sempronius cannot remember whether he had sufficient attention in hearing Mass on Sunday. The presumptions are that Caia married validly and that Sempronius heard Mass properly, if they acted in good faith.

660. Reflex principles that may be used to settle negative and invincible doubts concerning law or obligation are the following:

(a) If no serious reasons can be found to prove or disprove the existence of a law, or its gravity or application to a present case, use may be made of the principle: "Invincible ignorance of the law excuses from sin." Example: Titus on an ember day consults all the sources of information he has to discover whether it is a fast day; but all he can learn is that some vigils are fast days, others are not.

(b) If no serious reasons can be found to prove or disprove that a law bears a certain meaning, recourse may be had to such principles as the following: "A law obliges only in so far as it is knowable"; "The interpretation may be made against the legislator who could have spoken more clearly"; "Things burdensome to the subjects of the law should be construed narrowly; things favorable, broadly." Example: Caius, who supervises workingmen, has no notion regarding the meaning of the word "workingman" as used in an indult on fasting— viz., whether it applies to supervisors of work or exclusively to laborers.

(c) If no serious reasons can be found to prove or directly disprove that a certain law has ceased or been abrogated, the principle to be followed is: "In doubt decide for that which has the presumption." In this case the presumption is for the continuance of the law, since it was certainly made, and there is no probability for its non-continuance. Example: Sempronius learns that certain mitigations have been made in the law of fasting, and wonders whether the same is true as regards the law of abstinence; but he has no reason to think that any change has been made on this latter point.

661. In the above cases negative doubt was solved generally in favor of non-obligation as against obligation. But there are two cases in which negative doubt must be settled in favor of obligation, according to the rule: "In doubt follow that which is safer." The two cases are:

(a) Negative doubt must be settled in favor of obligation, when the doubt is about a matter of such importance that it does not permit the taking of risks in its performance, as when there is question of laws that safeguard the supreme rights of man, or of laws that prescribe the essentials to be used in the administration of the Sacraments. Example: Sempronius adopts a newly-born infant abandoned at his door. As there is nothing to indicate whether the baby has been baptized or not, Sempronius takes the safer course and has it baptized.

(b) Negative doubt must be settled in favor of obligation when it persists because no reflex principle is found, or none that seems to be suitable for the case. Example: Titus wavers between uncertainties about the existence of a law; he can discover no reasons pro or con, and he knows no principle or presumption to guide himself by in his difficulty. He does not know or even think that he may act as if the law were non-existent, and hence he must inquire further, or else act as if the law did exist.

662. Opinion.—The duty of one whose state of mind is opinion is as follows:

(a) If he is able to remove every objection against his judgment or to make unimportant such objection or objections as remain, his opinion has become moral certainty (see above, 644 Sqq.), and he may follow it as a safe guide. Example: Caius promises to marry Sempronia, but his parents forbid the marriage. Caius opines that he should keep his promise, but to be sure he consults his pastor. The latter shows him that the opposition to his marriage is unreasonable, and thus sets at rest the difficulties of Caius.

(b) If a person is not able to remove one or more important objections against his judgment, his opinion has not become moral certitude, and he may not follow it as a safe guide. Example: If Caius' pastor holds that the parents are right and Caius wrong in the question of marriage with Scmpronia, so that Caius, while still thinking he should keep his promise, has serious fears that it would be a wrong step, the young man should not follow his own view.

663. Those who act when their state of mind is doubt, suspicion, or uncertain opinion are: (a) guilty of sin, for they do not act in good faith

(Rom, xiv. 22, 23), and they are imprudent and lovers of danger (Ecclus., iii. 27); (b) guilty of the species and gravity of sin which they fear may be in their act; for they interpretatively wish that to which they expose themselves. Example: If Titus takes an oath, fearing that his act is perjury, he is guilty of perjury before God, even though what he says is true.

664. Fears or objections against an opinion are unimportant as follows: (a) if they have only a slight probability (e.g., Titus opines that he is not obliged to say the second lessons, because he knows that he began them, and therefore must have said them; but he fears he may be obliged to say them, because he cannot remember the details of the lessons, and hence has probably not said them); (b) if they are improbable (e.g., Caius fears that he may have omitted Sext, although he recalls going to choir to chant at the regular times.)

665. Fears against an opinion are important, when they are not merely possible, but have such an appearance of truth that even a prudent man would consider them as worthy of support.

(a) Intrinsic signs of this solid probability are the good arguments by which the fear, or contrary of an opinion, is supported. Example: Titus after careful examination of conscience decides that he is not obliged to mention a theft in confession, because it happened just before his last confession; yet, he fears that he is obliged, because he does not remember having thought of restitution.

(b) Extrinsic signs of solid probability are the good authorities by whom the contrary of the opinion is defended. Example: Caius opines that he is not obliged to confess a calumny, because he is not certain that it is unconfessed; he fears that he is obliged, because St. Alphonsus, whose authority is great in Moral Theology, teaches that a grave sin must be confessed unless it is certain that it has been confessed already.

666. He who is moved by unimportant fears or difficulties is scrupulous, but not so he who hesitates in the face of an important difficulty. Examples: Balbus fears he may be guilty of murder, because he left a sick person for a moment and the latter unexpectedly died in his absence (scrupulous conscience). Sempronius fears he may be

bound to restitution, because by his ridicule he made Titus lose his means of livelihood (disturbed conscience).

667. What is to be done by one who holds an opinion as to what he may or may not do here and now, but who has a serious fear that his opinion is wrong?

(a) If the fear persists as serious, when the means to remove it (such as consideration and consultation) have been duly resorted to, he should delay, if this is possible, or follow the safer course, if delay is not possible. Example: Titus must go to confession now, but he cannot recall whether or not a past theft was ever confessed; he thinks he is not obliged to mention it now, but is far from feeling certain about this, because of a serious doubt which he cannot resolve. The thing for him to do is to resolve to confess the theft as one that was perhaps unconfessed before.

(b) If the fear is removed or made unimportant, by direct means (such as theological argument from moral principles) or by indirect means (such as consultation or the use of reflex principles), the opinion may be followed. Example: If Titus, mentioned above, learns from his confessor or deduces from reliable reflex principles that he is not obliged to confess the theft, he may act with a safe conscience in following this decision.

668. The authority that may be safely followed by a lay person who holds an opinion, but fears that the opposite may be true, is that of anyone whom he knows to be pious, instructed and prudent; for, as it is impossible for him either to settle the question for himself or to remain in perpetual uncertainty, he must acquire certainty here as in other important affairs by consulting those who are expert and reliable. Hence, if the conscience is merely opinionative, a dependable adviser should be conferred with to make it certain.

(a) In the case of an accusing or excusing conscience, it is at least advisable that the doubtful sin be mentioned in confession, and especially by those who are not strict in their lives and who are inclined to judge their own acts and motives with leniency.

(b) In case of a forbidding or permitting conscience, it is necessary that one seek reliable information where it can be had, as from parents or teachers, and if these cannot give it, from a pastor or confessor or other priest. Example: Sempronius thinks he has a right to drink a glass of wine now and then to be sociable; but he fears he has no right to do so, as the drink occasions excitement or foolish remarks, and sometimes makes it difficult for him to get to his home safely.

669. The authority that may be safely followed by confessors and other priests in resolving important doubts against a moral judgment is as follows:

(a) If the opinion is supported as morally certain by all or nearly all of the approved text-books on moral teaching, it may be followed; for surely there would not be such unanimity, if the objections were really formidable.

(b) If the opinion is supported as morally certain by a goodly number (say, six or seven) of those who are considered as preeminent in Moral Theology, and who independently arrived at the same conclusion, it may be followed; for the judgment of many is better than that of one, and the certainty of authorities should prevail over the doubt of one who has not the same authority.

(c) If the opinion has the support as certain of only one theologian, it may be followed without further investigation, if he has received special mention from the Church as an authority and a safe guide. Thus, the Holy See has expressly declared that the doctrine of St. Alphonsus may be safely followed by confessors, and the approbation given to St. Thomas Aquinas as Universal Doctor makes his word more convincing than a contrary argument based on one's own reasoning. Of course, this does not mean that these or any other private Doctors are infallible in their judgments, or that one should not depart from their teaching in a point where the Church has decided against them, or where there is a manifest reason for doing so; it simply means that they are so conspicuous among moralists for the correctness of their teaching that one who is in doubt may safely follow them unless the contrary is known to him.

670. But one may be unable to settle one's difficulty by appeal to authority, as such, as in the following instances: (a) when the particular case to be decided is not considered at all in text-books, or is not considered under the circumstances that exist; (b) when the authorities speak hesitatingly about the question, and say that the opinion in question is at most probable, etc.; (c) when the authorities are about equally divided, as when a few great names are opposed to many names of inferior rank, or when those who are equal in knowledge so disagree that half are on one side, half on the other. In counting authorities, however, it is not always easy to decide who should be included, as a writer may himself be arguing from the authority of an individual or of a school, and thus he is not a distinct witness in favor of what he holds.

671. When a priest or other person sufficiently instructed in theology is not able to change through recourse to authority an opinionative or doubtful conscience into a certain conscience, he can still obtain certitude: (a) directly, by reexamining the question diligently and with entire impartiality, until he has discovered reasons strong enough to settle it convincingly one way or the other; (b) indirectly, by submitting the question to the arbitrament of a reflex principle that really appears true to him, and permitting it to decide between the opinion and the objection, or between the contending doubts.

672. The Moral Systems.—There are two general systems regarding reflex moral principles:

(a) Tutiorism, which teaches that the only principle which can change uncertainty into certainty is: "When one is undecided between the safer and the less safe, he must always choose the safer," because only what is safer excludes the uncertainty of sinning;

(b) Anti-tutiorism, which teaches that the principle given above is true in a few exceptional cases on account of special reasons, but untrue as a rule. The general principle which it substitutes for that of Tutiorism is: "When one is undecided between the safer and the less safe, one may choose the less safe if it is morally certain."

673. Of two moral judgments that are compared, it must be noted:

(a) that one is safer which departs more from the danger of sin by deciding for the stricter side. Example: In doubt whether a law exists, whether it obliges in a present case, whether its obligation is grave, the safer opinion is that which holds for the affirmative;

(b) that moral judgment is more likely which is supported by stronger arguments. Example: That a law has ceased, or does not apply in a certain case, or does not oblige under sin, is a more likely opinion if the arguments in its favor outweigh those against it.

674. Thus, it may happen that an opinion which is safer is less likely. Example: The opinion that the precept of repentance obliges under pain of new sin from the moment a sin is committed is safer, but less likely than the opposite opinion.

675. Danger of sin is twofold. (a) Danger of formal sin (see 249, 258) is a risk taken which involves, not only that an act may be unlawful, but that the doing of it may be unlawful. Example: Caius eats meat, doubting whether the day is one of abstinence and whether he is obliged to abstain or not. (b) Danger of material sin (see 249, 258) is the danger that an act may be unlawful, not in the concrete or as to its performance, but in the abstract as to itself. Example: Titus is unable to discover whether this is a day of abstinence, but he is of the opinion that it is not. Hence, he takes meat, arguing that, while this may be a violation of the law, he himself is not guilty of sin, since he feels that he has a right to eat meat under the circumstances.

676. Tutiorism.—This system has been condemned by the Church, and with good reason, for the following motives:

(a) If by that which is safer, Tutiorism intends that which is better, it contradicts the Gospel, which distinguishes between counsel and precept (see 364 sqq.), commanding what is good, but only recommending what is better.

(b) If by that which is safer Tutiorism means that which favors law against liberty, it imposes an intolerable yoke on the consciences of men; for, while law obliges only in so far as it is promulgated and known, Tutiorism would bind one to observe, not only what was not known to be obligatory, but what was held to be most probably not obligatory.

677. A modified form of Tutiorism taught: "When one is undecided between the safer and the less safe, one must choose the safer, unless the less safe is most probable." This system has not been censured by the Church, but Catholic theologians with hardly an exception have rejected it, for the following reasons:

(a) Most probable, as understood by the defenders of this system, is that which has such likelihood and such appearance of truth as to remove every probable danger of even material sin. Thus, in reality this system requires absolute certitude and agrees with the rigorous tenet of Tutiorism that even a most probable opinion against the law may not be followed.

(b) Most probable, as commonly understood, is that side of a question which so far excels the other side that no answer can be given to any of its arguments, while all the arguments of the other side can be answered. To require this in moral difficulties is to require the impossible, for even the greatest theologians have to be content at times with less.

678. We are obliged always to follow a safe course, that is, not to expose ourselves to the danger of formal sin (see 249, 258); but Tutiorism errs when it teaches that we are also obliged always to follow the safer or safest course, that is, never to expose ourselves even to the danger of material sin. There are cases, however, when we are obliged (because some law requires it) to follow a safer course, that is, not to expose ourselves or others to some great harm. Thus, we must follow the safer side in the following cases:

(a) when there is question concerning something essential for the salvation of ourselves or of others, for the law of charity forbids that any risk be taken in this supremely important matter. Example: Titus instructs the dying Caius only concerning the existence of God and of the future life. He should also instruct him about the Trinity and the Incarnation, which is the safer course, since it is more probable that an explicit faith in these two mysteries is a condition of salvation;

(b) when there is question of some great spiritual loss or gain for ourselves or others, for justice or charity forbids that we take chances in such affairs. Examples: Sempronia doubts whether she is excused from the law of abstinence, and whether she will be guilty of sin if she eats meat. Caius doubts whether attendance at a certain school will do harm to the religion of his son. Balba doubts whether she is bound to inquire about the truth of her sect. As long as their serious doubts remain, these persons should follow the safer course;

(c) when there is question of the validity or invalidity of a Sacrament, for the virtue of religion requires that the Sacraments be administered with fidelity, and be not exposed to the peril of nullity. Example: It is not lawful to consecrate matter that has probably been substantially adulterated;

(d) when there is question of some temporal good or evil to oneself or another, and one is certainly obliged to promote the former or prevent the latter. Examples: Caius suspects that a drink before him is deadly poison; Titus suspects that an object at which he is preparing to shoot is a human being. Neither may disregard his suspicion, even if its contrary is more probable, because the safer side must here be taken. The Fifth Commandment forbids one needlessly to imperil one's own or another's life.

679. In emergency one may expose a Sacrament to nullity by taking a course that is less safe for the Sacrament, but safer for the subject, relying on the axiom that the Sacraments are for men, and not men for the Sacraments. Example: Titus is called to baptize the dying Caius. No water can be procured except rose water, whose sufficiency is doubtful. Titus not only may, but should, use the doubtful matter, since no other can be had.

680. Laxism.—The extreme opposite of Tutiorism is Laxism, whose principle is: "When one is undecided between the safer and the less safe, one may choose the less safe, if it is only slightly or uncertainly probable," because whatever seems at all probable may be prudently followed, and so forms a certain conscience. Example: According to Laxism, one would be justified in following an opinion, because it was defended by one theologian, even though he was of little authority.

681. This system has been condemned by the Church for the following reasons:

(a) It is contrary to the teaching of the Gospels and of the Fathers, which requires one to observe the laws of God with understanding and diligence;

(b) It leads to corruption of morals. The Laxists of the seventeenth century were called in derision those "who take away the sins of the world," and it was against their loose teachings that Pascal inveighed;

(c) Its argument is of no value, for no prudent person would feel that he should follow what was only slightly above the improbable, or that a law should be deemed uncertain because an opinion of uncertain probability could be quoted against it.

682. The true system of reflex principles will lie between the extremes of Tutiorism and Laxism. As already said, these two doctrines have been censured by the Church; but there are other systems that are moderate, and that are permitted by the Church and defended by theologians. These systems are:

(a) Probabiliorism, whose principle is: "When one is undecided between the safer and the less safe, one may choose the less safe only when it is more probable";

(b) Equiprobabilism, whose doctrine is: "When one is undecided between the safer and the less safe, one may choose the less safe only when it affirms the non-existence of the law, and is at least equally probable with the opposite";

(c) Probabilism, whose doctrine is: "When one is undecided between the safer and the less safe, one may choose the less safe whenever it is certainly and solidly probable";

(d) Compensationism, whose doctrine is: "When one is undecided between the safer and the less safe, one may choose the less safe whenever it is certainly and solidly probable, and there is a proportionate reason to compensate for the risk taken."

683. Probabiliorism.—The arguments in favor of Probabiliorism are as follows:

(a) extrinsic or from authority. This system is more ancient, and, when the controversy over systems began in the seventeenth century, this was the one that was most favored by the Church and theologians;

(b) intrinsic and direct. An essential note of certitude is that it should exclude all doubt, for as long as doubt remains there is only opinion. But one who is undecided cannot exclude all doubt, unless the arguments against the doubts not only balance, but outweigh the latter (i.e., unless one has greater probability on one's side). Hence, he who acts against the safer, which is always certain enough, when his own opinion is not more probable, acts with an uncertain conscience;

(c) intrinsic and indirect. In all other matters a man is not prudent if he assents to that which is less safe and less probable. Thus, in things speculative no scholar would think of accepting a theory which to his knowledge was further removed from the truth; in things practical no man of common sense would prefer a road that seemed less likely to lead to his destination. But we should not be less prudent about the good than we are about the true and the useful. Hence, in doubt we should always decide in favor of the law, unless the arguments for liberty are more convincing.

684. The answers given to the above arguments are:

(a) Probabiliorism is not more ancient as a system, since none of the moral systems were formulated before the sixteenth century; if Patristic and medieval authorities can be quoted who decided cases probabilioristically, others who were contemporary can be named who decided according to milder principles. Moreover, the passages cited are frequently obscure, and do not necessarily bear a Probabilioristic sense. That Probabiliorism enjoyed more favor at the beginning of the controversy is not wonderful, since other systems were more or less identified with Laxism, and the question at issue had not been studied thoroughly. Today Probabiliorism has few defenders.

(b) That which is more probable by far, or most probable, does overcome all doubt, and is even speculatively certain; but he who would require the more probable in this sense does not differ from the Tutiorists spoken of above. That which is more probable, but not to a notable extent, does not exclude all doubt, for the very definition of the more probable is "that judgment which appears more likely to be true than another, but which does not exclude all fear that the other may be true." Hence, if Probabiliorism calls for the notably more probable, it does not differ from Tutiorism; if it calls for the moderately more probable, it wrongly claims that there is no probability on the opposite side.

(c) The true is that which is in harmony with facts, the useful that which conduces to the obtaining of an end, the good that which is in conformity with law. Certainly, a man is not a prudent seeker of truth if he arbitrarily prefers the less to the more true-seeming, nor a prudent seeker of the useful if he chooses the less safe way of obtaining what is a necessary end; but a man can be a prudent seeker of the good, even though he prefers the less safe and less probable, when the law itself, the norm of good, does not demand more from him. Hence, one who makes a judgment according to the anti-Probabiliorist systems does not feel that he is yielding assent to what is speculatively less probable; but that he is making a decision that is practically certain; not that he is choosing a perilous way, but one that is absolutely safe.

685. Arguments against Probabiliorism.—(a) Theoretical Objection.— The principle of Probabiliorism that it is lawful to act against the safer side when the less safe side is more probable, cannot be justified except on the ground that invincible ignorance of obligation exists, and hence that the law does not oblige. But the same argument can be used in favor of milder systems; for even if the less safe side is only probable, it makes one invincibly ignorant that one is obliged. Hence, the basis of Probabiliorism is fatal to its own claims.

(b) Practical Objection.—A system for the direction of conscience should be so simple that it can be easily applied in the everyday affairs of life. Abstract questions may receive attention from moralists for days and months, but concrete cases have to be decided as a rule without delay. But Probabiliorism is such a complicated system that it is unsuited to everyday life. St. Alphonsus declares that he found by the experience of many years that this system cannot be profitably used in the guidance of souls, for it imposes an intolerable burden on both confessors and penitents. And how few are so skilled as to be able to decide quickly, without scruples, and correctly about the relative degrees of probability in opposite opinions!

686. Answers of the Probabiliorists.—(a) A probable opinion against the existence of obligation does not create invincible ignorance, but only doubt; nor does a more probable opinion against obligation create invincible ignorance, since it excludes the less probable opinion for obligation, and makes one assent unwaveringly and in good faith, even though erroneously, to the judgment that one is not bound.

(b) It is no more difficult to decide what is more probable than to decide what is equally probable, or truly and solidly probable; nor is the same skill and attention expected in all persons and cases, but each person must judge according to the best light he has, and each case must receive the measure of attention its importance calls for. If Probabiliorists may become scrupulous, may not Probabilists become lax?

687. The debate between Probabiliorism and its adversaries is not often heard today, as most modern moralists give their allegiance either to Equiprobabilism (a modified Probabiliorism) or to Probabilism.

688. Equiprobabilism.—The doctrine of Equiprobabilism is a middle way between Probabiliorism and Probabilism. Thus: (a) it agrees with Probabiliorism in holding that it is not lawful to follow the less safe, if the safer is more probable, or if the safer is equally probable, and the question is about the cessation of the law; (b) it agrees with Probabilism in holding that it is lawful to follow the less safe, if the safer is only equally probable, and the question is about the existence of the law.

689. The principle that "it is not lawful to follow the less safe, if the safer is equally probable and the question is about the cessation of the law," is defended as follows by Equiprobabilists:

(a) In real doubt we should decide in favor of that side which is possession. But, when doubt is about the cessation of a law, the law is in possession; for there is no question that it was made. Therefore, in such a doubt we should decide for the safer side, that is, that the law has not ceased.

(b) A certain obligation is not complied with by a doubtful fulfillment. But doubts about the cessation of the obligation of law usually arise from a probability that one has already fulfilled the law. Therefore in such cases we should decide that the law has not been fulfilled—that is, that its obligation has not ceased.

690. The Probabilists reply that: (a) it is not true that, in equiprobability about the cessation of law, the law is in possession; for liberty is naturally prior to law, and hence has possession in doubt; (b) nor is it true that an obligation that has probably been complied with or removed is certain.

691. The Equiprobabilists answer: (a) liberty was in possession, until it was dispossessed by the making of the law; (b) an obligation that certainly existed must be held as certainly in existence, until the contrary is proved; whereas a fact, such as dispensation, abrogation, or fulfillment, is not proved if it is only probable.

692. The principle that "it is lawful to follow the less safe side, if the safer is only equally probable and the question is about the existence of the law," is defended as follows by Equiprobabilists:

(a) In real doubt we should favor the side that is in possession. But when doubt is about the existence of a law, liberty is in possession; for liberty is prior to law. Therefore, in such doubt we may decide that there is no obligation.

(b) An uncertain law does not oblige, if one is invincibly ignorant of its existence. But, when there are equiprobable reasons against the existence of a law, one is invincibly ignorant of its existence. Therefore, in such cases one is not obliged.

693. The principle that "it is not lawful to follow the less safe side if the safer side is more probable," is defended as follows by Equiprobabilists:

(a) In doubt improperly so called—that is, in that condition of mind in which there is no fluctuation between equal arguments, but only some indecision between the more and the less probable—we should decide in favor of the more probable, as being morally certain. Hence, it is not lawful to follow what is less safe and less probable.

(b) A law sufficiently promulgated obliges. But, when it is more probable that a law was made or is in force, such law is sufficiently promulgated to the conscience. Hence, the safer side must be followed, if it is more probable.

694. Probabilist Criticism of the Foregoing Arguments.

(a) If the excess of the more probable over the less probable is so great that the latter is only slightly or doubtfully probable, the more probable is equivalent to certitude; for certitude is assent without fear of the opposite, and the fear of the opposite in such a case would be so slight that it may be considered as non-existent. If the excess is not so great, the less probable remains solidly and certainly probable, and the more probable is not certitude, but opinion (that is, assent with fear of the opposite). The Equiprobabilists are speaking of greater probability in the second sense, and hence they are wrong when they identify it with certitude (see above, 654).

(b) A law must be so promulgated to the conscience that one knows the law or could know it with sufficient diligence; it does not suffice that one can get no further than opinion. It would be unreasonable to oblige one to observe not only what is the law, but also what seems to be the law. Now, he who has only more probable opinion that he is bound by some law, does not know that such obligation exists; he only knows that it seems to exist.

695. Reply of the Equiprobabilists.-(a) The more probable always removes the appearance of truth from the less probable. Hence, he who recognizes an opinion as more probable can assent to it without any fear of error.

(b) One who holds it as more probable that he is obliged by a certain law, does not know for certain that he is obliged by reason of that law; but he does know for certain that he is obliged by reason of a higher law. Superior to every particular law is the general law that nothing may be done that will deprive law of its efficacy. But law loses its efficacy if each one is free to decide that he is not bound even when the greater weight of probability is to the contrary.

696. General Arguments in Favor of Equiprobabilism.—(a) From Authority.—St. Alphonsus Liguori, who holds a unique place in the Church as a moralist, preferred Equiprobabilism to every other moral system; and his views are followed not only by his own Congregation, the Redemptorists, but by many others.

(b) From Comparison with Other Systems.—Truth lies midway between extremes; for truth is lost either by exaggeration or by defect. But Equiprobabilism is a happy medium between Probabiliorism inclining to Rigorism, and Probabilism inclining towards Laxism. Hence, the relation of Equiprobabilism to other systems is in its favor.

(c) From the Character of Its Teaching.—According to principles of justice universally admitted as true, a judge should pronounce sentence in favor of the more probable when there is evidence of unequal weight and in favor of that which is in possession when there is evidence of equal weight. But these principles ought to be of universal application. Therefore, Equiprobabilism does right in making these the guiding principles for the court of conscience.

697. Probabilist Criticism of these Arguments.—(a) St. Alphonsus is one of the greatest moral theologians of the Church. Whether in his later years (1762-1787) he taught Equiprobabilism, is a matter of dispute among those who are familiar with his writings. But there is no doubt that in his mature age (1749-1762), when he wrote his Moral Theology, he was a Probabilist.

(b) Probabilism can likewise claim that it stands midway between the extremes of Rigorism (represented by Probabiliorism and Equiprobabilism), on the one side, and of Laxism, on the other side.

(c) The principle of possession invoked by Equiprobabilism applies to matters of justice, because there is a presumption that he who holds property has a right to it, and also because human laws must favor him who is in possession, lest property rights be left uncertain and disputes be multiplied. The principle of possession does not apply, however, to other matters; if the law obliged one yesterday, how can that create a presumption that it obliges one today, if one has good reasons for thinking the obligation has ceased? And as for human ordinances, while they have jurisdiction over external goods and may award them in case of doubt to the possessor, they have not, and have never claimed, the right to make the principle of possession a rule for solving all difficulties about duty.

The principle of Probabiliorism for which the Equiprobabilists claim the authority of judicial practice certainly does not apply to criminal cases, for in these preponderance of evidence against an accused is not to be followed if there is a reasonable doubt. In civil cases judges apply the principle of probabiliorism, but it does not follow that conscience should do the same, for the circumstances are different. The judge is seeking to decide which of two litigants has the more likely claim, and hence he is bound to declare for the side that has stronger evidence. Conscience is seeking to decide whether an obligation is certain or uncertain, and hence it is not obliged to decide for obligation when this is more probable, but still not certain.

698. Answer of Equiprobabilists to this Criticism.—(a) Granted that St. Alphonsus once held Probabilism, he rejected it later emphatically, and when dying declared that his former defense of Probabilism was the only thing that gave him anxiety.

(b) Equiprobabilism is further removed from Rigorism than Probabilism is from Laxism. It hears both sides of the question—that for liberty and that for law—before it decides. Probabilism is satisfied to hear one side, that for liberty; or at least it does not compare the two sides.

(c) The principle of possession is applied more strictly in cases of justice; for, since justice implies a more exact equality and a more rigorous right than other virtues (see 154), disputes in matters of justice demand stronger proofs. But every virtue renders to someone his due, and hence there is no reason why principles applicable to justice should not be applicable to other virtues also. The principle of Probabiliorism, likewise, is just as applicable to the court of conscience as to the civil court, since in both courts the aim is to get the truth as nearly as possible.

699. General Arguments Against Equiprobabilism.—(a) Theoretical Objection.—If we judge Equiprobabilism by its arguments, we find it unconvincing, for that which is old in it does not agree with that which is new, and that which is new argues equally well for Probabilism. Thus, the old arguments for Probabiliorism mean in the last analysis that the greater probability deprives the opposite side of all solid probability; logically, then, one should conclude that equal probability deprives both sides of all solid probability, since one neutralizes the other. The new arguments are drawn from the principles that in doubt one should decide in favor of the side in possession, that a doubtful law does not oblige, etc.—all of which principles, as we shall see, favor Probabilism.

(b) Practical Objection.—If we judge Equiprobabilism by its adaptibility for use, we find it wanting. A moral system should be one that can be easily understood and applied, otherwise it is unworkable and useless. But Equiprobabilism is so complicated and abstruse that even the professional theologians who hold it are often at a loss how to apply it, and are found to give inconsistent decisions. How can it be expected, then, that anyone else will be able to decide whether the law or liberty is is possession, whether the degree of probability on one side is greater than or equal to that on the other, whether the question has to do with the existence of the law or its cessation, etc.?

700. Replies of the Equiprobabilists.—(a) The old (i.e., probabilioristic) principles of Equiprobabilism are not contrary to the new. A more probable opinion not only balances the opposition by its equal arguments, and thus puts away doubt, but it also wins assent by the surplus in its favor, and thus certitude is had. When the two opposites are equally probable, there is a state of true doubt, but certitude is had by recourse to the principles of possession and doubtful law. These principles proper to Equiprobabilism do not favor Probabilism, if one is impartial in one's use of them, and willing to use them against as well as for liberty.

(b) Equiprobabilism is not more difficult in its application than Probabilism. It does not require that one determine minutely and exactly the greater or equal probability of the arguments for law and for liberty, or that one devote extraordinary diligence to the solution of the problem. All it requires is that one consider the matter seriously, weigh the arguments on both sides impartially, and decide to the best of one's ability which side appears to be more probable or to have the presumption in its favor.

701. Probabilism.—The meaning of Probabilism can be seen from a comparison with the opposite systems. (a) Unlike Probabiliorism and Equiprobabilism, Probabilism does not require a greater or equal probability, but permits one to follow what is less probable; (b) unlike Laxism, it does not allow one to follow what is only slightly or uncertainly probable, or to apply the system to all cases of doubt.

702. A judgment is probable when it is supported by arguments that make it seem true, although there may remain reasons for doubt. Examples are conclusions based on analogy, on hypothesis, on the opinions of others, or on the calculus of probabilities.

703. Probability is of various kinds. (a) It is absolute or relative, according as the supporting reasons are grave, either when considered alone, or when compared with the objections. Even the Probabiliorists admit that an opinion that is merely probable may be followed, if it is solidly probable and there is no argument against it (see 649). (b) We have solid or slight probability, according as the supporting motives are or are not such as would move, if not convince, a prudent man—that is, a man who shows good judgment in most things. (c) We have certain or uncertain probability, according as a person is sure or not, after reasonable consideration, that the arguments seem valid and the opinion likely. (d) Probability is internal or external, according as the arguments are drawn from the matter at issue itself (i.e., from its nature, properties, causes, effects, etc.) or from the authority of the doctors who have defended an opinion.

704. Relative probability according to logicians remains even when a lesser is compared with a greater probability. (a) If the opposing arguments are drawn from different sources, the more probable does not attack the less probable, and hence does not weaken its probability. Example: An intrinsic argument has more weight than a mere appeal to authority, but it does not attack the opposite argument, and hence does not diminish its probability. (b) If the opposing arguments are drawn from the same source, each one weakens the opposite, since there is

direct opposition. But the more probable does not destroy the less probable, since, in spite of the greater appearance of truth on the one side, there still remains room for the possibility that the other side may be true.

705. A moral judgment is solidly probable when the following conditions are present:

(a) For the judgment there must be an intrinsic or extrinsic argument that would be considered weighty by a prudent man. Example: An opinion that has the support of a universally acknowledged authority is strongly probable, whereas, if it has only the support of one obscure writer, it is only slightly probable.

(b) Against the judgment there must be no decisive argument from authority or reason. Example; The judgment that a certain course of action is lawful because St. Alphonsus permits it, is ordinarily solidly probable; it is not probable, however, if the opinion of St. Alphonsus (e.g., that Catholics may act as sponsors in non-Catholic baptisms) has been disallowed by the Church, or if the argument he uses (e.g., that concerning the amount that constitutes grave matter in theft, which reasons from conditions in his day) is not strong.

(c) The arguments for the judgment must retain their probability, if they are set over against the arguments for the opposite. Manifestly, if the arguments are all satisfactorily answered by the opposite side, the judgment based on them ceases to retain the appearance of truth. Probabilism does not require, however, that one determine the relative degrees of probability in opposite opinions.

706. It is not sufficient according to the Probabilists that another be certain of the probability of an opinion; but the person who follows the opinion must himself be certain that it is solidly probable.

707. Regarding the kind of authority necessary to make an opinion solidly probable from external evidence, Probabilism teaches:

(a) that absolute probability (that is, such a weight of authority as would appear strong even to the most learned) ought to be estimated by quality rather than quantity—by the learning, prudence, impartiality, and independent study of the authors, rather than by their numbers. If five distinguished moralists arrive by separate study at the same conclusion (i.e., that an opinion is probable), or if one of special reputation in a matter under question supports the probability of an opinion, the argument from authority is strong;

(b) that relative probability (that is, such a weight of authority as suffices for one who is unlearned, such as a child, a halfwit, an uneducated person) is had sufficiently through the word of only one person who is looked up to as a guide or instructor, such as a parent, confessor, or teacher.

708. Probabilism supposes that one regards the opinion one follows as truly probable, and that one is convinced that it is lawful to follow such an opinion. Hence, the system does not apply in certain cases.

(a) It does not apply to cases in which there is no probability on either side—that is, to cases of negative doubt (see 656 sqq.), whether the doubt be of law or of fact.

(b) Probabilism does not apply to cases in which there is only slight or uncertain probability for the less safe side. Example: Caius has heard that a certain novel opinion is defended by a recent author, but he is uncertain of the author's standing as a theologian, and he realizes that the fact that a man has written a book does not make his ideas solidly probable.

(c) Probabilism does not apply to cases in which there is solid probability for the less safe side, but one doubts whether one can lawfully follow it; for it is always sinful to act with a doubtful conscience (see 641 sqq.). Example: Caius has read in a reliable work of theology that a person in certain circumstances, which are his own, is probably excused from Mass. But the word "probably" makes him uncertain whether he can follow this opinion.

709. For the above-mentioned cases, to which their principle does not apply, Probabilists refer to the rules for a doubtful conscience (see 656 sqq.). The following special rules are given for cases of negative doubt:

(a) If the doubt is one of law and insoluble, one is free to act; for it is a general principle that an act may be considered lawful, as long as there is no serious reason to the contrary. Example: Sempronius goes out into the country on Sunday afternoon. An opportunity to fish presents itself, but Sempronius begins to doubt whether there is or is not a church law against fishing on Sundays. As no argument for either side is known to him, he may act on the general principle that what is not forbidden is lawful.

(b) If the doubt is one of fact and insoluble, and a prohibitory law is involved, one is free to act; for it is commonly admitted that legislators do not intend their prohibitions, which are restrictions of liberty, to be interpreted with the utmost rigor. Example: Titus is eating a chicken dinner late on Thursday night when his watch stops. As he has no way of discovering the time, he does not know whether Friday or the end of the dinner will arrive first. He may continue the meal, making no undue delays.

(c) If the doubt is one of fact, and a preceptive law is in question, one must take reasonable precautions to settle the doubt; for the lawgiver wills that those who are subject to the law should make use of the ordinary means to learn the facts on which obligation depends (see above, 384). If the doubt remains insoluble, one may decide in favor of liberty; for it may reasonably be presumed that the legislator does not intend to obligate those whose obligation remains uncertain. Example: Caius doubts whether he has reached the age of sixty, when the obligation of fasting ends. He should try to discover his real age; but, if he can find no real proofs either for or against the age of sixty, he may decide in favor of sixty, if there are some indications that he is of that age.

710. The solutions given above for cases of negative doubt suppose that there is no other or higher law that forbids one to take the risk of deciding in favor of liberty. Hence, in the following instances one must decide against liberty:

(a) in negative doubts when the validity of acts is at stake. Example: Titus is uncertain whether the law requires the age of fourteen for a valid contract of marriage; he is also uncertain whether he is fourteen years old. The doubt of law and of fact does not excuse Titus from the law, if he wishes to marry. He must clear up the doubts, and if necessary he must secure a dispensation.

(b) in negative doubts when reasons of charity or justice forbid one to take risks. Example: Caius is uncertain whether he paid Sempronius for work done for him. He is bound to make inquiries about the matter.

711. Probabilism cannot be applied, therefore, when the mental state of the subject is doubt, weakly founded opinion, or practical uncertainty. But, even when one holds an opinion as solidly and certainly probable, one may not follow it as a moral guide, if there is something in the nature of the object or matter itself which forbids this.

(a) A probability of law favoring liberty may not be followed in those matters in which some natural, divine or human law requires one to follow the safer side (see cases enumerated above, 678, 661). Example: The following opinions are probable; that instruction regarding the Trinity and the Incarnation is not indispensable for salvation; that rye-bread is valid matter for the Eucharist. But in practice it would be unlawful to take the risk of following these opinions, except in cases of extreme necessity, when nothing else can be done.

(b) A probability of fact favoring liberty may not be followed so long as there remains nothing more than probability of fact; for, while the will of the lawgiver may on account of probability of non-obligation change one's relation to the law from obligation to non-obligation, it does not change facts. Examples: On Friday Titus doubts whether a dish before him is meat or fish; probably it is meat on account of its appearance, probably it is fish on account of its odor. At night Fr. Caius is much fatigued, and doubts whether he has said Vespers. Probably he did not, because he cannot recall what feast will be celebrated tomorrow; probably he did, because he remembers having said Compline.

712. For probabilities of fact, to which as such their system does not apply, Probabilists offer the following solutions:

(a) In certain cases one may take from the doubt of fact its bearing on obligation, by recourse to the manifest will of the legislator as declared in the law itself or expressed through dispensation. Examples: While hearing confessions, Sempronius doubts whether his jurisdiction has already expired. He cannot recall the date of expiration, but, thinking the matter over, he sees that probably the date has not arrived. His difficulty is therefore solved, for the Code (Canon 209) supplies jurisdiction in cases of probability of fact. Titus and Caia wish to marry. There is a doubt whether or not they are first cousins, but it seems that probably they are not so related. Their difficulty is solved by obtaining a dispensation.

(b) In other cases one may change the probability of fact into a probability of law by recourse to a probable opinion or argument that under the existing doubt of fact the legislator does not wish the law to oblige. Examples: Titus, who has what is probably lawful food before him, argues with himself that it is not likely that the Church wills to put him to the expense, trouble, and loss of time required to order other food. Fr. Titus, who has probably said Vespers, argues that theologians of authority teach that, when there is a serious reason for thinking one has performed such an obligation, it may be presumed that the Church does not require more.

713. If a case of probability of fact on which obligation hinges cannot be solved by recourse to the expressed or inferred will of the lawgiver, one has no choice but to follow the safer side, for then, though it is probable that a certain thing is a fact, it is not probable that one has a right to act. Example: Sempronius, while hunting, sees an object moving in the bushes. The probabilities are that it is not a human being, but it is not probable that Sempronius has the right to risk homicide by firing at it.

714. Not all Probabilists use the principle of the presumptive will of the lawgiver for all cases of negative doubt; some employ different principles for different kinds of doubt, and sometimes arrive at other decisions than those given in the preceding paragraphs. Thus, they give such rules as the following:

(a) In negative doubt of law regarding the lawfulness of an act, use the principle that law or liberty should be followed according as one or the other is in possession (see 660). Example: He who has only slight reasons for thinking that a law exists, or that it is of grave obligation, or that it extends to his case, etc., may decide against the law. But he who has only slight reasons for thinking that a law has been abrogated, or that a dispensation has been granted, etc., must decide for obligation.

(b) In negative doubt of law regarding the validity of a past act, use the principle *that what was done is to be held as rightly done.* Example: He who has no reasons, or only trifling ones, for thinking that a Sacrament was not administered validly or received validly, should decide for validity.

(c) In negative doubts of fact, use the principles that one should judge according to what usually happens, or that facts must not be taken for granted but must be established, or that presumption favors that which has possession. Examples: If there is no good reason to think that a conscientious person gave consent to a temptation, one may decide for the negative, since that would usually be true. If there is no good reason to think that one has made a vow, one may decide for the negative, since the burden of proof is with the other side. If, in a question about fast and abstinence, it is uncertain whether or not a person has reached twenty-one years, or whether Friday has commenced, the presumption is for the negative, since liberty has been in possession; but if it is uncertain whether a person has reached the age of sixty or whether Friday has ended, the presumption is for the negative, since the law has been in possession.

715. Having discussed the cases to which Probabilism is not extended, we pass on to the cases to which it is applied. Probabilism is used in any and every case where speculative certainty as to what is lawful or unlawful is not had, but where there is only speculative probability against an opposite probability.

(a) Probabilism is used not only in probability of law, but also in probability of fact that can be reduced to probability of law, as was explained above (see 712).

(b) Probabilism is used in probability of law, whether or not the question be about the existence or the cessation of the law. There is probability against existence of law, when one has good reason to think that a law was not made or not promulgated, or that the time when it goes into force has not arrived, or that it does not apply to certain persons or circumstances, etc.; there is probability for cessation of law, when it is certain that a law did exist, but one has good reason to think that it ceased or was abrogated, that one is excused or dispensed from it.

(c) Probabilism is used in probability of law, whether the law in question be natural, divine or human—that is, in every case of law where invincible ignorance is possible (see 319 sqq., 356).

716. The claim of Probabilism is that, in all the cases given above, he who follows an opinion excusing him from obligation, may act with a practically certain conscience and be free of all moral guilt, if the opinion is theoretically and seriously probable. The arguments for this thesis are of two kinds: (a) extrinsic proofs, from the approval given Probabilism by the Church and the favor it has enjoyed among moralists; (b) intrinsic proofs, from the nature of law and obligation, and the superiority of Probabilism in practice.

717. Extrinsic Arguments.—(a) The Church gave explicit approval to Probabilism by praising the theological works of St. Alphonsus in which Probabilism is defended; she gave and continues to give implicit approval by the freedom she has granted to the teachers of this system from the days of Bartholomew Medina, its first expounder (1527-1581), down to the present. The Church even makes use of the principles of Probabilism in interpreting her own laws, as is evidenced by such rules of law as the following in the Decretals: "Things that are odious should be understood strictly, things that are favorable widely" (Rule 15); "Where the law is doubtful, follow the minimum" (Rule 30); "Where the lawgiver could have spoken more clearly, the interpretation should be against him" (Rule 57); "The kinder interpretation should be given penal laws" (Rule 89).

(b) In the Patristic and medieval periods Probabilism had not been scientifically formulated, but many of the Fathers and early Doctors solved cases probabilistically, and there are not a few passages in the great theologians before the sixteenth century which enunciate the same principles as those advocated by Probabilists. When the system was formulated by Medina in 1577, it met with universal favor among Catholic moralists, and, though it suffered an eclipse from the middle of the seventeenth to the middle of the eighteenth century, it has been growing in influence since the days of St. Alphonsus, and appears today to have recovered its former preeminence. Among its adherents are some of the greatest names in the history of theology, and it is not confined to any particular school or body.

718. Objections of Equiprobabilists.—(a) The praise given to St. Alphonsus by the Church reflects no glory on Probabilism, since the Saint rejected Probabilism and professed Equiprobabilism. Further, more than one Pope, and especially Innocent XI (1676-1689), has expressed a dislike for Probabilism, while the silence of others does not mean more than toleration. The legal axioms used by canonists apply to the external forum, and cannot be used equally in the forum of conscience. (b) Probabiliorism had the field before Probabilism, having been formulated and defended before Medina appeared, and it is that more ancient system that is represented today in a milder form as Equiprobabilism.

719. Answer of the Probabilists.—(a) St. Alphonsus teaches Probabilism in his Moral Theology, which is his chief work; if later, in his old age, he was an Equiprobabilist, it can be shown that the change was not free, but under compulsion. As to Pope Innocent XI, he is the only Pope who expressed disapproval of Probabilism, and even he refrained from any official pronouncement. The fact that hundreds of works written by Probabilists since the sixteenth century have not been censured or forbidden by the Church authorities, indicates more than mere toleration.

(b) Probabiliorism, as a systematized method, preceded Probabilism as a systematized method only by a brief interval, if at all. Before the 16th century neither of these systems had been formulated, and neither can make much of the argument of priority in time. As for Equiprobabilism, it is first seen in the writings of Christopher Rassler (about 1713) and of Eusebius Amort (1692-1775).

720. Intrinsic Arguments for Probabilism.—(a) Theoretical Argument.—An uncertain law does not oblige. But a law is uncertain if there is a solidly probable opinion against its existence, or for its cessation, even though the other side be equally or more probable.

Therefore, he who follows such an opinion does not violate any obligation.

(b) Practical Argument.—Probabiliorism and Equiprobabilism impose on confessors and the faithful impossible burdens, since, as was explained above (see 683 sqq.), they require that one compare and weigh probabilities, decide whether or not possession is had by the law or by liberty, etc.; whereas Probabilism is simple and easily applied, requiring only that one be convinced that one's opinion is really probable, and that one use it in good faith.

721. The proposition that an uncertain law does not oblige (saving cases of validity, etc., as above, 678), is defended as follows:

(a) If the uncertainty arises from the law itself, because it has not been clearly worded or sufficiently promulgated, the truth of the proposition is manifest, for the very nature of law requires that it be brought to the knowledge of those for whom it is made (see 285).

(b) If the uncertainty arises from the invincible ignorance of one who is subject to the law, the proposition is true in the sense that no one is a transgressor in the internal forum who fails against a law unwittingly (see 327, 489 sqq.). But an act that transgresses no law is lawful in conscience, for all that is not forbidden is lawful.

722. The adversaries of Probabilism offer the following criticism:

(a) As to the proposition that "an uncertain law does not oblige," the use of this principle by Probabilism may be considered as a begging of the whole question; for what is in dispute is whether, in case a law is uncertain, there is or is not a higher law that requires one to decide for obligation. It can be shown, however, that there is such a higher law; for the legislator cannot be willing that his ordinances be at the mercy of every uncertainty or loophole which subtle minds can devise, and God cannot be willing that those who are subject to laws should expose themselves to sin by deciding against a law because it appears to them to be of doubtful obligation.

(b) As to the proofs given for that proposition, they proceed from an incomplete enumeration, for a law can be doubtful on account of vincible ignorance, as well as for the reasons given. And no one will maintain that vincible ignorance excuses.

723. The Probabilists reply: (a) The principle that "an uncertain law does not oblige," cannot render law nugatory, since there is question here only of honest doubt, not of pretended or responsible ignorance. Neither can that principle expose one to the danger of formal sin (see 249), since it is supposed that he who follows it is convinced that it is true, and that he has the right to regulate his conduct by it. It does expose to the danger of material sin (see 249), since the law about which there is uncertainty may be existent; but we are not obliged to avoid every danger of material sin, else we should be under the intolerable necessity of fulfilling not only all certain, but all uncertain duties. Moreover, the danger of material sin is not avoided by any moral system except Tutiorism, since even equiprobable and more probable opinions may be false.

(b) The enumeration of cases of doubtful law is sufficient; for, as just remarked, only those cases are being considered in which one is judging about one's duty in good faith.

724. The second proposition used above as the Minor of the argument for Probabilism—that "a law is uncertain whenever there is a solidly probable opinion against its existence or for its cessation"—is defended by the very definition of the term "uncertain."

A thing is said to be accepted as certain when one yields it firm assent and has no serious misgivings that it may be false; hence, the uncertain is that which is not assented to firmly (the doubtful), or that which does not exclude serious doubts about its truth (matter of opinion). Now, a law whose existence or obligation seems likely, but against which there militates a solidly probable argument, is not so firmly established as to inhibit every prudent doubt. In other words, such a law is uncertain.

725. Criticism of the Argument in the Preceding Paragraph.—(a) The supposition on which the argument rests is false. It supposes that the interpretation of the legal axiom that "a doubtful law does not oblige," should be drawn from the philosophical definition of the terms, whereas it should be drawn from the sense given it by other rules of law. Now, there are canonical rules which declare that in doubt one

should follow that which has possession, or that which seems more probable. Hence, the axiom quoted by the Probabilists refers only to cases of negative doubt; the other two rules refer to cases of doubt in the wide sense, or to cases of opinion; otherwise, we should have to admit that these legal maxims are contradictory, one to the other. Thus, it appears that Probabilism is based on a principle formulated to solve difficulties of an entirely different kind from those which the system deals with.

(b) The argumentation itself is fallacious. It takes for granted that an opinion is certainly and solidly probable, not only when it has no opposite or when its opposite is less probable, but also when its opposite is equally or more probable. This cannot be. Solid probability on the other side of a question must create doubt about an opinion held, and so make it at best uncertainly probable or probably probable; while greater likelihood or presumption on the other side must make one's own opinion appear imprudent and unworthy of a rational being, and therefore not solidly probable.

726. The Probabilists answer: (a) The two principles with reference to doubtful law are understood and proved by Probabilism by an analysis of the notions of obligation and incertitude (see 285, 654), and hence they apply to every case that is restricted to the question of probable lawfulness or unlawfulness.

The rules quoted against Probabilism—there are some that might also be quoted against Probabiliorism and Equiprobabilism—are opposed to it only in appearance, since they deal with matters that are outside its sphere (see 697). Thus, in civil cases when both ownership and possession are doubtful, the decision must be given for the more probable side, since the issue is not what is lawful, but what seems to be true. As to the principle of possession, it is not, as supposed, unfavorable, but favorable to Probabilism; since liberty, inasmuch as it is presupposed by obligation (for only those who have freedom can receive obligation), has priority and must be given the benefit of the doubt, whenever a strictly probable reason in its favor cannot be refuted.

(b) Solid probability for the law creates doubt of the truth of the opinion for liberty, but it does not create doubt of its probability; for truth is the agreement of one's judgment with the facts, probability the appearance of such agreement on account of the arguments by which the judgment is supported. Hence, greater probability for law does not make uncertain the probability there is for liberty. Neither is it a sign of imprudence to accept the less probable, if one has sincerely and diligently sought the truth; for even the more probable may not be true, and the great majority of moralists hold that one is not obliged to follow it.

727. Criticism of the Pragmatic Test Offered by Probabilists.— Probabilism boasts of the ease with which it can be used (see 700, 720); but the ease with which it can be misused is greater still.

(a) Persons not inclined to piety must quickly fall into Laxism, if they make use of this system, for they will accustom themselves to find every sort of pretext to escape unwelcome duties by raising doubts and dignifying them with the name of probable opinions; they will follow, now one opinion, now its contrary, according as it suits their interests; they will become stubborn in their own views, and unwilling to change or accept instruction.

(b) Persons inclined to piety, if guided by Probabilist principles, will soon lose all interest in what is higher and better, and content themselves with the minimum; for in every case of uncertainty Probabilism permits one to choose what is less safe and less probable.

728. General Answer of the Probabilists to the Objections of the Preceding Paragraph.—(a) The history of Probabilism contradicts these objections. From its beginning to the present day it has been defended and followed by men noted for piety, who used kindness towards others, but were severe with themselves. While the principles of stricter systems have proved a torture both to confessors and penitents, no detriment to holiness is observed from the use of Probabilism.

(b) The nature of Probabilism refutes the objections in question. There is no system so good that it may not be perverted and turned to evil, and stricter systems have been converted into Tutiorism or Rigorism. But the logical and usual results of Probabilism are not a lowering of moral standards. If these evils follow it, they do so only when it is not rightly understood or not rightly applied.

729. The charges of a tendency to Laxism are thus answered:

(a) Probabilism holds that only learned theologians are judges of internal probability. Others must not decide for themselves, but must seek instruction from their spiritual guides who have competent knowledge. The moralists themselves must not be so wedded to their opinions that they are not always ready to change when they find they are wrong or learn that the Church does not admit their view.

(b) Probabilism permits one to use contrary probable opinions in different instances (e.g., to use for one will or testament the opinion that informality makes it invalid, and for another will the opinion that informality does not make it invalid); but it does not permit contrary opinions to be used in the same case for one's advantage (e.g., to use the opinion that an informal will is valid, in order to secure an inheritance, and at the same time to use the opinion that it is invalid, in order to escape the payment of legacies).

(c) Probabilism does not sanction the use of a probable opinion, unless it has been examined without prejudice, and has been honestly judged to be of certain and solid value (see 708 sqq.). Neither does it approve of the conduct of those who put themselves voluntarily in a state of doubt. On the contrary, it considers such conduct as sinful, and as gravely so, if the matter be serious and if this occur frequently. Example; Titus is uncertain whether three hours remain before Communion time, and yet he takes some refreshment, and thus makes it doubtful whether he has the right to receive Communion. The principle that a doubtful law does not oblige will enable Titus to receive Communion, but it does not excuse him from venial sin in putting himself without cause in a state of doubt and in danger of material sin.

730. The charge of a tendency to minimism in spiritual matters is thus answered: Probabilism deals only with what is lawful, not with what is better; it aims to show only what one may do without sin, not what one ought to do in order to become perfect. Hence, it is used when there is question of imposing obligations, or of deciding whether a certain course is lawful; for in these matters one must be kind, lest by

exceeding one's authority one drive others to sin; but it is not used when there is question of giving spiritual advice and direction, for here all should be exhorted to seek after progress in holiness.

731. Compensationism.—Between 1850 and 1880 a number of theologians, feeling that there were serious difficulties against all the systems up to then considered, developed a reformed or restricted Probabilism, which would not be open to the criticisms made against ordinary Probabilism, and yet would have those good qualities that make it preferable to the stricter systems. This new doctrine is called Compensationism, because it permits one to follow a probable opinion against the law only when there is present a sufficient reason to compensate for this course of action.

732. The following rules are, therefore, given as restrictions on the use of Probabilism: (a) the more serious or the more probable the doubtful law, the greater the reason must be to justify one in acting against it; (b) the higher and greater the good to be obtained from the exercise of freedom against a doubtful law, the less the reason that suffices for exercising freedom.

733. Illustrations of the Use of Compensationism.—(a) Titus, a poor man, is in uncertainty, through no fault of his own, about two debts. He thinks it more probable that he owes $10 to Sempronius, and 10 cents to Caius; but he believes it is really probable that he has paid both debts. He foresees that, if he offers the money to Sempronius, he will be subjected to serious quarrels and vexations, or at least that very bad use will be made of the money; while, if he offers to pay Caius, the latter may take some slight offense. He decides that there are proportionate reasons in each case to justify his following the less probable opinion.

(b) Fr. Titus thinks that a penitent is more probably bound to ask pardon of one whom he has offended. But he knows that, if he imposes the obligation, the present good faith of the penitent will be changed to bad faith, and he will refuse to do what is imposed. Fr. Titus decides, therefore, that it will be more profitable for the penitent if the less probable opinion—that there is no obligation—be followed.

734. The two chief arguments for Compensationism, which are also the two chief objections it makes against ordinary Probabilism, are:

(a) The obligation of a law depends on the knowledge one has about it. If one knows that the law exists, there is certain obligation; if one knows that the law does not exist, there is no obligation; if one holds it as probable that the law exists, there is probable obligation. Now, since one may not be excused from obligation unless there is a reason proportionate to the obligation itself (see 495), he who is under probable or more probable obligation must have a graver reason for using freedom than he who is under no obligation (against Probabilism), but he need not have as grave a reason as one who is under a certain obligation (against Probabiliorism). Hence, one may not act against a probable law, unless by so doing there is some good secured that compensates for the danger to which the right of the law is exposed.

(b) It is lawful to perform a good act from which an evil effect will result, only if one has a proportionally grave cause for permitting the evil effect (see 102 sqq.). But he who follows the opinion for liberty against a more probable or equally probable opinion for law, performs an act from which will probably result the evil of a material transgression of law. Therefore, one may not use Probabilism unless by so doing there is some good secured that compensates for the danger of material sin to which one exposes oneself.

735. Criticisms from the Probabilists.—(a) The dictum that a doubtful law obliges doubtfully cannot be applied, for in actual life there is no middle way between decision for the law and decision for liberty, unless it be indecision. The principle of Compensationism must mean, then, that we must always decide for a doubtful law (which is Tutiorism), or remain in suspense (which is no help to the one in doubt).

(b) The supposition that there must always be some special reason of good to offset the evil of the danger of material sin is not correct. For there always exists a compensation proportionate to the danger, namely, the exercise of liberty, a great gift of God, and the avoidance of the burden of fulfilling all uncertain obligations.

736. Reply of the Compensationists.—(a) The principle that a doubtful law obliges doubtfully means only that the reasons in favor of the law deserve some consideration, and should not be put aside unless one has some better reason than mere arbitrariness, self-will, or the intention to take always the easier way. There is no question of either Tutiorism or hesitation, but only of a prudent and honest facing of the fact that there are two sides to one's doubt.

(b) It is not true that the exercise of liberty and the escape from the burden of uncertain obligations are always a sufficient compensation for the danger of material sin. For material sin is not only an evil in itself, as being a violation of law; it is also the source of many and great evils both to the individual and society, such as wrong habits acquired, scandal given, etc. Liberty is a great gift, but it should not become a cloak for malice. Neither is the foregoing of liberty so great an evil that one should not be willing to suffer it now and then in order to prevent the greater evils spoken of just above.

737. Other Objections Against the System of Compensation.

(a) From Authority.—Compensationism is of very recent origin, and it cannot be admitted that the right solution of moral difficulties was unknown before this new system appeared.

(b) From Reason.—It runs counter to the principle commonly accepted in the controversies of the systems, namely, that the decisive factor as to obligation in doubt is knowledge. For it introduces a new factor, that of sufficient reason or compensation.

(c) From Serviceability.—It is easy to say in the abstract that one should always have a suitable reason for adopting a probable opinion in favor of liberty. But, when one attempts to apply this rule to actual cases, difficulties innumerable arise (searchings of motives, comparison of probabilities, measuring of consequences, etc.), so that for use Compensationism is impossible, or impracticable.

738. Reply of Compensationists.—(a) Compensationism is an example of doctrinal progression from the implicit to the explicit. The principles on which it is based are found in the teaching and practice of the most ancient authorities.

(b) Sufficient reason is not a new principle, since it is admitted by all moralists for the case of double effect (see above, 102 Sqq.); its application to the solution of doubts of conscience is not an innovation, since the cases of doubt and of double effect are analogous.

(c) Compensationism is not intended as a system to be applied by those who have not sufficient theological training, but as a guide for moralists, directors and confessors. That it is not difficult, is clear from the fact that it is only an application of the commonly accepted principle of double effect, and that Probabilists themselves recommend it and make very general use of it, as if they instinctively recognized its necessity.

739. Practical Conclusions.—From the foregoing discussions one may deduce three rules for the guidance of those who are not expert theologians:

(a) If your state of conscience is certitude (i.e., if you are firmly convinced which way your duty lies), entertain no fears or scrupulous doubts, and, having done your part to understand your obligations, you need not hesitate to follow your conscience.

(b) If your state of conscience is imprudent assent (i.e., the acceptance of what you recognize as unlikely), or if it is suspended assent (i.e., a wavering between opposites), do not act blindly, but seek truth and decision.

(c) If your state of conscience is opinion (i.e., the acceptance of what you regard as likely though uncertain), consult your confessor or another competent theologian; if there is no time for this, decide for any course that seems true and prudent (see on perplexed conscience, 611 sqq.).

740. Regarding the respective merits and the use of the rival systems of conscience, the following conclusions may be drawn:

(a) If there is question of what is to be counselled, one should be a "Meliorist," for the better and more perfect is more advisable than what is merely good or lawful. All Christians should be directed to aspire after holiness, but, if one is unwilling to follow a counsel, it should not be imposed on him as a precept. Naturally, of those in higher station higher things are required.

(b) As between doubt and certitude regarding obligations, one must be a "Certitudinist," that is, one must resolve doubts or slight probabilities into direct or indirect certitude (as was explained above in 641 sqq.). If a doubt remains, one must for that case be a Tutiorist, that is, one must follow the safer side (as explained in 661).

(c) As between the safer and the less safe, one must be a Tutiorist, when some law requires this, as is the case when validity or supreme rights are at stake (as explained in 678, 679).

(d) As between the more likely and the less likely, one must be a Probabiliorist, when this is according to law, as is the case in civil suits where the preponderance of evidence must be followed (see 697).

(e) One may not follow either Tutiorism (see above, 676) as a general moral system, nor Laxism (see above, 681).

(f) If a probable opinion for liberty is opposed by no contrary probable opinion or by none whose arguments cannot be overcome, one is free to follow that opinion, as explained in 649, 703.

(g) If a probable opinion for liberty is opposed by an opinion that is less, equally or more probable, one is free to act according to the principles of Probabiliorism, Equiprobabilism, Probabilism or Compensationism, according to conviction.

741. As for the use of moral systems by confessors, the two following rules are generally admitted:

(a) If a penitent has formed his conscience according to one moral system, the confessor has no right to impose on him the opinion of a different moral system; for the Church allows liberty.

(b) If a penitent has not formed his conscience according to any moral system and seeks the answer to a moral doubt, the confessor should decide, not necessarily for what his own system declares lawful, but for what appears, all the circumstances being considered, to be most advantageous spiritually for the penitent. Example: Fr. Titus is a

Probabilist, and he usually advises questioners to follow opinions that are less probable; while Fr. Caius, who is a Probabiliorist, always requires that such persons follow the more probable opinions. Both act unwisely. For persons who are better disposed, it will often be more profitable to follow what is more probable or favorable to obligation; for those Whose dispositions are less good, milder opinions may be recommended, lest the smoking flax of goodness that is in them be entirely extinguished. Neither is it right to impose as certain an obligation which the penitent, if he were acquainted with Moral Theology, would see is controverted.

742. In case of disagreement between confessor and penitent as to whether absolution may be given, whose opinion should prevail? (a) If the disagreement is concerned with matters about which the confessor himself has to judge (e.g., the disposition of the penitent, the requisite matter for absolution, etc.), the opinion of the confessor must prevail; for the act of judging is his own, and he must be guided therefore by his own conviction.

(b) If the disagreement is concerned with matters about which the confessor is not the judge (such as the controversies of schools and theologians), the confessor may not refuse absolution to a well-disposed penitent, just because the latter will not accept the opinion of his school or system. If it be manifest that the penitent's opinion is false or improbable, absolution may be denied him, unless it seems more prudent to leave him in good faith.

PART II
SPECIAL MORAL THEOLOGY

743. In the First Part of this work, the means to man's Last End were spoken of in a general way; the features that are common to all good acts—that they be human, morally deserving, directed according to law and conscience—were treated. In the present Part the means to the Last End will be discussed in particular, and we shall consider in turn the kinds of duties that are owed by all men and those owed by persons in special states of life.

Question I
THE DUTIES OF ALL CLASSES OF MEN

THE INFUSED VIRTURES

744. Good habits, specifically different, are all reducible to seven most general virtues (see 150, 151), and hence in studying these seven virtues, we shall at the same time study all the common duties of man.

745. The properties of the seven infused virtues are chiefly four:

(a) In the first place, these virtues may be increased: "This I pray, that your charity may more and more abound" (Phil, i. 9). The increase takes place *ex opere operato* through the Sacraments, or *ex opere operantis* through meritorious works—that is, whenever sanctifying grace, their root, is increased.

(b) A second property of the infused virtues is that they may be lost: "I have somewhat against thee, because thou hast left thy first charity" (Apoc., ii. 4); "Some have made shipwreck concerning the faith" (I Tim., i. 19). The loss is caused by the contrary of the virtue: faith is lost by disbelief, hope by despair; charity and the moral virtues are lost by any mortal sin, for they are built on sanctifying grace, which mortal sin destroys.

(c) A third property of the infused virtues is that they cannot be diminished directly. If we leave out of consideration their opposites (which, as just said, remove these virtues entirely), there is nothing else that can act directly upon them. Mere failure to exercise them cannot lessen them, since they are caused by divine infusion, not by human exercise; venial sin cannot lessen them, since it does not lessen grace on which they depend.

(d) A fourth property of the infused virtues is that they are diminished indirectly. Failure to practise them or venial sin does diminish the ease and fervor with which the acts of these virtues are exercised; and thus indirectly—that is, by preparing the way for acts that are directly contrary—neglect or venial sin diminishes the habits themselves.

Art. 1: THE VIRTUE OF FAITH

(*Summa Theologica*, II-II, qq. 1-9.)

746. The order of the theological virtues here followed is that given by St. Paul in I Cor., xiii. 13—viz., faith, hope, charity. The order of these virtues is twofold: (a) according to dignity the order is charity, hope, faith; (b) according to time, the order is that of I Cor., xiii. The habits of these three virtues are infused at the same time (i.e., at the moment when grace is conferred), but their acts are not simultaneous, and one must believe before one can hope or love.

747. Excellence of the Virtue of Faith.—(a) Faith is the beginning of the supernatural life, the foundation and the root of justification, without which it is impossible to please God and arrive at fellowship with Him. (b) It is an anticipation of the end of the supernatural life, for by faith we believe that which we shall behold in the beatific vision: "All these died according to faith, not having received the promises, but beholding them afar off, and saluting them and confessing that they are pilgrims and strangers on the earth" (Heb., xi. 13).

748. Utility of Faith for the Individual.—(a) Through faith the intellect receives a new light, which discloses to it a higher world—"the wisdom of God in a mystery" (I Cor., ii. 7)—and which illuminates even this lower world with a heavenly brightness, that man may know more quickly, more surely, and more perfectly the natural truths that pertain to God and duty. (b) The will is strengthened to perform duties valiantly through the motives and examples which faith offers: the patriarchs of old "by faith conquered kingdoms, wrought justice, obtained promises, recovered strength from weakness" (Heb., xi. 33). In adversity faith is a stay and a consolation: "For what things soever were written, were written for our learning, that through patience and the comfort of the scriptures, we might have hope" (Rom., xv. 4).

749. Utility of Faith for Society.—(a) Domestic society is defended in its security and happiness by faith, which teaches the sacramental character of marriage, which offers the model of the Holy Family to Christian homes, which never ceases to declare in the name of God the duties of husbands and wives, parents and children. (b) Without faith and religion civil society cannot be maintained in strength and prosperity. It is faith in God more than laws or armies that gives security to life, reputation, and property, with order and peace at home and abroad.

750. The Meaning of Faith.—In Holy Scripture and other religious writings the word *faith* has various meanings.

(a) Sometimes it stands for a promise, or for the quality of being true to one's promises. Examples: St. Paul condemns widows who remarry against their word, "because they have made void their first faith (promise)" (I Tim., v. 12). Speaking of the unbelief of the Jews, he says: "Shall their unbelief make the faith (i.e., fidelity to promise or faithfulness) of God without effect? God forbid. But God is true" (Rom, iii. 3, 4).

(b) Sometimes the term *faith* stands for good reputation, or for confidence in another. Examples: "He that discloseth the secret of a friend loseth his faith (credit, reputation), and shall never find a friend to his mind" (Ecclus., xxvii. 17); "O thou of little faith (trust, confidence), why didst thou doubt?" (Matt., xiv. 31).

(c) Sometimes *faith* stands for truths or doctrines offered for one's belief, or for the assent of the mind to the judgment of conscience or to the revelation of God. Examples: "Thou has not denied My faith" (that is, "the truths revealed by Me," Apoc. ii. 13); "All that is not of faith (i.e., from the firm conviction of conscience) is sin" (Rom, xiv. 23); "Without faith (i.e., assent to the unseen on the word of God) it is impossible to please God; for he that cometh to God must believe" (Heb., xi. 6).

751. It is faith only in the last sense that is known as the theological virtue of faith, and hence with it alone we are here concerned. St. Paul describes this faith as follows: "Faith is the substance of things to be hoped for, the evidence of things that appear not" (Heb., xi. 1). This verse is variously interpreted. (a) According to St. Chrysostom, the meaning is: Faith is the subsistence or anticipated existence in the soul of future blessings that are hoped for, through the firm confidence it gives; it is the conviction of the reality of the unseen. (b) According to St. Thomas, the meaning is: Faith is the substance or basis on which is built the hope of blessedness, or on which rests as on its foundation the whole work of justification; it is an argument producing certainty of that which is not seen. The elements of St. Thomas' interpretation have been incorporated into the Vatican Council's definition: "The Catholic

Church professes that this faith which is the beginning of human salvation is a supernatural virtue by which we, with the aid and inspiration of the grace of God, believe that the things revealed by Him are true, not because the intrinsic truth of these things has been perceived by the natural light of reason, but because of the authorityof God Himself revealing, who can neither deceive nor be deceived" (Sess. 3, chap. 3, Denz. 1789).

752. Thus, faith is an intellectual habit and act, but it differs from all other intellectual habits and acts as follows: (a) it differs from science, vision, understanding, for its object is "the things that appear not"; (b) it differs from opinion, doubt, suspicion, for it is a firm "substance," a certain "evidence"; (c) it differs from human faith or belief resting on man's word and promises, for it is the pledge, beginning and cornerstone of the happiness promised by God Himself.

753. Faith will now be considered according to two aspects: (a) objectively, as regards the things that are believed by him who has faith; (b) subjectively, as regards the habit and act of the believer which put him in contact with these truths of the unseen world.

754. The Object of Faith.—There is a twofold object of faith, viz., material and formal.

(a) The material object, or the truth that is believed, includes all that is contained in the Word of God, whether written or handed down by tradition. The principal material object is God Himself as the Deity, or Supreme Truth in Being (*prima veritas in essendo*); the secondary material object embraces all other revealed truths.

(b) The formal object of faith, or the motive that prompts one to give assent to the material object, is the authority of God, who is Supreme Truth in Knowing and Speaking (*prima veritas in cognoscendo et dicendo*), and hence He can neither be deceived nor deceive.

755. The material object of faith includes all truths revealed by God; but, since it belongs to the Church to teach those truths, there is a distinction of truths that are revealed by God but not defined by the Church, and truths that are revealed by God and defined by the Church as revealed. Thus: (a) divine faith is belief in revealed truth that has not

been declared by the Church as revealed; (b) divine and Catholic faith is belief in a revealed truth that has been proposed as such by the Church, either solemnly or ordinarily. Example: Dogmas contained in creeds, definitions of Popes or general councils. The Vatican Council has determined the object of this faith: By divine and Catholic faith all those things must be believed which are contained in the written word of God and in tradition, and which are proposed by the Church, either by a solemn pronouncement or by her ordinary and universal magisterium, to be believed as divinely revealed (Ibid., Denz. 1792).

756. The formal object of faith extends to all truths that have been revealed and to no others. Theologians discuss the status of certain truths connected with revelation concerning which the Church is guaranteed infallibility on account of her teaching office. Special difficulties arise in relation to: a) dogmatic facts, that is, definitions concerning particular facts closely related to dogma (e.g., that Anglican orders are invalid; that a particular book contains a sense contrary to revelation; that this Supreme Pontiff, legitimately elected, is the successor of St. Peter in the primacy and consequently infallible); b) theological conclusions, that is, deductions drawn from revealed truth.

Many theologians teach that both dogmatic facts and theological conclusions when defined by the Church constitute a special object of faith distinct from divine and Catholic faith, namely, ecclesiastical faith. Accordingly, for them, ecclesiastical faith is the internal assent given to truths connected with revelation and defined by the Church as true, the motive of assent being the infallibility of the Church in her teaching office.

Others deny the existence of such faith and insist a) that dogmatic facts are contained in revealed doctrine implicitly as singulars in universals and hence are believed before definition by divine faith implicitly, and after definition by divine and Catholic faith, b) that theological conclusions before definition are held by theological assent, afterwards by divine and Catholic faith. Some also have maintained that before definition such conclusions belong to divine faith. (For a summary of the various teachings on this problem see Reginaldo-Maria Schultes, O.P., *Introductio in Historiam Dogmatum*, pp. 46 ff.; Marin-Sola, O.P., *L'Evolution homogene du Dogme Catholique*).

757. Private revelations, even when approved by the Church, are not an object of divine and Catholic faith, for they form no part of the revelation given to the whole human race that was closed with the death of the Apostles and committed to the Church. Hence: (a) if they are negatively approved by the Church, the approval means only that such revelations contain nothing contrary to faith and morals, and are useful and edifying; (b) if they are approved positively (as is the case with the revelations of St. Hildegarde, St. Brigit, and St. Catherine of Siena), the approval means that they appear to be true divine revelations and may be prudently accepted as such.

758. The assent to be given to private revelations, therefore, is as follows:

(a) Such revelations should receive the assent of divine faith, if it is certain that they are genuine. This applies to those to whom and for whom they were given, and probably to others also. It rarely happens, however, that the genuineness of a private revelation can be critically established, and the Church does not require that such revelations be accepted by all the faithful. To refuse assent, therefore, to a private revelation is not generally an offense against divine faith.

(b) Private revelations cannot receive the assent of Catholic faith, since, even when approved by the Church, they are not proposed as a part of the Christian revelation committed to her care. To dissent from them, therefore, is not a sin against Catholic faith, unless in rejecting them one would also reject defined dogma (e.g., by denying the possibility of revelation).

(c) Private revelations are not offered for the assent of ecclesiastical faith, since in approving them the Church does not propose them as necessarily connected with the exercise of her teaching office or under guarantee of infallibility. To dissent from them, therefore, is not a sin against ecclesiastical faith, unless other errors (e.g., against the authority of the Church in matters connected with revelation) are also involved.

(d) Private revelations are offered for the assent of human faith, since the Church proposes them to the faithful, if approved, as matters of pious opinion, which are according to the rules of prudence truly probable on account of traditions in their favor, supported by suitable testimony and documents (Benedict XIV, *De Canonizatione Sanctorum*, lib. II, cap. 23; III, cap. ult.; Sacred Cong. Rites, May 12, 1877, n. 3419, ad 2). The Church permits, but does not exact belief in these revelations. One would not be excused, however, who rejected them through pride or contempt, or without sufficient reason.

759. Similarly, although the Church offers for human faith alone certain particular facts of history, one who rejects them may easily be guilty of contempt or temerity. Such particular facts are: (a) apparitions of heavenly beings in post-Biblical times, such as the appearance of the Archangel Michael in Monte Gargano about 525 and the appearance of the Blessed Virgin at Lourdes in 1858, for which the Church has instituted feasts; (b) deeds related in the legends of the Saints, such as the victory of St. Catherine of Alexandria over the pagan philosophers and the carrying of her body to Mt. Sinai by Angels, which the Church inserts in the Breviary lessons; (c) the authenticity of relics. In granting certificates of genuineness, the Church guarantees only that there is sufficient historical evidence or probability for the belief that particular bones or other objects belonged to a particular Saint.

760. Many tenets of the Church, indeed, have not the prerogative of infallibility—for example, decrees of the Popes not given *ex cathedra*, decisions of Congregations made with Papal approval, teachings of Bishops to particular members of the Church, doctrines commonly held by Catholics as theological truths or certain conclusions. These decrees, decisions, etc., receive not the assent of Catholic faith, but what is called religious assent, which includes two things, viz., external and internal assent.

(a) External assent should be given such teachings—that is, the homage of respectful silence due to public authority. This does not forbid the submission of difficulties to the teaching authority, or the scientific examination of objections that seem very strong.

(b) Internal assent should be given such teaching—that is, the submission of the judgment of the individual to the judgment of the teacher who has the authority from Christ and assistance from the Holy Spirit. This internal assent differs, however, from the assent of faith, inasmuch as it excludes fear of error, but not of the possibility of error, and it may later on be suspended, called into doubt, or even revoked. Pope Pius X in his *Motu proprio*, "Praestantia scripturae Sacrae" (Nov. 18, 1907), indicated the binding force of the decrees both of the Pontifical Biblical Commission and of all doctrinal decrees: All are bound in conscience to submit to the decisions of the Biblical Commission which have been given in the past and which shall be given in the future, in the same way as to the decrees which appertain to doctrine, issued by the Sacred Congregations and approved by the Supreme Pontiff; nor can they escape the stigma both of disobedience and temerity, nor be free from grave guilt as often as they impugn their decisions either in word or writing; and this over and above the scandal which they give and the sins of which they may be the cause before God by making other statements on these matters which are very frequently both rash and false. (Reaffirmed by the Biblical Commission on Feb. 27, 1934.)

761. The objects, therefore, which formally or reductively pertain to the virtue of faith, are as follows:

(a) Divine faith has for its object all the truths revealed by God as contained in the Canonical scriptures approved by the Church, and in the teachings received by the Apostles from Christ or the Holy Spirit and handed down to the Church as Tradition. Private revelations in exceptional cases may also be the object of divine faith.

(b) Catholic faith has for its object all the truths formally revealed in scripture and Tradition that have been defined as such by the Church. The definitions of the Church are either solemn (e.g., those given in the Creeds, *ex cathedra* definitions of the Popes, decisions of Ecumenical Councils) or ordinary (e.g., those contained in the universal preaching, practice or belief of the Church, encyclical letters [see *Humani Generis*, n.20]). Equivalent to definitions are the condemnations of error opposed to revealed truths.

(c) According to some theologians ecclesiastical faith has for its object all infallible decisions of the Church about matters not revealed, but connected with revelation, or necessary for the exercise of the teaching office of the Church. Such are: (i) definitions, that is, definitive declarations of theological conclusions or of dogmatic facts, disciplinary laws made for the entire Church, canonization of the saints, solemn approbation of religious Orders, express or special recognition of Doctors of the Church, declaration of the relation of private revelations to the public revelation; and (ii) censures, that is, condemnations of teachings, on account of falsity, as heretical, near to heresy, savoring of heresy, erroneous, rash, etc.; on account of their expression, as equivocal, ambiguous, presumptuous, captious, suspected, ill-sounding, offensive to pious ears, etc.; on account of their tendency, as scandalous, schismatical, seditious, unsafe, etc. Examples: The definitions concerning the sense of the book *Augustinus*, the suitability of the terms "consubstantial" and "transubstantiation," the agreement of the Vulgate with the original scriptures, the lawfulness of the insertion of the *Filioque*.

(d) Religious assent has for its object all doctrinal pronouncements of the Church that are not infallible, but are yet official and authoritative. Examples are ordinary instructions and condemnations given by Pontifical Congregations and Commissions. The Syllabus of Modern Errors issued by Pius IX was most likely not an infallible or definitive document, although many of the errors it rejects are contrary to dogma, and hence, even apart from the Syllabus, they are to be rejected as opposed to Catholic faith. Likewise, many of its tenets are drawn from encyclical letters. Papal allocutions, radio addresses, and the doctrinal parts of Apostolic Constitutions, in themselves, are in this class.

(e) Respect is due to the judgment of the Church even in non-doctrinal matters and where no obligation is imposed by her, on account of her position and the careful examination given before decision. Example: It would be disrespectful to reject without good reason a pious belief which the Church after mature deliberation has permitted to be held.

762. Though the truths of faiths are many, the duty of believing imposes no great burden on the believer. Thus: (a) it is not required that explicit belief be given to all the teachings of faith; (b) it is not required that one distinguish the particular kind of assent in case of uncertainty, but it suffices to yield assent according to the mind and intention of the Church. Example: When a group of propositions is condemned under various censures, no indication being made of the censure that applies to particular propositions, it suffices to hold that all

of them are false, and that to each of them applies one or more of the censures listed.

763. Faith is divided into explicit and implicit, according as the object believed is unfolded or not to the mind.

(a) Faith is explicit regarding any truth, when assent is given to that truth as known in itself and expressed in terms proper to itself. Example: He has explicit faith in the Eucharist who has been instructed concerning the meaning of the mystery, and who assents to it according to that distinct knowledge.

(b) Faith is implicit regarding any truth, when that truth is not known or not accepted in itself, but is accepted in another truth. Example: He has implicit faith in the Eucharist who has not yet heard of it, but who accepts all the teachings of the Church, even those he does not know.

764. Faith is implicit as follows:

(a) Improperly, faith is implicit, if one does not give assent, but is prepared to give it, if necessary, or wishes to give it. These pious dispositions are not the act of faith itself, but they are its beginnings, or preparations leading up to it; they are good, but not sufficient. Example: A pagan who says he would accept the Christian creed, if he thought it were true, or who wishes that he could believe it.

(b) Properly, faith is implicit, if one gives assent to a truth by accepting another in which it is contained, as a particular is contained in a universal (e.g., he who explicitly accepts all the truths of Christianity, implicitly accepts the Eucharist, even when in good faith he thinks it is not revealed), or as an instrument is involved in its principal cause (e.g., he who explicitly believes in the Redemption implicity believes in Baptism, which is the instrument by which Redemption is applied), or as means are contained in their end (e.g., he who explicitly believes that eternal life is a reward, implicitly believes that good works must be performed as a means to that end), or as the reality is expressed in the figure (e.g., those in the Old Testament who explicitly believed in the Paschal Lamb, implicitly believed in the sacrifice of Christ of which the Paschal Lamb was the figure), or as the assent of the disciple is bound up with the assent of the teacher (e.g., the child who explicitly accepts as true the doctrines of faith taught by his pastor, implicitly believes the sense and implications contained in the latter's instructions).

765. The points about which explicit faith is required can be reduced to four heads (see Catechism of the Council of Trent). These heads are:

(a) The things to be believed: "Preach the Gospel to every creature. He that believeth shall be saved" (Mark, xvi. 15). The Gospel doctrine is summarized in the Apostles' Creed;

(b) The things to be done: "Teach them to observe all things whatsoever I have commanded you" (Matt., xxviii. 20). The Ten Commandments (see Vol. II) are called the epitome of the whole law;

(c) The ordinances to be observed; "Baptize them in the name of the Father, and of the Son, and of the Holy Ghost" (Matt, xxviii. 19). The Seven Sacraments are the sacred instruments through which the merits of the Passion of Christ are applied to the soul;

(d) The petitions to be made to God: "Thus shall you pray: Our Father, etc." (Matt., vi. 9). The prayer (see Vol. II) given us by Christ teaches us both the manner of prayer and the requests that should be offered.

766. Faith in the revelation given by God is necessary for salvation (Heb., xi. 6), but in the usual providence of God faith cannot be had or safeguarded without short formulas of its principal doctrines.

(a) Faith cannot be received without such formulas, because, its doctrines being many and frequently difficult and the study of all scripture and Tradition being impossible for most persons, a list of short and clear propositions of revealed truths (Creed) is needed that the faith may be proposed and accepted.

(b) Faith cannot be retained without such formulas, because, being unchanging in itself and yet for all times and places, its doctrines would be easily corrupted if there were not an official standard (Symbol) by which both truth and error could be at once recognized (I Cor., i. 10; II Tim., i. 13).

767. The formulas of Christian teaching as summarized in the Creeds, since they must be brief and orderly, are divided into short and

connected propositions, which are therefore known as articles. Brevity being the character of Creeds, not all revealed truths are expressed in them as articles, but only those that have the following characteristics:

(a) An article of the Creed deals with one of the two main objects of belief, namely, the end of man, which is eternal life (Heb., xi. 1), and the means thereto, which is Jesus Christ (John, xvii. 3). Other things, which are proposed for faith, not for their own sake, but only on account of their relation to these two main objects (e.g., the wandering of the Israelites in the desert, the details of the journeys of St. Paul, etc.), are not mentioned in the Creeds.

(b) An article of the Creed deals only with those doctrines concerning eternal life and Christ which are in a special manner unseen or difficult, for faith is "the evidence of things that appear not" (Heb., xi. 1). Other doctrines which have no special difficulty of their own are considered as implicit in those that express the general mysteries, and hence they are not mentioned. Thus, the three Persons of the Trinity are given distinct articles, because the mysteriousness of the Triune God cannot be reduced to any more general mystery, whereas the Eucharist is not mentioned, as having no mystery that is not implied in the articles on the divine omnipotence and the sanctification of man through Christ.

768. Has there been an increase in the articles of faith?

(a) If by increase is meant the addition through new revelation of main beliefs not contained in the primitive revelation, there has never been an increase in the articles of faith; for from the beginning God made known His own being, which includes the eternal things of God and the end or happiness of man, and His providence, which includes the temporal dispensations of God and the means for the salvation of man (Heb., xi. 6).

(b) If by increase is meant the addition of new revelations that brought out more clearly and definitely things contained in previous revelation, there was an increase in the articles of faith from the beginning of revelations down to the end of the Apostolic age. Thus, the nature of God and His purpose as regards the redemption of humanity were brought out ever more distinctly by new revelations in Old Testament times (Exod., vi. 2), and were given in final and complete form by the revelation of Christ (Heb., i. 1; Eph., iii. 5; Heb., xii. 27, 28; II Tim., i. 13).

(c) If by increase is meant a clearer and fuller explanation of the revelation once delivered to the Saints, there has been and always can be an increase of articles of faith. Thus, in the Council of Nicæa the Apostles' Creed was amplified; in the Council of Constantinople the Creed of Nicæa was added to, and similarly today or tomorrow the Pope could add new explanations or developments to the Creed, if new heresies or necessities required that the true sense of revelation already given should be brought out more clearly or fully.

769. There are three principal Creeds used by the Church:

(a) the Apostles' Creed, which according to an early tradition was composed by the Apostles themselves before they separated to preach the Gospel. It was in use from the first centuries in the Roman Church, which required that the catechumens learn and recite it before receiving Baptism. It is divided into twelve articles;

(b) the Nicene Creed, which is used in the Mass and was drawn up at the Council of Nicæa (325) against the Arian denial of the divinity of Christ, and was revised by the Council of Constantinople (381) against the Macedonians, who refused to acknowledge the divinity of the Holy Ghost;

(c) the Athanasian Creed, which is used in the Office of Prime and is a résumé of the teaching of St. Athanasius on the Trinity and Incarnation. It was composed in the West some time after the beginning of the fifth century.

770. Summary of the teaching of the First Article of the Creed: "I believe in God, the Father Almighty, Creator of heaven and earth."— (a) "I believe," i.e., I give unhesitating assent to God revealing His mysterious truths; (b) "in God," i.e., the Supreme Being, one in nature and three in persons; (c) "the Father," i.e., our Maker and Provider, from whom also we receive the spirit of adoption of sons; (d) "almighty," i.e., all-powerful, and therefore all-wise and endowed with every other perfection in the highest degree; (e) "Creator," i.e., who freely produced the world out of nothing, without external model or

effort of any sort, and who preserves, rules and moves all creatures; (f) "of heaven and earth," i.e., of the world of pure spirits, of matter, and of man, who is at the confines of matter and spirit—in other words, of all finite things, visible and invisible.

771. Summary of the Second Article: "And in Jesus Christ, His only Son, our Lord."—(a) "Jesus," a name given by command of God and meaning "Saviour"; (b) "Christ," i.e., "the anointed," because He was King, Priest, and Prophet; (c) "His only Son," i.e., born of the Father before all ages, God of God, Light of Light, true God of true God, begotten not made, consubstantial with the Father, by whom all things were made; (d) "our Lord," for as God He shares all the perfections of the divine nature, as man He has redeemed us and thus deservedly acquired the title of Lord over us, while as the God-man He is the Lord of all created things. It should be noted that there is nothing imperfect or carnal in the generation of the Son, or in the procession of the Holy Ghost, for God is a spirit and all-perfect.

772. Summary of the Third Article: "Who was conceived by the Holy Ghost, born of the Virgin Mary."—(a) "Who was conceived." The Only-begotten Son, the second Person of the Trinity, for us men and for our salvation, became incarnate and was made man. Thus, the same Divine Person is in both the divine and human natures, and the union preserves the properties and the actions of both natures. (b) "By the Holy Ghost." At the moment when Mary consented to the announcement of the angel, the body of Christ was formed in her womb from her flesh, the rational soul was infused, and the divine and human natures were united in the Person of the Word. Thus, Mary is truly the Mother of God. This conception was miraculous, accomplished without the aid of man, through the sole operation of the three Persons of the Trinity. Being an external work of God in which love towards us is especially manifested, the Incarnation is attributed to the Holy Ghost, who in the internal life of the Deity proceeds as the mutual love of Father and Son. (c) "Born of the Virgin Mary." Mary was ever a virgin, before, during, and after childbirth; immaculate and holy in soul; the spiritual Mother of whom Christians are born in holiness.

773. Summary of the Fourth Article: "Suffered under Pontius Pilate, was crucified, dead and buried."—(a) The effect of that which is contained in this article is expressed in the words of the Nicene Creed, "for us." The passion and death of Christ, willed by Himself, accomplished our salvation, as satisfaction, sacrifice and redemption; (b) The manner in which this was brought about is declared in the words above quoted. In His human nature Christ suffered agony and pain of body; He was sentenced to death by the Roman governor and nailed to the cross. His soul and body were separated in death, although the Divinity never departed from either, and His dead body was laid in the tomb.

774. Summary of the Fifth Article: "He descended into hell; the third day He rose again from the dead."—(a) "He descended." After His death the soul of Christ went to the abode of the departed, to liberate those who were there. (b) "Into hell." The name hell is applied in a wide sense to all those secret abodes in which are detained the souls of those who have not obtained the happiness of heaven—viz., the hell of the damned, in which the impenitent suffer eternal pain of loss and sense; purgatory, in which the souls of just men are cleansed by temporary punishments; limbo, where the fathers of the Old Testament awaited in peaceful repose the coming of Christ. It was this last abode into which the soul of Christ entered. (c) "The third day"—i.e., on Sunday morning, the third day after His burial. (d) "He rose again." As He had laid down His life by His own power, so He took it up again by His own power. (e) "From the dead." Christ not only returned to life, He also conquered death; He rose to die no more, and thus He is first in the final resurrection. (f) "According to the scriptures." These words are added in the Creed of Constantinople, to call attention to the fact that the resurrection is the attestation of the truth of our Lord's claims and doctrine (I Cor., xv. 14, 17; Matt., xii. 39, 40).

775. Summary of the Sixth Article: "He ascended into heaven, sitteth at the right hand of God, the Father almighty."—(a) "He ascended." By His own power as God and man Christ ascended into heaven. (b) "Into heaven." As God, He never forsook heaven, the Divinity being omnipresent; but as man, body and soul, He ascended to the abode of glory forty days after the resurrection. (c) "Sitteth at the right hand of God the Father Almighty." Christ is said to stand at the right hand of

God, inasmuch as He is our Mediator with the Father (Acts, vii. 55; Heb., vii. 25; John, xiv. 2); He is said to sit at the right hand of the Father to express the permanent possession of royal and supreme power and glory (Eph., i. 20-22; Heb., i. 13).

776. Summary of the Seventh Article: "From thence He shall come to judge the living and the dead."—There is a particular judgment at death; at the end of the World, of which the time is uncertain, there will be a general judgment, both of the living and the dead. Christ will come a second time, and as Judge will pass sentence either of eternal loss and pain or of eternal happiness.

777. Summary of the Eighth Article: "I believe in the Holy Ghost."— The Third Person of the Trinity is equal to the Father and the Son, proceeds from them both as their mutual love, and is spoken of, therefore, by appropriation, as the Author of works of grace and sanctification, in which especially the charity of God is manifested: "The Holy Ghost, the Lord and Giver of life, who proceedeth from the Father and the Son, who together with the Father and the Son is adored and glorified, who spoke by the prophets" (Creed of Constantinople).

778. Summary of the Ninth Article: "I believe the Holy Catholic Church; the Communion of Saints."—(a) The Church pertains to the material, not the formal object of divine faith (see 754), and hence it is not said: "I believe in the Church." We believe of the Church that she is the visible society made up of the faithful scattered throughout the world, called also the house of God (I Tim., iii. 15), the flock of Christ, the spouse of Christ (II Cor., xi. 2), the body of Christ (Eph., i. 23; Col., i. 24); that besides the Church militant on earth, composed of both the good and the bad, and outside of which are unbelievers and the excommunicated, there is the Church triumphant in heaven and the Church suffering in purgatory; that there are four marks by which the true Church may be recognized—viz., that she is one, holy, Catholic, and Apostolic; that she is divine in her origin and possesses divinely given powers. (b) "The Communion of Saints." The members of the Church have different offices, but there is among them a community of spiritual goods, the Sacraments being a bond of union, and each one profiting according to his condition in the good works done by others,

The Church suffering is assisted by our suffrages, while we in turn are helped by the intercessions of the Church triumphant.

779. Summary of the Tenth Article: "The forgiveness of sins."—God forgives all sins, when they are truly repented of, either through Baptism (in case of sins before Baptism) or through the due exercise of the power of the keys given the Church (in case of sins after Baptism). Venial sins may be forgiven by private repentance.

780. Summary of the Eleventh Article: "The resurrection of the body."—The soul is immortal, the body mortal. But at the end of the world the bodies of all the dead, even though corrupted, shall be restored and reunited with their principle of life—i.e., the soul to which they belonged. Substantially, the risen body will be identical with the mortal body, but it will have certain new qualities corresponding to its new state.

781. Summary of the Twelfth Article: "Life everlasting."—Those who die in the friendship of God will be received into unending happiness, in which they will be exempted from all evil and enjoy the beatific vision and other divine gifts.

782. The Acts of Faith.—According to St. Paul, there are two acts of faith, one internal, the other external: "With the heart we believe unto justice, but with the mouth confession is made unto salvation" (Rom., x. 10). (a) The internal act of faith is the firm and constant judgment of the intellect assenting to divine revelation (II Cor., x. 5), but freely and under the command of the will (Mark, xvi. 16), being moved thereto by divine grace (Eph., ii. 5). (b) The external act of faith is the profession before the world by signs, such as words or deeds, of the internal assent given to divine revelation.

783. The internal act of faith is one, but it has a threefold relationship: (a) it believes about God, if we consider the intellect as assenting to the material object; (b) it believes God, if we consider the intellect as assenting to the formal object; (c) it believes in God, if we consider the will as moving the intellect to assent, and tending towards God as the Last End.

784. The truths to which the assent of faith is given are either supernatural or natural. (a) Supernatural truths or mysteries (e.g., the Trinity of Persons in God) are revealed for faith, that man may know, desire and work for the supernatural destiny to which he has been raised. (b) Natural truths (e.g., the Oneness of God) are revealed for faith, so that mankind may obtain more quickly, more generally, and more certainly the knowledge of divine things which reason can afford. It is impossible, however, that an act of faith and an act of knowledge should coexist in the same individual about the same truth, for faith is of things that appear not.

785. The act of faith is a necessary preliminary to other supernatural acts, for we do not tend towards the supernatural, unless we first accept it by belief; hence, faith is necessary. But the act of faith may also be made after other supernatural acts, like those of hope and charity; and so it may be meritorious. (a) The act of faith is necessary, both as a means and as a precept (see 360). The necessity of means will be treated now, the necessity of precept later, when we speak of the commandments of faith (see 913 sqq.). (b) The act of faith before justification is meritorious congruously and in a wide sense; but after justification it has condign merit (see 110).

786. For all adults the act of faith is necessary for salvation as a necessity of means (see 360), for the Apostle says: "Without faith it is impossible to please God" (Heb., xi. 6). The truths which must be believed under necessity of means are of two kinds. (a) One must believe with implicit faith all revealed truths which one does not know and is not bound to know. An act of implicit faith is contained in the formula: "O my God, I firmly believe all the truths the Catholic Church teaches, because Thou hast revealed them." (b) One must believe with explicit faith all the truths which one is bound to know. An act of explicit faith in all the truths necessary by necessity of means is contained in the Apostles' Creed. Other truths that must be explicitly believed on account of a necessity of precept will be discussed in 918, 920.

787. What specifically are the truths just referred to that all are bound to know as a necessary means? (a) Theologians generally agree that it has always been necessary for adults to know and accept two basic

mysteries—God's existence, as the supernatural End or happiness of man, and His providence as exercised in supplying the means necessary for supernatural salvation (see 768). Without such belief, supernatural hope and charity, at all times necessary, are impossible. (b) A majority of theologians hold, and with greater probability it seems, that since the promulgation of the Gospel it is necessary for adults to know and accept the two basic mysteries of Chrisitanity—viz., that in God, who is our beatitude, there are three persons (the Trinity), and that the way to our beatitude is through Christ our Redeemer (the Incarnation).

788. Even before the Gospel, it was always necessary as a means that one believe explicitly in God as our supernatural happiness and as the provider of the means thereto. Thus, the Apostle, speaking of the ancient patriarchs, says: "He that cometh to God, must believe that He is, and is a rewarder to them that seek Him" (Heb., xi. 6). He that would come to God (i.e., be saved), must believe in God as the Author of glory and of grace. Hence, one must believe: (a) that God exists, who is not ashamed to be called our God, and who prepares for us a better, that is, a heavenly country (Heb., xi. 6); (b) that God is a remunerator, from whom must be expected the working out of His promises and the helps to attain the reward, as well as the meting out of justice. In this faith is included implicitly a faith in Christ, and thus in the Old Testament a belief, at least implicit, in the Messiah to come was always necessary: "Man is not justified by the works of the law, but by the faith of Jesus Christ" (Gal., ii. 16).

789. Since the promulgation of the Gospel (see 342, 354), it is also necessary as a means that one believe explicitly in the mysteries of the Trinity and Incarnation. For he who does not accept these, does not accept the Gospel, whereas Christ says: "Go ye into the whole world, and preach the Gospel to every creature. He that believeth not shall be condemned" (Mark, xvi. 15, 16).

(a) Theoretically, this opinion seems more probable than the opposite opinion; but chiefly on account of the difficulty about negative infidels, which is discussed in dogmatic treatises on Predestination and Grace, many theologians either reject it (e.g., those who say that belief in the two great Christian mysteries is necessary only as a precept, or that implicit faith suffices), or modify it (e.g., those who say that belief in these two mysteries is not necessary as a means for justification, but only for glorification, and those who say that regularly such faith is a necessary means, but that an exception is allowed for invincible ignorance, or for the insufficient promulgation of the Gospel in many regions).

(b) Practically, this opinion is safer, and hence all theologians, even Probabilists, hold that one must act as if it were true and certain, whenever it is possible to give instruction on the Trinity and Incarnation.

790. Knowledge about the mysteries of faith is either substantial (by which one knows the essentials of a mystery) or scientific (by which one knows also its circumstances and details, and is able to give a more profound explanation of it). Scientific knowledge is required, on account of their office, in those who are bound to teach the faith, but substantial knowledge suffices for salvation. Hence, for an adult to be saved, it suffices that he have the following kind of knowledge about the four great mysteries:

(a) There is a God who has spoken to us, promising freely that He will take us to Himself as our reward. It is not necessary that one understand such theological concepts as the essence of deity, the definition of supernaturality, the formal and material objects of beatitude, etc.; for many persons are incapable of understanding them.

(b) This God, who will be our reward, is one, but there are three divine Persons—the Father, the Son and the Holy Ghost, really distinct and equal. It is not necessary that one understand the distinction between nature and person, nor subtle questions about the processions and properties.

(c) God provides for us, giving us the helps we need, and also, if we serve Him, the reward He has promised. It is not necessary that one understand the theology of providence, grace, and merit.

(d) Jesus Christ, who is God the Son, became man, suffered and died for us, thus saving us from sin and winning back for us the right to heaven. It is not necessary that one understand scientifically that in

Christ there are two natures united hypostatically in the one Person of the Word.

791. Since Baptism is fruitless without due faith in the recipient, it is not lawful as a rule to baptize those who lack substantial knowledge of the four mysteries just mentioned. (a) Outside of danger of death, it is never lawful to baptize a person, adult in mind, who is in substantial ignorance of any of these four mysteries. Such a person must first receive instruction. (b) In danger of death, when instruction cannot be given, an adult in substantial ignorance about the Trinity and the Incarnation may be baptized conditionally; for it is probable that explicit knowledge of those two mysteries is not a necessity of means (see 789; Canon 752, §2).

792. Since absolution is invalid if the person absolved is incapable of receiving grace, and since acts of faith in the four chief mysteries are an essential means to justification in adults, absolution given to one who is in substantial ignorance about one of the four mysteries above mentioned is certainly or probably invalid, as the case may be. Absolution certainly invalid is never lawful, but absolution probably valid may in certain cases be regarded as lawful before administration, and as valid after administration. Hence, the following cases must be distinguished:

(a) Outside of danger of death, it is not lawful to absolve one who is in substantial ignorance about any of those four mysteries. Such a person should be sent away for further instruction, or given a brief instruction then and there, if there is time.

(b) In danger of death, when instruction cannot be given, an adult in substantial ignorance about the Trinity and Incarnation may be absolved conditionally, for the reason given in the similar case of Baptism.

(c) After the fact, absolution given to one who was in substantial ignorance of the Trinity and Incarnation, may be regarded as valid, since the opinion that explicit knowledge of these mysteries is not a necessary means, is at least probable. Hence, according to the principles of Probabilism a penitent who made confessions While ignorant of those two mysteries is not obliged to repeat his confessions, since he has probably satisfied his obligation.

793. In the following cases (which would be rare, it seems) Baptism or absolution cannot be administered, even to the dying who are unable to receive instruction: (a) when it is certain that the dying person is substantially ignorant about the existence of God, the Author of grace and glory; (b) when it is certain that the dying person is substantially ignorant of the Trinity and Incarnation through his own fault, and is unwilling to hear about them.

794. Practical rules for granting the Sacraments in case of doubt or urgency to those who seem to be indisposed on account of substantial ignorance are the following:

(a) In danger of death, when instruction is out of the question, if there is doubt about his ignorance, the dying person should be given the benefit of the doubt.

(b) In danger of death, and when instruction is impossible, if there is doubt about the mental ability of the dying person and his obligation to have explicit faith, he should receive the benefit of the doubt.

(c) In danger of death or other urgent necessity, when instruction is needed and possible, it should be given briefly as follows: "Let us say the act of faith: I believe in one God, the Father, Son and Holy Ghost, who has promised to take to Himself after this life all those that love Him, and who punishes the wicked. I hope to have the happiness of being received into His companionship through the help of Jesus Christ, the Son of God, who became man and died for my salvation." This or a similar instruction should be given by the priest or lay person present in baptizing an adult who is about to die. When there is not immediate danger of death, a person who is baptized or absolved after short instruction on account of emergency, should be admonished of the duty of receiving fuller instruction later on.

795. Faith is the free exercise of the free assent of the intellect to the unseen, an acceptance of obligations and tasks hard to human nature. It is, therefore, an act of homage to the authority of God, and is meritorious: "By faith the ancient patriarchs obtained the promises"

(Heb., xi. 33). Is the freedom and meritoriousness of this act of faith lessened if one seeks for other arguments than the authority of God in giving one's assent to revelation? (a) The merit of the act of faith is not lessened, when one seeks human arguments for the assent of credibility which is prior to the assent of faith; for it is only the part of prudence that one should first assure oneself of the fact that a revelation has been made, before one assents on faith to the doctrines contained in that revelation. Now, the arguments by which one assures oneself of the fact of a revelation are human arguments, such as proofs that revelation is possible and suitable, that there are miracles, prophecies and other signs to guarantee the divine mission of those who delivered the revelation, etc.

(b) The merit of the act of faith is not lessened if one seeks human arguments for the preambles of faith, that is, for those divine truths that can be established by natural reason (such as the existence of God, His infinite knowledge and truthfulness). The person who demonstrates these preambles by philosophical proofs, has knowledge, not belief, about them; but the merit of faith is not lost, if, while knowing these truths, he remains willing to accept them on the authority of revelation.

(c) The merit of faith is not lessened, if one seeks human arguments for the mysteries of faith, that is, for those truths of revelation that are above human reason (such as the Trinity and the Incarnation), provided these arguments are sought not for the demonstration, but for the confirmation or defense of dogma. Nay, a person ought, in so far as he is able, to use his reason in the service of faith, and to do so is a sign, not of little, but of great faith. "Be ready always," says St. Peter (I Peter, iii. 15), "to satisfy everyone that asketh you a reason of that hope which is in you." And St. Anselm says: "It appears to me a sign of carelessness, if, having been confirmed in the faith, we do not take pains to understand what we believe." St. Thomas writes: "When a man is willing to believe, he loves the truth, meditates upon it, and takes to heart whatever reasons he can find in support thereof; and with regard to this, human reason does not exclude the merit of faith, but is a sign of greater merit."

(d) The merit of faith is lessened if one seeks human arguments as the formal object, that is, as the motive on which faith is grounded; for then one does not wish to believe, or to believe so readily, on the word of God alone, but feels one must call in other testimony to support it.

The attempt to understand mysteries or to establish them by natural reason is opposed to the humble assent of faith: "He that is a searcher of majesty, shall be overwhelmed by glory" (Prov., xxv. 27); "Seek not the things that are too high for thee, and search not into things above thy ability" (Ecclus., iii. 22); "Faith loses its merit, if it is put to the test of reason" (St. Gregory the Great, Hom. xxvi).

796. Besides the internal act of acceptance of revealed truth, faith has also external acts. (a) It commands the external acts of the other virtues, that is, acts directed to the specific ends of those virtues. Hence, one who fasts exercises an external act of the virtue of temperance, but it is his faith in the virtue that commands the fast. (b) Faith elicits the external act of profession of faith as its own proper external act directed to its own specific end: "I believed, for which cause I have spoken" (Ps. cxv. 10; II Cor., iv. 13). External profession of faith, therefore, is not an act proceeding from faith; it is an act of faith. The necessity of this act will be considered below in the article about the commandments of faith.

797. The Habit of Faith.—Faith is not only an act that passes, but it is also a permanent quality or habit conferred by God, one of the "most great and perfect promises" which man must make use of (II Peter, i. 3 sqq.), a charism that is not for a time but for all this life, just like hope and charity (I Cor., xiii. 13). God, who does all things sweetly (Wis., viii. 1), and who has provided for His natural creatures internal powers by which they incline and move themselves towards the ends of their activities, has not done less for those whom He moves to a supernatural destiny; and, in justifying the sinner, He infuses along with grace the supernatural virtues of faith, hope and charity (Council of Trent, Sess. VI, Cap. 6).

798. The virtue of faith is thus defined by the Council of the Vatican: "Faith is a supernatural virtue, by which, with the help of God's grace, we believe the truths revealed by Him, not on account of an intrinsic evidence of the truths themselves, perceived by natural reason, but on account of the authority of God who revealed them."

799. Hence, the virtue of faith has the following properties:

(a) It is supernatural, not only because its object and motive are supernatural, but because it proceeds from a supernatural principle, i.e., grace (John, vi, 29; Eph., ii. 8).

(b) It is obscure, because the believer assents to that which has no intrinsic evidence for him. He does not see its truth as the blessed see God, for "we see now through a glass in a dark manner, but then face to face" (I Cor., xiii. 12). He does not know its truth as he knows evident or naturally demonstrated propositions, for faith is about truths that surpass reason—things "that appear not." This, of course, does not mean that faith is not rightly called a new light added to the mind, and that the motives which call for the acceptance of faith are not evidently credible.

(c) It is free, because, although one cannot dissent from that which is evident intrinsically (e.g., that two and two make four), one is able to dissent from that which is obscure.

(d) It is not a process of reasoning, but a simple act of assent, in which one accepts at the same time the authority of the Revealer and the truth of His revelation. "Jesus said to her (Martha): I am the resurrection and the life .... Believest thou this? She saith to Him: Yea, Lord, I have believed that Thou art the Christ, etc." (John, xi. 25-27).

(e) It is firm and unshaken in a far higher degree than the assent of understanding and science, since it rests on the infallible authority of God (I Thess., ii. 13).

800. Before justification, faith exists, it seems, only as an act performed under the influence of actual or transitory grace. After the infusion of habitual grace, faith is a habit or infused virtue. But there are two modes of existence characteristic of this one habit, and hence the distinction of living and dead faith (Gal., v. 6; James, ii. 26).

(a) Living faith is that which is informed or animated by charity. This latter virtue is called the soul of all the other virtues, inasmuch as it directs them to their supreme end, divine friendship, and gives meritorious value to their works. All those have living faith who join to belief a life in agreement with belief—that is, the state of grace, love of God and good works.

(b) Dead faith is that which is separated from charity. It is a true virtue, because it directs the assent of the intellect to its proper end; but it is an imperfect virtue, because its acts are not directed to the Last End, and are not meritorious of eternal life. All those who believe, but who do not live up to their belief in matters of importance, who neglect serious duties to God or others, have dead faith. Examples are those who call themselves Catholics, but neglect attendance at church and the reception of the Sacraments.

801. Those who have, or who had faith, are the following:

(a) the Angels in the state of probation and our first parents in Paradise, for faith is necessary as a means in every condition short of the beatific vision (see 785, 158); (b) those in this life who are in the friendship of God, and also those believers who are not in the friendship of God, the former having living, and the latter dead faith (see 800); (c) the souls in purgatory, the ancient patriarchs in limbo.

802. Those who have not faith are the following: (a) those who have vision of the truths of faith, that is, the Saints in heaven and Christ while on earth (I Cor., xiii. 10); (b) those who reject obstinately even one doctrine of faith, for, if individual judgment is put above the authority of God even in one point, the motive or keystone of faith, and therefore faith itself, is no longer assented to; (c) the lost, for, being cut off entirely from grace, these possess no virtue infused by God. "The devils believe and tremble" (James, ii. 19), but their belief is not supernatural or free, but natural and unwilling.

803. Of those who have faith, some have greater, and some less faith. Thus, our Lord reproved St. Peter for his little faith (Matt., xiv. 31), and praised the Woman of Canaan for her great faith (Matt., xv. 28). But since all are obliged to have supreme confidence in God and to accept all He teaches, how is there room for different degrees of faith?

(a) Faith must be supreme appreciatively, that is, all must put the formal object of faith, the motive of its assent, above every other motive of assent, for the First Truth speaking deserves more adherence than any other authority. In this respect, therefore, and in the exclusion of every doubt, the faith of all is equal. But faith need not be supreme intensively, that is, it is not required that the intellect should feel the assent of faith more than the assent given to natural truth, or that the will must experience the highest alacrity, devotion and confidence; for the truths that are nearer to us move us more vehemently than do higher and invisible truths. Hence, in this respect the faith of one may be more firm or fervent than the faith of another, according as one is more childlike, more loving, more intense in his acceptance of God's Word than another.

(b) Faith must be universal, that is, we must accept the entire material object of revelation, and none may pick and choose according to his likes or fancies, for all of revelation has God for its Author. In this respect the faith of all is equal, all believers accepting twelve articles, while those who accept eleven or six or one or none, are not believers. But faith need not be explicit as to all its doctrines, and hence, while one believer who is not thoroughly instructed may know only the twelve articles of the Creed, another believer who is better instructed may know the hundreds of other truths that are contained in the articles. In this way the faith of one is greater extensively.

804. Can faith grow or decline in the same person? (a) If there is question of acts of faith, the later acts can be more or less firm or fervent than those that preceded, in the way explained in the previous paragraph. In this sense we may understand the Apostles to have asked of our Lord a higher degree of faith, that they might work miracles in His name (Luke, xvii. 5). (b) If there is question of the habit of faith, it itself is increased at every increase of sanctifying grace (see 745). St. Paul writes to the Corinthians (II Cor., x. 15) that he has hope of their "increasing faith." Moreover, by repeated acts of faith the ease and delight with which the habit is exercised increases, as is the case with acquired habits. But the habit of faith is not diminished directly as was explained regarding the infused virtues in general (see 745).

805. The means of growing in faith are: (a) prayer to the Father of lights: "Lord, increase our faith" (Luke, xvii. 5); (b) reading of the scriptures, the Lives of the Saints and other similar works, and attendance at spiritual instructions; (c) frequent acts of faith in the

world we see not and its coming rewards; (d) exercise of faith, by directing our thoughts, words, and actions according to the teaching of faith, rather than according to the maxims of the world; for "the just man liveth by faith" (Heb., x. 38), and "faith without works is dead" (James, ii. 20).

806. The cause of faith is God. (a) It is God who directly through revelation, or indirectly through the Church, the evangelists, preachers, etc., "brings the message before man" (Rom., x. 15); (b) it is God who "causes the mind of man to assent" to His message. No matter how persuasive the teacher or how well disposed or learned the hearer may be, faith will not come unless the light of grace leads the way (Eph., ii. 8).

807. The effects of faith are fear of God and purification of the heart. (a) Dead faith causes one to fear the penalties of divine justice, that is, to have servile fear (James, ii. 19): living faith causes one to fear sin itself, that is, to have filial fear. (b) Faith, by elevating man to higher things, purifies his soul from the defilements of lower things (Acts, xv. 9): if faith is dead, it at least purifies the intellect from error; if it is living, it also purifies the will from evil.

808. The Gifts of Understanding and Knowledge.—As was said above (see 159), the Gifts of the Holy Ghost are intended as means for perfecting the theological virtues. There are two Gifts that serve the virtue of faith, namely, the Gifts of Understanding and Knowledge.

(a) Faith, being assent, must have a right idea of what is proposed for acceptance; but, as it is obscure (see 799), and as there are things apart from faith that may corrupt our notion of it, the Gift of Understanding is conferred, a simple perception and divine intuition through which one receives a correct notion of the mysteries of faith.

(b) Faith, being the starting point of all supernatural activities, must be the norm by which we judge of what we should think and do in the affairs of life; but, as it is a simple act of assent (see 799) and as the creatures of the world are a temptation and a snare (Wis., xiv. 11), the Gift of Knowledge is given, through which one receives a correct judgment about the things of this world. These then take on a new and fuller significance in the light of the teachings of faith.

809. The Gift of Understanding must not be confused with the Beatific Vision. (a) A perfect penetration of the mysteries, which enables one to perceive their essence and causes (e.g., the how and the why of the Trinity), is given by the Beatific Vision; but such understanding removes all obscurity, and is therefore insociable with faith. (b) An imperfect penetration of the teachings of faith, which does not take away the obscurity and mysteriousness, is given by the Gift of Understanding, and is therefore sociable with faith. The effects of this Gift are: it distinguishes the truths of faith from false doctrines; it conveys a clear view of the credibility of the mystery of faith against all difficulties and objections; it gives knowledge of the supernatural import of the secondary truths of faith, that is, of those revealed happenings and facts that are not themselves supernatural (Luke, xxiv. 32); it gives understanding of the practical aspect of a mystery—for example, that the intratrinitarian relations of the Divine Persons are a model for the regulation of the Christian life, in knowledge and love of divine things.

810. The Gift of Knowledge, which like the other Gifts is had by all the just, must not be confused with sacred knowledge or theology, nor with the extraordinary gifts of infused knowledge and the charism of knowledge.

(a) The Gift of Knowledge resembles theology in that it reproduces objectively what reason does when it argues from the visible world to the invisible Creator; but, while subjectively theology is the result of study in which one passes successively from premise to conclusion. Knowledge is the result of a divine light that may be found even in the illiterate, and it takes in at a glance all that is contained in a process of argumentation. Through this Gift the wonders of nature, the events of history, the arguments of philosophy, lead one firmly and spontaneously to the Last End and the supernatural realities of faith.

(b) Infused knowledge may have for its object things purely natural (such as truths of philosophy and the ability to speak foreign languages), while the Gift of Knowledge is concerned only with faith, judging what is to be believed or done according to faith.

(c) The charism of knowledge (I Cor., xii. 8) is a grace given one for the benefit of others, by which one is able to communicate to them successfully the teachings of faith; the Gift of Knowledge, on the contrary, proceeds from the habit of sanctifying grace, and is intended for the benefit of its recipient.

811. To each of the Gifts of the Holy Ghost correspond Beatitudes and Fruits (see 159).

(a) To the Gift of Understanding corresponds the Sixth Beatitude: "Blessed are the pure of heart, for they shall see God." For by Understanding the mind is pure from wrong ideas of truth, and sees that God is above all that the intellect can comprehend. The two fruits that proceed from Understanding are faith (i.e., conviction about revealed truth) and ultimately joy, in union with God through charity. (b) To the Gift of Knowledge corresponds the Third Beatitude: "Blessed are they that mourn, for they shall be comforted." For by Knowledge one judges rightly about created things, grieves over the wrong use made of them, and is comforted when they are turned to their proper end.

Art. 2: THE SINS AGAINST FAITH

(*Summa Theologica*, II-II, qq. 10-15.)

812. The sins against faith can all be reduced to four heads: (a) sins of unbelief (see 813-886), which are opposed to the internal act of faith; (b) sins of blasphemy (see 887-903), which are opposed to the external act of faith; (c) sins of ignorance (see 904-911), which are opposed to the Gift of Knowledge; (d) sins of blindness and dullness (912), which are opposed to the Gift of Understanding.

813. The Sin of Unbelief.—Unbelief in general is a want of faith. It is of two kinds, negative and positive.

(a) Negative unbelief is the absence of faith in a person who has never heard of it at all, or only insufficiently. Thus, the Indians in America before the coming of Christian missionaries were negative unbelievers. This kind of unbelief is a punishment, since it results from original sin; but it is not a sin itself, and those who die in negative unbelief are lost,

not on account of this, but on account of sins against the natural law
(John, xv. 22; Rom., x. 14). With this kind of unbelief we are not here
concerned.

(b) Positive unbelief is the absence of faith in one who has heard it
sufficiently, so that the lack of it is due to his own fault. This kind of
unbelief is, of course, a sin, for it supposes that one is acting against the
light one has received.

814. Positive unbelief is either a refusal or a renouncement of faith. (a)
Ordinary unbelief is a refusal of faith, that is, non-acceptance of faith
by one who has never had faith; (b) apostasy, or desertion, is the
abandonment of faith by one who formerly accepted it. This is not a
distinct kind of unbelief, since, like ordinary unbelief, it has for its
object or term the denial of revealed truth; but it is an aggravating
circumstance of unbelief (II Peter, ii. 21).

815. The sin of unbelief is, committed either directly or indirectly. (a) It
is committed directly, when one rejects what pertains to faith (its acts,
objects or motive); (b) it is committed indirectly, when one guiltily
places oneself or others in the occasion or danger of unbelief. The
dangers against faith will be considered after the sins of unbelief (see
848-886).

816. Direct sins of unbelief are those opposed to the elements that
belong to the nature of faith and that are contained in its definition (see
751, 798). (a) Opposed to the act of assent are sins of non-assent or
dissent (see 817-839); (b) opposed to the certitude and firmness of
assent are sins of doubt (840-846); (c) opposed to the right object of
faith are sins of credulity (847); (d) opposed to the motive of faith is
rationalism (847).

817. Sins of non-assent are those by which one omits to make an act of
faith when one should. This kind of sin will be treated when we come
to the commandments of faith as to its internal and external acts (see
925 sqq.)

818. Sins of dissent are sins of commission, and are of two kinds: (a)
privative unbelief, which is the want of faith in one who has heard the
faith sufficiently and should realize the obligation of embracing it, but

who refuses to believe, although he makes no opposition to faith; (b) contrary unbelief, which is the want of faith in one who has heard the faith and its motives of credibility sufficiently to know the duty of embracing it, and who not only refuses to believe, but even accepts the errors opposed to faith.

819. What is the gravity of sins of dissent, doubt, and rationalism? (a) From their nature, these sins are always mortal, for they refuse to God the homage of the intellect and will that is due Him, deprive man of the beginning of spiritual life, and lead to eternal condemnation (Mark, xvi. 16). (b) From their circumstances, these and other sins against faith may be venial (see 180-184). Thus, if a man refuses to believe or accepts error, not having sufficient knowledge of his obligation or not fully consenting to the sin, his fault is venial subjectively or formally.

820. Are sins against faith more serious than all other kinds of sin? (a) From their nature, sins against faith are worse than sins against the moral virtues, for the former offend directly against God Himself, but not so the latter. Hatred of God, however, is a greater sin than sins of unbelief, as will be shown when we treat of sins against charity. (b) From their circumstances, sins against faith may be less serious than sins against the moral virtues. Example: A venial sin against faith is less serious than a mortal sin against justice.

821. With regard to the effect of sins against faith on good acts it should be noted: (a) an unbeliever is able to perform works that are ethically or naturally good (Rom., ii. 14), and the Church has condemned the opposite teaching of Baius (Denzinger, *Enchiridion*, n. 1025). (b) an unbeliever is not able to perform works that are supernaturally good and meritorious (see 112).

822. Contrary unbelief (see 818), which not only refuses to believe but also assents to contrary errors, has three degrees according to the greater or less number of truths denied or errors admitted in these three degrees. Some theologians see different species of unbelief, while other theologians regard them as only accidental modes or circumstances of the one species of sin.

(a) The most extensive denial of faith is found in infidelity, which rejects both Christ and His revelation. To this form of unbelief belong atheism, agnosticism, pantheism, paganism, polytheism, animism, and denials of Christ and Christianity. The chief religious bodies today that profess such errors are: Confucianism, Taoism and Shintoism (founded in China and Japan), which are polytheistic and practise idolatry and ancestor worship; Brahmanism (founded about 14 centuries before Christ), which is polytheistic or animistic: Buddhism (founded 6th century B.C. in India), which is polytheistic and practises idolatry; Zoroastrianism (founded in Persia about the 7th century B.C.), which is dualistic; Mohammedanism (founded in Arabia in the 6th century A.D.), which makes Mohammed and his religion superior to Christ and Christianity, and rejects the Trinity and the Incarnation. (b) A less complete departure from faith is found when Christ and His revelation are accepted as contained in the figures and prophecies of the Old Testament, but rejected in their fulfillment and development in Jesus and the New Testament. This is the error of Judaism, which today has about 15 million adherents.

(c) A still smaller degree of rejection of faith exists when Christ is recognized as leader and teacher, but not all of His revelation is accepted. This kind of error is called heresy, and those bodies which profess it are known as sects. The chief heresies in times past were Gnosticism and Manicheism in the first centuries; Arianism and Macedonianism in the fourth century; Nestorianism, Monophysism and Pelagianism in the fifth century; Monothelism in the seventh century; Iconoclasm in the eighth century; Photianism in the ninth century; Albigensianism in the eleventh century; Waldensianism in the twelfth century; Wicliffism in the fourteenth century; Hussism in the fifteenth century; Protestantism in the sixteenth century, and Modernism in the twentieth century. Today, the erring Christian groups outside the Church are the Orientals, called Orthodox, and the Protestants.

823. Since error is not consistent, false teachings are found that accept all the above-mentioned degrees of unbelief, or borrow impartially from all.

(a) Indifferentism or Latitudinarianism holds that all forms of religion are equally true, and that it makes no difference whether one is Buddhist, Jew or Christian. In a modified form, Indifferentism teaches that any form of Christian belief, provided it suits the inclinations of the individual concerned, may be followed, and hence it is left to each one to decide whether he prefers Catholicism or one of the bodies of the Orthodox Church or of Protestantism. Many who profess a denominational creed or confession are Indifferentists in belief.

(b) Syncretism holds that there are truths in all separate religions, but that none of them has all the truth, and hence that one must select what is good from each, rejecting the evil. Thus, the Judaizers of the first century borrowed from Judaism, the Gnostics and Manicheans from paganism, while today Freemasonry, Theosophy, Christian Science and Spiritism accept, along with the Gospel, ancient pagan, Buddhistic, Brahmanistic and Mohammedan theories; finally, Mormonism endeavors to unite characteristics of the Old and the New Testament dispensations. In a restricted form, religious Syncretism teaches the doctrine of Pan-Christianism—that is, that truth is scattered among the various Christian denominations, and that all should confederate as equals on the basis of more important doctrines to be agreed on by all.

824. What is the order of gravity in unbelief, as between infidelity, Judaism, heresy?

(a) The gravity of a sin against faith is to be determined primarily from the subjective resistance made to faith, so that he sins more against the light to whom greater light was given. The sin of unbelief in one who has received the Gospel (heresy), is greater than the same sin in one who has accepted only the Old Testament (Judaism); in one who has received the revelation of the Old Testament (Judaism) the sin of unbelief is more serious than the same sin in one who has not received that revelation (infidelity).

(b) The gravity of unbelief is measured secondarily from the objective opposition of error to truth, so that he is farther away from faith who is farther away from Christ and the Gospel. Thus, a Buddhist denies Christian truths more radically than a Jew, and a Jew more radically than a Protestant. Hence, of three apostates, one to Protestantism, another to Judaism and a third to Buddhism, the second sins more grievously than the first, the third more grievously than the second.

825. If we leave out of consideration the radical truth of divine revelation (formal object of faith), it is possible that a heretic, in spite of

his acceptance of Christ and the scriptures, should be farther away objectively from faith than an infidel—that is, that he should deny more revealed truths (material objects of faith). Thus, the Manicheans called themselves followers and disciples of Christ, but their teaching on God contains more errors than does the doctrine of many pagans.

826. Heresy.—Heresy is defined as "an error manifestly opposed to faith and assented to obstinately by one who had sincerely embraced the faith of Christ."

(a) It is called "error," that is, positive assent given to error, or dissent from truth. Hence, those who merely act or speak as if they do not believe, but who internally do believe, are not heretics, although in the external forum they may fall under the presumption of heresy. Similarly, those who have doubts or difficulties in matters of faith, but who do not allow these to sway their judgment, are not guilty of heresy, since they give no positive assent to error (see 842 sqq.). Examples: Titus is internally convinced of the truth of the Church's teaching; but he attends Protestant services, says he does not believe the Trinity, refuses to make a profession of faith required by the Church, separates himself from obedience to the authorities of the Church, and calls himself an independent. By his former external acts he makes himself guilty of disobedience and falls under the suspicion of heresy, and by his last external act he incurs the guilt of schism; but, since internally he does not disbelieve, he is not a heretic. Balbus has doubts before his mind from his reading or conversation, but he must immediately give his whole attention to a very pressing matter of business, and so gives neither assent nor dissent to the doubts. He is not guilty of heresy, since he formed no positive erroneous judgment.

(b) Heresy is "opposed to faith." By faith here is understood divine faith, especially divine and Catholic faith (see 755). Hence, an error opposed to what one held to be a genuine private revelation, or to the public revelation, especially when dogmatically defined by the Church, is heretical. On the contrary, an error opposed to ecclesiastical faith alone, to human faith, or to human science, is not of itself heretical. Examples: The Saints who received special private revelations from Christ with proofs of their genuineness would have been guilty of heresy, had they refused to believe. Sempronius refuses to believe some

Biblical teachings about things not pertaining to faith and morals and not expressly defined by the Church (e.g., chronological, physical, geographical, statistical data). If he really believes that what he denies is contained in the Bible, he is guilty of heresy. Balbus admits the infallibility and authority of the Church, but he does not believe that a certain Saint solemnly canonized is in heaven, that a certain non-infallible decision of a Roman Congregation is true, that certain second lessons of the Breviary or certain relics are genuine. He is not a heretic, since, as supposed, he denies no revealed truth; but in his first unbelief he sins against ecclesiastical faith; in his second unbelief, if the contrary of the decision has not been clearly established, he sins against the duty of religious assent; in his third unbelief, he sins against prudence, if he has no good grounds for his opinion, or against the respect due the Church, if he is moved by contempt for its judgment. In a conversation between A, B, C, D and E, the following opinions are defended. A thinks that any use of natural knowledge with reference to matters of faith is wrong; B, that the theologian should employ mathematics and physical science, but avoid reasoning and philosophy; C, that the method and principles of Scholasticism are not suited to our age or to all peoples; D, that the psychology and cosmology of the Scholastics should be remade entirely; E, that many hypotheses of Aristotle in physics have been proved false. The opinion of A contains heresies condemned in the Vatican Council regarding the preambles of faith and the motives of credibility. The opinions of B and C are at least contrary to the religious assent due the authority of the Church (see Denzinger, Enchiridion, nn. 1652, 1680, 1713, Code of Canon Law, Canon 1366, §2, *Humani Generis*, n. 11-14). The opinion of D, as it stands, contains a denial of several doctrines of faith, such as the immortality of the soul and the creation of the world, and is thus implicitly heretical. The opinion of E is true and admitted by all.

(c) By "opposed" to faith is meant any judgment which, according to the logical rules of opposition between propositions, is irreconcilable with the truth of a formula of dogma or of a censure of heresy. Examples: The Council of Trent defined that "all sins committed after Baptism can be forgiven in the Sacrament of Penance." It would be heretical, therefore, to hold that "no sins committed after Baptism can be pardoned in the Sacrament of Penance" (contrary opposition), or that "some sins committed after Baptism cannot be absolved" (contradictory opposition), Similarly, the Council of Trent (Sess. VI, Can. 7) rejected the proposition that "all Works done before justification are sinful," and hence according to Logic the contradictory—viz., that "some works before justification are not sinful"—is of faith, for two contradictories cannot both be false; the contrary—viz., that "no works before justification are sinful"—is not, however, defined, for two contraries can both be false.

(d) Heresy is "manifestly opposed to faith." He who denies what is only probably a matter of faith, is not guilty of heresy. Example: The Instruction of Eugenius IV on the matter of the Sacraments is held by some authorities of note not to be a definition, and hence those who accept opposite theories are not on that account heretical.

(e) Heresy is "assented to obstinately," This is the distinctive note of heresy, and hence those who assent to error through ignorance, whether vincible or invincible, are not heretics, if they are willing to accept the truth when known. A heretic, therefore, is one who knowingly refuses to admit a truth proposed by the Church, whether his motive be pride, desire of contradicting, or any other vice.

(f) Heresy is held "by one who had sincerely embraced the faith of Christ." This includes only catechumens and the baptized, for others who deny the truths of faith are Jews or infidels, not heretics.

827. The sin of heresy (heresy before God), as just defined, differs from the canonical crime of heresy (heresy before the Church), since it is more inclusive. (a) These two differ as regards the error in the intellect, for one is guilty of the sin, but not of the crime, even without error— that is, if one denies what is really false, thinking it to be defined doctrine; (b) they differ as regards the obstinacy in the will, for one is guilty of the sin, but not of the crime, if one is prepared in mind and purpose to deny a truth not yet defined, if it is ever defined; (c) they differ as regards the truths rejected, for one is guilty of the sin, but not of the crime, if one rejects divinely revealed truths not defined as such by the Church; (d) they differ as regards the person who denies, for not everyone who merely accepted the faith of Christ can be guilty of the crime of heresy, but only those who after Baptism retain the name of Christian (Canon 1325, §2).

828. Various Kinds of Heresy.—(a) Heresy is positive when error is accepted (e.g., the doctrine of consubstantiation); it is negative when truth is denied (e.g., the doctrine of transubstantiation).

(b) Heresy is internal, when it is in the mind alone and not externally professed. It is external, when expressed in an external way (i.e., by words, signs, acts or circumstances that clearly indicate present heresy), if this is done not for a good purpose, such as that of asking advice, but for the purpose of professing error.

(c) External heresy is occult, when it is made known to no one, or only to a few; it is public or notorious, when it is made known before a large number and cannot be concealed. Example: One who calls himself a Catholic and is known as such, but who in conversation with a few intimate friends declares himself a Modernist, is an occult heretic. One who declares in public addresses or articles that he agrees with Modernism, or who joins openly an heretical sect or has always belonged to one, is a public heretic.

(d) Occult and public heresy may be either formal or material, according as one is in good or bad faith. Heresy is formal, if its malice is known and willed by the one in error; if its malice is not known by him, it is material.

829. Heresy is not formal unless one pertinaciously rejects the truth, knowing his error and consenting to it.

(a) One must know that one's belief is opposed to divine revelation or to Catholic faith. Hence, those who were born and brought up in Protestantism, and who in good faith accept the confession of their denomination, are not formal but material heretics. Even those who are ignorant of their errors through grave fault and who hold to them firmly, are guilty, not of formal heresy, but of sinful ignorance (see 904 sqq.)

(b) One must willingly consent to the error. But for formal heresy it is not required that a person give his assent out of malice, or that he continue in obstinate rejection for a long time, or that he refuse to heed admonitions given him. Pertinacity here means true consent to recognized error, and this can proceed from weakness (e.g., from anger or other passion); it can be given in an instant, and does not presuppose an admonition disregarded. Hence, if one sees the truth of the Catholic Church, but fears that assent will involve many obligations and out of weakness turns away from the truth, one then and there pertinaciously consents to error.

830. Examples of material heresy are: (a) Catholics who deny certain dogmas of faith, because they have not been well instructed, but who are ready to correct their errors, whenever the Church's teaching is brought home to them; (b) non-Catholics who do not accept the Catholic Church, but who have never had any misgivings about the tenets of their own denomination, or who in doubts have searched for the truth to the best of their ability.

831. The sinfulness of heresy is as follows: (a) formal heresy is a grave sin, as was said above regarding unbelief in general (see 819; Tit., iii. 10); (b) material heresy is no sin at all, if the ignorance is invincible; it is a grave or a venial sin, according to the amount of negligence, if the ignorance is vincible.

832. Circumstances of the sin of heresy are of various kinds. (a) Circumstances that change the species. Most theologians hold that the particular article denied, or the particular sect adhered to, does not constitute a particular species of heresy, and hence that in confession it suffices for one to accuse oneself generically of heresy. (b) Circumstances that aggravate the sin. The facts that heresy is external, that it is manifested to a large number, that it is joined with apostasy and adhesion to an heretical sect, etc., increase the accidental malice of this sin. (c) Circumstances that multiply the number of sins. It seems that when several articles or defined truths are denied at the same time, so many numerically distinct sins are committed (see 219). Example: Titus says: "I do not accept the Resurrection, either of Christ or of the dead." The act is one, but two sins are committed.

833. Various penalties and inhabilities are incurred through heresy, for example, excommunication *latæ sententiæ* reserved to the Pope (Canon 2314), loss of the power of suffrage (Canon 167, §1, n.4), irregularity (Canon 984, n. 5; 985), inability for the office of sponsor (Canons 765, 795), deprivation of ecclesiastical burial (Canon 1240, §1, n. 1). The

excommunication which perhaps had been incurred by those who now wish to join the Church is absolved according to the form for the reception of converts prescribed by the Congregation of the Holy Office, July 20, 1859, and found in rituals. Rituals published after March, 1942, contain the formula of profession of faith and abjuration approved by the Holy Office.

834. If a confessor should meet with a case of heresy, his procedure will be as follows: (a) If the heresy was merely internal, no censure was incurred, and every confessor has power to absolve from the sin, no matter how serious it was. (b) If the heresy was external, but the person was in good faith, or even in affected ignorance of the sin, or inculpably ignorant of the penalty, no censure was incurred; for the excommunication attaches only to formal heresy, and contumacity (Canon 2242). (c) If the heresy was external and formal, but not notorious (i.e., the party did not publicly join an heretical sect), ordinarily the case should be brought before the bishop for absolution in the external or internal forum. But in urgent cases every confessor has power to absolve as prescribed in Canon 2254. (d) If the heresy was public and notorious (i.e., if the party joined officially an heretical sect), absolution is regularly to be given in both the external and internal forums. The case should be submitted first to the Ordinary, unless there is urgency (Cfr. Canon 2254), or the confessor has special powers from Rome. The Ordinary can absolve in the external forum. Afterwards, the heretic can be absolved by any confessor in the forum of conscience (see Canon 2314, §2.)

835. Apostasy.—Apostasy (etymologically, desertion) has various meanings in theology.

(a) In a special sense, it means the abandonment of the religious or clerical state; but in its usual sense it means the abandonment of the Christian religion.

(b) Apostasy from faith in a wide sense includes both partial abandonment (heresy) and total abandonment; but, in the strict sense, it means only total abandonment of Christianity.

Example: A Christian who denies one article of the Creed becomes a heretic and an apostate in a wide sense; if he rejects the entire Creed, he becomes an infidel and an apostate in the strict sense.

(c) Apostasy which extends to infidelity is also twofold: before God and before the Church. The first kind is committed by any person who really had faith, even though unbaptized or not a Catholic; the second kind is committed only by those who were baptized and were Catholics. Examples: A catechumen who accepted Christianity and asked for Baptism, becomes an apostate before God if he abandons his belief and purpose and goes back to paganism. Similarly, a person brought up as a Lutheran becomes an apostate before God, if he abandons all belief in Christianity. But the crime of apostasy of which the Church takes cognizance is the desertion of Christianity by a baptized Catholic.

(d) A Catholic apostatizes from Christianity, either privatively (by merely renouncing all belief in Christ), or contrarily (by taking up some form of unbelief, such as indifferentism or free thought, or by joining some infidel sect, such as Mohammedanism or Confucianism).

836. What was said above regarding the gravity, divisions, penalties and absolution of heresy, can be applied also to apostasy.

887. As to the comparative gravity of sins of apostasy, the following should be noted. (a) Apostasy is not a species of sin distinct from heresy, since both are essentially the same in malice, being rejections of the authority of divine revelation; but it is a circumstance that aggravates the malice of unbelief, since it is more sweeping than heresy (see 822, 824). (b) Apostasy into one form of infidelity is not specifically different from apostasy into another, but the form of infidelity is an aggravating or extenuating circumstance. Example: Paganism is further from faith than Mohammedanism; atheism further than paganism.

838. Could one ever have a just reason for abandoning the Catholic Church or remaining outside its faith? (a) Objectively speaking, there can never be a just cause for giving up Catholicism or for refusing to embrace it. For the Catholic Church is the only true Church, and it is the will of Christ that all should join it. (b) Subjectively speaking, there may be a just cause for leaving or not entering the Church, namely, the

fact that a person, ignorant in this matter but in good faith, believes that the Catholic Church is not the true Church. For one is obliged to follow an erroneous conscience, and, if the error is invincible, one is excused from sin (see 581-583). Examples: A Protestant taught to believe that the teachings of the Church are idolatrous, superstitious and absurd, is not blamed for not accepting them. A Catholic, poorly instructed in religion and thrown in with non-Catholic and anti-Catholic associates, might become really persuaded, and without sinning against faith itself, that it was his duty to become a Protestant.

839. Apostasy is committed not only by those who leave the Church and join some contrary religion (e.g., Mormonism), but also by those who, while professing to be Catholics, assent to the non-Catholic principles of some society that claims to be philosophical, charitable, economic, patriotic, etc. Much more are those apostates who join societies that openly conspire against the Church. Such are: (a) Societies that are really non-Catholic sects, because they have an infidel or heretical creed—e.g., Freemasonry (which, according to its own authorities, is a brotherhood based on Egyptian mysteries and claiming superiority to Christianity), Theosophy (which is a conglomeration of nonsensical ideas about the Deity, Christ and Redemption), the Red International, whose aims are the destruction of property rights, etc; (b) Societies that are anti-Catholic sects, because their creed is hatred of the Church—e.g., the Orangemen's Society, the Grand Orient, the Ku Klux Klan, Junior Order, etc.

840. The Sin of Doubt.—Faith as explained above must be firm assent, excluding doubt (see 752, 799), and hence the saying: "He who doubts is an unbeliever." The word "doubt," however, has many meanings, and in some of those meanings it is not opposed to firm assent, or has not the voluntariness or acceptance of error that the unbelief of heresy or infidelity includes. To begin with, doubt is either methodical or real.

(a) Methodical doubt in matters of faith is an inquiry into the motives of credibility of religion and the reasons that support dogma, made by one who has not the slightest fear that reason or science can ever contradict faith, but who consults them for the purpose of clarifying his knowledge and of strengthening his own faith or that of others. This kind of doubt is employed by St. Thomas Aquinas, who questions about each dogma in turn (e.g., "Whether God is good"), and examines the objections of unbelievers against it; but unlike his namesake, the doubting Apostle, he does not withhold assent until reason has answered the objectors, but answers his own questions by an act of faith: "In spite of all difficulties, God is good, for His Word says: 'The Lord is good to them that hope in Him, to the soul that seeketh Him' (Lament, iii. 25)."

(b) Real doubt, on the contrary, entertains fears that the teachings of revelation or of the Church may be untrue, or that the opposite teachings may be true.

841. Real doubt in matters of faith is always unjustifiable in itself, for there is never any just reason for doubting God's word; but it is not always a sin of heresy or of infidelity. There are two kinds of real doubt, viz., the involuntary and the voluntary. (a) Doubt is involuntary, when it is without or contrary to the inclination of the will, or when it proceeds from lack of knowledge (see 40-55 on the Impediments to Voluntariness). Example: Indeliberate doubts, and doubts that persist in spite of one, lack the inclination of the will, while doubts that proceed from invincible ignorance lack knowledge. (b) Doubt is voluntary, when it is according to inclination and with sufficient knowledge.

842. Involuntary doubt in matters of faith is neither heretical nor sinful, for an act is not sinful, unless it is willed (see 99).

(a) Indeliberate doubts arise in the mind before they are adverted to and without any responsibility of one's own for their appearance. From what was said above on first motions of the soul (see 129), it is clear that such doubts are not sinful.

(b) Unwelcome doubts persist in the mind after they have been adverted to, and, since faith is obscure (see 752, 799), it is not possible to exclude all conscious doubts, or even to prevent them from occurring often or lasting a considerable time. From what was said above on temptation (see 253 sqq.), it is clear that, if the person troubled with unwished doubts makes prompt and sufficient resistance, he not only does not sin, but gains merit. But, if his resistance is not all it should be, and there is no danger of consent to the temptation, he sins venially.

(c) Ignorant doubts occur in persons who have not received sufficient religious instruction, through no fault of their own, and who therefore regard the doctrines of faith as matters of opinion, or at least look upon doubts as not sinful. From what was said above on invincible ignorance (see 30), it is clear that such persons do not sin by their doubts.

843. Voluntary doubt is entertained either in ignorance for which one is responsible, or in full knowledge; in the former case it is indirectly voluntary, in the latter, directly voluntary.

(a) The doubts of one who is responsible for them because he did not use the means to instruct himself in the faith, are a sin of willful ignorance proportionate to the negligence of which he was guilty; but, if he is willing on better knowledge to put aside his doubts and accept the teaching of the Church, he is not pertinacious, and hence not guilty of heresy or infidelity.

(b) The doubts of one who is responsible for them, and not uninstructed or ignorant in faith, are sometimes positive, sometimes negative. Neither of these kinds of doubt is equivalent to heresy or infidelity in every case.

844. Negative doubt is the state of mind in which one remains suspended between the truth contained in an article of faith and its opposite, without forming any positive judgment either of assent to or dissent from the article, or its certainty or uncertainty.

(a) If this suspension of decision results from a wrong motive of the will, which directs one not to give assent on the plea that the intellect, while not judging, offers such formidable difficulties that deception is possible, then it seems that the doubter is guilty of implicit heresy, or at least puts himself in the immediate danger of heresy.

(b) If this suspension of judgment results from some other motive of the will (e.g., from the wish to give attention here and now to other matters), the guilt of heresy is not incurred, for no positive judgment is formed. Neither does it seem, apart from the danger of consent to positive doubt or from the obligation of an affirmative precept of faith then and there (see 925), that any serious sin in matters of faith is committed by such a suspension of judgment. Examples: Titus, being scandalized by the sinful conduct of certain Catholics, is tempted to doubt the divinity of the Church. He does not yield to the temptation by deciding that the divinity of the Church is really doubtful, but the difficulty has so impressed him that he decides to hold his judgment in abeyance. It seems that there is here an implicit judgment (i.e., one contained in the motive of the doubt) in favor of the uncertainty of the divinity of the Church. Balbus has the same difficulty as Titus, and it prevents him from eliciting an act of faith on various occasions. But the reason for this is that an urgent business matter comes up and he turns his attention to it, or that he does not wish at the time to weary his brain by considering such an important question as that of faith, or that he thinks he can conquer a temptation more easily by diverting his thoughts to other subjects (see 257), or that he puts off till a more favorable moment the rejection of the difficulty. In these cases there is not heretical doubt, since Balbus forms no positive judgment, even implicitly, but there may be a sin against faith. Thus, Balbus would sin seriously if his suspension of assent should place him in immediate danger of positive doubt; he would sin venially, if that suspension be due to some slight carelessness.

845. Positive doubt is the state of mind in which one decides, on account of some difficulty against faith, that the latter is really doubtful and uncertain, and that assent cannot be given to either side. With regard to such a state of mind note: (a) If this judgment is formed by a Catholic, it is heretical; for his faith, as he knows andadmits, is the true faith, revealed and proposed as absolutely certain. Hence, although he does not deny the faith, he does positively judge that what is revealed by God and proposed infallibly by the Church as certain, is not certain, and thus in his intellect there is pertinacious error.

(b) If this judgment is formed by a non-Catholic, it is likewise heretical, if the truth doubted belongs to divine or Catholic faith, for we are now considering the formal heretic who belongs to a non-Catholic sect against conviction; but it is not heretical, if the doctrine doubted belongs only to what is wrongly considered in his sect as divine faith, or to what may be called Protestant faith (i.e., the official confession of his religion), for he does not profess to accept his church as an infallible interpreter.

846. The doubts We have been just discussing are the passing doubts that come to those who are believers, or who consider themselves believers. There are also doubts that are permanent, and that are held by those who class themselves, not as believers, but as doubters or agnostics. Some of these sceptics doubt all religious creeds, holding that it is works and not beliefs that matter. This doctrine amounts to infidelity, since it rejects Christian faith entirely. Others profess Fundamentalism, which accepts a few Christian beliefs and considers the others as optional, pretending that the true faith cannot be recognized amid so much diversity of opinions. This doctrine is heretical, since it accepts some and rejects others of the articles of faith.

847. Credulity and Rationalism.—Opposed in special ways to the material and formal objects of faith are credulity and errors about the existence and nature of revelation.

(a) Other sins against faith are opposed to its material object (i.e., the articles of belief), inasmuch as they subtract from it by denying this or that article. Credulity, on the contrary, adds to the material object of faith by accepting a doctrine as revealed when there is no prudent reason for so doing, contrary to the teaching of scripture that "he who is hasty to believe is light of heart" (Ecclus., xix. 4). This sin is opposed rather to prudence, inasmuch as it causes one to neglect the consideration of the reasons on which a prudent judgment rests (see Vol. II), and hence it does not destroy the virtue of faith. It is, nevertheless, injurious to faith, since it brings Christianity into contempt, keeps others from embracing the teachings of the Church, and leads to superstition, the "twin-sister of unbelief." Examples: Sempronia, who is not well educated, accepts as matters of faith every pious legend, every marvellous report of miracle no matter from what source it comes or how suspicious may be its appearance. Titus holds many views considered by good authorities as improbable or false, or as at best only opinions, but he gives them out as doctrines of the Church that must be accepted, or as infallible or revealed teaching. The credulity of Sempronia is excusable imprudence on account of her ignorance, if she has not neglected instruction; but that of Titus is blameworthy, for he ought to inform himself better before attempting to instruct others.

(b) Other kinds of unbelief are opposed to the formal object of faith (i.e., to the authority of revelation as the motive of belief); for implicitly at least they substitute private judgment for authority. The various systems of Naturalism, such as Deism, go farther and openly attack supernatural revelation as the ground of belief. Some of these systems deny the fact of revelation (e.g., Deism), others its character (e.g., Modernism, which makes revelation to consist in the internal experience of the believer), others its necessity (e.g., Rationalism). These heterodox teachings pertain, some to infidelity (e.g., Deism), some to heresy (c.g., Modernism). The great majority of Protestants nowadays cannot be said to have faith, declares Cardinal Newman, since they deduce from scripture, instead of believing a teacher. What looks like faith is mere hereditary persuasion.

848. Dangers to Faith.—One becomes guilty of heresy, infidelity, doubts against faith, etc., indirectly, by placing oneself in the danger of those sins (see 258 sqq., on the Dangers of Sin). Dangers of this kind are partly internal, partly external.

(a) Internal dangers to faith are especially the following: intellectual pride or an excessive spirit of independence, which makes one unwilling to accept authority; love of pleasure, which sets one at odds with the precepts of faith; neglect of prayer and piety, particularly in time of temptation.

(b) External dangers to faith are especially as follows: literature opposed to religion; schools where unbelief is defended; mixed marriages; association with unbelievers in religious matters; certain societies.

849. Dangerous Reading.—There is a threefold prohibition against the reading of literature dangerous to faith.

(a) The natural law forbids one to read or hear read written matter of any description which one knows is dangerous to one's faith, even though it is not dangerous to others and not forbidden by the law of the Church. For a similar reason one may not keep such material in one's possession. Example: Titus and Balbus read the letters of a friend on Evolution. Titus finds nothing unsound in the letters, and is not troubled by reading them; but they fill the mind of Balbus with doubts and perplexities, as the subject is above him. This reading is naturally dangerous for Balbus, but not for Titus.

(b) The law of the Church forbids the use of certain kinds of writings or representations dangerous to faith (Canon 1399), as well as of those individual writings that have been denounced to the Holy See and placed on the Index, or forbidden by other ecclesiastical authorities. (See Appendix I for Summary of Common Law on Prohibition of Books.)

(c) The law of the Church also pronounces ipso facto excommunication against those who make use of works written by unbelievers in favor of their errors (Canon 2318).

850. As regards the kind of sin committed by using writings dangerous to faith, the following points must be noted:

(a) If a writing is dangerous and forbidden under natural law, the sin committed is of itself grave whenever the danger itself is serious and proximate; it is venial, when the danger is slight or remote. The sin committed depends, therefore, not on the time spent in reading or the number of pages covered, but on the danger (see 260-261, on the Dangers of Sin). No sin at all is committed, if the danger is slight or remote, and there is reason for reading the writing in question (e.g., the defense of truth).

(b) If the writing is forbidden under ecclesiastical law, the sin committed is of itself grave, even though the danger to an individual is not serious or proximate, for the law is based on the presumption of a common and great danger (see 460). The sin is not grave, however, when the prohibition is generally regarded as not binding under grave sin, or when the use made of the writing is inconsiderable. No sin at all is committed, if one has obtained the necessary permission to read forbidden works, and is not exposed to spiritual danger in using the permission.

851. There are two cases in which the use of writings forbidden by the Church is only a venial sin. (a) When a writing, which in itself is not dangerous or only slightly dangerous, is forbidden, not on account of its contents, but only on account of its lack of ecclesiastical approval, it

is not ordinarily regarded as forbidden under grave sin (e.g., Catholic Translations of scripture that have not received the Imprimatur). (b) When a writing has been condemned on account of its contents or manner of presentation, one does not sin mortally, if the use one makes of it is only slight.

852. What constitutes notable use of forbidden matter is not determined by law, but recent moralists, bearing in mind the character of the law and what would prove proximately dangerous to faith for the generality today, offer the following rules: (a) notable matter in reading a book is three or four pages from the more dangerous parts, from thirty to sixty pages from the slightly dangerous parts; (b) notable matter in reading a paper or periodical is habitual use of it, or even one very bitter article; (c) notable matter in retention of forbidden writings is a period in excess of the reasonable time (say, a month) for securing permission or for delivering the writings to those who have a right to have them.

853. It is more difficult to decide what is notable matter, when a book has been condemned on account of its general tendency. (a) Under the natural law, of course, even a page or less is notable matter, if it places an individual in proximate danger; (b) under the positive law, perhaps anything in excess of one-tenth of the book would place one in proximate danger. But, as we are dealing now with the general tendency of a writing, this may have its effect on the reader before he has read one-tenth, if the book is large, or the treatment is very seductive. Hence, "one-tenth" is an approximation, rather than a rule.

854. The kinds of printed matter forbidden by the Code (Canon 1399) are as follows: (a) the prohibition extends to books, to other published matter (such as magazines and newspapers), and to illustrations that attack religion and what are called "holy pictures" (i.e., images of our Lord and the Saints), if opposed to the mind of the Church; (b) the prohibition extends to published matter dangerous to faith, and therefore to the following; to writings or caricatures that attack the existence of God, miracles or other foundations of natural or revealed religion, Catholic dogma, worship or discipline, the ecclesiastical hierarchy as such, or the clerical or religious state; to those that defend heresy, schism, superstition, condemned errors, subversive societies, or

suicide, duelling, divorce; to non-Catholic publications of the Bible and to non-Catholic works on religion that are not clearly free from opposition to Catholic faith; to liturgical works that do not agree with the authentic texts; to books that publish apocryphal indulgences and to printed images of holy persons that would be the occasion of error (e.g., the representation of the Holy Ghost in human form).

855. The mere presence, however, of condemned matter in a writing does not cause it to fall under prohibition.

(a) Some works are not forbidden unless the author's purpose to teach error or attack the truth is known. Hence, books on religion written by non-Catholics which contain errors against the Catholic Faith are not forbidden, unless they deal with religion *ex professo* (i.e., not incidentally or cursorily, but clearly for the purpose of teaching). It is not necessary, however, that religion be the main theme of the book, Similarly, books that attack religion are forbidden, not when attacks are casual or by the way, but when they are made purposely; and the same is true as regards books that insult the clerical state. The purpose is recognized from the declaration of the author, from the nature of the work, from the systematic treatment, length or frequency of argumentation or attack, etc.

(b) Other works are not forbidden, unless they contain not only agreement with error, but also argument in defense of error. Thus, books in favor of heresy, schism, suicide, duelling, divorce, Freemasonry, etc., are forbidden when they champion wrong causes by disputing in their behalf.

(c) Other works are forbidden, not because they state, but because they approve of error. Such are books that attack or ridicule the foundations of religion or the dogmas of faith, those that disparage worship, those that are subversive of discipline, those that defend proscribed propositions, those that teach and favor superstition, etc.

856. Books that deal with religion *ex professo* (i.e., of set purpose), or *obiter* (i.e., incidentally), are as follows: (a) Books that are *ex professo* religious are manuals of theology, works of sermons, treatises on the Bible, instructions on religious duties, works of piety, text-books of church history. Works of a profane character, such as scientific books,

may also teach religion *ex professo*, but it is not easy as a rule to perceive the intention of teaching religion in works of this kind. (b) Books that deal with religion only *obiter* are works of a profane character, in which the subject of religion is introduced only briefly (e.g., by way of illustration).

857. Books dealing *ex professo* with religion and written by non-Catholics are: (a) forbidden, if they contain matter contrary to Catholic faith; (b) not forbidden, if it is clear to one (e.g., from a competent review) that they contain nothing contrary to Catholic faith.

858. How is one to know in a particular case whether a book falls under one of the foregoing classes forbidden by the Code? (a) If the Holy See has made a declaration, the matter is of course clear; (b) if no declaration has been made, and one is competent to judge for oneself, one may read as much as is necessary to decide whether the book is one of those proscribed by the Code; but if a person has not received the education that would fit him for judging, he should consult some person more skilled than himself, such as his parish priest or confessor.

859. Is it lawful to read newspapers, magazines, or reference works (such as encyclopedias), which contain some articles contrary to faith, and others that are good or indifferent, if these papers or books have not been condemned? (a) If the reading or consultation, on account of one's individual character, will subject one to grave temptations, then according to natural law it should be avoided. (b) If there is no serious danger or temptation, but the policy of the works or journals in question is anti-religious or anti-Catholic, as appears from the space given to hostile attack, their frequency or bitterness of spirit, then, according to the law of the Code just mentioned, one should avoid such reading matter. Examples of this kind of literature are papers devoted to atheistic or bolshevistic propaganda, anti-Catholic sheets, etc. (c) If there is no danger to the individual, and the editorial policy is not hostile, one may use such matter as is good and useful, while passing over any elaborate or systematic attack on truth or defense of error.

860. Individual books are forbidden by name to all Catholics by the Holy See and to their own subjects by Ordinaries and other local or

particular councils (Canon 1395). Books condemned by the Apostolic See must be considered as forbidden everywhere and in whatsoever language they may be translated into (Canon 1396).

(a) If a book is forbidden, one may not read even the harmless parts of it, for there is the danger that, if one part is read, the other parts will also be read. But, if the part that occasioned the prohibition be removed, the prohibition ceases as regards the remainder of the book.

(b) If a work is forbidden, one may not read any volume, if all the volumes deal with the same subject. But, if the volumes treat of different subjects or of one subject that is divisible (e.g., universal history), one may read such volumes as do not contain the danger that occasioned the prohibition.

(c) If all the works of an author are condemned, the prohibition is understood to apply only to books (i.e., not to smaller works), and only to books dealing with religion, unless it appears that the other kinds of writings are also included; but the prohibition is to be presumed to include works that appear after the condemnation, unless the contrary is manifest.

861. Some outstanding works that have been condemned are the following: (a) In English: *Decline and Fall of The Roman Empire* (Gibbons);*Myth, Ritual, and Religion* (Andrew Lang); *History of England*(Goldsmith); *The Roman Popes* (Ranke); *The Life and Pontificate of Leo X* (Roscoe); *Constitutional History of England* (Hallam);*Political Economy* (Mill); *Happiness in Hell* (Mivart); *History of English Literature* (Taine); *Reign of Charles V* (Robertson);*Zoonomia*, or The Laws of Organic Life (Darwin).

(b) In French: *Notre Dame de Paris* (Hugo); *Life of Jesus* and eighteen other works of Renan; all the works of Anatole France; *The Social Contract* and four works of Rousseau; nearly all the works of Voltaire; *The Gospel and the Church, Gospel Studies, The Fourth Gospel, Apropos of a Little Book, The Religion of Israel* (Loisy); all the works of Jean Paul Sartre; *La Deuxieme Sexe* and *Les Mandarins*by Simone de Beauvoir.

862. What is meant by "use" of forbidden writings? (a) In the first place, those "use" a writing who read it—that is, who go over it with

their eyes, understanding the meaning therein contained. Hence, a person does not violate the church law against forbidden books if he merely listens to another read; although he might sin against the natural law, and even against the church law, if he induced the other to read to him; neither does a person violate the church law, if he merely glances at the characters, without understanding the sense expressed. Example: Titus, a professor of theology, has permission to read forbidden books, and he sometimes reads to his class doctrinal passages from works on the Index in order to explain and refute errors. Balbus examines very carefully the pages of a beautifully printed copy of a forbidden work, but he understands hardly a word of it, since it is in a foreign language. Neither Titus' class nor Balbus are guilty of reading as forbidden by the Church, for strict interpretation is given to penal laws (see 485).

(b) In the second place, those "use" a forbidden writing who retain it— that is, who keep it in their home as belonging to themselves or borrowed from another, or who give it for safekeeping to another, even though they are not able to read it. Hence, a librarian who has forbidden books on his shelves does not break the law, since the books are not his property, nor are they kept in his home. A bookbinder also who receives forbidden books is considered as excused through *epieikeia* for the time the books are in his shop, especially if his customer has the permission to read those books. Example: Sempronius bought an expensive work and then discovered that it is on the Index. Is he obliged to destroy it? No, if he does not wish to destroy it, he may, if he does not delay beyond a month, either give it to someone who has permission to keep it, or obtain that permission for himself.

(c) In the third place, those "use" a forbidden writing who communicate it to others—for example, those who make presents of works that are on the Index, who lend such books to others, or place them where others will read them, who read to others passages or write out excerpts for them. It is lawful, however, for professors in theological and other classes of sacred science to read from forbidden works to their student body, if a suitable explanation and refutation exclude all danger.

(d) Lastly, those fall under the law as violators who co-operate in the production or distribution of forbidden literature—for example,

870. The danger to faith is necessary when there is no Catholic school, or none that is sufficient for the needs of individual students, and their parents are unable to send them elsewhere. In such a case it is lawful to attend a school that is neutral, but means must be used to make the proximate danger remote. Such means are the following: (a) religious instruction must be taken outside of school, as in special week-day classes, Sunday school, home study, etc.; (b) special attention must be given to the strengthening of faith on those points that are attacked or slighted in the neutral school; (c) parents, guardians, or others responsible must see that the reading and the associates of their wards in the neutral schools are good, and that they are faithful to their religious duties.

871. Is attendance at non-Catholic schools sometimes unlawful, even when there are serious reasons in its favor?

(a) It is unlawful, if the schools are sectarian, and then no excuse can justify such attendance; for, in addition to scandal and coöperation in false worship, there is present a proximate danger to faith that is not made remote. Parents or guardians who knowingly send their children to schools for education in a non-Catholic religion are suspected of heresy and incur excommunication *ipso facto*, reserved to the Ordinary (see Canon 2319). Example: Titus sends his daughter to a sectarian academy because it is nearer and cheaper than the Catholic academy. He claims that she is old enough not to lose her religion, that opposition will make her faith stronger, etc. Titus' arguments are fallacious and his conduct gravely sinful.

(b) Attendance at non-Catholic schools is unlawful, if the schools are neutral in theory, but so dangerous in practice that loss of faith is practically certain if one attends. Example: Balbus sends his son to an undenominational university which is regarded as a hotbed of atheism, and whose students practically to a man lose all religion.

872. Absolution should be denied in some cases to those who send their children to non-Catholic schools, if they refuse to change.

(a) Absolution should be denied on account of lack of faith in the parents themselves, if they send their children to non-Catholic schools on account of their own ideas that are contrary to the teachings of the

Church. Example: Sempronius refuses to send his children to parochial schools, because he thinks each one should judge about religion for himself, and not receive it from instructors.

(b) Absolution should be denied on account of the danger caused to the faith of the children, when the children are sent to sectarian schools, or when they are sent to neutral schools and sufficient efforts are not used to counteract the evil influence there felt.

(c) Absolution should be refused on account of scandal or coöperation in evil, if, while the parents themselves are sound in faith and prevent all danger of perversion of their children, they send them to non-Catholic schools without sufficient reason, to the grave disedification of others, or the great assistance of unchristian education.

873. Absolution should not be denied in the following cases: (a) when the parents have a sufficient reason for sending their children to non-Catholic schools (i.e., a reason approved by the local Ordinary as sufficient). It belongs only to the Ordinary to decide in what circumstances and with what precautions attendance at such schools is allowable (Canon 1374; for application to the United States, see Holy Office, 24 Nov., 1875; Council of Baltimore, III, n. 199, in regard to elementary and high schools. As to colleges and universities, see *S.C.Prop.Fid.*, 7 Apr., 1860; *Fontes*, n. 4649, Vol VII, p. 381; n.4868, Vol. VII, p.405; also S.C.Prop.Fid., 6 Aug., 1867); (b) when the parents have no sufficient reason, but there is no lack of faith on their part, no danger of perversion of the children, no grave scandal or sinful co-operation in evil.

874. The presence of Catholics as teachers in non-Catholic schools is beneficial, since it lessens to some extent the evil influence of such schools; but there is also the danger that it may cause scandal or create the impression that attendance at Catholic schools is not necessary. Hence, it has been permitted by the Church in certain cases but only when danger of scandal or wrong impression is absent. (a) The secular sciences may be taught by laymen in non-Catholic schools of higher or lower education, if there is no scandal, no unlawful coöperation, and no immediate danger of perversion. (b) Christian doctrine may be taught by priests to Catholic students of neutral schools, either in the school

building or elsewhere (as in a church), and certain priests may be appointed as chaplains for this work (Sacred Congregation of the Holy Office to Bishops of Switzerland, March 26, 1866).

875. Dangerous Marriages.—The following kinds of marriage are dangerous to the faith of Catholics: (a) marriage with non-Catholics, unbaptized or bigoted persons (mixed marriages); (b) marriage with fallen-away Catholics (that is, with those who have given up the Catholic religion, although they have not joined another), or with those who belong to societies forbidden by the Church.

876. The danger to faith in the aforesaid kinds of marriage are serious and proximate, and hence such unions are forbidden by divine law, as long as the danger is not removed or made remote through the use of precautions. The dangers are for the Catholic party and the children.

(a) The Catholic party is in serious danger of losing the faith (i.e., of joining the religion or sharing the ideas of the other party), or of doubting the truth of the Church, or of taking refuge in Indifferentism. For, if domestic life is peaceful, the Catholic may easily be led in time to regard with favor the other party's religion or views; if it is not peaceful, the Catholic through fear or annoyance may make compromises or sacrifices in matters of faith, or else suffer temptations that could have been avoided.

(b) The children born are in serious danger of being deprived of the faith (i.e., of not being brought up as Catholics), or of having their faith weakened by the example of parents who do not agree in the matter of religion. If the non-Catholic or fallen-away Catholic interferes with the religion of the children, their baptism, religious education, attendance at church, etc., will be forbidden or impeded; if that party does not interfere, there will be at least the example during impressionable years of one parent who does not accept the Catholic faith or who disregards its requirements. Statistics indicate that one of the chief sources of leakage in the Church today is mixed marriages.

877. Dangerous marriages are also forbidden by the law of the Church. (a) Lack of baptism in the non-Catholic party causes the diriment impediment of disparity of worship (Canon 1070); (b) membership of the non-Catholic party in an heretical or schismatical sect causes the

prohibitive impediment of mixed religion (Canon 1060); (c) unworthiness of one of the parties, on account of notorious apostasy or affiliation with forbidden societies (see 945 sqq.), prevents the pastor from assisting at the marriage without permission from the Ordinary (Canon 1065).

878. No one may enter into any of the dangerous marriages here considered, unless the requirements of the natural and ecclesiastical laws be complied with. (a) The natural law requires under pain of grave sin that the danger of perversion be removed, that no non-Catholic ceremony take place, and that the Catholic spouse work prudently for the conversion of the other party. (b) The ecclesiastical law requires under grave sin that guarantees be given that the requirements of the natural law shall be fulfilled (Canons 1061, 1071); that there be grave and urgent reasons for the marriage (ibid.); that dispensations from the impediments be obtained, or permission, in the case of unworthiness of one of the parties, to assist at the marriage be granted by the Ordinary (Canons 1036, 1065).

879. The canonical consequences of dangerous marriages illegally contracted are as follows: (a) Those who knowingly contract a mixed marriage without dispensation are *ipso facto* excluded from legitimate ecclesiastical acts, (e.g., the office of godparent), and from the use of sacramentals, until a dispensation has been obtained from the Ordinary (Canon 2375). Marriage contracted with the impediment of disparity of worship is invalid, whether the parties are in ignorance or not (Canon 1070, §16). (b) Catholics who enter into marriage before a non-Catholic minister acting in a religious capacity or who contract marriage with the implicit or explicit understanding that any or all of the children will be educated outside the Church incur excommunication *latæ sententiæ* reserved to the Ordinary (Canon 2319).

880. The prenuptial guarantees required by church law in case of mixed or other dangerous marriages are as follows: (a) According to the Code, no dispensation for mixed marriages will be granted unless the non-Catholic party gives a guarantee that the danger of perversion for the Catholic party shall be removed, and both parties promise that all the children shall be baptized and brought up only in the Catholic faith. There must be moral certainty that the promises will be kept, and as a

rule they should be demanded in writing (Canons 1061, 1071). The permission for marriage with fallen-away Catholics is not granted until the Ordinary has satisfied himself that the danger to the Catholic and the children has been removed (Canon 1065, §2). (b) The pre-Code legislation further required that both parties promise that there would be no non-Catholic ceremony and that the Catholic promise to work for the conversion of the other party. Canons 1062-1063 speak of these obligations, but do not exact promises.

881. Remedies against mixed and other dangerous marriages are the following: (a) Before engagement Catholics should be instructed and encouraged to marry those of their own faith. Thus, confessors can discourage company-keeping with non-Catholics, parents can provide their children with opportunities for meeting suitable Catholics, and, above all, pastors should frequently speak and preach to old and young on the evils of mixed marriages. (b) After engagement to a non-Catholic has been made, the non-Catholic should be persuaded to accept the Catholic religion, if he or she can do this with sincerity; otherwise, the Catholic should be warned of the danger of the marriage, and the pastor should refuse to seek a dispensation unless there is a really serious cause (see Canon 1064; II Plenary Council of Baltimore, n. 336; III Plenary Council of Baltimore, n. 133).

882. Dangerous Communication.—Mixed marriages are mentioned specially among the communications with non-Catholic that are dangerous to faith, because marriage is a lifelong and intimate association. But there are other communications with unbelievers that can easily corrupt faith, the less dangerous being communication in matters that are not religious, and the more dangerous being communication in religious matters. (a) Non-religious or civil communication is association with non-Catholics in secular affairs, such as business, social life, education, politics. (b) Religious communication is association with non-Catholics in sacred services or divine worship.

883. Non-religious communication is sinful as follows: (a) It is sinful according to natural law, when in a particular case it would be a proximate danger of perversion freely chosen, or an involuntary danger against which one does not employ sufficient precaution. Examples: Titus chooses infidels and freethinkers for his friends and intimates,

understanding their character and bad influence. Balba on account of her poverty is obliged to work in a place where all her companions are unbelievers who scoff at religion and try in every way to win her over to their errors; yet she is not concerned to arm herself more strongly in faith.

(b) According to ecclesiastical law, civil communication is forbidden with those who have been excommunicated as persons to be avoided (Canon 2267). Such persons are those who lay violent hands on the Roman Pontiff (Canon 2343), or who have been excommunicated by individual name and as persons to be avoided through public decree or sentence of the Apostolic See (Canon 2258). Exception is made, however, for husband and wife, children, servants, subjects, and for others in case of necessity.

884. Religious communication is sinful on account of danger in the following cases:

(a) If it is a proximate and voluntary occasion of sin against faith. Examples: Sempronius goes to a non-Catholic church to hear a minister who attacks the divinity of Christ and other articles of the Creed. The purpose of Sempronius is to benefit himself as a public speaker, but he knows that his faith suffers, because he admires the orator. Balbus chooses to listen over the radio to attacks on religion and Christianity, which cause serious temptations to him.

(b) If it is a necessary occasion of sin and one does not employ sufficient precautions against it, religious communication becomes sinful. Example: Titus, a prisoner, has to listen at times to a jail chaplain, who teaches that there are errors in the Bible, that man evolved from the ape, etc. Titus feels himself drawn sympathetically to these teachings, but makes no effort to strengthen his faith.

885. Communication with unbelievers that is a remote occasion of sin, is not sinful, for "otherwise one must needs go out of this world" (I Cor., v. 9). On the contrary, reasons of justice or charity frequently make it necessary and commendable to have friendly dealings with those of other or no religious conviction. (a) Reasons of justice. It is necessary to coöperate with non-Catholic fellow-citizens in what pertains to the welfare of our common country, state, city, and

neighborhood; to be just and fair in business relations with those outside the Church, etc. (b) Reasons of charity. Catholics should be courteous and kind to all (Heb., xii. 14), and be willing to assist, temporarily and spiritually, those outside the Church. Thus, St. Paul, without sacrificing principle or doctrine, made himself all things to all men, in order to gain all (I Cor., ix. 19). Indeed, the mission of the Church would suffer, if Catholics today kept aloof from all that goes on about them. The Church must teach, by example as well as precept, must be a salt, a light, a leaven, an example of the Gospel in practice; and surely this ministry will be weakened if her children aim at complete isolation and exclusivism.

886. Societies that are purely civil or profane—e.g., social clubs, charitable organizations, temperance societies, labor unions, that are not identified with any church and are neutral in religion—may be dangerous to faith. (a) There may be danger on account of the membership, even when the nature of the society is purely indifferent or good. Example: It would be dangerous to faith to join a convivial society whose members were mostly aggressive infidels, even though the purpose of the organization was only recreation. (b) There may be danger to faith on account of certain methods or principles of the society. Example: A Boys' or Girls' Club whose purpose is to train young people for good citizenship is dangerous to faith, if it acts as though the natural virtues were sufficient, or as though moral education belonged to itself exclusively or principally.

887. The Sin of Blasphemy.—So far we have spoken of the sins of unbelief that are contrary to the internal act of faith. We now come to the sins that are contrary to the external act, or profession of faith. These sins are of two kinds: (a) The less serious sin is that of ordinary denial of the faith, that is, the assertion that some article of faith is false, or that some contrary error is true. This sin will be treated below in 913 sqq. on the commandments of faith. (b) The more serious sin is blasphemy, that is, the denial to God of something that is His; or the ascription to God of what does not belong to Him. Of this sin we shall speak now.

888. Blasphemy etymologically is from the Greek, and signifies damage done to reputation or character; theologically, it is applied only to

insults or calumnies offered to God, and is threefold according to the three stages of sin described above (see 168). (a) Blasphemy of the heart is internal, committed only in thought and will. So "the wicked man said in his heart: There is no God" (Ps. xviii. 1), and the demons and lost souls blasphemed God without words (Apoc., xvi. 9). (b) Blasphemy of the mouth is external, committed in spoken words, or in their written or printed representations. (c) Blasphemy of deeds is also external, committed by acts or gestures. The action of Julian the Apostate in casting his blood towards heaven was intended as a sign of contempt for Christ.

889. Internal blasphemy does not differ from unbelief or disrespect for God. We are concerned here, therefore, only with external blasphemy, which is contrary to the external profession of faith. External blasphemy is opposed to faith either directly (by denying what is of faith) or indirectly (by showing disrespect to what is of faith), and hence it is either heretical or non-heretical.

(a) Heretical blasphemy affirms about God something false, or denies about Him something true. The false affirmation is made directly, when some created imperfection is attributed to God, or indirectly, when some divine perfection is attributed to a creature. Example: It is heretical blasphemy to affirm that God is a tyrant or the cause of sin, or that man is able to overcome God. It is also heretical blasphemy to deny that God is able to perform miracles, that His testimony is true, etc.

(b) Non-heretical blasphemy affirms or denies something about God according to truth, but in a mocking or blaming way. This sin is opposed, therefore, to reverence rather than to faith, and will be treated later among the sins against the virtue of religion (see Vol. II). Example: A person in anger at God says scornfully: "God is good!"

890. The nature of heretical blasphemy will better appear, if we compare it with other kinds of speech disrespectful to God.

(a) It differs from maledictions or curses, (e.g., "May God destroy you!"), because the one directly offended in blasphemy is God Himself, while in a curse it is some creature of God.

(b) It differs from non-heretical blasphemy, from perjury and disregard of vow, from vain use of the name of God, because none of these necessarily proceeds from a lack of faith, as does heretical blasphemy. Non-heretical blasphemy proceeds from hatred or contempt of God, perjury from presumption, disregard of vow from disobedience, vain use of the Divine Name from irreverence.

(c) Heretical blasphemy differs from temptation of God (e.g., "God must help me now if He can," said by one who exposes himself rashly to danger), for, while temptation of God implies doubt, it is directly an act of irreverence by which one presumes to put God Himself to proof, whereas heretical blasphemy is directly an act of denial of truth.

891. Heretical blasphemy calumniates God, either in His own attributes and perfections, or in those created persons or things that are specially His by reason of friendship or consecration. Thus, we have: (a) blasphemy that attacks the Divine Being Himself, as was explained above; (b) blasphemy that attacks what is especially dear to God, which consists in remarks or acts derogatory to the Blessed Virgin, the Saints, the Sacraments, the crucifix, the Bible, etc.

892. Unlike God, creatures are subject to imperfections, moral or physical, and thus it is not always erroneous or blasphemous to attribute imperfections to the Saints or sacred things.

(a) If sacred persons or things are spoken ill of precisely on account of their relation to God, or in such a way that the evil said of them reverts on God Himself, blasphemy is committed. Example: It is blasphemous to say that the Mother of God was not a Virgin, that St. Peter was a reprobate, that St. Anthony and St. Simeon Stylites were snobbish or eccentric, that the Sacraments are nonsense, that relics are an imposture, etc.

(b) If sacred persons or things are criticized precisely on account of their human or finite imperfections, real or alleged, the sin of irreverence is committed, when the criticism is prompted by malice or levity. No sin at all is committed, if one is stating facts with due respect for the character of the persons or things spoken of. Examples: To call a Doctor of the Church an ignoramus out of anger at a theological opinion defended by him, would be of itself a serious sin of disrespect.

To speak of a Saint as a dirty tramp or idle visionary, if the intention is to insult, is also a serious sin of disrespect. But, if one were to say in joke that St. Peter was a baldhead, St. Charles Borromeo a big nose, the sin of irreverence would be only slight. No sin would be committed, if one, describing a religious painting from the artistic standpoint, called it an abomination.

893. Heretical blasphemy is expressed not only by sentences that are complete and in the indicative mood, but also by phrases or interjections, by wishes, commands, or even signs.

(a) Blasphemy is expressed optatively, imperatively, or interrogatively. Examples: "Away with God!" is equivalent to the assertion that God is not eternal. "Come down from the cross, if Thou be the Son of God" (Matt., xxvii. 40), is equivalent to the statement that Christ is not the Son of God. The question put to the Psalmist, "Where is thy God?" (Ps. xli. 4.), meant in the mouth of the Psalmist's enemies that Jehovah did not exist, or was powerless.

(b) Blasphemy is expressed even by short words, or by a grunt or snort of contempt. Example: To utter the name of our Lord in a contumelious way signifies that one regards Him as of no account. The word "hocus-pocus" is sometimes used in derision of the Mass or other sacred rites.

(c) Blasphemy is expressed by acts that signify disbelief and dishonor, for example, to spit or shake one's fist at heaven, to turn up the nose or make a wry face at the mention of God, to trample in the dust a crucifix, etc.

894. Rules for Interpreting Cases of Doubtful Blasphemy.—(a) Custom or usage is a better guide than etymology or grammar in discovering whether a blasphemous meaning is contained in certain common expressions of an ambiguous character. Examples: According to signification the phrase, "Sacred Name of God," is harmless and might be a pious ejaculation, but according to the sense in which it is taken in French it curses God and is blasphemous. According to signification, the expression "Ye gods" in English, "Thousand names of God" in French, "Thousand Sacraments" in German, are blasphemous; but according to the sense in which they are used by the people they merely

express surprise, and are at most a venial sin of irreverence. The English language as a whole is singularly free from blasphemous expressions, just as English classic literature as a whole is singularly free from obscenity.

(b) The dispositions or feelings of the user are a better index of the presence or absence of blasphemy than the mere words, if the latter are capable of various senses. If doubt persists about the sense of an ambiguous expression that could be blasphemous, it may be held that no blasphemy was intended. Examples: Titus, a good man, is so annoyed trying to correct his children that he exclaims: "Why did the Lord ever send me such pests?" Balbus, who is a hater of religion, answers him: "Who is to blame if they are pests?" Since Titus is habitually religious and Balbus habitually irreligious, the question of the former sounds like irritation, the question of the latter like blasphemy. Claudius is a very religious-minded man, but he meets with a series of calamities which so stun him that he exclaims: "I must be only a step-child of God. Certainly, He cares little for me. Why did He ever create me?" The sentiment seems to be one of grief and wonder rather than of insult to God. Balbus is very devoted to his mother, and often addresses her in hyperbolic language, saying that he adores her, that she is the goddess at Whose shrine he worships, his supreme beatitude, etc. Taken literally, these expressions are blasphemous, but as used by Balbus they are harmless.

895. The Sinfulness of Blasphemy.—(a) From its very nature (i.e., from the importance of the rights it attacks and the goods it injures), blasphemy is a mortal sin, since it outrages the Majesty of God, and destroys the virtues of religion, love of God, and frequently faith itself. In the Old Testament it was punished with death (Lev., xxiv. 15 sqq.), and Canon 2323 of the Code prescribes that blasphemy be punished as the Ordinary shall decide. It is also a crime at common law and generally by statute, as tending to a breach of the peace and being a public nuisance or destructive of the foundations of civil society; when printed, it is a libel.

(b) Unbelief is the greatest of sins after hatred of God (see 820). But blasphemy is the greatest of the sins against faith, since to inner unbelief it adds external denial and insult.

(c) Blasphemy cannot become a venial sin on account of the smallness of the matter involved, for even slight slander or scorn becomes great when its object is God Himself. Example: It is blasphemous to say that our Lord was not above small or venial imperfections, or to show contempt for even one of the least of the Saints as such.

(d) Blasphemy cannot become a venial sin on account of unpremeditation, if at the time it is committed one is aware of its character, just as murder does not become a venial sin, because one killed another in a sudden fit of anger. Example: Sempronius has the habit when driving his refractory mules of shouting at them: "You creatures of the devil!" A priest on hearing this admonishes Sempronius that the expression is blasphemous. But Sempronius continues to use it whenever the mules irritate him, making no effort to improve.

896. There are some cases in which blasphemy is only a venial sin or no sin on account of the lack of deliberation.

(a) If there is no advertence or only semi-advertence to the act itself, the blasphemy pronounced, unless it be voluntary in its cause (see 102, 196), is not a mortal sin. In the former case, there is no sin at all, for the act is not human (see 33); in the latter case there cannot be mortal sin, for there is no full reflection on the deed (see 175). Example: Balbus now and then catches himself humming blasphemous songs that he heard years ago, but he always stops as soon as he thinks of what he is saying. Titus, coming out of the ether after an operation, makes a few blasphemous remarks, but he is so dazed that he hardly knows who is speaking. Sempronius makes himself drunk, foreseeing that he will blaspheme while out of his senses. Balbus commits no sin, Titus may be guilty of venial sin, but Sempronius is guilty of mortal sin in blaspheming.

(b) If there is no advertence or only semi-advertence to the malice of the act, the blasphemy pronounced, if it is not voluntary in its cause, is not a mortal sin; for one is not responsible for more than one knows or should know (see 99-100, on imputability). Examples: Titus, a foreigner, has been taught to repeat certain blasphemous phrases, whose real meaning he does not suspect. Balbus has the habit when angry of blaspheming at his mules, but he is doing his best to use more suitable language. Sempronius unawares gets into a tipsy condition in which he realizes his acts, but is confused about moral distinctions, and hence uses blasphemous expressions which he would abhor if he were in his normal state. Caius, a boy, blasphemes, thinking that he is committing only a venial sin of "cussing."

897. Different kinds of blasphemy must be noted with reference to the duty of confession.

[a] There are three distinct species of blasphemy—non-heretical, which is opposed to the virtue of religion; heretical, which is opposed to religion and faith; diabolical, which is opposed to religion, faith and the precept to love God. These species should be distinguished in confession. Examples: Titus, angered because his Patron Saint did not obtain a favor for him, ironically turns the Saint's picture to the wall, saying: "You have great influence with God!" (non-heretical blasphemy). Balbus in similar circumstances said: "I have lost all faith in Saints" (heretical blasphemy). Sempronia, Whose child has just died, rebels against God and calls Him a cruel monster (diabolical blasphemy).

(b) Circumstances may aggravate the malice of blasphemy. Blasphemy that is directly against God Himself is worse than blasphemy against the Saints; blasphemy against the Blessed Virgin is worse than blasphemy against other friends of God; blasphemy that ascribes evil to God is greater than blasphemy that denies Him some perfection; blasphemy that excuses itself or boasts is worse than blasphemy that is more concealed; blasphemy that expressly intends to dishonor God is graver than blasphemy that only implicitly intends this. Some authors require that aggravating circumstances be mentioned in confession, but others say this is not necessary (see Vol. II).

898. According to the causes from which they proceed (see 250), blasphemies are divided into three kinds: (a) blasphemy against the Father, which is contumely spoken against God out of passion or weakness, as when one being annoyed uses what he knows to be blasphemy; (b) blasphemy against the Son, which is contumely against God spoken out of ignorance. Thus, St. Paul said of himself that he had been a blasphemer, and a persecutor, and contumelious, but that he

obtained mercy, because he did it ignorantly in unbelief (I Tim., i. 12, 13); (c) blasphemy against the Holy Ghost, which is contumely against God spoken out of sheer malice. Such was the sin of the Jews, who attributed the divine works of Christ to the prince of demons (Matt, xii. 31).

899. To the Holy Ghost are appropriated the supernatural gifts of God that prevent or remove sin; and, as these can be reduced to six, there are also six sins against the Holy Ghost (i.e., six kinds of contemptuous disregard of spiritual life). The expression of this inner contempt is a blasphemy.

(a) Man is kept from sin by the hope mingled with fear which the thought of God, as both merciful and just, excites in him. Hence, despair and presumption which remove these divine preventives of sin are blasphemies against the Holy Ghost.

(b) Man is kept from sin, next, by the light God gives him to know the truth and by the grace He diffuses that all may perform good. Hence, resistance to the known truth and displeasure at the progress of God's kingdom are also sins against the Spirit of truth and holiness.

(c) Man is kept from sin by the shamefulness of sin itself and the nothingness of the passing satisfaction it affords; for the former inclines him to be ashamed of sin committed, or to repent, while the latter tends to make him tire of sin and give it up. Hence, the resolve not to grieve over sin and obstinate adherence to such a resolve are also sins against the Holy Ghost.

900. There is no sin which, if repented of, cannot be forgiven in this life. How then does our Lord say that the blasphemy against the Holy Spirit shall not be forgiven, neither in this world nor in the world to come (Matt., xii. 31)?

(a) The sins against the Holy Ghost are unpardonable according to their nature, just as some diseases are incurable according to their nature, because not only do they set up an evil condition, but they also remove or resist those things that could lead to betterment. Thus, if one despairs, or presumes, or resists truth or good, or determines not to abandon error or evil, one shuts out the remedy of repentance, which is necessary for pardon; whereas, if one sins through passion or ignorance, faith and hope remain and help one to repentance.

(b) The sins against the Holy Ghost are not unpardonable, if we consider the omnipotence of God. Just as God can cure miraculously a disease that is humanly incurable, so can He pardon a sin which, according to its nature, is unpardonable; for He is able to bring hope and repentance to those who were in despair, for example. Hence, we repeat, there is no sin which, if repented of, cannot be forgiven in this life.

901. Does one arrive at the state of malicious sin or blasphemy suddenly or gradually? (a) Malice in sin (i.e., the willing choice of evil by one who is not weakened by ignorance or passion) is sometimes due to a disorder in the will itself which has a strong inclination towards wrong, as when long-continued habit has made sin attractive. It is clear that in such cases one does not arrive at blasphemy suddenly, Example: Titus blasphemes with readiness and without remorse. This argues that he is an adept and not a beginner, for readiness and strong attachment are signs of practice. (b) Malice in sin is sometimes due to the fact that the will has lost certain protections against sin, and hence chooses sin readily and gladly, as happens when a sin against the Holy Ghost has been committed. Generally, the contempt of God's gifts contained in sins against the Holy Ghost does not come suddenly, but follows as the climax of a progressive deterioration (Prov., xviii. 3); but, since man is free and sin very alluring, it is not impossible that one should suddenly become a blasphemer, especially if one had not been careful before in other matters. It is next to impossible, however, that a religious-minded man should all at once become a blasphemer or malicious sinner.

902. Remedies Against Blasphemy.—(a) Those who blaspheme maliciously should be admonished of the enormity of their sin, as well as the absurdity of defying the Almighty (Ps. ii. 1, 4). Prayers and ejaculations in praise of God are a suitable penance for them. (b) Those who blaspheme through habit or out of sudden anger or passion should be told that at least they cause great scandal, and make themselves ridiculous. A good practice for overcoming habit or sudden outbursts is that some mortification or almsdeed or litany should be performed each time blasphemy is uttered.

903. Absolution of Blasphemers.—(a) If blasphemy is not heretical, no censure or reservation is incurred under the general law, and every confessor may absolve; (b) if blasphemy is heretical, excommunication is incurred under the conditions given above in 834, and absolution may be granted as explained there.

904. Sins of Ignorance, Blindness, Dullness.—After the sins against faith itself come the sins against the Gifts of the Holy Ghost that serve faith (see 808): (a) against the Gift of Knowledge is the sin of ignorance; (b) against the Gift of Understanding are the sins of blindness of heart and dullness of understanding.

905. Ignorance (as explained in 28 and 249) is a cause of sin—of material sin, if the ignorance is antecedent, of formal sin, if the ignorance is consequent. But ignorance is also a sin itself, in the sense now to be explained.

(a) Ignorance may be considered in itself (i.e., precisely as it is the absence of knowledge), and in this sense it is not called a sin, since under this aspect it is not opposed to moral virtue, but to knowledge, the perfection of the intellect.

(b) Ignorance may be considered in relation to the will (i.e., precisely as it is a voluntary defect), and in this sense it is a sin, since under this aspect it is opposed to the moral virtue of studiosity (i.e., the part of temperance which moderates the desire of learning and keeps the golden mean between curiosity and negligence). This sin of ignorance pertains to neglect, and is twofold; it is called affected ignorance, if the will is strongly desirous of the lack of due knowledge, and is called careless ignorance, if the will is remiss in desiring due knowledge. Affected ignorance is a sin of commission, careless ignorance a sin of omission.

(c) Ignorance may be considered in relation to obligatory acts (i.e., precisely as it makes one voluntarily incapable of fulfilling one's duties), and in this sense it partakes of various kinds of sinfulness, inasmuch as he who is voluntarily ignorant of his duty is responsible for the mistakes he will make. Thus, he who is sinfully ignorant in matters of faith, will fail against the precepts of that virtue; he who does not know what his state of life as judge, lawyer, physician, etc., requires, will fail against justice; he who does not know what charity demands of him, will sin against charity.

906. The malice of the sin of ignorance in matters of faith is as follows: (a) Vincible ignorance of the truths one is obliged to know, whether the obligation be of means or of precept (see 360, 786 sqq.), is a grave sin, for faith in these truths is commanded under pain of losing salvation (Mark, xvi. 15, 16). (b) The sin committed is but one sin, regardless of length of time, and is incurred at the time one omits due diligence in acquiring knowledge, as is the case with other sins of omission. Hence, he who remains in culpable ignorance of Christian doctrine for a year commits one sin, but the length of time is an aggravating circumstance.

907. Culpable ignorance regarding truths of faith, as a distinct sin, is as follows:

(a) It is not distinct from its cause (i.e., negligence), for ignorance is not a sin at all, except in so far as it proceeds from negligence. Hence, one would not be obliged to accuse oneself of the sins of omission in regard to instruction in Christian doctrine and of ignorance in Christian doctrine, for these are but one sin.

(b) Culpable ignorance is not distinct from its effect (i.e., from a sin committed on account of the ignorance), if the truth one is ignorant of has to be known only on account of some passing duty that must be performed here and now; for in such a case the knowledge is required, not for its own sake, but for the sake of the duty. Hence, ignorance of fact or of a particular law is not distinct as a sin from the sin that results from it. Examples: Titus knows that he should not take money that belongs to another; but through his own carelessness he is ignorant of the fact that the money before him belongs to another, and takes the money. Balbus knows that the precept of the Church on fasting is obligatory; but through his own negligence he is unaware that today is a fast day, and does not fast. Titus and Balbus committed one sin apiece.

(c) Culpable ignorance is distinct from its effect, if the truth one is ignorant of has to be known for its own sake; for in such a case one sins against the virtue of studiosity (see 905) by not knowing something which one should know habitually, and also against some other virtue by violating its precepts as a result of one's sinful ignorance. Truths one is obliged to know for their own sake are the mysteries of faith, the Commandments of the Decalogue, the Precepts of the Church, and the duties of one's own state. Examples: Sempronius through his own carelessness does not know the mystery of the Incarnation, and as a result blasphemes Christ. Titus does not know that stealing is a sin, and therefore he steals. In both cases two sins are committed, the sin of ignorance and the sin that resulted from ignorance.

908. Cases in which ignorance in matters of faith is not culpable are the following: (a) if one has used sufficient diligence to acquire knowledge, one is not responsible for one's ignorance; (b) if one has not used sufficient diligence to acquire knowledge, one is not responsible for one's ignorance, if the lack of diligence is not one's fault.

909. Sufficient diligence is a broad term and has to be understood with relation to the mental ability of the person and the importance and difficulty of the truth in question. What is sufficient diligence in an illiterate person, or with regard to a matter of minor importance, would be insufficient in a learned person, or in a matter of greater importance. However, the following general rules can be given:

(a) To be sufficient, diligence need not be as a rule supreme (i.e., it is not necessary that one employ every possible means to acquire instruction), for even the most conscientious persons feel they have used sufficient diligence when they have employed the usual means for obtaining religious instruction;

(b) To be sufficient, diligence should equal that which is employed by good people in similar circumstances. Thus, the unlearned who consult the learned or frequent the instructions provided for them, the learned who devote themselves to study as ordered and who seek assistance in doubts, are sufficiently diligent.

910. One who has not used sufficient diligence is sometimes responsible, sometimes not responsible.

(a) A person is not responsible for his ignorance and lack of sufficient diligence, if he conscientiously desires to have the proper amount of instruction, and has not even a suspicion that his studies and knowledge are not sufficient. Example: Titus, having gone through a very small catechism, thought that he understood Christian doctrine sufficiently and had done all that was required. But some years later he discovered, when examined, that he was ignorant of many important matters, and had entirely misunderstood others.

(b) A person is responsible for his lack of diligence and knowledge, if at heart he does not care to know, even though no fears or doubts about his ignorance disturb him. Examples: Balbus always felt religion a bore. At Sunday school he was daydreaming; now during sermons on Sunday he falls asleep. The result is that he has many infidel ideas, but doesn't know it, and is not much concerned. Caius secured for himself an office, for which he is unfitted on account of his ignorance. But he enjoys his position so much, and cares so little about its responsibilities, that he does not even dream of his incompetence, and would not try to change things if he did.

911. Similar to negligence about the truths of faith itself is negligence about truths connected with faith. (a) An unbeliever is guilty of negligence when against conscience he fails to pray for light and to inquire or inform himself about the credentials of religion, revelation, and the Church; (b) a believer is guilty of negligence if he fails to seek answers to objections against faith, when thrown much in the company of objectors.

912. Like to sins of ignorance are the two sins opposed to the Gift of Understanding. (a) Dullness of understanding is a weakness of mind as regards spiritual things which makes it very difficult for one to consider or understand them. It is sinful inasmuch as it arises from over-affection for carnal things, especially the delights of eating and drinking. (b) Blindness of mind is a complete lack of knowledge of divine things due to the fact that one refuses to consider them lest one feel obligated to do good, or to the fact that one is so wedded to passion that one gives it all one's attention (Ps. xxv. 4). Blindness is sometimes a punishment (Is., vi. 10; Wis., ii. 21); it is a sin when it is voluntary—that is, when carnal delights, especially lust, make one disgusted or negligent as to the things of faith. Abstinence and chastity are two means that greatly aid spiritual understanding, as is seen in the example of Daniel and his companions (Dan. i. 17).

Art. 3: THE COMMANDMENTS OF FAITH

(Summa Theologica, II-II, q. 16.)

913. Unlike the commandments of justice, which are summed up in the Decalogue, the commandments of faith are not given in any one place of scripture; but they may be reduced to three: (a) one must acquire knowledge and understanding of one's faith according to one's state in life and duties; (b) one must believe internally the truths of faith; (c) one must profess externally one's belief.

914. The Commandment of Knowledge.—The first of the foregoing commandments includes three things. (a) The doctrines of faith must be taught and must be listened to—"These words thou shalt tell to thy children" (Deut., vi. 6), "Teach ye all nations" (Matt, xxviii. 19), "He that heareth you heareth Me, and he that despiseth you despiseth Me" (Luke, x. 16). (b) One must apply oneself to understand what one hears—"Thou shalt meditate on these words, sitting in thy house, and walking on thy journey, sleeping and rising" (Deut., vi. 7), "Meditate upon these things, be wholly in these things. Take heed to thyself and doctrine" (I Tim., iv, 15, 16). (c) One must retain what one has learned—"Thou shalt bind the words of the law as a sign on thy hand, and they shall be and shall move between thy eyes. And thou shalt write them in the entry and on the doors of thy house" (Deut., vi. 8, 9); "Have in mind in what manner thou hast received and heard" (Apoc., iii. 3).

915. The means of communicating a knowledge of the faith to unbelievers are as follows:

(a) The remote means is to get a hearing from those who have not the true faith, and this supposes that one secure their good will through edifying example and charity towards them: "Be without offense to the Jews and the Gentiles, and to the church of God; as I also in all things please all men, not seeking that which is profitable to myself, but to many that they may be saved" (I Cor., x. 32, 33); "Let us work good to all men" (Gal., vi. 10).

(b) The proximate means of communicating a knowledge of faith is the declaration of the faith to non-Catholics who are willing to hear,

through missionaries sent to foreign countries, Catholic literature given
to those who are well-disposed, invitations to Catholic instructions,
public lectures on the faith, the question box at missions, etc. (see
Canons 1350, 1351). coöperation with Catholic schools and
publications, foreign and home missions, etc., makes one a sharer in the
work of the apostles who are bearing the burden of the day.

916. The means appointed by the Church for communicating the
doctrines of faith to Catholics are as follows:

(a) For the Laity.—From childhood religious and moral training should
have the first place in education, and should not be confined to
elementary schools, but continued in secondary and higher schools
(Canons 1372, 1373). Pastors are obliged to give catechetical
instructions, and parents must see that their children attend them
(Canons 1329-1336).

(b) For the Clergy.—Aspirants to the priesthood must follow the
courses prescribed for preparatory and higher seminaries or houses of
studies (Canons 1352-1371, 587-592), and no one is admitted to Orders
who has not passed canonical examinations (Canons 996, 997, 389, §2).
The faculties for hearing confessions and preaching also presuppose
examinations (Canons 1340, 877), and no one is to be promoted to
ecclesiastical offices, such as that of parish priest, unless he is judged
competent in knowledge (Canons 459, 149). The clergy are encouraged
to take university studies and degrees (Canons 1380, 1378).

917. A person applies himself sufficiently to the understanding of the
teaching of faith when he takes care that, both extensively or in quantity
and intensively or in quality, his knowledge is all that is required of him.

(a) Extensively, the knowledge should be such as to include at least all
those truths that have to be known, because explicit faith in them is
necessary; (b) intensively, the knowledge should be more or less perfect
according to the greater or less intelligence, rank or responsibility of the
person.

918. The truths that have to be known by all capable of the knowledge
are as follows:

(a) All must know, from the necessity of the case (necessity of means), that they have a supernatural destiny and that Christ is the Way that leads to it; for one cannot tend to a destination, if one is unaware of its existence and of the road that will bring one there. Hence, all must know the four basic truths: God our Last End, the Trinity, the Incarnation, God the Remunerator (see 787).

(b) All must know, from the will of Christ (necessity of precept), the other truths to which He wishes them expressly to assent, and the duties, general or particular, that He wishes them to fulfill (Mark, xvi. 16); that is, they must know the doctrine contained in the Creed, the commandments and ordinances of Christ concerning the Sacraments and prayer, and the special obligations of each one's particular state or office.

919. As to the degree of knowledge that one must possess intensively (i.e., as to its quality and perfection), it is clear that knowledge ought to be more perfect in those who are more intelligent or whose duties call for a more excellent learning.

(a) Knowledge of the truths that should be known by all the faithful ought to be of a more developed kind in those whose minds are more mature. A scientific and theological understanding of religion is not required in any lay person; nor should we expect the same knowledge in a child as in an adult, or in a subnormal person as in one who is normal mentally. Examples: No religious instruction is necessary for an idiot (i.e., a grown-up person who has the mind of a two-year-old child), for such a one cannot reason. A child of seven or an imbecile (i.e., a grown-up person whose mentality is on a par with that of a child of seven) may be received to Communion, after such a child or imbecile has learned in a simple way that the God-Man is received in the Eucharist and that it is not common food. A child who is between ten and twelve and a moron (i.e., a grown-up who is not mentally such a child's superior) should receive more instruction than an imbecile.

(b) Knowledge of sacred doctrine naturally should be greater in priests than in the laity; for in religious things priests are the teachers, the people their pupils (Mal., ii. 7). A mediocre knowledge of theology in a priest is not sufficient, especially in these days when the laity are educated, when theological questions are debated on all sides, and when so many outside the Church as well as in it are looking for help and light. A profound knowledge of abstruse questions, however, is not demanded of all priests in an equal degree: more is expected of a bishop than of his parish priests, more of a parish priest than of one who has not the care of souls or office of teaching, more of one who has to speak to or write for the better educated than of one who has to do these things for those who are less educated, etc. Knowledge should include not only learning, but also prudence (i.e., good judgment and practical ability to use learning well), for a priest learns, not for his own sake alone, but also for the benefit of others.

920. Scientific or complete knowledge is not required of those who are not theologians, as was said about the four basic truths (see 790). It suffices for lay persons that they know in a simple way, according to their age and capacity, the substance of the truths they must believe. Thus, they should know:

(a) The Creed.—One should know about God, that He is but one and that there are three divine Persons, Father, Son and Holy Ghost; that God is the maker of the world, and that He will reward everyone according to his deeds. One should know about Christ, that He is the Son of God and God Himself; that He was miraculously born of the Blessed Virgin Mary; that He suffered and died for our salvation; that He rose from the dead and by His own power ascended into glory and will come again after the general resurrection to judge all. One should know about the Church, that it is the one true Church founded by Christ, in which are found the communication of spiritual goods and the forgiveness of sins.

(b) The Decalogue.—One should know the general meaning of the Commandments so as to be able to regulate one's own conduct by them. It is not necessary that a child should know all the kinds of crimes and vices that are forbidden by the Commandments. In fact, it is better for such not to know much about evil. Nor is it required that a layman should know how to make correct applications of the Commandments to complicated situations that require much previous study.

(c) The Virtues.—One should know enough to be able to apply to one's own life, for ordinary cases, what a virtuous life demands. It is not necessary that a child should know the requirements of prudence as well as an experienced person, or that a layman should be able to settle doubts of conscience as well as a priest. But each should know enough to fulfill what is required of one of his age and condition. Both old and young should know in substance the acts of faith, hope, charity and contrition; for to these all are bound. The young should know the laws of the Church that apply to them (e.g., the law of abstinence); the older people should understand the law of fasting which they are bound to observe, etc.

(d) The Sacraments.—One should know substantially the doctrine of the Sacraments that are necessary for all, namely, Baptism, Penance and the Eucharist. Since all the faithful have the duty of baptizing in case of necessity, all should know how to administer lay Baptism properly and fruitfully. When the time comes for receiving a Sacrament, the recipient should know enough to receive it validly, licitly, and devoutly, although less knowledge is required in children and in the dying who cannot be fully instructed (see Canons 752, 854, 1330, 1331, 1020).

(e) Special Duties.—One should know the essentials of one's condition or state of life and the right way to perform its ordinary duties. Children should understand the obligations of pupils and of subjects; the married, religious and priests should know the duties of their respective states; citizens, the loyalty owed to the community; officials, judges, lawyers, physicians, teachers, etc., the responsibilities to the public which their own professions imply.

(f) The Lord's Prayer.—The substance of this form of prayer should be known by all, namely, that God is to be glorified, and that we should ask of Him with confidence goods of soul and body and deliverance from evil. Though Christ is the only necessary Mediator (I Tim., ii. 5), it is most suitable that all should know substantially the Hail Mary, namely, that we should ask the intercession of her who is the Mother of God and our Mother (John, xix, 27).

921. Is a person guilty of sin who does not know what to do in some manner that pertains to his state of life? (a) If he is blamably ignorant of

the nature of a state he has undertaken or of the ordinary duties that it imposes, he is guilty of sin; for he is, in a sense, unjust to himself by obligating himself to what he does not understand, and to others by promising what he cannot fulfill. Examples: A young person who marries without understanding the meaning of the contract, or becomes a religious without knowing the meaning of the vows, would be ignorant of the nature of the state embraced. A priest occupied in the ministry, who does not know how to administer the Sacraments validly, how to explain the Gospels correctly, how to judge usual cases in confession rightly, etc., would be ignorant of the ordinary duties of his office. A ruler who habitually acts beyond his authority, a lawyer who regularly gives wrong advice, and a teacher who makes mistakes in the elements of his specialty, would also be ignorant of their ordinary duties.

(b) If a person understands the nature of his state and his everyday duties, but is ignorant of recondite points or extraordinary cases, he is not guilty; otherwise, no one could undertake with a safe conscience the office of pastor, physician, judge, etc.; for, even when a person has devoted a lifetime to a calling, he has to admit that he finds difficulties or problems that he cannot solve offhand. Example: Father Titus gave an incorrect solution about a case of restitution, because he had to express an opinion at once, and there were so many angles and circumstances that some of them were overlooked.

922. The means appointed by the Church for the retention of knowledge in matters of faith are:

(a) For the Laity.—The course of Christian doctrine should not be discontinued with the parochial school or Sunday school, but should be continued in the higher schools (Canon 1373). Moreover, for adults catechetical instruction is given on Sundays and feast days (Canon 1332), and the people are exhorted to attend sermons on matters of faith and morals that are preached at parochial Masses (Canons 1337-1348).

(b) For the Clergy.—The clergy are admonished not to give up study after ordination (Canon 129), and the law requires that the junior clergy should take examinations annually during the first three or five years after ordination to the priesthood (Canons 130, 590), and that all the clergy should take part in theological conferences several times a year (Canon 131).

923. What has been learned by heart is more easily retained in the memory, and hence the common practice of committing the Catechism to memory is to be recommended. Some believe that it is obligatory to memorize the Creed and other points mentioned above (see 920); but this is unlikely, since even the form of the Decalogue and of the Lord's Prayer is not identical in different parts of scripture. In the early centuries the catechumens were obliged to learn the Creed and the Lord's Prayer by heart before Baptism, but there is no general law that requires this at the present time.

(a) According to positive law, one is not obliged to memorize the words and order of the Creed and other formulas, and it may be considered an indication that a person has retained sufficiently what was learned, if he is able to reply correctly to questions put to him (e.g., to explain the first article of the Creed by stating the direct and simple signification of its terms, and so on with the rest).

(b) According to natural law, one is obliged to learn by rote ithe formulas of faith, if this is possible and there is danger of spiritual detriment when it is not done. There is hardly anyone who cannot by practice commit to memory the Our Father, the Apostles' Creed, and short forms of acts of faith, hope, charity, and contrition; and, if none of them is thus known, it is practically certain that the grave duty of prayer will be neglected. Hence, it seems that there is a serious obligation of memorizing at least the Our Father. Feebleminded persons are not obliged to memorize, or even to know, the truths of faith, if they are incapable.

924. Confessors should examine in religion penitents who show signs of ignorance (e.g., in the manner of making their confession), and should grant or deny absolution according to the case.

(a) If the ignorance is about the truths that are necessary as a means of justification (see 790), the penitents should be dealt with as explained in 792.

(b) If the ignorance is about the truths that are necessary because commanded and there is urgent need of absolution (e.g., on account of mortal sin committed), the penitent may be absolved, if he is truly contrite and promises to repair his negligence by studying his religion, attending Sunday school, instructions, etc.

(c) If the ignorance is about the truths necessary because commanded, and there is no urgent necessity of absolution, the penitents may be sent away without absolution. Thus, children who have no serious sins to confess and who do not know how to say the act of contrition or other prayers, or who cannot answer simple questions of the Catechism, should be sent away with a blessing and told to study these things and return when they know them better.

925. The Commandment of Internal Acts of Faith.—The second commandment of faith mentioned above (see 913) is both negative and affirmative. (a) As negative, it forbids at any time disbelief or doubt concerning that which God proposes for faith. This aspect has been treated above in discussing the sins against faith (see 813 sqq., 840 sqq.). (b) As affirmative, it commands that one at certain times should give assent to the truths revealed by God. This aspect of the commandment will be considered now.

926. The existence of the command that one should elicit a positive act of assent to divine truth is taught in both Testaments. (a) In the Old Testament, implicit faith in all scripture was required; for lawgivers, prophets, and inspired writers spoke as delivering a message from God. Moreover, explicit faith in God and His Providence was commanded (see 788). (b) In the New Testament, implicit faith in all revealed doctrine is required, whether delivered in writing or as tradition (II Thess., ii. 15). Moreover, there is a command of explicit faith in the Gospel: "This is His commandment that we should believe in the name of His Son, Jesus Christ, and love one another, as He hath given commandment unto us" (I John, iii. 23).

927. This commandment obliges adults under grave sin as to all revealed truths. (a) The primary truths of revelation, truths of faith and morals to which all are commanded to give assent (i.e., to believe explicitly), are so important that those who refuse to believe them merit

condemnation (Mark, xvi. 16). (b) The secondary truths of revelation—
i.e., those that were made known by God, not for their own sake, but
on account of their relation to the primary truths (e.g., the names of the
patriarchs, the size of Saul, the complexion of David and thousands of
similar facts)—need not be known by all, for that is impossible. But all
are seriously obliged to believe that everything contained in the Word
of God is true, and to be ready to give assent even to the truths that are
not known. Hence, the minor truths of revelation must be believed
under pain of grave sin—implicitly, if they are not known, explicitly,
when they become known.

928. The obligation of explicit faith in the primary truths or articles of
faith is not grave with reference to every detail contained in those
truths. (a) Some details, on account of their difficulty, oblige to explicit
faith only under venial sin. Such are (in the Creed) the descent into
Limbo, the procession of the Holy Ghost, the mode of the
Communion of Saints. (b) Other details, on account of less importance,
do not oblige to explicit faith under any sin. Such are the facts that it
was Pilate under whom Christ suffered, that it was the third day when
Christ rose from the dead.

929. An affirmative commandment "obliges at all times, but not for all
times" (see 371). Hence, the question: How often or when must one
give internal assent to the teachings of faith, in order to fulfill the law?
Before answering this question, let us distinguish three kinds of laws
that may oblige one to an act of faith: (a) the divine law expressly
prescribing an act of faith; (b) the divine law prescribing an act of some
other virtue, which presupposes an act of faith; (e) human law
prescribing something that at least presupposes or includes an act of
faith.

930. The divine law expressly prescribing an act of faith (about which
we spoke in 925), obliges in the following cases: (a) at the time when
the commandment is first presented to one, and one recognizes its
obligation: "Preach the Gospel to every creature. He that believeth and
is baptized shall be saved; he that believeth not shall be condemned"
(Mark, xvi. 16); (b) it also obliges at other times during life; for "the just
man liveth by faith" (Rom, i. 17). The Church has rejected the

Jansenistic teaching that an act of faith once in a lifetime suffices (see Denzinger-Banwart, nn. 1101, 1167, 1215).

931. The commandment of internal belief is brought before one for the first time, either of one's whole life or for the first time after loss of faith, as follows:

(a) It is brought before a person for the first time in his life, when he first hears the truths of faith, or first realizes his duty of accepting them. Examples: A Catholic child who has just reached the age of reason and has been told in Sunday school that he must believe the Creed and other truths he has been taught; an adult Catholic who hears for the first time of transubstantiation, or of some other dogma just defined by the Church; a non-Catholic who has just perceived the truth of the Catholic Church.

(b) The commandment of internal belief is brought before one for the first time after loss of faith, as soon as the duty of returning to belief occurs to the mind.

932. Does this commandment require that, as soon as the obligation of faith dawns on one, one is obliged without an instant's delay to make a formal and explicit act of faith?

(a) As regards children, on account of the imperfection of their understanding, it can easily happen that they do not perceive that the obligation binds them there and then, or that it binds under sin, and thus some time may elapse after the use of reason, or after knowledge of the command of faith, before the omission of the act of belief would become a sin. Practically every child of Catholic education complies with the command when, having learned the truths that must be known, he says devoutly the act of faith, either in his own words or according to the form given in the Catechism.

(b) As regards adults, while the entrance of converts into the Church admits of some delay for necessary preparation, the act of faith itself should not be postponed for an instant, once the necessity of making it is perceived as certain.

933. As to its frequency or the times when the act of faith should be renewed, there are various opinions, but in actual life the question presents no difficulty.

(a) As to theory, the theologians are divided, some holding that the act of faith should be made at least once a year, others holding for once a month, still others for all Sundays and holydays. There is no solid support for any of these opinions, and it seems that the time and frequency of acts of faith are not determined by divine law.

(b) As to practice, the theologians agree that one who fulfills the usual religious duties of a Catholic, has also fulfilled the command to renew the act of faith. Thus, those who attend Mass and receive the Sacraments, as the law of the Church prescribes, make acts of faith in doing so, which satisfy the divine law of faith.

934. Those who omit to make an act of faith in time of temptation against faith, are also guilty of sin, if the omission is through sinful neglect.

(a) If the act of faith is the only means by which the temptation can be overcome (a rare contingency, outside the danger of death), one is of course gravely bound to elicit the act. The sin committed by one who would neglect the act of faith in such a circumstance is by some considered as opposed to the negative command, that one do not dissent; by others as opposed to the affirmative command, that one assent to faith. Example: Caius is very much tempted to blasphemy, and finds that the best remedy is an act of faith in the Majesty of God.

(b) If the act of faith would be harmful, as prolonging or intensifying the temptation (a thing that is not infrequent), it is better to struggle against the temptation indirectly by turning the attention to other matters (see 257, 844).

935. Other cases in which one is obliged to make an internal act of faith are as follows:

(a) By reason of a divine commandment of some virtue other than faith, it is sometimes necessary to make an act of faith also. Examples: When a sinner is preparing himself for the state of grace, of which faith is the prerequisite; when one is tempted against hope, justice, etc., and needs to call on faith to resist the tempter; when one is near to death and must make an act of charity in preparing to meet God. In these cases there are divine precepts of repentance, hope, justice, charity, and virtually of faith, which is presupposed.

(b) One must at times make an internal act of faith by reason of a human commandment enjoining some external act or virtue which supposes faith. Examples: The command to swear on the Bible, or by some mystery of religion, supposes an act of faith. The commands to receive Communion at Easter (Canon 859), to make meditation and spiritual retreats (Canons 125, 126, 595, 1001), to apply the intention of Mass (Canons 339, § 1, 466, § 1), all include virtually the command of an act of faith, for the things required (Communion, retreat, Mass) cannot be rightly performed without such an act.

936. The act of faith is either formal or virtual, according as it is made in itself, or in the act of another virtue that supposes it.

(a) The act of faith is formal, when one mentally accepts the truths of revelation on account of divine authority, even though one does not express the assent in words or according to any set formula. This kind of act of faith is necessary when one passes from non-belief or unbelief to belief, for none of the acts prior to faith contains supernatural assent to revelation. Hence, the commandment of faith requires in children or in converts from unbelief a formal act.

(b) The act of faith is virtual, when one elicits the act of some other supernatural virtue without thinking expressly about faith; for faith is presupposed by all other supernatural virtues, since one cannot wish what one does not believe. Thus, the acts of hope, charity, and contrition are virtually acts of faith. It seems that commandments of other virtues and of the renewal of faith itself do not require that one make a formal act of faith, although of course this would be the better thing to do. Thus, to fulfill the Easter precept of yearly Confession and Communion well, it is not required that one make a formal act of faith before Confession, since faith is included in the act of contrition. It is not necessary, then, that the penitent should say: "I believe in the forgiveness of sins, etc.," for in his purpose to receive forgiveness he makes a virtual act of faith in the tenth article of the Creed and in the Sacrament of Penance, as well as in the other mysteries of faith.

937. Practically, there is no difficulty for confessors about the violation of the commandment regarding internal acts of faith.

(a) If penitents are instructed and practical Catholics, they have made at some time a formal act of faith, even though they do not remember the time, for the act of faith precedes the acts of other virtues they are exercising. True, this act of faith may not have been made as soon as the age of reason was attained or the duty of faith perceived, but invincible ignorance excuses those who were in good faith about the matter. Regularity in prayer and other duties is an index that the act of faith is being renewed in such a way as to comply with the commandment. Hence, there is no necessity of questioning this class of penitents about the act of faith.

(b) If penitents are very ignorant Catholics (e.g., young children), it is clear that they have not made an act of faith as they should, for no one believes what he does not know. They should, therefore, be instructed that it is their duty to acquire more knowledge, and to make an act of faith along with their other prayers. Regarding absolution, see 924.

(c) If penitents are instructed but not practical, the confession that they have neglected prayer, Mass, and the Sacraments, means that they have also neglected the command of making acts of faith. It is not necessary, therefore, that the confessor interrogate or instruct them about this command, and he may absolve them, if they are resolved to amend. It is well, however, to recommend daily acts of faith, hope, charity and contrition to careless Catholics, especially to those who cannot attend Mass or receive the Sacraments often.

938. The Commandment of External Profession of Faith.—The third commandment of faith given above (see 913) is both negative and affirmative: (a) as negative, it forbids denial of the faith or profession of error opposed to faith; (b) as affirmative, it commands that one make open profession of one's faith.

939. The existence of a prohibition against denial of the faith or profession of error is taught in scripture and the sinfulness of such

denial is clear from its nature. (a) "He that shall deny Me before men, I will also deny him before My Father who is in Heaven" (Matt., x. 33). Denial of Christ is a grievous sin, for it entails denial by Christ. (b) He who denies the faith is a heretic or infidel, if he means what he says; he lies, if he does not mean what he says, and his lie is a grave injury to God, whose truth is called into question, and against the neighbor, who is scandalized.

940. With reference to its voluntariness, denial of faith is either direct or indirect. (a) It is direct, when one intends to deny the faith; (b) it is indirect, when one does not intend to deny the faith, but wills to use words, acts, etc., which either from their signification or use, or from the meaning that will or may be given them by others, will in the circumstances express a denial of the faith. Examples: A convert from paganism conceals a crucifix in the idol of a temple and then joins the pagans in their customary bows of reverence, while intending only adoration to Christ crucified and detesting the idol. Titus takes off his hat when passing any church, as a mark of respect for the good they do. Balbus, a convert from Nestorianism, recites the names of Nestorius and Dioscurus at Mass, intending only to honor the patron Saints of those two heresiarchs.

941. There are three ways of denying the faith: (a) by words, spoken or written, as when one says: "I am not a Catholic," "I do not believe in miracles"; (b) by acts, as when one dissuades persons of good faith from entering the Church, or moves them to abandon it, or refuses to genuflect before the Blessed Sacrament, or studiously excludes scapulars, pictures and all religious symbols; (c) by omission, as when one fails to answer calumnies against faith, which one could profitably answer, or fails to protest when another speaks of oneself as a non-Catholic.

942. There are various ways in which error opposed to faith is professed: (a) by words, as when one says that one is a freethinker or Christian Scientist; (b) by acts, as when one offers incense to an idol, or receives the Lord's Supper in a Lutheran church, or cheers an anti-religious address; (c) by signs, as when one uses the Masonic grip, wears the robes of a Buddhist bonze, takes a Mohammedan or pagan name, etc., in order to pass oneself off as a non-Catholic; (d) by omission, as

when one is silent when introduced as a Rationalist, or makes no protest when Indifferentism is being advocated by one's companions.

943. The following are not a denial of faith or profession of error:

(a) Words that deny, not one's allegiance to religion, but one's acceptance of it as qualified by some calumnious designation. Examples: Titus denies that he is a "Papist," because he wishes his questioner to use a term that is not intended to be an insult. Balbus, entering a pagan region where the name Christian has the meaning of criminal or enemy on account of crimes committed there by white men in past times, says to the tribesmen that he is not a Christian, but a follower of Jesus and a Catholic.

(b) Words that conceal one's rank or state in the Church, are not against faith, because one can hold the faith without being in a certain rank or state in the Church, Thus, St. Peter's denial that he was a follower of Jesus, that he had ever known Him, etc., was, according to some authorities, not a denial of the Divinity of Jesus or of the truth of His teaching. Example: A Catholic who hides or denies his character of priest or religious, his membership in a Catholic family, organization, race, does not thereby necessarily deny his faith.

(c) Deeds that are contrary to practices of religion, but not to the profession of faith, are not denial of belief; for one may be very much attached to one's religion, even ready to fight for it, but not willing to follow its requirements. Example: Caius is careless about church duties, misses Mass, eats meat on Fridays, and never goes to the Sacraments; but he always calls himself a Catholic and wishes to be considered one.

(d) Signs that have some association with non-Catholic religion, but do not necessarily represent it (since they are indifferent in themselves and have other and legitimate uses), do not deny the faith, when not used as symbols of false religion. Similarly, the omission of signs that are associated with Catholicity, but which are optional, is not a denial of the faith. Examples: Titus, when travelling in the Orient, makes use of the national salutation of the pagan peoples among whom he lives. Balbus builds a church with architectural features borrowed from pagan temples. Caius wears a fez or turban in Mohammedan regions where it is not looked on as a religious headgear. Sempronius practises circumcision as a hygienic measure. Claudius does not say grace at meals when dining in public, and does not wear scapulars when bathing at the seashore.

(e) Omission of profession of faith, when it is not obligatory, is not a denial of faith; for no one is bound to make known his affairs and convictions to every acquaintance. Example: Titus works in an office where most of the clerks are non-Catholics. But no one ever speaks about religion, and hence it is not known that he is a Catholic.

944. Dangers of Profession of Unbelief.—The principal dangers of making external profession of false religion, if not of losing faith itself, are the following: (a) membership in forbidden societies; (b) communication in sectarian services; (c) coöperation in activities whose tendency or principles are erroneous.

945. Forbidden Societies.—Societies are forbidden by the Church when they are intrinsically or extrinsically evil. (a) A society is intrinsically evil, when it has an evil purpose, or uses evil means to obtain even an honest end. Thus, societies or parties that conspire against Church or State, or that seek to undermine Christian doctrines or morals, have an evil purpose; while those that demand absolute secrecy or oaths of blind obedience to unknown persons, that favor cremation, use a sectarian ritual, promote evil literature, etc., are employing evil means, no matter what may be the end in view. (b) A society is extrinsically evil, when its end and means are good, but membership in it is dangerous to faith or morals on account of circumstances (e.g., on account of the bad type of individuals who make up the society or control it).

946. The Code (Canon 684) mentions the following kinds of societies as banned for Catholics:

(a) secret societies, that is, those which demand of members that certain things which the society considers secrets be told absolutely to no one outside the society, or certain degrees of the society, not even to those who may legitimately inquire about them, such as the bishop or civil superior in the external forum, parents with regard to their children not emancipated, pastors and confessors in the internal forum. Those societies are also secret which demand blind and absolute obedience to unknown leaders;

(b) condemned societies, that is, such as have been censured by the Church, or simply forbidden. Canon 2335 decrees *ipso facto* excommunication reserved to the Holy See against all those who join Masonic or similar associations which plot against the Church or lawful civil authority. Among the societies forbidden without censure are: various Biblical societies, societies for the promotion of cremation, the Knights of Pythias, the Odd Fellows, the Sons of Temperance, the Independent Order of Good Templars, Theosophical societies, the Y.M.C.A. Female societies affiliated with these are also condemned, since they are branches of the main society—for example, the Rebeccas, the Eastern Star, the Pythian Sisters.

Worthy of detailed consideration is the condemnation of the Communist
Party and the penalties attached to membership in, or defense, or propagation of the Party. The following questions were asked of the Holy Office:

1. Whether it is licit to join the Communist Party or to favor it.

Reply: In the negative; for Communism is materialistic and anti-Christian; and the leaders of the Communists, although they sometimes verbally profess that they are not attacking religion, in fact, nevertheless, by doctrine and action show themselves to be enemies of God and of the true religion and the Church of Christ.

2. Whether it is licit to publish, propagate, or read books, periodicals, daily papers, or sheets which promote the doctrine or action of Communists, or to write in them.

Reply: In the negative: for they are forbidden *ipso iure* (see Canon 1399).

3. Whether the faithful who knowingly and freely do the acts mentioned in 1 and 2 can be admitted to the sacraments.

Reply: In the negative, according to the ordinary principles governing the refusal of the sacraments to those who are not properly disposed.

4. Whether the faithful who profess the materialistic and anti-Christian doctrine of Communists, and especially those who defend or propagate it, incur *ipso facto* as apostates from the Catholic faith the excommunication specially reserved to the Holy See.

Reply: In the affirmative (Decree of the Holy Office, July 1, 1949).

The sanction of excommunication specially reserved to the Holy See was imposed also upon those who teach boys and girls in associations set up by the Communists to imbue youth with principles and training which are materialistic and contrary to Christian morality and faith. The associations themselves are subject to the sanctions of the decree of July 1, 1949. Moreover parents or guardians who send their children to such associations, and the children themselves, as long as they have part in these associations, cannot be admitted to the reception of the sacraments (Monitum of the Holy Office, July 28, 1950).

(c) seditious societies, that is, those organizations, even though not secret, which aim at the overthrow of family and property rights;

(d) suspect societies, that is, those whose principles or methods have the appearance of being unsound. On January 11, 1951 the Holy Office in response to the question: "Whether Catholics may join the 'Rotary Club'?" issued the following decree: "It is not licit for clerics to join the Association 'Rotary Club' or to be present at its meetings; the laypeople are to be urged to preserve the prescript of Canon 684." The decree seems to have taken many English-speaking people by surprise, one paper describing it as "a bewildering document." The surprise flowed from personal experience of Rotary Clubs as social clubs dedicated to bonhomie and community improvement. Nevertheless, the decree was in accord with the general trend of Church policy in regard to undenominational societies. They are not approved; they are not condemned as Masonry has been condemned. What is their position? The response that layfolk are to be exhorted to observe Canon 684 is indicative of the attitude of the Church in regard to such societies. The canon instructs them to "beware of secret, condemned, seditious and suspect societies." Since Rotary Clubs are seldom considered to be secret and never as condemned nor as seditious, the implication is that they are suspect. Such was the interpretation of the decree given in the *Osservatore Romano* of Jan. 27, 1951.

In regard to clerics, the effect of the decree was to make illicit what was formerly simply inexpedient; for the Sacred Consistory had replied on February 4th, 1929, that it was not expedient for Ordinaries to permit clerics to join Rotary Clubs, or to take part in their meetings. Moreover, as the *Osservatore* article indicates, the prohibition is limited to meetings of members only and does not extend to meetings at which non-members may be present, provided the purpose of such meetings befits priestly activity.

The exhortation to layfolk in regard to "Rotary" simply reaffirms the Church's general attitude to all secular associations. As early as November 5, 1920 the Holy Office, referring specifically to Y.M.C.A., warned the Ordinaries that the note of "suspicion" attaches to all secular societies. Their efforts to promote good works and good moral standards independent of religious authority tend to foster the spirit of religious indifferentism and moral naturalism. Both the Spanish hierarchy (1929) and the Dutch hierarchy (1930) have so judged Rotary. However, the degree of suspicion to be attached to each Rotary Club is a question of fact to be determined in specific instances by the proper local Ordinary. Where evidence of suspicion is available, exhortatious not to join the clubs must be made; in the lack of such evidence, the ordinaries may maintain discreet silence.

(e) societies that aim to elude the lawful vigilance of religious authority.

947. The following organizations fall under the censure against Masonic societies:

(a) all varieties and degrees of Freemasonry, for all the Masonic sects are included in the Canon. The fact that American, English and Irish Masons have many excellent individuals in their ranks, and lack the irreligious and revolutionary character of the Masonry of Continental Europe or Latin countries, does not exempt them from the censure.

(b) all organizations similar to Masonry, that is, secret societies that conspire against lawful authority. Such are societies like the Carbonari, the Fenians, anarchists and nihilists.

948. The sin committed by membership in forbidden societies is grave, since the purpose of the law—viz., the safeguarding of faith against serious danger—is itself grave. Such membership is interpreted also as a profession of false religion, when one joins oneself to a body which in its branches or degrees has a false creed of its own. (a) Even though the branch or degree to which one belongs does not require assent to such a creed, membership expresses a fellowship with those who do accept it; (b) similarly, participation in the ritual of the lodges is a communication in ceremonies expressive of false religion; for, though their externals may appear good or even Christian, the internal meaning known to the adepts is anti-Catholic or anti-Christian.

949. Absolution of Those Who Belong to Forbidden Societies.—(a) The sin cannot be absolved unless there is repentance, and hence absolution cannot be granted those who without sufficient reason refuse to withdraw from membership, or who refuse to discontinue participation in false rites.

(b) The excommunication is not incurred by those who joined forbidden societies in ignorance of the law or of the penalty, provided the ignorance was not crass or supine. If the censure was actually incurred, the mode of absolution will depend on the nature of the case: if the case is occult (i.e., if it is not known and not likely to become known that the penitent belonged to a society forbidden under pain of excommunication), the Ordinary may absolve or grant faculties to absolve (Canon 2237); if the case is a public one, and it would be very inconvenient to await faculties from Rome, absolution is given under the condition of recourse to the proper authority within a month (Canon 2254). Many Ordinaries have by Indult faculties to absolve members of secret societies.

950. Nominal membership and temporary attendance at meetings may be permitted as an exception when there are sufficient reasons.

(a) Nominal membership means that one leaves one's name on the roster of the society and continues to pay its assessments, but does not communicate with the society or attend its meetings. In 1896 the Holy Office replied to the American Bishops that this kind of membership in the Odd Fellows, Sons of Temperance and Knights of Pythias might be permitted under certain conditions, if there was a sufficient reason (viz., that grave material loss would be incurred by withdrawal). (b) Temporary attendance at meetings means that for a short time, and not for longer than absolutely necessary, one is present at gatherings of the society, but takes no active part in its false cult.

951. The following conditions were laid down for permission of nominal membership in the Odd Fellows, Sons of Temperance, etc.: (a) that the penitent joined the society in good faith, before knowing that it was condemned; (b) that there be no danger of scandal, or that it be removed by the declaration that membership is only nominal and only for the purpose of avoiding temporal losses; (c) that there be no danger of perversion of the party himself or of his family, in case of sickness or of death, and no danger of a non-Catholic funeral.

952. Procedure of the confessor with a penitent who has incurred excommunication on account of membership in the Masons or other like society should be as follows: (a) the faculty to absolve must be obtained (see 949), (b) the following promises must be exacted from the penitent—that he will withdraw entirely from the sect and that he will repair, as well as he can, the scandal he may have caused; (c) the penitent must be required to renounce the sect, at least in the presence of the confessor, and to deliver over to him the books, manuscripts, insignia, and other objects that are distinctive of it (the confessor should give these objects to the Ordinary as soon as he prudently can, but, if grave reasons prevent this, he should burn them); (d) a salutary penance should be given and frequent confession urged.

953. Procedure of the confessor with a penitent who belongs to the Odd Fellows or other society forbidden by name, but without censure, should be as follows: (a) if the penitent is contrite and promises to leave the society, he can be absolved without special faculties; (b) if the penitent is contrite but wishes to retain nominal membership, the case must be referred to the Archbishop of the Province or to the Apostolic Delegate; (c) if the penitent wishes to retain full membership, he is not repentant and cannot be absolved.

954. Procedure of the confessor with a penitent who belongs to a society not condemned by name, but which the confessor himself

regards as evil should be as follows: (a) if the confessor is certain that the society is one of those condemned implicitly by the Church, because it exacts inviolable secrecy or blind obedience to its leaders, or has Masonic characteristics, etc., he should treat it in the same way as the societies condemned by name; (b) if the confessor is certain that the society is condemned by natural law for the penitent before him (e.g., on account of the evil associates and moral dangers it contains), he should treat it as any other occasion of sin, but it should be noted that no priest or local Ordinary has authority to condemn publicly and by name any society not condemned by the Church; (c) if the confessor is in doubt, he should proceed according to the rules for an uncertain conscience (see 678, 679, 742), and for the prudent administration of the Sacraments (see Vol. II).

955. As one of the chief remedies against evil societies is the formation of Catholic societies, the Code (Canon 684) praises those of the faithful who enroll as members in associations established or recommended by the Church. Catholic societies distinct from religious Orders or Congregations are of two kinds.

(a) Distinctly religious societies are those instituted for the purpose of promoting a more Christian life among their members, or of fostering works of piety and charity, or of contributing to the solemnity of public worship. Such are the Secular Third Orders, Confraternities of the Blessed Sacrament and of Christian Doctrine, and other pious unions.

(b) Societies that are not distinctly religious, but whose membership and spirit are Catholic, are of many kinds. Such are the Knights of Columbus, Ancient Order of Hibernians, Catholic Daughters of America, Volksverein, Young Men's Institute, etc.

956. Communication in Worship.—Communication with non-Catholics (as was said above in 882) is either religious or non-religious. It is clear that communication in non-religious matters does not contain a profession of error, but the same cannot be said of communication in religious services, since these are not only acts of worship, but also expressions of faith in the creed of a certain religion. We must distinguish, however, between private and public communication.

(a) Communication is private, when a Catholic and non-Catholic offer together the Lord's Prayer or other similar prayer as a private devotion, not as an act of official worship. Private devotion is not the expression of a sectarian creed, and, if there is nothing false in it and no danger of scandal or perversion from communication between Catholic and non-Catholic in such devotion, this kind of communication is not unlawful. In the following paragraphs there will be question of public communication.

(b) Communication is public, when the rites performed are the official services of the Catholic Church or of some non-Catholic sect (e.g., the Mass, the Lord's Supper of the Lutherans, the Evensong of the Anglicans, the prayer-meeting of other sects). Thus, public communication takes place either when non-Catholics take part in Catholic worship, or Catholics take part in non-Catholic worship.

957. Participation of non-Catholics in Catholic services is either by mere presence, or by reception or performance of Catholic rites.

(a) Mere presence consists in a purely material attendance at a service, as when non-Catholics assist at Mass and sit, rise and kneel with the congregation or remain seated throughout. There is no objection whatever to this kind of participation; on the contrary, non-Catholics should be invited to Catholic sermons and services, and made to feel welcome, for in what better way can the divine command of working for their conversion be complied with? Only excommunicated persons are excluded from the offices of the Church (Canon 2269, §1). It is also allowed that Catholic bishops and clergy accompany a non-Catholic ruler to the church, and assign him and his escort an honorable place therein.

(b) Reception of Catholic rites is had when non-Catholics, without performing any liturgical function, receive some spiritual favor through the rites of the Church, as when a non-Catholic receives a priest's blessing.

(c) Performance of Catholic rites exists when a non-Catholic exercises some office in a liturgical function of the Catholic Church, as when a Protestant acts as sponsor at a Catholic Baptism.

958. Cases of reception of Catholic rites by non-Catholics permitted by law are the following:

(a) Reception of Sacramentals.—Since the purpose of these rites and objects is to implore graces and temporal favors with a view to the illumination and salvation of the recipient, and since our Lord Himself blessed and cured even the pagans, the Church permits blessings and exorcisms to be conferred on non-Catholics (Canons 1149, 1152). Similarly, blessed candles, palms, ashes and other real sacramentals may be given to them. Examples: The Church has permitted priests to visit the homes of Mohammedans to bless and pray over the sick, and also to bless the houses of schismatics, provided they were summoned and avoided all communication in prayer.

(b) Reception of Sacraments.-Since it is possible that the salvation of a dying person may depend on absolution, good moralists, relying on decisions of Roman Congregations, hold that conditional absolution may be given to a heretic or schismatic who is dying and unconscious, or even to one such who is dying and conscious, provided he is in good faith and contrite, and danger of scandal has been removed.

(c) Reception of Fruits of the Mass.—Since Christ died for all, there is nothing in the nature of things to prevent the application of Mass to any persons who are living or in Purgatory; and from Canon 809 it appears that Mass may be offered for any living person, and also for any deceased person about whose salvation we may entertain hope. Hence, neither the divine nor the ecclesiastical law forbids the application of Mass for heretics, schismatics, or infidels. The Church also permits Mass to be said privately, all scandal removed, for excommunicated persons. Under these same conditions, then, Mass may be said for non-Catholics, both living and dead (Canon 2262, §2, n. 2).

(d) Reception of the Suffrages of the Church.—Since God wishes all to be saved and public peace to be maintained (I Tim., ii), and since the Church desires that Ordinaries and pastors should have at heart the conversion of non-Catholics (Canon 1350), public prayers for the prosperity of non-Catholic rulers and officials—likewise sermons, missions and other works for the conversion of unbelievers—are not only allowed, but recommended and required.

959. Non-Catholics have not the same right as Catholics to receive the rites of the Church, and hence when they are admitted to them, there are certain restrictions to be observed.

(a) Restrictions as to Sacred Things.—As admission of non-Catholics to sacramentals, etc., is a favor, not a right, it should be confined to cases allowed by the Church. Thus, it is forbidden to grant indulgences or to give the nuptial blessing to non-Catholics, and only in very exceptional cases may any ceremonies be permitted at mixed marriages (Canons 1102, 1109). Non-Catholics may not receive the Pax; may not be invited to take part in the solemn services of receiving ashes on Ash Wednesday, palms on Palm Sunday and candles on Candlemas Day; may not receive ecclesiastical burial (Holy Office, June 8, 1859). Children sent by their parents to non-Catholic services may not be confirmed (Holy Office, August 28, 1780); a Catholic priest is not allowed to supply for a non-Catholic minister, by accompanying the body of a non-Catholic from the home to the graveyard, even though the body be not brought to Church, nor the bell tolled (Holy Office, January 26, 1886). It is not permissible to lend a Catholic church to non-Catholics for their services.

(b) Restrictions as to Persons.—As superstition and irreverence have to be avoided, the sacramentals may not be administered or given at all to non-Catholics about whose good faith and purpose there is doubt.

(c) Restrictions as to Mode.—The Church, while she wishes to help and benefit non-Catholics, must avoid anything that would cause scandal or have the appearance of equal recognition of believers and unbelievers. Thus, when Mass is offered for outsiders, the same publicity and pomp is not permitted as when there is question of Catholics.

960. As regards the performance of Catholic rites by non-Catholics, the Church disapproves of every kind of such participation, but does not refuse to tolerate the more remote kind, when there is grave necessity and no scandal is caused.

(a) By more remote participation we understand such as scarcely differs from passive assistance (e.g., to act as witness at a marriage), or such as carries with it no recognition as an official of the Church (e.g., to act as substitute or temporary organist). Hence, the Church has permitted this kind of participation in particular cases, when the authorities decided that there was urgent necessity and no scandal. Examples: Moralists hold that, when a heretic or schismatic has been designated as sponsor at Baptism and cannot be refused without grave offense, he may be allowed to act as witness. The Holy Office has also declared that heretics should not be used as witnesses at marriage, but may be tolerated as such by the Ordinary, when there is a grave reason and no scandal (August 18, 1891); that a non-Catholic organist may be employed temporarily, if it is impossible to secure one who is a Catholic, and no scandal is caused (February 23, 1820); that in certain special circumstances girls belonging to a schismatical sect might be allowed to sing with the Catholics at church functions, especially at Exposition and Benediction of the Blessed Sacrament (January 25, 1906).

(b) Proximate participation is the exercise of functions connected with a sacred rite (e.g., to act as server at Mass), or that imply a recognition of the religion of the one who participates (e.g., to act as representative of some sect at a funeral and receive liturgical honors). The Church has always refused to tolerate this kind of participation. Examples: Non-Catholics may not act as sponsors at Baptism or Confirmation under pain of invalidity of sponsorship (Canons 765, 795), nor chant the Office in choir (Holy Office, June 8, 1859), nor be employed as singers of the liturgical music (Holy Office, May 1, 1889), nor carry torches or lights in church ceremonies (Holy Office, November 20, 1850). Likewise, non-Catholics may not become members of Catholic confraternities, nor assist at Catholic services as official representatives of some sect or sectarian society.

961. Participation of Catholics in non-Catholic services may happen today in so many ways, and it is so difficult at times to draw the line between lawful and unlawful communication, that it is well before considering these cases to state the general rules that apply here.

(a) It is lawful to perform an act from which two effects follow, one good and the other bad, if the act in itself is good or indifferent, if there is a sufficiently grave reason for performing it, if the evil effect is not intended, and if the evil effect be not prior to the good effect (see 104).

(b) Circumstances vary in different localities and countries, and communication that would signify unity of belief in a place where Catholics and non-Catholics are very unequal numerically might be very harmless in a place where there is no great numerical difference. Offense to non-Catholics should not be given needlessly.

(c) In doubtful cases the decision whether or not a particular kind of communication is lawful or unlawful pertains to the Ordinary (Canon 1258).

962. Participation of Catholics in non-Catholic services is either active or passive. (a) Participation is active when one takes a part or fulfills some function in an act that is an official expression of the worship and belief of a sect, even though this takes place outside a church, or is not open to the general public.

(b) Participation is passive, if one merely assists as a spectator, and not as a worshipper, at something pertaining to non-Catholic worship.

963. Sacred things in which communication is possible are of three classes:

(a) the chief acts of divine worship (i.e., Sacrifices, Sacraments, sacramentals);

(b) the secondary acts of divine worship (such as prayers, processions, vows, oaths, the Divine Office, hymn singing, scripture reading, etc.). In the Protestant denominations some one or other of these is, as a rule, the central or distinctive service, although some have other proper features of their own, such as the silent meeting of the Quakers, the seance of the Spiritualists, the march of the Salvation Army, the charity kiss of the Dunkards;

(c) places (e.g., churches, lodge rooms, cemeteries), times (e.g., days of feast or fast), and objects (e.g., images, badges, aprons, banners, robes), pertaining to divine worship.

964. It is unlawful for Catholics in any way to assist actively at or take part in the worship of non-Catholics (Canon 1258). Such assistance is intrinsically and gravely evil; for (a) if the worship is non-Catholic in its form (e.g., Mohammedan ablutions, the Jewish paschal meal, revivalistic "hitting the trail," the right hand of fellowship, etc.), it expresses a belief in the false creed symbolized; (b) if the worship is Catholic in form, but is under the auspices of a non-Catholic body (e.g., Baptism as administered by a Protestant minister, or Mass as celebrated by a schismatical priest), it expresses either faith in a false religious body or rebellion against the true Church.

965. It is unlawful for Catholics to simulate active assistance in the worship of non-Catholics, for, while the non-Catholic rite would be avoided, something which appeared to be that rite would be done, and thus profession of faith in it would be given.

(a) Hence, it is not lawful to do an indifferent act which bystanders from the circumstances will have to conclude is an act of false worship. Thus, Eleazar would not eat lawful meat which was put before him in order that he might pretend to eat the meat of sacrifice after the manner of the heathen (II Mach., vi).

(b) It is not lawful to accept a false certificate of participation in false worship. Hence, the early Church condemned as apostates the Libellatics (i.e., those Christians, who, to protect themselves in time of persecution, obtained by bribery or otherwise a forged or genuine magistrate's certificate that they had sacrificed to the heathen gods).

966. It is unlawful for Catholics to assist passively at non-Catholic worship, unless there are present the conditions requisite for performing an act that has two results, one good and the other evil (see 104); for even passive assistance frequently involves sin.

(a) Hence, the assistance itself must be really indifferent, that is, it must be a merely passive presence without any active participation in the service. Examples: A person who stands in the rear of a Quaker meeting house as an onlooker assists passively; but one who sits quietly among the others present, as if in meditation, assists actively. A person who sits in a pew during a revival in order to see what is going on, assists passively; but, if he joins with the congregation in bowing, groaning, etc., he assists actively.

(b) The evil effect that may result from assistance (such as scandal and danger of perversion) must not be prior to the good effect; otherwise, evil would be done for the sake of good. Examples: Titus, a non-Catholic, goes to Mass as a spectator, with his Catholic friend Balbus. He then asks Balbus to assist as a spectator at the services of his denomination, and thus see for himself that the latter is better. Balbus, in order to be courteous, consents. Here Balbus aims to show politeness, which is good, but the means he uses—namely, the impression he gives that he is not convinced of the superiority of his own religion—is bad.

(c) The evil effect (i.e., remote danger of perversion, unavoidable scandal) must not be intended or approved, but only permitted. Example: Caius, a Catholic public official, has to attend funerals and weddings in Protestant churches as a mark of the public respect for notable persons. He knows that a few will take scandal at his action, but he wishes only to do his duty as an official, and not to offend anyone (see on Scandal).

(d) The cause of assistance must be in proportion to the kind of assistance. Hence, a greater reason is required for assistance on several occasions than on one, for assistance at infidel than at heretical services, for assistance at the primary than at the secondary act of worship, for assistance by a priest than for assistance by a layman, etc. Example: Graver reason would be necessary to justify assistance at a non-Catholic funeral, if there were signs of anti-Catholicism manifested (e.g., flower designs and regalia of a hostile sect placed on the coffin), than if the service contained nothing offensive.

967. Cases of communication in false sacrificial rites are as follows: (a) Active participation is had in such acts as the slaying and offering of victims, the burning of incense before idols, the eating of sacrificial

banquets; (b) Passive participation is had when one merely watches the rite of sacrifice without taking any part therein.

968. Cases of communication in the Sacrifice of the Mass are as follows: (a) Active participation is had in such acts as taking the part of deacon in a schismatical Mass, assisting at a schismatical Mass with the intention of hearing Mass formally (i.e., of offering it with the priest). If on Sunday, one is where there is only a schismatical church, one is excused from the obligation of hearing Mass, and may not hear Mass in that church (Holy Office, December 5, 1608; August 7, 1704). (b) Passive participation is had when one is present merely as a spectator, kneeling before the Blessed Sacrament, but giving no other signs of religious devotion. This is permissible under the conditions mentioned above (see 966), if there is no scandal, or danger of perversion (Holy Office, April 24, 1894).

969. Cases of participation in the Sacraments or sacramentals, real or reputed, are as follows: (a) Active participation takes place when one receives a Sacrament from a non-Catholic minister, or offers one's child to receive a Sacrament from such a minister, or contracts marriage in the presence of such a minister, or acts as sponsor at a non-Catholic baptism or confirmation or as the religious witness at a non-Catholic marriage, or answers in public non-Catholic prayers, or takes ashes blessed by schismatics. (b) Passive participation is had when one merely looks on at the administration of a Sacrament or sacramental by a non-Catholic minister, without signs of approval or union in what is being done.

970. There are certain cases that seem to be active participations in Sacraments with non-Catholics, and yet are permitted by the Code. In reality, however, there is no active communication in those cases.

(a) Canons 886 and 905 allow the faithful to receive communion and absolution according to a Rite different from their own, so that one who belongs to the Latin Rite may lawfully receive in Communion a Host consecrated according to the Greek Rite, or go to confession to an Oriental priest. But in these Canons there is question of different Rites within the Catholic Church, not of those of non-Catholics.

(b) Canons 742 and 882 allow those who are in danger of death to receive Baptism and absolution from an heretical or schismatical minister, and theologians apply the same principle to Extreme Unction and the Viaticum. But there is no communication in non-Catholic ceremonies in these cases, for the Sacraments belong to the Catholic Church, and for the sake of the dying she authorizes non-Catholic ministers to act as her representatives, provided there is no scandal or danger of perversion.

971. Cases of participation in non-sacramental rites are as follows:

(a) Oaths and Vows.—Participation is active when one swears in words or by other signs which, according to local usage, manifest belief in the creed of some sect; it is not active, when the manner of the oath does not signify adherence to a false creed; Example: If one is required to swear, by touching or kissing the non-Catholic Bible, as a sign of approval of Protestantism or Masonry, one may not consent. But, if the Government presents a non-Catholic Bible with no thought of Protestantism, there is no approval of Protestantism in the one who swears on that Bible, although, if the custom is not general, there might be scandal if no protest were made. A Catholic may bring his own Bible with him, or ask for a copy of the Catholic Bible.

(b) Services—Participation is active when one marches in an Anglican procession, plays the organ or sings at Y.M.C.A. services, joins in the prayers or responses offered in a Protestant church, etc. (Holy Office, July 6, 1889). Participation is passive if one looks on during a rare visit, or listens by radio to the musical program broadcast from Protestant services, or if one is obliged to attend non-Catholic services habitually, not as a profession of faith, but as a matter of civil duty or of domestic discipline, as happens with soldiers or with inmates of public institutions. Participation is not active if one adores the Blessed Sacrament carried in a schismatical procession which one meets by chance and unavoidably. Examples: Titus belongs to the honorary guard of a state ruler, and has to accompany the latter to non-Catholic services on certain state occasions. Balbus is tutor in a non-Catholic family, and is expected to take his charges to their church and back home on Sundays. Claudia is a maid in a non-Catholic family, and is ordered to hold one of the children while it is being baptized by the non-Catholic minister. In all these cases the presence at the services is purely passive, since the intention of the Catholic present is not to perform any religious duty, but only some civil or domestic service (see IV Kings, v. 18). But, on the other hand, the martyrs during the reigns of Elizabeth and her successors refused to attend the Anglican services, because this was required by law as a sign of conformity to the Established Church—that is, an active presence was prescribed.

972. Cases of participation in religious places, times and objects are as follows:

(a) Places.—Participation is active when one orders one's body to be buried in a sectarian graveyard, when one enters a schismatical or heretical church privately in order to visit the Blessed Sacrament or pray, when one offers up Catholic services in a non-Catholic temple, if these things are looked upon by the public as indications of identity of belief between Catholics and non-Catholics. Participation is merely passive, if one visits non-Catholic places of worship out of curiosity in order to look at the pictures, hear the music or listen to or take part in a political lecture or debate. In case of necessity, the Church permits Catholic services to be performed in the same building as that wherein non-Catholic rites are held, e.g., the Church of the Holy Sepulchre at Jerusalem which is used by various denominations (Holy Office, 12 April, 1704).

(b) Times.—Participation is active if one observes new moons, sabbaths, and days of fast as prescribed in the Old Law.

(c) Objects.—Participation is active if one wears the uniform of a condemned society, the ring or other emblem of Freemasonry, etc., or makes use of other insignia whose sole purpose is to indicate membership in some sect, unless it be evident that these are used for some other purpose (e.g., in order to act a certain part in a play).

973. Cases of participation through attendance at non-Catholic religious instructions are as follows:

(a) Active participation in worship is had when one listens to a preacher, Sunday school teacher, etc., and signifies approval by joining in "Amens" or other acclamations.

(b) Participation is merely passive, if at church or over the radio, one listens out of curiosity, or in order to be able to refute errors, or for the sake of perfecting oneself in diction or eloquence, or of showing respect to a person whose funeral oration is being delivered, etc. But, even though there be no active participation, it will usually be unlawful to listen to these sectarian discourses on account of the danger of perversion to the listener or of scandal to others. Catholics who are scientifically trained and staunch in faith may for good reasons hear sectarian sermons, but the greater number would be disturbed or unsettled (see the principles given above on dangerous books and schools, 854-857, 868). Moreover, even those who have a right to listen to non-Catholic religious talks have to be on their guard against scandal, for outsiders may regard their attention as approval of doctrine or participation in cult, and Catholics not sufficiently instructed may regard their example as an encouragement to imitate (cfr. 979, 981).

974. Participation in non-Catholic assemblages or occasions whose character is of a mixed kind (partly religious and partly non»religious) are permitted by the Church, when due regard is had for avoidance of scandal, perversion, denial of faith, etc.

(a) Some of these occasions are chiefly religious, but are also looked on as family or civic solemnities, such as christenings, weddings, funerals. Hence, it is allowed to assist at the religious part of the occasion in a passive way for the sake of courtesy, or to exercise some function which is looked upon as belonging to the non-religious part of the occasion. Caution must be taken to ensure that the particular sect involved does not consider the exercise of the particular function as participating in the religious aspect of the ceremony. Likewise, on condition that the possibility of scandal, perversion, etc., has been removed, the following functions may be performed. One may act as a witness at the christening of a near relative who is not a Catholic; however, it is forbidden to be a sponsor, even by proxy, at baptisms performed by a heretical minister (Holy Office, decr., May 10, 1770). To be pallbearer or undertaker at a funeral, to be an usher at a wedding, to be an extra bridesmaid, etc., may be permitted. (If the function of best man or maid of honor be considered as merely attendants to the bride or groom, such participation in itself would not be illicit; but since the danger of scandal might often be present, such participation is dangerous. It is lawful for a Catholic pastor to attend the funeral of a non-Catholic friend or relative, provided he does not wear his sacred garb and takes no part in the ceremonies. Canon 1258, §2 establishes the general norm regulative of these cases: a passive or merely material presence may be, for a serious reason, tolerated as a mark of esteem or social courtesy at funerals, weddings, and similar functions, provided there is involved no danger of perversion or scandal; in a doubtful case, the serious reason for this presence must be approved by the local Ordinary.

(b) Other occasions are chiefly non-religious in character, but are also partly religious, or have the appearance of being religious. Such are, for example, the coronation, birthday, wedding, or funeral of a ruler, school commencements, political conventions, patriotic meetings, civil marriage before a magistrate who is also a non-Catholic minister. When these exercises are chiefly non-religious or entirely civil, even though conducted in non-Catholic churches or by non-Catholic ministers, the Church grants permission to participate in them to some extent, if there is sufficient reason.

975. Among the mixed occasions just mentioned are not included such as have an anti-Catholic or anti-religious spirit, such as funerals from which all manifestations of religion are excluded on account of hatred of religion, entertainments held by forbidden societies in which the members are present in regalia, picnics under the auspices of the Orangemen, etc.

976. Coöperation in Religious Activities.—A third danger of making external profession of a false religion is coöperation in activities whose tendency or principles are erroneous (see 944). Coöperation in a false religion is of two kinds, immediate and mediate. (a) Coöperation is immediate, when one takes a part in an act of a false religion itself (e.g., by worshipping an idol). This kind of coöperation was discussed above, as participation or communication (see 956-975). (b) Coöperation is mediate, when one takes part, not in an act of a false religion, but in some other act which is a preparation for a help to the act of a false religion. This is the kind of coöperation we are now considering.

977. Mediate coöperation is of various kinds. (a) It is proximate or remote, according as the preparation or help afforded to false religion is near to or far from the religious act. Thus, to make ready the lights, incense, flowers, etc. in front of an idol is proximate coöperation; to give money to an idolatrous priest or bonze is remote coöperation. (b) Mediate coöperation is material or formal, according as the intention of the coöperator is to share in or help error itself, or merely to help those who are in error, while disapproving of their error. Thus, if one prepares a pagan temple for worship or contributes money towards its maintenance because one's sympathies are with its idolatry, one's coöperation is formal; if one does these things only in order to make a living or to show friendship to an individual pagan, one's coöperation is material. It is clear that formal coöperation is a grave sin against faith, and hence we shall speak now only of material coöperation.

978. The principles governing the lawfulness of material coöperation will be treated at length below in their proper place among the sins opposed to charity. But since, on account of the mixed conditions of society today, there are innumerable cases of material coöperation in religion, it will be useful to state in advance in this place the principles bearing on material coöperation and their application to cases on religion and worship. The principles are the same as those given for an act that has two effects, one good and the other bad. Hence, material coöperation is not lawful, except when the following conditions are present:

(a) The action of him who coöperates must be good in itself or at least indifferent, for of course, if it is evil, it is not lawful. Thus, if a person were to give to one pagan temple objects he had stolen from another temple, his action would be intrinsically sinful on account of the theft. Similarly, if a person were to contribute to a collection list as "sympathizer" with a school for the propagation of atheism or as "beneficiary" from the sacrifices to be offered an idol, his act would be intrinsically sinful as being a promotion of error or superstition, even though he were not really a sympathizer with atheism or a believer in idols.

(b) The intention of him who coöperates must be good; for, if he wills to help a false religion, he is guilty of formal coöperation; if he wills some other wrong end, he is guilty of some other species of sin. Thus, if one who does not believe in idolatry contributes to it on account of sympathy with anti-Christian movements, he is guilty of enmity to the truth.

(c) There must be a reason for the coöperation proportionate to the gravity of the sin which will be committed by others, to the proximity and necessity of the coöperation, and to the obligation which one has of preventing the sin of others. Examples: To contribute to a sect which plots the downfall of legitimate authority is never lawful, for there is no reason of temporal or private good that can be a compensation for the destruction of the public good. To contribute to the building of a Mohammedan mosque does not require so serious a reason as to contribute to the building of a pagan temple, for mosques are not used for idolatry. A graver reason is needed to justify ringing the bell or ushering the people to their seats for a service of false worship than to justify sweeping and dusting the temple the day before the service, for in the former case the coöperation is closer. A greater reason is required to build a house of false worship, when there is no one else to build it, than when there are many others who will gladly build it if one refuses, for in the former case one's coöperation is so necessary that without it the false worship cannot take place, but not so in the latter case. A much more serious reason would be required to justify parents conducting their children to a place of false worship than would be required to justify a public chauffeur in taking passengers thither; for the parents have a special duty to guard the religion of their children.

979. The above principles on mediate coöperation are clear enough, but it is frequently very difficult to apply them on account of the uncertainty as to whether or not a particular act of coöperation is indifferent in itself, or whether a particular reason for coöperation is sufficient. But the following rules will help:

(a) An act is indifferent or good, when it does not tend to evil from its very nature or the circumstances, but has purposes that are not bad. It is bad when either intrinsically (i.e., from its nature) or extrinsically (i.e., from circumstances) it tends necessarily to evil. Examples: A derisory image of Christ and the manual of an obscene cult are intrinsically evil, inasmuch as they necessarily convey error or immorality. To draw up plans for a temple of idolaters in a Christian country would have the appearance of favoring the propagation of idolatry; to work on the construction of a temple in a pagan country where the lending of one's labor is regarded as a sign of acceptance of paganism, to help build a meeting house for a sect that plots the overthrow of government or religion—all these acts are indifferent in themselves (for one may also draw plans and put up walls for good or indifferent purposes), but from the circumstances they are evil in the cases given.

(b) Reasons for coöperation may be ranked as great, greater and greatest according to the kinds of goods that are at stake, and their sufficiency or insufficiency may be determined by measuring them with the gravity of the coöperation that is given. Great reasons are: fear of serious suffering, or of the wrath of husband or other superior, or of loss of an opportunity to make a considerable profit. Greater reasons are: fear of loss of position, or of notable detriment to reputation or fortune, or of severe imprisonment. Among the greatest reasons for coöperation in the worship of a false religion are the following: danger of loss of life or limb, of perpetual imprisonment, of great dishonor, of loss of all one's earthly possessions, of disturbance of the public peace.

980. Cases of coöperation in false religion that occur most frequently are: (a) contributions made to schools, churches, institutions; (b) labor given to buildings and objects of worship or instruction; (c) labor given to acts of worship or instruction.

981. Contributions to false worship are unlawful, even apart from scandal, danger of perversion, and the bad intention of the coöperator in the following cases:

(a) When on account of circumstances the contributions are signs of sympathy with religious errors. Examples: Titus gives many stipends for Masses to a schismatical priest. Balbus, when asked, contributes liberally to a fund for the building of a hall under the auspices of atheists. Caius, without being asked, gives a small donation towards the erection of a pagan temple. Claudius sends in a subscription to the treasury of a political organization whose purpose is anti-religious, and promises to support their ticket.

(b) Contributions, even though they manifest no sympathy with religious error, are unlawful, when there is no reason for the coöperation, or only an insufficient reason. Examples: Caius contributes to a pagan temple for no other reason than that he has not the heart to refuse anyone. Titus advertises constantly in an antireligious paper in order to help his business (cfr. 1530).

982. If there is no bad intention on the part of the contributor, and if the danger of scandal or perversion is excluded, contributions are permitted under the following conditions, of which both must be present:

(a) The contribution must not be a mark of sympathy with religious error. This condition will be fulfilled more readily in countries of mixed religion, where Catholics and non-Catholics have been long associated together, and where non-Catholic denominations are engaged in many things other than the preaching of their doctrines, such as works of benevolence. Example: Balbus contributes at times to the building or maintenance of Protestant orphan asylums, hospitals, and schools, in a locality where these institutions are open to all and a contribution is not regarded as a sign of agreement with sectarian purposes.

(b) There must be a sufficient reason for making the contribution, such as the common good or great private necessity. Examples: Claudius contributes to the building of a non-Catholic church, in order that Catholics may thus obtain exclusive use of a church till then used by Catholics and non-Catholics alike. Titus buys tickets for bazaars, lawn fêtes, oyster suppers, dances, picnics and other entertainments held for the benefit of non-Catholic churches, since, if he does not do this, he will lose trade and his business will be injured.

983. The building of houses of false worship, the production and sale of articles used in false worship, are unlawful also in two cases:

(a) when, on account of circumstances, they are a mark of approval of the false worship. Examples: Christians of Japan were forbidden by the Church to coöperate in the erection of altars or temples to idols, even if threatened with death or exile, and the reason of the prohibition seems to have been in each instance that such work was looked on and demanded as a profession of faith in paganism. Similarly, the construction of non-Catholic edifices in a Catholic country, of a pagan temple in a Christian country, or of an atheistic hall, would be signs of approbation of error. It is difficult to see how one who sells idols to those who request them for purposes of idolatry does not show favor to false worship, although he might be excused if, under threat of great harm, he delivered them with a protest that he was acting under compulsion;

(b) when there is no reason, or no sufficient reason, for coöperation with false worship. Example: Balbus helps to build non-Catholic places of worship for no other reason than that he is asked to do so, or that he receives good pay.

984. Building non-Catholic temples or furnishing the appurtenances of worship, scandal and other evil being avoided, are lawful under two conditions as above:

(a) the work must not be regarded as a sign of approval of false worship. Examples: The Church has permitted Christians to assist in the construction of Mohammedan mosques, when this was done unwillingly by them and under compulsion. The manufacture of statues of Buddha or of other idols is not a sign that one approves of idolatry, because these objects have legitimate uses, such as adornment of palaces or art galleries. Similarly, the production and distribution of emblems of a non-Catholic sect or secret society is regarded as being in itself an indifferent sect, on account of the various uses to which such objects may be put;

(b) there must be a reason sufficiently grave for doing this kind of work. Hence, a greater reason is needed to build a pagan temple than a Mohammedan mosque, and graver reason to build a mosque than an heretical place of worship; likewise, greater reason is required to coöperate as architect than as hirer and supervisor of labor, greater reason to coöperate as supervisor of labor than as stonecutter, bricklayer, etc.; greater reason is required to justify selling than making idols; greater reason to justify selling altar cloths and breads for the Lord's Supper than for selling pews and stained glass windows. Examples: Since lights, benches, bells, tables, cloths, etc., are not necessarily intended for direct use in acts of worship, a sufficient reason for selling them to non-Catholic churches is the profit that will be made. But, since vestments and chalices pertain directly to worship, a more serious reason is required for selling them than business gains.

985. Making the preparations for non-Catholic services is unlawful in the two cases given above, that is, when there is approval or insufficient reason. (a) If the work manifests an approval of the services, it is unlawful. Such positions as sexton, sacristan, usher, beadle, church-warden, and trustee, imply recognition of the worship or membership in the congregation, although the same does not seem to be true of membership in the civil corporation of a church, nor of external offices such as janitor, caretaker, and attorney. Examples: Balba, an Anglican who is sick, wishes her minister to bring her communion. She asks her nurse, Titia, who is a Catholic, to telephone the minister to bring communion, and also directs Titia to prepare an altar and assist the minister on his arrival by lighting the candles, making responses, etc. Titia may not consent, for such immediate coöperation would mean approval of and participation in Anglican rites. Claudius, a Catholic, is hired by the minister of a Protestant church to take care of the yard and garden about the church and parsonage. Sometimes the minister asks Claudius to play the chimes in his church tower which call the people to the services. The gardening work is indifferent, but the playing of the chimes seems at least an unlawful coöperation, since it is an invitation to non-Catholic worship.

(b) If there is no sufficient reason for the work, it is unlawful. Examples: Gaia, a Catholic, acts as scrubwoman and cleaner in a schismatical church for no other reason than friendship for members of the altar society. On certain feast days her husband, Caius, a Catholic, takes pilgrims to the schismatical church in a bus, only because he makes considerable profit.

986. Making preparations for non-Catholic services, scandal and other danger being avoided, is lawful when the two conditions given above are present. (a) Hence, the preparations must contain no indication of approval of the services. Examples: If Titia, the nurse mentioned in the previous paragraph, called in an Anglican nurse to receive and fulfill the orders of Balba, she would show that she did not herself approve of the rites, and her act would be indifferent in itself. If she could not avoid

telephoning the minister without serious consequences, it would not be unlawful for her to tell him that Balba wished him to call. She might even in great necessity prepare the table herself, but could take no part in the rite. The acts of telling the minister that a visit from him was desired and of preparing the table would not be, in the circumstances, approving of the rite that followed. If Claudius mentioned in the foregoing paragraph wound up the clock in the church tower, or rang the bell at certain times to indicate the hour of the day, his acts would be indifferent, since they have no necessary reference to worship.

(b) There must be a reason sufficiently grave for engaging in the work that prepares for the services. Examples: If Caia mentioned in the preceding paragraph were in great poverty and could find no other employment, this would be a sufficient reason for her coöperation. Likewise, if her husband drove a bus that carried passengers to whatever destination they desired, and he could not refuse to let them off at the church without being dismissed or causing other like inconveniences, he would have sufficient reason for his coöperation.

987. The Commandment of External Profession of Faith.—The third commandment of faith (mentioned in 918) has been considered so far in its negative aspect—that is, as a prohibition against the denial of truth or the profession of error. It remains to consider it in its affirmative aspect—that is, as a precept of profession of faith or of denial of error.

988. The ways of making profession of faith are various: (a) It is made implicitly, if one performs acts that suppose faith; explicitly, if one declares in words one's internal belief. Thus, a Catholic professes his faith implicitly by observing the precepts of the Church; explicitly, by reciting before others an act of faith or the Creed.

(b) The declaration of one's faith in words is made in ordinary ways, if one affirms it to others, privately or publicly, or if one teaches it or defends it in debate; it is made solemnly, if it is recited according to a prescribed form as a ceremony. Thus, a Catholic who answers to a questioner that he is a Catholic, or who explains the truths of faith to an inquirer, or who replies to the objections of an unbeliever, makes an ordinary profession of faith; one who reads before the bishop or other designated authority a formula prescribed by the Church, makes solemn profession of faith. The solemn profession of faith is usually made before the altar, on which candles are lighted; and he who makes profession of faith kneels before the authority who receives it. Sometimes witnesses are present and the profession is signed.

(c) The solemn profession of faith is sometimes an abjuration (i.e., a declaration of one's adherence to the faith of the Church and a recantation of previous errors); sometimes it is a declaration or oath that one rejects errors or accepts truths. Thus, converts before reception into the Church abjure the errors they formerly held; officials in the Church before assuming authority make a profession of faith in which they reprobate Modernism and express their belief in the Creed and the teachings of the Church.

989. The existence of a divine precept of profession of faith is proved from revelation and intrinsic reasons, as follows:

(a) "If thou confess with thy mouth the Lord Jesus, and believe in thy heart that God hath raised Him up from the dead, thou shalt be saved. For with the heart we believe unto justice, but with the mouth confession is made unto salvation" (Rom., x. 9, 10). This precept obliges under grave sin, since it is required for salvation.

(b) The first reason for external profession of faith is the honor of God; for it is a mark of disrespect to God to be ashamed or afraid to acknowledge oneself as a believer in His Word or a witness to its truth, on account of what others may think or say or do.

(c) A second reason for the external profession of faith is one's own good. It is well known that faith is strengthened by external acts, and that it grows weak and decays among Catholics who have no priests or churches or means of practising their faith.

(d) A third reason for profession of faith is the good of others, for the confession of faith is an encouragement to those who are strong in faith, an example to those whose faith is weak, and a light to those who have not the faith.

990. The divine precept of profession of faith, since it is affirmative, does not call for fulfillment at every moment. It obliges only at those times when the honor of God, the Revealer of Truth, or the needs of our neighbor, who is called to the truth, demand that one declare externally one's internal belief. (a) The honor of God demands a confession of faith, when a refusal to give it signifies that one does not accept the truths revealed by God, that revelation contains error, etc. (b) The needs of our neighbor demand a confession of faith, when a refusal to give it will prevent another from embracing the faith, or will cause him to lose it or give up its practices, etc.

991. The honor of God or the good of the neighbor calls for an external profession of faith at the following times: (a) when a person is joining the Church or returning to it, for the Church is a visible society and membership in it should be visible; (b) when a Catholic is interrogated about his faith, for here the honor of God and the good of others require that he be not ashamed of Christ or His Words (Luke, ix. 26), and that he should cause his light to shine before men (Matt., v. 16); (c) when a Catholic is in the company of others who are ridiculing or calumniating the faith, and a protest is looked for from him on account of his authority, knowledge, etc.

992. The profession of faith made by one who is joining the Church must be external, but the same publicity is not necessary for every case.

(a) Secret profession of faith is made when the reception of a convert is known only to himself and the priest who received him. This is permitted only in grave necessity, when the spiritual good of the convert requires it, and no injury is done to the honor of God or the Welfare of the neighbor. Example: Titus is dying and wishes to be baptized, but for an important reason he is unwilling to have the fact of his conversion disclosed. Father Balbus, therefore, baptizes without witnesses.

(b) Private profession of faith is made when the reception of a convert is made before the priest and two witnesses, but the fact of the conversion is not made known to others on account of circumstances. This is permitted only for a short time and for serious reasons (see 932, 993), as the task of concealing one's faith for a long time is most difficult and is dangerous to faith itself. Example: Caius is a pagan who wishes to become a Catholic, but is kept back on account of dangers from his fellow-pagans, who will persecute him as an apostate. He, therefore, asks to be received as a secret Christian, with liberty to profess no religion externally. This may be permitted for a time, until Caius can move to some other place, but it cannot be permitted permanently.

(c) Public profession of faith is made when the reception of a convert is made before the priest and two witnesses, and the convert thereafter makes it known that he is a Catholic by attending Mass, receiving the Sacraments, etc. This kind of profession of faith is ordinarily required, but there is no law making it necessary for a convert to publish the news of his conversion.

993. A difficult case occurs when one who wishes to become a convert is unable to make public profession of Catholicity without suffering very great detriment, and is unable to make private profession without continuing in external practices of the non-Catholic religion. An example of this would be a non-Catholic girl who is threatened with destitution by her parents if she becomes a Catholic openly, and who knows that she will be forced to go to church with them if she becomes a Catholic privately. There are three courses in such a case: (a) public profession of Catholicism at once could be advised if the party showed signs of a special divine call and of a heroism equal to the difficulties the public profession would entail; (b) private profession of Catholicism could be tolerated for a time, if the party was of such age and circumstances as to appear able to cope successfully with the temptations and perplexities that beset this course; (c) delay of Baptism until things take a better turn would be the most prudent plan, if the deprivation of spiritual advantages would in the long run prove a lesser evil than the inconveniences of public or private profession of Catholicism.

994. Examination about one's religious status refers either to one's faith, or to something not necessarily connected with faith. (a) When a person is examined about his faith (e.g., whether he is a Catholic, whether he believes in the doctrine of the Real Presence, or in Papal Infallibility), profession of faith is obligatory, if its omission is

equivalent to denial. (b) When he is examined about something not necessarily connected with faith, denial or concealment of the truth would not be denial of faith, and concealment might be lawful, if the question were unfair. Evasion would be sinful, if the denial or concealment contained a lie or caused scandal. Examples: If a missionary in England or Ireland in the sixteenth century had refused to admit that he was a priest or religious, or a layman had refused to confess that he had harbored a priest in his house or had assisted at Mass, these denials would not necessarily contain a denial of the faith.

995. Examination about one's faith is made either by a private person or by public authority.

(a) When a person is questioned about his religious belief by a private person, he is not bound by reason of the question itself to make a profession of his faith, for a private person has no authority to call upon one in the capacity of a solemn and public witness; but he is bound to make a profession of faith by reason of circumstances, if the honor of God or the good of his neighbor requires that he declare his belief. Examples: Titius is known as a very iniquisitive and meddlesome character, who is continually asking others about their personal affairs and putting silly questions. Wherefore, those who know him are accustomed to pay no attention to his questions, or to tell him to mind his business, or to give him some humorous reply. One day Titius asked Balbus, whom he knew very well to be a Catholic: "What is your religion?" Balbus retorted: "What is yours?" and left him. Caius is studying Christianity with a view to embracing it, and asks Sempronius' opinion on miracles. Sempronius, fearing the ridicule of some others present if he admits belief in miracles, says that he knows nothing about that subject. Balbus had a right to deny an answer to his questioner; but Sempronius should have replied for the edification of Caius and the honor of God.

(b) When a person is questioned about his religious belief by public authority, his obligation to make a profession of faith is certain, if the questioner has the right according to law to ask the question, and if it is made to one individually and out of hatred of the faith; for to this case apply the words of Christ: "You shall be brought before governors and kings for My sake, for a testimony to them and to the Gentiles" (Matt., x. 18).

996. In the following cases, one is not bound to confession of faith on account of the public authority that puts the question, although one may be bound on account of the circumstances:

(a) When the question is not put to an individual, but to a whole community, by a law which requires them in time of persecution to deliver themselves up as Christians or Catholics, there is no obligation to comply with this law, since it is unjust, and neither the honor of God nor the good of others requires one to make the profession of faith it demands (see 377, 552).

(b) When the question is put to an individual by one in authority but contrary to the law of the land, there is no obligation to answer. Thus, if according to civil law the magistrates have no right to examine about matters of conscience and one of them should nevertheless do so, the party questioned could treat the question as out of order and deny any answer.

(c) When the question is made according to law, but does not proceed from hatred of the faith, one is not obliged positively to profess one's faith, unless the omission would seem to those present to be a denial of faith. Thus, a person might remain silent, or say that he did not wish to answer, that he did not wish to say what his belief was, etc., and in the circumstances it would seem that he would not be denying his faith, but merely for some reason refusing to discuss it when he thought there was no necessity.

997. The third case mentioned above (see 991), in which one is obliged to profess one's faith publicly, is when the faith is. being attacked in one's presence. The honor of God and the good of the neighbor then require one to speak out. (a) Thus, if the doctrines of the faith are being blasphemed or ridiculed, one should defend them, if one is able. Otherwise, one should protest or leave the company, if this will be advantageous to religion. (b) If sacred things are being profaned, one should resist physically, if one is able to prevent what is going on.

998. Debates on religion between Catholics and non-Catholics are not in themselves wrong, but as a rule they are useless and inexpedient.

(a) That such debates are not essentially wrong, is clear from the fact that a suitable defender of the faith is able by argumentation to show the misconceptions that are entertained about the faith and the fallacious objections that are made against it. This is honorable to God and profitable to the neighbor: "Saul confounded the Jews that dwelt at Damascus, affirming that this is the Christ …. He spoke also to the Gentiles and disputed with the Greeks" (Acts, ix. 22, 29).

(b) That controversy is generally unprofitable is a matter of experience. Religious debates often lead to bitterness, and seldom effect conversions. There is, moreover, an ever-present danger that the sophistry or eloquence of an adversary may give him the appearance of victory to the discredit of the faith, for even a foolish person can raise difficulties which only a wise man can answer.

999. Consequently the rule governing religious disputations is that they should be avoided, unless ecclesiastical authority deems them useful at times. (a) If no provocation is offered, or if no good seems likely to result from a debate, it should be avoided. (b) If one is attacked and it seems that the honor of God and the good of souls will be served by a debate, then capable and prudent speakers are permitted by the Church to defend the faith, provided permission is secured from the Holy See, or, in case of urgency, from the local Ordinary (Canon 1325, §3). The prescriptions of this Canon were reaffirmed recently by the Holy Office and applied especially to "ecumenical" conventions convoked to promote church unity. Catholics, both lay and clerical, may in no way be present at such meetings without the previous consent of the Holy See (Holy Office, Monitum, June 5, 1948). See Appendix II.

1000. The divine precept of profession of faith so far considered obliges on account of the virtue of faith itself, that is, on account of the external honor or service due to the Word of God. There is also a divine precept of profession of faith which obliges on account of other virtues that may require such a profession of faith to be made (e.g., on account of charity or justice). The omission of the profession of faith in these cases, however, is not a sin against faith, but against the other virtues, and should be confessed as such.

(a) Justice requires a profession of faith when, by reason of his office, a person has the duty of teaching others in the faith, for to teach the faith is to manifest one's own belief in it. Hence, bishops and other pastors are obliged to preach: "Woe is unto me, if I preach not the Gospel" (I Cor., ix. 16); and their teaching is a manifestation of faith: "Having the same spirit of faith, as it is written: I believed, for which cause I have spoken; we also believe, and therefore we speak also" (II Cor., iv., 13).

(b) Charity requires a profession of faith when a person has not the office of teacher, but has a suitable opportunity to impart instruction to one who is in great ignorance about religion. For, as charity requires one to perform corporal works of mercy for the suffering and destitute, so it requires one to perform spiritual works of mercy for the spiritually indigent, such as to instruct the ignorant, to counsel the doubtful. Thus, a lay person who can prudently do so (the circumstances of time, place, person, etc., being duly considered), ought in charity to instruct in faith and morals the neglected children around him.

1001. One is not bound to give instruction about matters of faith or morals when this would lead to more harm than good; but misrepresentation must be avoided.

(a) The purpose of instruction is to fulfill the will of God and to benefit others; therefore, if these ends are not obtained but rather defeated by an instruction, it should be omitted. The truth is always good in itself, but its communication may not be expedient on account of the recipient, who, being immature, may be harmed by the wrong impression he will receive, or who, being badly disposed, may use knowledge as a means to wrongdoing. Strong meat should not be given to infants (Heb., vi. 11-14); pearls should not be cast before swine (Matt., vii. 6). Examples: The mysteries of the faith (e.g., transubstantiation), should be explained with caution to those who are not well instructed, lest they be overwhelmed with the brightness and misunderstand. Difficult matters (such as predestination) or dangerous subjects (such as sex duties) should not be discussed indiscriminately with all kinds of persons. It is not right to instruct those who are in ignorance of their duty, if this is not absolutely necessary and one foresees that instruction will not prevent them from continuing in evil ways but will only add to their guilt. It is wrong to put the Bible into the hands of those who will use it for bad purposes.

(b) Misrepresentation or suppression is a lie, and in matters of doctrine a denial of faith; hence, it is never lawful. The rule to be followed, therefore, in teaching the faith is that one communicate the same doctrine to all, but according to the capacity of his hearers—to some in outline and to others more fully. This was the method of Christ, who "with many parables spoke to them the word, according as they were able to hear" (Mark, iv. 33).

1002. The Church has the duty not only of keeping the faith untarnished among Catholics, but also of spreading it among non-Catholics, Protestants, Jews and infidels, as far as circumstances will allow. For God "Will have all men to be saved, and to come to the knowledge of the truth" (I Tim., ii. 4). Those, therefore, who assist missionary work for unbelievers at home or abroad, do a work thrice blest, for (a) it is a thanksgiving offering to God, testifying our appreciation of the gift of faith which we have received from Him, (b) it is a work of charity to ourselves, for by helping others to receive the faith we strengthen our own faith, and (c) it is an act of supreme mercy to those who are sitting in darkness and the shadow of death.

1003, In addition to the divine precepts, there are also ecclesiastical laws prescribing profession of faith.

(a) Ecclesiastical precepts of profession of faith for various officials are contained in Canon 1406 and in the *Sacrorum Antistitum* of Pius X (September 1, 1910), and Canon 2403 decrees that those who contumaciously refuse to make the profession of faith of Canon 1406 may be deprived of their office. Converts to the faith who are received without absolute Baptism make an abjuration (Holy Office, July 20, 1859), and persons who have incurred excommunication on account of apostasy, heresy or schism are absolved in the external forum after juridical abjuration (Canon 2314).

(b) The purpose of these ecclesiastical laws is to prevent the acceptance of spiritual or temporal jurisdiction or authority in the Church, or the commission of teaching or the benefits of membership by those who are unbelievers. Hence, the purpose is grave, and the laws themselves are held to bind under grave sin.

(c) The persons bound by these ecclesiastical laws are both ecclesiastics and laymen, namely, those who are about to be received into or reconciled with the Church, and those who are about to be admitted to some dignity, order, office or function (such as candidates for the ranks of Cardinal, bishop, canon, parish priest, religious superior, professor, preacher, confessor, doctor, etc).

(d) The form of the profession of faith is the Tridentine or Pian given in the Bull of Pius IV, *Injunctum Nobis*, of November 13, 1564, with additions referring to the Vatican Council. The oath against Modernism prescribed in the *Sacrorum Antistitum* of Pius X, of September 1, 1910, is also obligatory.

(e) The times when these professions of faith must be made are at admission into the Church and at the reception or renewal of an office.

1004. The affirmative precepts of profession of faith, divine and ecclesiastical, oblige only at the proper time and place, and therefore on other occasions one is not obliged to make profession of faith. (a) Hence, one may avoid a profession of faith by evading interrogation in time of persecution—for example, through the payment of money to be exempted from examination, or through flight. As these acts indicate that the person is unwilling to deny his faith, but has reasons for wishing to preserve his life or to avoid the danger of apostasy, they are not of themselves unlawful, and may be a duty. (b) One may omit a profession of faith by concealing one's religion, when prudence calls for concealment rather than publication.

1005. Flight in time of persecution is lawful or unlawful according to circumstances, since in itself it is something indifferent, being simply the act of moving from one place to another.

(a) Flight is unlawful, if one's circumstances are such that one will do an injury to justice or charity by departure. Hence, a pastor would sin against justice if he fled in time of persecution, leaving his flock who stood in need of his presence: "The good shepherd giveth his life for his sheep. But the hireling and he that is not the shepherd, seeth the wolf coming, and leaveth the sheep and flieth" (John, x. 11, 12). Hence also, one who has no care of souls but whose presence is necessary to a persecuted community should prefer out of charity their spiritual good to his own bodily safety: "We ought to lay down our lives for the brethren" (I John, iii. 16).

(b) Flight is necessary, if one's circumstances are such that one will do an injury to justice or charity by remaining. Hence, if a pastor's life is necessary for his flock, while his absence can be supplied by others who will take his place, justice to his subjects requires that he save his life for their sake. Thus, for the good of souls St. Peter escaped from prison (Acts, xii. 17 sqq.); St. Paul fled from Damascus (Acts, ix. 24, 25); our Lord Himself hid when the Jews took up stones to cast at Him (John, viii. 59). Similarly, if a person is very fearful lest his courage may fail him if he is brought before the persecutors, charity to self requires that he take flight so as to escape the danger of apostasy.

(c) Flight is permissible, if there is no duty to remain and no duty to depart: "When they shall persecute you in this city, flee into another" (Matt., x. 23). Hence, if one's presence is useful but not necessary in time of persecution, it is lawful for one to flee. Some authorities hold that the desertion of Jesus by the disciples during the Passion was not sinful flight.

1006. To refuse to flee when flight is permissible, is usually not advisable, for this is dangerous for most persons. It would be advisable, however, if a person had strong and prudent confidence of his victory, had the right intention, and used the means to prepare himself for the struggle.

1007. Concealment of one's faith is lawful, if the requisite conditions are present.

(a) Thus, it is not lawful to conceal one's faith at times when a profession of it is called for by divine or ecclesiastical law (see 991, 1003); at other times it is lawful. Example: Titus is travelling in a country where there are no Catholic churches, and where no one ever asks him about his religion. He never tells anyone what he is.

(b) It is not lawful to conceal one's faith from a dishonest motive. Example: If Titus conceals his religion in order not to be unjustly discriminated against, his motive is good; but if he wishes to be taken for a non-Catholic, his motive is evil.

(c) It is not lawful to conceal one's faith in a sinful way. Example: If the means of concealment employed by Titus imply deception or denial of the faith (such as lying about his origin and active participation in non-Catholic worship), he is guilty of sinful concealment. But, if the means employed are permissible (such as silence about himself, omission of grace before and after meals, eating meat on Fridays in virtue of dispensation, etc.), his method of concealment is not sinful.

1008. Generally speaking, concealment of one's religion is not advisable. (a) The reasons for concealment are often imaginary, rather than real. We see that Catholics who are not ashamed of their religion, or afraid to have it known that they practise it, are respected for their sincerity and conscientiousness even in bigoted regions, while on the contrary those who are apologetic or who do not live up to their religion are looked down on as cowards or hypocrites. (b) The means employed for concealment will cause endless doubts and scruples, for it is often difficult to decide what means are lawful and what unlawful.

Art. 4: THE VIRTUE OF HOPE

(*Summa Theologica*, II-II, qq. 17-22.)

1009. Definition.—The word "hope" is variously used. (a) In a wide and improper sense, it signifies the expectation of some wished-for evil, or desire without expectation. Hence, colloquially one hopes for misfortune to another (hope of a future evil), or that another has succeeded or is in good health (hope of past or present good), or that some unlooked-for fortune will turn up (hope without expectation). (b) In its strict and proper sense, hope signifies the expectation of some desired good in the future. Thus, one hopes to pass an examination, or to recover from illness.

1010. Hope, strictly understood, is of various kinds. (a) It is an emotion or an affection, according as it proceeds from the sensitive or the rational appetite. The emotion of hope is an inclination of the irascible appetite to possess some object known through the senses and apprehended as good and attainable, and is found both in man and in the brutes. The affection of hope is a spiritual inclination, tending to good as known through the reason.

(b) Hope is either natural or supernatural, according as it tends either to goods that are temporal and within the power of man to acquire, or to goods that are eternal and above the unaided powers of creatures. It is in this latter sense that hope is now taken.

1011. Supernatural hope is understood, sometimes in a wide sense, sometimes in a strict sense. (a) In a wide sense, it is used objectively to designate the object, material or formal, of hope. Thus, St. Paul is speaking of the material object of hope (i.e., of the things hoped for), when he says: "Hope that is seen is not hope" (Rom., viii. 24), "Looking for the blessed hope" (Tit., ii. 13); while the Psalmist is speaking of the formal object of hope (i.e., the motive of hope), when he says: "Thou hast been my hope, a tower of strength against the face of the enemy" (Ps. lx. 4). (b) In a strict sense, hope is used subjectively to designate the act or habit of hope. The act of hope is spoken of in the following texts: "We are saved by hope" (Rom., viii. 24); "Rejoicing in hope" (Rom., vii. 12). The habit of hope is indicated in these verses from Job and St. Paul: "This my hope is laid up in my bosom" (Job, xix. 27); "There remain faith, hope, charity, these three" (I Cor., xiii. 13). Hope is now taken in the strict sense, as a virtue or infused habit, from which proceed supernatural acts.

1012. The virtue of hope is defined: "An infused habit, by which we confidently expect to obtain, through the help of God, the reward of everlasting life."

(a) It is "an infused habit." These words express the genus to which hope belongs, and they set it apart from the emotion and the affection of hope, as well as from any acquired habit of hoping for purely natural goods. A natural virtue of hope, strengthening the will with reference to natural happiness, is not necessary in any state of man, fallen or unfallen, for the will does not stand in need of a superadded virtue with respect to those things that fall within its proper sphere of action.

(b) Hope is a habit "by which we expect, etc." These words express the specific subjective elements of hope, that is, the powers of the soul in which it resides and the kinds of acts it performs.

(c) "Through the help of God." These words express the formal object or motive of hope.

(d) "The rewards of eternal life." These words express the material object of hope, that is, the thing that is hoped for.

1013. There is a general similarity between the virtue of hope and natural hope as regards their objects and acts.

(a) Natural hope is the result of a love of some good, and so differs from fear, which is the dread of some evil. Similarly, the virtue of hope springs from a love of heavenly goods (Rom., viii. 24, 25).

(b) Natural hope has to do with a good that is absent, and it is therefore desire, not enjoyment. Similarly, the virtue of hope looks forward to goods not as yet attained: "We hope for that which we see not, we wait for it with patience" (Rom, viii. 25).

(c) Natural hope, unlike mere desire, seeks a good whose attainment is not certain or easy, and hence it presupposes courage. Similarly, the virtue of hope demands strength of soul: "Do ye manfully and let your heart be strengthened, all ye that hope in the Lord" (Ps. xxx. 25).

(d) Natural hope tends towards an objective, which, while difficult, is not impossible; hence, it expects with confidence, for, when an object of desire is impossible, one does not hope for it, but despairs. The virtue of hope also is confident: "Hold fast the glory and confidence of hope unto the end" (Heb. iii. 6).

1014. Christian hope is superior to natural hope, because it is a supernatural virtue.

(a) It is a virtue, since its acts are commanded by God, and through it the will is directed to its beatitude and the secure means of realizing its lofty aspirations: "I have inclined my heart to do Thy justifications for ever, for the reward" (Ps. cxviii. 112); "Trust in the Lord, and do good" (Ps, xxxvi. 3).

(b) Christian hope is a supernatural virtue, since through it man is sanctified and saved: "I (Wisdom) am the mother of holy hope" (Ecclus., xxiv. 24); God "hath regenerated us into a lively hope" (I Pet., i. 3); "We are saved by hope" (Rom., viii. 24); "Everyone that hath this hope in Him sanctifieth himself" (I John, iii. 3).

1015. Though hope seeks its own reward, it is not therefore mercenary or egotistic. Experience shows that hope produces idealism and self-sacrifice, while the lack of it leads to engrossment in the things of time and sense and to selfishness. (a) Thus, the hope of the just man is not separated from charity, and hence he loves God above all,and his neighbor as himself: "I have inclined my heart to do Thy justifications forever, for the reward" (Ps. cxviii. 112). (b) The hope of the sinner is a preparation for charity, since he must desire charity as a means to the beatitude he wishes: "He that hopeth in the Lord shall be healed" (Prov., xxviii. 25).

1016. Just as faith is divided into living and dead faith, so hope is divided into animated and inanimated hope. (a) Animated hope is that to which is joined the state of grace and charity, and which is thereby perfect as a virtue and meritorious. This hope is stronger, because we hope more confidently from friends. An act of animated hope is more perfect when commanded by the virtue of charity, less perfect when not so commanded—that is, he who makes an act of hope out of love of God performs a better work than he who makes an act of hope out of some other motive (such as self-encouragement). (b) Inanimated hope is that to which the state of grace and charity is not joined, and which therefore is an imperfect virtue and not meritorious.

1017. The following divisions of hope made by the Quietists are not admissible:

(a) The division of hope into natural hope (which seeks its own good, and which is permitted to the ordinary faithful) and supernatural hope (which is entirely disinterested, and which is necessary for the perfect) contains Rigorism; for since natural hope is of no avail towards justification or for merit, it would follow that without disinterested love of God one could not obtain forgiveness, nor could an act be meritorious.

(b) The division of hope into two supernatural species, the one disinterested (which desires heavenly goods for the glory of God alone) and the other interested (which desires heavenly goods for the advantage of self), is useless; for acts of disinterested love belong to charity, not to hope (Denz., 1327-1349).

1018. The Object of Hope.—By the object of hope we mean three things: (a) the good that is hoped for (material object, the end which is intended); (b) the person for whom that good is hoped (the end for whom); (c) the ground or foundation of hope (formal object).

1019. The material object of hope is twofold, namely, the primary object, which is desired for its own sake, and the secondary, which is desired on account of the primary object.

(a) The primary object of hope is God Himself, the infinite good, considered as our Last End and Beatitude (Ps. lxxii. 25). Connoted in this object is the beatific vision, the finite act by means of which the creature attains to the possession of God. The primary object of our hope is the imperishable crown (I Cor., ix. 25), glory (Col., i. 27), the glory of the children of God (Rom., v. 2), salvation (I Thess., v. 8), eternal life (Tit., i. 2), entrance into the holy of holies (Heli, x. 19, 23), the inheritance incorruptible and undefiled that cannot fade, reserved in heaven (I Pet., i. 4), the vision of God (I John, iii. 3). It is this object especially that distinguishes supernatural from natural hope (I Cor., xv. 19). "From God," says St. Thomas (II-II, q. 17, a. 2), "we should expect nothing less than God Himself."

(b) The secondary object of hope embraces all those created things that assist one to attain one's Last End. We may hope for all those things for which we may pray, as St. Augustine remarks.

1020. The primary object of hope includes: (a) essential beatitude, that is, the beatific vision; (b) accessory beatitude, that is, all resultant joys, such as glory of soul and body, the companionship of the Saints, security from harm, and the like.

1021. The secondary object of hope includes: (a) spiritual goods, such as graces; (b) temporal goods, such as health and the means that will enable us, at least indirectly, to work for the life to come and acquire merit; (c) deliverance from evils that would hinder spiritual goods; (d) all that promotes one's salvation, such as labors for God.

1022. The person for whom eternal life is hoped may be either oneself or one's neighbor. (a) Absolutely speaking (i.e., apart from the supposition of friendship towards a neighbor), a person can hope only for himself; for the salvation of others is not attained by him, but by them; and thus, if there is no bond of affection, it cannot arouse in him that feeling of courageous confidence which belongs to hope. (b) Accidentally (i.e., on the supposition of friendship or charity towards others), one can hope for them; for love makes a person regard the good of others as his own. Thus, St. Paul is hopeful for the perseverance of the Philippians (Phil., i. 6), and he labors for the Corinthians that his hope for them may be steadfast (II Cor., i. 7).

1023. The formal object of hope is twofold, namely, the primary object, which is the principal cause that effects our salvation, and the secondary object, which is a secondary or instrumental cause of salvation. (a) The primary motive of hope is God Himself, the Author of salvation, and hence it is said: "Cursed be the man that trusteth in man" (Jer, xvii. 5). (b) The secondary motive of hope are creatures by whom one is assisted in obtaining the means for salvation (such as the Saints, who aid us by their intercessions). Thus, in the *Salve Regina*, our Lady is addressed as "our hope." The merits of Christ and our own merits, since they are instruments used by God, are motives of hope.

1024. On what divine attribute is the virtue of hope based?

(a) Essentially, hope is based on God's character of omnipotent helper; for the specific and differentiating note of this virtue is its courageous confidence, and this, in view of the surpassing height one expects to attain and the feebleness of all created efforts, must rely on the assistance of One who is equal to the task: "The Lord is my rock and my strength. God is my strong One, in Him will I trust" (II Kings, xxii. 2, 3); "You have hoped in the Lord Mighty forever" (Is., xxvi. 4); "The name of the Lord is a strong tower; the just runneth to it and shall be exalted" (Prov. xviii. 10).

(b) Secondary (i.e., as regards acts that it presupposes, or that are connected with it), hope is concerned with other divine attributes.

Thus, a person does not hope unless he first believes that God has promised beatitude and that He is true to His promises, unless he regards beatitude as something desirable; and so he who hopes has placed his dependence on the loyalty of God to His given word, and on the desirability of God as the prize of life's efforts: "Let us hold fast the confession of our hope without wavering, for He is faithful that hath promised" (Heb., x. 23); "Unto the hope of life everlasting, which God, who lieth not, hath promised before the times of the world" (Tit., i. 2); "The Lord is my portion, therefore will I wait for Him" (Lam., iii. 24); "Fear not, I am thy reward, exceeding great" (Gen., xv. 1). Just as faith presupposes a beginning of belief and a pious inclination towards it, so does hope presuppose faith and the love of God, as He is our beatitude.

1025. Omnipotent divine help as the foundation of hope can be understood in two senses:

(a) It may be taken for some created help, that is, for some gift of God possessed by us (such as habitual or actual grace, merits, virtues, etc). It is not in this sense that divine help is called the motive of hope; for even a sinner can and should hope, and the just man's merits, while they are dispositions for beatitude, are not a principal cause that will conduct him to it.

(b) This divine help may be taken for uncreated help, that is, for the act by which God confers His gifts upon us. In this sense only is divine aid the basis of hope. For if a person is asked why he is confident of salvation, he will not answer, "Because I am in the state of grace and do good works," but "Because I know that God will help me."

1026. The divine perfections included in the title of helper now given to God are:

(a) essentially, the almighty power of God; for this is the immediate and sufficient reason for the confident expectation that one will at last possess the same object of felicity as God Himself. The higher and more difficult the goal one sets before oneself, the greater must be the resources on which one counts for success;

(b) secondarily, these perfections include the infinite kindness of God; for it is the goodness of God that prompts Him to employ His omnipotence in assisting creatures to attain their Last End. Man has hope, therefore, of attaining supreme felicity, because he relies on supreme power to aid him, while this supreme power aids him, because it is directed by infinite goodness and mercy. Thus, the Psalmist says: "I have trusted in Thy mercy" (Ps. xii. 6). Just as faith rests proximately on the reliability of God and remotely on His perfection of being, so hope rests proximately on God's almighty power and radically on His goodness and perfection.

1027. The Excellence of Hope.—Hope is a theological virtue, and is therefore superior to the moral virtues.

(a) It is a theological virtue, inasmuch as it tends immediately to God Himself. As was said above (see 1019, 1023), we hope for God and we hope in God: "In God is my salvation and my glory. He is the God of my help, and my hope is in God" (Ps. lxi. 8); "What is my hope? Is it not the Lord?" (Ps. xxxviii. 8); "In Thee, O Lord, have I hoped" (Ps. xxx. 1). Hence, the Apostle numbers hope along with the other theological virtues (I Cor., xiii. 13). "By faith the house of God receives its foundations, by hope it is reared, by charity it is completed" (St. Augustine, Serm. xxvii., 1).

(b) The two moral virtues that most resemble hope are longsuffering and magnanimity, for the former is the expectation of good that is distant, while the latter is the readiness to encounter difficulties in the quest of high ideals. But these two virtues belong to courage, rather than to hope; for the goods they seek are finite, and the difficulty they encounter is external struggle, whereas the good which hope seeks is infinite, and the difficulty lies in the very greatness of that good.

1028. There are various points of view from which virtues may be compared one with another.

(a) One virtue is prior to another in duration, when it precedes the latter in time. Thus, the natural virtues that pagans have before their conversion are prior in duration to the supernatural virtues that are received in Baptism.

(b) One virtue is prior to another by nature, or in the order of generation, when it is the necessary preparation or disposition for that other, which essentially presupposes it. Thus, the intellectual virtues are naturally prior to justice, for a man cannot will to give others their due, unless he first knows that this is his duty.

(c) One virtue is prior to another virtue in excellence as a habit, when it has an object that is more elevated and comprehensive, and when it is fitted to be the guide of the other virtue. For the standard of comparison of habits must be taken from the objects to which they tend, and from which they derive their specific character (see 134). Thus, the habit of philosophizing is in itself more noble than the habit of accumulating wealth, for truth is better than money.

(d) One virtue is prior to another in excellence according to the general concept of virtue, when it does more to set the will right. For the standard of comparison then is to be taken from the influence exercised on one's acts (as the word "virtue" or "power" intimates), and the will is the motor power that sets the other faculties in motion. Thus, for one who has debts to pay, it is better that he give his time to earning money than to storing his mind with the lore of scientists; justice has more of a claim on him than knowledge.

1029. Comparison of Hope with Faith.—(a) These virtues are not the same, for, while faith makes us cling to God as the giver of truth and assent to what is obscure to us, hope makes up turn to Him as the author of beatitude and strive for that which is difficult for us.

(b) Faith and hope are normally equal in duration, since as a rule they are infused at the same time (as in Baptism). Accidentally, however, faith may precede hope, as when one who preserves his faith loses hope on account of despair, and later recovers it.

(c) They are unequal as to natural precedence, faith being prior to hope, since both glory and grace—the objects of hope—must be known through faith (Heb., xi. 6).

(d) They are unequal in their excellence as habits, faith being superior to hope, as the intellectual habits are superior to the moral; for faith is regulative and directive of hope, and has an object more abstract and universal.

(e) They are unequal in their excellence according to the general concept of virtue, hope being superior to faith, as the moral virtues are superior to the intellectual (see 156). For hope includes a rightness of the will towards God that is not included in the concept of faith, which is chiefly intellectual, and it is the will that moves the other powers to action.

1030. Comparison of Hope with Charity.—(a) These virtues are not the same, for, while faith and hope adhere to God as the principle from which one derives truth or goodness, charity adheres to God for His own sake. Hope tends towards God as our good, from whom beatitude and the means thereto are to be expected; but charity unites us to God so that we live for God rather than for self.

(b) Hope and charity are normally equal as to duration, but accidentally hope may precede charity, as when one commits a mortal sin, but retains his hope of salvation, and later recovers charity. There is question now only of the habits, because the acts of the sinner leading up to charity—faith, fear, hope, contrition, etc.—are for the most part successive, although in a sudden conversion hope may be virtually included in charity.

(c) They are unequal as to natural precedence, hope being prior to charity, for, just as fear naturally leads to interested love such as is contained in hope, so does this interested love prepare one for a higher love that is disinterested: "The end of the commandment is charity from a pure heart" (I Tim., i. 5). We speak here of hope unanimated by charity; for animated or living hope trusts in God as a friend, and hence presupposes charity.

(d) They are unequal in excellence, for hope proceeds from imperfect love, which desires God for the sake of the one who loves, while charity is perfect love and desires God for His sake.

1031. Hope, as said above (see 1015-1017), is good and virtuous even when separated from charity, or when exercised without the actual motive of charity. But imperfect or less perfect hope must not be confused with the following acts, which have only the appearance of hope: (a) acts that remove the material object of hope, which are such as look for all beatitude in something different from God (e.g., in secondary joys of heaven); (b) acts that do injury to the objects of hope, such as those that subordinate them to lesser goods (e.g., hope which puts self above God or delight above virtue).

1082. Three types of the latter kind of pseudo-hope may be distinguished:

(a) Egotistical hope is that which places the end for which beatitude is hoped (i.e., self, as was said in 1022) above the end which is beatitude (i.e., God the Last End, as was said in 1019 sqq.), or which places subjective beatitude (i.e., the act of intuitive vision by which beatitude is attained) above objective beatitude (i.e., God as the object in which beatitude consists). Just as the intellect is in error when it mistakes the conclusion for the premise, so is the will in disorder when it takes a means for the end. Hence, while there is nothing inordinate in a man's hoping for food on account of eating and in his eating on account of health (since in reality health is the purpose of eating, and eating the purpose of food), it is extremely inordinate to hope for God on account of the beatific vision or on account of self, since God is the End of all, and the beatific vision is only the condition for attaining to this Last End, and self merely the subject to whom God and the beatific vision are to be given for its perfection through them.

(b) Epicurean hope is that which places pleasure above the other elements that pertain to subjective beatitude. The subjective happiness of man consists essentially in the act that is highest and distinctly human—namely, in the act of the intellect seeing God intuitively; hence, pleasure—even the chief spiritual pleasures-should be esteemed as something secondary and consequent.

(c) Utilitarian hope is that which places reward above virtue, as if the latter were merely a means, as when one says: "If there were no heaven, I would practise no virtue." There are three kinds of good: (i) useful good, or that which is desirable only because it serves as a means to something else (e.g., bitter medicine, which is wished, not for its own sake, but for the sake of health); (ii) moral good, or that which is desired for its own sake, as being agreeable to the rational nature of man (such as virtue); (iii) delightful good, that is, the repose or satisfaction of the will in possession of that which is desirable for its own sake. It is a mistake, therefore, to regard virtue as merely a useful good, something that is disagreeable in itself and cannot be practised on account of its inherent goodness. It is also a mistake to consider heaven as something above and apart from virtue; for eternal life is the perfect flowering and fruitage of the moral life that has been planted and developed here on earth. The things of this world are only means to virtue, and virtue reaches its climax in the beatific vision. The delights of heaven are results of that vision, not its end.

1033. Hope, therefore, must seek God as the chief good; it must not prefer the lesser to the greater, and it must not hold virtue as good only in view of the reward. But, on the other hand, hope seeks God as its own good, and it need not be joined to disinterested love, in order to be a true virtue.

(a) Hence, it is not necessary that one hope with the proviso that, in the impossible hypothesis that God were unwilling to reward virtue, the reward would not be expected; for it is not necessary to consider chimerical cases.

(b) It is not necessary that hope be elicited by the act of charity (i.e., that one always direct one's desire of salvation to the end that God may be glorified), for thus the motive of hope would cease to be active, and the lesser virtue would be absorbed in charity.

(c) It is not necessary that hope be commanded by the act of charity (i.e., that one hope for salvation as one's own good, only when a previous act of charity has bidden that this be done as a mark of love towards God), for to desire that which God wishes one to desire is in itself good and laudable, and stands in need of no other act to justify it.

1034. Discouragement and aridity occur even in the lives of great Saints, and at such times, when pure love of God seems almost impossible, hope comes to the rescue by offering encouragement and spurring on to activity. Hence, the importance of this virtue in the spiritual life; for (a) hope is an anchor of the soul in times of tempest, since it offers reasons for patience and good cheer (Heb, vi. 19; Ecclus.,

iii. 9; Rom., xii. 12, viii 25; I Thess., v. 8); (b) hope gives wings to the soul in times of weariness, since the motives it presents are inducements to courage and good works (Is., xl. 31, xxx. 15; Ps. cxviii. 32; Heb., X. xi).

1035. The following means are recommended for growth in hope: (a) to ask this from God: "Grant us, O Lord, an increase of faith, hope, and charity" (Missal, 13th Sunday after Pentecost); (b) to meditate on the rewards of heaven and the motives of hope, and to make corresponding acts (II Cor., iv. 18; Ecclus., ii. 11-13); (c) to have recourse to God in all our needs, casting all our care on Him (I Pet., v. 7); (d) to work courageously for salvation and to preserve purity of conscience (Ps. xxvi. 14; I John, iii. 21, 22).

1036. The Subject of Hope.—By the subject of hope we mean the power of the soul to which this virtue belongs and also the persons who are capable of hope. (a) The faculty of the soul in which hope resides is the will, for this virtue seeks the good, not the true. (b) The persons capable of hope are all those who have not yet received their final reward or punishment.

1037. The virtue of hope does not remain in the blessed. (a) They cannot hope for the principal object of bliss, since they already enjoy it: "Hope that is seen is not hope. For what a man seeth, why doth he hope for?" (Rom., viii. 24). (b) The blessed can desire secondary objects, such as the continuance of their state, the glorification of their bodies, the salvation of those who are still on earth, etc.; but this desire belongs to the virtue of charity, since with the blessed there is no longer the struggle and expectation of the future that is contained in the desire of hope. Moreover, the desire of objects other than God does not constitute the theological virtue of hope, which tends directly to God.

1038. As to the departed who are not in heaven, we must distinguish between those in hell and those in purgatory.

(a) Those who are in hell, whether demons or men, cannot hope; for it is part of their punishment that they know their loss is eternal (Matt., xxv. 41; Prov., xi. 7). Dante expresses this truth when he says that on the gates of hell it is written: "Hope abandon ye that enter here." Only in an improper sense can the lost be said to hope, inasmuch as they desire evils, or things other than heaven. Unbaptized infants either do not know their loss, or else are not tormented by the thought that heaven is for them unattainable, realizing that its privation has resulted from no personal fault of their own.

(b) Those who are in purgatory have hope; for, although they are certain of their salvation, it still remains true that they must ascend through difficulties to their reward. Hence, in the Mass the Church prays for the departed "who sleep the sleep of peace"—that is, who are secure about their salvation. The Fathers in limbo also had hope before their introduction into heaven: "All these died according to faith, not having received the promises, but beholding them afar off and saluting them, and confessing that they are pilgrims and strangers on the earth.... They desire a better, that is to say a heavenly country" (Heb., xi. 13, 16).

1039. As to those who have not yet passed from this mortal life, some have hope, others have it not.

(a) Those who have no hope are unbelievers and those believers who have rejected hope. Unbelievers have no theological hope, since faith is "the substance (i.e., basis) of things to be hoped for" (Heb., xi. 1). Hence, even though one accepts the Article of the Creed, "I look for the resurrection of the dead and the life of the world to come," one's hope is not real, if one culpably rejects some other Article; for then one expects the end without the necessary means (Heb. xi. 6). Believers who despair of salvation, or who do not look to God for it, have not the virtue of hope; for, just as faith is lost if its object or motive is not accepted, so also hope perishes if its object is not expected or its motive is not relied on.

(b) Those who have hope are all believers not guilty of a sin contrary to hope. Sinners cannot expect to be saved if they continue in sin, but they can expect through the grace of God to be freed from sin and to merit eternal life; indeed, they are bound to believe that God wishes their salvation and to hope for it.

1040. The certainty of hope does not exclude the uncertainty of fear; on the contrary, man must both hope and fear, as regards his salvation.

(a) If a person looks to the motives of hope (i.e., God's power and mercy), he has the assurance of faith that God can and will help him to attain salvation; and thus there arises in him a firm and unshaken hope: "I know whom I have believed, and I am certain that He is able to keep that which I have committed unto Him, against that day" (II Tim., i. 12; cfr. Heb., vi. 18; Ps. xxiv. 2; Ps. xxx. 2.; Rom., xiv. 4)

(b) But, if a person looks to his own frailty and remembers that others have hoped and yet have been lost, he is not certain that he will coöperate with God and be saved, and hence he must fear (Eccles., ix. 1 sqq.; I Cor., iv. 4, ix. 27). The Council of Trent declares that no one can promise himself with absolute certainty that he will persevere (Sess. VI, Cap. 13). Therefore, it is written: "He that thinketh himself to stand, let him take heed lest he fall" (I Cor., x. 12); "With fear and trembling, work out your salvation" (Phil., ii. 12).

1041. The Gift of Fear of the Lord.—The Gift of the Holy Ghost that perfects the virtue of hope is Fear of the Lord (see 159 sqq.); for (a) hope is the root from which the Gift of Fear is derived, since hope joins the affections to God, and fear acts upon the soul that is thus tending towards its beatitude—we fear to lose what we hope for; (b) fear assists hope, since it makes us dread, not the loss of beatitude or of divine help, but the lack of coöperation on our own part with the assistance given by God.

1042. Not every kind of fear pertains to the Gift called Fear of the Lord. In the first place, we must distinguish between physical and moral fear. (a) Fear, physically considered, is the emotion treated above (see 41 sqq., 120), which manifests itself in aversion, bashfulness, shame, dismay, alarm, horror, etc. This kind of fear, like the other passions (see 121), is morally indifferent in itself. (b) Fear, morally considered, is a dread of imminent evil as leading one to God or away from Him. In this sense fear is now discussed.

1043. The object of fear is always some evil, for the good does not repel, but attracts. The motive of fear, however, is something good; for one dreads evil on account of some good one wishes to obtain or retain. By reason of the motive, then, fear may be divided into two moral species, namely, fear of the world and fear of God.

(a) Fear of the world is that which dreads creatures more than God, because it sets more store by the things of time than by those of eternity. Thus, St. Peter's denial of Christ was prompted by fear of the world. When the object of this fear is loss of the esteem of men, it is called human respect.

(b) Fear of God is that which dreads the Creator more than creatures, because it prizes Him above all. Thus, St. Peter's death for Christ proceeded from his fear of God.

1044. Fear of the world is always sinful, because it makes one offend, or be willing to offend, God for the sake of escaping some temporal evil. It is forbidden by our Lord: "Fear ye not them that kill the body and are not able to kill the soul, but rather fear Him that can destroy both body and soul in hell" (Matt, x. 28). Elias (or Eliseus) is praised because of his freedom from fear of the world: "In his days he feared not the prince" (Ecclus., xlviii. 13). We should note, however, the distinction between habitual fear, on the one hand, and actual or virtual fear, on the other hand.

(a) Habitual worldly fear is a state, not an act—that is, the condition of those who are in mortal sin, and have therefore preferred self to God as the supreme end of life. It is a matter of faith that not all the acts of sinners or unbelievers are bad, for they are able to seek certain particular or natural goods.

(b) Actual fear of the world is a deliberate choice of sin out of fear of some temporal evil; virtual fear is a deliberate act proceeding from such a choice though without advertence to the choice or fear. In both these kinds of fear there is sin, for actual fear commands evil, virtual fear executes it. Examples: Sempronius internally resolves to be guided by his fear of imprisonment rather than by the law of God against perjury (actual fear). He then proceeds to perjure himself, adverting to what he says, but not thinking about his previous fear (virtual fear).

1045. The species of sin to which worldly fear belongs are as follows:

(a) The theological species of this sin depends on the disposition of the person. He sins mortally, if on account of fear he is ready to offend God seriously; he sins venially, if on account of fear he is prepared to commit only a venial sin. Examples: Titus, in order to escape imprisonment or exile, swears falsely. Balbus, having been absent from his office without leave, tells a little lie to escape reproof for this misdemeanor. Titus' fear is a grave sin, that of Balbus a venial sin.

(b) The moral species of worldly fear is, as a rule, the same as the species of the sin to which it leads, so that but one sin is committed and need be confessed. The reason is that generally the object of fear is something that deserves to be dreaded, and that the aversion from it is not wrong except in so far as it is carried to the extreme of using sin as a means of escape. Example: Caius is wrongly suspected of theft. To free his reputation he swears falsely about a circumstance that appears incriminating. His fear of losing his good name is not a sin in itself, and hence he is guilty of the one sin of perjury.

1046. There are exceptional cases when fear is a distinct sin from the sin to which it leads.

(a) If the fear of losing some temporal good is so great that one is prepared to commit any sin to escape the loss, and if later by reason of this fear one swears falsely, two sins are committed—one against charity, because a temporal good was preferred to God, and the other against religion, because God was called on to witness to falsehood.

(b) If the fear is that one will not be able to commit one kind of sin, and this induces one to commit another kind of sin, evidently two sins are committed. Example: Balbus wishes to calumniate Caius, but is not able to do so himself. Fearing that Caius will escape his vengeance, he steals money and offers it to Sempronius as an inducement to calumniate Caius. The two sins, calumny and theft, are committed.

1047. Not every fear of man or of temporal evil falls under worldly and sinful fear. (a) To fear or reverence man in those things in which he represents the authority of God is a duty: "Render to all men their dues . . . fear to whom fear, honor to whom honor" (Rom., xiii. 7). (b) To fear temporal evils (such as loss of life, reputation, liberty, property) in a moderate and reasonable manner, is good. Hence, our Lord bids us pray for deliverance from evil.

1048. Fear of God is of two specifically distinct kinds, according as the object one dreads is offense of God or punishments from God. (a) Servile fear, that of a servant with regard to his master, dreads sin because of the punishment it entails; (b) filial fear, that of a son with regard to his father, dreads sin because of the offense to God that is contained in it.

1049. Servile fear may be considered either as to its substance or as to its accidents. (a) The substance or essence of servile fear is derived from its object (see 71), that is, from the evil of penalty which it entails; (b) the accidents of servile fear are its circumstances (see 72), such as the state of the person who has the fear, the manner in which he fears, etc.

1050. Servile fear in itself is good and supernatural.

(a) That servile fear is good, is a dogma of faith defined in the Council of Trent (Sess. VI, Can. 8; Sess. XXIV, Can. 5). Our Lord recommends this fear when he says: "I will show you whom ye shall fear. Fear ye Him who after He hath killed, hath power to cast into hell. Yea, I say to you, fear Him" (Luke, xii. 5). the object of this fear is penalty, which is an evil, and consequently something that ought to be dreaded.

(b) That servile fear is supernatural, follows from the fact that its acts are supernatural. It comes from the Holy Ghost that man may prepare himself for grace; it is "the beginning of wisdom" (Ps. cx. 10), because through it the wisdom of faith first becomes effective as a rule of action, causing man to depart from sin on account of the justice of God which it makes known to him. Servile fear is thus far superior to that natural fear of pain and suffering which all have.

1051. Though servile fear is good, useful and praiseworthy, it is not perfect. (a) It is inferior to filial fear; for, while servile fear looks upon God as a powerful master who cannot be offended with impunity, filial fear regards Him as a loving Father whom one does not wish to offend. Hence, the Old Law, given amid the thunder of Sinai and with many threats against transgressions, is less perfect than the New Law, which relies more on love than on fear (Rom., viii. 15; Heb., xii. 18-25; Gal., iv. 22 sqq.). (b) Servile fear, although it is regarded by some theologians as an infused habit, is not a Gift of the Holy Ghost, since it may coexist with mortal sin. It seems that it is not even a virtue, since it turns man away, not from moral, but from physical evil; but a number of authorities consider it as a secondary act of the virtue of hope.

1052. Servile fear, as to its circumstances, may be evil. (a) The circumstance of the state of the person who has servile fear is good, when the person is a friend of God; it is evil, when that person is an enemy of God. (b) The circumstance of the manner in which servile fear is elic[i]ted is good, if punishment is not feared as the greatest evil; it is bad, if punishment is feared as the greatest evil, for then one makes self the principal end of life, and would be disposed to sin without restraint, were there no punishment.

1053. The effect of evil circumstances on servile fear itself is as follows:

(a) Servile fear is not rendered evil because of the evil state of the person who fears. Just as a person who is habitually foolish may actually say or do something wise, so a person who is habitually wicked may perform virtuous acts. Mortal sin is no more a defect of servile fear in a sinner than it is a defect of faith or hope in one who has faith or hope without works; neither faith nor hope nor fear is to be blamed for the state of mortal sin, but the person who has those gifts of God is at fault. True, the sinner, by reason of his lack of love of God, does not put fear of sin above fear of punishment. But from this it does not follow that he puts fear of punishment above fear of sin, for he may fear punishment absolutely (i.e., without making any comparison between the evil of sin and the evil of punishment). The fear which makes no comparisons is good, or else we must say that only filial fear avails, which, as said above, is not true.

(b) Servile fear is rendered evil as to the manner in which it is performed, when one compares sin and punishment, dislikes only the latter, and avoids sin only to escape punishment. This kind of fear is slavish, for it makes one do something good unwillingly, like a slave forced to labor against his wishes, whereas God is pleased only with service that comes from a willing spirit (I Par., xxviii. 9).

1054. Hence, we must distinguish the following cases of servile fear:

(a) Fear of punishment is purely servile when it makes a person avoid sin, but does not make him put away his love of God.

(b) Fear of punishment is not purely servile, when it causes a sinner not only to cease from sin, but to give up his affection for sin; this fear is distinct from charity, but prepares for it: "The fear of the Lord driveth out sin" (Ecclus., i. 27).

(c) Still less is the fear of punishment purely servile, when it leads a just man, who already detests sin as an offense against God, to detest it as involving punishment from God. This fear exists along with charity, for the love of God and the right love of self are not exclusive. But, as charity increases, servile fear must decrease; the more a person loves God, the less is he concerned about his own good, the more confidently does he hope in God, and hence the less does he fear penalty.

1055. There are two degrees of filial fear to be distinguished:

(a) Initial fear is that of beginners in charity. On account of past sins, they fear punishments from God; on account of their present love of God, they fear they may be again separated from Him. The second fear is stronger with them, and it commands that the first fear be aroused to hold the will more firmly against whatever might separate from love. Of this fear it is said: "The fear of God is the beginning of His love" (Ecclus., xxv. 16).

(b) Perfected fear is that of those who are established in charity. The more the love of God sways the heart, the more is every other love, that of self included, subjugated to the love of God, and the less is one troubled by the thoughts of evils that may befall self. Even in this present life some souls are so strong in the love of God that all servile fear disappears: "I am sure that neither death nor life ...shall be able to separate us from the love of God" (Rom., viii. 38, 39); "Perfect charity casteth out fear, because fear hath pain, and he that feareth is not perfected in charity" (I John, iv. 18).

1056. The perfected fear of God has two acts:

(a) In the present life, where it is possible that one may offend God and lose His friendship, one dreads the commission of offense and the loss of friendship. This fear should be always with us: "Keep His fear and grow old therein" (Ecclus., ii. 6). With the growth of charity there is a corresponding growth in the fear of separation from God, because the more ardently God is loved, the more one realizes the greatness of the loss sustained through sin.

(b) In eternal life, where sin and separation from God are impossible, the blessed do not fear these evils: "He that shall hear Me, shall rest without terror, and shall enjoy abundance without fear of evils" (Prov., i. 33). But in the presence of the Divine Majesty the Angels and Saints are filled with awe and reverence: "I saw them that had overcome the beast, singing: Who shall not fear Thee, O Lord, and magnify Thy name?" (Apoc., xv. 3, 4); "The pillars of heaven tremble and dread at His beck" (Job, xxvi. 11); "Through whom (Christ) the Angels praise Thy majesty, the Dominations worship it, the Powers are in awe" (Preface of the Mass). This holy fear is unending, for the infinite distance between God and His creatures, His incomprehensibility to them, will never cease: "The fear of the Lord is holy, enduring forever and ever" (Ps. xviii. 10).

1057. The filial fear of God is identical with the Gift of fear of the Lord, spoken of in scripture: "He shall be filled with the spirit of the fear of the Lord" (Is., xi. 3). The function of the Gifts is to make the soul docile to the inspirations of the Holy Spirit, and to supplement or serve the habits of virtue, and both these benefits are conferred by filial fear.

(a) This fear makes the soul ready to follow impulses prompted by God, for through it we subject ourselves to God as our Father, revering His wondrous majesty and fearing to stray from Him. Indeed, this is the first of the Gifts, for the realization of one's nothingness before God is the starting-point of promptitude in receiving His teaching and guidance.

(b) Filial fear is a principle from which proceed acts of all the moral virtues, inasmuch as the reverence for God's surpassing majesty and respect for His almighty power and justice incline one to lay aside pride, intemperance, and every vice, and exercise good works that are pleasing to Him: "The root of wisdom is to fear the Lord, and the branches thereof are long-lived" (Ecclus., i. 27).

(c) Filial fear is especially and primarily related to the virtue of hope, for these two complement each other, as do the emotions of hope and fear. Hope aspires to conquer the heights of heaven, and feels that God is on its side; fear reminds one of the greatness of God and of the dangers of over-confidence. Each then is necessary to balance the other: "The Lord taketh pleasure in them that fear Him, and in them that hope in His mercy" (Ps. cxlvi. 11).

1058. To the Gift of Fear correspond the first Beatitude and the fruits of modesty, continency and chastity. (a) Filial fear makes one realize that all but God is as nothing, and hence that true greatness must be sought, not in the self-esteem of pride, nor in the external pomp of riches and honors, but in God alone: "Some trust in chariots, and some in horses; but we will call upon the name of the Lord our God" (Ps. xix. 8). This is the disposition of soul to which is promised the First Beatitude: "Blessed are the poor in spirit, for theirs is the kingdom of heaven" (Matt, v. 3). To the first of the Gifts, in the order of preparation, corresponds the first of the Beatitudes. (b) Filial fear makes one dread the thought of separation from God, and hence it leads one to use temporal things with moderation, or to abstain from them entirely, To it, then, pertain the Fruits of the Spirit, which St. Paul names "modesty, continency, chastity" (Gal, v. 23).

1059. The Sins Against Hope.—There are two sins contrary to hope: (a) despair, which is the opposite of hope by defect; (b) presumption, which is the opposite of hope by excess.

1060. Since hope has many elements of which it is composed, despair—or the falling short of hope—may happen in various ways. (a) Hope is a turning of the soul towards beatitude, and so the omission of the act of hope may be called despair (negative despair). (b) Hope regards beatitude as its good, and so aversion from divine things may be called despair (despair improperly so-called). (c) Hope pursues a good that is difficult of attainment, and so he who is dejected by the difficulty is said to despair. (d) Hope firmly believes that its goal may be reached, and hence one who doubts the possibility of success in the quest of heaven is in despair. (e) Hope has the expectation of one day entering into eternal life, and hence he is guilty of despair who admits that salvation will be secured by others, but denies that he himself should expect it.

1061. Definition of Despair.—Leaving out of consideration negative despair and despair improperly so-called, the sin we are now considering may be defined as follows: "Despair is an act of the will by which one turns away from the beatitude one desires, not under the aspect in which it appears as good, but because one apprehends it as impossible, or too difficult, or never to be realized, and under this aspect as evil."

(a) Despair is an "act of the will," and as such it differs from the intellectual sin of unbelief. The Novatians, who rejected the forgiveness of sins, and a heretic who denies the future life, are guilty by these acts of sin against faith, though of course one who disbelieves must also despair (see 1029, 751).

(b) Despair is a positive "turning away from beatitude." It differs, therefore, from the mere omission of the act of hope or from an act of feeble hope, as well as from the sins against the moral virtues, which consist primarily in a turning towards some created good.

(c) Despair turns away "from God," and thus it differs from despondency about other things.

(d) Despair turns away from God "apprehended as good and desired as the beatitude of man," for no one is said to despair of what he considers evil or undesirable. Hence, despair differs from aversions and fears; such as hatred of God (which regards Him as evil) or fear of God (which thinks of Him, not as a rewarder, but as the author of chastisement).

(e) Despair, however, does not reject God, because He is good and desirable, but because He is apprehended as a "beatitude that is impossible," or too difficult for one, or as a good that one will never attain to. For a person does not turn away from that which he regards as the object of his happiness, unless he considers that there is some inconvenience in seeking after it.

1062. Is despondency about things other than God a sin? (a) It is the sin of pusillanimity, when it makes a person abandon hope of something which he is capable of attaining and which he should aim at, as when students, on account of the labor required, give up hope of learning a certain subject which they have been assigned. This sin will be treated in the section on Fortitude.

(b) It is no sin, if a person gives up the expectation of something about which he has no reason to hope, or which he is not obliged to hope for. Examples: Caius gives up the hope of getting an education, because he lacks money to pay the expenses. Balbus ceases to pray for health, because he thinks it is not God's will to grant that request. Titus abandons the expectation of a long life, and even at times wishes for death.

1063. To wish for death may include despair of salvation or other sin.

(a) If this wish means that one has no desire for any kind of existence (as when one desires extinction), manifestly eternal life is not looked for, and hence there is despair. It should be noted, however, that such expressions as, "Would that I had never been born!" "Would that I were out of existence!" often signify nothing more than weariness of life on earth, or disgust with conditions.

(b)If the wish is not for annihilation, but only that God send death, it is not a sin of despair; but if the wish is inordinate, some other species of sin is committed—for example, if the person wishing to die is not resigned or submissive to God's will in the matter, he is guilty of rebellion against Providence, and his sin is grave, if there is sufficient reflection and consent.

(c) If the wish is merely for death and is not inordinate, it may be an act of virtue, as when, out of a longing for heaven, one deliberately desires to be taken from this world, if this be pleasing to God. Thus, St. Paul said that he desired "to be dissolved and to be with Christ" (Philip., i. 23).

1064. Certain acts of fear or sadness must not be mistaken for despair: (a) acts that are praiseworthy, like servile and filial fear spoken of above (see 1048 sqq.), grief over sin, etc.; (b) acts that are a trial from God, such as spiritual desolations in holy persons, scruples about forgiveness of sins, anxieties about predestination, perseverance, or the Judgment; (c) acts that are sinful, such as worldly fear, fear of God that is purely servile, timidity (i.e., an excessive dread of death or other evils). Those who fear that, on account of their frailty, they may not acquire a good habit or overcome an evil one, are guilty of pusillanimity. Those who, on account of sadness, neglect prayer are guilty of spiritual sloth.

1065. There are two species of despair, namely, the despair of unbelief and the despair that is found even in those that have faith.

(a) The despair of unbelief arises from a judgment contrary to faith, as when one holds as general principles that salvation is impossible, that God is not merciful to sinners, that all sins or certain sins cannot be forgiven. Thus, St. Paul designates the pagans who do not accept the Final Resurrection as those "who have no hope" (I Thess., iv. 12).

(b) The despair of believers arises from a judgment formed by them which is not directly opposed to faith, but which is erroneous, and is induced by some wicked habit or passion. Example: Titus lives a very disorderly life, and so thinks that he is predestined to hell, or that he is too weak to repent and persevere. Since his predestination and perseverance are not matters of faith, he is not guilty of unbelief by his judgment about them, but the judgment itself is wrong, and one which he has no right to form or act on.

1066. Signs which indicate that a penitent suffering depression has not been guilty of despair are: (a) if he retains the faith and has not abandoned the usual practices of religion and piety; (b) if he retains the faith, but has given up some of its practices through discouragement or weakness, but intends to repent. His sin is sloth or cowardice or attachment to some vice.

1067. Hence, the erroneous judgment that precedes despair is similar to that which precedes every act of sin, namely, it is always practically erroneous, though not always speculatively so.

(a) Judgment is speculatively erroneous with regard to duty, when one decides that in general something is lawful which is unlawful; or vice versa, as when one thinks that lying is pleasing to God. It is clear that this kind of error need not precede sin, or else all sinners would err against the faith.

(b) Judgment is practically erroneous about duty, when a person decides that here and now he should do something which in fact he should not do, as when he knows well that lying is displeasing to God, and yet makes up his mind that, all things considered, he ought to tell a lie. It is clear that this kind of error precedes every sin, for no one wills something unless his judgment has first told him that he ought to will it. The sinner first judges in a particular case that he should prefer the good of pleasure or of utility to the good of virtue, or he first neglects to consider the right manner in which he should act: "They err that work evil" (Prov., xiv. 22).

1068. The Malice of Despair.—(a) Despair is a sin, for Holy Scripture declares woe to the fainthearted, who trust not God and lose patience (Ecclus., ii. 15, 16), and it holds up the despair of Cain and Judas for reprehension. The malice of despair appears in this, that it is based on a perverse judgment that one ought not to labor for salvation in confident expectation, despite God's promise and command to the contrary. (b) It is a mortal sin according to its nature, for it destroys the theological virtue of hope, turns man away from God his Last End, and leads to irreparable loss.

1069. In the following cases despair is not a mortal sin, nor at times even a venial sin. (a) When there is not sufficient reflection, despair is not a grave sin. Examples: Those who are ignorant of the sinfulness of despair, those who on account of great discouragement or fear do not fully advert to their despair of amendment, do not sin gravely. Despair is often a result of insanity. (b) When there is not full consent of the will, despair is not a grave sin. Examples: Those who, on account of a melancholy disposition, inclination to pessimism, past sins, etc., are tempted to give up the hope of salvation, are not guilty of sin, provided they fight against these suggestions of the mind or imagination.

1070. The gravity of despair as compared with other sins is as follows:

(a) Despair is a greater sin than offenses against the moral virtues, for the chief inclination of despair is aversion from God, whereas the chief inclination of the latter kind of sins is conversion towards creatures. Thus, a person who drinks excessively does not primarily intend offense against God, but his own enjoyment or escape from certain worries.

(b) Despair in itself is less serious than the sins of unbelief and hatred of God; for, while despair is opposed to God as He is our good, the other two sins are opposed to God's own truth and goodness.

(c) Despair is more serious than the sins of unbelief and hatred of God with reference to the danger it contains for the sinner; for it paralyzes effort and resists remedies: "Why is my sorrow become perpetual and my wound desperate, so as to refuse to be healed?" (Jer., xv. 18) "If thou lose hope, being weary in the day of distress, thy strength shall be diminished" (Prov., xxiv. 10). Despair is, therefore, a sin against the Holy Ghost, a sort of attempt at spiritual suicide. But (see 900) it is not unpardonable and may be overcome by divine grace.

1071. It is important to know the causes of despair, for this knowledge enables us to distinguish it from the mystical state known as "the dark night of the soul," and to prescribe suitable remedies. Despair comes from one's own fault, whereas mystical purgation from God is a preparation for a higher state of divine union. The causes of despair can be reduced to two, luxury and sloth.

(a) The secondary characteristic of a hopeful pursuit of heaven is courage, the adventurous spirit which foregoes ease and comfort for the sake of higher things, despising the danger and difficulty. Hence, the vice of lust, since it makes one love bodily delights and disregard or underestimate those that are spiritual, is a cause of despair, as well as of other sins opposed to the spiritual life (Gal., v. 17).

(b) The chief and most distinctive characteristic of hope is its cheerful confidence of success. Hence, the vice of sloth, since it is sadness weighing down the soul and making it unwilling to think rightly or to exert itself, is the principal cause of despair (Prov., xvii. 22).

1072. The apparent despair that is a trial to holy persons can be distinguished, therefore, from the sin of despair, especially by two signs: (a) though they are spiritually desolate and find no joy in religious practices, these persons do not turn to unlawful delights for consolation, but retain their dislike for lower pleasures; (b) though overcome with dismay at the thought of their own imperfection and of God's holiness, they do not so lose heart as to give over their exercises of piety (cf. St. John of the Cross, *The Dark Night*, Bk. I, e. 9 ff.).

1073. Spiritual writers make the following recommendations for cases of spiritual desolation: (a) the afflicted persons should understand that the deprivation of former sensible devotion is a sign of God's love and has been experienced by the Saints, and should, therefore, possess their souls in peace, leaving to God the time and manner of His heavenly visitation; (b) they should not burden themselves with new and heavier mortifications, lest they be overcome by too great sorrow, but should go on with their accustomed good works, and realize that, though bitter to them, these works are now all the more pleasing to God (Ibid., c. 10).

1074. Some Remedies for the Sin of Despair.—(a) If the cause is lust, one should learn that spiritual joys are nobler and more enduring than the joys of the flesh, and should take the means to sacrifice the lower in favor of the higher.

(b) If the cause of despair is spiritual sloth, one should meditate on the greatness of God's power, mercy and love, and should avoid whatever fosters undue sadness, "lest he be swallowed up with over-much sorrow" (II Cor., ii. 7). Thus, those who are tormented by the thoughts of past sins or future temptations must subject their scruples to direction, and remember the mercy shown to the good thief, to Magdalene, and other penitents; those who have lost courage because they read spiritual books of a rigorous or terrifying nature, or have been advised to attempt that for which they were unsuited, should seek more prudent instruction and counsel; those who are naturally nervous or melancholy, should employ such therapeutical or preventive measures as are useful or necessary. All should follow the direction of St. Peter to labor the more, that by good works they may make sure their calling and election (II Pet., i. 10).

1075. Presumption is the name given to certain acts of the intellect. (a) Sometimes it signifies an arrogant self-esteem, as when an ignorant person thinks he is able to dispute with a learned scholar. (b) Sometimes it is a judgment about the affairs of others made rashly or out of fear: "A troubled conscience always presumeth grievous things" (Wis., xvii. 10). (c) Sometimes it is a conclusion based on probable evidence, and which by jurists is called violent, strong, or weak presumption according to the evidence (see 658).

1076. Presumption is also a name given to various acts of the will. (a) It is used, in a good sense, to signify an excellent confidence or hope, which seems rash according to human standards, but is really well founded, since it rests on the immensity of the divine goodness. Thus, Judith prayed: "O God of the heavens, Creator of the waters and Lord of the whole creation, hear me a poor wretch, making supplication to Thee, and presuming on Thy mercy" (Jud., ix. 17). Thus, too, Abraham hoped against hope (Rom., iv. 18). (b) Generally, however, the word "presumption" is applied to acts of the will in a bad sense, and indicates the purpose to do what exceeds one's powers.

1077. Here we are concerned only with presumption as it is an act of the will choosing to do what exceeds one's power. "Power" may be understood in three ways, and thus there are three kinds of sins all bearing the name of presumption.

(a) If a person chooses to overstep his moral power (i.e., his right of action), he is guilty of the general sin of presumption, which is not a special category of sin, but a circumstance common to any kind of sin in which one acts with full knowledge, and without subjection to any fear or coercion. Hence, in Canon Law it is said in various places: "If anyone shall presume to transgress" (i.e., if anyone shall coldbloodedly transgress).

(b) If a person wishes to accomplish by his own efforts something so great and difficult that it surpasses his physical powers, he is guilty of the special sin of presumption that is opposed to the moral virtue of magnanimity or greatness of soul, which attempts great things for which it is suited. Thus, he is presumptuous who undertakes a profession, when he has no sufficient knowledge of its duties (cf. Luke, xiv. 28 sqq.). This may be called the moral sin of presumption.

(c) If one wishes to obtain through divine aid something that surpasses even the divine power to confer, one is guilty of the special sin of presumption that is opposed to the theological virtue of hope, which expects from God only such things as are worthy of God and as God has promised. Thus, he who looks forward to a free admission into eternal bliss, without repentance or obedience, does injury both to the character of God and to the virtue of hope. It is this special sin of presumption that we are now considering. It may be called the theological sin of presumption.

1078. Definition of Presumption.—The theological sin of presumption may be defined as follows: "An act of the will by which one rashly expects to obtain eternal happiness or the means thereto." (a) It is an act of the will, and hence is distinct from intellectual sins, such as disbelief in the justice of God or the necessity of repentance. (b) It is an act of pleasing expectation, and so differs generically from fear, which is an act of dreadful expectation. (c) It is a rash expectation, and so is specifically opposed to hope, which is well-founded expectation.

1079. The objects of presumption are material and formal.

(a) The material object is eternal happiness and the means thereto, such as forgiveness of sin, observance of the Commandments, etc. This object by extension would include also such extraordinary supernatural gifts as the hypostatic union, equality in glory with the Mother of God, etc.; for it would be rash to expect against His will what God has made unique privileges.

(b) The formal object, or motive, of presumption is divine mercy not joined with justice, or divine power not regulated by wisdom, as when one hopes for heaven because one reasons that God is too merciful to be a just judge of sinners. The motive by extension would include also the unaided power of human nature relied on as equal to the task of working out salvation, as when a man feels so confident of his own virtue and his security against temptation that he thinks he can dispense with prayer and all appointed means of grace and yet save his soul. Similarly, a person is presumptuous if he feels that it is absolutely impossible for him to be lost, because he has received Baptism or other Sacraments.

1080. Presumption is rash, therefore, for the following reasons: (a) because it leads one to expect what is impossible according to the absolute or ordinary power of God (e.g., to share in some divine attribute, to sit at the right hand of Christ in glory), or (b) because it makes one expect to obtain supernatural goods in ways other than those ordained by God (e.g., to obtain forgiveness without repentance, to obtain glory without merits or grace).

1081. The nature of presumption as compared with temptation of God and blasphemous hope is as follows: (a) they are alike, inasmuch as all three wrongly expect something from God; (b) they differ, for presumption looks towards salvation and one's own happiness, whereas temptation of God seeks rashly some sign from God as a proof that He is wise, good, powerful, etc., or that the person is innocent, holy, etc., and blasphemous hope expects that God will help one in working revenge or committing other sin.

1082. The Malice of Presumption.-(a) It is a sin, because it is an act of the will agreeable to false intellectual judgments, namely, that God will pardon the impenitent or grant eternal life to those who have not labored for it. (b) It is a mortal sin, since it does grave injury to the divine attributes. We cannot hope too much in God, but we can expect what a perfect God cannot grant; in this latter respect—that is, in its contempt of God's majesty and justice—consists the offense of presumption. (c) It is a sin against the Holy Ghost, because it makes one despise the grace of God, repentance, etc., as if they were not necessary.

1083. The gravity of presumption as compared with other sins, is as follows:

(a) It is graver than sins against the moral virtues, because it is directly against God. Thus, theological presumption, being injurious to the power of God, is a more serious offense than moral presumption, which is an exaggeration of the power of man.

(b) It is less grave than despair, for, while presumption is a disregard of God's vindictive justice, despair is a disregard of His mercy, and God's vindictive justice is due to the sins of man, His mercy to His own goodness.

(c) Presumption is less grave, therefore, than unbelief and hatred of God, which, as said above, are more wicked than despair (see 1070).

1084. Presumption and Unbelief.—(a) Presumption is joined with unbelief whenever it proceeds from a speculatively false judgment about matters of faith. Persons, however, who are in error (e.g., Pelagians, Lutherans, Calvinists, etc.), may be in good faith, and hence guiltless of the formal sin of presumption. Examples: Caius expects to win heaven by his own unaided efforts (Pelagian presumption). Balbus expects to be equal in glory to the greatest Saints, and to be saved by the merits of Christ without repentance or observance of the Commandments (Lutheran presumption). Titus expects to be saved on the strength of wearing scapulars, practising certain devotions, or giving alms, while he wholly disregards church duties and important Commandments (Pharisaic presumption). Sempronius thinks that all members of his sect are predestined, and hence concerns himself little about the Commandments, being persuaded that all must end well with the elect (Calvinistic presumption).

(b) Presumption is committed without unbelief, when it proceeds from a practical judgment that one should act as if salvation were obtainable without merits or repentance, or as if natural efforts were alone sufficient, although speculatively one does not accept such errors (see 1067). The same is true when presumption springs from a failure to consider the divine justice or the established means of obtaining salvation.

1085. Presumption and Loss of the Virtue of Hope.—(a) Presumption properly so-called (i.e., hope of the impossible) takes away the virtue of hope, for it removes the motive and reasonableness of the virtue; now, the essence of true hope is a reasonable expectation, just as the essence of faith is assent to divine authority. Hence, he who expects future blessedness unreasonably (i.e., through his own efforts alone or through exaggerated mercy exercised by God), is not hopeful, but presumptuous.

(b) Presumption improperly so-called (i.e., hope of the uncertain) does not take away the virtue of hope, since it does not remove the motive of hope. Thus, one who commits sin, trusting to go to confession and to make restitution after he has enjoyed the benefits of wrongdoing, is presumptuous in the sense that he puts himself in a state of sin, for it is uncertain whether the time to repent will be granted him. However, he is relying on the mercy of God, which never abandons man during life, and not on his own efforts, or on pardon given freely. He is guilty of a want of charity towards self, and of injustice to his neighbor, rather than of a want of hope.

1086. Presumption properly so-called is a sin rarely committed by Catholics. For (a) the presumption of unbelief is excluded by their faith in the justice of God and in the necessity of repentance and good works; (b) the presumption that is not the offspring of erroneous doctrines is also unusual, because even those who go on sinning with the expectation of being saved in the end, generally have the purpose of repenting at some future date.

1087. Is a sin worse because committed with the hope that later it will be pardoned? (a) If, at the moment of sin, a person has the intention to continue in sin, though he hopes for pardon, he is guilty of presumption, and his sin is made worse. (b) If he has the intention of sinning, but hopes for pardon, and is resolved to repent later on as a means to pardon, he is not guilty of presumption. The intention not to continue in sin diminishes the sin, for it shows that one is not so strongly attached to evil.

1088. The intention to sin now and repent later varies in malice according to circumstances.

(a) If the hope of obtaining forgiveness is concomitant as regards the sin now committed—that is, if one sins with the hope, but not because of the hope of pardon-one is less guilty. Example: Titus while on a tour indulges in much drunkenness, because he has the opportunity and is not known; but he intends to repent on his return home.

(b) If the hope of obtaining forgiveness is antecedent as regards the sin—that is, if one sins because of the hope of pardon—one is more guilty. Example: Balbus stays away from Mass most Sundays, because he reasons with himself that God is kind and it will be easy to obtain pardon. Caius, when urged to repent, always replies that it will be a simple matter to turn over a new leaf at the hour of death. Sempronius goes on multiplying sins from day to day, because he argues that it is just as easy to be pardoned late as early, just as easy to repent of a hundred sins as of ten.

1089. In the following cases presumption is not a grave sin: (a) no mortal sin is committed, if there is not sufficient reflection; for example, a person who is invincibly ignorant of the seriousness of presumption, or who on account of immaturity has exaggerated ideas of his own strength, does not sin gravely if he presumes on God's mercy or his own power; (b) no mortal sin is committed, if there is not full consent of the will. For example, Titus is a self-made man, and hence is inclined at times to feel that he can work out even his salvation without any assistance, but he rids his mind of this presumptuous thought as soon as he takes notice of it.

1090. Are there cases in which presumption and despair are transformed into venial sin, not on account of the imperfect knowledge or consent of the subject, but on account of the slightness of the matter involved? (a) If there is question of presumption and despair properly so-called, they are never venial on account of the lightness of the matter, for the matter, man's eternal destiny, must always be an affair of the utmost moment. (b) If there is question of presumption and despair in a wider sense, these sins may be venial on account of smallness of matter; for they may be understood with reference to things other than salvation. Examples: Titus despairs of his success in overcoming a habit of arriving late for his meals or of talking too much. Balbus imprudently trusts to his own efforts to get up promptly in the morning, or to fight against some slight distraction in prayer.

1091. The causes of presumption are as follows: (a) the presumption which depends too much on one's own powers arises from vainglory, for, the more one desires glory, the more is one inclined to attempt things that are above one, especially such as are new and will attract applause; (b) the presumption that depends rashly on divine assistance seems to result from pride, for a person who desires and expects pardon without repentance, or heaven without merits, must have a very exaggerated opinion of his own importance.

1092. The Commandments of Hope and of Fear.—Since hope is a necessary preparation for justification, and since man should tend towards the supernatural beatitude prepared for him by God, we cannot be surprised that scripture in many places inculcates the duty of hope.

(a) In the first legislation, given in the Decalogue, neither faith nor hope are enjoined by distinct Commandments, for, unless man already believed and hoped in God, it would be useless to give him commandments from God. Hence, in the Decalogue faith and hope are presupposed, faith being enjoined only in so far as it is taught, as when the law begins with the words: "I am the Lord thy God" (Exod., xx. 2), and hope being prescribed only in so far as promises are added to the precepts, as in the First and Fourth Commandments.

(b) In the later laws there are given distinct commandments about hope, in order to remind man that he must observe not only the law, but also that which the law presupposes. Thus, we read: "Hope in Him, all ye congregation of people" (Ps. lxi. 9); "Charge the rich of this world not to be high-minded, nor to hope in the uncertainty of riches, but in the living God" (I Tim., vi. 17).

1093. Since acts of hope are obligatory for all adults in this life, the Quietists were in error when they defended disinterested love and absolute holy indifference (Denzinger, 1221 ff., 1327-1349). (a) Hence, man can at times make acts of pure love of God, in which self is not thought about, or even acts of renunciation of beatitude on condition that that were possible and necessary; but the habitual state of pure love, in which self-interest is entirely lost sight of, cannot be admitted (Philip., iii. 14; II Tim., iv, 8). (b) Indifference to the happenings of life, sin excluded, is good; but it is not lawful to be indifferent about one's own salvation, or the means thereto. Indifference about salvation is not holy, but unholy.

1094. Is it lawful to desire to surrender beatitude for the sake of another's spiritual good? (a) If there is question of beatitude itself, this is not lawful. The prayer of Moses that he be stricken from God's book (Exod., xxxiii. 31, 32), and of St. Paul that he suffer loss of Messianic benefits (Rom., ix. 3), were only velleities or hyperbolical expressions of their great love for their race. (b) If there is question, not of beatitude itself, but of something that refers to it (such as the time of receiving it, present certainty about its possession), one may be willing to sacrifice this good for the benefit of his neighbor. Thus, St. Martin of Tours was willing to have his entrance into heaven delayed for the sake of his flock (cfr. Philip., i. 22 sqq.), and St. Ignatius Loyola would have preferred to remain uncertain of salvation and labor for souls, rather than to be certain of salvation and die at once.

1095. At what times does the commandment of hope oblige? (a) In its negative, or prohibitory aspect, this commandment obliges for all times and at all times (see 371). Hence, it is not lawful to despair, even when things are darkest, nor to presume, even when they are brightest. (b) In its affirmative, or preceptive aspect, this commandment obliges for all times, but not at all times. Hence, the law of hope remains always in force, but one is not obliged at every instant to make acts of hope.

1096. By reason of the virtue of hope itself (i.e., on account of the response one should make to the promises of God concerning eternal life), an act of hope is obligatory on the following occasions:

(a) Such an act is obligatory at the beginning of the moral life, that is, at the time when one first realizes that one must choose between God and creatures as the object of one's happiness. This moment occurs for all when the age of reason is attained, and to it we may apply in this connection the words of Christ: "Seek ye first the kingdom of God and His justice" (Matt, vi. 33). This moment occurs for those who are in the state of sin as soon as they perceive the necessity of turning from creatures towards God: "Delay not to be converted to the Lord, and defer it not from day to day" (Ecclus, v. 8).

(b) During the course of the moral life, one is also bound to renew the act of hope: "The grace of God our Saviour hath appeared to all men, instructing us that we should live soberly, and justly, and godly in this world, looking for the blessed hope" (Titus, ii. 11, 12), "Serving the Lord, rejoicing in hope" (Rom., xii. 11, 12); "He that plougheth, should plough in hope" (I Cor., ix. 10). Even those who are more perfect must have on "the helmet of hope" (I Thess., v. 8), for by hope all are saved (Rom, viii. 25).

(c) It seems that at the end of life one is especially bound to elicit an act of hope, as on that moment eternity depends (Heb., iii. vi). But, if one has received the Last Sacraments or is otherwise well prepared for death and undisturbed by temptations to despair, there is no manifest need of making an express act of hope (cfr. 930).

1097. How frequently should acts of hope be made during life? (a) About the theoretical question, there is the same diversity of opinion as with regard to the act of faith (see 933). (b) But, practically, there is agreement among theologians that the commandment is fulfilled by all those who make an act of hope when this is necessary to preserve the virtue on account of danger of presumption or despair, and who comply with the duties of a Christian life, such as attendance at Mass and the reception of the Sacraments.

1098. How should the act of hope be made? (a) The act is made explicitly, when one expresses one's confident expectation, the objects expected and the basis of the expectation, as when one prays according to the formulas of the Catechism or prayer books: "O my God, relying on Thy all-powerful assistance and merciful promises, I firmly hope to obtain pardon for my sins, obedience to Thy commandments, and life everlasting." This form of the act of hope is recommended, since it expresses the essential elements of the virtue. (b) The act of hope is made implicitly, when one offers petitions to God as one ought; for the confidence that accompanies every good prayer makes it an expression of hope of God and of hope in God. Thus, the words, "Thy Kingdom come," utter the soul's expectation of bliss and its reliance on God. The implicit act of hope satisfies the commandment, and hence those who comply with the duty of prayer, comply also with the duty of hope.

1099. By reason of some virtue other than hope (cfr. 935), there also arises at times an obligation of making an act of hope. (a) If another virtue will be lost or endangered without the assistance of hope, one is bound to make an act of hope. Examples: Titus is so discouraged by the difficulties of his duties that he will not perform them, unless he stirs up his will by thinking of the reward. Balba, on account of aridity, finds prayer so hard that she will give it up, unless the motive of future blessedness is before her mind. (b) If another commandment presupposes an act of hope, one is bound to the act of hope, although it may be made virtually or implicitly, as being contained in another virtue. Example: Sempronius is in the state of sin, and therefore obliged to repentance. Since repentance presupposes hope of pardon as a means to salvation, Sempronius must not only grieve over his sins, but must also have confidence in the divine mercy.

1100. Do those persons sin against hope by omission who wish they could remain in the enjoyment of the present life forever?

(a) If those persons are so disposed that they would willingly forego heaven for earth, they are guilty of a neglect of the precept of hope (I Tim., vi. 17). Hope requires that God be the chief object of our desires, but these persons give the first place to creatures (see 1019, 1031).

(b) If such persons are not willing to relinquish heaven, and their wish to remain here forever merely denotes an over-fondness for life or its goods or an exceeding dread of death, hope is not excluded, but they are guilty, slightly or seriously according to the case, of inordinate love of creatures.

(c) If such persons mean by their wish only that they are very much attached to something of earth and wish to retain it as long as God will allow, there is no sin committed. Thus, man and wife happily mated or other friends sometimes express the wish that both might live forever, meaning only that the thought of any separation is unpleasant.

1101. So far we have spoken of the necessity of precept of the act of hope. But there is also a necessity of means, as was said above about faith (see 785, 918), as regards both the act and the habit of hope.

(a) The act of hope is an indispensable condition of salvation for all adults. The unjustified man cannot prepare himself for pardon unless he hopes in God's mercy; he cannot resolve on amendment of life unless he relies on the necessary divine help. The justified man must earn heaven by his works and must pray to God in his necessities—things that are impossible without the firm confidence of hope (Rom., vi. 23).

(b) The habit of hope is an indispensable condition of salvation for all, infants included. For it is by justification, in which the soul and its various powers are sanctified (Rom., v. 6), that one is elevated to the supernatural sphere and made ready for the beatific vision.

1102. The habit of hope is not lost by every sin against hope.

(a) It is not lost by sins of omission, for it depends on divine infusion, not on human acts (see 745).

(b) It is not lost by sins of commission that do not remove its formal object or motive, such as sins against charity and the moral virtues. For it is possible for one to expect external happiness and at the same time not love God for His own sake, or not regulate one's conduct conformably to the happiness desired, just as it is possible for one to believe and yet not practise one's belief (see 1016, 1030).

(c) Hope is lost by sins of commission that remove its foundation or its formal object. Hence, sins of unbelief (since they remove the foundation of hope) and sins of desperation and despair (since they take away the formal object of hope) are destructive of this virtue. It should be noted, however, that sins which only in a wider sense are named presumption and despair, do not remove the object, nor consequently the virtue of hope. Examples: Titus does not believe in a future life, and hence does not expect it. Claudius believes in a future life, but he is so weak in virtue that he has given up all expectation of its rewards for himself. Balbus, on the contrary, is living on stolen property and intends to continue to do so, but he hopes that somehow all will turn out well in the end. Sempronius, who is associated with Balbus, intends to make a deathbed repentance and restitution. The sins of the first three are ruinous to hope, since by reason of them there is no expectation of salvation, or only an expectation that is not based on divine power. The sin of Sempronius is presumptuous, since it risks a most grave danger imprudently; but it is not theological presumption, since it expects forgiveness through divine power and in a way that does not exceed divine power. It is not contrary to, but beyond theological hope.

1103. Divine Commandments Concerning Fear.—(a) Servile fear was not commanded in the Decalogue by any distinct precept, for fear of punishment is supposed in those who received the law; it was, however, commanded there implicitly, inasmuch as penalties were attached to transgressions. Later, in order to keep man more strictly to the law already given, instructions or commandments about the necessity of fear were given. Thus, Job says: "I feared all my works, knowing that Thou didst not spare the offender" (Job, ix. 28), and the Psalmist prays: "Pierce Thou my flesh with Thy fear, for I am afraid of Thy judgments" (Ps. cxviii. 120); our Lord commands: "Fear Him that can destroy both soul and body in hell" (Matt, x. 28).

(b) Filial fear, on the contrary (i.e., reverential love of God), since it is the principle from which proceed the external acts of respect and homage enjoined in the Decalogue, was inculcated at the time the first law was given. "What doth the Lord thy God require of thee, but that thou fear the Lord thy God, and walk in His ways, and love Him, and serve the Lord thy God?" (Deut., x. 12).

1104. As to the times and frequency of obligation, the principles and conclusions given above for hope can be applied also to fear.

Art. 5: THE VIRTUE OF CHARITY

(*Summa Theologica*, II-II, qq. 23-27.)

1105. Definition.—The word "charity" (*carum*, what is held dear, highly esteemed) is used either in a more general, or in a particular sense.

(a) In its more general sense, it is applied to acts or feelings of a kindly nature towards others, whether or not God be concerned in them as the object or motive. Thus, it is applied to kindly judgments about others, to a benevolent disposition towards their welfare, to gratuitous relief of the needy or suffering, to the bestowal of gifts for public benefit, and the like. In scripture the word is sometimes applied to friendship: "It is better to be invited to herbs with charity than to a fatted calf with hatred" (Prov., xv. 17).

(b) In its particular sense, charity refers to divine love, that is, to the love of God for man or the love of man for God. Here we are considering charity as the virtue by which the creature loves God for His own sake, and others on account of God.

1106. Love in general is the inclination towards a suitable good, or what is considered as one's good. It is the root of all appetites of the soul, and hence the importance that the object of love be a true good.

(a) Every attraction is based on the recognition of some suitability in a certain good that attracts, and so is based on love. Example: Love may result from desire, as when from a desire of money springs love of the giver of money; but in the last analysis it will be found that the desire itself came from a previous love, for a person would not wish for money, unless he saw in it some advantage which inclined him towards its possession.

(b) Every repulsion is based on the fact that a certain thing is opposed to that which is suitable for self, and hence results from love. Example: Love sometimes is an effect of hate, as when one loves A because he hates A's enemies; nevertheless, hate is basically always the result of some love, for one hates only those things that impede or destroy what one loves.

(c) Every satisfaction is due to the possession or presence of something helpful or congenial, and so it presupposes love. Example: A particular satisfaction may cause love, as when one loves a person because his company is entertaining; but the satisfaction is due to the love one has of being entertained.

1107. The effects of love are two; (a) union of affection, for the lover regards the object of love as another self and desires its presence; he delights to think of it and wishes what it wishes; (b) separation from other things, for the lover's thoughts are on the object of his love, and he is jealous of anything that might take it from him.

1108. Several degrees of love may be distinguished:

(a) Natural love is the tendency of things to their ends which results, not from knowledge, but from nature, and which is found in the irrational and inanimate as well as in higher forms of being. Thus, we may say that fire loves to burn, that every being loves its own existence;

(b) Sense love (*amor*) is the attraction that follows on knowledge obtained through the senses, and that exists in the brutes as well as in man. Thus, a dog loves bones, a cat loves fish. Sex-attraction is a species of sense love;

(c) Rational love (*dilectio*) arises from the reflection of the mind, and is a choice based on the judgment of the reason concerning the worth of the beloved object.

1109. Rational love is of two kinds: (a) love of desire (*amor concupiscentiæ*), which is affection for an object which one desires for oneself or for another, in such a way that good is not wished for the object, but the goodness of the object is wished for something else (thus, one loves food or money with the love of desire, because one does not wish good for them, but from them); (b) love of benevolence (*amor benevolentiæ*), which is had for an object to which one wishes good (thus, one loves a poor person with the love of benevolence when one wishes to give him food or money).

1110. The love of benevolence is called friendship when the following conditions exist: (a) when the love is mutual, for, if one party who is loved does not reciprocate the other party's affection, they are not considered friends; (b) when the love is based on some similarity which is a bond of union, for friendship supposes that the parties have common interests and that they delight in each other's company, which is impossible without congeniality (see Ecclus., xiii. 19). Thus, there is friendship of relative for relative, of citizen for citizen, of soldier for soldier, of scholar for scholar. True, those who belong to the same state in life are often enemies; but this is due, not to the similarity of their life, but to some individual dissimilarity, as when one is successful and the other unsuccessful, one rich and the other poor. Aristotle remarked that potters never got along together, and Proverbs, xiii. 10, says that between the proud there are always quarrels; for each potter saw in the other potter one who took away profits, and each proud man sees in another proud man an obstacle to personal glory. Unfriendly feeling may exist, then, among those who are alike, but friendship is impossible when the parties have nothing special in common.

1111. Two kinds of friendship must be distinguished. (a) The friendship of utility or of pleasure is that by which one desires good for one's friend, not for the friend's sake, but for one's own advantage or gratification. Hence, friendships of this kind contain some love of benevolence, but they are prompted by love of desire. On account of this admixture of selfishness, they fall short of friendship in the truest sense. Examples: Titus cultivates the friendship of Balbus, because the latter is wealthy and will patronize his business; Balbus, on his part, returns the friendship of Titus, because he finds his prices cheaper (a friendship of convenience or utility). Caius and Claudius associate together much and help each other gladly, but the only thing that draws them together is the amusement they get out of each other's companionship (a friendship of pleasure).

(b) The friendship of virtue is that by which one desires good for another, and by which the cause of attraction is the virtue of the friends. This is true friendship, because it is unselfish and has the highest motive; it is naturally lasting, since it is built on moral goodness, the real good of an intelligent being (Ecclus., vi. 14-16). Example: David and Jonathan became friends because each recognized the other's virtue.

1112. Charity is a true friendship between God and His intellectual creature, for in scripture the just are called the friends of God (John, xv. 15; James, ii. 23; Ps. cxxxviii. 17), and the conditions of true friendship are affirmed about their relation to God. (a) There is a mutual love of benevolence between God and the just: "I love them that love Me" (Prov., viii. 20); "He that loveth Me shall be loved of My Father, and I will love him" (John, xiv. 21). (b) There is a common bond; for, while according to nature God and man are infinitely distant, according to grace man is an adopted son of God and the heir to glory in which he will share happiness with God.

1113. Charity is twofold, namely, uncreated and created. (a) Uncreated charity is God Himself. The entire Trinity is called charity, just as It is also called truth, wisdom, etc.: "God is charity, and he that abideth in charity, abideth in God" (I John, iv. 8). The Holy Ghost especially is called charity, because he proceeds in the Trinity as love. Hence, in the *Veni Creator* He is addressed as "Fount of life, fire, charity, and spiritual anointing." (b) Created charity is a supernatural habit added to the will, inclining it to the exercise of love of God and enabling it to act with promptness and delight: "The charity of God is poured out in our hearts by the Holy Ghost who is given to us" (Rom., v. 5). We are concerned here only with created charity.

1114. Created charity is defined: "A supernatural virtue infused by God, through which we love with friendship God, the author of our beatitude, on account of His own goodness, and our neighbor, on account of God." Charity is given with sanctifying grace, but differs from it, inasmuch as grace is a principle of being and makes man himself holy, whereas charity is a principle of acting and makes acts holy.

1115. The Excellence of Charity.—Human friendship of the lower kind is not a virtue, while that which is higher is rather the extension or result of virtue than a virtue in itself. The divine friendship, however, constitutes the theological virtue of charity.

(a) Thus, charity is a virtue, since through it our acts are regulated by their supreme standard and our affections united to the divine goodness.

(b) Charity, although it exercises a sway over the other virtues, is distinct from them; for it has its own proper object, namely, the divine goodness, all-perfect in itself: "These three: faith, hope and charity" (I Cor., xiii. 13).

(c) Charity, although it includes our neighbor as well as God among the objects of love, is but one virtue, since it has but one end (i.e., the goodness of God), and it is based on but one fellowship (i.e., the beatific vision to be bestowed by God).

1116. Charity is less perfect than the act of the intellect by which God is seen intuitively in the beatific vision, but it is preeminent among the virtues of this life. (a) Thus, it is superior to the normal virtues, for while they regulate actions by the inferior rule of reason, charity regulates them by the supreme rule, which is God Himself. (b) It is superior to the other theological virtues, since it tends to God in Himself, whereas faith and hope tend to God as He is the principle whence we derive truth and blessedness: "The greatest of these is charity" (I Cor., xiii. 13).

1117. The other virtues require charity for their perfection.

(a) Without charity the other virtues are either false virtues, or true but imperfect virtues; for they are then directed, not to the universal and last End, but at most to some particular and proximate good end. Nor are they meritorious without charity, for "if I should distribute all my goods to feed the poor, and if I should deliver my body to be burned, and have not charity, it profiteth me nothing" (I Cor., xiii. 3).

(b) With charity the other virtues become true and perfect virtues. Examples: Titus gives alms to the poor in order to win them to infidelity (false charity). Caius avoids drunkenness, not because he dislikes it, but because he is a miser and dislikes to spend money (false temperance). Balbus has no religion, but is very faithful to his family duties (imperfect justice). Claudius discharges his duties to his family and neighbors out of love for God (perfect justice).

1118. The influence of charity on the other virtues is expressed by various titles.

(a) Charity is called the informing principle of the other virtues. This does not mean that charity is the type on which the other virtues are modelled, or the internal character that makes them what they are; otherwise, all the virtues would be absorbed in the one virtue of charity. It means, then, that the other virtues derive the quality of perfect virtue from charity, through which they are directed to the Last End.

(b) Charity is called the foundation and root of virtues (Eph., iii. 17), not in the sense that it is a material part of them, but in the sense that it supports and nourishes them.

(c) It is also spoken of as the end and the mother of the other virtues, because it directs the other virtues to the Last End, and produces their acts by commanding their exercise: "The end of the commandment is charity" (I Tim., i. 5).

1119. Charity causes the other virtues, negatively by forbidding evil, affirmatively by commanding good (I Cor., xiii, 4-7).

(a) It forbids that evil be done the neighbor, either in desire or in deed: "Charity envieth not, dealeth not perversely."

(b) It forbids evil passions by which one is injured in oneself, such as pride, ambition, greed, anger: "Charity is not puffed up, is not ambitious, seeketh not her own, is not provoked to anger."

(c) It forbids that one harm one's own soul by thoughts or desires of wrong: "Charity thinketh no evil, rejoiceth not in iniquity."

(d) It commands that good be done the neighbor, bears with his defects, rejoices over his good and bestows benefits upon him: "Charity is patient, is kind; rejoiceth with the truth, beareth all things."

(e) It commands that good be done towards God by the practice of the theological virtues of faith and hope, and by continuance in them: "Charity believeth all things, hopeth all things, endureth all things."

1120. Direction is given by charity to the other virtues that makes them perfect and meritorious.

(a) Actual direction—that is, the intention here and now to believe, or hope, etc., out of love for God—though more perfect, is not required for merit in faith, hope and other virtues: otherwise, merit would become extremely difficult and rare.

(b) Habitual direction—that is, the mere fact that one has the habit of charity, though it in no way influences an act of faith, or of hope, etc, now made—does not suffice; otherwise, it would follow that an act of faith recited by a person in the state of charity, but here and now unconscious, is meritorious, which would make merit too easy.

(c) Virtual direction—that is, the influence of an intention, once made and never retracted, of acting out of love for God, which continues, though it is not adverted to, while one believes, hopes, etc.—at least is necessary; otherwise, one would make oneself deserving of the Last End, without ever having desired it, for the other virtues do not tend to the Last End in itself. In practice, however, there is no person in the state of grace who does not perform all his acts that are human and virtuous under the direction of charity, actual or virtual.

1121. Production of Charity.—The virtue of charity belongs to the appetitive part of the soul, but supposes a judgment by which its exercise is regulated. (a) Thus, the power of the soul in which charity dwells is the will, for its object is good apprehended by the intellect; but (b) the judgment by which it is regulated is not human reason, as is the case with the moral virtues, but divine wisdom (Eph., iii. 19).

1122. The Origin of Charity.—(a) Charity is not caused by nature, nor acquired by the powers of nature. Natural love of God, indeed, is possible without grace; but charity is a supernatural friendship based on a fellowship in the beatitude of God. (b) It is introduced or begotten by other virtues, in the sense that they prepare one to receive it from God (I Tim., i. 5).

1123. The cause of charity, then, is God, who infuses it into the soul: "The charity of God is poured forth in our hearts by the Holy Ghost, who is given to us" (Rom., v. 5). The measure according to which God infuses the gift of charity depends on His will and bounty.

(a) The Angels received charity at their creation, according to their natural rank, so that those who were higher excelled those who were lower, both in nature and in grace.

(b) Those who receive charity through infant baptism have it according "to the measure of the giving of Christ" (Eph., iv. 7; cfr. John, iii. 8; I Cor., xii. 2).

(c) Those who receive charity through repentance, have it, "everyone according to his proper ability" (Matt., xxv. 15), that is, according to the disposition with which he has prepared himself. But the preparation itself depends on the grace of God (Col., i. 12).

1124. Charity may be increased: "I pray that your charity may more and more abound" (Philip., i. 9). It must, however, be noted that: (a) the increase is not in the motive of charity, for the goodness of God is supreme and incapable of increase, nor is it in the objects of charity, for even the lowest degree of this virtue extends to all those things that must be loved on account of God; (b) the increase, then, is in the manner in which charity exists in the soul, in that it becomes more deeply rooted and takes stronger hold of the will, whose acts of love become correspondingly more intense and fervent. Just as knowledge grows as it becomes clearer and more certain, so does charity progress to higher degrees as it exists more firmly in its subject.

1125. With reference to the increase of charity, acts of love are of two kinds: (a) the less fervent are those that do not surpass the degree of charity one already possesses; (b) the more fervent are those that surpass the degree of charity one has. Example: If one has ten degrees of habitual charity, an act of five degrees is less fervent, an act of fifteen degrees is more fervent.

1126. Every act of charity, even the less fervent, contributes to an increase of the charity one already possesses. This is true whether the act be elicited by charity (i.e., an act of love of God), or commanded by charity (i.e., an act of some other virtue performed out of love for God). Every act of charity merits from God an increase of the habit of charity (see Council of Trent, Sess. VI, Can. 32). Even a cup of cold water given in the name of a disciple shall not go without its reward (Matt., X. 42).

1127. As to the manner and time in which the increase takes place, there are various opinions, but the following points sum up what seems more probable:

(a) The increase of the habit of charity merited by a more fervent act is conferred at once, for God confers His gifts when one is disposed for their reception. Example: Titus, who has habitually ten degrees of charity, makes an act of charity whose degree is fifteen; he thereby merits the increase of the habit, and it is conferred at once.

(b) The increase of the habit of charity merited by less fervent acts is not conferred until the moment one enters into heaven or purgatory, for there is no time during life on earth when one has a disposition equal to the added quantity contained in less fervent acts, since, as just said, more fervent acts are rewarded at once by the increase that corresponds to them, while less fervent acts do not dispose one for an increase then and there. But the increase must be conferred when one enters into glory; otherwise, one would lose the degree of beatitude one merited during life. Hence, those who make many—even though less fervent—acts of charity during life, will receive a very high degree of reward for them hereafter.

1128. The increase of charity will come to an end in the future life, when one has attained the degree of perfection to which one was predestined by God (Philip, iii. 12). But, as long as a person lives here below, he may continually grow in charity, for each increase makes him capable of receiving from the infinite power of God a further participation in the infinite charity, which is the Holy Ghost (II Cor., vi. 11).

1129. Charity is absolutely perfect, when it loves God in the same degree in which He is lovable—that is, infinitely; but it is clear that so great charity is possible only to God. Charity is relatively perfect, when one loves God as much as one can. This relatively perfect charity is possible to man (Matt, v. 48; I John, ii. 5, iv. 12, 17); but it has three degrees:

(a) The perfect charity of heaven, which is not possible in this life, consists in this, that one is constantly occupied in thinking of God and loving Him.

(b) The perfect charity of earth, which is special to some of the just, consists in this, that one gives all one's time to divine things, as far as the necessities of mortal existence allow.

(c) The perfect charity of earth that is common to all the just, consists in this, that habitually one gives one's whole heart to God, permitting no thought or desire opposed to the divine love.

1130. Those who are growing in charity are divided into three classes: (a) the beginners, or those whose chief care is freedom from sin and resistance to what is contrary to divine love; (b) the proficients, or those who must still fight against temptation, but whose chief attention is given to progress along the way of virtue; (c) the perfect, or those who are progressing in holiness, but whose chief desire is to reach the end of the journey and be with the object of their love (Philip., i. 13).

1131. The Decline of Charity.—(a) Actual charity can decline, in the sense that subsequent acts can be less fervent than those that preceded (Apoc., ii. 4). (b) Habitual charity cannot grow less in itself. The only causes that can be supposed for a decline in habitual charity are omission of the act of charity and commission of venial sin; the former, however, cannot lessen charity, since this habit, being infused, does not depend on human acts; the latter, which is a disorder about the means to the end, does not contradict charity, which is the right order of man with reference to his Last End itself. Thus, charity differs from human friendships, which grow cold through neglect or slights. (c) Habitual charity can be lessened, first, with reference to the disposition that makes for its preservation and increase (as when one commits numerous and dangerous venial sins), and secondly, with reference to itself (as when one rising from sin has less charity than he had before). But in neither of these cases does the same numerical habit decrease.

1132. The Loss of Charity.—(a) The charity of the blessed cannot be lost, because they see God as He is, and are constantly occupied in loving Him. But the charity of earth, since it proceeds from a less perfect knowledge and is not always in use, may be surrendered by man's free will (see Council of Trent, Sess. VI, Cap. 12, 13, 14, Can. 23). (b) The habit of charity is lost, not only by any sin against the love of God, but by any other mortal sin opposed to other virtues (see Council of Trent, Sess. VI, Cap. 15). Every mortal sin is a turning away from the Last End, and so is incompatible with charity, which is a turning to God, the Last End: "He that hath My commandments and keepeth them, he it is that loveth Me" (John, xiv. 21). Venial sin diminishes the fervor of charity, but does not remove charity itself.

1133. The Object of Charity.—There is a threefold object of charity: (a) the formal object, that is, the reason for love, which is the infinite amiability of God in Himself, as known from the supernatural illumination of faith; (b) the primary material object, that is, the chief thing which charity loves, which is God (i.e., the divine Essence, the divine Persons, the divine attributes): "Thou shalt love the Lord, Thy God. This is the greatest and the first commandment" (Matt, xxii. 37,

38); (c) the secondary material object, that is, the thing loved because of God, which is self and the neighbor: "And the second is like to this: Thou shalt love thy neighbor as thyself" (ibid, 39).

1134. The love of creatures is not always an act of the virtue of charity. (a) Sinful love of creatures, by which one loves them more than God or inordinately, destroys or deviates from charity. Hence, St. John says: "Love not the world, nor the things that are in the world" (I John, ii. 15). (b) Natural love of creatures, by which one loves them on account of reasons apart from love of God (such as the benefits one derives from them or the excellences they possess), is not charity, even though good. Thus, gratitude which sees in another only a benefactor, friendship which sees in another only a congenial spirit, and philanthropy which sees in another only a fellow-man, differ from charity, although they are good in themselves. (c) Supernatural love of creatures, by which one loves them on account of the divine that is in them, inasmuch as they are friends of God or made for the glory of one's divine Friend, does not differ specifically from love of God, for in both loves there is the same motive (viz, the amiability of God Himself).

1135. Since charity is friendship, it does not include among its objects those things that are loved with the love of desire (see 1109), that is, those things whose good is desired, but for another.

(a) Hence, charity itself is not an object of charity, for it is loved not as a friend, but as a good that one wishes for one's friends. The same applies to other virtues and to beatitudes.

(b) Irrational creatures are not objects of charity, for a fellowship with them in friendship, and especially in the beatific vision, is impossible. We can love them out of charity, however, inasmuch as we desire their preservation for the sake of those whom we love with charity (e.g., desiring that they be preserved for the glory of God or the use of man).

1136. Love of self is of various kinds.

(a) Sinful self-love is that by which a person loves himself according to his lower and corrupt nature, and not according to his higher or rational nature, or loves himself egotistically to the hurt of others. Of those who indulge their passions it is said: "In the last days shall come dangerous times. Men shall be lovers of themselves" (II Tim., iii. 1, 2); of those who love themselves selfishly it is said: "All seek the things that are their own, not the things that are Jesus Christ's" (Philip., ii. 21); whereas charity seeketh not her own (I Cor., xiii.) to the exclusion of others, but desires what is for the advantage of the neighbor (I Cor., x. 33).

(b) Natural self-love is that necessary desire which each one has for his own good, happiness, existence, etc. (II Cor., v. 4), or any desire for reasonable self-improvement that is not prompted by a supernatural love of God. This love is stronger than love for another, for it implies not merely union, but unity. It is not friendship, but the root of friendship, for one is said to be friendly towards another when one holds him as another self.

(c) Supernatural self-love is that love which one has for God, and consequently for self as a friend of God.

1137. If by "self" we understand the substance and nature of man, as composed of soul and body, then both good and bad understand aright the meaning of self and desire its preservation. But if by "self" we mean principally the inward man and secondarily the outward man (II Cor., iv. 16), then only the good understand what self is, and have a true love for it, whereas the wicked hate their own souls (Ps. x. 6). For the five marks of true friendship are shown to the inner man by the good, to the outward man by the sinner: (a) the good are solicitous for the life of the soul, the wicked for that of the body; (b) the good desire spiritual treasures for the soul, the wicked carnal delights for the body; (c) the good labor to provide for the needs of the soul, the wicked work only for the needs of the body; (d) the good are pleased to converse with their souls, finding there thoughts of past, present and future good things to delight them, while the wicked seek to distract themselves from wholesome thought by pleasure; (e) the good are at peace with their souls, whereas the wicked are troubled by conscience.

1138. Supernatural love of self, which pertains to charity, extends not only to the soul, but also to the body; for (a) according to its nature, the body is good, since it is from God and may be employed for His service (Rom., vi. 13), and hence it may be loved out of charity with the love of desire on account of the honor it may give to God and the service it may render in good works; (b) according to grace, the body is capable of sharing in secondary beatitude, through glorification with the soul, and hence it may be loved with charity and with the love of benevolence, inasmuch as we desire for it a share in beatitude: "We would not be unclothed, but clothed over, that that which is mortal may be swallowed up by life" (II Cor., v. 4); (e) according to the consequences of sin that are in it, the body is a drag on the soul, or a hindrance to it, and one should not love but rather desire the removal of its imperfections. Hence, St. Paul desired to be freed from the body (Rom., vii. 24; Philip,, i. 23), and the Saints have shown their hatred of the body's corruption by the mortifications to which they subjected it (John, xii. 25).

1139. Love of neighbor is of three kinds: (a) sinful love, which is all love that is excessive, irregulated, or directed to what is evil in others; (b) natural love, which is all love that is attracted by some excellence of a human or created kind, such as knowledge or skill; (c) supernatural love, which is that by which one is drawn towards another on account of the divine in him, such as his gifts of grace and of heavenly calling.

1140. Hence, it seems that there is no such thing as a special and distinct virtue of human friendship. (a) Thus, friendships of utility or of pleasure are clearly not virtues, since they are not caused by attraction towards moral good. (b) Virtuous friendships are the consequences of virtues rather than virtues, for the attraction one has for one's friend arises from the attraction for the virtue one sees in him. Thus, friendship for another because he is not the slave of passion, is an exercise of the virtue of temperance. (c) Supernatural friendships are not distinct from the virtue of charity, for the gifts and graces which evoke them are participations of God's goodness, which is the object of charity.

1141. The neighbors whom we are to love according to charity are all those who can have with us the relation of supernatural friendship, that is, all rational creatures. (a) Hence, the Angels are objects of this love, and in the resurrection men will be fellow-citizens with them (Heb., xii, 22); (b) our fellow-men are objects of this love, for they also are called to the heavenly companionship (ibid., 23).

1142. Charity for Sinners.—Should we love with charity those who are sinners and enemies of God? (a) If we consider sinners precisely as enemies of God, we may not love them, for their sin is an evil, an offense to God and a hurt to themselves. On the contrary, we should hate even in those who are nearest to us whatever is opposed to love of God (Luke, xiv. 26). (b) If we consider sinners precisely as creatures of God, we may not love them with charity or as friends, if they are demons or lost souls; for in their case fellowship with us in beatitude is out of the question. We may, however, love their nature out of charity towards God, desiring that it be preserved by Him for His glory. (c) If we consider sinners precisely as creatures of God, we may love them with charity or as friends, if they are still in the present life; for we should wish that God may be glorified in them by their conversion and salvation. The commandment of love of neighbor was not restricted to loving the just.

1143. If sinners be considered precisely as they are enemies of God, is it lawful to hate them and wish evil to them? (a) It is lawful to hate the evil that is in sinners, but not their persons. He who hates their sin, loves themselves, for their sin is against their own interests. In this way the Psalmist hated sinners (Ps. cxviii. 113, cxxxviii. 32). (b) It is lawful to wish that punishment overtake sinners, if one is actuated, not by a spirit of malevolence, but by love of justice (Ps. lvii. 11; Wis., i. 13; Ps. x. 8). It is also lawful to wish that the sinfulness that is in them may be destroyed, that they themselves may be saved. In this sense we may understand some of the imprecations that are met in scripture (Ps. ciii. 35). Thus, a judge sentences a criminal, not because he hates the man before him, but because he wishes to reform him, or to protect society, or to do an act of justice.

1144. The evils of punishment or of destruction of sin are in a broader view not evils, but goods. But the following punishments may not be desired: (a) that anyone living lose his soul and be condemned to hell, for charity requires that we desire the salvation of sinners; (b) that a sinner be punished by blindness of heart and go from bad to worse. He who wishes sin approves of the offense to God; but it does not seem unlawful to wish that God permit a person to fall into sin, as a means to a spiritual awakening.

1145. Association with Sinners.—(a) It is never lawful to associate with sinners in their sins, for thus one becomes a sharer in their guilt. Hence, St. Paul says: "Go out from among them and be ye separate" (II Cor., vi. 17). (b) It is not lawful to associate with sinners even in matters indifferent or good, if one is weak and apt to be led away by them into sin (see 258 sqq.). (c) It is lawful to associate with sinners in things not forbidden, if one is not endangered, and if one aims to convert them to better ways. Thus, our Lord ate with sinners, because He came to call them to repentance (Matt., ix. 10-13).

1146. Friendship with Sinners.-(a) If this means that we like and dislike the same things as the sinners, it is an evil friendship, and it should be discontinued; (b) if it means that we seek to bring the sinner to imitate our good likes and dislikes, the friendship pertains to charity (Jer, xv. 19).

1147. Should one continue to show signs of special regard to a friend who has taken to ways of sin? (a) As long as there is hope of betterment, one should not deny the other the benefits of friendship. If it would be wrong to desert a friend because he was perishing from starvation, much more would it be wrong to desert him because he was perishing morally. (b) But if all hope of betterment has gone, one should give up a companionship which is not profitable to either party, and may prove harmful.

1148. Charity towards Enemies.—Enemies can be considered in two senses: precisely as enemies, or precisely as human beings destined for beatitude. (a) If considered as enemies, they are not to be loved with charity—that is, it should be displeasing to us that they are enemies and opposed to us, for it would be contrary to charity to love in a neighbor that which is evil in him. (b) If considered as human beings, enemies should be loved with charity—that is, their nature created by God and capable of receiving grace and glory should be pleasing to us, for love of God should make us love all that belongs to Him, even that which is not well disposed towards ourselves.

1149. The precept of love of enemies did not originate with the law of Christ. (a) It pertains to the natural law, for (i) it follows from the natural principle: "Do unto others as you would have them do unto you," and (ii) it was known by natural reason (e.g., Plato and Cicero knew it). (b) Love of enemies was commanded in the Old Law, being the second great commandment of that law (Matt., xxii. 39), and was taught in various Old Testament books (Lev., xix. 17, 18; Exod., xxiii 4, 5; Prov., xxi. 21, 22). (c) It was renewed by Christ, who corrected the false interpretation of Leviticus, xix. 18, given by the scribes and Pharisees, who taught: "Thou shalt love thy friend and hate thy enemy." In the Sermon on the Mount our Lord declares: "I say to you: Love your enemies: do good to them that hate you: that you may be the children of your Father who is in heaven" (Matt., v. 44, 45).

1150. The following examples of love of one's enemies are found in the Bible: (a) in the Old Testament, Joseph forgave his brethren who had sold him into Egypt, David spared the life of his persecutor Saul and wept over the ungrateful Absalom, and Moses prayed for the people who had rebelled against him; (b) in the New Testament our Lord mourned over Jerusalem which had rejected Him, and on the Cross prayed for His enemies.

1151. What kind of love must we entertain for enemies?

(a) A general love of enemies is that which extends to all neighbors for the love of God, no exception being made as regards enemies. This kind of love is required. Example: Caius makes an act of love in which he declares his love for his neighbor, but mentions no names. Titus makes this act of love: "I love all except Caius." The act of love made by Caius is sufficient, that of Titus is insufficient.

(b) A special love of enemies is that which extends to them in particular, not as included in the human race or the community, but as individuals, as when one expressly mentions the name of an enemy in his act of love. This kind of love of enemies is not required at all times.

1152. Is there an obligation of special love of enemies? (a) In cases of necessity (e.g., when the omission of a special love would bring on hate), one is bound to special love. (b) Outside of cases of necessity, one is bound to be willing to love an enemy in particular, if the necessity should arise. (c) Outside of necessity, one is not bound to love an enemy in particular, for it is impossible to give such attention even to all those who are not enemies. But to give an enemy more love than is required is a sign of perfect charity.

1153. The principles just given as to internal love of enemies apply also to external love, or to the signs by which internal love is manifested. For St. John says: "Let us not love in word, nor in tongue, but in deed, and in truth" (I John, iii. 18).

(a) Hence, it is not lawful to deny to an enemy the common signs of charity (i.e., such benefits as are bestowed on his community or class as a whole), for to do so would be to signify a desire for revenge (Lev., xix. 18). Consequently, he who excludes his enemies from prayers offered for his neighbor sins against charity.

(b) In cases of necessity, as when an enemy is in great need as to life, fame, fortune or salvation, one is bound to show special signs of charity, such as salutation, conversation, assistance, etc. Thus, we are told: "If thy enemy be hungry, give him to eat; if he be thirsty, give him to drink" (Prov., xxv. 21).

(c) Outside of cases of necessity, one is bound to be ready to assist an enemy, should there be need.

(d) Outside of necessity, one is not bound actually to manifest particular love for an enemy, by speaking to him, trading with him, visiting him, etc. Hence, David, although he had pardoned Absalom, would not meet him (II Kings, xiv. 24). To confer special benefits on an enemy when there is no obligation is a counsel of perfection: "Do good to those that hate you" (Matt., v. 24). This heaps coals of fire upon the head of the enemy, curing him by the salutary pain of repentance, and so overcomes evil by good (Rom., xii. 20, 21).

1154. The common signs of charity are not limited to those that are shown to all mankind, but include also such as are usually shown by one Christian to another Christian, by one citizen to a fellow-citizen, by a relative to a relative, etc. Thus, to make a social call, though it would be a sign of special regard in the case of one not a relative, might be only a common sign of charity in the case of a relative.

(a) Hence, it is against charity to deny an enemy signs of charity that are customarily shown to all men. Example: Titus dislikes Balbus, and therefore refuses to sell to him, does not return his salutations, speaks to all others in company, while ignoring Balbus, and will not even answer if Balbus addresses him.

(b) It is against charity to deny an enemy signs of charity that are commonly shown to all those to whom one is similarly related. Examples: Claudia calls on her other children frequently and makes them presents, but she keeps away from one daughter, even when the latter is sick and poor and she is calling next door. Sempronius habitually invites to his house for family festivities all his relatives except his brother.

(c) It is against charity to deny to an enemy some benefit not commonly shown, but which one has bestowed out of liberality on the group to which the latter belongs. In such a case a special sign of charity becomes common. Example: Titus prepares a banquet for a neighboring institution, and purposely sends no invitation to two members whom he dislikes.

1155. The rule that common signs of charity must be shown does not apply, if some higher or more urgent duty requires that they be omitted: however, internal charity must persist all the while.

(a) Thus, by reason of charity owed to self or to the better interests of an offender, one should at times omit the common signs of charity. Examples: Caius avoids Balbus, with whom he has had a quarrel, because he knows well that Balbus is seeking some pretext to get revenge. Titus has a surly way of speaking, and his mother, in order to cure him, does not answer until he has spoken civilly.

(b) By reason of justice, the signs of charity should sometimes be denied as a punishment. Examples: Claudia punishes her children, when they are disobedient, by refusing them for a time privileges given the other children. For the same reason she refuses to call on a daughter who ran away from home and married a worthless fellow.

(c) By reason of justice, the signs of charity should be refused, when this is required for the protection of one's own rights. Example: Titus goes about defaming Sempronius and his family, but appears very affable when he meets Sempronius; the latter knows all this, and hence is very cool with Titus, to show that the injuries are not held as light.

1156. The following are the rules for judging whether (apart from scandal to others) sin has been committed through refusal of the signs of charity:

(a) If internally there is hatred (i.e., a contempt for one's neighbor, as if he were unworthy of common charity), or malevolence (i.e., a will to exercise spite), then one is guilty of grave uncharitableness, unless the smallness of the matter makes it only a venial sin.

(b) If externally the denial of charity is such that in the judgment of a prudent man it indicates real hatred, and the injured party perceives this and is scandalized or hurt thereby, the sin of uncharitableness is committed, even though there be no internal hatred. The gravity depends on the scandal or offense caused the other party. Example: Claudius and Balbus, once very friendly, have had a disagreement. Now, when Claudius sees Balbus coming in his direction, he turns off by a side street, not to show hatred, but to avoid a meeting. If Balbus does not know this, or does not care, no sin—or at most only a venial sin—is committed; but if Balbus is deeply wounded or scandalized by this conduct, Claudius sins seriously against charity.

1157. Refusal of Greetings.—(a) To refuse to exchange a bow or salutation (such as "Good morning") indicates a want of charity, when such mutual courtesy is expected according to custom; not, however, when custom does not require it, Example: In Balba's office the girls employed usually salute one another on arrival and departure, but Balba never salutes Titia, and hence is regarded as her enemy. On Caius' street the neighbors are of a very mixed kind, and it is not customary to speak to everybody. Hence, the fact that Caius never salutes certain neighbors, whom he dislikes, does not signify any uncharitableness on his part.

(b) To refuse to salute another first, where custom expects this, is a mark of uncharity, unless one has a sufficient excuse. Examples: Claudius has a grudge against Sempronius, an elderly man who is much his senior, and says he will never salute him as others do. Titus refuses to greet Balbus, his acquaintance, when they meet, because in the past Balbus has treated his greetings with contempt, and shows that he does not care to notice Titus.

(c) To refuse to return a salutation sincerely given indicates a want of charity.

1158. The Order of Charity.—Charity not only requires that we love God, ourselves, and our neighbors, but it also obliges us to love these objects according to a certain order, some being preferred to others.

(a) God must be loved above all, more than self (Matt., xvi. 24), more than father and mother (Matt., x. 37; Luke, xiv. 26), for He is the common good of all, and the source of all good.

(b) Other things being equal, one should love self more than one's neighbor, for the love of self is the model for the love of neighbor (Matt., xxii. 39), and nature itself inclines to this in accordance with the saying: "Charity begins at home."

(c) Among neighbors those should be loved more who have more of a claim on account of their greater nearness to God or to ourselves.

1159. Love can become greater in two ways: (a) objectively, when the person loved is esteemed as of greater worth, or has more titles to affection, or has a more enduring right to be loved; (b) subjectively, when the person loving is more touched and moved in his feelings, even though the object be not more amiable in itself.

1160. The Character of our Love of God.—(a) It must be supreme objectively, since He is infinite perfection and has the highest of all claims on our love. Hence, one should be disposed to suffer any loss rather than abandon God. (b) It must be supreme subjectively, in our desire, that is, realizing that God is the highest good, we should at least wish to give Him the utmost of our fervor and ardor. (c) It need not be supreme subjectively, in fact; for we are not always masters of our feelings, and things that are nearer to us affect us more than those that are more important, but remote from sense. Hence, it is not against charity that one should be more moved sensibly at the thoughtof a dear human friend than at the thought of God, provided the will places God above all.

1161. Regarding the love of God for the sake of reward, we must note: (a) If there is question of the eternal reward, one may love and serve God for the sake of reward, provided one makes the reward the end of one's service, but not the end of God; for salvation is really the end of our faith (I Pet., i. 9), but God is the end of all, and He is to be preferred to all. This love of God for the sake of reward coexists with charity, for one may love a friend for his own sake, and at the same time expect benefits from the friendship, provided the love of benevolence is uppermost. (b) If there is question of a temporal reward, one may love and serve God for the sake of the reward, not in the sense that spiritual things are made a means and temporal things their end, but in the sense that one hopes one's service of God will be so blessed that one will have health, strength and opportunity, so as to be enabled to continue and progress in that service.

1162. Regarding the love of self (i.e., of the inner man, or our spiritual nature), we should note: (a) Objectively, one esteems others who are higher in sanctity than oneself (e.g., the Blessed Virgin), as more worthy of love. But one may desire for self according to charity such progress in virtue that one will pass some others who are now better than oneself; for the virtue of charity is given us that we may perfect ourselves. (b) Subjectively, one holds self as being nearer than other persons, and thus loves oneself with a greater intensity.

1163. Is it lawful to sacrifice one's own spiritual goods for the benefit of a neighbor?

(a) One may not sacrifice necessary spiritual goods for the benefit, spiritual or temporal, of any one, not even of the whole world; for in so doing one inflicts a wound on one's own soul and prefers the good of others to one's own spiritual welfare. Hence, it is not lawful to wish to be damned in place of another; to commit sin, mortal or venial, to prevent another from sinning; or to expose oneself to the certain and proximate danger of sin for the sake of another's spiritual progress.

(b) One may, however, sacrifice unnecessary or less necessary spiritual goods for the benefit, spiritual or temporal, of a neighbor; for, by doing this, one chooses the course which God wishes, and does not lessen but rather increases one's own profit. Thus, a priest should interrupt his devotions to hear the confession of a penitent; a daughter should give up the idea of becoming a nun as long as her parents need her; a lay person should stay away from Mass on Sunday, if an invalid has to be cared for, or a dying person must be baptized; it is laudable to make the heroic act of charity, by which one transfers the satisfactory value of one's good works to the souls in purgatory; one may expose oneself to a remote danger of sin in order to perform a great service of charity, as in waiting on a sick person who on account of irritability is a great temptation to anger; one may wish that one's entrance into heaven be delayed, so that one may labor longer for souls (Philip., i. 23, 24).

1164. The Love of the Body.—(a) One should prefer the spiritual welfare of one's neighbor to one's own bodily welfare, for our neighbor is called to be a partaker with us in the beatific vision, while the body will share only in accidental glory. (b) One should prefer one's own bodily welfare to that of another, all other things being equal, for it has more of a claim on one.

1165. There are three kinds of spiritual necessity in which a neighbor may be placed, and in which one might be called on to sacrifice one's bodily welfare for the other's good (cfr. 1236), Thus, there is: (a) extreme spiritual need, or that in which a neighbor will perish eternally unless help is given him, as when an infant is about to die without baptism; (b) grave spiritual need, or that in which a neighbor runs grave danger of losing his soul unless help is given, as when a dying person, who is in mortal sin, asks for a confessor, because he is scarcely able to make an act of perfect contrition; (c) ordinary spiritual need, or that in which a neighbor is in remote danger of damnation, or in proximate danger of sin, but can easily help himself, as is the case with those who from choice live in occasions of sin.

1166. For a neighbor who is in extreme spiritual need, one should risk death (I John, iii. 16) or lesser evils, if the following conditions are present: (a) if there is a good prospect of success in helping the needy one (e.g., a mother is not obliged to undergo an operation dangerous to her life, in order to secure the baptism of her child, if it is uncertain that the baptism can be administered); (b) if there is no one else who can and will give the needed help; (c) if there is no reason of public good that stands in the way; thus, if by helping one in extreme need a person would lose his life, and so deprive of his aid a large number who are also in extreme need, he should prefer to help the many rather than the one.

1167. For a neighbor who is in grave spiritual necessity, the same risk is not required of all. (a) The risk of death itself is required of pastors of souls (John, x. 11), since they have bound themselves to this. Hence, a pastor who would refuse to go to a parishioner dying of pestilence and needing absolution and Extreme Unction, would offend against justice, while another priest who would go to such a dying person would practise the perfection of charity; for the dying person can help himself by an act of contrition, and the strange priest is not bound by office to care for him. (b) The risk of some great corporal evil (such as a sickness or impairment of health) should be taken even by those who are not pastors of the person in need, if there is no one else to help. Thus, if a pastor were sick, another priest ought to visit a dying person, even at the risk of catching a severe cold.

1168. For a neighbor who is in ordinary spiritual necessity charity requires that something be done (Ecclus, xvii. 12). (a) But it does not require the risk of life or of serious bodily loss, for the person in danger can easily and better help himself. Thus, it is not necessary that one should penetrate into the haunts of criminals and endanger one's life, in order to drag away one who chooses to go to such places. (b) It does require that one be willing to undergo a slight bodily inconvenience or deprivation. Thus, an ordinary headache or the loss of a meal ought not to stop one from counselling another in order to keep him away from bad company.

1169. If only corporal good (life, health, liberty, etc.) is compared with corporal good of the same kind, then, as said above, one should prefer one's own good to that of another. Thus, it is not lawful to offer oneself as substitute for a condemned criminal, or to put one's family into bankruptcy to save another family from bankruptcy. But, if a neighbor's corporal good is of a more important kind or is connected with higher goods, then one may sacrifice one's own good for that of another.

(a) Thus, one may prefer a greater corporal good of a neighbor to a lesser corporal good of one's own. Examples: One may weaken one's health to save another's life. One may give of one's blood for a transfusion to assist another who is in danger of death.

(b) One may prefer an equal corporal good of a neighbor to an equal corporal good of one's own, if the common good requires this; for the good of all is preferable to that of an individual. Thus, one may expose oneself to the peril of death in order to protect a public person whose life is very important to the nation. Thus, policemen and firemen, soldiers and sailors, are daily imperilling their own safety for the safety of the public.

(c) One may prefer an equal corporal good of another, who is only a private individual, to one's own equal good, if the intention is to practise virtue, to assist a person in need, or to give edification. At least, it is more probable that this is lawful, for the good of virtue is a higher good than the good of the body, and the Fathers praise holy men who sold themselves into slavery, or who gave themselves as hostages to barbarians, for the liberation of captives; and they hold up for admiration Damon and Pythias, each of whom was ready to die for the other. Hence, it is not against the charity owed to self to jump into a river and risk one's life in order to rescue a drowning person, for heroic charity is a hotter adornment to self than mere, ordinary charity. Similarly, if two explorers in a wilderness have only enough provisions for one to reach civilization, one of them may surrender his rations to the other, that both may not be lost.

1170. There are two exceptions to the rules just given: (a) A person should not risk his life for another's life, if he thereby endangers his own salvation (e.g., if he is in a state of sin and cannot reconcile himself to God). But this case is theoretical, for it is admitted that one who makes the supreme sacrifice of giving his life with a virtuous intention, has not only charity, but the perfection of charity (John, xv. 13), which will certainly purify him even from a multitude of sins. (b) One should not risk one's life for the life of another, if a third party has a higher claim on him. Thus, a married man, who has a dependent wife and children, may not throw away his life for the sake of a friend.

1171. The order of charity between different neighbors is as follows: (a) as to good in general (e.g., the attainment of salvation), we should love all neighbors alike, for we should desire salvation for all; (b) as to good in particular (e.g., the degree of beatitude), we should love some more than others. Thus, we should desire a higher degree of glory for the Blessed Virgin than for the Saints.

1172. The reasons for loving one neighbor more than another can be reduced to two. (a) One neighbor may be nearer to God than another, and hence more deserving of love—for example, a saintly acquaintance may be nearer to God than a sinful relative. (b) One neighbor may be nearer to ourselves on account of relationship by blood or marriage, friendship, civil or professional ties, etc. Thus, a cousin is nearer by nature to his cousin than another person who is not a relative.

1173. The order of charity as between those nearer to God and those nearer to self is as follows:

(a) Objectively, we should esteem more those who are better, and desire for them that higher degree of God's favor which belongs to their merits. But we may desire for those nearer to ourselves that they will finally surpass in holiness those now better than they are, and thus attain to a greater beatitude. Moreover, while we prefer in one respect (i.e., that of holiness) a saintly person, who is a stranger, we prefer in many respects (e.g., on account of relationship, friendship, gratitude) another who is less holy.

(b) Subjectively, the love for those nearer to self is greater, that is, more intense, more vividly felt. The preferences for those nearer to self, therefore, far from being wrong or the expression of mere natural love, are expressions of charity itself. For it is God's will that more love should be shown to those who are nearer to us: "If any man have not care of his own, and especially of those of his house, he hath denied the faith, and is worse than an infidel" (I Tim., v. 8). Hence, charity itself inclines one to have more love for one's own, and it supernaturalizes filial piety, patriotism, and friendship.

1174. The order to be followed in the manifestation of charity will correspond with the order of charity itself. (a) To those to whom greater objective love is due, on account of their holiness, more respect due to their excellence should be shown. (b) To those to whom greater return of love is due on account of the benefits they have shown (as parents, friends, etc.), more assistance should be given spiritually and temporally. That is, if one had to choose between helping either a relative or a stranger who was more virtuous, one would have to decide in favor of the relative. (c) To those to whom greater subjective love is due, more signs of affection (such as visits) should be given.

1175. Exceptions to the above are the following cases, in which the good of the better person should be preferred:

(a) if the common good requires such a preference. Thus, public interest demands that in conferring positions, making appointments, or voting for candidates, one should not be guided by family affections or private friendships, but only by the common welfare; and one should decide in favor of the better man;

(b) if the person nearer to self has forfeited his claims to preference. Thus, a son who has treated his father with contempt and is a wastrel, may be deprived of his share of the family goods in favor of strangers who are self-sacrificing and who promote some holy cause.

1176. The order of charity between various kinds of natural relationships is as follows: (a) the relationship that arises from consanguinity is prior and more stable, since it arises from nature itself and cannot be removed; (b) the relationship of friendship, since it arises from one's own choice, may be more congenial and may be preferred even to kinship, when there is question of society and companionship (Prov., xviii. 24).

1177. In practice, other things being equal, one should manifest more love to a relative in those things that belong to the relationship.

(a) To those who are related by blood, corporal or temporal assistance is more due. If one has to choose between helping one's indigent parents or an indigent friend, one should rather help one's parents.

(b) To those who are spiritually related (e.g., pastor and parishioner, director and penitent, god-parent and god-child), more spiritual assistance in instruction, advice and prayer is due. Thus, a pastor is supposed to be more solicitous about instructing his congregation than his relatives who belong to another congregation.

(c) To those who are related by some special tie, political, military, religious, etc., more is due in things political, military, religious, etc., than to others. Thus, a soldier owes obedience to his officer, and not to his father, in matters that pertain to army life; a priest owes deference to an ecclesiastical superior in clerical matters, not to his parents.

1178. Kinship, as being an older and more fundamental relationship, should have precedence in assistance over any other kind of private relationship in case of conflict and extreme necessity. (a) Thus, as regards spiritual matters (e.g., calling a priest to give absolution), if a parent and a spiritual father were both in extreme necessity, one's first duty would be to one's parent. (b) As regards temporal matters, if one has to choose between assisting one's needy parents and remaining in some relationship in which one cannot help them, one should give up the relationship, if possible. Thus, a Religious is allowed to return to the world, if his parents require his support.

1179. The order of charity as between kinsfolk gives preference of course to the nearer relatives-parents, children, wife. Between these nearer relatives there is also an order of preference, as follows :(a) objectively (or with reference to the greater or less claim to respect and honor), the order is: father, mother, wife, children; (b) subjectively (or with reference to the greater or less intensity of affection), the order is the reverse, namely: children, wife, parents.

1180. The following should be noted about this order of preference between the members of one's family: (a) the basis of preference given is only kinship, and hence there may be other considerations to change the order given (e.g., a pious mother is rightly more respected and honored by her children than a worthless father); (b) there is no notable excess in the claim of one member of the family over that of another, and hence those whose affections do not follow the order given are not guilty of serious sin.

1181. The order in which relatives have a claim on assistance when several are in equal need is as follows: (a) in cases of ordinary need the order is, first, the wife, for a man leaves his parents for his wife (Gen.,

ii. 24), second, the children, for ordinarily parents must provide for children, and not children for parents (II Cor., xii. 14), third, parents; after these come in order, brothers and sisters, other relatives, friends, fellow-citizens of the same locality or country, all others; (b) in case of extreme need, however, parents are to be preferred to all others, even to wife, children or creditors, since one receives life from parents.

1182. The order of charity is also observed in heaven. (a) Thus, God is loved above all, not only objectively, but also subjectively, for His amiability is better understood and is not for a moment neglected. (b) Self is loved less, objectively, than those who are higher, and more, objectively, than those who are lower in glory: for the state of the blessed is fixed, and each of them desires that which God wills. But, subjectively, each loves self with a more intense love, since charity itself inclines that one first direct self towards God, and then wish the same for others. (c) Among neighbors, since love of them will be entirely divine, the reason of earthly preferences (such as dependence of one on another) having ceased, those who are more perfect in holiness will be loved with deeper appreciation and affection than those who are nearer by kinship or friendship.

1183. The Acts of Charity.—The principal act of the virtue of charity is love. It is sometimes spoken of as benevolence, but in reality the love of charity includes more than mere benevolence. (a) Thus, benevolence wishes well to another according to a right judgment, and so it pertains to charity, which rejoices in the perfections of God and wishes beatitude to man; but (b) love is a union of affection with another, which makes one regard him as another self, and so it pertains to charity, which, as said above, is a supernatural friendship, One can be benevolent towards a stranger and for a passing moment, but love is intimate and lasting, from its nature.

1184. Exercise of the Act of Love.—(a) From benevolence proceed gladness at the perfections of God (I Pet., i. 8), zeal for His external glory (I Pet., iv. 11), grief over sin committed against Him (Ps. lxxii. 3), obedience to His commandments (John, xiv. 15, 21, 23). (b) From the union of affection proceed a warmth of inclination and a personal interest in the things of God, so that one rejoices over the divine perfections, not merely because one knows that this is a duty, but because one feels the attachment of a friend for all that pertains to God.

1185. Charity loves God: (a) for His own sake; (b) immediately; (c) entirely; (d) without measure.

1186. We love God for His own sake, in the sense that there is nothing distinct from God that causes Him to be loved. (a) Thus, there is no ulterior end on account of which He is loved, for He is the Last End of all; (b) there is no perfection different from His nature that makes Him lovable, since He is perfection itself; (c) there is no source of His goodness on account of which He is loved, since He is the Primal Source.

1187. We may love God for the sake of reward (see 1161), on account of benefits, and for fear of punishment, in the following senses: (a) the eternal reward is the proximate end of our love of God: "Receiving the end of your faith, even the salvation of your souls" (I Pet., i. 9); but the end of salvation itself, and the Last End of love of God, is God Himself; (b) temporal rewards, benefits received, and the wish to avoid punishment, are dispositions that lead up to love of God, or to progress in His love; but they are not the end of the act of love.

1188. Charity loves God immediately, and so differs from natural love of God. (a) Thus, natural love of God rises from love of neighbor whom we see to love of God whom we do not see, just as natural knowledge rises from the creature to the Creator. (b) Charity, on the contrary, tends to God first, and by reason of Him includes the neighbor in its love.

1189. Charity loves God entirely. (a) But this does not mean that the creature's love is adequate to the amiability of God, for God is infinite, whereas love in the most perfect creature must be finite. (b) It means, with reference to the object of love, that charity loves everything that pertains to God—each of the Divine Persons, all of the divine perfections. (e) It means, with reference to the person who loves, that he loves God to the best of his ability, by subordinating all else to God and preferring His love to other loves. On earth, charity gives to God the greatest objective love; in heaven, it also gives Him the greatest subjective love (see 1129): "Thou shalt love the Lord, thy God, with thy whole heart" (Deut., vi. 5).

1190. Charity loves God without measure, as St. Bernard says (*De diligendo Deo*, cap. 1). God has fixed a degree of perfection in charity beyond which a soul will not progress, but no one should set a limit for himself, for love has to do with God, who is not measured, but is the measure of all things.

(a) Hence, in the internal act of love, there is no possibility of excess, since the Object is infinitely amiable and the End of all, and so the greater the charity, the better it is.

(b) In external acts proceeding from charity, however, there is a possibility of excess, since these acts are a means to an end, and have to be measured by charity and reason. Thus, it would be excessive to give more to strangers than to one's needy parents, for this act would not be according to the rule of charity. It would also be excessive to perform works of charity, when one ought to be attending to household duties, for reason requires that everything be done at its proper time and place.

1191. The love of an enemy may be a better act than the love of a friend, when there are special excellencies in the former love that are not found in the latter. (a) Thus, if the enemy, all things considered, is a better person than the friend, and if he is for that reason objectively preferred, this is as it should be (see 1173). (b) If the parties are of equal merit, an act of love towards the enemy on account of supernatural charity is better than an act of love towards the friend on account of natural affection: "If you love them that love you, what reward shall you have? do not even the publicans this?" (Matt, v. 46).

1192. If all other things are equal, the love of the friend is essentially better, while the love of the enemy is better in some minor respects. (a) Thus, the love of the friend has a better object, for the friend who loves us is better than the enemy who hates us; it has also an object that has a greater claim on charity, as being nearer to self. Hence, it is essentially a better and more meritorious act. (b) The love of the enemy is more difficult, and may thus be a more convincing sign that one really loves God. But the fact that an act is more difficult does not suffice to make it more meritorious, or else we should have to say that the love of neighbor is more meritorious than the love of God.

Art. 6: THE EFFECTS OF CHARITY

(Summa Theologica, II-II, qq. 28-33.)

1193. Internal Effects of Charity.—There are three acts of the soul that result from love, viz., joy, peace, mercy. (a) The joy of charity is a repose or delight of the soul in the perfections of God and in the union of self and the neighbor with Him: "The fruit of the Spirit is charity, joy" (Gal., v. 22). (b) The peace of charity is the harmony of man with God, self and the neighbor: "There is much peace to those that love Thy law" (Ps. cxviii. 165). (c) Mercy is an inclination of the will to relieve the misery of another; it follows from charity, for love of the brotherhood "weeps with them that weep" (Rom., xii. 10, 15).

1194. Joy.—The precept of charity includes a precept of joy, and hence the Apostle says: "Rejoice in the Lord always; again, I say, rejoice" (Philip., iv. 4, 5). This joy of charity has the following properties: (a) it is about good, not about iniquity, and it is not unrestrained; it rejoices "in the Lord"; (b) it should not be discontinued or interrupted by sin, but should rejoice "always." It may, however, be mixed with sorrow over sin or the delay of entrance into the presence of God (Rom., xii. 15; Ps. cxix. 5), for only in heaven will joy be filled (John, xv. 11). St. Paul spoke of himself as "sorrowful, yet always rejoicing" (II Cor., vi. 10).

1195. Peace.—The precept of charity also includes a precept of peace, and our Lord commands: "Have peace among yourselves" (Mark, ix. 49). Peace, like joy, has two properties: (a) it should be genuine (i.e., it should be a contentment and agreement based on right), for there is a false peace, of which Christ says: "I am not come to bring peace" (Matt, x. 34), which rests in a good that is only apparent, and which does not exclude great evil and anxiety (Wis., xiv. 22), (b) peace is constant, for, as long as charity remains, there are friendly relations with God and man, and order in the interior of the soul. Perfect tranquility, it is true, is found only in heaven. On earth, disturbances may arise in the lower part of the soul, or from without, but the will continues in the peace of God (II Cor., i. 4).

1196. Reconciliation of a sinner to God is effected through an act of perfect charity: "He who loves Me, will be loved by My Father and I will love him" (John, xiv. 21). (a) Thus, sin is washed away, even before Baptism or absolution, when the sinner makes an act of love of God joined with a desire, at least implicit, of receiving the Sacrament of Baptism or Penance. The act of love is not the cause, but the final disposition introducing justification. (b) The punishment of sin is forgiven, when one makes an act of love, or performs a good deed out of love of God; but the degree of remission corresponds to the fervor of the charity.

1197. Does the precept of peace demand unanimity of judgments?

(a) In matters of greater importance, there should be agreement in judgments; else, there will not be that harmony of wills, desiring the same things and disliking the same things, which constitute peace. In necessary things, therefore, there should be unity of judgments: "I beseech of you, brethren, by the name of our Lord Jesus Christ, that you all speak the same thing, and that there be no schisms among you, but that you be perfect in the same mind and in the same judgment" (I Cor., i. 10).

(b) In matters of slight importance, difference of opinion does not remove friendship, for each one thinks that his judgment will better serve the good that is sought alike by all. We find that even very holy men have disagreed on matters of opinion—for example, Paul and Barnabas on the question whether or not Mark should be taken on the second missionary journey (Acts, xv. 37), Jerome and Augustine on the status of Mosaic observances after the death of Christ. Disputes may offend against charity, however, if they become too personal or too heated, as sometimes happens even to minds occupied with heavenly things (e.g., theologians, spiritual writers).

1198. Reconciliation with enemies is necessary, in order that peace may be maintained. It includes: (a) internally, the putting away of thoughts and feelings contrary to concord; (b) externally, signs of renewed charity, if there has been an open breach.

1199. The duty of reconciliation does not necessitate the forgiveness of every kind of wrong suffered from an enemy—that is, it does not always oblige one freely to remit the consequences of an enemy's acts. There are three kinds of wrong: (a) offenses, which are such contradictions offered to the will of another as do not trespass on any strict right or occasion any damage. Example: Balbus, who is in great distress, asks his friend Titus to secure employment for him. Titus could easily do this favor, but he refuses; (b) injuries, which are violations of the strict right of another, but without damage. Example: Claudia addresses Caia in very disrespectful language when no witnesses are present; (c) damages, which are the taking from another of what is his, or harm done to him as regards his soul, his life, his fame, or his fortune. Examples are theft, scandal, assault and slander.

1200. Whether an offender asks pardon or not, one is obliged to forgive the offense—that is, to put aside all aversion, indignation and hatred: "Forgive us our trespasses, as we forgive them that trespass against us" (Matt., vi. 12). But, granting that one desires salvation for the offender as for others, shows the common signs of charity, and is not prompted by hatred, the following are not required: (a) that one so pardon the offense as to take the offender back to the same special friendship as may have existed before; (b) that one overlook an injury so as not to require satisfaction (and hence, without acting against charity, Gaia may insist on an apology from Claudia for the disrespectful language used by the latter); and (c) that one renounce restitution or reparation for damage done one. No one is obliged to give to another what is one's own, and, if there is no other way of securing one's rights, one may have recourse to court. If the result of prosecution will be punishment of the offender rather than restitution (as in case of libel or slander), it is not uncharitable to prosecutethe offender, if one's motive is the fulfillment of justice, the prevention of the same wrong to others, or the honor of one's family (Lev., xix. 17).

1201. There are cases, however, in which charity requires one to forgive a debt of satisfaction or restitution, namely, when this would impose too heavy a burden on the offender, compared with the benefit that would be derived therefrom. (a) Thus, restitution should not be insisted on, when the offender is repentant and can ill afford to pay the debt, and the party offended can easily get along without the payment. (b) Punishment should not be insisted on, if the harm done the offender or his family will be out of proportion to any good that may result. (c)

Prosecution should not be used, if a wrong can be amicably adjusted out of court (I Cor., vi. 1).

1202. Who should make the advances towards reconciliation after a rupture of charitable relations? (a) If only one party was the offender, he should normally make the first move towards reconciliation. It is of counsel, but not of precept, that the innocent party ask for reconciliation, unless the circumstances require that he should do so, as when the offended party can much more easily make the advances, or when great scandal will arise, or when the offender will become hardened in hate and lose his soul, if the party offended does not make efforts for peace. (b) If both parties were offenders, he who offended more seriously should make the advances. (c) If both offended equally, he who was first to disturb the peace should also be first to work for its restoration. (d) If it does not appear which of the parties was more to blame in any of the foregoing ways, both are equally bound.

1203. The manner of seeking reconciliation is as follows: (a) Reconciliation can be sought either in person, or through an intermediary who is a friend to both parties. (b) It can be sought either explicitly (by expressing regret and asking pardon), or implicitly (by a friendly conversation or favors shown). Generally speaking, an inferior (e.g., a child) should explicitly request reconciliation with a superior (e.g., a parent); but it will suffice for a superior to seek forgiveness from an inferior implicitly.

1204. The time for seeking reconciliation is the earliest possible moment: "If thou offer thy gift at the altar, and there thou remember that thy brother hath anything against thee, leave there thy offering before the altar, and go first to be reconciled to thy brother, and then coming thou shalt offer thy gift" (Matt, v. 23, 24). (a) Thus, internal reconciliation (i.e., repentance on the part of the offender and forgiveness on the part of the one offended) should not be delayed, and should precede any sacred action, such as offering a gift to God, if this latter is to be acceptable and meritorious. (b) External reconciliation (i.e., asking pardon and making satisfaction) and the manifestation of forgiveness should be attended to as soon as the circumstances of time and place permit. The resolve to be reconciled externally is included in internal reconciliation, but prudence dictates that one wait for the suitable occasion, lest precipitation make matters worse.

1205. Mercy.—From charity results mercy, for he who loves his neighbor as a friend in God, must grieve over the latter's sorrows as if they were his own. Our Lord commands: "Be ye merciful, as your Heavenly Father is also merciful" (Luke, vi. 36). But not all compassion is true mercy or supernatural.

(a) Thus, as regards the object that causes sorrow, true mercy grieves over the evils that befall another against his will, such as sickness, failure in an enterprise, or undeserved misfortune. But wilful evil, such as sin, provokes not mercy, but rather indignation, although one may compassionate sinners on account of the ills their sins bring on them (Matt., ix. 36).

(b) As regards the internal cause of sorrow or sympathy, supernatural mercy arises from the love of charity for the one suffering; natural mercy, from the fear one has that a similar evil may overtake oneself, or that oneself may suffer loss on account of another's misfortune.

(c) As regards the act of mercy, it is to be noted that it proceeds from the will, regulates the emotions, and is itself regulated by reason. Thus, mercy differs from the sensible distress a refined person experiences at the sight of suffering, which, though good in itself, may never lead to a wish to alleviate sorrow. Thus, also, it differs from unregulated sympathy, which bestows help or forgiveness indiscriminately, without thought of the greater evils that may result; it differs from sentimentality, which does not restrain tears and other emotional expressions within due bounds. The virtue of mercy has a care for the interests of justice, but mere pity, like prejudice, blinds the mind to what is true and right.

1206. The causes of an unmerciful spirit are: (a) lack of charity towards one who is in misery; (b) pride or too much prosperity, which makes one feel that others suffer justly, or that one is above their condition (Prov., xxviii. 4); (c) great misfortunes or fears that have hardened one's disposition, or made one self-centered.

1207. Mercy Compared with the Other Moral Virtues.—(a) Mercy, if taken for the emotion of sympathy as regulated by reason, is inferior to prudence and justice, which are perfections of the higher powers of the soul (i.e., of the intellect and will). (b) Mercy, if taken for an act of the will disliking the misery of another and moving one to remove that misery, surpasses the other moral virtues; indeed, it may be said to be something divine, and hence more than a virtue. Certainly, it is the greatest of the virtues that have to do with the neighbor, for of its nature it implies freedom from some defect and the relief of that defect in others, which is not the case with other virtues. Thus, while prudence directs acts and justice renders to others their due, these do not of themselves remove ignorance or destitution in a neighbor.

1208. Mercy Compared with Charity.—(a) In itself (i.e., considered precisely as to its essential notes of freedom from misery and relief given to the miserable), mercy is the greatest of the virtues. For, carried to its highest development, freedom from defect means infinite perfection; while relief of defect in others means that, out of infinite love for the Supreme Good, relief is poured out by God on His creatures. Thus, in God mercy is an extension of the love God has towards His own goodness, for the benefit of creatures, and is greater than charity: "The mercy of God is above all His works" (Ps. cxliv. 9).

(b) In its subject (i.e., considered precisely as to the perfection it brings to its possessor), mercy is inferior in creatures to charity. For it is better to be united by love to the Supreme Good than to remove evil in a creature: "Above all these things have charity" (Col, iii. 14). Mercy is the sum of the Christian religion as far as external works are concerned, but charity is the sum of Christianity as regards internal acts.

1209. The Obligation of Mercy.-(a) The natural law itself inculcates mercy, but those not influenced by divine revelation have not highly esteemed it or practised it. Thus, Plato wished that all the poor might be sent into exile. Virgil thought that freedom from pity was a sign of wisdom; Seneca called mercy a vice of the soul; Nietzsche taught that compassion has no place in the morality of the superman.

(b) The divine law commands mercy, especially in the New Testament. Assistance of the poor, the widows, the orphans, the sick, the captives, the slaves and other unfortunates is everywhere insisted on: "I will show thee what the Lord requireth of thee: verily to do justice, and to love mercy, and to walk solicitous with thy God" (Mich., vi. 8).

1210. External Effects of Charity.—Three external effects of charity will now be considered-beneficence, almsgiving and fraternal correction. These are not distinct virtues, but only separate acts pertaining to the virtue of charity and proceeding—like love, joy and peace—from the same motive of love of God. (a) Thus, beneficence naturally results from charity, since one of the acts of friendship is to do good to one's friend; (b) almsgiving is one of the special ways in which beneficence is exercised; (c) fraternal correction is a species of spiritual almsgiving.

1211. Beneficence.—Not every act of helping others is virtuous, nor is all virtuous assistance called beneficence. (a) Thus, to assist others in evil is maleficence, nor is it virtuous to help them with an evil purpose. Examples: To give money to criminals to help them defeat the law is participation in crime. To give presents to others in order to receive a return of favor from them is cupidity (Luke, xiv. 12). (b) To assist others or to give to them out of compassion for misery, is mercy; to do so out of a sense of obligation, is justice; to do so out of love of God, is beneficence.

1212. Beneficence is a duty, and like charity should be universal: "While we have time, let us work good to all men" (Gal., vi. 10); "Do good to them that hate you" (Matt., v. 44). But this does not mean that no discrimination is to be used in beneficence, or that impossibilities are required.

(a) Not every kind of activity in which others are engaged is deserving of assistance, not every kind of suffering of others may be removed. Examples: Criminals or enemies of the State are not to be assisted in their wrongdoing, but one may attempt to bring them to better conduct; one who has been justly sentenced to prison may not be aided to escape, but he may be visited and consoled and given religious assistance.

(b) Not all can be helped individually; even the richest and most generous person can benefit only a small percentage of those who are deserving. Charity requires, however, that one be so disposed that one would help all individually, if it were possible, and that one does help all generally, by praying for both Catholics and non-Catholics.

1213. Since it is impossible to help all individually, beneficence should be regulated by the order of charity (see 1174 sqq.), and particular good should be done to those with whom on account of conditions of time or place one is more closely associated. Hence, the following general rules are given:

(a) In benefits that pertain to a particular kind of relationship; one should give the preference, other things being equal, to those with whom one has that relationship. Examples: To make a banquet for another is a benefit pertaining to friendship, and hence should be shown to one who is a friend, rather than to one who is a business associate, but not an intimate. To support another person is a benefit pertaining to kinship, and hence should be shown to a parent, rather than to a stranger.

(b) In benefits given to those with whom one has the same kind of relationship, one should give the preference, other things being equal, to those nearer in relationship. Example: In dispensing alms, one should help one's own family rather than distant relatives.

1214. If other things are not equal, the foregoing rules must sometimes be reversed.

(a) When the common good is involved, preference should be given those who represent it, even though others are nearer to one as regards private good. Hence, a citizen should help the fortunes of his adopted country rather than those of his mother country; in a civil war one should aid rather one's comrades than one's kinsmen who are on the opposite side.

(b) When a supreme good of a private person is at stake, one should prefer to help him, even if a stranger, rather than another who is a friend, or relative, but who is not in the same distress. Example: One should give one's loaf to a man dying of starvation rather than to one's own father, who is hungry but not starving.

(c) When the means with which a benefit is bestowable belong to another, one must prefer to give back what belongs to the other, even if this person is a stranger, rather than use it for the good of a friend or relative. Thus, if a person has stolen money or has borrowed money from a stranger, he must return it to the owner, rather than make a present of it to his own wife. An exception would be the case in which the wife was in dire necessity, whereas the owner was not; but the duty of restitution would remain for the future.

1215. No general rule can be laid down for all cases in which one party is nearer to self and the other party more in need, and many such cases have to be decided according to prudent judgment in view of all the circumstances. It should be noted that, though wife and children are nearer to one than parents, the latter have a greater claim on charity when they are in equally extreme necessity, on account of the supreme benefit of life received from them. But ordinarily one is bound rather to provide for one's children (II Cor., xii. 14).

1216. Almsgiving.—Almsgiving is defined: "Assistance to one who is in need, given out of compassion and for the love of God." Hence, this act pertains to various virtues. (a) It is elicited by the virtue of mercy, which means that compassion for misery is the immediate principle which produces almsgiving. (b) It is commanded by the virtue of charity, which means that love of God is the remote principle or end of an alms, for, as said above (see 1205), mercy itself is an effect of charity (I John, iii. 17). (c) Secondarily, it may also be commanded by other virtues. Thus, if a person gives an alms to satisfy for his sins, he performs an act of justice; if he gives in order to honor God, he performs an act of religion; if he gives without undue grief over the loss of what he gives, he practises liberality.

1217. Qualities Recommended for Almsgiving.—(a) Alms should not be given ostentatiously (Matt, vi. 2 sqq.), though it is often edifying that they receive publicity (Matt., v. 16); (b) they should be given cheerfully (II Cor., ix. 7).

1218. Forms of Almsgiving.—(a) In the strict sense, an alms is a gift made without any obligation of payment or return; (b) in a wide sense, almsgiving includes selling on credit as a favor to a poor customer, a loan granted at a low rate of interest or without interest, help in securing employment, etc. Thus, if a poor man is sufficiently helped by the use of an article, there is no need of making him a present of it.

1219. Almsgiving is to be distinguished, also, from mere giving. (a) Thus, assistance given the poor out of a bad motive (e.g., to lead them away from their religion, to induce them to crime) is sinful; (b) assistance given the poor out of a merely natural good motive (e.g., pity for their sufferings) is philanthropy, but not charity (I Cor., xiii. 3), and may coexist with the state of hatred of God.

1220. Corporal alms, in the form of bodily necessaries given freely in themselves or in their money equivalent, are of as many kinds as there are bodily needs. (a) Hence, the common necessities of food, drink, clothing and shelter should be provided as alms to the starving and to those who lack sufficient clothing, or who are without a home. (b) Special necessities, whether internal (such as sickness) or external (such as persecution or imprisonment), should be relieved or assuaged by remedies, visits, protection or relief. (c) The necessity of the body after death is that it be cared for with the honor which the memory of the deceased deserves, and hence burial of the dead is numbered among the corporal alms.

1221. Thus, there are seven corporal works of mercy. (a) Those that pertain to the needs of the body during life are mentioned by our Lord in Matt., xxv. 35, 36. (b) The burial of the dead is praised in scripture as a good work, as we see in the cases of Tobias (Tob., i, ii, xii), and of those who buried our Lord (Matt, xxvi. 12, xxvii. 57 sqq.).

1222. Spiritual alms, consisting of assistance given those who suffer want in mind or spirit, are either prayers, by which divine aid is asked for them, or various acts by which human aid is conferred. These acts are also of two kinds, and constitute seven spiritual works of mercy.

(a) The defects from which a soul suffers, and which are not moral, include ignorance in the intellect, doubt in the practical judgment, and sadness in the affections; and hence the acts of almsgiving for such cases are instruction, counsel, and comfort.

(b) The defects of soul which are moral are the guilt of sin and its consequences—that is, the offense given and the burdens that result for the sinner or others. The corresponding spiritual alms are admonition against sin, pardon of the offense done to self, patience in bearing with the difficult ways of others, especially if they err through infirmity, or willingness in helping them to bear the consequences of their errors (Rom., xv. 1).

1223. The giving of spiritual alms may suppose superiority or authority in the giver over the receiver, or a certain procedure to be followed; hence, in the administration of spiritual benefits, the due order of time, place and persons has to be remembered. (a) Thus, in the instruction of the ignorant, it is not every kind of ignorance that is a defect, but only the ignorance of things one must know; and it is not every person who is to give the needed instruction. (b) In the correction of sinners, it is not every kind of reproof that is to be used, but gentleness and secret admonition should be employed where possible (Prov., xxvii. 6).

1224. Comparison of Corporal and Spiritual Alms.—(a) Spiritual alms are better, because their nature is higher and they are of greater benefit to the recipient, even though he appreciates them less. Thus, it is better to enjoy peace of mind than to feast sumptuously. (b) Corporal alms are sometimes more necessary in a particular case, and hence they should be attended to first. Thus, for one suffering from hunger food is more necessary than words of comfort (James, ii. 15, 16).

1225. Though corporal alms are not spiritual in the assistance they give, they are spiritual in their effects. (a) Thus, they bless the recipient corporally, by relieving his hunger or other need; (b) they bless the giver spiritually, since God will reward his charity (Ecclus., xxiv, 13, 14), and the person helped will pray for his benefactor (ibid., 15).

1226. The Duty of Giving Alms.—(a) The natural law requires that we do to others as we would be done by, and there is no one who does not wish that help be rendered him if he falls into need. Moreover, the common welfare requires that the rich assist the poor, for otherwise there will be discontent and disorder. Hence, even unbelievers are not exempt from the obligation of almsgiving. (b) The divine law, in both Old and New Testaments, commands almsgiving: "Give alms out of thy substance, and turn not away thy face from any poor person" (Tob., iv. 7); "Depart from Me, you cursed, into everlasting fire, for I was hungry, and you gave Me not to eat" (Matt., xxv. 41-42); "Let us love, not in word, nor in tongue, but in deed and in truth" (I John, iii. 18). Tobias, Dorcas, Cornelius, and Zacheus are praised for their charitable gifts.

1227. Almsgiving, being an affirmative commandment, does not oblige for every moment of time, but only when right reason calls for it on account of the state of the giver or of the receiver.

(a) The state of the giver requires him to give alms only when he has a superfluity of goods, for no one is bound to deprive himself of what is necessary for his own use (see 1164, 1169). John the Baptist said to the people: "He that hath two coats, let him give to him that hath none; and he that hath meat, let him do in like manner" (Luke, iii. 11). "That which remaineth," says our Lord, "give as alms" (Luke, xi. 41).

(b) The state of the receiver gives him a claim on charity, when he is in necessity and unable to help himself. Temporal goods, according to the will of God, are for the benefit of the whole human race; and, while the ownership of particular goods belongs to the rightful possessor, he should not withhold the use of them from those who are in need, when he has more than he needs for his own use. Neither is it necessary that one be asked for an alms; one is obliged to give it when one knows that one's neighbor is in want, though unable or ashamed to beg for help.

1228. It is not a precept, therefore, but only a counsel, that one give alms in other cases. (a) Thus, when one is in equal need oneself and has no superfluous goods, one may give to another; (b) when one's neighbor is not in need, or is able to help himself, one may still give to him out of charity, if he is deserving (see 1169).

1229. Superfluities are those goods that remain over and above what are necessary for life, or the maintenance of one's state of life justly acquired and socially useful.

(a) Necessaries of life are the goods one must have to provide food, clothing and home for oneself and one's family. Among necessaries of life we may include what one has to set aside for old age, sickness, increase of family, and the future sustenance of dependents who will need it (II Cor., xii. 14). But they should not be extended to include imaginary cases, or all the possible cases of personal need that may arise in the future; otherwise, one is guilty of that exaggerated solicitude for the morrow which our Lord forbids (Matt, vi. 34).

(b) Necessaries of state are the goods a person must have to keep up his position and that of his family according to the standard of living of his class. This includes provision for the education and advancement of one's children, for hospitality, adornment of home, and the care and improvement of one's business; but it does not include provision for excessive pleasures or luxuries, or improbable future opportunities of bettering one's condition; otherwise, even the wealthiest person might say that all his money was tied up and that he had no superfluous goods.

1230. What is necessary for the decency of particular stations in life? (a) This does not consist in any fixed amount, for, even when considerable additions to or subtractions from a person's wealth have been made, he may retain and support the same social rank. (b) It consists, therefore, in the amount sufficient for him to maintain, according to the opinion of prudent men, what is becoming in one of his class. Thus, one's position may require that one do much entertaining or keep up an expensive household, or it may require only that one live moderately.

1231. The giving in alms of goods for which the giver himself has need is governed by the following rules:

(a) Necessaries of life should be given away to another, as a matter of precept, if the common good is bound up with the life of that other, but not with one's own life; they may be given away to another, as a matter of counsel, when the common good does not require it, but the higher good of virtue invites one to sacrifice one's life for one's neighbor (probable opinion). Examples: One should give away one's last loaf to save the life of a leader on whom the salvation of his people depends. One may make the same sacrifice, if one is single and without dependents, and another is married and has a dependent family. But one may not give away what is necessary for the life of one's family (I Tim., v. 8).

(b) Necessaries of state, at least in part (see 1251), should be given away to another, as a matter of precept, if the public good or the life of a private individual are at stake, or if that which is given in alms can be easily recovered and will now prevent a very grave calamity; they may he given away, as a matter of counsel, if the higher good of virtue invites one to embrace voluntary poverty: "If thou wouldst be perfect, go sell all that thou hast and give to the poor" (Matt., xix. 21). Examples: One should offer one's fortunes in support of one's government, if in some crisis the nation cannot otherwise be saved. One may give up riches and become poor in order to follow Christ in the religious life.

1232. Superfluities of one's state are the goods from which the precept of almsgiving requires that assistance ordinarily be given. But the mere fact that one has a superfluity does not oblige one to give alms. As in every virtuous act, so also in almsgiving there must be not only an object according to reason, but also circumstances according to reason. Hence, one who has a superfluity is bound to give alms only when the proper conditions of time, place, person, etc., are present. (a) As regards time, a person is not obliged to devote to almsgiving the time that is needed for other duties. (b) As to persons, a person is not obliged to give alms, if there is no needy person known to him.

1233. As to need, we may distinguish three classes of persons:

(a) Those in apparent need are such as pretend poverty, sickness, or misfortune, in order to get sympathy and financial aid (e.g., professional beggars). Alms should not be given persons of this kind, since they take what would be given to the really poor and needy. Rather they should be exposed and punished.

(b) Those in real need through choice should not be helped, if they take to begging because they are too lazy to work, or find it profitable to live off others; for they have no right to beg, being able to help themselves, and it would be wrong to encourage them in idleness and an imposition on others (II Thess., iii. 10). But those who are voluntarily poor for Christ's sake, whether they belong to a religious order or not, are worthy of respect and it is meritorious to assist them.

(c) Those who are in real need against their will, should be assisted; for, even though they became destitute through their own fault, they are in fact unable to help themselves now.

1234. Regarding money obtained under the false pretense of poverty and the duty of restitution, the following rules may be given: (a) If a person obtains considerable alms by pretending to be blind, disabled, in great want, etc., and he is not afflicted or in need, he should give back the money to the donors or, if this is impossible, to the poor, since the donors wished to help the poor, not to encourage idlers. (b) If one obtains only a small amount under a false pretense of poverty, some moralists say there is no duty of restitution, since the donor may be presumed to give unconditionally in the case of minute sums; likewise, if a beggar is really poor but exaggerates his need, it does not seem that he is bound to restitution, for those who give alms expect a certain amount of romancing from tramps and other professional beggars.

1235. What is one's duty in cases of doubtful need? (a) Minute inquiries are inexpedient, since the really deserving are often unwilling to publish their needs; (b) refusal of alms except in cases where one is certain of the need, is not a good general rule to follow, since it is a less evil that an unworthy person be helped than that a worthy one be refused.

1236. There are three degrees of corporal need (cfr. 1165). (a) A person is said to be in extreme need, when he is in manifest danger of losing his life, if help is not given him at once. This does not mean, however, that a person is not in extreme need until he is breathing his last breath; for at that moment he is beyond the reach of human aid. (b) A person is in grave need, when he is in probable danger of death, or is in manifest danger of some very serious misfortune, such as severe sickness, amputation of some member, long and bitter imprisonment, insanity, loss of good name, reduction from wealth to poverty, destruction of home by fire, etc. (c) A person is in common need, when he suffers the inconvenience of poverty, such as being obliged to beg, to deprive himself of many things, to wear poor clothes or to eat ordinary victuals, but is not in danger of any serious loss.

1237. Rules on Giving Alms from the Superfluities of One's State.—(a) To those who are in extreme or grave necessity alms must be given in each individual case, for these cases are rare, and the persons in need have a personal claim on one's charity when this is the sole means of saving them from death or other great evil. Example: Last year Titus saved a mother from death and her child from disease by giving his money and services free of charge. This would not exempt him from the duty of doing a like charity, if a like necessity presents itself now.

(b) To those who are in common necessity alms must be given from time to time—now to one, now to another, as prudence dictates—but there is no obligation for an individual case. Even the richest man could not give to all who are in common need, and their want is not so pressing that any one of them can be said to have an individual claim.

1238. Gravity of the Obligations to Give Alms.—(a) For cases of extreme and grave necessity, the obligation of almsgiving is grave. There is general agreement among theologians on this point, since the loss suffered by the neighbor is serious and the withholding of help indicates a lack of charity (I John, iii. 17). Example: The priest and the levite who passed by the wounded man on the road to Jericho were guilty, from the nature of their act, of mortal sin.

(b) For cases of common necessity, the obligation of almsgiving, as it appears, is also grave; for it seldom happens that one is called on to assist those who are in extreme or grave necessity, whereas almsgiving is inculcated as an ordinary duty, and the reasons given by our Lord in Matt., xxv. 41-46, for exclusion from heaven seem to be neglect of alms in common necessity. But some theologians hold that the obligation is only light, since the need is light; and, since these authorities are numerous and of repute, a confessor could not refuse absolution to a rich man who refused on principle to give anything to those in common necessity. Such a one should be advised, rather than reproved, on this point.

1239. From what was said above, the following conclusions may be drawn about the gravity of the sin of refusing alms: (a) It is certainly a mortal sin to refuse alms to one in extreme or grave need, and probably also a grave sin to refuse ever to give alms to those in common need, (b) It is not a mortal sin to refuse an alms in a particular case, if one is not sure of the obligation (e.g., if there is doubt about one's ability to give the alms or the other's need), or if it seems that others will give assistance, or that the need will disappear, or that one will suffer some serious inconvenience by giving, etc.

1240. Refusal of Alms and Restitution.—(a) The mere refusal of an alms does not oblige one to make restitution. For restitution is the giving back to another of what strictly belongs to him, and it cannot be said that a poor person has a strict right to a gift from another. A violation of charity may be gravely sinful, and yet not oblige to restitution. (b) The refusal of an alms, if joined with injustice, does oblige one to make restitution. Thus, if by threats or force one prevents a starving man from taking the food that has been denied him, injustice is committed; for in extreme necessity one has the strict right to take what is necessary, and reparation should be made if this is prevented.

1241. Alms given from ill-gotten goods are sometimes lawful, sometimes unlawful.

(a) If the acquisition of the goods was unjust, because they belong to another and the present possessor has no right to keep them, it is not lawful to give them as alms, for they must be returned to the owner. An exception would have to be made, however, for the case of extreme necessity, for in such a case the person in danger of death would have a right prior to that of the owner not in need. Example: It is unlawful to give stolen money as an alms to the poor, when one is able to restore it to the rightful owner.

(b) If the acquisition of the goods was unjust, because both giver and receiver acted against law and forfeited their rights to possession, the former has no claim to restitution, nor the latter to retention, and the goods ought to be devoted to alms. Example: If a simoniacal transaction is forbidden under pain of loss of the price paid and received, the receiver is obliged to give the money to the poor.

(c) If the acquisition was not unlawful, but the manner through which it was made was unlawful, the gain is shameful, but still it belongs to the one who has earned it, and may be devoted to alms. Example: Titus hired Balbus to work on Sundays. The violation of the Sunday law was a sin, but the labor given was serviceable to Titus and difficult to

Balbus. Hence, the latter is not bound to give back the money, but may keep it and use it for a good purpose.

1242. Though shameful gain may be used for almsgiving, it should not be devoted to sacred purposes, when this will cause scandal or be irreverent to religion. Thus, the chief priests would not accept the "blood money" of Judas for the use of the temple (Matt., xxvii. 6), because the law forbade the offering of gifts that were an abomination to the Lord (Deut., xxiii. 18; Ecclus., xxxiv. 23).

1243. The Proceeds of Gambling and Almsgiving.—(a) Profits made from gambling may not be used for alms, when one is bound to restore them to the loser. Thus, according to natural law he who wins money at cards or similar games from a minor or other person who has not the right to dispose of money, or who wins through fraud, must give back the winnings. Likewise, restitution is due according to some, if the civil law makes such aleatory contracts null and void; but others deny this. (b) Profits made from gambling may be devoted to alms, when according to law one has a right to them, as when one has played for recreation, with moderation and with fairness to the loser.

1244. Persons who may give alms are all those who have a right to dispose of goods as gifts. Others who have no such general right (e.g., religious, wives, children and servants), may also give alms as follows: (a) They may give alms from any goods that belong to them, and of which they have the control. Thus, a wife may give alms from money which is her own, by inheritance, earnings, etc. (b) They may give alms from such goods as are placed in their charge and dispensation. Thus, the procurator of a religious house has the right to give alms with permission of his superior and according to his Constitution (Canon 537). A religious who is a parish priest may administer and dispense parish alms (Canon 630, §4). (c) They may give alms with express or implied permission. Thus, children may give articles of food to the poor, when their parents consent. (d) They may give alms without permission in a case of extreme need. Thus, a wife could make use of her husband's money without his consent, if this should be necessary to save a life.

1245. The right of a wife to give alms from her husband's earnings is as follows: (a) from the money given her for the support of herself and the family, the wife may give reasonable alms; (b) from the common money of the family she may give alms with her husband's express or presumed consent. But, if he is miserly and unwilling to give alms, she may nevertheless use what is reasonable according to the family resources for almsgiving (e.g., in helping her impoverished parents).

1246. The right of servants to give alms from the goods of their employer is as follows: (a) the rule is that servants have no right to give away anything that belongs to their employer without his express permission, for, if permission could be presumed, the property of employers would not be safe; (b) an exception to the rule is made for such things as are to be thrown away (e.g., leavings of the table), since if they are given in alms the proprietor suffers no loss.

1247. Since charity should be universal, no class of persons, such as strangers, unbelievers or sinners, may be excluded from the benefit of almsgiving (Matt, v. 45). However, charity is also well ordered, and hence there is a preference to be observed, as follows:

(a) Other things being equal, one should favor those who are nearer to oneself by bonds of kinship, friendship, etc., since their claim on one's charity is greater. Charity begins at home.

(b) If other things (such as worthiness, need or public utility) are on the side of those not related by kinship, friendship, etc., the order of preference may be reversed. Thus, if a person had to choose between helping a distant relative for whom he was not specially responsible, and who was a worthless fellow, or who was not in great need or who was not of great value to the community, and helping a stranger, who was most deserving, or in dire distress, or of great value to the community, the latter should be assisted rather than the former.

(c) In case of two strangers in equal poverty, one should help first the one who is more worthy or who feels his distress more. Thus, a person who is poor through misfortune is more deserving than one who gambled his money away; those who were once wealthy feel the sufferings of poverty more than those who are inured to a life of privation.

1248. Is it permissible for one appointed to distribute alms to keep some himself, if he is really poor? (a) If the persons are designated to whom the alms are to be given, the distributor must give only to them; (b) if it is left to the discretion of the distributor, he may keep a reasonable alms for himself.

1249. The amount that should be given in alms has to be measured according to the income of the giver and the need of the receiver.

(a) As to the income of the giver, he should give in proportion to his income: "According to thy ability be merciful. If thou have much, give abundantly; if thou have little, take care even so to bestow willingly a little" (Tob., iv. 9). A rich man who spends more in the barber shop on cosmetics, etc., than he gives to the poor, and a poor man who gives more towards alms than to the feeding of his own family, are not giving according to their means.

(b) As to the need of the receiver, a person should give his share towards providing for the case before him. Thus, if there is no one else who can or will give, and a neighbor is in grave necessity, a charitable person will bear the whole expense, as was done by the good Samaritan. But if the necessity is ordinary (as in the case of street beggars), or there are others who will help, a smaller alms suffices. Steady employment is a better charity than temporary doles, inasmuch as it gives permanent assistance.

1250. Hence, in the following cases alms are excessive: (a) When, outside the instances given in 1231, one gives away all the necessaries of one's life or station. The poor widow who gave all her living (Luke, xxi. 1-4) is praised, but doubtless she was able somehow to obtain enough to provide for her own life. (b) Alms are excessive when one gives from one's superfluities so much that the recipients are spoiled and encouraged to do nothing for themselves, For the purpose of almsgiving is not that those who have wealth be impoverished and others enabled to live in luxury, but that the poor be relieved of suffering and the rich gain the merit of charity (II Cor., viii. 13).

1251. Regarding the obligation of giving all the goods of one's station in life or of one's superfluities, the following points should be noted:

(a) Some theologians hold that, in a case of extreme necessity, one is bound to give all the goods necessary to one's state of life, since a neighbor's life is a more important good than one's own position in life. Others deny this on the ground that one is not bound, even for preserving one's own life, to have recourse to extraordinary means and so lose the rank and style of living one has. Thus, a self-supporting workingman would not be obliged to reduce himself to beggary in order to prolong the life of a dying person. A well-to-do person is not obliged to sell his office, conveyance, books, and other things needed for his business or profession, in order to rescue a captive held for ransom by bandits.

(b) There are theologians who hold that one is bound to give away all one's superfluous wealth in alms, even apart from cases of extreme or grave necessity; but others teach that, while this is of counsel, it is not obligatory, since the needs of the poor will be sufficiently relieved if all who have means give something from their superfluities. Moreover, the retention of some superfluous goods is necessary for the promotion of industrial and commercial enterprises, and, by increasing national wealth, this policy indirectly benefits the poor.

1252. Ecclesiastical law, however, requires all clerics who enjoy a benefice to give all that remains over and above from the returns of the benefice, after they have provided for their own decent maintenance, to the poor or to pious causes. This obligation is held as grave. It will be treated below when we come to the special duties of the clergy.

1253. Is there any definite amount or percentage, then, which should be contributed to alms?

(a) For a case of extreme or grave necessity, one should contribute enough, according to one's ability, either in conjunction with others or alone (if others will not help), to give relief. Thus, if a neighbor is about to die of starvation, a charitable man will give food free of charge. If a poor man is about to be treated unjustly, a charitable lawyer will give him advice without charge. But it is not necessary that one provide extraordinary remedies or helps—for example, that one pay the expenses of a trip to Europe for a poor person whose health would be benefitted by the travel.

(b) For cases of common necessity, St. Alphonsus held that one should give two per cent of what remains from the yearly income after the necessities of life and station have been taken care of. But other moralists believe that today the amount cannot be fixed mathematically, and that only the general direction can be given that one should be generous according to one's means, and regulate one's yearly alms according to the prevalence of poverty.

1254. Is it better to give a little to many, or much to one person in need? (a) If the one person is in great need, and others are only in slight need, it is better to give to the one in great need. Example: If one has ten dollars to give in alms, it is better to buy an overcoat for Titus who is shivering from the cold, than to give ten one-dollar bills to ten men who need new collars and neckties. (b) If the need is equal, it is better to divide the alms, for thus more distress is alleviated and the danger of spoiling a recipient with overmuch bounty is avoided. Example: Caius has $30,000 to give in charity and there are three deserving institutions of charity known to him, all of which are in great need—a hospital, an orphan asylum and a school. He ought to divide his money between the three.

1255. The Time for Giving Alms.-(a) One should give at one time all the amount of one's alms for a certain period, if one is able to do this, and there is a need that calls for it—"He gives twice who gives quickly" (Prov., iii. 28)—for the poor may perish or may be driven to acts of desperation or violence, if help is postponed. (b) One may distribute one's almsgiving if there is no urgent call for it—that is, one may make partial contributions at various times, retaining meanwhile money for almsdeeds in order to invest it for future charities, or to await greater needs to which it may be applied, etc.

1256. The Manner of Giving Alms.—(a) One gives alms directly when one ministers relief personally to the needy, giving food to the starving and medicine to the sick, helping to put out a fire, etc. (b) One gives alms indirectly when one pays taxes for the support of alms-houses, public hospitals, orphan asylums, homes for the aged, the insane, etc.; when one contributes to charitable collections or drives or to organizations for relief (such as the St. Vincent de Paul Society); when one assists or promotes movements for the free education of those who cannot pay, for the betterment of living and working condition of laborers, for security against loss of employment, pensions for the aged, etc.

1257. Public charity done by the State is useful and necessary under the conditions of modern life, but it does not and cannot take the place of charity done by the Church or by private individuals.

(a) State-administered charity does not reach all, or even the most deserving, cases of need. Hence, those who pay their taxes for the support of state charities are not thereby exempted from the obligation of contributing to cases they may meet, especially of extreme or grave necessity. The payment of these taxes, however, diminishes need, and so it also diminishes the amount one is bound to give in alms.

(b) State charity provides for the corporal needs of the recipient, and it is imposed as compulsory on the giver. Hence, it cannot take the place of alms given by the Church or by individuals that will care for both soul and body, and that are given cheerfully and received gratefully.

1258. Fraternal Correction.—Fraternal correction is defined: "An act of charity and mercy by which one uses suitable words or other means in order to convert one's neighbor from sin to virtue."

(a) Thus, it is an act of charity, for it is a love of our neighbor and the desire of his spiritual welfare that prompts this correction. Hence, the admonition of a sinner for his own good differs from a correction administered to a wrongdoer for the good of another or of the public; the former is fraternal correction and is an act of charity, while the latter is judicial correction and is an act of justice.

(b) Fraternal correction is an act of mercy, for, just as feeding the hungry and other corporal alms remove bodily misery, so does admonition of sinners remove spiritual misery.

(c) Fraternal correction uses suitable words or other means, for while it proceeds from charity and mercy, it must be regulated by prudence. It is not an easy matter to correct another successfully, and hence the need of good judgment as to the means to be employed, whether they shall be words or equivalent signs (e.g., sad looks, a gesture of disapproval, a change of subject of a sinful conversation, or refusal of help), and whether one shall use reproof, instruction, counsel, or warning.

(d) Fraternal correction aims at turning a neighbor from sin to virtue. It is the proper remedy for sins of negligence, as judicial correction is for sins of malice. It is applied, also, chiefly to the cure of sin that has already been committed; but it should be extended so as to include the prevention of sin in the future, since there is no less an obligation of preventing than of removing sin. Hence, those who are in dangerous occasions receive fraternal correction when a charitable warning is given.

(e) Fraternal correction is given to a neighbor (i.e., to an individual), and so it differs from the general censure of vice that is given by preachers, whose duty it is to correct sins that are prevalent, provided this be done prudently, in such a way as to effect good and not harm. Unpopularity or other such handicaps do not excuse a preacher from the duty of correction.

1259. Fraternal correction is a grave duty, and more important than that of almsgiving. (a) The natural law requires that a person should do unto others as he would wish them to do unto himself, and everyone ought to wish that, if he needs correction, it will be given him. Even the pagans proclaimed the need of correction. Seneca desired to have a monitor who, by advice and reproof, would guard him against the dangers of evil examples and conversations; and Plautus said that a friend who refuses to chide the faults of his friend is himself worthy of blame.

(b) The divine positive law also commands that one should correct one's brother in order to save him from another offense (Ecclus., xix. 13, 14), and to win him back to good (Matt. xviii. 15), that the spiritual should instruct with mildness those who have committed some transgression (Gal, vi. 1), that a sinner should not be treated as an enemy, but admonished as a brother (II Thess., iii. 15).

1260. Does the duty of fraternal correction oblige one to go out and seek a person who is living a life of sin? (a) If the sinner is under one's care, so that one is responsible for him, there is a duty to seek him as long as there is hope of amendment; for the good shepherd goes after the lost sheep (Matt., xviii. 12, 13). Hence, parents, pastors and superiors must try to win back their subjects from the ways of sin. (b) If the sinner is not under one's care, there is no duty to seek him out; for obligations that are owed to our neighbor in general, but not to any determinate person, do not require that we go out to look for the persons to be aided, but only that we aid those whom we meet. Hence, a private person is not obliged to frequent the haunts of vice and crime in order to reform those who are there; but the community at large has duties regarding such cases.

1261. Since the precept of fraternal correction is affirmative, it does not oblige for every time and place; acts of virtue must be so performed that not only the object and the motive shall be good, but the circumstances also should be suitable. But the object and motive of correction (viz., the conversion of a sinner) are primary, and the circumstances of time, place, etc., secondary considerations. (a) Hence, correction is good and a duty when it will serve to convert or improve a sinner, now or later, although it may be imperfect as to some of the circumstances. (b) Correction is not good, nor a duty, when it will not serve to convert the sinner, even though other circumstances would seem to call for it (Ecclus., xxxii. 6). Consequently, a person ought not to correct when either he or the other person is under the influence of anger, lest matters be made worse. This, of course, is said of fraternal, not of judicial correction; for a judge or other superior must condemn even when the culprit will not be made better, in order to restrain him from evil and to provide for the common good, the protection of justice, and the avoidance of scandal.

1262. In the following cases fraternal correction defeats its own purpose: (a) when the sinner will not be bettered by the correction, for his continuance in sin will become graver by reason of his rejection of the admonition; (b) when the sinner will become hardened and embittered by correction, and as a result commit more numerous or more serious sins. Thus, if one knows that a blasphemer is only made worse by scolding or remonstrances, it is a sin to attempt to correct him as to those ways: "Rebuke not a scorner lest he hate thee" (Prov., ix. 8).

1263. The duty of fraternal correction depends, therefore, on the knowledge or opinion one has about the success it will have. Hence, the following cases may occur: (a) If one is certain that the correction will be beneficial, one should give it; if one is certain it will not be beneficial, one should omit it. (b) If it is likely that the admonition will be profitable, and certain that it will not be positively harmful, it should be given, for a physician in order to help a sick person should give a remedy that is harmless, even though only probably beneficial, if there is nothing else that can be done. (c) If it is doubtful whether the admonition will do any good, and also doubtful whether it will do harm (e.g., when one is dealing with a stranger, whose character one does not know), one should weigh the good and the evil and decide accordingly, as will be explained in the next paragraph.

1264. Cases of doubt concerning the advantage of a fraternal correction may occur as follows: (a) If the good expected is superior to the evil that is feared, one should give the correction. Example: If it seems that a sinner, if admonished, may suffer great confusion or be for a time estranged, but may also be finally converted, the good result of conversion is to be preferred to prevention of confusion or estrangement. If it seems doubtful whether correction will help or hurt a dying man, the good of his salvation should be preferred to the good of freedom from a new sin. (b) If the good expected and the evil feared are about equal, the correction should be omitted, since the negative precept of not injuring a neighbor outweighs the affirmative precept of doing him a service.

1265. When is sin committed by omitting fraternal correction? (a) If the correction is omitted out of charity, the omission is good and meritorious. Example: Titus omits to correct Sempronius, because he thinks the reproof would do harm to the latter or to others, or because he awaits a more favorable occasion. (b) If the correction is omitted contrary to charity (i.e., because a person hates his neighbor or disregards his spiritual welfare), the omission is a mortal sin. Example: Caius neglects to correct Sempronius, because he prefers to see Sempronius go to ruin rather than lose his friendship or incur his enmity. (c) If the correction is omitted in spite of charity, the omission is a venial sin. Example: Balbus, who is not a superior, fails to correct Sempronius, because through frailty he fears to give offense, or to be considered over-bold, but he prefers the latter's spiritual welfare to his own human fears and interests, and would give the correction, if he felt that it was absolutely necessary.

1266. The sin committed by delaying fraternal correction is to be judged according to the rules just given about omission of correction. But is it lawful to put off correction in the hope that the sinner, through experience of the evil effects of sin, may become more tractable? (a) If there is hope of present amendment through correction, this should not be delayed; otherwise, one is careless about the honor of God, the edification of others, and the possible hardening of the sinner or his death in the midst of his sins. (b) If there is no probability of present amendment through correction, one can only wait in the hope that the experience of the evils of sin may bring the prodigal back to God.

1267. It is not often necessary for one who is not a superior to make fraternal correction, since there are many conditions that must exist before one is obliged to it. These conditions include the purpose to be attained, of which we have just spoken, and the proper circumstances, which are as follows: (a) the fault to be corrected should be a known and serious sin; (b) the person to give the correction should be one who has the right and duty to correct; (c) the manner of giving the correction should be such as will promote the end in view.

1268. One should not attempt to correct a fault, unless one is morally sure that a fault has been committed, or is about to be committed. For this reason the scrupulous, who are inclined to suspect or see evil where there is none, are generally excused from the duty of making corrections. Reasons why doubt, fear, suspicion or rumor do not suffice, are: (a) correction is not pleasant to the one corrected, and, if his guilt is not provable, he will be able to argue with the corrector, and so quarrels and enmities will result; (b) charity bids us to give the benefit of the doubt to a neighbor, and, if this is not done, the one who is being corrected will be able to correct the corrector on account of uncharitable suspicions.

1269. Is one obliged, therefore, to make inquiries into the conduct of those whom one suspects of wrongdoing?

(a) If there is question of judicial correction, the public authority is bound in justice to examine juridically into matters of doubt before acting.

(b) If there is question of fraternal correction, a parent or other superior is bound in charity to make paternal inquiries into the conduct of his subjects; for, as a father does not wait until his children ask for corporal goods but inquires about their needs, so neither should he wait until their spiritual distress is brought to his attention. The superior here should avoid the extremes of suspicion, on the one hand, which will lead him to act rashly and win for him the hatred of his subjects, and of over-trustfulness, on the other hand, which will foster all kinds of secret irregularities. Likewise, he should not betray a special watchfulness about one individual that will be harmful to the latter's reputation.

(c) If there is question of fraternal correction, private individuals should not inquire into the affairs of others. Those who go about spying on or shadowing others, even if their purpose is to reform, are acting against charity to themselves and to the persons they wish to improve; their own affairs will suffer, since the number who need reformation is large, and the person who is being investigated will be annoyed or otherwise injured: "Lie not in wait, nor seek after wickedness in the house of the just, nor spoil his rest" (Prov., xxiv. 15).

1270. The kinds of faults that call for fraternal correction are as follows: (a) grave sins should be corrected, for otherwise one allows a soul to perish that might have been saved (Matt., xviii. 14, 15), (b) slight sins or transgressions of rules should also be corrected, when they are the occasion of grave scandal or disorder in a community, and superiors who are negligent about this commit mortal sin; (c) slight sins or transgressions should not be corrected in ordinary cases, for these faults are so numerous that, if one had to correct them, an intolerable burden would be laid on everyone, Persons who scold and lecture over every trifling misdeed are regarded as pests and do more harm than good.

1271. The purpose of fraternal correction is to save one who is in danger of losing his soul. Hence, it should not be restricted to those sins that are an offense to the corrector, but it should extend also to sins that are against God, the neighbor, or the offender himself.

1272. Since fraternal correction is given for the purpose of converting a sinner from the evil of his ways, it is not called for when one's neighbor is not a sinner, strictly speaking, or has already reformed. Thus, there is no need of this correction in the following cases: (a) when a person sins through ignorance and is not guilty of formal sin; (b) when a person who was a sinner in the past has given up his old ways.

1273. A person who sins from vincible ignorance should not be corrected unless the two following conditions are present: (a) there must be hope of amendment, otherwise the admonition would only aggravate the sinner's guilt; (b) there must be no greater evil that will result from the admonition and correction.

1274. A person who sins from invincible ignorance is not guilty of formal sin, and hence, as said above, he is not a subject for fraternal correction. But charity often requires that he be instructed especially by superiors, confessors, etc., with a view to the prevention of various evils. These evils are of the following kinds: (a) injury to God, as when a person unacquainted with the language uses expressions that are blasphemous; (b) injury to self, as when a child not understanding the power of liquor becomes intoxicated; (c) injury to the neighbor, as when a person who does not know that it is a fast day causes scandal by not keeping the fast.

1275. If there is hope that the instruction will have a good result, one should instruct the invincibly ignorant in order to prevent injury to God, themselves, or their neighbor; but, if it seems that an instruction will do only harm or more harm than good, it should be omitted. The duty of instruction rests especially on superiors, such as parents, teachers, confessors. These principles are applied to various cases as follows:

(a) A material sin may have been committed in the past. Titus through inadvertence ate meat on a day of abstinence, but gave no scandal; Balbus did the same thing, and this caused considerable scandal. Now, there might be an obligation of telling Balbus what he did in order to repair the scandal, but no such obligation would exist in the case of

Titus. Sempronius and Caius both married invalidly, but are in good faith. If Sempronius is told about his marriage, matters can be easily rectified; but if Caius is informed that his marriage is null, he will abandon his putative wife and his family, and there will be serious discords and scandals. Hence, Sempronius should be told, but not Caius.

(b) Material sin may be about to be committed against the natural or divine law. Titus is about to destroy what he thinks is an abandoned and useless picture, but which is in reality a very valuable work of art belonging to Balbus. Caius is going to the altar to be married; Claudius knows of a diriment impediment to the marriage, but cannot make it known without causing a scene and giving great scandal. Titus should be instructed, but it is a duty to say nothing to Caius.

(c) Material sin may be about to be committed against human law. Sempronius sees Claudius and others eating meat on a day of abstinence, which they have forgotten. He also sees Father Balbus, who has forgotten to put on an alb or a chasuble, going to the altar to say Mass. There is no obligation to call the attention of Claudius to the day of abstinence, but for the sake of respect to divine worship the attention of Father Balbus should be directed to the missing vestments.

1276. Certain past sins do not demand fraternal correction: (a) those sins that have been repented of, especially if there is no danger of a relapse (e.g., a wife should not be always reminding her now sober husband that he was addicted to drink before he met her); (b) those sins that will in all probability be remedied shortly without one's intervention. Hence, it is not necessary to reprove Titus because he drank too much, if he is not careless about his salvation and will soon approach the Sacraments, or if his parents or wife are better fitted to make the correction and will not fail to do so.

1277. To what persons may correction be given? (a) Judicial correction can be given only to one's subjects, since it supposes authority; (b) fraternal correction can be given, not only to inferiors and equals, but also to superiors. For charity should be shown to all those who are in need of assistance, and, the higher the office, the greater the danger. Superiors who are giving scandal or doing harm to others should be remonstrated with by their equals, or, if need be, by their subjects. Fraternal correction among the clergy is especially advantageous.

1278. When fraternal correction is given to a superior: (a) the superior should take a proper correction with gratitude and humility, imitating St. Peter when reproved by St. Paul (Gal., ii. 11); (b) the inferior should give the correction without boldness or harshness, but respectfully and mildly: "An elderly man rebuke not, but entreat him as a father" (I Tim., v. 1). It is better that the person giving the correction be himself of some standing, lest the act seem to proceed from contempt, and so only embitter the superior who is at fault. Example: Children should plead with parents who steal, get drunk or neglect religion, to mend their ways.

1279. What persons may administer correction? (a) Judicial correction as just said can be given only by a superior; (b) fraternal correction may be given by any person who is not so unfitted that a correction from him will necessarily be useless or harmful. It is not required, however, that one be immaculate, for if immunity from all sin were necessary in a corrector, who could reprove delinquents (I John, i. 8)?

1280. The fact that a person is known to be a sinner, or not in the state of grace, or guilty of the same things he reproves, does not unfit him for giving a fraternal correction; because, in spite of his own sinfulness, he may retain a right judgment and so be able to correct wrongdoing. In the following cases, however, correction made by a sinner is reprehensible, on account of circumstances other than that of the person: (a) the motive of the correction is sinful, when the sinner corrects only in order to distract attention from himself, to conceal bad deeds by good words, to practise revenge, etc.; (b) the mode of the correction is sinful when the sinner corrects with pride, as if he himself were above correction: "Wherein thou judgest another thou condemnest thyself, for thou dost the same things which thou judgest" (Rom, ii. 1); (c) the consequences of correction made by a sinner are an evil circumstance, as when scandal results. Thus, if a person who is guilty of far greater sins corrects his neighbor, this has a demoralizing effect, when the impression is given that good words rather than good deeds are important.

1281. One who prefers his neighbor's conversion to his own deviates from the right order of charity, since he should love himself more. But a person may without any transgression against the precept of fraternal correction seek to correct his neighbor before he has corrected himself.

(a) Thus, from the nature of correction itself or from the provisions of the commandment, there does not seem to be any obligation of correcting self before correcting others; for a humble correction made by a sinner with acknowledgment of his unworthiness to censure others, or by a sinner who is thought to be good or to have reformed, may be just as efficacious as a correction made by a truly virtuous man. But it is of counsel that one correct oneself as a means towards the better correction of another.

(b) Because of special reasons, a person may be otherwise obliged to correct himself before he attempts to correct another, as when self-correction is the only means towards obtaining some necessary end. Thus, a superior who cannot enforce discipline because he is unobservant himself, the friend of a dying man who cannot convert the latter unless he gives evidence of his own conversion, a person who cannot repair the scandal he has given unless he manifests repentance—all these should begin by correcting themselves. One should take the beam out of one's own eye, if otherwise one cannot remove the mote from a neighbor's eye (Matt, vii. 5).

1282. All suitable persons, then, are bound by the duty of fraternal correction: "He gave to every one of them commandment concerning his neighbor" (Ecclus., xvii. 12). But the duty rests more heavily on some than on others. (a) Thus, bishops and other pastors are held out of justice to fraternal correction, and even at the peril of life. (b) Other prelates, confessors, parents, husbands, masters, teachers and guardians, are held to fraternal correction from charity and by reason of their office; but they are not held to this duty when there is grave personal danger to themselves. (c) Private persons are held out of charity, but their obligation is less than in the case of those whose office requires them to make corrections.

1283. A person is not bound to make a correction for the sole reason that he is able to make it successfully. For he is excused: (a) if correction by him is not necessary, as when parents or others better able than himself will attend to the matter; (b) if his correction will bring on himself evils which he is not obliged to incur.

1284. An obligation of making a correction even when this will cause an injury to the corrector, exists in the following cases: (a) If the correction is necessary to avert extreme spiritual evil (i.e., damnation), one should be prepared to make a sacrifice, even of life itself, to give the correction (see 1165). Example: Titus is dying of a contagious disease, and will lose his soul, if Balbus does not come to advise him. (b) If the correction is necessary to avert grave spiritual evil, a pastor should be willing to risk his life, and another person should be willing to risk the loss of money, and even some injury to health. But a subject is not bound to correct his superior, when this will bring on him persecutions; a scrupulous person is not bound to correct, for this would cause him worries and suffering.

1285. The manner of making a correction is as follows:

(a) The internal dispositions should include charity towards the one corrected and humility as regards one's own fitness. For fraternal correction is not opposed to the commands of bearing with the weaknesses of others (Gal, vi. 2), and of not proudly preferring self to others (Philip., ii. 3). One should correct inferiors paternally, equals kindly, and superiors respectfully. In every correction there should be seriousness mingled with mildness.

(b) The external order to be followed is that given by our Lord in Matt., xviii. 15-18, namely, that, when possible, admonition should be given privately, and that one should not proceed to accusation before superiors until other means, such as the calling in of witnesses, have proved unavailing. The order to be followed in fraternal correction is not only of the positive divine law, but it is also of the natural law. For the natural law requires that we do for others what we wish done for ourselves, and there is no one who does not desire that correction be given him in such a way that the least possible injury be done to his feelings and to his good name.

1286. In what cases should secret admonition be used?

(a) For public sins (i.e., real sins known or soon to be known to the larger part of the community), no secret admonition is required, since the guilt is already publicly known; a public correction, on the contrary, is necessary to remedy the scandal: "Them that sin reprove before all, that the rest also may have fear" (I Tim., v. 20).

(b) For occult sins that are against the common good or the good of a third person no secret admonition is required, but one should denounce them immediately; for the spiritual or corporal welfare of the multitude or of an innocent private individual is a greater good than the reputation of the guilty person. Exception should be made, however, for the case in which one is certain that by a secret admonition one can correct the sinner and prevent the harm that threatens others. Examples: If Titus knows that there is a plot to rob the house of Balbus, and that any effort to dissuade the criminals would only bring him into danger, he ought to warn Balbus or the authorities. If Claudius knows that in his school a certain student is teaching the other boys to steal and become drunk, he should make this known, and hence cannot be absolved if he refuses. But the seal of the confessional must be observed.

(c) For occult sins that are not against the common good or that of a third person, one should have recourse to secret admonition before making the sins known. This will save the sinner from loss of reputation and from consequent hardness in sin; it will also save others from a share in his infamy, or from the scandal caused by publicity.

1287. What is the obligation of reporting an occult sin that is doing harm in a community, when the person who reports will suffer for telling what he knows? (a) If harm to the community will result from silence, one is obliged even at the cost of great inconvenience to speak (see 1284). Example: Claudius knows that a fellow-student has a bad influence over his companions, and is leading more and more of them into stealing, with the result that a large number will be corrupted and the institution disgraced. But he cannot speak without serious harm to himself, because he also has been implicated, or because informers are regarded and treated as traitors. (b) If some private harm will result from silence, one is not bound at the cost of great inconvenience to speak. Example: If Claudius knows that only one or two are being led astray, he is not bound to implicate himself or to incur the ignominy of being regarded as a spy.

1288. There are exceptional cases in which occult faults, not injurious to others, are reproved publicly, without previous private admonition. (a) God as the supreme ruler has the right to publish hidden sins, although He admonishes men secretly through the voice of conscience or through external preaching or other means. St. Peter, in making known the sin of Ananias and Saphira, acted as the instrument of God's justice and in virtue of a revelation given him (Acts, v. 3, 4, 9). (b) Members of a society who are agreed to remind one another publicly of transgressions of their regulations, do not violate the order of fraternal correction given by Christ, if there is nothing defamatory in these reminders. Example: The proclamations made in the chapter of faults in religious orders.

1289. May a prelate (e.g., in a visitation) oblige his subjects to carry to him, without a previous secret admonition of the person to be accused, information about the secret sins of fellow-subjects that are not harmful to others?

(a) If a sin is entirely secret, and the subjects have not renounced their right to reputation in the sight of the prelate, the latter has no right to give orders that he be informed at once, since the rule given by Christ requires that a fraternal correction be first given. A subject would be bound, therefore, if such orders were given, to obey the divine injunction, rather than that of the prelate (Acts, v. 3, 4, 9).

(b) If a sin is entirely secret, but subjects have renounced their right to receive first a private admonition, a prelate may require that information be brought to him at once. This is the rule in certain religious societies; but even in them a sin should not be reported to the prelate if the sinner has already amended, nor should the higher superior be informed if the immediate superior can take care of the matter sufficiently. These religious have a right to their reputation.

(e) If a sin is not entirely secret, because there are some indications (such as ill-repute or grounds for suspicion), a prelate may require that information be brought to him immediately.

1290. If, after several private admonitions have been made, there is no hope of success by this method, what should be done? (a) If it appears that the other means prescribed by our Lord will be successful, they should be tried, just as a physician has recourse to new remedies when old ones have failed. (b) If it appears that any further efforts will do harm rather than good, the attempt to correct a private sin that harms only the sinner should be given up.

1291. The order to be followed in fraternal correction, after personal reproof or remonstrance has failed, is as follows:

(a) One should enlist the services of one or two others to assist in making the brotherly correction. The conversion of the culprit is more important than his reputation with these others; whereas their knowledge of the matter safeguards the corrector from the charge of being a mischievous talebearer, should things go further, and it should arouse the culprit to the need of correcting himself, before his case is brought before the superior for correction.

(b) When other things have failed, recourse should be had to the superior of the person at fault, if there is hope that this will prove successful. If the superior is imprudent or given to wrath or is known to dislike the person to be corrected, or if the latter would only be enraged by a reproof from this superior, charity would urge one to say nothing about the matter. Example: Titus makes himself intoxicated from time to time. Balbus is the only one who knows this, and he tries to correct Titus. But, as the latter denies the accusation, Balbus asks Caius and Sempronius, friends of Titus, to be witnesses; and all three of them make an effort to convert Titus. This correction also has no effect, and so Balbus and the other two make the matter known to the parents of Titus, that they may watch their son more carefully and keep him away from occasions of drink.

1292. What are the duties of a superior to whom a subject has been reported for fraternal correction? (a) He should try to discover the truth of the matter. Means to this end are a consideration of the character and motives of the accuser, the reply which the accused makes in his own defense, and in case of necessity a confrontation of accuser and accused, a cross-examination, etc. (I Cor., i. xi; Dan., xiii. 5). Those who make a practice of gladly carrying tales to superiors are disturbers of peace, and they should be given to understand that their accusations are not wanted, and that they should mind their own business.

(b) If the superior has reason to believe that the accusation in question is true, he should use moderate remedial measures, while at the same time preserving the good name of the person to be corrected. For the information has been brought before him, not as judge, but as father of the person accused, and hence public punishments or corrections injurious to reputation must be avoided. Removal from an office, a change of place and special vigilance may be used, when this can be done prudently.

1293. Cases in which a subject may be reported to his superior for fraternal correction without previous admonitions are not impossible; for the law given by Christ concerning the order to be followed is affirmative, and hence obliges only under the proper circumstances. (a) Thus, if previous admonitions would be harmful, whereas an admonition by the superior will be beneficial, recourse should be had at once to the superior. (b) If an admonition by the superior will be more advantageous, the other admonitions may be omitted. Thus, if the superior is more revered by the person to be corrected and will be listened to more readily, or if there is danger of delay in making previous admonitions, it is better that the matter be brought before the superior at once. What is said of the superior can be applied also to some other pious and prudent person from whom a correction would be better received.

1294. The obligation of fraternal correction by private individuals may be summed up as follows: (a) One is bound to correct when one is certain about a grave sin which will not be corrected except by oneself, and when one has good reason to hope that the correction will be profitable to the sinner and not unreasonably harmful to the corrector. Those who interfere when these conditions are not present are meddlesome or imprudent, rather than charitable. (b) One is bound to report to a superior when one is certain about a grave sin which is harmful to the community or which cannot be corrected so well by private admonition, if one believes that it will not be reported except by oneself, and that one's report will be for the good of others and not an undue detriment to oneself. Those who report of their own choice when these conditions are not existent, are malicious tale-bearers or rash news-carriers, rather than charitable accusers.

Art. 7: THE SINS AGAINST LOVE AND JOY

(*Summa Theologica*, II-II, qq. 34-36.)

1295. The sins against charity and its subordinate virtues can be reduced to the following: (a) hatred, which is opposed to love; (b) sloth and envy, which are contrary to the joy of charity; (c) discord and schism, which are opposed to the peace of charity; (d) scandal, which is the opposite of beneficence and fraternal correction.

1296. Hate.—Hate is an aversion of the will to something which the intellect judges evil, that is, contrary to self. As there are two kinds of love, so there are also two kinds of hate. (a) Hatred of dislike (*odium abominationis*) is the opposite of love of desire, for, as this love inclines to something as suitable and advantageous for self, so hatred of dislike turns away from something, as being considered unsuitable and harmful to self. (b) Hatred of enmity (*odium inimicitiæ*) is the opposite of love of benevolence, for, as this love wishes good to the object of its affection, so hatred of enmity wishes evil to the object of its dislike.

1297. Hatred of God.-A thing cannot be hated unless it is looked upon as evil, and hence God cannot be hated except by those who regard Him as evil to themselves.

(a) Thus, those who see the Divine Essence (i.e., the blessed), cannot hate God, for His Essence is goodness itself, and, therefore, the blessed can see in God only reasons for love. (b) Those who see God obscurely through the things made by Him (i.e., wayfarers on earth), cannot hate God considered as the author of effects that are in no way displeasing to the will, such as existence, life, intelligence; but they can hate God as the author of effects displeasing to their will, such as law and punishment. Thus, no one can hate God because God has given him being, for existence of itself is something good and desirable; but a depraved will can hate God for having forbidden sin, or for inflicting chastisements, or for permitting some evils to accompany the blessings of life. That hatred of God is not a mere possibility, the scriptures in many places attest: "The pride of them that hate Thee ascendeth forever" (Ps, lxiii. 23), "Now they have seen and hated both Me and My Father" (John, xv. 24).

1298. It should not be inferred from what has just been said that it is not God in Himself that is hated, but only His works; nor that it is a sin against God to dislike evils or even divine punishments.

(a) Thus, God Himself is not the principle or motive cause of the hatred directed against Him, for in God there is no evil that can produce dislike; but God is the term or object of the hatred aroused in the sinner by the divine effects that displease him, as the texts given above from scripture indicate. For example, a man hates his neighbor on account of certain defects he perceives or thinks he perceives; the defects are the principle, but the neighbor is the term of the hatred.

(b) Dislike of the evils that are in the world, or of chastisements sent by God, is not dislike of God Himself, since God does not ask us to love evil, but only to endure such evils as cannot be cured. Even murmurs against Providence are usually manifestations of impatience, not of hatred of Providence. It is only the sinner that dislikes God Himself for permitting or inflicting evils, who is guilty of hatred of God.

1299. Hatred of God of various kinds. (a) As regards the intention, it is either interpretative or formal. Interpretative hatred is aversion that is not intended directly or for its own sake, but only indirectly and by reason of something else whose love is preferred. Formal hatred is an aversion that is intended directly and expressly in itself. Every mortal sin is an act of interpretative hatred of God, since mortal sin consists in placing one's own pleasure or interest above the friendship of God; but it is only the special sin which attacks God directly that constitutes formal hate. Thus, he who murders his enemy does not directly intend dislike of God, but revenge; whereas the condemned murderer who blasphemes God, because he is to be executed, directly dislikes God. (b) As regards the degree of malice it contains, formal hatred of God is either dislike or enmity. Dislike of God is the sin of those who do not like some attribute of God; enmity towards God is the sin of those who wish some evil to God. Thus, one who deliberately wishes that God would sanction injustice dislikes the divine attribute of justice, while an unjust man who wishes he might be rid of God and His judgment is guilty of enmity to God.

1300. Hatred of God as a Special Sin.—(a) Interpretative hatred of God is not a special sin but a general circumstance of every mortal sin; but formal hatred is a special sin, and indeed one that is comparatively rare, and that must be specially mentioned in confession. This is a sin which is distinct, not only from the sins against the other theological virtues (e.g., unbelief, despair), but also from the sins against the other objects of charity (e.g., hatred of the neighbor).

(b) Formal hatred of God is not a special sin against the Holy Ghost (see 899); but its malice pervades every such sin, and it is thus a general sin against the Holy Ghost. For example, presumption is a dislike of God's law which requires that one must attain salvation through the observance of the commandments; rejection of the known truth is a dislike of God's revelation.

1301. The Gravity of Hatred of God.-(a) It is a mortal sin from its nature, and can never be venial on account of the smallness of the injury, but only on account of lack of deliberation or consent. Dislike of even one attribute of God is a grave injury, for everything pertaining to God is perfect and infinitely lovable. (b) Hatred of God is the worst of all mortal sins; for it is directly opposed to God (the supreme good) and to charity (the most excellent virtue in a creature), whereas other mortal sins offend against these goods only indirectly.

1302. The comparison just made between hatred of God and other sins supposes that the other sins do not include hatred of God, for it is clear that simple hatred of God existing in the will is less serious than a composite sin, such as external blasphemy uttered to manifest internal hatred of God. (a) Thus, hatred of God without unbelief is worse than unbelief without hatred of God; (b) hatred of God without hatred of the neighbor is worse than hatred of the neighbor without hatred of God.

1303. Degrees of Malice in Hatred of God.—(a) A new species of sin is added to hatred of God, when out of hatred one proceeds to sin against creatures, or to commit other offenses against God Himself. Example: Titus hates God, and therefore persecutes those who believe in God, and also blasphemes God. (b) A new degree of malice is added to hatred of God when one proceeds from dislike to enmity, or when the circumstances of person, place, manner, etc., aggravate the malice. Example: Hatred of God outwardly manifested adds the evil of scandal; not so hatred of God that is concealed.

1304. Hatred of Creatures.—All dislike of God is sinful, because there is nothing in God that merits dislike. But in creatures imperfections are found as well as perfections.

(a) Hence, dislike of the imperfections of our neighbor (i.e., of all that is the work of the devil or of his own sinfulness), is not against charity, but according to charity; for it is the same thing to dislike another's evil as to wish his good. Thus, God Himself is said to hate detractors, that is, detraction (Rom., i. 30), and Christ bids His followers hate their parents who would be an impediment to their progress in holiness, that is, the sinful opposition of those parents (Luke, xiv. 26). Only when dislike is carried beyond reason is it sinful. Thus, a wife who dislikes her husband's habit of drunkenness so much that she will not give him a necessary medicine on account of the alcohol it contains, carries her dislike to extremes.

(b) Dislike of the perfections of nature or of grace in our neighbor (i.e., of anything that is the work of God in him), is contrary to charity. Thus, God does not hate the detractor himself, nor should children ever hate the person of a parent, or the natural relationship he holds to themselves, no matter how bad the parent may be. As St. Augustine says: "One should love the sinner, but hate his vices."

1305. The same principles apply to dislike of self. (a) Thus, one should dislike one's own imperfections, for they are the enemies of one's soul. So, contrition is defined as a hatred and detestation of one's vices, and it is a virtue and an act of charity to self. (b) One should not dislike the good one has, except in so far as it is associated with evil. Thus, one should not regret one's honesty, even if by reason of it one loses an opportunity to make a large sum of money; but one may regret having married, if one's choice has been unfortunate and has made one's life miserable.

1306. Should a person dislike in others their opposition to himself? (a) If their opposition is unjust, he should dislike it, for it is then a sin in them and an injury to himself, and charity to them and to self requires that he should dislike what is harmful to all concerned. (b) If their opposition is just, he should like it, for it is virtuous in them and beneficial to himself: "Better are the wounds of a friend than the deceitful kisses of an enemy" (Prov., xxvii. 6).

1307. Direct enmity to self is not possible, for nature inclines each one so strongly to love of self that it is impossible for anyone to wish evil to himself as evil: "No one hateth his own flesh" (Ephes., v. 29). But indirectly a person may be at enmity with himself, inasmuch as he wishes evil under the guise of good; and hence St. Augustine, commenting on the words, "He that loveth his life shall lose it" (John, xii, 25), says: "If you love self wrongly, you hate it; if you hate self rightly, you love it." This indirect enmity to self happens in two ways. (a) A person sometimes wishes himself what is not a true, but only an apparent good, as when he chooses the satisfaction of revenge rather than that of pardon of injuries. (b) A person sometimes chooses what is good, not for his true, but for his lower self, as when he decides to gratify the body at the expense of the soul.

1308. Is it ever lawful to wish evil to self or to others? (a) It is not lawful to wish anyone evil as evil, for even God in punishing the lost does not will their punishment as it is evil to them, but as it contains the good of justice. Hence, it is contrary to charity to wish that a criminal be put to death, if one's wish does not go beyond the sufferings and loss of life the criminal will endure. (b) It is lawful to wish evil as good, or, in other words, to wish misfortunes that are blessings in disguise. Thus, one may wish that a neighbor lose his arm, if this is necessary to save his life.

1309. One may easily be self-deceived in wishing evil to one's neighbor under the pretext that it is really good one desires, for the true intention may be hatred or revenge. Hence, the following conditions must be present when one wishes evil as good:

(a) On the part of the subject (i.e., of the person who wills the evil), the intention must be sincerely charitable, proceeding from a desire that the neighbor be benefitted. Thus, it is lawful to wish that a gambler may meet with reverses, if what is intended is, not his loss, but his awakening to the need of a new kind of amusement. St. Paul rejoiced that he had made the Corinthians sorrowful, because their sorrow worked repentance in them (II Cor., vii. 7-11). Of course, the desire of a neighbor's good does not confer the right to wrong him, for the end does not justify the means.

(b) On the part of the object (i.e., of the evil which is wished to another), it must he compensated for by the good which is intended. It is not lawful to desire the death of another on account of the property one expects to inherit, for the neighbor's life is more important than private gain; but it is lawful to wish, out of interest in the common welfare, that a criminal be captured and punished, for it is only by the vindication of law that public tranquillity can be secured (Gal., v. 12).

1310. Is it lawful to wish the death of self or of a neighbor for some private good of the one whose death is wished? (a) If the good is a spiritual one and more important than the spiritual good contained in the desire to live, it is lawful to desire death. Thus, it is lawful to wish to die in order to enter into a better life, or to be freed from the temptations and sinfulness of life on earth. But it is not lawful to wish to die in order to spare a few individuals the scandal they take from one's life, if that life is needed by others as a source of edification (Philip., i. 21 sqq.). (b) If the good is a temporal one but sufficiently important, it does not seem unlawful to desire death. Thus, we should not blame a person suffering from a painful and incurable disease, which makes him a burden to himself and to others, if, with resignation to the divine will, he prays for the release of death; for "death is better than a bitter life" (Ecclus., xxx, 17). But lack of perfect health or a feeling of weariness is not a good reason for wishing to die, especially if one has dependents, or is useful to others.

1311. Is it ever lawful to wish spiritual evil to anyone? (a) Spiritual evil of iniquity may never be desired, for the desire of sin, mortal or venial, is a sin itself (see 242), and it cannot be charitable, for charity rejoiceth not with iniquity (I Cor., xiii. 6). It is wrong, therefore, to wish that our neighbor fall into sin, offend God, diminish or forfeit his grace, or lose his soul. On the contrary, we are commanded to pray that he be delivered from such evils. (b) The good that God draws out of spiritual evil may be desired. Some are permitted to fall into sin, or be tempted, that they may become more humble, more charitable, more vigilant, more fervent. It seems that the permission of sin in the case of the elect is one of the benefits of God's predestination, inasmuch as God intends it to be an occasion of greater virtue and stronger perseverance. It is not lawful to wish that God permit anyone to fall into sin, but it is lawful to wish that, if God has permitted sin, good will follow after it.

1312. Gravity of the Sin of Hatred of Neighbor.—(a) Hatred, whether of dislike or of enmity, is from its nature a mortal sin, since it is directly opposed to the virtue of charity, which is the life of the soul.

(b) Dislike, if enmity is not joined to it, is rarely in fact a mortal sin. Aversions and antipathies for others usually are either indeliberate, or have to do with what are real or fancied defects in others. Dislike is a mortal sin only when one despises another so much that one deliberately loathes even that which is of divine provenance in the other, or dislikes a real imperfection so immoderately as to inflict serious injury (e.g., by refusing pardon or the common signs of charity, by giving grave scandal, etc.)

(c) Enmity in fact is often only a venial sin, either because one wishes only a small harm (e.g., the loss of a small sum of money), or because one wishes harm, even a great harm (e.g., the commission of mortal sin), without full deliberation. Enmity is a mortal sin, however, when one deliberately wishes a grave evil (e.g., mortal sin or the loss of reputation) to one's neighbor.

1313. Hatred Compared with Other Sins Against the Neighbor.—(a) Hatred is a graver sin than other internal sins against the neighbor, such as envy, anger; for, while each of these latter attacks some particular kind of good of the neighbor or only to a limited degree, hatred may be directed against any good and knows no measure. Thus, covetousness is directed against the external goods or possessions of a neighbor, whilehate may extend to either internal or external goods. Envy is opposed to the neighbor's good relatively, in so far as it is considered an obstacle to one's own glory, but hate detests another's good absolutely. The hater finds his satisfaction, not in any profit derived for self, but in his aversion for another's good, and the harm that is wished his neighbor. This comparison here made should be understood, other things being equal, so that hatred of another's life is contrasted with envy of his life, etc.; for, if the goods are not the same, hatred may be a lesser sin, as when hatred of a neighbor's temporal good is compared with envy of his spiritual good. (b) Hatred of a neighbor is a more serious sin than external offenses done against him, for hatred sets the will wrong, and it is in the will that sin takes root: "He who hates his brother is a murderer" (I John, iii. 15). The external act, on the contrary (e.g., killing an innocent man), is not a formal sin when the will is guiltless. (c) Hatred is a less harmful sin to the neighbor than external offenses; for example, internal dislike and malevolence will not break any bones, as may happen from a severe blow.

1314. Why is hatred not numbered among the capital vices? As was said above (see 269), a capital vice is one from which naturally and usually other species of sin take their origin. Now, hatred of God or the neighbor, in the natural and usual course of sin, does not precede, but rather follows other sins. Hence, hatred is not a capital sin. This will appear more clearly if we distinguish two kinds of hatred:

(a) Hate of that which is truly evil and opposed to the true good of man (e.g., hate of vice), is naturally prior to other disinclinations, since rational nature first inclines one to love its good and hate its evil (see 1106).

(b) Hate of that which is not evil (as hate of God or of the neighbor), is naturally subsequent to other sins, for it is only a nature already corrupt that detests true goodness. This does not mean, however, that the whole catalogue of lesser sins must have been committed before hatred is arrived at, nor that in individual cases a sinner has not the freedom to hate before he has committed less grave sins.

1315. In a certain wide sense, however, it may be said that hatred of the neighbor goes before all other sins against the neighbor, just as was remarked above (1299) concerning sins against God.

(a) Hence, interpretative hate—i.e., a feeling against another that makes one act in effect as if there were hatred—does precede the other sins. Thus, if Titus, who bore no ill-will to Balbus, becomes enraged against him and inflicts death, the murder is traced back to anger, but this anger may be called hate, inasmuch as dislike of the life of Balbus is included in the desire of revenge.

(b) Formal hate—i.e., dislike of another that is absolute, and not modified by such considerations as desire of revenge or sorrow over one's own inferiority—does not precede, but rather follows the other sins, as was explained in the previous paragraph. It is only this sin of formal hate that is a special sin. Titus in the example murdered Balbus, not because he had an absolute dislike for him, but because the thirst for revenge made Balbus displeasing to him.

1316. The causes of the sin of hatred are as follows: (a) causes that dispose one to hate are anger and envy, for to desire evil to another, for revenge or on account of one's own glory, prepares the way to desire evil to him absolutely, which is hatred. Envy, however, disposes to hate more than anger, since it is more akin to hatred: anger wishes evil to another as something owed to justice, but both envy and hatred look upon the neighbor's good as a thing distasteful. (b) The cause that induces sinful hatred of the neighbor is envy; for one cannot hate that which is good unless one regards it as in some way disagreeable, and it is the vice of envy that makes one regard one's neighbor's good as one's own evil. Hatred of God also indirectly results from envy, for, while the creature does not envy God, his envy of his neighbor breeds hatred of his fellow-man, and this in turn may produce hatred of God.

1317. Various Species of the Sin of Hatred.—(a) Hatred of God and hatred of the neighbor are sins specifically distinct, and hence to be declared specifically in confession. They are opposed to the same virtue of charity, but, on account of the generical difference of sin against God and sin against the creature, they must be classed as different species of sin.

(b) Hatred of the neighbor in itself is but one species of sin, since all its acts have this one essential character in common, that evil is wished to a neighbor as evil—that is, one wishes another evil in general or every kind of evil, but does not specify particular evils, such as damnation or death.

(c) Hatred of the neighbor on account of its circumstances or results may be connected with sins of other species. Thus, he who hates his neighbor because the latter is pious, adds irreligion to his hatred; he who out of hatred wishes the death of his neighbor, adds the guilt of murder to hatred; he who out of hatred wishes to destroy his neighbor's property, adds the guilt of injustice to his hatred: he who hates his parents, adds impiety to uncharitableness; he who calls down a curse on another, adds malediction to hate.

1318. Penitents who accuse themselves of hatred often have in mind a sin specifically distinct from the sin of hatred, or an act not sinful at all.

(a) Thus, "hatred of God" is sometimes used to signify a want of resignation to the divine will.

(b) "Dislike of the neighbor" is sometimes used to signify uncongeniality on account of difference of character, etc., or positive disapproval of qualities or acts that deserve dislike or censure. Thus, a penitent who always feels ill at ease in the company of a neighbor on account of some natural incompatibility or of some fear which he himself does not understand, or who dreads meeting an individual whose manners are boorish or whose conversation is distasteful, may accuse himself of sinful dislike.

(c) "Wishing evil to the neighbor" is sometimes used to signify one's desire that justice take its course or that the order of charity be observed. Thus, a penitent who wished for the common good that a criminal be punished, or according to charity that his friend would defeat others in competition for a prize, may accuse himself that he wished harm to the criminal or had luck to the competitors against his friend.

1319. Circumstances of hatred should be mentioned in confession as follows: (a) when they add a new species—thus, the person hated (e.g., one's father) or the evil wished (e.g., a fall into mortal sin, loss of reputation, death, etc.) may add a new sin to that of hate; (b) when they multiply the number of sins within the species of hate, as when one hates a large number of persons (see 219).

1320. The Sin of Sloth.—Sloth is a sadness or dejection of the will about the divine good one possesses, and arises from a want of esteem for one's Last End and the means thereto.

(a) Sloth is a sadness of the will. Hence, the sin of sloth differs from the passion of sadness, and also from bodily weariness. The passions (as said in 121) are not evil in themselves, but become evil when exercised immoderately, or turned to an evil object. Weakness or weariness of body is not sinful, but it disposes one for the passion of sadness, and this in turn may tempt the will to sloth, when duties owed to God are to be attended to.

(b) Sloth is a sadness about good, and so it differs from sadness about the smallness of one's good. Humility demands that one be sensible of one's own shortcomings and of the greater merits of those who are better. But it is not humility but ingratitude and sloth to depreciate and grieve over the good which one has received from God, such as the gift of faith, membership in the Church, etc.

(c) Sloth is sadness about the divine good, which is loved by charity. Thus, the sin of sloth differs from the circumstance of sloth, which is found in every sin. There is no sin that does not contain a sadness or disgust about the act of the opposite virtue; the very thought of moderation is depressing to the glutton, and religion is associated with gloom by the irreligious. But what is special to the sin of sloth is, that it grieves about that divine good itself over which charity rejoices, and which is the end of all the other virtues.

(d) Sloth is a sadness about the divine good as shared by self, that is, about the end offered oneself and the means thereto, such as eternal beatitude, the friendship of God, the Sacraments, the Commandments, good works and other divine gifts which should be esteemed and received with gladness. Sloth thus differs from hatred of God, which is a sadness over God's own goodness; and from envy, which is a sadness over the good of the neighbor.

(e) Sloth is a sadness over the divine good, which is considered by one as an evil. The sin of sloth looks upon the joys of heaven or the practice of virtue with contempt; it directly spurns them as unworthy of love (cfr. Num., xxi. 4). Hence, sloth differs from laziness or idleness,

528

for this latter sin dislikes the exercise of virtue, not because it considers virtue as evil, but because it has a dread of the labor and exertion which virtue entails, and is overmuch in love with repose and ease.

1321. Sloth is a sin. (a) It is forbidden by God: "Bow down thy shoulder and bear wisdom, and be not grieved with her bands" (Ecclus., vi. 26). (b) It is an evil sorrow, for it grieves over good. (c) It has evil effects, since it keeps man from his duty, swallowing him up with overmuch sorrow (II Cor., ii. 7).

1322. Qualities of the Sin of Sloth.—(a) Sloth is a special sin, since, as explained above, its individual objects differentiate it from the general slothfulness that is found in every sin, as well as from hatred, envy and laziness. But it is a sin, by comparison, rarely committed. (b) It is a mortal sin, from its nature, since it is a horror and detestation for the divine good. It is implicitly forbidden in the Third Commandment, (c) It is a capital sin (i.e., a vice naturally productive of others), for sadness inclines man to many evils as means of escape from sorrow or of consolation in sorrow.

1323. In the following cases sloth is not a mortal sin. (a) It is not a mortal sin if in the object there is not grave matter. When a person is grieved at the thought that he will be forced to some spiritual good which is not of precept but of counsel, he does not sin thereby, for one does not sin by not choosing the counsels. Strictly speaking, however, this grief is not the sin of sloth, which is a sorrow over the divine good that one is bound to accept with joy. (b) Sloth is not a mortal sin, if in the subject there is not sufficient reflection or full consent. Hence, mere bodily weariness in serving God, is no sin at all, and a feeling of disgust for spiritual things, not consented to, is only a struggle of the flesh against the spirit, and at most a venial sin.

1324. Sins that Spring from Sloth.—(a) To escape his sadness about divine things, the slothful man avoids or flees the things that sadden him—his last end (sin of despair) and the means thereto (sins of cowardice and carelessness). He also attacks the causes of his grief—the persons who would lead him to God (sin of rancor) or the spiritual things themselves (sin of malice). (b) To console himself for the want of joy in spiritual things, he seeks comfort in forbidden things: his mind is unquiet and curious about that which does not concern him, his talk is excessive, his bodily movements are restless, and he must be continually moving from place to place.

1325. The Conquest of Sloth.—(a) Flight is a suitable form of resistance to temptation, whenever the temptation grows stronger by thinking over the matter, as is the case with temptations against purity (I Cor., vi. 18). (b) Attack is a suitable form of resistance, when the temptation becomes weaker as one thinks over the matter (see 257). This is the case with sloth, for, the more one gives oneself to the consideration of spiritual things, the more pleasing do they become.

1326. Laziness, as distinct from the capital vice of sloth, is a generic name given to a number of sins or circumstances of sin, and hence it will be treated in several places.

(a) Thus, negligence is a want of prompt decision about duties to be performed. It is opposed to the virtue of diligence or solicitude, which pertains to prudence. Hence, negligence will be considered among the sins against prudence.

(b) Sluggishness (*pigritia*) is a tardy performance of duty, and will be considered among the sins opposed to diligence.

(c) Carelessness (*torpor*) is a perfunctory discharge of duties, without thought or love. It is one of the consequences of sloth given above (see 1324), and hence it is a sin against charity.

(d) Indolence is an excessive dislike of labor or exertion, caused by an inordinate love of recreation or bodily rest. It will be considered when we treat the sin of softness or delicacy, which is opposed to fortitude.

(e) Idleness is the actual omission of one's duty on account of indolence, and hence it is considered among the sins against the various precepts. Thus, under the precepts of charity and of justice will be discussed the omission of labor to which one is bound.

1327. The sin of carelessness about the service of God is also known as tepidity or lukewarmness. It consists in a want of fervor, and causes one to live in spiritual languor, wishing on the one hand to live holily and avoid sin, but fearing on the other hand the effort and generosity required for the practice of virtue and the struggle against evil. It is, therefore, most dangerous.

(a) Even if it is only internal, it may be more dangerous to the one concerned than grave sin itself, since threats and promises that move a sinner are often unavailing with one who is tepid and moving on to grave sin. Thus, we read: "I know thy works, that thou art neither cold, nor hot. I would that thou wert cold or hot. But because thou art lukewarm, and neither cold, nor hot, I will begin to vomit thee out of my mouth" (Apoc., iii. 15, 16).

(b) If it is external, this sin is a danger to others who witness the disrespectful way in which one prays or exercises other duties owed to God.

1328. The Sin of Envy.—Envy is a sadness at the good of a neighbor, which one considers as a detriment to one's own excellence or glory, and therefore as an evil to self.

(a) Envy is a species of sadness, that is, it is a displeasure of the will at the presence of what one regards as an evil. In this way envy differs from the sin of rejoicing at the evils of others, which, as will be said below (see 1342), is one of the consequences of envy, although both are of the same species. Thus also, envy differs from pride and vainglory (which are not aversions but inclinations), and from covetousness (which is the desire of what belongs to another).

(b) Envy is about some good, especially about those goods from which men obtain the esteem and honor of others, such as virtue, ability, rank, success, prosperity. Thus, envy differs from sorrow about evil or the evil effects of good, such as repentance for one's sins, regret that one is not as good as others, displeasure at the bad use that men make of health or wealth.

(c) Envy is about the good of a neighbor, for only an insane person would feel chagrin at the superiority of God, and self-envy is a contradiction in terms. Thus, envy differs from sorrow at the good of God (hatred of God), and from sorrow at the good of self (sloth). A person may be said, however, to envy God in the sense that he is mortified at the external glory of God, if he feels himself an antagonist of that glory. In this way the devil is said to envy the attributes of God, because they overcome his efforts to promote impiety, and man is said to envy the Holy Ghost, when he is discontented at the progress of holiness in the souls of men.

(d) The envious man considers his neighbor's good as a detriment to his own good. This is the distinctive trait of envy which sets it apart from other forms of repining at another's good fortune. Thus, displeasure at the excellence or glory of another without reference to detriment to self is not envy, but hatred; with reference to the unworthiness of another, it is not envy, but indignation.

(e) Hence, envy looks on the neighbor's prosperity as a calamity to self, as a sort of punishment and the contradiction of one's own desires. Here envy stands in contrast with mercy, for, while the merciful regard the misfortunes of neighbors as the misfortunes of themselves, the envious regard the prosperity of others as their own misfortune.

1329. The Objects of Envy.—(a) The material objects are many, but they are reduced to excellence and glory. Excellence includes every kind of desirable quality. Glory is the honor, fame and praise that follow on public knowledge of one's excellence. As a rule, envy is concerned with the excellence of glory, but it may also be about internal or objective excellence. Thus, if two disputants are alone, the less able will perhaps envy the greater knowledge of the more able; but, if there is an audience, the more able will perhaps envy the greater applause received by his less able opponent.

(b) The formal object of envy is one, namely, the detriment to the excellence or glory of self which the envious person sees in the excellence or glory of another. Detriment must not be understood absolutely here, as if the envious person lost something or failed to obtain something on account of the other person. It must be understood relatively, in the sense that the envious person feels that the situation between himself and the other person is no longer the same, that the latter has gained on him or passed him, and has thus lessened his excellence.

1330. The Subjects of Envy.—(a) The persons most inclined to envy are of two quite different types, namely, the ambitious and the pusillanimous. The ambitious man ardently covets honors, and he is correspondingly saddened when others surpass him, especially if he already enjoys repute or is not far removed from the object of his desires. The pusillanimous man, being petty, holds every small advancement of others as great and as a blow to his own prestige. He is, therefore, filled with intense envy, where a different person would see little or no cause for such a feeling. On the contrary, those who recognize their own unsuitability for what is above them, and those who are great of soul, are not so much inclined to envy. There are few, however, even among the most perfect, who are not tempted to envy in some form.

(b) The persons who are most likely to be envied are those who in some way or other are one's likes or equals, for one does not feel that one is thrown into the shade by a person who is always far above one, or by those who are far removed in time, place, age, etc. Thus, a beggar will envy a fellow-beggar who becomes a millionaire, but not those acquaintances who were always rich, and still less the fortunate persons whom he knows only from hearsay. The elder son envied his brother, not his father (Luke, xv. 28). Many exceptions to this are only apparent. Thus, persons sometimes are envious of those far above them, but it is because these have advanced at their expense, as when a poor person envies those who have the property he once owned. Persons are sometimes envious of their equals who have not surpassed them, but it is because these latter have obtained with little or no effort what they themselves have gained only by hard work. Persons are sometimes envious of their inferiors, but this is because they make a comparison from some viewpoint in which there is equality, as when an old man envies a youth the advantages that were not enjoyed in his own youth, or the present promotion that surpasses his own.

1331. It was said above (see 1313) that hatred differs from other sins against charity, inasmuch as it dislikes another's good unqualifiedly, whereas these other sins dislike his good with some qualification. Hence, envy differs from hate, because envy is a qualified displeasure. It differs from other kinds of displeasure over the prosperity of others, because the qualification in each case is different.

(a) Thus, emulation is displeased at the thought of a neighbor's prosperity, not because it does not like his success, but because it dislikes the unsuccess of self. Example: Titus is grieved when he thinks of the virtue of Balbus, because he himself lacks virtue.

(b) Fear dislikes the prosperity or superiority of another, not on account of the prosperity or superiority in itself, but on account of the evil results it apprehends from that prosperity. Example: Caius is displeased at the elevation of Claudius, because he knows the latter is his enemy and will persecute him. He is also displeased that, in spite of his own greater learning and soundness, he has not the influence possessed by Balbus, who misleads many by long-winded sophistry.

(c) Indignation (*nemesis*) is displeased that a neighbor has a certain good, of which he is unworthy. Example: Sempronius is angry because Titus, who is dishonest, succeeds in business.

(d) Envy grieves over a neighbor's prosperity, not because it thinks this prosperity will actually bring about a lessening of the honor of self, but because it regards the very fact of that prosperity, in itself and apart from any consequences, as a change in one's relationship to the neighbor, and to that extent an obscuration of the glory of self. Example: Balbus is grieved at the prosperity of Claudius, because he knows Claudius will use his resources to defame him. Caius is grieved at Claudius' prosperity, because he regards it as a reflection on his own fame, since he is less prosperous. Balbus fears, Caius envies.

1332. Is emulation a sin? (a) If emulation is about spiritual things, it is not sinful, but praiseworthy. St. Paul encourages a holy rivalry among the Corinthians for the higher gifts of God (I Cor., xii. 31). St. Jerome writes to Læta that her daughter should be associated with other girls as fellow-pupils, that the progress of the latter and the praises they receive may act as a spur to the daughter not to be outdone. One who equals or surpasses the virtue or knowledge of another does not take away or lessen the other's good, but improves his own good; and thus emulation is not harmful, but beneficial in spiritual matters. (b) If emulation is about temporal things, it is also lawful to be sorry at their absence. But, if the desire is inordinate, then emulation is sinful. Example: Sempronius is not inferior in ability to Titus, and hence, while not desiring monopoly or disliking competition, he is sorry that he has not attained an equal success in business. Balbus is very deficient in education, in initiative and in character, while Caius excels in all these qualities; and yet Balbus is discontented that he does not hold the responsible position of Caius, or one of equal importance. The emulation of Sempronius is reasonable, that of Balbus is unreasonable.

1333. Rivalry is called jealousy, when it proceeds from a love so ardent that it wishes to have exclusive possession of the object loved. This jealousy is lawful or unlawful, according as the person who loves has or has not exclusive rights.

(a) Jealousy is unlawful in a mother who is vexed because her child loves his father as well as herself. The child ought to love both parents, and it is an evil jealousy that makes the mother grieve when the child does this.

(b) Jealousy is lawful in a wife who grieves because her husband gives to others the affection he promised would be hers alone. Scripture speaks of God Himself as jealous of the fidelity of His creatures, and declares that He will suffer no rival, but must have sole dominion over the heart (Josue, xxiv. 19 sqq.); and St. Paul tells the Corinthians that he is jealous of them, with the jealousy of God, because they have not been faithful to his preaching, but have been friendly to false teachers (II Cor., xi).

1334. Is grief at the prosperity of another a sin, when it is caused by fear of the harm he will do?

(a) If it is clear that the other will use his prosperity to act against justice or charity or the like, it is not a sin to grieve over the prosperity. For, since it is right to deprive a neighbor of the means of sinning when one has the power to do so, it is not wrong to wish that he lacked those means. Thus, it is not a sin to grieve over the election of an official who will promote lawbreakers and persecute the law-abiding: "When just men increase, the people shall rejoice; when the wicked shall bear rule, the people shall mourn" (Prov., xxix. 2). St. Gregory the Great declares that, as it is not uncharitable to rejoice at the downfall of an enemy, neither is it envious to be saddened at his success; since his downfall is a blessing to the oppressed, while his success means injustice to many.

(b) If it is clear that the other will use his power, wealth, or other goods to inflict evils that are deserved or not unjust, it is wrong to be sorry that he has the power, wealth, etc., just as it would be wrong to deprive him of them. Thus, it is wrong to grieve over the election of an honest official who will correct abuses and punish lawbreakers. It is not unlawful, however, for a lawbreaker to be sorry for himself at the prospect of the penalty he will receive.

(c) If it is uncertain whether the other will use his prosperity to do injury to oneself or to others, it is lawful to fear and to be on one's guard, but it is not lawful to grieve unconditionally at the prosperity, just as it is not lawful in the circumstances to deprive the other of his prosperity.

1335. Is grief at the prosperity of another sinful, when it is caused by his unworthiness of prosperity? (a) If the indignation could be about spiritual things, of course it would be sinful; but this is not possible, for it is precisely spiritual goods (such as virtues) that make one deserving. Indignation, then, is about temporal goods, which are enjoyed by the bad, as well as the good. (b) If the indignation is about temporal things owned by the wicked, and one grieves that they have prosperity, sin is committed. For it is God who distributes to the undeserving the goods they have; His purpose is just, namely, that these goods may be for the correction or the punishment of the wicked; those who grieve over the prosperity of the unworthy overlook the fact that eternal goods are a reward to man, temporal goods only a trust to be administered. Hence, the Psalmist says: "Be not emulous of evil-doers, nor envy them that work iniquity, for they shall shortly wither away as grass" (Ps. xxxvi. 1).

1336. Two special cases of sorrow over the prosperity of the wicked must be considered. (a) If one sorrows precisely because the prosperity is had by an undeserving person, and is not thinking of the divine cause and purpose in human affairs, it does not seem that one sins; for, abstracting from Divine Providence, there does appear an unsuitability in the prosperity enjoyed by the wicked, and hence it is something to be sorry about. But such sorrow is at least a preparation for the sin spoken of in the previous paragraph, and so it should be shunned: "My feet were almost moved, my steps had well-nigh slipped, in anger at the wicked, seeing the prosperity of sinners" (Ps. lxxii. 2, 3). (b) If one sorrows precisely because the sinner will use his prosperity in such a way as to become more wicked and to incur chastisement, the sorrow is not uncharitable, but charitable.

1337. Sorrow at being surpassed by another on account of the relative loss of glory to self, with the wish that the other had not the good that makes him superior, is envy, as explained above. This sorrow is a sin. (a) Thus, it is condemned in scripture: "Let us not be made desirous of vainglory, envying one another" (Gal, v. 26); "The patriarchs through envy sold Joseph into Egypt" (Acts, vii. 9), "Charity envieth not" (I Cor., xiii. 4). (b) It is not reasonable to be grieved at the prosperity of others, since prosperity is something good and an object of joy rather than of sorrow.

1338. From its nature envy is a mortal sin. (a) Thus, it is directly opposed to the principal acts of charity, which are love of the neighbor, desire of his good, and joy over his prosperity; and charity is the life of the soul (I John, iii. 14). Secondary acts of charity, such as kissing the sores of a leper, may be omitted without loss of love, but envy destroys love itself. (b) Envy is directly contrary to mercy; for, while mercy grieves at the evil of others, envy grieves at their good. The envious are not merciful, neither are the merciful envious.

1339. Envy is a greater sin than the other kinds of sorrow at a neighbor's good. (a) Thus, envy grieves over the neighbor's good (even if he is worthy), and is greater or less in proportion to that good; (b) emulation grieves over one's own deficiency, fear over the consequences of the other's good, indignation over the prosperity of one who is unworthy.

1340. Envy is not a mortal sin in the following cases: (a) if the object is not grave, as when one is envious about some trifle (such as good looks); (b) if the subject does not give sufficient reflection or full consent, as when infants are jealous of one another, or adults feel the stirrings of envy. Even holy men are not above the first movements or inclinations towards envy, and very many envious thoughts are not mortal, because not fully adverted to.

1341. Degrees of Gravity in Sins of Envy.—(a) There are no different species of envy of the neighbor, for all acts of envy have the one essential trait that they are sorrow over the excellence of another, viewed, not absolutely in itself, but relatively as a lessening of one's own excellence. We should distinguish, however, the envy which is a sin against God (viz., envy at another's spiritual good, or sorrow at the diffusion of grace) from the envy which is a sin against the neighbor.

(b) There are different degrees of envy within the species, according to the greater or less excellence of the good which is envied. Thus, it is a greater sin to be envious about spiritual things (e.g., another's influence for good) than about temporal things (e.g., another's ability to get money); it is a greater sin to be envious about the wellbeing of the body than about dress, style, etc.

1342. Envy is one of the capital vices, that is, it is an evil tree which from its very nature yields the evil fruits of other sins. The fruits of envy are progressive in evil.

(a) Thus, in the beginning of envy, one tries to diminish the glory of the person one envies, either secretly (sin of whispering) or openly (sin of detraction).

(b) In its progress, envy rejoices at the adversity of the neighbor, if its attempt to injure succeeds; or it sorrows over his continued prosperity, if its effort at blackening has failed. Rejoicing at a neighbor's adversity is not different specifically from envy; but the affliction over the neighbor's prosperity now spoken of is of the same species as the vice which sought to undermine the neighbor. Thus, if the envious person resorted in vain to detraction, his grief at the failure of his efforts is in guilt a sin of detraction.

(c) In its consummation, envy becomes hatred, as was said above on the causes of hate (see 1316).

1343. Envy is not the first of the seven capital vices. (a) Thus, it is caused by pride, for one who inordinately desires his own excellence will easily grieve over what he regards as the lessening of that excellence by the excellence of another. (b) It is caused by vainglory, for one who inordinately longs for fame and honors, will easily be grieved over the fame and honors enjoyed by others.

1344. In what way is envy preeminent among sins? (a) Envy is not the most enormous vice, for, as said above (see 1301), hatred of God is from its nature the worst of all sins. But there is one kind of envy—namely, envy of a brother's spiritual good—which has a place among those gravest offenses called "sins against the Holy Ghost" (see 899).

(b) Envy is most like to the sin that brought all woe into the world, for "by the envy of the devil death entered the world" (Wis., ii. 24). It was sorrow at the gifts bestowed upon our first parents that moved the demon to tempt them, and accordingly his envy led to their fall and to the loss of original justice by the Whole race.

1345. Useful Considerations against Envy.—(a) Envy is useless, since it does not obtain that on which one's heart is set, or obtains it only by the sacrifice of charity, which is something better. (b) Envy is harmful, since it carries its own torment with it (Gen., iv. 5; Wis., vi. 25; Prov., xiv. 30), and brings on many sins against the neighbor. Through envy the first murder was committed (Gen., iv. 8), and it was envy that brought about the crucifixion of Christ (Matt, xxvii. 18).

1346. Useful practices against envy are: (a) the uprooting of its causes, pride and vainglory; (b) the cultivation of an unselfish charity and of emulation of what is best in others: "So that by all means, whether by occasion, or by truth, Christ be preached, in this I rejoice, yea, and will rejoice" (Philip., i. 18); "Let us consider one another, to provoke unto charity and to good works" (Heb., x. 24).

Art. 8: THE SINS AGAINST PEACE

(*Summa Theologica*, II-II, qq. 37-42.)

1347. The following sins are opposed to the peace of charity: (a) discord, which is opposed to peace in wills; (b) contention or quarreling, which is opposed to peace in words; (e) schism, war, fights and sedition, which are opposed to peace in works.

1348. Discord.—As here understood, discord is a disagreement in the wills of two or more persons in matters pertaining to the divine good, or the good of the neighbor, and concerning which charity requires that they be in agreement.

(a) Discord is a disagreement in wills, that is, in wishes and desires. Hence, it is not the same as difference of opinion (see 1197), which is a disagreement in judgments.

(b) It is about matters in which agreement is necessary, that is, in which the law of God requires that all wish the same things, and have but one heart and soul. Thus, discord differs from disagreement about matters of supererogation. Examples: Titus and his wife are at variance, because Titus is unwilling to give any alms. Balbus and his wife are at variance, because she wishes him to give away in alms more than is strictly necessary. In the first husband there is discord, but not in the second.

(c) Discord is opposed to the divine good, or the good of the neighbor. Thus, it differs from a disagreement with another who is attacking the divine good or the good of the neighbor. The standard of concord is the divine will, and he only of the persons at variance is discordant who is not in harmony with the divine will.

(d) Discord is confined to those matters in which charity calls for agreement. If it be some other virtue that demands unanimity (e.g., justice), the disagreement is not discord in the special sense now employed, Thus, he whose will refuses consent to the command of a superior is disobedient; he whose will refuses to pay the debt due a creditor is dishonest.

1349. There are two kinds of discord: (a) intentional discord, which is the act of one who knowingly and purposely contradicts in a matter about which charity requires that he agree;

(b) unintentional discord, which is a disagreement between persons, who both intend the divine good or the good of the neighbor, but who are divided in opinion as to what that good here and now requires.

1350. Sinfulness of Intentional Discord.—(a) From its nature, this species of discord is a mortal sin, since it directly excludes charity. Hence, those who are guilty of discord shall not obtain the kingdom of heaven (Gal, v. 21). (b) From the lack of sufficient reflection or consent, the first impulses towards discord are not mortal sins.

1351. Sinfulness of Unintentional Discord.—(a) From its nature, this kind of discord is not opposed to charity, nor is it sinful; for the concord of charity consists in a union of wills, not in a union of opinions. Thus, the disagreement between Paul and Barnabas about John Mark (Acts, xv. 39) was not sinful, although the difference of judgment indicated their human limitations. (b) From its circumstances, this kind of discord may be sinful, as when it is caused by culpable ignorance in matters of faith, or is carried on with obstinacy.

1352. By whom is the sin of discord committed? (a) It is committed sometimes by one party only, as when one knowingly resists the will of another who wishes to perform a necessary act of charity. (b) It is committed at other times by both parties, as when each in defending his own good infringes knowingly on the charity due the other.

1353. Is it lawful to promote divisions, when one's purpose and the result will be good? (a) To promote division that takes away the concord of charity is never lawful, but a mortal sin: "There are six things the Lord hates, and a seventh which His soul detests, a sower of discord among brethren" (Prov., vi. 16, 19). (b) To promote division that takes away a concord of malice is lawful and praiseworthy. Thus, St. Paul introduced a dissension between the Pharisees and the Sadducees, who had been in agreement against him (Acts, xxiii. 6, 7). But the intention of the Apostle was to win the Pharisees to the defense of the Resurrection and of himself, not to incite the Sadducees to a denial of the Resurrection, and so there was no question of his using evil means for a good end.

1354. The Origin of Discord.—(a) The disagreement with the will of a neighbor arises from envy. For he who considers the excellence of his neighbor as a lessening of his own excellence, is inclined to contradict the wishes of the neighbor, even if he recognizes them as good. (b) The preference of one's own will and persistence in it are due to pride and vainglory. For he who unduly desires his own excellence or fame does not wish to yield to others or change his purposes. He feels that, even though he is in the wrong, he must not take what he regards as a position of inferiority.

1355. Contention.—Contention is discord carried into words or equivalent signs, (i.e., a dispute or altercation), in which one denies what the other affirms. It is divided as follows: (a) by reason of the intention, it is either an investigation of the truth, a defense of the truth, or an attack on the truth; (b) by reason of the manner in which it is conducted, it is either suitable or unsuitable to the persons and the matter in question.

1356. Contention whose aim is the discovery of the truth is lawful as follows. (a) Such contention is lawful and useful in itself, for it is a means of acquiring useful knowledge, of seeing both sides of a question, and of sharpening the mind for the refutation of error. Hence, a contest in a court of justice, a controversy in a scientific journal, a public debate on some important matter, and a theological disputation are according to their nature lawful, and may be necessary. Even to argue against the truth, for the sake of practice in discussion or to bring out the truth more clearly and forcibly, is, apart from danger, scandal, or prohibition, not unuseful.

(b) Debate is unlawful in its manner when a disputant does not argue according to the rules, appeals to prejudice or ignorance, uses an insulting tone or unparliamentary language, etc.

1357. The Sin of Contention.—Contention is a sin when its aim is the concealment or discomfiture of the truth. (a) From its nature this kind of contention is a mortal sin, for it is the external expression of internal discord in matters about which charity requires concord and the same speech. Hence, the Apostle numbers contention among the works of the flesh that exclude from the kingdom of God (Gal, v. 20). (b) From the lightness of the matter or the imperfection of the consent, this kind of contention is very often, if not usually, only a venial sin, or no sin at all. Examples: A person argues against what he knows is true, but the matter is trivial (e.g., his weight); or he is distracted by the heat of dispute or the tactics of the other party.

1358. Mortal sin is not committed by contention, therefore, unless the truths against which one contends are of a serious kind. Such truths are: (a) truths of a religious or moral character, such as the doctrines of faith and the commandments of God; (b) natural truths of a universal

character, the knowledge of which pertains to the perfection of the
intellect, such as first principles; (c) natural truths of a particular
character in which important rights are involved. Example: An historian
who writes against some deservedly revered person of the past, or a
lawyer who attempts to prove against an accused what he knows is not
a fact, are guilty of the sin of contention.

1359. Hence, one may be defending one kind of truth and contending
against another kind of truth at the same time. St. Paul, accordingly,
makes the distinction between announcement of the truth out of
charity and announcement of the truth out of contention (Philip, i, 15
sqq.). (a) The truth is defended out of charity when one does not use
truth as a means for the defense of error; (b) it is defended out of
contention when one makes use of it as a means for the propagation of
error. Thus, while St. Paul was imprisoned at Rome in 61, certain
personal enemies preached Christ, but at the same time spoke or hinted
falsehoods against St. Paul in order to undermine his authority or add
to the bitterness of his captivity. Similarly, if one defends the truth to
make oneself appear different or better than one is, one speaks from
contention.

1360. Ways in which one is guilty of the mortal sin of contention: (a)
when one contends formally against the truth, that is, when one knows
the truth and intends to overcome it or suppress it; (b) when one
contends virtually against the truth, that is, when one is so bent on
carrying one's point that one does not care whether it is true or false.
Thus, the Sophists aimed to win, right or wrong.

1361. When the aim of contention is the overthrow of error: (a) in
itself, such contention is good and praiseworthy, and at times necessary;
(b) by reason of circumstances, it may be a venial or a mortal sin.
Examples: A dispute on a matter that is unbecoming, such as which of
the disputants is greater (Luke, xxii. 24); dispute with greater warmth
than the case requires; a dispute that leads to scandal or other evil
consequences, as in religious controversies (I Tim., ii. 14).

1362. The Causes of Sinful Contention.—(a) The cause of that which is
principal in contention—namely, the departure from the truth held by
another and the stand made for error—is envy, pride and vainglory, as

said above (see 1854) concerning discord. (b) The cause of that which is secondary in contention—namely, the wrangling or bawling manner and the shouts or screams of the contenders—is anger.

1363. The sins in act against the peace of charity are the following: (a) schism which is opposed to the peace of the spiritual society, the Church; (b) war, which is opposed to international peace, and sedition, which is opposed to national peace; (c) fighting, which is opposed to peace between individuals.

1364. Schism.—Schism (etymologically, a split, rent) is defined: "A voluntary separation of oneself from the unity of the Church."

(a) Schism is a voluntary separation, that is, a separation intended for its own sake. Every sinner in a sense separates himself from unity, for sin divides one from God (Is., lix. 2); but it is only the schismatic who expressly intends separation as such. Other sinners expressly intend some inordinate gratification. Moreover, schism is not the same thing as the state of the unbaptized, who have not separated themselves from unity, or of the excommunicated, whom the Church herself rejected from her body on account of some sin other than schism.

(b) Schism is a separation from unity, and so it differs from disbelief in unity (heresy) and dislike of unity (hatred). One may separate oneself from unity, although one believes in it. One may hate unity, and yet not separate oneself from it. Further, schism does not necessarily include affiliation with some schismatical body or the setting up of such a body.

(c) Schism is a separation of oneself from unity—that is, schism does not deprive the Church of the note of unity, but separates the schismatic himself from that unity which is in the Church. The schismatic may wish to take away the unity of the Church, but he accomplishes only the loss of union of himself with the Church.

(d) Schism is a separation from unity, that is, from fellowship in the mystical body of Christ (I Cor., xii). It is a refusal to recognize the authority of the head of the Church, or to communicate with those subject to him. Thus, schism differs from disobedience to the head of the Church or to particular prelates in the Church, for one may disobey orders and still recognize the authority of him who gives the orders.

(e) Schism is a separation from the unity of the Church, that is, of the spiritual kingdom of Christ on earth. Hence, rebellion in matters purely civil against a churchman who has civil authority, is not schism, but is unjust war or sedition. Schism is possible only in the Church Militant, for the members of the Church Suffering and the Church Triumphant cannot fall away from unity.

1365. The Principal Schismatical Movements.—(a) In Apostolic times there were local factions and dissensions, though not real schisms, at Corinth (I Cor., i. 10 sqq.) and in Asia Minor (III John, i. 10). (b) In post-Apostolic times there have been numerous schisms, such as that of the Novatians at Rome in the third century, that of the Meletians in Egypt in the fourth century, that of the Donatists in Africa in the fourth century, that of the Acacians in the East in the fifth century. The most lamentable of all the schisms, because of the number of those whom it led away from unity, was the Eastern Schism, begun by Photius in the ninth century and made permanent under Michael Cærularius in the eleventh century.

1366. Schism is voluntary in two ways: (a) directly, when one intends schism itself, wishing to separate oneself from the head or members of the Church; (b) indirectly, when one intends to do that from which schism follows. Thus, a person who prefers to act as if he were not a member of the Church rather than desist from his design of calling or presiding over an unauthorized Council, is guilty of schism, even though he does not directly intend separation from the Church. His case is similar to that of one who does not wish to kill his neighbor, and yet is determined to do something from which the neighbor's death will surely result.

1367. There is a threefold unity of the Church, as follows: (a) unity in the theological virtues and in the Sacraments. All the faithful have the same faith, hope, charity, Sacraments, and thus there is a unity of similarity; (b) unity between head and members. There is but one head of the Church, Christ in heaven and the Vicar of Christ an earth. Thus, there is a unity of subordination; (c) unity between the members of the Church. All the faithful form but one society, and all are parts of one great whole. Thus, there is a collective unity.

1368. The sin of schism is committed in two ways (Canon 1325, n. 2). (a) It is committed by separation from the head of the Church on earth and the keystone of unity, that is, the Pope (Col., ii. 18, 19). The mere fact that a man is in rebellion against his bishop does not make him a schismatic, if he continues to acknowledge subjection to the Holy See. But such rebellion is often the first step towards schism. (b) The sin of schism is also committed by separation from the members of the Church. Thus, one who refuses to communicate with Catholics in matters of faith or worship, choosing to act as an independent in those things, is a schismatic.

1369. Rejection of a decision or command of the Pope can happen in three ways:

(a) The reason for rejecting the decision may be the thing commanded, and not the one who gave the command, as when a person refuses to keep a fast or make a restitution commanded by the Pope, because he considers it too difficult. In this case the person is guilty of disobedience, but not of schism, even though he persists in his refusal; for he rejects a commandment of the Church, not the head of the Church.

(b) The reason for rejecting the command may be the one who gave the command, considered as a private individual. As the Pope in his personal relations is not above human weakness, he may be swayed by hatred, prejudice or impulsiveness in issuing commands to or forming judgments about individual subjects. Hence, if we suppose that it is reasonably certain that a Pope is unfavorable to an individual, and that the latter accordingly is unwilling to have a case in which he is concerned fall under the immediate decision of that Pope, neither schism nor any other sin is committed; for it is natural that the person should wish to protect his own interests against unfairness.

(c) The reason for rejecting the Pope's judgment may be the one who gave the command considered in his official capacity as Pope. In this case the person is guilty of schism, since he disobeys, not because the thing ordered is difficult or because he fears that the individual will be unjust, but because he does not wish to recognize the authority of Pope in him who issued the judgment.

1370. Comparison of Heresy and Schism.—(a) These sins are not the same, since heresy is opposed to faith, schism to charity. A person who really believes that the Church is one in its head and its body, may nevertheless out of pride, hatred, ambition, interest, self-sufficiency, etc., decide not to recognize the authority of the head, or not to communicate with the body. (b) There is an intimate union between heresy and schism, since every heretic separates himself from the unity of faith, while schism is always found to adopt some heresy as a justification for its separation (I Tim., i. 6). Thus, the Eastern Schism soon trumped up charges of heresy against the Church, and history shows that schism almost invariably leads to a denial of papal primacy.

1371. The Opposition between Schism and Charity.—(a) Charity in itself is a spiritual bond of unity between the soul and God, for love is unitive. One who sins against this unity by offending God or his neighbor, is not thereby a schismatic, since one may hate an individual, for example, without hating the Church. (b) Charity in its effect is the communion of all the faithful in one mystical body of Christ, for charity inspires the desire to love, not only individuals, but also the spiritual society formed of individuals in the entire world. One who sins against the unity and peace of the Church is a schismatic.

1372. The Sinfulness of Schism.—(a) Schism has a special seriousness, since it is opposed to the union and peace of mankind as a whole in the universal spiritual society which is the Church. It seems to be the greatest sin against the neighbor; for other sins are against the individual or against the multitude in temporal things, while this sin is against the multitude and in spiritual things. Scripture (cfr. I Cor., i. 10) and Tradition (e.g., St. Clement of Rome, St. Ignatius of Antioch, St. Irenæus, St. Cyprian, St. Augustine) energetically condemn the sin of schism.

(b) Objectively, it is not as serious as unbelief, since unbelief is against God, schism against the neighbor; but subjectively, or in its consequences, it may be greater than unbelief, as when a schismatic sins with greater contempt than an unbeliever, or is an occasion of more danger to others.

1373. Schism, like heresy, may be either formal or material (see 828). (a) Formal schism is that described above, in which one wishes to separate oneself from the unity of the Church, and is in culpable revolt. It is a mortal sin. (b) Material schism is that in which one is in fact separated from the unity of the Church, but is in good faith. An example is the Great Schism of the West (1378-1417), when there were rival claimants for the Papacy, and invincible ignorance among the people as to who was the true head. This kind of schism is not a mortal sin.

1374. The Spiritual Powers of Schismatics.—(a) The power of Orders is not lost through schism, for that power is conferred through a consecration, and the consecrations of the Church are permanent. Hence, a schismatical priest can perform validly the acts that pertain to the power of Orders, such as the celebration of Mass and administration of the Sacraments; but he does not perform those acts lawfully, unless the Church permits, for the power of Orders should not be used by an inferior except as permitted by the superior.

(b) The power of jurisdiction may be lost through schism, for that power depends on a commission received from a superior, which may be withdrawn by him. Hence, a schismatical priest deprived of jurisdiction could not absolve, excommunicate, grant indulgences, or perform other acts that pertain to the power of jurisdiction.

1375. The law of the church on the powers of schismatics is as follows:

(a) All schismatics incur *ipso facto* excommunication, as well as various inhabilities and penalties (Canon 2314). It is fitting that those who separate themselves should be declared outside the communion of the faithful, and this is what Moses commanded to be done at the time of the schism of Core: "Depart from the tent of these wicked men and touch nothing of theirs, lest you be involved in their sin" (Num., xvi. 26).

(b) The excommunicated are forbidden the celebration of Mass and the active use and administration of the Sacraments and sacramentals, except when the faithful apply to them or when there is danger of death, as declared in Canon 2261.

(c) The excommunicated are denied the power of jurisdiction except in certain cases where the Church grants it for the sake of the common good. Thus, they may give absolution in danger of death (Canon 882), or in common error (Canon 209), or at request, if they are not *vitandi* or sentenced (Canon 2261). It is the teaching of learned authorities that the Roman Church for the good of souls has allowed ecclesiastical jurisdiction to remain in the schismatic Oriental Churches for the conferring of the Sacraments.

1376. War.—War is defined as a state of conflict between two or more sovereign nations carried on by force of arms.

(a) It is a state of conflict, and so differs from passing conflicts, such as battles, skirmishes, campaigns. The enemy in war is not only those with whom one is actually fighting, but all those who side with them, as counsellors, helpers, etc.

(b) War is between sovereign nations, and so differs from civil war, sedition, riots, duels. Moreover, war is made by nation against nation, not against particular individuals or groups of individuals within a nation.

(c) It is carried on by force of arms, and so differs from trade war, rivalry in preparedness for war, embargo, blockade, breach of diplomatic relations, etc.

1377. There are two kinds of war, just and unjust. (a) War is just when undertaken for a right cause (e.g., the independence of the nation); (b) it is unjust when undertaken for a wrong cause (e.g., the enslavement of a nation).

1378. Just war is either offensive or defensive. (a) Offensive war is attack made on an enemy in order to avenge an injury or enforce a right (e.g., invasion of the enemy's territory to obtain compensation for damages inflicted by him); (b) defensive war is resistance to unjust attack made or menaced by an enemy (e.g., war made on the invader of one's country).

1379. Just war is called defensive in two senses. (a) In the strict sense, it is defensive when the nation whose rights are unjustly attacked does not initiate hostilities, that is, does not declare or begin the war. (b) In a less strict sense, it is defensive when the nation unjustly attacked declares war or strikes the first blow. Thus, if the innocent nation knew that the enemy was secretly preparing war against its independence, it would be on the defensive, even though it declared war.

1380. War is not against the law of God. (a) Under the law of nature Melchisedech blessed Abraham returning from victory over the four kings (Gen., xiv. 18-20). (b) Under the written law, God many times ordered or approved of war, as can be seen from Exodus and following books in numerous places. (c) Under the New Law, John the Baptist acknowledged the lawfulness of the soldier's profession (Luke, iii. 14), a centurion was praised by Christ (Matt, viii. 10), Acts, x. 2, speaks of the officer Cornelius as a religious man, and St. Paul lauds warriors of the Old Testament such as Gedeon, Barac, Samson, etc. (Heb, xi. 32-34). Our Lord Himself used physical force against evildoers (John, ii. 14 sqq.).

1381. Certain sayings of our Lord—for example, that those who take the sword shall perish by the sword (Matt, xxvi. 52), and that one should not resist evil (Matt, v. 39)—are not an endorsement of extreme pacifism, but are respectively a condemnation of those who without due authority have recourse to violence, and a counsel of perfection, when this serves better the honor of God or the good of the neighbor. Moreover, these words of Christ were addressed, not to states, which are responsible for the welfare of their members, but to individuals. The Quakers have done excellent service for the cause of world peace, but their teaching that all war is contrary to the law of Christ cannot be admitted. The spirit of the Gospel includes justice as well as love.

1382. War is not against the law of the Church. (a) The Church has never condemned war as such. She has always labored for the promotion of peace or for the lessening of the evils of wars that could not be prevented; but her official declarations and the writings of the Fathers and Doctors show that she recognized that recourse to arms by nations is not necessarily sinful. (b) The Church has put her approval on some wars as necessary and laudable. Thus, the Crusades, to which the salvation of Christian civilization is due, were promoted by the Church; military orders for the defense of the Holy Sepulchre were instituted by her, and she has raised to the honors of the altar soldiers like Sebastian, Maurice, and Martin of Tours.

1383. War is not against the law of nature. (a) As the law of nature allows even a private individual to use force to drive off an unjust aggressor, it cannot be unlawful for a nation to have recourse to defensive war when its rights are invaded. (b) As the law of nature allows the individual to seek satisfaction for injury and restitution for loss, it cannot be unlawful for a nation to make offensive war when another nation will not make reparation, unless compelled to it by force. If physical coercion were unlawful, a conscienceless nation would take advantage of this at the expense of other nations, and thus a premium would be set on iniquity.

1384. Like every other act, war is not morally good, unless its object, its purpose and its circumstances are in accord with right. War is not lawful, therefore, unless the three following conditions exist:

(a) Hostilities must be authorized by the public authority, for the care of the State against internal and external disturbances has been committed to the ruler (Rom., xii. 4; Ps. lxxxi. 4), and the individual or the subject state can have recourse for protection of its rights to the higher authority.

(b) There must be a just cause for war, that is, some fault on the side of the other nation; for, if a nation may not use force against its own subjects without sufficient reason, much less may it do so against those who are not its subjects.

(c) There must be a right intention, that is, the desire to obtain some good or to ward off some evil. Even if war is declared by the proper authority and there is a sufficient reason for it, those who take part in the war are guilty of sin if they have evil motives, such as the exercise of cruelty, revenge, pride, or avarice. To delight in war because one loves excitement or wishes to show one's skill or get promotion, is not a right frame of mind.

1385. What public authority has the right to declare war? (a) Ordinarily, only the sovereign power—that is, the person or body in whom the chief authority is vested according to the constitution of the nation—

can make war. War is an act of the nation, and hence only the authority that represents the nation can make war. Subordinate bodies in a confederation or union of states have the right to make war, if custom or law allows it.

(b) In extraordinary circumstances, an inferior power can authorize war, as when war is necessary and it is impossible to await a declaration from the sovereign power. Thus, if a province were suddenly invaded, it would be lawful for the head of the province to make war on the invaders at once. It seems, indeed, that the head of a province could justly authorize the invasion of a neighboring state, to protect such province against aggressions, if the central authority would do nothing; for such a war would be really defensive.

1386. In order that the cause of war be just, it is necessary that the enemy nation has done or now menaces an injury which cannot be repaired without war, and which is so serious that the evils of war are less than that of toleration.

(a) Thus, a serious injury or grave dishonor inflicted by another nation is the only just cause for the armed conflict which constitutes war, for war is exercised as a punishment or a compulsion, and these are unjust if no grave and formal fault is supposed.

(b) Only an injury that cannot be otherwise repaired is a just cause for war, because a state has no right to use force against another sovereign state except as a last resort. Hence, if the country at fault has already made satisfaction or has promised to make satisfaction, war should not be declared.

(c) Only an injury so grave that it outweighs the risks and losses of war is a justification for making war, for when two effects, one good and one evil, follow from an act, there must be a proportionately grave reason for permitting the evil effect before acting (see 104, 105). It would be wrong to avenge some small insult or some isolated injury at the expense of immense treasure and enormous loss of life. Modern warfare is so devastating that only the gravest reasons known to society can authorize it. For, according to scientists, a single H-bomb may cause death and destruction over a wide area, perhaps the space of a hundred square miles. In view of the havoc which is foreseen to outweigh the benefits of victory, it could happen that a nation with justice on its side and the potential to wage war would nevertheless not be justified in waging war (see 1410). This destructive power of modern weapons, however, need not imply a sweeping condemnation of all warfare. Spiritual values, e.g., freedom from tyranny, freedom to worship God, still hold primacy over material values and can be deemed so precious as to outweigh the great loss of lives and property involved in defending them or recovering them through modern warfare. "A people menaced by, or already victims of unjust aggression, if it desires to think and to act in a Christian manner, cannot remain in passive indifference" (Pope Pius XII, Christmas Message of 1948).

1387. In comparing the advantages and disadvantages of war, one should take into consideration, not only the losses oneself will suffer, but also the losses that will be suffered by others. (a) Thus, if the enemy nation will be ruined as the price of one's obtaining some small right, charity would urge that one abstain from war. (b) If the world in general or posterity will suffer greater evils materially or spiritually than a nation is now suffering from the denial of some non-essential right, charity at least should rule out a declaration of war.

1388. Is there a just reason for war, when a fault has been committed on both sides? (a) If the injuries are about equal and still in being, there is no reason for war, for neither nation is in a position to accuse the other of injustice. (b) If the injuries are quite unequal or one nation has shown a willingness to cease from injury, the less guilty nation has a right to make war; but it should first clear itself of injustice, before it proceeds to chastise injustice in the other.

1389. Sufficient causes for making war are: (a) grave injury to the honor of a nation, such as insult to its ruler or ambassadors (II Kings, x.); (b) injury to the natural right of the nation to existence, self-preservation, property, free action within its own sphere; thus, a people may make war to defend their independence (I Mach., iii. 59), to recover territory taken from them unjustly, to resist a violation of neutrality (II Kings, viii. 5), to protect their own citizens and commerce; (c) injury to the rights of the nation under positive law. Thus, a nation may make war to uphold important international agreements, to enforce the observance of treaties, and the like.

1390. Injury done to a third nation or to the subjects of a third nation may also be a sufficient reason for war. (a) Thus, out of justice, a nation is obliged to help its allies in a just war; for to help those with whose interests one's own interests are involved is only self-defense. (b) Out of charity, a nation that has the right of intervention may lawfully go to war to protect a weaker nation against a stronger and bullying nation, to assist a government unjustly attacked by its subjects, or to help innocent subjects who are tyrannized over by their government.

1391. Is it lawful to go to war over religion or morality?

(a) Error in the religion or immorality in the practices of another people is not a sufficient reason for making war on them. No one can be forced to believe, says St. Augustine; and it is likewise true that no one can be forced to love virtue, whereas external conformity without conviction or love is hypocritical. Moreover, a nation has no authority to correct the sins of those not subject to it. Hence, it would not be right to attack a people for the sole reason that it was pagan or polygamous.

(b) Interference, however, with the religious rights of others or sinful practices that are injurious to others are a sufficient reason for war. No war ever had a more legitimate cause than the Crusades, which were undertaken to defend the Christian religion against the unspeakable atrocities of infidels. The cause of humanity justifies a war to put an end to such evils as cannibalism or human sacrifice.

1392. Is it lawful to make war on another nation in order to bring to it the benefits of modern civilization? (a) If the uncivilized nation lacks a government and suffers from disorder, it is an act of charity for a civilized nation to set up a government there which will act for the benefit of the people of the country. It is also lawful to make war on those who resist the government thus established. (b) If the uncivilized nation has its own orderly form of government and is at peace, no other nation has the right to interfere under pretext of introducing a higher type of government. Colonial expansion is not a sufficient reason for war in such circumstances.

1393. The following causes for war are not sufficient:

(a) Motives clearly sinful are such as do not suppose any injury done by the other nation, but rather some evil passion of pride, greed, jealousy, suspicion, or selfishness on one's own side. Hence, it is not lawful to go to war for the glory of a ruler or of the nation, for the enlargement of one's territory, for the advantage that may be gained over a commercial rival, for the preservation of the balance of power, or for the prevention of difficulties at home.

(b) Motives apparently just, but really sinful, are injuries done by another, if one has secretly provoked them in order to have a pretext for war. It is not right to make war on a people because of attacks made by their citizens, if these attacks were purposely caused by one's own citizens.

(c) Motives of displeasure with another nation are not sufficient as motives for war, if the other nation has violated no right of justice, but only acted in a way not consonant with charity or friendship. Thus, the fact that one nation denies another financial assistance or the tariff advantages granted to a third nation is not a *casus belli*; for in matters of benevolence or privilege there is no strict claim or title, and hence no right to have recourse to arms.

1394. Is war lawful when the justice of the cause is doubtful? (a) The government may not declare war, unless it is morally certain that right is on its side. The consequences of war are so dreadful, and the use of force against another nation is such an extreme measure, that one should refrain from hostilities as long as one's moral right is uncertain.

(b) Volunteers not already enlisted may not offer their services to a belligerent, unless they are morally certain that his cause is just. They participate in war from choice, and they should assure themselves that their choice is correct.

(c) Subjects called to the colors should fight for their country, even if they are in doubt about the justice of the cause, for the presumption is on the side of the government. This does not mean, however, that one should be willing to fight for one's country, right or wrong. nor that one would be obliged to fight for a cause manifestly unjust, or to obey an order flagrantly wrong.

1395. What is the meaning of "moral certitude" in the previous paragraph? (a) Some moralists believe that a high degree of probability of the righteousness of his cause suffices in order that a ruler may take steps towards war. (b) The greater number of moralists, however, hold that no degree of probability suffices. The justifying reasons must be clearer than day, and the state which goes to war must not entertain a single doubt that its cause is right. This opinion we prefer; for, if a jury may not sentence an accused to death as long as there is a reasonable doubt of his innocence, neither ought a nation to pass what is really a death sentence on hundreds or thousands of citizens as long as there exists a doubt of a compelling reason for such a course. It should, however, be observed that a ruler who has only probable evidence that an injury has been done already, may have certainty that it will be done, if it is not prevented by war.

1396. Is it possible that the cause of war should be just on both sides? (a) Materially or objectively, the cause of war is just only on one side, for, if one nation has the right to demand satisfaction or restitution, manifestly the other nation has no right to refuse or resist. (b) Formally or subjectively, the cause of war is just only on one side, if the facts and obligations are known to both disputants, for the nation that knows the right of the other side and yet opposes it, does not act in good faith. (c) Formally or subjectively, the cause of war is just on both sides, if the nation that is objectively in the wrong is subjectively persuaded that it is in the right. And, even though a government is in bad faith, its people as a rule will be in good faith as a result of not understanding the facts or merits of the controversy.

1397. It is possible that there should be objective justice and injustice on the same side. (a) Thus, the side which is just as regards the cause of the war, may be unjust in its conduct of the war on account of the unlawful means it employs to win, or its continuation of a hopeless struggle. (b) The side which was just as regards the original cause of the war, may be unjust as regards a new cause that appears. Thus, a nation which goes to war to regain a lost territory, but which continues to fight for the sake of conquest after the legitimate end has been achieved, contends for a just cause at the beginning, but for an unjust cause later on. (c) The side whose grounds are justifiable from the immediate point of view may be in the wrong if causes are traced farther back.

1398. What are the duties before the beginning of war, according to natural law?

(a) Examination of the Cause of War.—It is clear that those charged with the declaration of war are bound to examine diligently and prayerfully into the dispute, weighing the reasons on both sides, and asking light from on high. To this end they should seek the counsel, not of a few, but of many—not merely among those who are experts in the diplomatic, legal, economic, and military aspects of the question, but also among those who will look at the matter from its ethical side and who are guided by fairness and justice. Since it is the people who have to bear the burdens of war, it seems that many wars in the past would have been prevented, had the wishes of the people been consulted.

(b) Judgment about the Merits of the Controversy.—It is also clear that those who have to decide for war or peace should be impartial in their judgment. Hence, they have to be on their guard against jingoism, yellow journalism, and war interests, as well as against the pacifist or the favorer of a foreign country at the expense of his own. They should not proceed to offensive war, if their cause remains doubtful, unless the other side provokes war by refusing peaceful settlement; but, if they are in possession, they have the right to make defensive war.

(c) Judgment about the Feasibility of War.—Prudence demands that, even when a nation is convinced that it has a just cause to make war, it should nevertheless refrain from this, unless it has a well-grounded expectation that war will improve matters (Luke, xiv. 31, 32). Statesmen who plunge their people into adventures whose end they cannot at all foresee, are criminals.

(d) Efforts at Peaceful Solution.—Even if the cause is just and the war feasible, hostilities should not be resorted to except as a last means. Hence, pacific means—such as direct negotiation, mediation, arbitration, judicial settlement, or pressure through trade embargoes, boycotts, breach of diplomatic intercourse, etc.—should be tried in the first place.

1399. The Chief Duties before Beginning War, According to International Law.—(a) Before war is declared, an ultimatum should be issued to the other nation, offering it final terms and a last opportunity to make apology or satisfaction. (b) Foreigners who are in one's territory should be given an opportunity to settle their affairs and leave the country within a reasonable time. (c) Ambassadors and other representatives of the enemy should be provided with passports.

1400. In itself, as said above (see 1380 sqq.), war is not unlawful. But in the light of the conditions required for a just war and of circumstances as they are today, can war at the present time be ever justifiable? (a) If the supreme interests of a nation are at stake (such as its independence, the policies or interests vital to its existence, its obligations under covenant or treaty of peace), war can still be lawful today, for a nation cannot surrender its right to self-defense, or betray its solemn engagements of coöperative defense. (b) If less than supreme interests are at stake, war today seems unjustifiable, for what proportion is there between the minor interests of a single or several nations and the enormous destruction of modern war and the dislocation of international security? Efforts of statesmen to secure a world pact, outlawing or renouncing war as a means of national policy, indicates progress for this view.

1401. What are the duties during war? (a) One should use every lawful means, according to one's position, to secure victory for one's country. Fighting to gain only a "stalemate," in itself, is immoral. (b) One should avoid such means as are opposed to natural or international law.

1402. It is not true that all is fair in war, for even a just cause cannot sanction unjust means. The commandments of God and the laws of nations retain their force even amid the clash of arms. Examples of acts of war that are unlawful, as being opposed to the natural law are the following: (a) acts of irreligion, such as wanton destruction of churches or monasteries; (b) attempts to seduce enemy soldiers from the obedience or loyalty owed their commanders; (c) murder, that is, the direct killing of innocent and unarmed persons, as when one refuses quarter to soldiers who wish to surrender, fires on an officer bearing a flag of truce, sinks passenger ships not engaged on errands of war, massacres the civil population by raids from the air, places a defenceless population at the mercy of savages or criminals employed as soldiers; (d) the dishonoring of women, the establishment of brothels for soldiers; (e) stealing, such as the unauthorized pillage of a town or countryside; (f) lying, such as breaking treaties, not keeping faith with the foe, entering into perjured agreements, circulating false stories of atrocities, forging of documents, etc.

1403. Just war is resistance to unjust aggression, and so the same means are lawful in warfare as are lawful in private aggression. (a) Thus, the means used against an aggressor must not be evil in themselves, as when a person protects himself against a murderer by making an innocent person a shield. Hence, in war one may not use any means that is opposed to the law of God, or to human contracts or other obligations. (b) The means employed must be such as are really necessary for overpowering the aggressor. Thus, it is not lawful to kill a burglar when wounding him will suffice for the protection of one's property. Likewise, in war it is not lawful to exterminate or depopulate an enemy, if the end of war can be attained by depriving the enemy of his weapons.

1404. The principal classes of acts of war from the moral standpoint are: (a) acts in which violence is done to things connected with religion; (b) acts of violence against persons; (c) acts of violence against property; (d) acts used to conceal truth.

1405. Acts of War and Sacred Times.—(a) It is lawful to carry on warfare, offensively or defensively, on feasts, when this is necessary, just as it is lawful to do servile work on those days in case of necessity (I Mach., ii. 41; John, vii. 23). (b) But if a suspension of hostilities can be arranged for feast days (especially for the greater ones, such as Christmas and Easter), warfare should be discontinued at those times.

1406. Acts of War and Sacred Places.—(a) It is lawful to attack a church building, if it is certainly being used for military purposes. It is also lawful to attack fortifications, and thus unintentionally to harm adjacent church buildings. (b) It is not lawful, apart from these reasons of real military necessity, to injure sacred places or edifices.

1407. Acts of War and Sacred Persons.—(a) It is lawful for clerics to coöperate in a just war in spiritual ways, as by exhortations, prayers, and religious ministrations. Moses prayed for the armies of Israel during battle (Exod., xvii. 8 sqq.), the priests accompanied Josue around the wall of Jericho (Jos., vi. 4), and St. Bernard and other holy men preached crusades. (b) It is not lawful, apart from necessity (as in case of conscription), for clerics to take part in actual fighting. Warfare is unbecoming in a cleric, because he is enrolled for a spiritual warfare (II Tim., ii. 4), and because his leader, Christ, shed His own blood, not that of others (Matt, xxvi. 52). Hence, the Church forbids clerics to volunteer as soldiers (Canon 141).

1408. The persons to whom violence is done during war are: (a) Combatants, that is, all those who are engaged in the actual promotion of the war. Direct combatants are the fighters, such as the officers and privates of army, navy, and air force; indirect combatants are the unarmed auxiliaries of the soldiers in military ways, such as makers of munition, transporters of supplies, and those in the communication service. (b) Non-combatants are enemy subjects who are neither fighters nor auxiliaries of the armed forces, such as chaplains and members of the medical service in the army, persons in civil life and occupation, old men, women, and children. (c) Neutrals are those who are not subject to either of the warring contenders, and who take no part in the hostilities, although they may sympathize with one side.

1409. The Killing or Wounding of Enemy Combatants.—(a) According to natural law, it is lawful to kill or wound the enemy in battle, or to starve him by blockade, just as it is lawful in self-defense to kill or wound an unjust aggressor. (b) According to international law, it was expressly forbidden to attack in ways that make war more cruel without hastening the decision.

1410. The Killing or Wounding of Non-Combatants.—(a) The indirect killing of non-combatants (i.e., killing which is unintentional and unavoidable) is lawful, according to the rules given for double effect (see 103, 104). Hence, it is lawful to bombard the fortifications, arsenals, munition works, and barracks of a town, to sink passenger liners that are carrying arms or stores to the enemy, to cut off food supplies from a town or country in order to starve out its troops, although these measures will entail the deaths of some civilians as well as of combatants. Humanity requires, however, that an effort be made to spare the non-combatants, when possible, as by serving warning of attack, so that they may be removed to safety. When it is a question, however, of the use of modern weapons (the atom, hydrogen or cobalt bombs) on military targets in the vicinity of large cities, where it is foreseen that many thousands of civilians will be killed or severely wounded, then the principle of double effect seems to rule out the lawfulness of using such devastating weapons. The immediate evil effect, the slaughter of the innocents, could hardly be called incidental and only reluctantly permitted. Concretely, the inevitable results of the use of such weapons would have to be intended directly, if not as an end, at least as a means.

(b) The direct killing of non-combatants (i.e., killing which is intentional) is unlawful and constitutes the sin of murder. Obliteration bombing, the dropping of H-bombs or atom bombs on a residential section of a city containing no military objectives, are of this character; for they are attacks on civilians. It can not be argued that such an attack would probably break down the morale of the citizens to such an extent that they would force their rulers to make peace and so save many thousands of lives. For this argument is based on the principle that a good end justifies evil means.

Occasionally it is argued that modern "total" warfare demands that all citizens contribute to the war effort and that consequently everyone is a combatant. The argument can hardly be sustained, for Catholic doctrine insists that those whose participation is only remote and accidental are not to be classified as combatants. In a well-documented article on "The Morality of Obliteration Bombing," by John C. Ford, S.J. (*Theological Studies*, V, 1944, pp. 261-309), the validity of the distinction between combatants and innocent non-combatants, even in the condition of modern war, is upheld. Fr. Ford shows that in an industrial city, as found in the United States, three-fourths of the population belong to the non-combatant category, and he lists more than a hundred trades or professions which, according to the natural law, exclude their members from the category of combatants. Direct attacks on such a population clearly would constitute unjustifiable killing or wounding of non-combatants.

1411. The Sentence of Death for Military Crimes.—(a) It is lawful to sentence to death persons guilty of international crime, such as those who approach when warned to halt, civilians who fire on the troops, guerrillas, pirates, spies and deserters. (b) It is not lawful to sentence to death persons not guilty of international crime. Thus, a private soldier should not be executed because under orders he killed a non-combatant; a hostage, not guilty of any capital crime, should not be put to death, because his fellow-citizens for whom he is held rebel or break faith.

1412. Imprisonment and Restraint.—(a) Combatants may be made prisoners of war, non-combatants are subject to the restrictions of military rules when their territory is occupied, and in very exceptional cases they may be transported behind their enemy's lines. (b) Prisoners of war and inhabitants of occupied territory are to be treated as human beings, but not better than the soldiers of one's own army. They may not be reduced to slavery, held as hostages, tortured or starved to death, or placed in front trenches as a shield to one's own forces.

1413. The Destruction or Seizure of Property During War.—(a) The military property of the enemy nation or of its subjects may be confiscated or destroyed, just as an individual has the right to destroy the weapon of an unjust aggressor. Hence, a commander may demolish fortifications, war factories, airships, warships, weapons and artillery; he may cut off or seize supplies and provisions of money, food or drink.

(b) The public, non-military property of the enemy may be occupied by a successful invader. He may appropriate movable goods (works of art and some others are excepted by international law), and he may use immovable goods (public places of worship, museums, etc., are excepted by law).

(c) As to private property of enemy subjects on land, international law requires that immovables generally be respected, and movables can be seized only for some necessary purpose of war. Requisitions and contributions may be exacted and soldiers may be billeted in the homes of citizens, but only so much may be levied as is needed for army maintenance and civil administration, and compensation must be made, or a receipt be given for future compensation. War is made, not against private persons, but against the state.

(d) As to private property on sea, the usage has been that the merchant ships of the enemy may be captured and made a lawful prize.

(e) The property of neutrals on land must not be molested, unless it is not really neutral, as when it is being used by the enemy. As regards the ships and shipping of neutrals on the high seas, they are not up to the present protected by international agreement. Rather the naval powers are divided between the theories of command of the seas and freedom of the seas. Thus, Great Britain claims the right to search, seize and hold the vessels or cargoes of neutrals who carry contraband or attempt to trade with the enemy in the face of a blockade.

1414. It is an axiom that booty taken in war belongs, not to the private soldiers, but to their government. Hence, the question arises: Are private soldiers, who take the goods of citizens without authorization from their officers, bound to make restitution? (a) If they take what is necessary for their own sustenance, they act against military discipline, but not against justice, and are not bound to restore. (b) If they take other things, they are bound to restore, since international agreements make this a duty of justice. But, if neither of the belligerents observed this agreement, the obligation of restitution cannot be insisted on as grave.

1415. Is it lawful to give over a city to be looted by the soldiery? (a) In ancient times, this was sometimes permissible, as when compensation and victory in a just war was otherwise impossible. (b) In modern times and according to present international law, looting is strictly forbidden. Violation of agreements by city heads gives no right to attack the property of the citizens who are not responsible, and valiant defense of the city by its troops does not forfeit the rights of the inhabitants to their goods.

1416. Stratagems in War.—(a) It is lawful to use various artifices for concealing one's plans from the enemy, such as camouflage, smoke screens, censored reports of engagements, etc. Thus, Josue by command of the Lord prepared an ambush for the citizens of Hai (Jos., viii. 2). (b) It is lawful also to conceal one's identity by wearing the uniforms of the enemy in order to obtain information about his plans. The Lord commanded Moses to send out men to spy on the land of Chanaan (Num., xiii. 1). While it is not lawful to tell or signify untruth, it is lawful to conceal the truth from those who have no right to know it.

1417. Reprisals are acts of retaliation by which one replies to unlawful aggressions of the enemy by equivalent aggressions against him. Their morality depends on circumstances. (a) Thus, if the act of the enemy is opposed only to international law, it is not unlawful to use the same act against him, for, since he has broken faith, the treaty obligation no longer binds the other side. For example, if the enemy, contrary to agreement, uses poison gas in warfare, it is lawful to use poison gas against him. Reprisals should not be made, however, without authorization from the proper authority. (b) If the act of the enemy is opposed to natural law, it is not permissible to retaliate by the same kind of acts. Two wrongs do not make a right. But one may retaliate in lawful ways, or else issue a protest and await compensation at the conclusion of the war. Thus, if the enemy murders the civil population, this does not justify one in murdering enemy citizens who are in one's power.

1418. Duties of the Nation Victorious in War.—(a) The victorious nation must not prolong the war after victory has been gained, or after the enemy has sued in good faith for peace or armistice. (b) It must not exact from the defeated foe more than it has a just right to.

1419. The Rights of the Victor.—(a) If the cause of the victorious nation was unjust, its victory gives it no claim, for might does not make right. On the contrary, it may be obliged to make restitution to the defeated nation for the losses it has suffered. (b) If the cause of the victor was just, the victorious nation has a claim to three things: (i) to the satisfaction or restitution for the sake of which the war was undertaken; (ii) to compensation for damages caused by the enemy during the war, and (iii) to guarantees against a recurrence of the former injury. Supervision of peace treaties by an impartial tribunal has much to recommend it, since victors are prone to disregard charity and justice when treating with a conquered foe, and to extort from him forced agreements.

1420. The Obligation of a Victor Whose Cause was Unjust.—(a) If the victorious nation fought in good faith, and only later perceived the injustice of its cause, it is bound to restore only those things which it has not consumed, and which make it better off than it was before the war. (b) If it fought in bad faith, it should restore all. Victory does not prove that one was right, but only that one was stronger. It does not make a bad cause good.

1421. The Obligation of a Victor Who Fought Without Due Authorization, or with a Wrong Purpose.—(a) Soldiers who inflict damage on the enemy against the orders of the commanders (e.g., by burning dwellings, robbing private citizens, murdering, etc.), are obliged to restitution for those injuries, for such acts are not war, but brigandage. (b) Soldiers who fight with a wrong motive (e.g., out of hatred), are not obliged to restitution, since they have not committed injustice; for similarly a judge, who sentences a convicted criminal, sins if his motive is hate, but he is not held to restitution.

1422. What Indemnity may be Imposed on the Vanquished?—(a) According to justice, one may exact compensation for the losses and expenses one has sustained on account of war, since the enemy is responsible for these. (b) According to charity, one may be obliged to relinquish part of what is owed, or to grant easier terms of payment, or to cancel a debt, as when the enemy is greatly impoverished, or cannot easily pay at present.

1423. In cases of doubt, as when counter claims are made and neither party is entirely victorious, or when a vanquished nation denies its ability to pay what is demanded, recourse may be had to other ways of settlement. (a) Thus, in the former case a compromise or mutual condonation of claims, especially if both sides are exhausted by the war, seems the reasonable solution. (b) In the latter case submission to an impartial tribunal of arbitration would benefit the victors as well as the vanquished, since in the long run it is not to the advantage of the former that the latter be deprived of its goods and productivity.

1424. Guarantees for the Future.—(a) One may insist on such guarantees as will insure against a probable renewal of the offense committed by the conquered nation. Hence, one may require that it destroy or deliver over fortifications and munition plants, sink warships, reduce its military force, punish certain individuals, or depose certain rulers.

(b) One may not insist on such guarantees as will make a renewal of war by the enemy, now or in the future, absolutely impossible. As said above, a nation has the right to go to war to defend itself against aggression, but it has no right to work at destroying equality or competition on the part of other nations. Hence, it is not lawful to demand that the conquered nation surrender its independence or the management of its affairs, or that one be allowed to annex all the territory taken during war, if one's rights or reasonable security does not require these conditions. Subjugation or temporary occupation are lawful, however, if there is no other way of obtaining redress or securities.

1425. Punishment of Enemy Soldiers for Crimes Committed during War.—(a) Special crimes committed during war (e.g., massacres of non-combatants) may be punished, but the punishment should be visited on those responsible, not on those who merely executed orders. (b) The crime of the war itself should not be revenged on private soldiers, for it is unjust to punish subjects for the madness of their officers and rulers. As to the latter, moral guilt is not easily established. The Nurenberg trials held commanders and high officers responsible for crimes against humanity, and not without precedent.

1426. Preparation for Future Wars.—(a) Reasonable preparedness is not only lawful, but a duty of the state to its own people. A nation should have such a military establishment or such alliances as will safeguard its right against probable attack. (b) Unreasonable preparedness is unlawful since it burdens the people and prepares the way for war. Examples of unreasonable preparations: maintenance of an army or navy far in excess of those nations of similar rank; oppressive military expenses or burdens; maneuvers offensive to other governments or too dangerous for the troops engaged; ruinous competition in armaments.

1427. Preparation for peace or against war is a duty no less obligatory than preparation for defensive war. Two chief ways of preparing for peace: (a) will for peace; (b) work for peace.

(a) The will for peace is promoted when the nations educate their people to a realization of the brotherhood of man, of the wrongfulness and folly of a narrow nationalism, of the sinfulness of war which has not all the conditions of a just war in its favor. Without the will for peace, conferences and treaties will effect little.

(b) Work for peace is done by all who give their service to practical plans for the prevention of war and the preservation of lasting world amity. Among these plans are agreements among nations to substitute moral right for material force, to abolish conscription and armaments, to establish international tribunals, associations and world courts, to make arbitration of disputes among themselves compulsory, to codify international law. History bears witness to the many and great services to humanity which the Popes have rendered by acting as arbiters between nations that were on the point of war. If jealousies prevent agreement among governments, the peoples of the world should nevertheless continue to work for peace and by constitutional means make their wishes prevail among the governments. With the Church we should pray: "From pestilence, famine and war, deliver us, O Lord."

1428. Fighting.—Fighting is an angry conflict between two or more persons carried on by means of physical violence.

(a) Thus, it is an angry conflict, and so differs from contests of strength or skill made for the sake of sport, amusement, recreation, health, exercise and training. Hence, wrestling and boxing matches, football games, fencing and similar athletic contests, in which fair play and a sportsmanlike spirit prevail, are not fighting as here understood. Similarly, the tournaments of the medieval knights were sports or spectacles, rather than fights.

(b) It is a conflict, and so differs from punishment inflicted by lawful authority, as when a police officer uses his club to prevent a crime, a parent or teacher chastises insubordinate children, or a sober man scuffles with an inebriate to take away his flask or with a lunatic to deprive him of a weapon.

(c) It is a conflict between two or more individuals, and so differs from war and sedition, which are conflicts between nations or parts of a multitude.

(d) It is conducted by means of physical violence, that is by the infliction of bodily injuries or harm. Thus, fighting differs from quarreling, which is a dispute in words. It makes no difference whether the attack be made by fists, fingernails or teeth, or by weapons or missiles, or whether the bodily harm be direct (e.g., a blackened eye) or indirect (e.g., a hat knocked off the head).

1429. Kinds of Fighting.—(a) As to its origin, fighting is provoked or unprovoked, according as one who fights is attacking another or defending himself against attack. (b) As to its manner, it is an ordinary fight or a duel, according as it takes place without or with previous arrangement and stipulated conditions. (c) As to its eject, the civil law distinguishes between assault and battery. Assault is a show of violence against the person of another, as when one lifts one's fist or cane in a threatening manner to put another in fear of bodily harm. Battery is the actual infliction of personal violence, as when one strikes, pushes, scratches, bites, or spits on another.

1430. The Sinfulness of Fighting.—(a) Unprovoked fighting is from its nature a mortal sin. It is classed among the works of the flesh that exclude from the kingdom of heaven (Gal, v. 20, 21), and it is essentially opposed to the charity owed to a neighbor. It is frequently only a venial sin, either because the act is not entirely deliberate, as when one fights in sudden anger, or because the violence is of a trifling kind, as when school-children pull one another's hair or throw snowballs.

(b) Fighting under provocation is no sin at all, when one intends only to defend one's rights and does not go beyond what is necessary for lawful defence, as when one struggles with a burglar who is trying to enter one's house, and pushes him through the door. It is a venial sin, when the person who is resisting aggression acts with some slight degree of hate or revengefulness, or inflicts a little more injury than is really necessary. It is a mortal sin, when the person who was attacked fights in a spirit of hate and revenge, or deliberately and needlessly seeks to kill or seriously maim the adversary.

1431. Causes of Fighting.—The remedy of sinful fighting is the removal of its causes. The sources of fighting are proximate and remote.

(a) The immediate cause is anger. The angry man provokes fights (Prov., xv. 18, xxix. 22), for anger, being a desire of revenge, is not content to injure another secretly, but wishes to punish him—that is, to injure him in such a way that he will know he is being punished and will feel grief on that account. Anger also blinds one to the foolishness of one's actions, and so leads one precipitately into quarrels and fights (Prov., xviii. 6).

(b) The remote cause of fighting is an inordinate desire of temporal things, such as wealth, power, ease: "Why are there wars and disputes among you? Is it not because of the desires that war among your members?" (James, iv. 1). Those who are overmuch concerned with their own interests, easily take offense at what they consider slights or insults or opposition, their rage bursts forth, and they proceed at once to visit revenge on those at whom they are offended. It was greed and envy that caused the herdsmen of Palestine to fill up the wells dug by Isaac and to fight with his servants for possession (Gen., xxvi. 14 sqq.).

1432. Hatred and Fighting.—(a) Hatred is not necessarily a cause of fighting. The hater wishes evil to his neighbor, not as punishment, but absolutely; his passion is calmer, more lasting, and more insatiable than that of the angry man. If it suits him, he will bide his time patiently, pretending friendship, but all the while plotting ruin to the one he hates. (b) Hatred at times does bring on fighting, for, if the hater sees that he can safely attack openly, he will use quarreling and fighting as a means to his purpose.

1433. Occasions that Frequently Bring On Fighting.—(a) Boasting about self or depreciation of others in the presence of persons who will take offense occasions fights, for "he that boasteth and puffeth himself up stirreth up quarrels" (Prov., xxviii. 25). Thus, disputes over the respective merits of nations or political parties often bring on bloody encounters. (b) Drunkenness occasions fights, for it so stupefies the mind that one minimizes one's danger and exaggerates one's own strength, and so is emboldened to attack others (Prov., xxiii. 29, 30).

1434. Evil Consequences of Fighting.—(a) Charity is wounded by fighting, wherefrom there often result lasting hates, discords, scandals. (b) Justice is wounded by fighting, as when a person unjustly maims or kills his neighbor, and is himself imprisoned or executed, to the disgrace and deprivation of his dependents.

1435. Duelling.—A duel is a prearranged combat between two persons fought with deadly weapons, for the purpose of settling a private quarrel.

(a) Thus, it is a combat, and hence the "suicide duel," in which the contenders draw lots with the understanding that the loser must kill himself within a specified time, is not properly a duel.

(b) A duel is prearranged, that is, the time, place, and weapons are determined in advance. Hence, if two feudists meet accidentally and proceed at once to shoot, their combat is not strictly a duel. It is not necessary, however, that a formal letter of challenge and a letter of acceptance precede the fight.

(c) It is between two persons, that is, a determinate combatant is matched against a determinate opponent. A true duel, however, might be carried on between many couples simultaneously, as in the fight between the twelve soldiers of Abner and the twelve soldiers of Joab (II Kings, ii. 13-17). The presence of seconds or witnesses is not essential to a duel.

(d) A duel is fought with deadly weapons, that is, with such arms as are capable of inflicting severe wounds, so that there is serious danger of grave wound or mutilation or death. There is no duel, therefore, if one fights with weapons that cannot do serious harm (such as fists, light sticks, mud), or if by agreement one uses dangerous weapons in a way that precludes injury (e.g., by padding the edge of one's sword, loading one's revolver with blanks, firing into the air, as in sham or mock duels). But academic duels, in which students try to stab each other in the face with small daggers, are true duels; for, while the fighters are well protected in vital parts and serious or fatal wounds rarely happen, it remains true that this manner of fighting is mortally dangerous. The same remark applies to duels fought on condition that only one or two rounds of shots shall be fired, or that fighting shall cease as soon as blood has been drawn.

(e) A duel is fought for the purpose of settling a private quarrel. A hand-to-hand combat during battle between two soldiers of contending armies is not a duel in the proper sense of the word, since there is no private quarrel between them, but only the public quarrel of their countries.

1436. The Morality of Duelling.—(a) Generally, the duel is mortally sinful. Like ordinary fighting, it is against charity, and in addition it includes a will to kill or gravely injure another, to expose one's own life or limb to chance, and to usurp the function of the State. This applies to the challenged as well as to the challenger, for one can decline the combat to which one is dared.

(b) Exceptionally, a duel would not be sinful, if it took on the character of a war, or of self-defense against an unjust aggressor. Thus, in order to shorten a war or to lessen the bloodshed, it might be lawful to make the whole issue depend on a single combat between the commanders or between champions chosen from opposing armies, as in the case of David and Goliath (I Kings, xvii); but in modern times such a practice has been abandoned. Again, if a person had to choose between certain death, if he refused a duel, and possible death, if he consented to a duel, it would seem that he is in the position of one attacked by an unjust aggressor; but it is not easy to picture such a case as happening in normal conditions.

1437. The Fallacy of the Arguments for Duelling.—(a) The amusement of the spectators was the purpose of the gladiatorial duels fought in ancient Rome. But today there is no one who would not grant that the butchering of human beings to make a holiday for the populace is savagery.

(b) The decision of doubtful cases before the courts was the purpose of the judicial duels fought among the Germans and Lombards in the early Middle Ages. But manifestly such duels are a temptation of God, since they rashly call on Him to disclose, through a duel between the litigants, what the evidence in court did not disclose. The outcome of the duel shows which party is stronger or more skilful, not which is in the right.

(c) Training in bravery and the termination of serious differences is the excuse offered for military and university duels. But to kill, cripple, or brutalize youth does not make the nation stronger, and the substitution of violence for law as a means of settling disputes is an encouragement to crime.

(d) Satisfaction for insults or other injury, or the avoidance of the reputation of being a coward, is the reason given for so-called affairs of honor. But is it not a superstition and a relic of barbarism to think that dishonor is wiped out by a dishonorable fight, or that a person shows himself brave because he lacks the moral bravery to act against the wrong opinions of the multitude?

1438. Penalties against Duelling.—(a) Church law deprives of ecclesiastical burial those who die as the result of a duel, if unrepentant (Canon 1240); it also declares excommunication reserved simply to the Holy See and infamy against duellists and their helpers (Canon 2351). (b) Civil law in English-speaking countries makes duelling a crime. If death results, it is regarded as murder, and the seconds are liable to punishment as accessories.

1439. What is the moral duty of restitution on account of injuries caused in a duel? (a) The challenger and his heirs have no right to restitution. (b) The challenged, if he accepted willingly, has no right to restitution, for his free acceptance of the fight implies the cession of such a right. (c) The challenged, if he accepted under grave compulsion, has the right to restitution. If he is wounded, the aggressor should pay the medical expense; if he is killed, the heirs should be compensated.

1440. Sedition.—Sedition is a discord between different factions of the same multitude so grave as to extend to physical conflict, and to the destruction of the unity of the State.

(a) It is a discord, that is, a disagreement of wills, and so it resembles schism, war and fighting. Difference of opinion in the political parties of a country is not sedition, since there is a unity of will and purpose in all of them with reference to the common good and the peace of the State (cfr. 1197, 1348). In fact, under a democratic system of government, the existence of some opposite parties has proved a useful, if not necessary means of stimulating the interest of citizens, and of expediting the business of legislation.

(b) Sedition is between different factions of the same multitude, that is, between different sections or groups of the same body politic. Thus, it differs from war (which is between states), and from fighting (which is between individuals).

(c) Sedition extends to physical conflict, that is, it tends from its character to break out into violence and to array the opposite factions in fight against one another. If not accompanied by actual hostilities, it is simple sedition. But, if fighting has begun, it is insurrection or rebellion, when the people seek to overthrow the government; it is civil war, if one part of the nation seeks to secede from or overcome the other.

(d) It is prejudicial to the civil unity and peace of the people, that is, it tends to the violent dismemberment of the State, or at least to the disturbance of the common good. Thus, sedition is more serious than riots, tumults, gang-warfare, and like particular disturbances, which are not directed against the State itself, or against the harmony of the whole body of the people. Sedition differs also from the peaceful separation of parts of a state, and from the lawful self-defense of the people against a tyrannical government.

1441. From the definition given above, it is plain that sedition is a special distinct species of sin. (a) It differs from spiritual discord, for unlike schism it is opposed, not to the unity of the Church, but to the unity of the State. (b) It differs from other kinds of temporal discord, for unlike war and fighting it is opposed, not to peace between nations or individuals, but to peace between the members of the same civil body. War takes away peace with foreigners, sedition takes away peace with fellow-citizens; fighting attacks a private person or persons, sedition attacks the public welfare of the country.

1442. Sedition in the strict meaning given it above is always sinful. (a) Thus, it is a mortal sin from its nature, since it is opposed to what is manifestly one of the greatest of temporal goods, namely, the unity of the State. (b) It is opposed to charity, as destroying the bond of peace; it is opposed to justice, as injuring a unity based on law and common utility, to which the nation has a strict right. (c) Sedition is graver in some persons than in others. Thus, the moral causes of sedition (i.e., those that sow discords or promote disaffection) are more responsible than those who are led and who carry out acts of violence. The gravity of the sin in each case depends on the amount of damage that is due to one's influence or acts.

1443. Is one who resists a tyrannical government guilty of the sin of sedition? (a) When resistance is made by legal and pacific means, such as the rejection of a bad government at the polls, there is no sedition. (b) When legal and pacific means are impossible and armed aggression against a tyrant will benefit the common good, a rebel is not guilty of the sin of sedition. In this case, it is rather the bad ruler who causes discords and is seditious against the common good, whereas the people only defend themselves according to the laws. Thus, the rebellion of the Machabees against their Syrian oppressors was not seditious. (c) When legal means are impossible but armed aggression will not benefit the common good, a rebel is guilty of the sin of sedition.

Art. 9: THE SINS AGAINST BENEFICENCE

(*Summa Theologica*, II-II, q. 43.)

1444. Having discussed in the preceding paragraphs the sins opposed to the internal acts of charity (love, joy and peace), we come now to treat of scandal and coöperation which are opposed to the external acts of charity—beneficence and brotherly correction.

1445. Scandal.—Scandal is derived from a Greek word signifying a snare or trap prepared for an enemy, or a stone or block laid in the road that he may stumble or trip over it. In use, it is applied in a wide or general sense, and in a strict or special sense. (a) In its wide sense, it refers to any kind of harm, especially of a spiritual or moral nature, that one brings on others. (b) In its strict sense, it refers to a fall into sin which one occasions for others by misconduct.

1446. The following are some examples of the word "scandal" as employed in its wide sense: (a) It is used to signify physical or natural injuries of various kinds. Thus, the servants of Pharaoh called the plagues brought on Egypt by Moses a scandal (Exod., x. 7), and the Psalmist says of the sinner that he laid a scandal (calamity) against his brother (Ps. xlix. 20). Those who spread defamatory gossip are called scandal-mongers, and "scandal" often signifies opprobrium or disgrace, as when Shakespeare speaks of the wrangling of nobles as a scandal to the crown. (b) The word "scandal" is also used to signify moral injuries distinct from inducement to sin. Thus, the shock and offense given to virtuous persons by blasphemous language spoken in their hearing is described as a scandal, and one who would prevent another from following some more perfect course or practice to which there is no obligation (such as entering religion, saying grace at meals, etc.), is sometimes said to scandalize.

1447. Definition of Scandal.—In the strict sense, scandal is defined as "any conduct that has at least the appearance of evil and that offers to a neighbor an occasion of spiritual ruin."

(a) By conduct is understood external behavior or manner of acting in the presence of others. Thus, scandal differs from sin, for sin is committed, not only by external acts done before others, but also by internal thoughts and desires and external acts that are secret.

(b) Scandal is conduct which is evil at least in appearance, that is, sinful, or from the circumstances seemingly sinful. Thus, an act is not scandalous, if it is morally indifferent or a less good, and is perceivable as being such.

(c) Scandal tends to spiritual ruin, that is, to a fall into sin, great or small. Here scandal strictly understood differs from scandal in the wide senses given in the previous paragraph.

(d) Scandal is an occasion of a fall into sin, that is, it sets an example of sin before the attention, and thus suggests to the will that the will imitate the sin. Scandal is not, however, the cause of sin, for a person causes his own sin in yielding consent to the suggestion offered by scandal.

(e) Scandal is to another. A person may be said to scandalize himself in the sense that by his looks or acts he puts himself in an occasion of sin (Matt., v. 29, 30), or inasmuch as he maliciously makes the acts of a virtuous neighbor an occasion of sin; but scandal is more properly understood of an occasion of sin prepared for one's neighbor.

1448. Causes of Scandal.—There are various divisions of scandal according to the kinds of external acts. (a) There is scandal in words, as profane language or calumnies spoken in a gathering of people. (b) There is scandal in acts, as when one is perceptibly drunk or fights in a city street. Scandal applies also to things, in so far as they are the result of acts or related to acts, such as disedifying books, pictures, dress. Thus, one gives scandal by having sinful objects on display, such as profane mottoes on one's wall, obscene advertisements or announcements on one's billboards. (c) There also may be scandal in omission, as when one is conspicuously absent from Mass on Sundays.

1449. The following kinds of sinful acts are not scandalous, for they are unknown to others, and hence cannot suggest sin: (a) internal acts, such as wicked thoughts, desires, emotions; (b) external acts concealed from others, such as inaudible profanity, intoxication not noticeable by others, omission of an obligatory penance about which others have no knowledge.

1450. There are, likewise, various divisions of scandal according to the internal purpose of the scandalizer. (a) Scandal is directly intentional, when the purpose of the scandalizer is to lead others to the guilt of sin (diabolical scandal). Example: Titus blasphemes religion before Caius in order that the latter may become irreligious, and thus be more easily persuaded to follow a life of crime. (b) Scandal is indirectly intentional when the purpose of the scandalizer is to perform some action whose nature is such that it will lead others to the guilt of sin, and he is determined to perform that action, although not directly willing the neighbor's guilt that will result. Example: Titus does not like to see his children drunk, but he likes to get drunk himself occasionally, knowing all the while that his example encourages them to drink.

1451. In the following cases there is no intention of scandal: (a) when one does an act that has no appearance of evil, and one neither directly nor indirectly wills that it should be an occasion of sin to anyone. Example: Balbus performs his duties faithfully, although he knows to his regret that his fidelity occasions envy and hatred in Claudius; (b) when one does an act that is evil or apparently evil, but is invincibly ignorant of the scandal it may give. Example: Sempronius and Titus converse together in a foreign tongue which they confidently think Caius does not understand. The conversation is disedifying, and Caius, who does understand, is shocked by what they say.

1452. The act of the scandalizer who intends, directly or indirectly, the spiritual ruin of his neighbor, is called active scandal, while the act of the person who takes occasion from the active scandal to incur spiritual ruin, is called passive scandal. Active and passive scandal are sometimes together, sometimes apart. (a) Thus, there is both active and passive scandal, when the scandalizer wills the fall of his neighbor, and the scandalized does fall. (b) There is active but not passive scandal, when the scandalizer wills the fall of his neighbor, but the latter does not fall into the snare. (c) There is passive but not active scandal, when one makes the good action rightly performed by another an occasion of sin. Thus, some made the life and passion of our Lord a pretext for not accepting Him (Matt., xiii. 57; John, vi. 62; I Cor., i. 23), and are said to have been scandalized at Him.

1453. As to the act that occasions the spiritual ruin of another, it must be wrong either in reality or in appearance. (a) The scandalous act is wrong in reality, when it is forbidden as a sin—for example, offering sacrifice in the temple of an idol, or diverting to personal use money collected for the poor. (b) The scandalous act is wrong in appearance, when on account of circumstances it seems to be an act forbidden as a sin. Thus, to take part in a banquet held in a pagan temple might seem like participation in sacrificial rites (I Cor., viii. 10), to expend secretly the money collected for the poor might have the appearance of improper use of funds (II Cor., viii. 20, 21). Hence, St. Paul directs; "From all appearance of evil refrain yourselves" (I Thess., v. 22).

1454. The acts wrong in reality or in appearance that give scandal are innumerable, since the whole world is seated in wickedness (I John, v. 19). But today there are a number of acts that should be specially mentioned, as they occasion sin oftener or for more persons than other acts. Among these are: (a) occasions of sin against faith, such as atheistical literature, as discussed in the section on faith; (b) occasions of sin against morals, such as obscenity in dress, pictures, plays, writings, and dances. These last-mentioned will be discussed now in separate paragraphs.

1455. Obscenity.—Obscenity is a quality of words, acts or objects by which impure thoughts are conveyed, or impure desires or actions suggested. We may consider it either internally (i.e., in the intention of the person who uses the words, acts or objects) or externally (i.e., in the nature of the things themselves which are used).

(a) Thus, internal obscenity, or the will to use what will corrupt the minds and morals of others, is of course a mortal sin. If the intention is to deprave another, the guilt of direct scandal is incurred; if the intention is only to satisfy one's own wish to use the sinful words, acts or objects, the guilt is that of indirect scandal. Thus, a woman who dresses fashionably in order to excite impure love is guilty of direct scandal; if she dresses immodestly, not to excite impure love, but to follow a fashion, she is guilty of indirect scandal.

(b) External obscenity is the tendency of words, acts or objects themselves to call up impure images in the mind, or to excite impure desires or actions in those to whom they are presented. The use of such words, acts, etc., is therefore a mortal sin. For, if the thing said or done is wrong in itself (such as obscene language), it is a scandalous sin against purity, if it is wrong on account of those who will be influenced (such as a talk on sex matters to immature or weak persons), it is a sin of scandal. Hence, a good or even religious motive (such as instruction, refutation of error, health, or mysticism) does not excuse the employment of what is clearly obscene, for the end does not justify the means.

1456. It is not always easy to determine in particular cases when a thing is obscene from its very nature, but the following general rules can be given:

(a) Pictures, statues and other images are obscene, when they represent scenes of immoral or sexual acts, or lascivious attitudes or postures; also, when they represent nude or partly nude human figures, ut quando depinguntur verenda adultorum vel pectora aut partes minus honestæ mulierum.

(b) Female dress or adornment is lascivious, when there is a notable display of the person through abbreviated skirts, necks, and sleeves; or a suggestiveness expressed in transparency of material or a closeness of fit that brings out the lines and curves of the figure; or in an extremity of fashion whose striking color or design will make the wearer conspicuous and direct special attention to her physical charms.

(c) Plays on the stage or moving picture screen are obscene by reason of the lesson taught (as when purity is derided or impurity condoned), by reason of the thing represented (as when the main theme is impurity, or when acts of impurity are represented or suggested, or when sexual passion is emphasized), or by reason of the players (as when they are noted for immorality, or when their dress is indecent, or their language objectionable).

(d) Dances are obscene in themselves when the postures, movements, or contact of the dancers is indecent; they are obscene by reason of the dancers, when these are indecently attired. Public dance halls, cabarets, road houses, and night clubs—where there is no supervision and young girls come unattended to dance until late hours with men unknown to them, and where there is intoxication and boisterousness—are the natural haunts of the obscene dance, but it may be found even in more respectable places.

(e) Books or other writings contain obscenity When they inculcate or recommend impure acts, or advise how these may be committed; when they treat sins of impurity or narrate immoral facts or stories in such a manner as to make vice seem alluring or pardonable to the intended reader; when an erotic composition by language, allusions, details, sympathetic treatment, etc., gives prominence to animal passion.

1457. As is stated elsewhere (see 1461 sqq.), scandal is not given unless the persons affected by one's conduct are susceptible to evil influence. Hence, there is no obscenity when on account of circumstances there is no suggestion of evil in things which under other conditions would be immoral and seductive.

(a) Images of the nude in the studio of an artist, and anatomical charts, figures or illustrations in a book intended for the instruction of medical men, are not classed as obscene, since the persons for whom they are made are supposed to be so much under the influence of the esthetic or scientific principles of their professions that no harm will be taken.

(b) The obscenity of dress is largely dependent on its novelty, for things that are usual cease to excite special attention. This we can see from the fact that styles that are conservative today would have been extreme ten years ago. And so the scanty attire of hot countries, the dress of the bathing beach, and the moderate decolleté tolerated in private gatherings are not obscene in their own proper times and places.

(c) Plays which contain gross or unseemly expressions or passages are not therefore obscene, if in the main they uphold decency and morality; otherwise, we should have to regard as immoral even the classic drama. Newman says of Shakespeare: "Often as he may offend against modesty, he is clear of a worse charge, sensuality, and hardly a passage can be instanced in all that he has written to seduce the imagination or to excite the passions." It is a simple matter to omit from plays of this kind the word or phrase that is offensive to modern ears or to the innocence of youth.

(d) The fact that some individuals find all dancing a strong stimulus to impure passion does not prove that every dance is obscene. Some types of dance, it is true, might be rightly called "the devil's march"; other dances, named after various animals, may also be suggestive. But there are also standard types of dance in which many experience not temptation, but innocent pastime, and which have also physical, esthetic and social values.

(e) To books and other writings should be applied what was said about plays, namely, that they are not to be classed as obscene on account of isolated passages unsuited for the reading of children or other susceptible persons, or excitable to prurient or impure minds. Even the Bible may seem objectionable to a prude, and the indecent will go through its pages with a fine-tooth comb in the search for indecent matter; but public opinion will rightly class as a lunatic the person who would endeavor to have the Bible rated as obscene.

1458. Persons Who Give Scandal on Account of Obscenity.—(a) In case of obscene pictures or statues, scandal is given by the artists, painters, sculptors or others who make the images, and by the responsible persons who place them in museums, galleries, parks or other places to which there is general admission.

(b) As regards female dress, the guilty parties are proximately the wearers, but remotely and principally the designers and society leaders who impose their will in making the fashions dangerous and in causing one extreme mode to follow quickly upon another.

(e) With respect to obscene plays, the scandal is given by playwrights, managers, actors and actresses, and those who patronize or applaud them. The public itself and the civil authorities share in the guilt, when they supinely tolerate the degradation of the stage and the corruption of morals.

(d) In the case of obscene dances, the givers of scandal are the proprietors of resorts where the dances are held, the musicians and singers (especially when the songs themselves are obscene), and the dancers, spectators and other patrons.

(e) In the case of salacious publications or writings, authors, publishers, printers, vendors, and the reading public share responsibility for the scandal. Government censorship of the press is not desirable, but government suppression of obscenity has always been the policy of countries of English origin. The private citizen, then, is not free of guilt if he takes no interest even when he sees piles of indecent magazines, pictures, etc., being sold openly on the newsstands. Canon Law (Canon 1404) forbids booksellers to sell, lend, or keep books that deal *ex professo* with obscenity, though there is no objection to expurgated editions, as in the case of classical works.

1459. Results of Scandal.—The spiritual ruin occasioned by scandal is sin.

(a) Thus, formal or material sin may be the result of scandal. Example: Titus blasphemed before a boy who did not understand the meaning of the word and before a youth who did understand, with the result that both repeated the same blasphemy. Thus, the scandal given by Titus produced material sin in the boy and formal sin in the youth.

(b) Mortal sin or venial sin may be the result of scandal, just as a stone in the road may cause either a fall or a stumble.

(c) Sin of the same species or sin of a different species from that committed by the scandal-giver may be the result of scandal. Thus, a calumny spoken against a neighbor may induce a hearer either to repeat the calumny, or to imitate the act imputed by the calumniator, or to give up religion.

(d) Sin already committed by the person scandalized or sin which is new to him, sin he had in mind to commit or sin he had not contemplated—any one of these results suffice for scandal. Example: It is scandal to recall to drunkenness by bad example a person who had reformed, or by bad example to bring back to another's mind and desire a sin on which he was once resolved.

1460. Scandal resembles solicitation and complicity, since like them it exercises an evil influence on others; but it is not identical with them.

(a) Thus, solicitation influences another to evil by counsel, persuasion, command, or invitation; scandal may influence to evil either in these ways or by mere example. Again, solicitation does not necessarily intend the fall of another into guilt, as does scandal. Thus, one may solicit another to get drunk who had already determined to get drunk, or one may persuade another that drunkenness is no sin, and then solicit him to drunkenness. But, if one who intends the demoralization and corruption of his neighbor solicits him to drunkenness, solicitation is joined with scandal.

(b) Complicity or coöperation influences another to evil by helping him in the commission of sin; scandal influences him to evil by suggesting that he commit sin. Example: Titus, an elderly man, gets drunk or praises drunkards in the presence of Balbus, a youth. Influenced by these acts and words, Balbus tells his acquaintance Claudius that he intends to get drunk, and Claudius supplies him with the intoxicants. Titus is guilty of scandal, Claudius of coöperation.

1461. The persons before whom disedifying words, deeds or omissions are done, are of two classes. (a) Persons apt to be scandalized are those who are not experienced either in vice (especially that to which the disedifying example would lead), or in virtue (especially the opposite virtue); for such persons are readily subject to bad influence. Thus, young persons Whose character is yet unformed, the ignorant and well-meaning persons who are weak, are peculiarly disposed to be led astray by example. (b) Persons not apt to be scandalized are those who are habitually so bad or so good that anything disedifying done before them is not calculated to influence their attitude towards evil.

1462. May a person hold himself guiltless of scandal, therefore, because his wrongdoing was committed before those who are not apt to be scandalized?

(a) If he is certain that the witnesses will not be weakened morally on his account, and if he does not intend their fall, he is free of the guilt of scandal. Thus, if one blasphemes in the presence of a lady renowned for piety, or of a rough crowd of men whose daily talk is interspersed with blasphemies, it is practically sure that no scandal is given.

(b) If a person is not certain that the witnesses will suffer no moral harm through his example, he cannot hold himself as not guilty of scandal. For, no matter how good or how bad the witnesses may appear to him, they may not be as fixed in character as he thinks, and his misconduct may be the starting point for them of a downward course or of a more rapid descent into evil. Generally speaking, there is this uncertainty about the influence of bad example, for the reading of character is no easy matter, and many sins are internal.

1463. There are two cases especially, when even the very good may become bad or the very bad become worse through force of evil example: (a) when the sin committed is from its nature very alluring. Sic auctores censent vix fieri posse quin in materia luxuriæ malum exemplum peccati motus cieat; (b) the second case is when the authority of the one who gives scandal is great. For the fact that he sides with or seems to side with evil, will demoralize the good and encourage the wicked in wrongdoing.

1464. Passive scandal (see 1452), that is, the spiritual fall consequent on the example of another, is of two kinds: (a) scandal given, which is a fall into sin occasioned by conduct really disedifying, as when a youth becomes drunk because he has seen his elders intoxicated; (b) scandal taken, which is a fall into sin occasioned by conduct irreproachable in itself, but wrongly interpreted, either out of malice (Pharisaic scandal), or out of ignorance or frailty (scandal of little ones). The Pharisees were scandalized at our Lord's dining with sinners, because they themselves were unmerciful (Matt., ix. 11 sqq.), and the weak brethren at Corinth were scandalized at the eating of certain meats, because their consciences were tender (I Cor., xi. 23 sqq.).

1465. Sinfulness of Scandal.—(a) Scandal in the wide sense is not necessarily a sin. Thus, St. Peter acted out of love for his Master when he wished to dissuade Him from the Passion, but our Lord, in order to correct more vigorously the wrong ideas of Peter, called them a scandal (Matt., xvi. 23).

(b) Passive scandal is always a sin in the one who falls because of the conduct of another; but it does not always suppose that the conduct which occasioned the fall was a sin, as is clear from the remarks made above on Pharisaic scandal and the scandal of little ones.

(c) Active scandal is always a sin in the one whose conduct occasions the fall of another, since that conduct is either sinful, or has such an appearance of sin that it should have been omitted. But it does not always suppose a sin in the person who witnesses the scandal, for he may proceed without a fall in spite of the obstacle placed in his path.

1466. Is scandal a distinct species of sin, or only a circumstance that may happen to any kind of sin?

(a) Passive scandal is not a special kind of sin. For the scandalized person may fall into any and every kind of sin, and the fact that example occasions his fall does not add any special or new opposition to the virtue against which he offends. Thus, he who breaks the fast because he saw others break the fast, is guilty of the same sin of intemperance as those who gave him scandal. But passive scandal may be an aggravating or an extenuating circumstance, aggravating if the scandal was taken, extenuating if the scandal was given.

(b) Active scandal, if it is only indirectly intentional (see 1450) and is offered by conduct evil in itself, is not a special sin. The reason is that in such scandal one does not specially intend the spiritual ruin of a neighbor, but only the satisfaction of one's own desire. Thus, he who breaks the fast before others to satisfy his own appetite, does not directly wish the corruption of those others, and hence his sin is that of intemperance with the added circumstance of bad example.

(c) Active scandal, if it is only indirectly intentional and is offered by conduct not evil but evil-appearing, is reductively the special sin of scandal, For, since all active scandal is sinful, and in this case there is no other species of sin, the conduct not being really evil initself, the sin in question must be reduced to scandal. Thus, one who is dispensed from the law of abstinence and who eats meat on a day of abstinence in the

presence of others who know he is a Catholic but do not know he is
dispensed, does not sin against temperance, but against edification. His
sin is that of scandal only reductively, since he does not directly will the
fall of others. There is also the circumstance that the law of abstinence
may suffer as a result of the scandal.

(d) Active scandal, if it is directly intentional (see 1450), is directly also
the special sin of scandal. For this kind of scandal directly intends the
spiritual ruin of a neighbor, and so is directly opposed to a special good
of another person and to the special charitable act of fraternal
correction. Hence, a person who breaks the fast in order to lead his
neighbor into a like transgression is guilty of both intemperance and
scandal; he who to make his neighbor sin appears to break the fast, is
guilty of scandal, but not of intemperance.

1467. Practical Applications of the Preceding Paragraph to
Confession.—(a) Species of Sins.—In case of passive scandal there is
only one species of sin to be confessed, namely, the intemperance
occasioned by bad example; in case of active scandal indirectly intended
and offered by evil conduct, there is only one species of sin, namely,
intemperance, with the circumstance of publicity or bad example; in
case of active scandal indirectly intended and offered by evil-seeming
conduct, there is only one species of sin, namely, scandal; in case of
active scandal directly intended, there is only the species of scandal, if
the conduct of the scandalizer is only evil-seeming, but there are several
species of sin, if his conduct is really evil, namely, his own intemperance
and the scandal he gives.

(b) Number of Sins.—As many sins of scandal are committed as there
are persons present to be scandalized, for scandal is given to those
present as individuals, not as parts of a group (see 219). Hence, one
commits more scandals by being drunk on a public street than by being
drunk with a roomful of companions; and by attacking religion before a
large assembly than by attacking it before a small circle.

(c) Circumstances of Intention and Conduct.—Those who give bad
example should confess especially the end and the means employed, for
on these depends the important distinction between directly intentional

and indirectly intentional scandal and the specific character of the sin committed, as explained in the preceding paragraph.

(d) Circumstance of Condition of the Persons Involved.—This should be mentioned in confessing scandal, if it adds a new malice. Thus, the fact that scandal is given by a superior bound by his office to give good example, adds to the violation of charity a violation of justice; the fact that the person whose ruin is intended is consecrated to God, or married, or a relative, adds to the malice of intentional scandal against chastity; the fact that a person is scandalized entirely against his will, makes the sin scandal rather than simple solicitation.

(e) Circumstance of the Result of Scandal.—The results of scandal should be confessed when they add a new malice to the sin or induce an obligation of restitution. This subject will be considered in the three following paragraphs.

1468. Is the scandalizer guilty of the species of sin to which his conduct is calculated to lead the scandalized? (a) If the scandal is directly intentional, that is, if the scandalizer intends that some special sin or sins shall be committed by the one scandalized, the former is guilty in desire of that which he intends that the latter shall be guilty of in reality (cfr. 96, 102). Hence, if by calumniating clerics or religious or church members one intends that one's listeners shall be induced to repeat these calumnies, or to do what the calumniated persons were said to do, or to abandon religion, one is guilty in desire of the particular sin or sins that one wills.

(b) If the scandal is only indirectly intentional, that is, if the scandalizer foresees but does not expressly will the fall of the scandalized (e.g., if he calumniates others to injure the calumniated and not those who hear the calumny), the matter is more difficult, and authorities differ in their opinions. Some moralists think that the scandalizer is guilty of the result he foresees, because he wills it interpretatively by offering the occasion for it. Others think that he is not guilty of the result foreseen, because he does not effect it, either in intention (for he does not desire it) or in reality (for he is not bound, except by charity, to prevent its accomplishment in others); he permits, but does not approve, the sin of his neighbor.

1469. A practical application of the previous paragraph to confession may be made as follows: (a) those who are guilty of direct scandal must confess not only their own sin, but also the sin to which their conduct leads their neighbor; (b) those who are guilty of indirect scandal are not obliged, according to the second opinion given above, to confess the species of sin to which their conduct incited the beholder, and hence, if their conduct was only evil-seeming, it suffices for them to confess that they gave scandal.

1470. Is the scandalizer responsible for the injuries to third parties resulting from the sins occasioned by his scandal?

(a) According to one opinion, he is bound to make his share of restitution for injustices occasioned by his own bad example, because it is admitted that he who counsels injustice is so bound, and example is more persuasive than words of counsel. Hence, one who steals from his employer before fellow-employees, and so brings on a custom of stealing among them, is bound to restore, not only what he took himself, but also a share of other losses not made good to the employer.

(b) According to the more common opinion, however, the scandalizer in the present case is not held to restitution, except as regards his own ill-gotten goods, even if there is question of scandal directly intended. For, either the scandalizer is not guilty of the injustice committed by the others, as not desiring it; or, at any rate, he is only the occasion, not the cause or coöperator in that injustice.

1471. If scandal amounts to incitation or coöperation, the guilt of the neighbor's sin and responsibility for injury the neighbor causes are incurred by the scandalizer.

(a) Thus, bad example may amount to incitation to sin, as when a person knows that others are directed to imitate him, and yet he gives them bad example. Even though he does not directly intend their fall into sin, he does intend his own conduct, while realizing that there is attached to it the circumstance that it is an invitation to sin; and hence it would seem that the guilt of this sin is also contracted.

(b) Bad example may amount to coöperation in sin, as when a person by his bad example shows others the way to commit sin, which they could not have learned without his example. Hence, if a person opens a safe to steal, knowing that other dishonest persons are observing in order to learn the combination and steal, it seems that to some extent he shares in the guilt and duty of restitution of the thieves who learn from him. There is no doubt that a defamer is bound to make reparation, not only before his immediate listeners, but also before others who have listened to them; for, by defaming before talkative persons, he virtually authorized them to spread his words.

1472. The Gravity of the Sin of Scandal.—(a) From its nature all active scandal is a mortal sin. It turns man away from Christ (I Cor., viii. 12); it is spiritual murder, destructive of the souls of others, and so contrary to the mercy and brotherly correction required by charity (Rom, xiv. 15); it brings on oneself the wrath of God (Matt., xviii. 6), and on one's family, friends and profession obloquy and disgrace.

(b) From the indeliberation of the act or from the smallness of the matter, active scandal may be venial, as will be seen in the following paragraph.

1473. Mortal and Venial Scandal.—(a) Passive scandal is always a sin, mortal or venial according to the fall occasioned by the conduct witnessed. But mortal sin may be occasioned by venial sin, as when an inferior takes the liberty to blaspheme, because his superior used profane language; and venial sin may be occasioned by mortal sin, as when the blasphemy of an infidel provokes his neighbor to use profane language against the blasphemer.

(b) Active scandal indirectly intended is sometimes a venial sin, as when the scandalous conduct is only a venial sin, or is no sin but has the appearance of a slight sin; sometimes it is a mortal sin, as when the scandalous conduct is a mortal sin, or when a person so despises the spiritual welfare of his neighbor that he chooses to do an evil-seeming act that will cause the neighbor to fall into serious sin.

(c) Active scandal directly intended is sometimes a venial sin, as when a person intends by conduct venially sinful to lead a neighbor into venial sin; sometimes it is a mortal sin, as when one intends to lead one's neighbor into mortal sin, or commits a mortal sin in order to lead one's neighbor into venial sin.

1474. Increase and decrease in gravity of scandal depends on the internal dispositions of the scandal-giver and the external influence he has on the person scandalized. (a) The internal factors on which the quantity of scandal depends are the amount of deliberation and the degree of intention. It is more serious to speak a scandalous word with premeditation than to speak it somewhat thoughtlessly; more scandalous to speak it when the hearer's spiritual ruin is directly intended, than when that ruin is not directly intended. (b) The external factors on which the quantity of scandal depends are the amount of influence the bad example has and the character of the evil to which it leads. It is more serious to corrupt A, who would not otherwise have been corrupted, than to corrupt B, who would have been corrupted even without one's bad example; it is more serious to cause another to commit mortal sin, than to cause him to commit venial sin.

1475. Persons Scandalized.—Is it possible to scandalize people who are firmly rooted in virtue?

(a) If the question be understood of scandal in a wide sense, even the perfect may be scandalized. They may be shocked and horrified at the evil example they witness; they may be hindered from performing the external good works they desire to accomplish (I Thess., ii. 18). But these things do not hinder them internally, or separate them from the love of God (Rom., viii. 38, 39).

(b) If the question be understood of possibility in an absolute sense, even the perfect may suffer real scandal, that is, they may be influenced to sin on account of the example witnessed. Since they are not confirmed in grace in this life, it is not repugnant that they commit sin and lose grace.

(c) If the question be understood of possibility in a relative sense—that is, if we consider what we should expect in view of the character of perfect men, and what does usually happen—the perfect cannot be scandalized, since they are so firmly united to God that the sayings or doings, no matter of whom, cannot cause them to sin (Ps. cxxiv. 1, 2), although they may at times be disturbed thereby (Ps. lxxii. 2).

1476. Is it possible that the perfect should give scandal?

(a) If the question be understood of absolute possibility, even the perfect may give scandal, since they are not immune from defect (I John, i. 8). (b) If the question be understood of relative possibility, as explained above, the perfect cannot scandalize, for their sins are mostly internal acts not entirely deliberate, while the external words or acts in which they fall short deviate so slightly from right as to offer no occasion of sinning to another. The perfect man is one who is on his guard, especially that he become not a stumbling-block to others, and it is therefore a rare exception when he causes scandal.

1477. Duty of Avoiding Scandal.—At times it is impossible to avoid giving scandal, unless one surrenders some spiritual or temporal good. Hence, on this point there are two questions to be considered: (a) When is one obliged to surrender spiritual goods for the sake of avoiding scandal? (b) When is one obliged to surrender temporal goods for the sake of avoiding scandal?

1478. The Surrender of Spiritual Goods in order to Avoid Scandal.—(a) Spiritual goods that are so necessary that one cannot give them up without committing sin may not be surrendered; for, according to the order of charity, one must be more solicitous to keep oneself from sin than to preserve others, and moreover a good end does not justify sinful means. Hence, it is not lawful to commit mortal or even venial sin to avoid giving scandal to another. Examples: One may not tone down the doctrine of right and wrong in order to keep another from blasphemy. One may not tell a slight lie to keep another from taking undeserved offense.

(b) Spiritual goods which can be put aside without sin are not to be neglected on account of malicious or Pharisaic scandal, as long as there is a good reason which calls for their use; for the person who takes malicious scandal from these spiritual things is in difficulty through his own fault and can rescue himself, and it is not reasonable that his malice should be permitted to impede the benefit of others. Thus, our Lord declared that no attention was to be given the scandal which the Pharisees took from His doctrine (Matt., xv. 14).

(c) Spiritual goods which can be put aside without sin should be neglected on account of Pharisaic scandal, if there is no great reason for their use; for one should not give another an occasion of sinning, even if the other is in bad faith, unless there is necessity. Thus, our Lord declared that the act of teaching truth to others should be omitted, if it would only provoke rejection (Matt, vii. 6). Example: A wife may omit saying grace aloud, if her prayer moves her husband to mimicry or to attempts to make the prayer a mockery.

(d) Spiritual goods which can be put aside without sin should be omitted on account of the scandal of little ones, as long as it remains scandal from weakness or ignorance; for charity requires that one assist those who are in spiritual need, and persons who are in danger of scandal through no fault, or through a slight fault of their own, are in spiritual need. Hence, one should conceal or delay the performance of good works that are not necessary, if they would scandalize the weak, or else one should explain to these persons the righteousness of such works. In any case, one should not do these works before those who without malice will be scandalized, but should await such a time as will give them better knowledge, or put them in bad faith. Examples: If a person knows that personal acts of piety which he performs seem to some well-meaning persons superstitious and will shake their faith, he should omit these acts when such persons are present. If parents are scandalized because a child wishes to leave them in order to become a priest or a religious, the child should delay for a while, if there is hope of a change of view on their part.

1479. As was said in the chapter on law (see 288 sqq.), the higher law has the preference in case of a conflict. Now, natural law itself requires that one avoid the scandal of the weak. Hence the following cases:

(a) Negative precepts of the natural law may not be contravened in order to avoid the scandal of the weak; for such contravention is necessarily sinful. Hence, one may not lie or commit perjury to prevent scandal.

(b) Affirmative precepts of the natural law should be contravened in order to avoid the scandal of the weak, but only when such scandal is a greater evil than the omission of the thing commanded. Thus, one should omit a fraternal correction or a punishment, if the one corrected would be made worse, or the punishment occasion a schism. But one may not neglect to help a person in extreme need because of scandal.

(c) Precepts of the divine law should be contravened on account of scandal of the weak, unless contravention of the law is a greater evil than permission of the scandal. Thus, the preaching of the Gospel is commanded by divine law, and yet it may be omitted to avoid scandal (Matt., vii. 6). Item integritas confessionis de jure divino est, et tamen poenitens deberet peccatum silere, si intelligeret confessarium cui ex necessitate confiteri deberet grave ex eo scandalum passurum. But it is not lawful to omit Baptism in order to avoid scandal to those who will be provoked to anger or blasphemy.

(d) Precepts of ecclesiastical law should be contravened, when otherwise there will arise a scandal of the weak which is a graver evil than the contravention of the precepts. Thus, a parish-priest should say Mass on Sunday, even though not fasting, if this is necessary in order to avoid great scandal among the people. A wife may omit Mass or a fast, in order to prevent her ignorant husband from using blasphemies or imprecations, or to avoid notable dissensions in the home. Puella quae scit juvenem infirmum ex suo aspectu scandalizari debet sacro omisso domi manere.

1480. In order that scandal of the weak may be considered a greater evil than contravention of a grave precept, it is necessary that the following conditions be verified:

(a) The evil of the scandal must be certain and grave, for an uncertain or slight scandal is not a greater evil than certain contravention of a grave precept. Thus, if one only has vague fears that scandal may be given, or if one has no determined person in mind and thinks only that someone or other will be harmed, there is no excuse for contravention of the precept.

(b) The evil of contravening the precept must not impose intolerable hardships or lead to greater scandals; for one is not required to attempt the impossible, or to give scandal in order to avoid scandal. Thus, it would be unreasonable to expect that a student should never read the classical poets or philosophers of Greece or Rome, lest scandal be given some person overstrict in this matter; that a wife absent herself from Mass permanently, lest her ignorant husband be provoked to rage; that a young lady be deprived of fresh air and exercise, lest an old relative be disedified. If we have to choose between occasioning irreligion in one person by attending Mass and occasioning irreligion in many persons by staying away from Mass, we should rather permit the scandal of the one. Moralists generally hold that scandal of the weak does not justify absence from obligatory Mass oftener than once or twice, and some hold that it does not require absence from Mass at all.

1481. Good works that are of counsel only (such as evangelical poverty), and those that are obligatory only under certain conditions (such as almsdeeds), may be more easily put aside in order to avoid scandal of the weak. It should be noted, however, that for some persons these works are of precept, and hence they are to be judged, as regards those persons, according to the rules given for contravention of precepts. (a) Thus, the counsels are obligatory for those who have vowed them (e.g., religious).

(b) Corporal and spiritual works of mercy are obligatory for prelates and other clerics because of their office.

1482. Spiritual goods, therefore, whether of precept or of counsel, are not to be surrendered entirely on account of any scandal, whether it be Pharisaic scandal or scandal of the weak. But, out of charity for others, these goods should not be made use of (apart from necessity) in a way that would occasion spiritual ruin to anyone. Hence, if there is danger of scandal: (a) they should be concealed, as when one goes to Mass early in the morning or by another way, so as not to occasion blasphemy in one's neighbor; (b) they should be delayed, as when one puts off a fraternal correction until the other person is in a frame of mind to be corrected with profit; (c) they may be used but should be explained, as when one is called to give Baptism to a person dying in a notorious resort and takes witnesses with him, or tells the bystanders the reason of his visit.

1483. When Should Temporal Goods be Surrendered for the Sake of Avoiding Scandal.—(a) Temporal goods of which one is not the owner, but only the custodian or administrator, may not be surrendered at will on account of scandal; for no one has the right to give away the property of others. Hence, rulers in Church or State may not arbitrarily surrender common property; guardians may not give up the property of their charges.

(b) Temporal goods of which one is owner should be surrendered on account of the scandal of little ones, unless a greater evil results from such surrender; for, as said above (see 1165 sqq.), one should be willing to suffer some detriment in temporal things to avert from one's neighbor detriment in spiritual things. Hence, one should abstain from a certain food, if one's eating of it will cause spiritual ruin to some innocent person (I Cor., viii. 13).

(c) Temporal goods are not to be surrendered on account of Pharisaic scandal; for this would be injurious to the common good, since it would encourage the wicked to despoil the conscientious, and it would also be injurious to the wicked themselves, since they would continue in sin by keeping what was not their own. Hence, one may demand money owed, even if the debtor is greedy and will use profane language.

1484. The surrender of temporal goods spoken of in the previous paragraph may be understood in a number of senses.

(a) It can be understood either of the act of giving another what is held by us and is our own property, or of the act of permitting another to keep that which is held by him but which belongs to us. Charity may call for either kind of surrender as a means to the avoidance of scandal. Example: Rather than have a bitter quarrel or lose a friendship over a few cents of change, it is better to let the other man keep what he owes you, or give him what you do not owe, if he is also in good faith.

(b) The surrender of temporal goods can also be understood either of the internal willingness to sacrifice temporal things for things spiritual, when necessity requires, or of the actual external sacrifice. Charity demands the internal willingness, but it does not always demand the actual sacrifice; for sometimes such a sacrifice would be harmful to the common welfare and the welfare of individuals. Thus, the saying of our Lord that we should not contend with a neighbor who wishes to take our coat, but should rather let him take our cloak as well (Matt., v. 40), and the saying of St. Paul that the Corinthians should prefer to suffer injury and fraud rather than have lawsuits against fellow-Christians (I Cor., vi. 7), are to be understood of a willingness to sacrifice temporal things in order to avoid scandal, when a greater good makes this necessary. But those texts do not mean that it is obligatory or advisable to make an actual sacrifice at other times.

(c) The surrender of temporal goods may be understood either of a giving over to others without protest or remonstrance, or of a yielding to them only after one has tried to prevent scandal without incurring temporal loss. Charity does not require, even when there is danger of scandal of the weak, that one should surrender one's goods without any effort to save them. Thus, if an ignorant Catholic is shocked because his priest asks for money to support the Church, the latter will do him a service by explaining the right the Church has to be supported and the duty of the members to contribute.

1485. Temporal goods may be understood here either of things of great value (e.g., necessaries of life) or of things of minor value (e.g., luxuries). (a) Thus, if scandal will place a neighbor in extreme spiritual need, even things of great value should be surrendered, if this is necessary to avoid scandal. (b) If scandal will not place him in extreme need, one is not obliged to surrender any except things of minor value (see 1165 sqq.). Thus, St. Paul does not ask that his converts give up all food in order to avoid scandalizing the weak, but only such food as they can get along without (Rom, xiv. 15; I Cor., viii. 13).

1486. Should church goods ever be surrendered in order to avoid scandal of the weak? (a) On the one hand, goods of the Church have a special sacredness, because they have been given and set apart for spiritual purposes and the common good of the Church. Hence, he would be an unfaithful steward who would devote them to merely temporal ends, such as the enrichment or exaltation of himself or of his friends, or who would alienate them without due authority. (b) On the other hand, the temporal goods of the Church are to serve spiritual ends, and the spiritual must not be subordinated to the temporal. Hence, one of the chief causes of scandal in the Church is the appearance of avarice in churchmen (even as regards goods that are not personal, but common), especially if they seem to put money before the salvation of the people. There are times, therefore, when to avoid scandal a prelate or priest ought to forego something really due the Church.

1487. Cases of Scandal and Renouncement of Church Goods.—(a) If there is question of Pharisaic scandal alone, one should not renounce the goods of which one is the custodian, but should resist spoliation as far as one is able. Thus, St. Thomas of Canterbury would not agree to the invasion of church rights by Henry II. So also a pastor should not neglect the collection of dues needed for the maintenance of the church, because some malcontents will take offense at this; neither should he yield to the extortionate demands of some hired person who will be scandalized because more is not paid.

(b) If there is question of the scandal of the weak, concessions should be made, lest spiritual things be made to suffer for the temporal. Thus, St. Paul would not accept any support for himself from persons newly converted to Christianity, lest this prove a hindrance to the preaching of the Gospel (I Cor., ix. 12). For the sake of the ignorant or the weak, therefore, the Church does not insist on dues and other payments, until these persons have had the opportunity of learning their duty. The faithful, indeed, are bound to contribute to the pastors who serve them, but the precept is an affirmative one, and obliges therefore not at all times, but when the conditions of time, place, person, etc., make this possible. It would be a real scandal of the weak, if a person were driven from church because he did not realize his duty of contributing, or if a poor person were taxed beyond his means, or if an affluent cleric were always asking for money and never giving to the needy, or if a priest were to talk collections instead of doctrine, or devoted most of his time to money-making enterprises. Anything that commercializes religion is also a scandal both to Catholics and non-Catholics.

1488. Duty of Repairing Scandal.-The paragraphs immediately preceding have spoken of the duty of avoiding scandal. There is also a duty of repairing scandal that has been given. (a) Thus, there is a duty of charity to repair the scandal one has given; for, if all are required to practise fraternal correction, those especially are bound to this who are responsible for the sins of others. (b) There is sometimes a duty of legal justice, as when superiors, who are bound from their office to give good example, give scandal to their subjects. (c) There is sometimes a duty of commutative justice, as when the scandalizer has employed unjust means (such as force, fear or traps) in order to lead another into scandal.

1489. Ways of Repairing Scandal.—(a) Scandal is repaired publicly or privately. Reparation is public, when it is made before the community, and private, when it is made before individuals. (b) Scandal is repaired explicitly or implicitly. Explicit reparation is made by retractation of one's words, by condemnation of one's acts, by the destruction of one's scandalous writings, by efforts to bring back to virtue those whom one has misled, etc. Implicit reparation is made by reformation of one's conduct, the abandonment of that which gave scandal, the practice of good example, prayer for the person scandalized, etc.

1490. Particular Kinds of Scandal to be Repaired.—(a) Scandal is public or private. Public scandal is given before the community at large, as when one openly apostatizes so that it is the talk of the whole neighborhood or town, or writes a signed article favoring atheism, or makes a disedifying speech before a gathering of people. Scandal is private, when it is given before a few persons, and when it does not tend to become generally known, as when husband and wife quarrel before their domestic circle.

(b) Scandal is ordinary or extraordinary. Ordinary scandal is given by bad example alone; extraordinary scandal adds to bad example injury or injustice, or the debt of punishment for a crime. Thus, one who becomes slightly intoxicated at a party gives ordinary scandal; while one who by trickery schemes to get another into a situation in which he will be effectually scandalized, or who strikes an inoffensive priest, or who spreads disedifying printed matter, is guilty of extraordinary scandal.

1491. It rests with the prudent judgment of the confessor or ecclesiastical authority to decide in particular instances the way in which scandals are to be repaired. But in general the following rules may be given:

(a) Public scandal should be repaired publicly, even though it has not actually seduced those who are aware of it; for otherwise the evil influence remains. Thus, a drunkard should take the pledge of total abstinence, or else give an example of sobriety; an apostate should renounce his errors as openly as he defended them.

(b) Private scandal may be repaired privately, that is, before the few persons who were scandalized. Thus, the husband and wife who quarrelled before their children make reparation when they tell the children not to quarrel, and when they strengthen this advice by good example.

(c) Ordinary scandal may be repaired implicitly, that is, by turning over a new leaf. Thus, one who has been away from Mass and the Sacraments for a long time makes reparation when he appears at church, goes to confession, and receives Communion; one who has been keeping bad company makes reparation when he separates from his former associates.

(d) Extraordinary scandal is repaired explicitly, that is, by making the restitution or satisfaction which justice demands, or by performing the penalty required by the law. Thus, if through treachery a person has seduced another from virtue, he must either himself or through others endeavor to recall the scandalized person to his former virtue; if a person has been guilty of laying violent hands on a cleric, he must perform the penance prescribed; if a person has distributed scandalous literature, he must try to stop its circulation, or to distribute contrary literature.

1492. When satisfaction requires public apology or retraction, this can be made in various ways. (a) Thus, one may withdraw through the press false statements publicly made; (b) one may apologize before a number of witnesses authorized to make this known; (c) one may retract before the pastor or confessor, with the understanding that the priest will later declare that all due satisfaction has been made.

1493. Denial of Sacraments in Cases of Scandal.—Is it lawful to administer the Sacraments to one who has not made satisfaction for public scandal?

(a) If the obligation of reparation is not grave, it is lawful to administer the Sacraments, since the person who gave the scandal is not subject to grave sin and unworthy of the Sacraments, and his admission to them will not be a new scandal.

(b) If the obligation of reparation is grave, it is lawful to admit the party in question to the Sacrament of Penance; for every person rightly disposed has a right to absolution, and the fact that a person who gave scandal goes to confession is edifying. But absolution should be given on condition that reparation for the scandal is seriously promised.

(c) If the obligation of reparation is grave, it is not lawful as a rule to admit to the other Sacraments, until the reparation has been actually performed. Thus, if it is notorious in a parish that a certain individual has been living in a serious occasion of sin or has been circulating impious doctrines, the occasion of sin should be removed or the doctrines should be retracted, before the individual is admitted to Communion, etc.; otherwise, a new scandal would be given the faithful from the apparent approval given the scandalizer by the minister of the Sacrament received.

1494. In certain cases, however, the Sacraments other than Penance may also be given before reparation for grave scandal has been made, namely, when the circumstances are such that the administration of the Sacraments will offer no scandal. (a) Thus, a dying person who is penitent but unable to perform some satisfaction for scandal given is granted the Sacraments. (b) A person who is well disposed, but who has not yet made satisfaction for scandal, may sometimes be given Communion privately. (c) A person who is not well disposed, and who will not make satisfaction for scandal, is sometimes permitted to contract marriage before the priest, namely, when there is a grave reason for marriage and scandal is precluded.

1495. Seduction.—Having discussed scandal, which leads others into sin by bad example, we shall now consider, first, solicitation or seduction, which leads others into sin by moral inducement, and, secondly, coöperation, which assists another to sin (see 1460).

1496. Seduction is some external act (words, writing, signs or gesture) by which one directly and explicitly seeks to win the consent of another to sin. There are various modes of solicitation.

(a) There is command to sin, which is an authoritative direction to commit sin imposed by a superior on his subject. Command is given expressly, as when a father tells his son to steal; or implicitly, as when he tells his son that it will please him if the son steals.

(b) There is counsel to sin, which is direct persuasion to do evil made through argument that sin is lawful, or through instruction on the ways of committing sin, or through advice, request, promises, threats, etc., as when one writes in praise of suicide to a person who is very discouraged, and recommends it.

(c) There is enticement which is an indirect persuasion to sin made through flattery, insinuation, calumny, narratives, etc. Thus, Absalom worked on the people of Israel and beguiled them into rebellion against his father (II Kings, xv. 1-6). Those who ridicule temperance and so lead others to drink excessively, entice to drunkenness. A host who offers little except fine meats on a Friday entices to the violation of abstinence.

1497. The Malice of Solicitation.—(a) The gravity of this sin according to its nature is mortal, but it may be venial on account of imperfect deliberation or smallness of matter (see 1473). Thus, it is a mortal sin to command one's son to commit grand larceny or perjury, a venial sin to command him to commit petty theft or tell a harmless lie. (b) The circumstances of the sin that aggravate or extenuate are the greater or less degree of deliberation and malice, the greater or less evil of the sin to which one induces one's neighbors, etc. (see 1473, 1474). (c) The species of the sin of solicitation is twofold; there is the sin of scandal, opposed to charity, inasmuch as a neighbor is led to sin, and there is also the sin which one persuades a neighbor to commit (see 1468 sqq.).

1498. Applications to Confession and Satisfaction.—(a) Since the seducer willed the species of sin to which he induced his neighbor, it does not suffice that he tell in confession that he induced another to sin; he must also tell the species of sin (e.g., theft), to which he induced or attempted to induce another. (b) Since the seducer is guilty of injustice against the person seduced, if he employed fraud, traps, violence, etc., it does not suffice in such cases merely to confess that he seduced; he must also tell that he used unjust means to seduce. (c) Since the seducer is guilty of spiritual damage, he is bound to make reparation for scandal given (see 1488 sqq.). (d) Since the seducer is responsible for temporal damages that are due to his influence (e.g., when he commands A to steal from or calumniate B), he is held to restitution for any such damages (see Vol. II on Justice).

1499. In confessing a sin whose nature implies an accomplice (e.g., obscene conversation), is it necessary to mention the circumstance that one seduced the other party? (a) If the seduction includes a special malice against charity or against justice, it should be mentioned. Thus, if the party seduced had been innocent and was scandalized, or was trapped into sin, the fact of seduction should be mentioned. (b) If the seduction includes no special malice against charity or justice, it seems there is no obligation to mention it. Thus, if the party solicited had been living a life of sin and consented to the solicitation without any detriment to ideals or any unwillingness, no scandal is given and no injustice committed by the solicitation, as far as that party is concerned, and there seems to be no reason why the circumstance of seduction must be confessed.

1500. Seduction is incitement to sin, and so differs from mere permission of sin in another. It is never lawful to incite to sin, but it is lawful for a sufficient reason to permit sin in others, as was said above in reference to Pharisaic scandal (see 1477, 1482, 1483). But, in applying this principle to concrete cases, it is sometimes difficult to draw the line between incitement and mere permission. We shall discuss now the following cases in which this difficulty occurs: (a) when one requests another to do something which one knows will be a sin for him; (b) when one advises another to commit a less rather than a greater evil; (e) when the opportunity for another to commit sin is not removed, or is prepared.

1501. Is it lawful to ask another to do something, when one knows that he will not consent without sinning?

(a) If the thing requested is sinful in itself, the request is also sinful. Hence, it is not lawful to ask a thief to sell the goods he has stolen, nor is it lawful to request absolution from a priest who lacks jurisdiction.

(b) If the thing requested is lawful in itself, but there is no sufficient reason for the request in view of the fact that the other will sin by granting it, the request is sinful. Hence, it is not lawful to ask baptism from a person who is in the state of sin, when one can easily obtain it from another person who is in the state of grace.

(c) If the thing requested is lawful, and there is a sufficient reason for the request, one does not sin by making the request. Hence, it is lawful for the sake of the common welfare to require that witnesses take an oath, even though one knows that one of them will commit perjury.

1502. Is it lawful to advise another to commit a less evil in preference to a greater evil?

(a) If the other has not made up his mind to commit either evil, it is not lawful to advise that he do either. Thus, to counsel another to steal, and to make his victims the rich rather than the poor, is a species of seduction.

(b) If the person has made up his mind to commit the greater evil and the lesser evil is virtually contained in the greater, it is lawful to advise that he omit the former for the latter. For in thus acting one prevents the greater evil and does not cause the lesser evil, since it is virtually contained in the greater evil which the other person had already decided on. Thus, if Titus is bent on stealing $100, Balbus is not guilty of seduction, if he persuades Titus to take only $10. We are supposing, of course, that Titus is so determined to steal that it is out of the question to deter him from taking at least a small amount.

(c) If the person in question has decided on the greater sin and the lesser is not virtually contained in the greater, it is not lawful to recommend that he commit the smaller instead of the greater sin. For, if one does this, one does not save the other from the internal guilt of the greater sin intended, while one does add the malice of the lesser sin which was not intended. Thus, if Titus plans to kill Caius, it is not lawful to advise that he rob him instead, or that he kill Claudius instead, for robbery is a specifically distinct sin from murder, and Claudius is a different person from Caius. But, if Titus planned to kill Caius in order to rob him, it would not be unlawful to point out that the robbery could be carried out without murder and to advise accordingly.

1503. Not all theologians accept the last solution just given. (a) Some reject it, and hold that, even when the lesser evil is not virtually contained in the greater, it is lawful to advise the lesser. They argue that what one does thereby is not to commit the lesser evil, to induce it or approve it, but only to permit it in order to lessen the harm that will be done, and they confirm their argument from scripture (Gen., xix. 8). According to this opinion, then, which has some good authorities in its favor, it would be lawful to advise robbery in order to dissuade another from the greater evil of murder. (b) Others modify the solution given in the previous paragraph, and hold that it is lawful to propose the lesser evil or mention it, provided one does not attempt to induce the other person to carry it into effect.

1504. Is it lawful so to prearrange circumstances that an occasion of sin will seem to offer itself to another?

(a) If the end and the means used are good, this is lawful; for there is no scandal or seduction, but sin or the danger of sin is permitted for a proportionately grave reason. Examples: Sempronius knows that someone is robbing his desk, and it is important that he discover the thief. He leaves the desk open and watches from concealment to see whether a suspected person who is coming to the room will steal. Claudius is quite certain that Titus is stealing his chickens, but he needs evidence in order to have Titus convicted and deterred from future stealing. So, he leaves doors open and hides himself with witnesses that Titus may be caught in the act.

(b) If the end or means is bad, it is not lawful to prepare an opportunity for sin, because in either case one intends something sinful. Examples: Sempronius knows that his wife Titia has been unfaithful and he threatens to leave her. She, wishing to have a countercharge to make or to secure evidence to discredit his word, hires various dissolute females to lay traps for him and his friends. Claudius out of revenge wishes that Caius be sent to jail, and he therefore employs agents to provoke Caius into something criminal in word or deed that will justify incarceration. Balbus knows that Mercurius is a dangerous character, and he frames a scheme by which Mercurius will be invited to participate in an act of banditry and be captured. Titia and Claudius sin, because their purpose is wrong; Balbus sins because he uses wrong means. All three are guilty of seduction, at least in intention.

1505. Seduction was described above (see 1496) as an inducement to sin through such manifest means as command, counsel, or enticement. But there is also a more subtle form of seduction, which does not appeal directly to the intellect or will, but makes a physical approach by acting upon the body, senses, or imagination. This is a more cunning, but none the less guilty form of seduction, examples of which are the following:

(a) Seduction through bodily states is exemplified in those who minister secretly to others drinks or drugs or foods that will produce emotional disturbances or mental confusion and make them more susceptible to temptation.

(b) Seduction through the senses is exemplified in those who surround others with pictures, companions, music, examples, etc., that continually speak of the desirability of vice or the undesirability of virtue.

(c) Seduction through the imagination is seen in hypnotism or suggestion when used to produce a vivid and strong impression of something dangerous to be thought on. A spirit of bigoted uniformity which demands that all dress, think and act alike even in matters where there should be liberty, may also be very seductive; for, rather than commit the unpardonable sin of seeming queer, a person may take to drunkenness or whatever vice is popular in his crowd or group.

1506. Coöperation in Sin.—Coöperation or participation in sin, strictly understood, is help afforded another, whom one has not seduced, to carry out his purpose of sinning.

(a) Hence, coöperation differs from scandal and solicitation, for these lead into sin one who had not decided on sin, while coöperation supposes that the other party had already made up his mind to sin. The scandalizer leads into sin, but does not help in its commission; the coöperator does not lead into sin but he helps in its commission.

(b) Coöperation, however, may include scandal and solicitation as regards future sins or as regards third parties. Example: Balbus, who had decided on his own initiative to steal, finds to his surprise that his conduct receives aid and comfort from Titus, a person of some authority. This coöperation will act as an example or incitement to Balbus to repeat the offense, and will likewise be an occasion of sin to others.

1507. Coöperation is also different from complicity as follows: (a) The coöperator acts as assistant or subordinate agent to the one who commits sin, providing him with moral or physical help, or supplying him with the means requisite for the act of sin. Thus, he whose services are commandeered by robbers and who carries away the stolen goods, or who puts a revolver into the hand of one bent on murder or obscene books into the hands of one bent on the corruption of youth, is a coöperator. (b) The accomplice acts as an equiprincipal or coordinate agent with another in the commission of the same sin, performing his own proper part or share of the joint act of sin. Thus, he who enlists as a member of a robber band and acts as their chauffeur or lookout at the time of "hold-ups," or who fights a duel, or who carries on an obscene dialogue, or listens willingly to obscene talk, is an accomplice. The accomplice is always guilty, but the coöperator may be guiltless.

1508. Kinds of Coöperation.—Divisions of Coöperation according to Different Kinds of Acts.—(a) From the viewpoint of the internal act, coöperation is either formal or material, according as one does or does not intend the sin whose external commission one is aiding. Examples: Caius offers a burglar information as to ways of climbing into a second-story window. Claudius, being covered by a revolver, makes no resistance or outcry while bandits are rifling his employer's office. Caius is an abettor of crime and a formal coöperator on account of his guilty intent; Claudius aids the commission of burglary, but he is only a material coöperator, since he does not intend what the criminals intend.

(b) From the viewpoint of the external act, coöperation is positive or negative, according as one does something to help the principal agent, or does nothing to impede him. In the examples given above, Caius was a positive, Claudius a negative coöperator. Positive coöperation is given in a moral manner, as when one votes for an unjust law or sentence, or cheers a sinful remark; or in a physical manner, as when one helps bandits to bind and gag their victims, or leaves doors and windows unfastened for the convenience of thieves.

1509. Divisions of Coöperation according to its Degree of Influence.— (a) From the viewpoint of its activity, coöperation is either occasional or effective. By occasional coöperation is understood that which leads another into sin, or allows him to be drawn into sin, but does not assist him to commit sin (e.g., scandalous example, failure to give a fraternal correction or admonition). By effective coöperation is understood assistance given another enabling him to carry out, or to carry out more easily, an act of sin on which he had resolved. As is clear from the explanation given above (see 1506), there is question here only of effective coöperation.

(b) From the viewpoint of its nearness to the act of the principal agent, coöperation is either immediate or mediate, according as one shares in the sinful act of the principal agent, or in some act that preceded or followed it. Thus, he who helps a thief to carry away stolen goods is an immediate coöperator, while he who supplied the thief with necessary keys before the theft, and he who offered refuge to the thief or concealment for the stolen goods after the theft, are mediate coöperators.

(c) From the viewpoint of the dependence on it of what is done, coöperation is either indispensable or not indispensable, according as the principal agent cannot act without it, or can. Example: Balbus supplies intoxicants to Titus and Sempronius, who are intemperate. Titus cannot secure intoxicants except from Balbus; Sempronius can secure them elsewhere. Balbus' coöperation is indispensable for Titus, but not for Sempronius.

1510. Coöperation is also divided from the viewpoint of responsibility or of the consequences incurred through it, into unjust coöperation and merely unlawful coöperation.

(a) Unjust coöperation is participation in the guilt of an injury done to a third party which involves the duty of restitution or strict reparation. Thus, those who act as "fences" or receivers of stolen goods, coöperate in injustice and are bound to restitution to the rightful owners.

(b) Unlawful coöperation is participation in a sin that contains no injustice to a third party, and that entails only the obligations of repentance and satisfaction, and, if the case requires it, of amends for scandal, proofs of sincerity, avoidance of dangers and submission to penalty. Thus, those who coöperate by marrying illegally, or by providing obscene literature to persons who demand it and insist on having it, are guilty of sin and also fall under various punishments prescribed in law. Coöperation, in so far as it is unjust, will be treated specially under the head of Justice (see Vol. II); here we are concerned with coöperation in general, and as it is a sin against charity.

1511. Formal coöperation is either explicit or implicit. (a) It is explicit, when the end intended by the coöperator (*finis operantis*) is the sin of the principal agent. Examples: Balbus gives incense money to an idolater, because he approves of idolatry and wishes to see idolatrous rites performed. Caius joins an anarchistic society because he agrees with its aims and wishes to help in their fulfillment.

(b) Formal coöperation is implicit, when the coöperator does not directly intend to associate himself with the sin of the principal agent, but the end of the external act (*finis operis*), which for the sake of some advantage or interest the coöperator docs intend, includes from its nature or from circumstances the guilt of the sin of the principal agent. Examples: Balbus detests idolatry, but in order to show courtesy he helps a pagan to burn incense before an idol, or he assists in the repairing of a pagan shrine, though his act is looked on as a sign of worship. Caius joins a freethinking society, not because he likes its principles, but because he wishes to obtain through membership certain social or financial advantages which he cannot obtain in any other way.

1512. Mediate coöperation is also subdivided into proximate and remote. (a) It is proximate or remote by reason of nearness, according as the act of sin will follow closely or otherwise on the act of coöperation. Thus, he who gives a ladder to a burglar coöperates in a remote preparation; he who holds the ladder while the burglar goes up coöperates in a proximate preparation. (b) Mediate coöperation is proximate or remote as to definiteness, according as the preparation points clearly or only vaguely to the commission of sin. Proximate coöperation is an action which, from its nature or circumstances, is regarded as morally connected with the evil action of the principal agent, while remote coöperation is an action that has no such moral connection with the sin that is committed. Thus, he who sells a revolver to a gunman who is preparing for a murder coöperates proximately, while he who sells the materials for this weapon coöperates only remotely. Again, if one sells to a burglar a "jimmy," a dark lantern, a mask, a revolver, and explosives, the coöperation is definite, since the circumstances indicate that robbery is contemplated. But if one sells a burglar a pair of soft-sounding shoes, the coöperation is indefinite, for the burglar may wish them in order to give no disturbance in his own home, and not in order to attract no attention in the homes of others.

1513. The Sinfulness of Coöperation.—The Sinfulness of Formal Coöperation.—(a) Formal coöperation is always sinful, for it includes the approval of the sin of another and the willing participation in the guilt of that sin.

(b) Formal coöperation is from its nature opposed to charity; for charity disapproves of the sins of others and strives to prevent them, while formal coöperation, on the contrary, approves and assists the sins of others.

(c) Formal coöperation is also opposed to the virtue violated by the sin of the principal agent, in so far as the will of the coöperator delights in or approves of the circumstance of help given to the sin of the other (see 1468). Thus, if one opens the door to a caller whom one suspects to be a burglar and at the same time mentally sympathizes with the act of burglary, one is guilty in will of the act one approves.

(d) Formal coöperation as to its external act is opposed to the virtue violated by the coöperator, when the external act has a malice of its own. Thus, if one swears falsely in order to conceal the presence of a burglar hidden in the house, one is guilty of perjury; if one disobeys the laws of the Church by marrying clandestinely, one is guilty of disobedience; if one scandalizes third parties by coöperating with sin, one is guilty of scandal; if one shares in fraud, one is guilty of injustice, etc. Hence, in confession it does not suffice to say that one has coöperated in sin, but one must also tell the sin committed and the necessary circumstances.

1514. The Sinfulness of Material Coöperation.—(a) Material coöperation, in itself, is sinful; for charity commands that one strive to prevent the sin of another, and much more therefore does it forbid one to help in the sin of another. (b) Material coöperation, in case of great necessity, is not sinful; for charity does not oblige under serious inconvenience to self, and it does not forbid one to coöperate by an indifferent act to prevent a neighbor from committing a greater evil than the evil he has in mind. He who coöperates materially through necessity does not cause sin, but uses his own right, which the bad will of the other abuses and makes an occasion of sin (see 1447 d).

1515. Lawfulness of Material Coöperation.—The conditions necessary in order that material coöperation be lawful are the same as for any other act that has a double result (see 104); for from the coöperation follow two results, one that is bad (viz., the sin of the other person) and one that is good (viz., the avoidance of loss or the retention of good). Two of the conditions required in the principle of double result need not be considered, however, since their presence is manifestly assured by the very fact that the coöperation is merely material. (a) Thus, the condition that the good effect must not be secured through the evil effect is verified; for, if one intends the sin of the other party as a means to the good end, coöperation is formal. Hence, if Balbus helps Claudius to get sinfully drunk, so that Claudius may go to confession the sooner, the coöperation of Balbus in the drunkenness of Claudius is formal. (b) The condition that the evil effect is not intended is also verified; for the very definition of material coöperation excludes the intention of the sin committed by the other party.

1516. Hence, we may confine our attention to the two remaining conditions stated in the principle of double effect, and conclude that material coöperation is lawful when and if the act of the coöperator is itself good or indifferent, and he has a reason sufficiently weighty for permitting the sin of the other party.

1517. The first condition of material coöperation is that the act of the coöperator must be good or at least indifferent; for, if it is evil, the coöperation becomes implicitly formal. But, since it is often difficult to determine in particular instances whether coöperation is intrinsically evil or merely indifferent, one must examine the nature and circumstances of the act.

(a) Thus, according to its nature, an act of coöperation is intrinsically evil, if it has no uses except such as are evil; it is indifferent, if, according to the intention of those who use it, it is now good, now evil. Hence, it is intrinsically wrong to assist in the manufacture or distribution of obscene books or pictures, or of drugs or instruments used exclusively for immoral purposes, since the only use to which such things can be put is sinful. It is also intrinsically wrong to take part even remotely in pagan superstitions, or to give any immediate assistance to an act which from its nature is opposed to the Sixth Commandment. But it is not intrinsically wrong to assist in the manufacture of firearms or poisons, which have many good uses, or to act as bodyguard to a person who fears harm from others.

(b) According to its circumstances, an act of coöperation is evil, if by reason of adjuncts it is wrong, as when it signifies approval of evil, gives scandal to others, endangers the faith or virtue of the coöperator, or violates a law of the Church. Thus, it is not from the nature of the act wrong to invite a pedestrian to ride in one's car; but it is wrong from the circumstances when the pedestrian asks to be taken to a spot where he intends to commit robbery. It is not wrong intrinsically to work at building a temple; but it is wrong from the circumstances, when this act is regarded by the public as a sign of adherence to a false religion, or when the act causes scandal (see 983). The laws of the Church on mixed marriage or neutral schools afford other examples of coöperation lawful in one set of circumstances, but unlawful in another on account of significance, scandal, danger, etc.

1518. But the circumstance that the coöperator knows for certain that the principal agent will use the coöperation for sinful purposes, or will take scandal to the extent of being strengthened in his evil designs by reason of the assistance given, does not necessarily make coöperation evil.

(a) Thus, the coöperator may know from the declaration of the principal agent just what is to be done, and yet have no will whatever to concur in the evil. Hence, if a person is forced at the point of a revolver to help in robbing his own guests, he knows very well what is being done, but he certainly does not approve of it.

(b) The coöperator may know that scandal will be occasioned by the coöperation, either to the principal agent or to others, but he may have sufficient reasons for permitting it (see 1478, 1482). Thus, if the employee of an undertaking establishment has orders to assist at the funeral of an anarchist, and will lose his means of livelihood if he does not comply, he is not obliged to suffer this great detriment to avoid Pharisaic scandal or even scandal of the weak. But he should, if possible, declare his want of sympathy with anarchy, if he knows of some anarchist present who regards his coöperation as a mark of sympathy for the principles of the deceased.

1519. The second condition for lawful material coöperation is that the coöperator should have a reason sufficiently weighty for permitting the evil connected with his coöperation. The standards for judging whether a reason is sufficiently weighty, are the rules given above onpermission of an evil effect (see 105).

(a) Hence, the graver the sin that will be committed, the graver the reason required for coöperation. Thus, a greater reason is required for coöperation in assault than for coöperation in theft.

(b) The nearer the coöperation is to the act of sin, the greater the reason required for coöperation. Thus, he who sells paper to the publisher of obscene books coöperates remotely; he who sets the type or reads the proofs of such books coöperates proximately. A greater reason is necessary for the latter than for the former coöperation.

(c) The greater the dependence of the evil act on one's coöperation, the greater the reason required for coöperation. Thus, a more serious reason is needed to justify giving intoxicants to a person who abuses liquors, if he is unable to procure them elsewhere, than if he can easily get them from others. But the fact that, if you deny intoxicants or other coöperation, another person will grant what you deny, is not of itself a sufficient reason for coöperation.

(d) The more certain the evil act, the greater the reason required for coöperation. Example: Titus gets drunk frequently, Balbus at intervals.

611

Hence, a greater reason is needed for providing liquor to Titus than to Balbus.

(e) The more obligation one is under to avoid the act of coöperation or to prevent the act of sin, the greater the reason must be for coöperation. Hence, a much greater reason is necessary for lawful coöperation by those who are bound *ex officio*, from piety or justice, to prevent a sin (such as parents, spiritual directors, and policemen) than on the part of those who are not so bound.

1520. Reasons for coöperation correspond in gravity with the importance of the goods or evils involved (see 1163 sqq.).

(a) Hence, a grave reason for coöperation exists when, if one refuses it, a great good will be lost or a great evil incurred. A day's wages or income is generally a great good; a severe or long-continued pain, great anger of an employer or other superior, things that bring on notable annoyance, shame, repugnance, etc., are examples of great evils.

(b) A very grave reason for coöperation is the gain or retention of a very great good or the avoidance of a very great evil. A notable percentage of the goods of one's station in life should be considered as a very great good. A severe and long-continued illness, unemployment on the part of the breadearner of a needy family, serious detriment to one's honor, reputation or peace of mind, etc., are examples of very great evils.

(c) Graver reasons for coöperation are those that surpass the very grave without being supreme, such as the loss of one's station in life, incurable disease, loss of an eye or other principal member, severe or perpetual imprisonment.

(d) Most grave reasons for coöperation are the public safety of Church or State, loss of all one's property, death, extreme disgrace, and the like.

1521. When the sin committed by the principal agent is grave, but contains no injustice to a third party, the reasons for coöperation need not be so serious as when the sin is grave and unjust.

(a) Thus, immediate and indispensable coöperation is justified in order to avoid grave loss to self; for example, one may ask absolution from an unworthy minister, in order to recover the state of grace more quickly.

(b) Immediate and not indispensable coöperation, or mediate and indispensable coöperation, is lawful when it is necessary in order to avoid a moderate loss. Examples: One may receive Communion from an unworthy minister in order to make the Easter duty more conveniently. One may supply intoxicants to a drunkard in order to avoid a brawl, if there is no time to call in the strong arm of the law to subdue the drunkard.

(c) Mediate and not indispensable coöperation is justified even by avoidance of a slight loss. Example: A butcher may sell meat on Friday to a cook who will serve it to some persons bound by abstinence, if the cook can easily get the meat from others and the profit will go elsewhere, unless the butcher sells her the meat.

1522. When the sin committed by the principal agent is a grave injustice to a private party, the reasons for coöperation need not be so serious as when the sin is against the public good.

(a) Thus, immediate and indispensable coöperation is permissible, if without it one cannot avoid a loss to self that is both certain and of a higher kind, or at least a greater one of the same kind than that which will be suffered by the injured party; for this latter would be unreasonable, if he expected one to suffer a greater loss in order to spare him. Example: Mercurius, a servant, is threatened with instant death if he does not open a safe of his employer, take from it certain papers, and deliver them to a burglar.

(b) Immediate and not indispensable coöperation, or mediate and indispensable coöperation, is allowed if necessary for the avoidance of an equal loss to self. Examples: The burglar mentioned above can blow open the safe if Mercurius refuses to open it, but, if he is put to this trouble, he will steal from Mercurius valuables comparable to the papers in the safe. Claudius, a servant, opens a backdoor, the only way through which a burglar can enter secretly, because he is taken by surprise, and refusal on his part will inevitably cost him the loss of papers equally as valuable as those the burglar wishes to secure.

Sempronius wishes to rob a house, but he cannot get there without the assistance of Caius, a chauffeur. Caius understands the purpose of Sempronius, but, if he refuses to take him to the house, Sempronius will give out information that will do almost as much harm to Caius as the robbery would do to the owner of the house.

(c) Mediate and not indispensable coöperation is justified by the avoidance of a loss to self less than the loss of the injured party, but in proportion to it, Example: Balbus is usually honest, but today he is going out to "fleece" a number of unsuspecting victims, and he gives orders to his servant Titus to get his coat and hat and open the door, and to his chauffeur Caius to drive him to the gambling place. Titus and Caius have an inkling of Balbus' plans, but no proofs. If they disobey his orders, other servants will do what Balbus asks, the swindling will not be stopped, but Titus will be demoted, and Caius thrown out of the position necessary for his livelihood.

1523. When the sin committed by the principal agent is against some good of a public character, though not against the common safety, still greater reasons are necessary for coöperation than those given above. (a) Thus, immediate and indispensable coöperation is allowed to avoid a greater public evil, or an equal public evil joined with grave loss to self; for it is lawful to permit a lesser in order to escape a greater evil. Thus, the law may tolerate certain evils for the sake of public tranquillity, if the attempt to suppress them would lead to serious disturbances. One may delay to denounce a practice that is doing harm to a family, if an immediate complaint would cause an equal harm to the family and bring on the maker of the complaint a serious evil.

(b) Immediate and not indispensable coöperation, or mediate and indispensable coöperation, is permitted when it is necessary to avoid an equal public evil, or a very serious personal evil proportionate according to prudent judgment to the public harm done. Thus, an actor who has a harmless part in a somewhat evil play may act it for a time, if the company can easily obtain substitutes but he cannot easily obtain other employment and needs his wages. Similarly, the owner of the only theatre in town may rent it to that company in order to be able to refuse it to another company that is worse.

(c) Mediate and not indispensable coöperation may be allowed when there is need of avoiding a grave loss to self which cannot be prevented except by coöperation. Thus, the ushers in the theatre who have no present way of supporting dependents except by the wages they are earning, may help patrons to seats, even when the play that is being shown is not morally unobjectionable.

1524. When the sin committed by another is directed against the necessary public welfare (i.e., against the common safety of Church or State), one may not coöperate, but should resist. In this case: (a) coöperation is unlawful, for there is no greater public good to justify it, and much less can it be justified by private good; (b) resistance should be made, if possible; for the individual should be willing to suffer loss, spoliation, and death itself to conserve the safety of the Church or of the State.

1525. In giving reasons sufficient for coöperation with sins injurious to the sinner alone or to some third party, we considered only the harm or loss to oneself that would result from a refusal to coöperate. But the good of others may also suffice for coöperation.

(a) Thus, the good of the sinner may justify one in coöperating, as when one assists in order to prevent the commission of a greater evil. It would not be wrong to give whisky to one who wished to make himself drunk, if otherwise he would take poisoned alcohol.

(b) The good of a third party may justify coöperation, as when one assists in perpetrating a minor injury against him in order to stop a major injury. It would not be wrong to bind and gag a man who was being robbed, if otherwise a burglar would murder him.

(c) The common good will often be a justifying reason. Thus, in political affairs it is at times necessary in indifferent matters to compromise with opponents, whose general policies one does not approve, in order to secure the election of good citizens or the passing of good laws, when these ends are very important for the general welfare. It is lawful to administer a Sacrament to one who is unworthy in order to avoid a public evil, such as disturbance or scandal among the people.

1526. Lawfulness of Immediate Coöperation.—(a) If one cannot coöperate immediately without performing an act that is intrinsically evil (see 1517), immediate coöperation is, of course, unlawful. Thus, if one helped a trembling assassin to administer poison or to stab or shoot to death the victim, one would be an accomplice in murder; if one assisted a decrepit pagan to burn incense before an idol, one would be an accomplice in false worship. (b) If one can coöperate immediately without performing an act intrinsically evil, immediate coöperation is held lawful by some authorities, but there are others who say that all immediate coöperation is sinful.

1527. Arguments for the Opposing Opinions on Immediate Coöperation.—(a) Those who deny the lawfulness of all immediate coöperation argue that immediate coöperation does not differ from complicity, and hence that it is always intrinsically wrong. If theft is the taking away of goods without the knowledge and consent of the owner, what shall we call the act of a servant who assists a thief by carrying out the family silver to a waiting automobile? The fact that the servant does this to save himself from wounds or death cannot change the moral character of the act, else we shall have to say that the end may justify the means. And what is said of theft, can be said likewise of other species of sin.

(b) Those who affirm the lawfulness of immediate coöperation in certain cases argue that circumstances may take away evil from an act of assistance given to a sinner, so that the act becomes indifferent or good. Thus, theft is the taking away of what belongs to another against the reasonable will of the owner. Now, the owner would be unreasonable if he were unwilling that one should coöperate in removing his goods, if one had to do so in order to protect one's life, at least if one had not engaged to defend his goods; for one is bound to protect one's life in preference to the goods of another. If a starving man may take a loaf of bread without the owner's consent, why may not one save one's life by assisting a desperate criminal to carry off money? Moreover, it is commonly admitted that a person in great need may lawfully ask a Sacrament from a minister who is unworthy and who will sin by conferring it; that is, one may coöperate immediately with the unworthy administration of a Sacrament and yet be free of guilt on account of the circumstances.

1528. Special Cases of Coöperation.—The cases of coöperation, like those involving scandal, are innumerable, but there are certain cases which occur today more frequently than others, namely, those of coöperation with evil publications, dances, and theatres, and those of the coöperation of merchants, innkeepers, renters, servants, and workingmen. Coöperation in sins against faith and sins against justice are treated in their proper places, but it will be useful here to speak of these other special kinds of coöperation, since they offer many difficulties and a consideration of them now will illustrate the general principles on coöperation just given. However, the following points should be noted:

(a) The application of the definitions and rules about coöperation to particular cases is one of the most difficult tasks of Moral Theology, and hence there will be found great diversity of opinion among theologians on particular points. Space forbids a discussion here of the opposing opinions, and we shall have to content ourselves, in some of the illustrations that follow, with solutions that are likely, but whose opposites are also likely.

(b) The cases that follow are treated according to the principles of coöperation. But frequently in actual life there will be other factors to be considered, such as the occasion of sin to oneself or scandal to others. It should be remembered, then, that when a particular kind of material coöperation is here said to be lawful, this must he understood as abstractly speaking; for in an individual instance there may be circumstances of danger or disedification which would make it unlawful—a thing that often happens.

1529. Formal Coöperation with Evil Reading Matter.—(a) Cases of formal coöperation on account of explicit intention to do harm are those of the managers, editors, ordinary collaborators and authors of periodicals, newspapers, books, etc., which are opposed *ex professo* to faith and good morals; for these persons are the brains which direct and select what is to be written and published, and the matter they are creating or putting on paper is evil, and has no direct purpose except evil.

(b) Cases of formal coöperation on account of implicit intention to do harm are those of the responsible heads of printing or publishing firms and their printers, who agree to publish such objectionable written matter; of booksellers, owners of newsstands, etc., who agree to sell it; for, as we suppose, these persons understand that the matter in question is intrinsically harmful and gravely forbidden.

1530. Coöperation with evil newspapers and other reading matter is material and lawful if the matter itself is not entirely evil, that is, if it has good uses as well as bad, and one has a reason for coöperation that is just and proportionate to the kind of coöperation. The following are examples of coöperation that may be merely material and lawful:

(a) Moral coöperation is given by writers of good matter who assist as collaborators; by those who offer small notices or advertisements; by readers who use a book, periodical, newspaper, etc., for the good matter it contains and skip the rest. For all these persons contribute in a greater or less degree, according to their influence, reputation, and ability, to the prestige and success of the journal, magazine or volume, with which their names are connected or which they patronize. Reasons sufficient to excuse in these cases, given by some authors, are the following: for a permanent contributor, a very grave reason, such as the need of support for his family which he cannot earn in any other way; for an occasional contributor, a rather grave reason, such as the opportunity of refuting error or of setting forth true principles (see Canon 1386, § 2); for the habitual reader, a reason somewhat grave, such as the advantage of reports useful for his business which cannot be found elsewhere; for the occasional reader, a slight reason, such as entertainment to be derived from reading a good story; for the small advertiser, a slight reason, such as profit in business. Those who by laudatory descriptions in advertisements or book reviews urge others to buy and read evil books are guilty of seduction, rather than coöperation (see 1495).

(b) Financial coöperation is given by those who endow or subsidize a publication, by shareholders, by large advertisers, by subscribers, etc. Reasons considered sufficient in these cases are as follows: for the original providers of capital, only a most grave reason; for the buyers of much stock or advertising space, only a very grave reason; for subscribers, a grave reason such as would suffice for habitual reading.

(c) Material assistance is given by those who produce or distribute a publication and by those who furnish necessary material. Among the producers, the proximate coöperators are, first, the managers of the printing company, and, secondly, the printers, the "readers" and the correctors; the remote coöperators are the typesetters, arrangers of ink and paper, binders, and machine operators. For proximate coöperation it is held that a most grave reason suffices, as when a printer cannot otherwise support himself and his family; for remote coöperation a grave reason is needed. Among the distributors, there are degrees of proximity in coöperation as follows: first, those who put the reading matter into the hands of others (e.g., by keeping it on the tables in their waiting rooms or offices); next, those who keep it for purchasers who may ask for it; finally, those who are employed as keepers of newsstands, newsboys, etc. We cannot think of any reason sufficient to excuse the first kind of coöperation, since there is no lack of good reading matter which doctors, lawyers, barbers, etc,, can provide for those who are waiting in their rooms; for the second kind of coöperation, a very grave reason suffices, such as loss of trade by a poor bookseller, if he would not supply his patrons with popular books or periodicals of a less elevated kind; for the third kind of coöperation, a grave reason suffices.

Among the suppliers are those who sell to the printer his ink, type, machinery, etc. These coöperate only remotely, and it is held that profit is a sufficient reason for their coöperation. This we admit, if the coöperation is not indispensable, but we do not think that profit alone would uniformly justify voluntary coöperation upon which depended the publication of pernicious matter.

1531. Formal Coöperation with Evil Dances or Plays.—(a) Cases of formal coöperation on account of explicit intention to do harm are those of the originators of sinful dances and the writers of indecent plays. (b) Cases of formal coöperation on account of implicit intention to do harm are those of the managements that produce bad shows, organize bad dances, or make the arrangements or issue the invitations for these affairs.

1532. Material Coöperation with Evil Dances or Plays.—Material coöperation is lawful, if the coöperation is not itself intrinsically wrong, and if there is a sufficient reason for permitting it.

(a) Cases of immediate material coöperation are those of players and dancers who have harmless parts in the performance. A very grave reason, such as avoidance of penury, is considered as sufficient excuse here, at least for a time.

(b) Cases of proximate material coöperation are those of musicians or singers, who do not perform lascivious music; of spectators, who show no approval of the evil that is done; of those who buy tickets but do not attend. A more serious reason is required in the musician at the dance than in the musician at the play, for the former directs the dance, while the latter only accompanies the play. Likewise, a more serious reason is required when one attends often, or when one's patronage is essential to the success of the occasion, than when one attends only rarely, or when the play or dance does not depend on one's presence or patronage.

(c) Cases of remote material coöperation are those of the owners who rent their theatres or dance-halls or cabarets, of ushers, guards, box-office employees, stage hands, etc. It is held that profit is a sufficient reason to justify the owners in renting their places, if the theatrical company or dance management can readily find other places in case they are sent away. The ushers, guards, and the like are excused, if they cannot easily find other employment; but this does not justify gazing on immodest spectacles or laughing at or applauding obscene jokes.

1533. Formal Coöperation by the Manufacture or Sale of Objects Whose Sole Purpose is Gravely or Venially Sinful.—(a) Cases of explicit coöperation are those of the inventor of contraceptives or of instruments that frustrate generation, of the designers of blasphemous representations or of tablets in honor of false deities, the authors of somewhat profane or irreverent cards, and the like. (b) Cases of implicit coöperation are those of persons who, for profit only, make or sell objects such as those just mentioned, while knowing that the purpose to which they naturally tend is the commission of sin.

1534. Material coöperation by the manufacture or sale of objects that are used for gravely or venially sinful purposes, is lawful under the conditions given in 1515. Hence, in the first place, the coöperation itself must not be intrinsically sinful, that is, the object made or sold must have good as well as evil uses. There are two classes of objects of this kind: (a) there are some objects which may have good uses, but which in fact are nearly always made to serve bad ends (e.g., idols, insignia of forbidden societies, pictures of the nude, ultra-fashionable dress, certain drugs or poisons, blackjacks, and pistol silencers); (b) there are other objects which are indifferent in themselves, although often employed for sinful uses (e.g., dice, playing cards and chips, rouge, lipsticks, necklaces and other feminine adornments, imitation jewelry, adulterated articles, and the like).

1535. The rules about proportionate cause for coöperation by the manufacture or sale of things that are employed in committing sin are those given above in 1519.

(a) Hence, the greater the sin that will be committed or the more harmful the consequences that will ensue from the use of an object, the greater the reason required for making, repairing or selling it. In some instances only a most grave reason will excuse, such as peril of instant death for refusal. Thus, one may not sell poison or drugs to a person who contemplates suicide, murder, or abortion. One may not sell narcotics to a person who asks for them in good faith and who cannot obtain them elsewhere, but who will become a drug-fiend if they are given him. One may not sell morphine, heroin, etc., to a person who is already a drug-addict and who will abuse the drugs, unless there is a very grave reason for not refusing, such as danger that refusal will lead him to set fire to the building. If one has all the playing cards in some remote hamlet, one should not sell them without grave reason to a customer who will spend a great part of the time at games to the neglect of serious duties, nor without a very grave reason to a customer who is a card sharper and who will swindle many innocent victims, or to a gambler who will waste the money due to his wife and family.

(b) The more closely related an object is with sinful uses, the graver must be the excuse for having part in its manufacture or sale. Thus, an ordinary reason (e.g., profit) might suffice for selling a lamb to a pagan or attractive ornaments of dress to a woman, where only a very grave or most grave reason would suffice for selling incense to a pagan or ornaments that are frequently used as amulets or charms. Generally speaking, it is seriously wrong and gravely sinful to make or sell articles whose ordinary use is gravely sinful.

(c) The more a customer depends on a determinate manufacturer or merchant to obtain such an object, the more serious must be the reason for making or selling it. Thus, a grave reason, such as a notable loss, is sufficient reason for selling a special fancy apparel to a notorious "vampire" (i.e., a woman who carries on scandalous flirtations in order to get presents), if the adornments can be obtained from other dressmakers or modistes or stores; but a much graver reason would be required, if the apparel could not be purchased except at one place. In the former case, refusal to sell would not prevent the activities of this woman; in the latter case, it would at least hinder her to some extent.

(d) The more certain it is that an object will be employed sinfully, the greater must be the reason for making, repairing or selling it. Examples: Sempronius, a curio dealer, is asked by three men for a statue of Joss along with joss-sticks and papers. The first customer says he intends to use these articles for religious rites; the second will not tell what his purpose is; the third wishes to present the articles to a museum. Sempronius may not sell to the first customer except for a most grave reason, such as fear of death if he refuses; he may not sell to the second customer without a very great reason, such as a very considerable loss to himself; he may sell to the third customer for an ordinary reason, such as the profit he makes from the sale. Titus, who sells firearms, knows that some of his customers, though he has no particular individuals in mind, will use these weapons unlawfully in poaching or shooting out of season. Since evil is not to be presumed of any particular individual, Titus has the right to sell to all for the usual reason of business profit.

1536. Is a merchant bound to inquire the use which a customer will make of an article that is often employed for sin?

(a) If the positive law requires that the merchant inform himself, he is bound to make inquiries necessary for obtaining the information. Thus, if the civil law forbids the sale of weapons without a permit or of poisons without a prescription, the merchant has to ask for the customer's authorization to buy.

(b) If the positive law has no such regulation, we should distinguish between articles that are frequently used for sin and articles that are generally used for sin. When an article of the former class is requested, there is no obligation to make inquiries, for such an obligation would be unduly burdensome; but, if an article of the latter class is desired, one should make inquiries, unless one is morally certain that the intention of the customer is good, or there is a very grave reason for seeking no information. Thus, one may sell a deck of cards to a stranger without asking for proofs that he is not a confidence man in disguise; but one may not sell deadly poison to an entire stranger merely on the strength of his word that he needs it for medical or other lawful purposes.

1537. Sinful Coöperation in Providers of Food and Drink.—(a) There is explicit formal coöperation with sins of gluttony, drunkenness, violation of fast or abstinence, whenever one gladly supplies the means for these sins to those who are about to commit them. Thus, if a host supplies a guest who is overdrinking with all the intoxicants the latter desires, and secretly wishes that the guest may make himself drunk, there is explicit coöperation. There is implicit formal coöperation when he who supplies the food or drink does not directly intend evil, but when the act of giving the food or drink is from the circumstances of the case an evil act, as when a person is given a meal which will not agree with him and will make him sick or aggravate a malady, or when a person who wishes to violate a fast ostentatiously to show contempt is furnished with the eatables he asks for. (b) There is unlawful material coöperation when one does not approve of the sin that will be committed, but nevertheless without sufficient reason supplies the food or drink. Thus, there is sinful coöperation when a restaurant owner gives meat on Friday to one not dispensed, for no other reason than the profit he himself will make.

1538. Material coöperation in providing food or drink to those who ask it, but have no right to take it, is lawful when one has the right to provide the food or drink, and there is a sufficient reason for coöperation. The sufficiency of the reason depends on circumstances, as explained in 1519.

(a) Hence, a greater reason is required when the sin that the other person will commit will be greater. Thus, a grave reason, such as indignation of a customer, might suffice for coöperation with a venial violation of temperance or abstinence; but a graver reason, such as a serious quarrel, is required if the violation will be mortally sinful. A graver reason is also necessary when the consequences will be more harmful (e.g., the fights of the drunkard, or the serious illness of one who has neglected his diet) than when they are less harmful (e.g., the foolish talk of the drunkard, or the stupefaction of the glutton).

(b) A greater reason is required when the coöperation is closer. Thus, in supplying meat the butcher coöperates only remotely, while the cook who prepares it and the waiter who serves it coöperate proximately.

(c) A greater reason is necessary when one's coöperation is essential to the commission of the sin. Thus, in a large town where there are many restaurants, the fact that a customer would quarrel if denied meat on a day of abstinence would excuse coöperation, whereas in a small village which has only one eating place, it seems there should be a more serious reason, such as blasphemies or boycott or strike against one's business which the refusal of meat might evoke.

(d) A greater reason is called for when the sin of the other person is more certain to follow. Thus, a restaurant-keeper who is patronized by strangers of all kinds, temperate and intemperate, Catholic and non-Catholic, may serve wine at meals, where this is allowed, and provide meat on days of abstinence for all comers; for the diners are not known to him, and it would not be possible for him to inform himself whether they are sober in their habits or exempted from the law of abstinence. But in a boarding house the landlady should not consent to have strong beverages on the table, when she knows that some of those present will thereby become intoxicated; neither should she agree to provide meat on Fridays for a Catholic who is not excused from abstinence, unless there is a serious reason, such as the loss of this boarder which she cannot afford on account of her poverty. Moreover, since dispensation is given from the laws of fast and abstinence but not from the law of temperance, there is less certainty about the intent to sin when one asks for meat on Friday than when one asks for a great quantity of liquor to be brought to one's table. Drunkenness is also more certain when a person who asks for drink is already somewhat under its influence.

1539. The sins with which one coöperates by supplying food or drink to others who have no right to it are more or less serious according as they violate the natural law or only positive human law.

(a) Thus, violation of fast and abstinence is opposed to the natural law when it is intended as a manifestation of hatred of religion. One may not coöperate with a violation of fast and abstinence which is manifestly of this character.

(b) Violation of temperance is also opposed to natural law, and doubly so when it leads to such evils as quarrels, fights, murders, blasphemies, etc. It is not lawful to coöperate with intemperance, unless this is necessary in order to prevent the commission of a greater sin by the other person, or a serious loss to oneself. Thus, it is not unlawful to supply whisky to a burglar who wishes to get drunk, if this is the only way one can prevent the robbery of a third party or serious injury to oneself.

(c) Violation of a fast or abstinence in itself is opposed only to positive law; and, since fasting is more difficult than abstinence, one is more easily excused from the observance of the former than from that of the latter. Hence, if there is a doubt whether a customer has a right to receive the food or drink he asks for, a restaurant-keeper can decide more readily in the customer's favor if there is question of fast or abstinence than if there is question of intemperance, and more readily still if there is question of fast than if there is question of abstinence. Generally speaking, a restaurant-keeper may supply meat on Friday to all who ask it, provided he has other substantial food indicated on his bill of fare and shows himself willing to serve that as well as meat.

1540. Renting of Houses or Rooms and coöperation in Sin.—(a) He who rents to persons who wish to carry on disorderly, immoral, idolatrous, unlawful, or other sinful occupations or practices, is guilty of formal or unlawful material coöperation, if he approves of the conduct of the renters or has no sufficient reason for renting to them. The same is true if in a similar way one permits persons bent on evil (e.g., pickpockets) to lounge in one's offices, hotels, etc.

(b) He who gives the use of his house, room, hall, field, etc., to persons who will employ them for evil, is only a material and not a guilty coöperator, if there is no prohibition of his act, and he has a sufficient reason for it.

1541. Examples of reasons sufficient for coöperation in renting are as follows:

(a) A very grave reason.—In civitatibus in quibus majoris mali vitandi causa permissum est, licet locare domum meretricibus, dummodo non sequatur grave nocumentum vicinis honestis vel major ansa peccandi ob domus situm, et adsit ratio proportionate gravis, utputa quod alii locatorii non adsint, dominus notabile damnum patiatur si domus non occupetur, et meretrices facile alium locatarium obtinere possint. Hodie vero quum constet meretrices plerasque invite vitam turpem exercere (white slavery) et morbis pessimis morteque præmatura affligi, meretricium vero nocumentum multigenum bono publico (the social evil) inferre, omnis vir probus abhorrebit a pretio locario ab administratoribus lupanarium oblato.

(b) A more grave reason.—Meetings whose purpose is contrary to the common good (e.g., anti-religious gatherings), even though permitted by civil law, should not be given the use of one's premises except in a rare case of the greatest necessity.

1542. Unlawful Coöperation of Servants, Employees, and Workingmen.—(a) Coöperation is formal if these intend the sin of their employer with which they coöperate, or if the act of coöperation is itself intrinsically evil. Thus, a bookkeeper does no wrong in merely keeping a record of receipts and expenses; but, if he notices many instances of great frauds and injustices done by his firm and keeps at his post in order that dishonesty may be covered up and continued, he becomes a formal coöperator. But a bookkeeper who falsifies or destroys records in order that his business may be able to issue an incorrect statement of its financial condition is involved in its guilt, even though his motive is pity or loyalty. Other examples of formal coöperation are those of a secretary who takes down dictation which contains blasphemous or obscene expressions, and of a taxi-driver who tells his passengers how to get to gambling dens, or who helps a criminal to get away by driving him through dark streets.

(b) Coöperation is material and unlawful, when the intention and the act itself are not evil, but when there is no sufficient reason for the coöperation. Thus, the following proposition was condemned by Innocent XI in 1679 as scandalous and pernicious: "Famulus qui submissis humeris scienter adjuvat herum suum ascendere per fenestras ad stuprandam virginem, et multoties eidem subservit deferendo scalam, aperiendo januam, aut quid simile coöperando, non peccat mortaliter, si id faciat metu notabilis detrimenti, puta ne a domino male tractetur, ne torvis oculis aspiciatur, ne domo expellatur" (Denzinger, n. 1201). Though the acts of coöperation of the servant here mentioned are not intrinsically evil, the coöperation is proximate and positive and habitual, and the wrong done so serious that only a most grave reason, such as fear of death, could justify the help given by the servant to his master.

1543. Lawful Coöperation of Servants, Workingmen, or Employees.— (a) If coöperation is remote and is not indispensable to the sin to be committed, the mere fact that one is employed by the principal cause will excuse; for the employee is not supposed to question the employer about the reasons of orders given, and he is not responsible for the intentions of the employer, but for the performance of what is assigned to himself. Hence, the following kinds of coöperation are held permissible for no other reason than that of service: carrying liquor or food to an employer who wishes to make himself drunk or to break the fast, buying and carrying to him papers which he should not read, giving him his hat and coat or getting his car ready as he starts out to attack an enemy, opening the door to a slanderer whom the mistress of the house wishes to employ. Also, a public taxi-driver may take his patrons to clubs or road-houses where they will become intoxicated, if he is in no way responsible for their intention and shows no approval of it, and they can go just as well without him.

(b) If coöperation is proximate, the mere fact that one is employed is not sufficient as an excuse for coöperation; there must be some other reason that is sufficiently weighty in view of the gravity of the sin and the other circumstances. Thus, to drive one's employer to the place where he is to receive stolen valuables is justifiable, if one is under threat of great bodily harm if one refuses. Item ob incommodum gravius evitandum permittitur famulo deferre litteras heri amatorias ad amasiam cum qua illicitum commercium habet, tempus et locum conveniendi amasiae nuntiare, excubias agere dum simul adsint. But a servant who is called on habitually to coöperate in these ways should secure another position, if possible.

1544. The principles given as to servants should be applied likewise to other persons who are subordinates, with due allowance made for the difference of circumstances.

(a) Thus, children, wives, pupils, etc., may be less excusable in coöperation than servants, since the former may be in a better position to remonstrate against what is ordered. Hence, if the master of the house who sometimes goes on a spree orders a servant to bring him his demijohn, disobedience might be more difficult than if the same order was given the wife.

(b) Children, wives, pupils, etc., may be more excusable, since unlike the servants they may be unable to go elsewhere. Those who agree to work at places known as vicious resorts, or who let their employer understand that they will not see or hear many things, or who habitually perform services proximately related to sin (what is called "dirty work"), are guilty of formal coöperation, at least when they can secure good employment elsewhere. Children, on the contrary, may be so dependent on a tyrannical father that they cannot refuse coöperation without serious consequences to themselves.

1545. Duties of Confessors.—Instruction should be given to penitents who are guilty of sinful coöperation. (a) The confessor should instruct ignorant penitents on the sinfulness of their coöperation, when there is a duty of justice to do this, as when the penitents ask to be instructed; or when there is a duty of charity, as when the sinfulness of the coöperation in question is known to many persons, or the penitents by reason of coöperation are giving great scandal or are in serious danger. (b) The confessor should not instruct ignorant penitents on the sinfulness of their coöperation—at least, not for a time—if they are in good faith and if graver evils would result from the instruction than from silence.

1546. Obligations to be Imposed on Penitents on Account of Sinful coöperation.—(a) Some cases of coöperation cause the culprit to fall under ecclesiastical penalties, for example, those who act as seconds or spectators at duels (Canon 2351). (b) Some cases entail a duty of reparation for scandal given, as when one has aided the diffusion of irreligious or obscene literature or whisperings among the people. (c) Some kinds of coöperation include dangerous occasions of sin which one is bound to avoid, as when one works for a man who produces adulterated wares or gets money under false pretenses.

Art. 10: THE COMMANDMENTS OF CHARITY

(*Summa Theologica*, II-II, q. 44.)

1547. There is no commandment concerning charity in the Decalogue, but charity is implicitly contained in all the commandments of other virtues; for charity is the end of every commandment (I Tim., i. 5). Thus, the commandments of the first table of the Law tend to the love of God; the commandments of the second table to the love of neighbor. On account of its supreme importance, however, charity was made the object of special commandments in both the Old and the New Testament.

(a) In the Old Testament, at the second giving of the tables of the Law, it is declared: "Now, Israel, what doth the Lord thy God require of thee, but that thou fear the Lord thy God, and walk in his ways, and love him, and serve the Lord thy God, with all thy heart and with all thy soul?" (Deut., x. 12).

(b) In the New Testament, our Lord, being asked which is the great commandment in the law, replied: "Thou shalt love the Lord, thy God, with thy whole heart, and with thy whole soul, and with thy whole mind. This is the greatest and the first commandment. And the second is like to this: Thou shalt love thy neighbor as thyself. On these two commandments dependeth the whole law and the prophets" (Matt, xxii. 37-40).

1548. Charity must come "from a pure heart, and a good conscience and faith unfeigned" (I Tim., i. 5), and these words may be used to indicate how all other commandments have charity for their purpose.

(a) "A pure heart" is had by the observance of the negative commandments of the natural law, which forbid evil, or of the commandments about the virtues regulative of the passions; and it is a disposition preparatory for the love of God, since an impure heart will be taken up with evil or with earthly things, and so turned away from the goodness of God.

(b) "A good conscience" is had by the observance of the affirmative commandments of the natural law, or of the commandments regulative of actions; and it too tends to charity as its goal, for a bad conscience fills one with dread and horror of the justice of God.

(c) "Faith unfeigned" is had by the observance of the supernatural law, or of the commandments about worship of the true God; and it leads up to charity, for a feigned faith, or false worship, separates one from the truth of God.

1549. Though charity is but one virtue (see 1115), it has two acts: one about love of God, which is the end, and another about love of neighbor, which is a means to that end.

(a) If all understood that the end includes the means and the means supposes the end, there would be no necessity for two distinct commandments; for there is no love of God without love of neighbor (I John, iv. 20), and he who loves his neighbor has fulfilled the law (Rom., xiii. 8).

(b) But since many would not perceive that one of the commandments of charity contains the other, it was necessary to propose these commandments separately: "We have this command from God that he who loves God love also his brother" (I John, iv. 21).

1550. Charity extends to other objects than God and the neighbor, namely, to self and one's own body (see 1133 sqq.); it also has other acts than that of love, such as the acts of joy, peace, beneficence (see 1193 sqq.), and the suppression of uncharitable hatred, sloth, envy (see

1295 sqq.), etc. Nevertheless, on the two commandments of love of God and love of neighbor depend the whole law and the prophets (Matt., xxii. 40), and other commandments about charity are not necessary.

(a) Thus, the objects of love are either the end or the means to the end, and, as the two commandments of charity refer to both of these, they omit nothing that is to be loved. It was not necessary to make express command of love of self, for nature inclines to that sufficiently, and the duty of keeping love of self within bounds is provided for in the commandments that God be loved above all and the neighbor as oneself.

(b) The acts of charity distinct from love result from love, and the acts opposed to charity are virtually forbidden in the commandments of their opposites. Hence, there was no need of explicit precepts about the secondary acts of charity or of explicit prohibitions of the sins against charity. But for the sake of those who might not perceive that the minor functions of charity are commanded and acts of uncharitableness forbidden in the two great commandments, special and explicit laws were given which enjoin peace, joy, etc., and forbid hatred, envy, etc.

1551. The precepts of the secondary acts of charity are: (a) joy: "Rejoice in the Lord always" (Phillip., iv. 4); (b) peace: "Follow peace with all men" (Heb., xii. 14); and (c) beneficence: "While we have time, let us do good to all" (Gal., vi. 10).

1552. The prohibitions of uncharitableness are as follows: (a) against hatred: "Thou shalt not hate thy brother in thy heart" (Lev, xix. IT); (b) against sloth: "Bow down thy shoulder and hear her (wisdom), and be not grieved with her bands" (Ecclus., vi. 26); (c) against envy: "Let us not be made desirous of vainglory, provoking one another, envying one another" (Gal., v. 26), (d) against discord: "Speak the same things and let there be no schisms among you" (I Cor., i. 10); and (e) against scandal: "Put not a stumbling-block or a scandal in your brother's way" (Rom., xiv. 13).

1553. The Commandment of Love of God.—In the commandment of love of God two things are expressed: (a) the matter of the commandment is God, the object of love; (b) the manner of the commandment is that God be loved as the Last End, to whose love all other love is to be subordinated.

1554. There is a twofold manner or mode of performing a virtuous act:

(a) The intrinsic mode is that which comes from the nature of the virtue commanded. Thus, in the Fourth Commandment is included not only the substance of an act (viz., that honor be shown), but also the mode of the act (i.e., that such honor and so much honor be shown as is owed to a parent by his child). The intrinsic mode is always included in a commandment along with the substance of the act prescribed (cfr. 480 sqq.).

(b) The extrinsic mode is that which belongs to some virtue different from the one commanded. This mode is not included in a commandment. Thus, if honor be shown to parents out of love of God, the mode of love of God is extrinsic to the commandment, for the commandment is concerned with the virtue of filial piety, and the mode of the act pertains to charity, which is a virtue distinct from filial piety.

1555. The intrinsic mode of performing an act of virtue is also twofold:

(a) The essential mode is that without which an act is not virtuous. Thus, he who gives to his indigent parents according to his means and their needs fulfills the essential mode of the Fourth Commandment, for, if he gave them less than he could afford and they needed, his act would not come up to the requirements of the commandment.

(b) The ideal mode of the performance of virtue is that which adds to the virtue greater goodness and value, and which is intended by a lawgiver as the end, but not as the object of his command. Thus, he who gives to his indigent parents not only sufficiently, but also with a great willingness and cheerfulness, fulfills the Fourth Commandment with greater perfection than another who supports his parents with less alacrity.

1556. The mode of the love of God prescribed in the first and great commandment is that God be loved with the whole heart, etc. But "to love with the whole heart, etc.," can be understood in various senses.

(a) Thus, it may be understood to mean a love that is subjectively or intensively great, as when one loves God with much fervor and affection. This mode of love is ideal, since the measure of loving God is to love Him without measure, but it is not essential. The end of the commandment is that we love God ever more and more, and perform what is required with ever greater promptitude and gladness; but the commandment does not fix any certain degree of intensity, although it would be inordinate to choose to love God less intensely than we love creatures (see 1160).

(b) "To love with the whole heart" may be understood to mean a love that is objectively or appreciatively great, as when one esteems and loves God as the Supreme Good. This mode of love is essential, and hence without it the commandment is not observed. However much one loves God, if one does not love Him as the Supreme Good, one does not love Him aright, and does not practise the virtue of charity that is commanded.

1557. Love of God from the whole heart, objectively or appreciatively understood, is either actual or habitual.

(a) Actually, one loves God with one's whole heart when there is never any interruption or distraction to one's love, and one is continually engaged in an act of loving God above all else. This is the ideal mode of fulfilling the commandment of love, and it is also the end to which the commandment is intended to lead. But it is only in heaven, where God will be all in all (I Cor., xv. 28), that this ideal fulfillment will take place.

(b) Habitually, one loves God with one's whole heart when one is in the state of grace, preferring the love of God to every contrary love, although it is only at intervals that one is able to make acts of love. This is the essential mode of fulfilling the command of love here on earth. The whole heart must be given to God to the exclusion of love for any mortal sin, for mortal sin separates from God.

1558. The mode of loving God is expressed in various places in scripture (Deut., vi. 5; Matt., xxii. 37; Mark, xii. 30; Luke, x. 27), and there are slightly different interpretations given to the words by which it is conveyed. Thus, some exegetes see in the expressions "heart," "soul," "mind," "strength," synonymous significations of the one thought that

God should be loved over all, and they think that different words are used only in order to give greater clearness and energy to the thought. But the following seems also a reliable explanation: (a) God must be loved with one's whole heart, that is, the will must not intend any Last End other than God; (b) God must be loved with one's whole mind, soul and strength, that is, the powers moved by the will—intellect, appetites and executive faculties—must be subject to God, must be regulated according to His will, and must carry out His commandments.

1559. Love of God with one's whole heart excludes, then, opposite loves, but it does not exclude other loves that are not opposite or other dispositions that are less perfect. (a) Thus, love of God with one's whole heart does not exclude love of self or of neighbor. (b) Love of God with one's whole heart does not exclude the use of acts in reference to God that do not reach the height of disinterested love, such as acts of hope, gratitude, or fear (see 1033, 1054, 1093).

1560. There are various degrees of perfection in the fulfillment of the commandment of love of God.

(a) The most perfect fulfillment is found in heaven, where there is no turning from the love of God by grave sin, no impediment to its exercise by venial sin, and no interruption of its act by other occupations.

(b) The more perfect fulfillment of this commandment found on earth is modelled on the love of God exercised by the Saints in heaven, and the nearer one approaches to the model, the better does one fulfill the commandment. Thus, he who avoids not only what is against charity (i.e., mortal sin), but also, as far as possible, what is aside from charity (i.e., venial sin), loves God more perfectly than one who is careless about venial sin; and he who shuns, not only things unlawful that are harmful to charity, but also things lawful that interrupt the exercise of charity, loves God more, other things being equal, than another who avoids the unlawful, but whose mind is greatly occupied with lawful temporal matters.

(c) The ordinarily perfect fulfillment of the commandment is found in all those who, both in their internal and in their external acts, avoid all that is contrary to the love of God, although they fall into venial sin and are mostly occupied with temporal affairs. Thus is charity the bond of perfection (Col, iii. 14), the tie that binds man to his highest good; those who keep the commandments for its sake are followers after perfection, those who embrace counsels for its sake are in the state of perfection.

1561. The Commandment of Love of Self.—Love of self is understood in many senses. (a) According to its moral character, love of self is either sinful or virtuous, and virtuous self-love is either natural or supernatural (as was explained in 1136). (b) According to its physical character, love of self is either innate or elicited. Innate love of self is the tendency of nature to desire what pertains to the perfection of self, such as existence and its preservation (see 1108). Elicited love of self is the choice on the part of the reason and will of an ultimate happiness for self and of the means thereto.

1562. Charity obliges each one capable of precept to an elicited supernatural love of self. The obligation is grave for the following reasons: (a) the love of God includes love of self, for we cannot love God truly unless we also love those things that are His, especially His rational creatures made to His image and destined for His society; (b) the love of neighbor supposes love of self, for the commandment of love (Matt., xxii. 39) offers love of self as the model for love of others.

1563. The goods which the law of charity to self requires one to desire and seek after, are all those things that are necessary for the attainment of one's happiness and due perfection.

(a) Thus, as to supernatural goods, one is bound to obtain for oneself things necessary for salvation. One is obliged, then, to acquire a sufficient knowledge of the faith; to enter into a state of life for which one is suited (e.g., matrimony or religion); to avoid sin and the occasions of sin; not to delay conversion for a notable length of time; to put oneself in the state of grace, especially at the hour of death. But one is not obliged to perform these duties with the motive of charity in mind, nor to elect for self works of supererogation or counsels of perfection.

(b) As to intellectual goods, one is bound to seek what is necessary for a proper fulfillment of the duties of one's station in life. Thus, one owes it in charity to oneself to seek the education and training that are presupposed in one's profession or occupation, and to bestow the necessary study and attention. See above, on the intellectual virtues (144 sqq.) and on the sin of ignorance (904 sqq.).

(c) As to corporal goods, one is obliged to use the ordinary means for preserving life and health (on the desire of death, see 1063). Hence, in matters of food, drink, clothing, and recreation, each one is in duty bound to follow the laws of hygiene.

(d) As to the external goods of person (i.e., honor and reputation), there is a strict duty of guarding them or of recovering them, as far as possible.

(e) As to external goods of fortune (i.e., wealth and possessions), one must aim to acquire as much as is necessary for one's subsistence and the fulfillment of duties to others. Hence the duty of labor for those who do not possess the necessary means. But charity to self does not demand that one aspire to reach the top of the ladder in the financial world or to accumulate a very large surplus. One may indeed lawfully seek to become a millionaire, or to become so wealthy as to be able to retire with leisure, if one goes about this lawfully; but there is no obligation to strive after more than is reasonably necessary.

1564. Man owes it to himself to put to good use the talents God has bestowed upon him for his self-improvement and self-development. It is a sin, therefore, greater or less according to circumstances, to neglect the care of the mind or of the mental culture one should possess.

(a) Thus, reason is the faculty that elevates man above the irrational world, and knowledge is the perfection and excellence of that faculty. What life or health is to the body, reason or knowledge is to the mind; and so, just as it is a sin against the body to neglect life or health, it is also a sin against the mind to neglect reason or knowledge. Persons predisposed to insanity who expose themselves to alienation of mind by the use of drugs or strong spirits or by practices or occupations that expose them to shocks (such as gambling), and others who value ignorance, scepticism, and error as if these infirmities were goods, sin against the mind, at least materially.

(b) Reason and knowledge are also necessary in numberless ways to man's bodily, social, cultural, and religious life. Without the elements of a general education in reading, writing and arithmetic, one is very seriously handicapped in making a bare living; and without the education of the high school, college or university, one is frequently under a disadvantage in seeking to better oneself or improve one's position. Besides these utilities for practical affairs, education has advantages of a loftier kind: it makes its possessor a more capable citizen, a more pleasant companion and friend, a more influential exponent of good causes, and a greater credit to the religion he practises; it gives enjoyment to leisure, comfort to rest, and dignity to success; the labor of acquiring it is a discipline of the will; the taste for higher things it imparts is a natural protection against much that is evil; the mental power and knowledge that are its gifts enable one to expose error and fallacy and to uphold the truth and the right. It is of precept, therefore, that one acquire the moral and mental training which one's salvation and calling in life make necessary; it is of counsel—and the counsel is one that should be much urged in our times—that one who has the opportunity of attaining to a higher proficiency, to the advantage of self and society, should avail himself of that opportunity.

1565. Examples of Sins Committed by Neglect of Necessary Education—(a) Directly, one sins against the duty of cultivation of the mind when through laziness or malice one slights the means of acquiring necessary knowledge—as when pupils absent themselves from school, or give no attention to the teacher or no preparation to their lessons; or when collegians sacrifice study to athletics and amusements.

(b) Indirectly one sins against the duty of knowledge, when one is responsible for habits that impede or prevent necessary concentration of mind, as when one goes about so much socially that the mind is always in a whirl, or reads so much light literature that everything serious becomes a bore, or overeats so much that the brain becomes sluggish, or pays no attention to the wise rule that a sound mind needs a sound body.

1566. The proper care of the body and of health is not merely a thing next to godliness; it is a moral duty, and so a part of godliness. God

Himself on Sinai gave to the Chosen People of old a sanitary code, and the faithful observance by orthodox Jews of those regulations has had much to do with the superior health and longevity of their race. Moral Theology, therefore, is not digressing from its proper subject-matter, if it gives some attention to rules of health. The duties owed to physical well-being can be reduced to the following: (a) to secure for the body the things needed for the maintenance and replenishment of its substance and vigor, such as food, air, sleep and exercise; (b) to ward off or remove those things that are injurious to or destructive of health, such as excessive heat or cold, waste matter, poisons, and disease; (c) to assist these physical means by psychical or spiritual ones, such as cheerfulness and the will to keep well and fit.

1567. Food and drink are naturally a prime requisite for life, since they furnish the material from which the body is built and renewed. They should be used, however, in such a way as to serve their purpose.

(a) Thus, the quantity and quality have to be regulated according to the needs of the individual and circumstances, and so will vary with climate, age, health, and occupation. The distinction of clean and unclean foods does not exist in the New Law (Rom., xiv. 14; Matt., xv. 17-20), but it is clear that the same kinds or amounts of food and drink do not agree with all constitutions; that overeating, undereating, and want of variety in diet are not conducive to good health. Physicians recommend that something raw be eaten every day and something indigestible at every meal, and that a person watch his weight, keeping a little overweight up to middle life and a little underweight after that age.

(b) The manner of eating is of first-rate importance, since the digestion is harmed if one eats without appetite or with mental preoccupation on deep subjects, or bolts the food, or makes excessive use of relishes or condiments.

1568. Fresh air, on which the production of pure blood and the continuance of vitality depend, is another necessity of life. Hence, we may well heed the following rules which hygienists lay down on this point: (a) let in fresh air and sunshine to the places where you live and work, and exclude dust and smoke; (b) wear light, loose and porous clothing, so that the skin may have air; (c) get out of doors in the open air part of the time every day, even though the weather is uninviting, for sunshine or natural light is also a requisite of good health; (d) breathe through the nose, and not through the mouth. Breathing should be deep, slow and regular, and one should take deep-breathing exercises several times a day; (e) sleep in a well-ventilated room, or out-of-doors if possible.

1569. Rest and relaxation are needful for body and mind alike, that the burdens of life may not bear too heavily, and nature may be allowed to exercise her ministries of renewal and restoration. But here, as in other things, the guiding rule must be moderation.

(a) Through excess, some harm their health by indulging in too much repose. A strong, healthy individual who remains in bed from midnight till noon, or who gives most of the afternoon to a prolonged nap, is storing up more energy than he or she needs, and will feel the worse for it. Similarly, persons whose life is one round of vacations or diversions pay for their aimless existence in various kinds of mental or nervous disorders, to say nothing of the moral dangers to which they are exposed (Ecclus., xxxiii. 29).

(b) Through defect, on the other hand, some injure their health by depriving themselves of the sleep or rest they ought to take. The time that should be given to repose differs with the individual. The young, brain-workers and the feeble are in greater need than others; but there is no one who can dispense with his proper share of rest. It is sinful, therefore, to reduce needed sleep by late retiring or early rising, or to work unremittingly to such an extent that the bodily powers and resistance become unequal to the demands made on them and unfitted for duties. According to physicians, seven hours out of every twenty-four should be spent in bed, and the hours before midnight are much more precious for rest than the early morning hours. Some holidays and vacations are a necessity in these days of rapid and strenuous life.

1570. Physical exercise is a factor of good health, for it stirs up the circulation of the blood, assists digestion, and rids the body of surplus weight. Moreover, it has great value for the mind (to which it gives diversion and refreshment) and for the soul (since it promotes temperance and chastity). If taken in the form of sports, physical exercise is a training in coöperation with others, in loyalty, discipline, and fairness. But health is impaired by excess as well as by defect in exercise.

(a) Examples of over-exercise are athletes who carry on endurance tests to the point of exhaustion, devotees of violent forms of contests or matches that overtax the heart, etc.

(b) Examples of under-exercise are ablebodied persons who prefer to lounge about the house all day rather than bestir themselves; also those who work indoors all day and who from choice ride rather than walk, no matter how short the distance they have to go, etc. Persons of sedentary life who can do so, should exercise every day, preferably out-of-doors, playing at some game like golf, taking a brisk walk of about five miles, or doing some manual labor, such as gardening or sawing wood. Regular gymnastics or setting-up exercises, and the habit of sitting, standing, and walking erect at all times are prescribed by experts on health as very important.

1571. Under the head of preventive or curative measures that ought to be attended to for the sake of bodily well-being are the following:

(a) In time of health sickness has to be guarded against. Suitable clothing and shelter must be used as protection against injurious effects of heat or cold; cleanliness must be cultivated by such means as daily baths, frequent ablutions, washing of teeth, tongue and gums; infections must be avoided; drugs or stimulants hurtful to one's health must not be indulged in, and attention must be given to daily, regular and natural elimination and to the exclusion of poisons from the system. According to authorities, one should drink at least six glasses of water a day, but warm water is often preferable to cold or hot.

(b) In time of sickness efforts must be made at restoration of health, if this is possible. It is of obligation to use the ordinary means to recover physical fitness, that is, to take remedies and medicines that are suitable, not on the advice of acquaintances or advertisements, but on the recommendation of a competent physician in whose knowledge and skill one has perfect confidence (Ecclus., xxxviii. 1 sqq.). But there is no obligation to have recourse to extraordinary means of recovery, such as a trip to a more balmy climate when one's purse cannot afford it.

Similarly, a very painful and uncertain operation or mutilation is not obligatory, unless one has dependents, and the danger to life from the operation is slight. In time of sickness, as well as in health, we should not omit to implore the divine aid.

1572. The state of mind has very much to do with good or bad health. It is well known, for instance, that a happy, cheerful attitude helps digestion and sleep; whereas worry, fear, anger or other emotional stress will bring on dyspepsia, insomnia, disease, and perhaps insanity. We should not overlook, therefore, the importance of the mental factor in our efforts to maintain good health.

(a) Natural means of cultivating an even temper and a buoyant disposition are: some kind of labor or occupation, avoidance of hurry and worry in one's affairs, cultivation of some interesting hobby or avocation that will vary the monotony of business or work, use of congenial recreations, whether of a more refined (e.g., conversation with friends, literature, music, art, the drama, travel to historic or beautiful scenes, etc.) or of a more material kind (e.g., reading tales of mystery or adventure, raising pet animals, witnessing baseball games, races, etc., playing billiards, cards, etc., smoking, attending banquets, picnics, etc.). A sense of humor and laughter in moderation are good for the health and not opposed to spirituality.

(b) Religious practices are all-important for cheerfulness of spirit. Christian Science, indeed, is in error when it holds that faith thinks or wills sorrow and disease and death out of existence, for evil is a reality; but virtue and a good conscience rid one of many enemies to peace, and there exist in the Church many supernatural and miraculous means that benefit body, mind and spirit.

1573. Persons who give exaggerated attention to their health cannot justify themselves by the commandment of charity to self; for this commandment has to be interpreted according to the order of charity as explained above (see 1164 sqq.). The bodily good has to be cared for, but with due subordination to higher goods (Matt, vi. 25; Rom., xiv. 16).

(a) Thus, spiritual goods are more important than those of the body, and it is lawful to practise mortifications by fastings, vigils, hair-shirts, and the like, which, though afflictive to the flesh, are refreshing to the spirit, provided all be done according to holy prudence.

(b) Intellectual goods are better than those of the body, and it is not sinful to devote oneself to studies, researches and other mental occupations in preference to manual labor or athletic exercises which would improve one's physique, but not one's mind. It is even lawful for the sake of mental improvement to suffer some slight detriment to health.

(c) Public good is greater than private good, and hence it is not only lawful but laudable to expose health, or even life, for the advancement of science or the welfare of the community. Many men and women in daily life do this as part of the day's work.

1574. Does charity to self oblige one to desire honors, such as dignities, titles, positions or rank, precedence, testimonials, eulogies, medals, decorations, monuments, and the like?

(a) Charity to self demands that one strive to acquire the excellence that is expected of one, and so to be deserving of honor. For we must let our light shine before men (Matt., v. 16; Rom., xii. 17; II Cor., vii. 21).

(b) Charity to self does not require that one actually secure honors. For one cannot force another to declare one's praises, since he may be prejudiced or ignorant, and it is not seemly to sing one's own greatness or merit (II Cor., x. 18), except in self-defense (II Cor., xii. 11).

(c) Charity to self would require one to seek after an honor, if the honor were necessary and the manner of seeking it honorable. Thus, it is a duty to self to seek to obtain a diploma or certificate of good character or proficiency, if this document is needed to exercise the profession for which one has trained.

(d) Charity to self would forbid one to seek after an honor, if the honor would prove harmful, or if it could not be obtained in a respectable way. Thus, if an honor rightfully belonged to another, or if it were bestowed in recognition of evil done, or if it would impose obligations for which one knows oneself to be unsuited, or if it could not be attained except by dishonesty, charity to self would urge one to fly from the honor.

(e) Charity to self in other cases would permit one either to seek an honor (as when a dignity will be useful and will be employed for good, and is not sought out of vainglory or hypocrisy) or to forego it (as when it is not necessary and one is moved to shun it, not out of contempt, but out of some virtuous motive).

1575. Does charity to self require one to desire a good name?

(a) Charity to self does require that one desire to be worthy of a good name, for one owes it to oneself as well as to others to be blameless (Phil., ii. 14-16) and to provide good things in the sight of men (Rom., xii. 17).

(b) Charity to self does require that one desire to have a good name. Spiritually, a good name is an advantage, for many a one is encouraged to continue in virtue by the good opinion which others have of him, while many another is discouraged from attempting or continuing a good life because he has a bad reputation. Temporally also, a good name is useful or necessary, for, if others do not trust us or respect us, we shall find it difficult to secure employment or position, or to exercise our office fruitfully. Hence, scripture admonishes: "Take care of a good name, for this shall continue with thee, more than a thousand treasures precious and great" (Ecclus., xli. 15).

(c) Charity to self does not require that one actually have a good name, since reputation may be lost through the work of detractors or through one's own unintentional imprudence, or through circumstances over which one has no control.

(d) Charity to self ordinarily requires that one seek to acquire a good name, if it has not yet been earned, also to preserve it, when gained, to recover it, when lost; for, as a rule, there is no greater good for which the good of reputation should be sacrificed. The means to be employed, however, should not be evil, as when one uses hypocritical pretense in order to pass as a man of piety, or has recourse to lying or duelling, to undermining or attacking another in order to recover one's reputation. A good name is built up by fidelity to the duties of one's calling and the avoidance of what may be offensive or scandalous to others; it is preserved or rebuilt by good deeds, especially those one is known or supposed to have lacked, and in case of need by words of self-defense, vindicating one's conduct, or refuting aspersions or false charges.

(e) Charity does not require one to seek after a good name, when this should or may be sacrificed for the sake of some higher good. St. Paul faithfully practised what he preached, that no dishonor might be reflected on the Gospel; and yet his enemies looked on him as a seducer and a nobody, as a melancholy and avaricious man. But the Apostle answered his traducers that neither honor nor dishonor, neither evil report nor good report, would move him from the exercise of his ministry (II Cor., vi. 4 sqq).

1576. Sacrifice of reputation is not lawful, however, unless there is a proportionately grave reason and the means are good.

(a) The end must be good and relatively important, not only if compared with the good of personal reputation, but also if compared with the public good and the rights of third parties. Examples: It would not be right to allow oneself to be defamed in order to cover up the tracks of a rascal who deserved punishment, or to distract attention from an evil that is being done; for the purpose would then be the defeat of justice or the success of some sinful plan. In such cases the end would not be good. Neither would it be right to allow the sacrifice of a good name for the notoriety and money profits to be gained in stage or book royalties. The practice of many young men of accepting imputed faults, of which they are not guilty, in order to be popular, or interesting, or attractive, is also sinful. Money cannot buy back a lost reputation, and popularity with the thoughtless is no compensation for disgrace before the judicious and loss of self-respect. In these cases the end is not important, if compared with the advantage of a good name. And even when an end is good and more important than one's fame, there will frequently be rights of others involved that forbid a sacrifice of reputation, as when a passive attitude in the face of calumny would give scandal or cast discredit on one's profession, office, work, religion, family, or friends.

(b) The means must be good. Examples: Even if the ambition to be "a good fellow" is praiseworthy, drunkenness and profanity are not suitable ways of winning esteem, and the same applies to pretending wickedness or accusing oneself of imaginary escapades and vices to please a circle which admires wildness in youth. The means used in these cases (drunkenness, profanity, lying) are evil in themselves. Again, the wish to cultivate humility does not justify one in giving scandal by consorting with evildoers as intimates, or by conducting oneself in such a way as to lower the esteem or respect that is entertained for one's position. The means used in those cases are at least evil-seeming and disedifying.

1577. Is self-detraction, that is, the revelation of some real fault or defect, lawful?

(a) If there is question of faults or defects that are of a public nature and generally known, a disclosure made in a good spirit and in a proper manner, and from which beneficial and not harmful results can be foreseen, is lawful, and sometimes obligatory. Example: Balbus has calumniated his neighbors, and he now admits the fact, not to boast about or excuse it, but to make satisfaction; he does not repeat the details of his defamatory remarks, but merely states that he wishes to retract what he had no right to say; he has every reason to think that his present course will undo the harm caused by the defamation. Balbus does right in thus acknowledging his mistake.

(b) If there is question of faults or defects not generally known, the reasons for mentioning them should be more serious, unless the sins are of a trifling nature. Examples: Caius once served a term in jail for dishonesty, but he is now a decent citizen. His family would be scandalized and would feel disgraced, if they knew this. But Caius thinks it would be a suitable reparation to tell them of his former guilt. Caius is wrong. To speak of his past experience would only add the sin of scandal to the old one, and there are other ways in which he can do penance in further expiation of dishonesty. Claudius wishes to marry Sempronia, but the latter insists that there must be no secrets between husband and wife, and that he must give her complete and accurate answers on certain questions about his past career—for example, whether he has ever been drunk, whether he has ever wished to be drunk, whether he has ever had questionable relations with other women, etc. Claudius should not deceive Sempronia, nor leave her in ignorance of any serious objection to the marriage, even if she forgot to mention it in her questions; but he owes it to himself not to put himself in her power by giving her information which she would probably use against him then or later. Titus has stolen a considerable sum, and, for the sake of getting advice and direction on how to make restitution, he consults a prudent friend who will regard his communication as confidential, just as if he were a confessor. Titus does not act against his own reputation by telling his case to this friend.

1578. **Confession of Sins against Charity Owed to Self.**—(a) It is not necessary to declare in confession that one has acted against the charity due to self, if there is question only of sins in which transgression of that charity was not directly intended; for to say that one has sinned against God by blasphemy, or against self by intemperance, or against the neighbor by injustice, is equivalent to saying that one has hurt one's own soul by sin. (b) It is necessary to declare a want of charity to self, if one has expressly intended such a sin. Thus, if a person who has been admonished to have care for his own soul is so enraged thereat that he vows to deliver his soul over to evil, and thereupon proceeds to commit various kinds of sin, he does not declare his true state of conscience by merely mentioning these latter sins. A case of this kind, however, is not usual (see 1307).

1579. **The Commandment of Love of Neighbor.**—Charity to fellow-creatures, especially to members of the chosen nation, was commanded in the Old Law. (a) Thus, internal love was made obligatory. The Lord forbade hatred, revenge, remembrance of injuries (Lev., xix. 17), and commanded love of fellow-citizens (ibid.) and kindness to foreigners dwelling in the land (Lev., xix. 33). (b) External love was also obligatory. Alms and help were to be given the needy (Deut., xxii. 1, 2, xv. 11), loans were to be made without interest (Deut., xxiii. 19), kindness was to be shown to widows, orphans, the blind, the crippled (Exod., xxii. 22, 23; Lev., xix. 14), part of each harvest was to be left for the poor, and in the third, seventh and fiftieth years special assistance was to be rendered the needy (Lev., xix. 9, xxv. 2-12; Deut., xiv. 28, 29).

1580. In the New Testament, which is the law of love, the precept of charity to neighbors is given with greater clearness and perfection. (a) Thus, internal love must be universal and modelled on the love which Christ had for humanity. Enemies are to be loved as well as friends, the bad as well as the good (Matt., v. 43-45), Gentiles as well as Jews, since there is one Lord of all (Rom., x. 12). The new commandment, whose observance will mark the faithful follower, is an imitation of the charity of Christ (John, xiii. 34, 35). (b) External charity must be practised, even at the cost of self-sacrifice (I John, iii. 16), for it will be regarded by Christ as done to Himself (Matt., xxv. 40), and will be the subject of interrogation and eulogy at the judgment (Matt., xxv. 34-46).

1581. In giving the commandment of love towards fellow-creatures, our Lord indicated both the reason for the love and the mode in which the love should be exercised: "Thou shalt love thy neighbor as thyself" (Matt, xxii. 39).

(a) The reason for this love is that a fellow-creature is our neighbor, or, as it is elsewhere expressed, our brother (I John, iv. 20, 21), our friend (Lev., xix. 18). He, like ourselves, is made to the image of God and is destined for the same beatitude.

(b) The mode of this love is that it should be similar, though not equal, to the love one has for oneself. Hence, the end of loving our neighbor should be God, that it may be a holy love; the rule to be followed in loving him should be that we agree with his wishes in good, but not in evil, that the love may be just; the manner of loving him should be that one wishes him well, not that one only seeks pleasure or advantage from him, and so the love will be sincere. For, as love of self must be holy, just and sincere, the same qualities are required in love of the neighbor.

1582. The following conditions must, therefore, be met in the love of neighbor which charity commands:

(a) Love must not be of a covetous or selfish or superficial kind, but must be sincerely benevolent and beneficent (see 1109). Those who wish to retain the companionship or association of a neighbor because this redounds to their own gain, on account of his wealth, influence, etc., while harming the neighbor, love themselves rather than the neighbor. Nor is love of neighbor genuine if it exists only in the emotions, or if it is manifested only in expressions of good will; for true love includes benevolence and will be translated into beneficence when the occasion presents itself (James, ii. 14 sqq.; I John, i. 22). Persons who are most ready to shed tears at the distress of others, or who are most profuse in compliments or good wishes, are frequently most unwilling to assist others, especially if some sacrifice is necessary.

(b) The love of the neighbor must not be a sinful benevolence or beneficence, but must desire for him and confer on him what are real, and not merely apparent goods, such as we ought to desire for ourselves (Matt., vii. 12). Those who secure for others lower and unnecessary goods at the sacrifice of those that are higher and necessary, putting wealth, pleasure, or position above virtue and a good conscience, have not the love of charity, for "what does it profit a man to gain the whole world, and lose his soul?" (Matt., viii. 36).

(c) The love of the neighbor must not be purely natural, but must wish for him and confer on him real goods out of a supernatural motive. This motive is the friendship one has for God, so that the neighbor is loved because God loves him and desires to communicate to him a share in the divine life through grace and glory. The motive of charity is absent, therefore, when one loves only one's friends, when one is kind to others out of pity, or generosity, or admiration for their good qualities, if there is no thought of God in this philanthropy or humanitarianism.

1583. The commandment of love of neighbor is sufficiently complied with as to its acts by all those who are leading a good Christian life. (a) Thus, the internal acts of sincere affection, peace, joy, and mercy are exercised by prayer for the living and the dead, or a devout recitation of the Lord's Prayer. (b) The external acts of spiritual and corporal mercy are performed by those who are giving according to their means and the necessities they meet.

1584. The commandment of love of neighbor is sufficiently complied with as to its motive, even though the supernatural motive is not actually present before the mind, or other and natural motives are also present. (a) Thus, the supernatural motive directs our love of neighbor, if it is present virtually, as will be explained in 1590. (b) Natural motives of love that are good in themselves (such as ties of relationship or nationality, common intellectual or other interests, the virtue or ability of a neighbor) do not detract from the supernaturality of love, provided their influence is subordinated to the divine friendship and the desire of beatitude for the neighbor. Even a certain amount of natural repugnance is not inconsistent with charity; on the contrary, charity is seen to be great, if for love of God one does good to implacable enemies, or waits on persons suffering from a loathsome disease.

1585. Fulfillment of the Commandments of Charity.—We speak now only of the commandment of love, in which the other commandments of charity are contained (see 1550 b). The love which is commanded must have the following qualities: (a) on the side of the subject who loves, it must be internal and made at the proper times—that is, one must love from the heart and affection, as well as in works and manifestations, and must make and renew the act of love as the law requires; (b) on the side of the object loved, it must be both universal and well-ordered; one must not only love all to whom charity is due (see 1133 sqq.), but one must also bestow love according to the rank of precedence in which charity is due (see 1158 sqq.).

1586. The act of charity can be made in various ways.

(a) It is made in itself, when one elicits or expresses love; it is made in its manifestations, when one performs an act of virtue distinct from charity. One who sincerely loves God with his whole heart will keep the commandments (John, xiv. 21), and hence acts of temperance, justice, fortitude, etc., may be called acts of love, in the sense that they are indications of love.

(b) The act of charity may be made internally or externally. Thus, affection for another as a friend in God, and a sincere desire of his good, are internal acts of love; while spiritual or temporal alms bestowed upon him, such as instruction or aid in time of sickness, are external acts of love.

(c) The act of charity may be made explicitly or implicitly. Charity is called explicit with reference to a person or object which is loved in itself, and not as included in another; it is called implicit with reference to a person or object loved as included in another, as when means and end involve each other, or a part is contained in the whole. Thus, he who loves God above all things loves God explicitly and his neighbor implicitly; he who loves his neighbor as a future co-sharer in bliss loves his neighbor explicitly and God implicitly (see 1549); he who includes all mankind in a common act of love, gives explicit love to the race collectively, and implicit love to individual members of the race not mentioned (e.g., enemies or strangers).

1587. For the fulfillment of the commandment of charity other acts of virtue are not enough. There must also be love. (a) Thus, as to charity towards God, our Lord declares that love of God is the great commandment on which the others depend, and St. Paul makes salvation depend on love: "If any man love not our Lord Jesus Christ, let him be anathema" (I Cor., xvi. 22). (b) As to charity towards the neighbor, the fulfillment of other commandments in his regard is inferior to the fulfillment of the commandment of fraternal love, and thus the commandments of justice to others are distinct from the commandment of love. Innocent XI condemned the proposition that we are not obliged to love our neighbor by a formal act of love (Denzinger, *Enchiridion*, n. 1160).

1588. For the fulfillment of the law of charity, external acts of love are not enough; there must also be internal love or affection.

(a) With regard to charity towards God, there can be no question of external charity through acts of beneficence, as is clear; but one is obliged to signify one's love of God, if silence would cause scandal or convey an expression of hatred of God. Mere lip-service, however, will not do, for God must be loved and served from the heart (Matt., xxii. 37; Eph., vi, 6; II Thess. iii., 5; etc.).

(b) With regard to charity towards the neighbor, external charity is commanded (see 1210 sqq. and 1551). But there must also be internal charity, for we are bidden to love our neighbor as we love ourselves (Matt, xxii. 39), as Christ loved us (John, xv. 12), from the heart (I Pet., i. 22). If a man distributed his goods to feed the poor, not out of love, but out of vanity or other sinful motives, his act would not be an exercise of charity. Innocent XI condemned the proposition that we may satisfy through external acts alone the precept of loving our neighbor (Denzinger, n. 1161).

1589. Must the internal act of love be explicit? (a) Love of God should be explicit, for the commandment of charity is that God be loved as the Last End, and the other commandments are to be observed as means to that End (see 1120, 1547). The Last End is that which is loved for its own sake, and hence distinctly, while the means are loved for the sake of the Last End. (b) Love of the neighbor is required to be explicit as regards all neighbors in general, when this is necessary for the preservation of charity towards God, or the fulfillment of obligations of charity towards man; it should be explicit as regards an individual, when this is necessary for the proper discharge of external works or other duties of charity, as when one will not be able to overcome a temptation to hatred unless one makes an act of charity which expressly includes the person one is tempted to hate. But one who loves his neighbor implicitly through an act of supernatural love of God, and neglects no external duty of charity towards others, is considered to have sufficiently complied with the law in ordinary circumstances.

1590. The Intention of Performing All Good Works out of Love for God.—(a) This intention is actual, when one expressly wills God as the Last End of one's actions. The commandment of loving God above all things does not require an actual reference of each good work to His love (see 1120, 85, 86).

(b) This intention is virtual but explicit, when previously a person had the actual intention and never retracted it, and now acts under the influence of that explicit and unretracted intention, though he does not advert to the Last End as he now acts. Thus, if an act of love of God above all things is made supernaturally by a Christian or naturally by a non-Christian, and later on by reason of the acts of love these persons give alms to the poor and do not think of God as they give the alms, their works are not actually, but virtually and explicitly done for His love. The commandment of love of God, as we shall see (1593 sqq.), obliges one at certain times to elicit an act of love of God as the Last End, loved above all things else (in unbelievers it must be an act of natural benevolence, and in believers an act of supernatural charity); and, since such an act includes a consecration of one's works to God, the commandment requires likewise at certain times a virtual and explicit reference of good works to the love of God.

(c) The intention is virtual and implicit, when there is no previous act of love of God influencing a present act, but this act itself is good, tending from its character and object to the Last End, and it is precisely its character and object that cause it to be chosen by the agent. Thus, if an infidel, who has made no offering of his works to God, gives an alms out of love of mercy, or honors his parents out of love of piety, or pays his debts out of love of justice, he has explicit love for virtue and implicit love for the Author and End of virtue. The commandment of love of God, being affirmative, does not oblige one at all times to elicit acts of love of God as the Supreme Good, and hence, apart from the occasions when that affirmative commandment calls for exercise, a virtual and implicit intention of acting for the sake of God suffices to excuse from sin.

1591. Applications of the Preceding Paragraph.—(a) A Christian who makes acts of love of God at the necessary times fulfills the commandment of loving God with his whole heart and the precepts of doing all things for the glory of God (I Cor., x. 31), and in charity (I Cor., xvi. 14), and in the name of Christ (Col., iii. 17).

(b) An infidel invincibly ignorant of the supernatural law, who makes acts of natural benevolence with reference to God when he should, does not sin against the precept of charity, and observes the law of natural love.

(c) A person who in no way refers a deliberate act to love of God, natural or supernatural, sins in that act. His sin is venial, if the evil intended is small (e.g., an alms given purely out of vainglory); it is mortal, if the evil is grave (e.g., an alms given for the purpose of seduction into serious sin).

1592. It should not be inferred from what has been said on the qualities which charity must have, or the influence it must exercise, that the duty of love of God is only for the perfect, or that it is with difficulty accomplished. (a) On the contrary, charity is a universal obligation, for it is the first commandment (Matt., xxii. 38), and he who does not love is accursed (I Cor., xvi. 22). (b) Neither is the commandment hard (I

John, v. 3), for nature itself inclines one to love the Supreme Good, and grace helps one to remove the impediments to a love of friendship that will cling to God above all. The observance of the commandments indicates that one is guided habitually by love, while a devout recitation of the Lord's Prayer is an actual expression of that love; and hence conscientious persons should not worry lest they may have been wanting in God's love.

1593. With reference to the times when the precepts of charity oblige, we should distinguish three kinds of precepts: (a) the negative precepts forbid sins against charity (such as hatred, envy, scandal, etc.), and they oblige at all times; (b) the positive precepts of external beneficence oblige when occasion requires, as was said above (see 1210 sqq.); (c) the positive precepts of internal love oblige at certain special times, as will now be explained.

1594. The precept of love of God obliges directly—that is, by reason of the virtue of charity itself—at the following times: (a) at the beginning of the moral life, that is, of the use of reason; (b) during life; (c) at the close of life, or when one is about to die (Denzinger, nn. 1101, 1289).

1595. The Obligation of an Act of Love of God at the Beginning of the Moral Life.—(a) The beginning of the moral life here signifies the moment when a child arrives at a full use of reason, and is able to deliberate on things of grave importance, such as the duty of having a supreme purpose in life and of doing good and avoiding evil. This moment does not coincide necessarily with any fixed period of the child's age (e.g., the seventh year), but depends on the gradual development of the moral conscience and may be earlier or later according to intelligence, surroundings, education, etc, (see 932).

(b) The act of love of God here signifies the turning to God as one's Last End, but it may be made either formally or virtually, according to the knowledge had. A formal act of love of God is made, when one has explicit knowledge, either through faith or through natural reason, concerning God as the Supreme Good and Last End, and when one loves Him as such. A virtual act of love of God consists in a resolution to direct one's life according to reason, or in a love of the goodness of virtue; for in such an act there is implied a love of the Author and End of moral good. The faithful who cannot remember having made this first act of charity when they came to the use of reason, should not disturb themselves at this, for the commandment was fulfilled by any service they freely offered to God.

(c) The reason for requiring an act of love at the beginning of the moral life is, that in that moment one has the choice placed before one of good or evil, and that faith, hope and charity, being fundamental precepts, should precede the other virtues of the law.

1596. Ignorance as Excusing from the Act of Love of God.—(a) Ignorance of God as the Author of the supernatural order excuses from the precept of supernatural love or charity, if it is invincible ignorance. Thus, a pagan who knows nothing of revelation does not sin by omitting an act of charity towards God.

(b) Ignorance of God as the Author of the order of nature does not excuse from a natural act of benevolence towards God, if the person in ignorance, though an infidel, has sufficient use of reason, for ignorance of God is then inexcusable (Rom., i. 20).

1597. The Obligation of the Act of Love of God throughout Life.—(a) The existence of an obligation to make frequent acts of love of God during life is a consequence of the preponderant part played by charity among the virtues (see 1115 sqq.), for how is one to regulate one's life according to the virtues, if one does not frequently renew that virtue which is the inspiration and direction of all the others? The Old Testament requires that one have the commandment of love of God frequently in one's thoughts (Deut., vi. 5-7), and in the New Testament it is called the commandment on which all the others depend (Matt., xxii. 37-40). The Church has condemned propositions that made infrequent performance of the act of love—such as once in a lifetime, once in five years—sufficient (Denzinger, nn. 1155-1157).

(b) The details of this obligation—that is, the frequency with which and the times at which the act of love of God must be made under pain of grave sin—is a matter of dispute among authorities. Some think once in three years sufficient; others, guided perhaps by the analogy of the precept of yearly Communion, regard once a year as sufficient; others, with St. Alphonsus, hold for once a month, basing their opinion on the difficulty of overcoming temptations if acts of love of God are omitted for more than a month; others, with Scotus, think the act of love of God should be made once a week, for, since the Sundays are set aside for the worship of God, the Church seems to have thereby determined with regard to the act of divine charity that which the law of God had left undetermined; finally, some teach that an act of love of God must be made daily, arguing that Christ commanded the Lord's Prayer to be said daily, and that its first petitions contain formal acts of love of God.

1598. None of the opposed opinions just given can be considered as demonstrated and theoretically certain. But in actual life this offers no difficulty, and the following are accepted as practical rules that may be acted on:

(a) Those who live habitually in the state of grace may be regarded as having fulfilled sufficiently the commandment of love of God, for "if any man love Me, he will keep My word" (John, xiv. 23).

(b) Those who live habitually in an occasion of sin or in sin itself, no doubt neglect the commandment of love of God; but it is not necessary that they accuse themselves of the omission to their confessor, since it is understood in the mention of the occasion of sin or bad habit. The confessor, however, ought to admonish careless penitents about the obligation of love of God, of recitation of the Our Father, etc. Mortal sin revokes the direction of one's works towards God, and, though one is not obliged to renew that direction immediately after repentance, a delay beyond four or five months according to some authors would be notable.

1599. Obligation of the Act of Love of God at the Close of Life.—The duty of making an act of love of God when one is at the point of death is admitted by all for the following cases: (a) the dying person is directly obliged to make an act of love of God when this is the only way in which he can secure justification, as when he is not in the state of grace and cannot receive the Sacraments; (b) the dying person is indirectly obliged to make an act of love of God when otherwise he cannot securely struggle against temptations to despair, doubt, etc.

1600. The duty of making an act of love of God at the time when death is near is considered as doubtful by some authorities when the following points are morally certain: (a) when the dying person has already sufficiently complied with the duty of making an act of love (e.g., when he made such an act just before he fell into danger of death), or is now in the state of grace (e.g., when he has received absolution with attrition just before or after the danger); and also (b) when the dying person will not expose himself on account of omission of the act of charity to the violation of any serious commandment.

1601. In practice, the priest who is attending the dying person should act as follows:

(a) He should remind the dying person of the obligation, if it appears certain, and should suggest to him the motives and assist him in pronouncing the form. In many manuals of the Ritual exhortations and aspirations suitable for this purpose are given.

(b) The priest should recommend the act of love of God, even though the obligation does not appear certain, if no harm will result from his doing so. For this will better prepare the dying person for entrance into eternity.

(c) He should not speak of the act of love of God, if the obligation is uncertain and harm would result from his doing so (e.g., if the dying person is in good faith, and would be much disturbed if told about the act of love to be made).

1602. Thus far we have spoken of the obligation which the precept of love of God imposes directly, or by reason of charity itself. There is also an obligation that is indirect, or by reason of some virtue or commandment distinct from charity.

(a) Thus, by reason of a virtue distinct from charity, one is bound to make an act of love of God, if this act is the only means of avoiding sin against that virtue. Example: Titus suffers severe temptations to injustice, and finds that only the love of God keeps him from injustice. In temptation, therefore, he should make an act of love of God.

(b) By reason of a commandment distinct from that of charity, one is bound to make an act of love of God, if otherwise one cannot fulfill rightly the commandment in question. Thus, if a person has to receive or administer a Sacrament of the living, or solemnly to administer a Sacrament, when he is not in the state of grace and has not the opportunity of receiving absolution, he is obliged to make an act of perfect contrition, which includes an act of love of God.

1603. An implicit love of neighbor is contained in every true act of love of God (see 1549, 1586). But in some cases love of neighbor must be explicit (see 1589).

(a) Thus, one is bound to explicit love directly (or by reason of charity itself), when the law of charity requires this. *Per accidens*, charity requires an internal act of love, when without this act some good commanded by charity (e.g., reconciliation with an enemy, alms to one in distress) will not be done, or some evil forbidden by charity (e.g., hatred, revenge) will not be overcome. *Per se*, it does not seem that charity requires explicit acts of love towards the neighbor, but only those implicit acts contained in the love of God; in practice, however, conscientious persons frequently make explicit acts of fraternal charity, as when they pray for the living and the dead, or say the Our Father with due attention and devotion.

(b) One is bound to explicit love indirectly (or by reason of some other virtue than charity), when apart from such explicit love that other virtue cannot be exercised as commanded. Example: Balbus is often tempted to defraud Caius, and does not resist the temptation successfully, unless he puts himself into a charitable disposition towards Caius.

1604. The Necessity of Charity.—(a) The habit of charity is necessary as a means (see 360, 785) for all persons, infants included, so that without it no one can be saved. For it is only with this virtue that one possesses the divine indwelling (I John, iv. 16), and is made a friend of God. Those who have not the wedding garment of charity are cast into the outer darkness (Matt., xxii. 13).

(b) The act of charity is also necessary as a means of salvation to all adults, for it is only by actual charity that they turn towards their Last End, and without actual charity they are in death (I John, iii. 14). A person who is justified through attrition joined with a Sacrament receives grace and the habit of charity, and by his voluntary acceptance he consents to the divine friendship and thus makes an act of charity.

(c) The act of charity is obligatory under grave precept at the beginning of the moral life, frequently during life, and at the hour of death (see 1594 sqq.).

1605. Is it possible that a sin against the love of God be only venial? (a) The imperfection of the act makes such a sin only venial, as when without full deliberation one wishes to omit an obligatory act of love. (b) The slightness of the matter makes such a sin venial, when it is aside from, but not contrary to, the love of God, as when one makes an act of love of God with culpable lukewarmness. Venial sin is not, strictly speaking, opposed to the commandment of love, since it does not destroy love.

1606. As the order of charity is commanded as a part of the law of charity, one is obliged not only to love those to whom love is commanded, but also to give greater love to those to whom greater love is due.

(a) God must be loved above all creatures, since He is to be loved with the whole heart (Deut., vi. 5; Matt., x. 37).

(b) Self must be loved more than the neighbor, for love of neighbor is commanded only as like to that of self (Matt., xxii. 9).

(c) One should love one's neighbor more than one's own body, since we ought to lay down our lives for the brethren (I John, iii. 16). The claims of self and of the neighbor to love are in the following order: the spiritual goods of self, the spiritual goods of the neighbor, the bodily goods of self, the bodily goods of the neighbor, the external goods of self, the external goods of the neighbor.

(d) Among neighbors, those who are better or more nearly related to self should be given the preference in love; for we should do good to all, but especially to those who are of the household of the faith (Gal, vi. 10), and those persons are specially blamed who have no care for their own and for those of their own house (I Tim., v. 8). The claims of neighbors on our help (as was explained in 1176 sqq.) rank in the following order: wife, children, parents, brothers and sisters, other relatives, friends, domestics, citizens of the same town, state, and country, and, finally, all others.

1607. The order of charity is commanded, because it is a mode intrinsic to the performance of the act of charity (see 1554); it is a circumstance without which the act of love is not in proportion to the person to whom it is shown. Thus, love given to God is not in proportion to His lovableness, if it is exceeded by the love given to a creature; love given to the members of one's family is not in proportion to their claims, if it is less than the love given to strangers.

(a) Hence, outside cases of a neighbor's need, the law of charity requires that one give him the amount of internal love that corresponds with the external charity due to him. Thus, love for a father should be in proportion to the external honor one is bound to show one's parent; love for a brother in proportion to the external marks of friendship that are due a brother. He who has no filial love for his parents, or fraternal love for his brethren, does not fulfill the law of charity.

(b) In cases of a neighbor's need, the law of charity requires that the internal love be in proportion to the external charitable assistance one should give. Thus, if a parent and a stranger are in equal necessity, more help and more love are due the parent; but if a stranger is in need, and a parent is not in need, more help and more corresponding love, as to that particular case, are due the stranger.

1608. It should be noted, however, that there is a twofold love of the neighbor.

(a) Obligatory love is that which is commanded, and which is due another as a debt, such as love for God, for a parent, for all neighbors in general, etc. The amount of love for fellow-creatures that is obligatory is, of course, not infinite, for no creature is infinitely lovable; neither is it mathematically fixed, for, as said above, it may be greater or less according to circumstances; but it is comparative or relative—that is, it should agree with the higher or lower claim to external charity that a neighbor has on one.

(b) Optional love, or love of supererogation, is that which is not commanded, but which may be given lawfully, such as special friendship outside a case of need for an enemy or stranger. As there is no precept regarding this kind of love, neither is there any precept regarding the order of love as between those to whom it is given, and one may invert the order that is obligatory as regards commanded love. Thus, if a brother and a cousin are both well-to-do, and one has property to bequeath to which neither of them has any right, it is not against charity to leave more to the cousin and less to the brother, or some to the cousin and none to the brother. This supposes, however, that in the matter of obligatory love the preference in order of charity has been shown the brother (as explained in 1158-1182).

Art. 11: THE GIFT OF WISDOM

(*Summa Theologica*, II-II, qq. 45, 46.)

1609. Wisdom is the Gift of the Holy Ghost which corresponds with and serves the virtue of charity (see 159 sqq., 808 sqq., 1041 sqq.), and hence it is discussed in this place.

The following points concerning Wisdom will be treated: (a) the Nature of the Gift of Wisdom; (b) the Persons who Possess the Gift of Wisdom; (c) the Beatitude of the Peacemakers, which pertains especially to Wisdom; (d) the Sin of Foolishness, which is opposed to Wisdom.

So far is it from being improper to give some space in Moral Theology to the Gifts of the Holy Ghost (as if they pertained only to higher mysticism), that it is even necessary to emphasize them. The Gifts are essential to salvation, and play a most important part in the daily spiritual life, whether in correcting or reinforcing the virtues, or in giving immediate direction from the Holy Spirit. Man, it is true, does not set them into action, but it is man's part to value them, to hold himself in readiness for them, and to hearken to their whispered enlightenment and counsel. The Gifts of the Holy Ghost are the very soul of Theology and of the Christian life.

1610. The Nature of the Gift of Wisdom.—Wisdom is defined as "a habit for judging things in the light of their First Cause, the Supreme Good, which is infused into the soul along with sanctifying grace."

(a) Wisdom is a habit, and so it differs from passing acts. Thus, a man in the state of sin who avoids idolatry, judges in the light of the highest cause that worship is not to be given to creatures; but he lacks the indwelling of the Holy Ghost, and therefore does not judge in virtue of that special instinct or power which originates from the abiding presence of the Holy Ghost.

(b) Wisdom judges, and this sets it apart from habits that belong to the will (e.g., the Gifts of Piety, Fortitude, and Fear), as well as from habits whose chief act is assent (e.g., the virtue of Faith) or penetration (e.g., the Gift of Understanding).

(c) The standard by which Wisdom judges things is the First Cause of all, or the Supreme Good, as when our Lord explained that the condition of the man born blind was due to the purpose of God to be glorified through that blindness (John, ix. 3). The wise man is he who goes back to first principles, to the origins of things, to ultimate purposes; but it is not every wisdom that estimates things according to the Supreme Good, and there is a false wisdom (see 1623) whose canon of excellence is the imperfect good opposed to Supreme Good. The Gift of Wisdom, therefore, is distinct from sinful wisdom, which is wise at doing evil (Jer., iv. 22); from particular wisdom, which understands well the theory and practice of some science, art, or profession, and is able therefore to decide correctly and to arrange successfully such matters as fall under a special kind of activity, as in medicine or architecture or strategy (I Cor., iii. 10).

(d) The things that make up the object of Wisdom are, in the first place, divine things (e.g., the attributes, plans, government, operations of God); and, in the second place, created things, whether in the speculative order (e.g., mind and matter, good and evil, science, religion, history), or in the practical order (i.e., human actions). Wisdom contemplates the divine as known from faith or the beatific vision, and then, with the things of God as its rule, it judges the things of earth and directs the conduct of men: "The spiritual man judgeth all things" (I Cor, ii, 15). Thus does Wisdom differ from the Gifts of Knowledge and of Counsel; for Knowledge is concerned directly with secondary causes and rises from the creature to the Creator, While Counsel is not a speculative but a practical Gift, and is a response to direction given by the Holy Spirit for the guidance of conduct.

(e) The Gift of Wisdom is an infused perfection of the intellect, "a wisdom descending from on high" (James, iii. 15). Hence, while it resembles the virtue of Wisdom, which also judges human and divine things through first causes (see 145), it differs from that virtue, even with reference to the same objects, on account of its different way of approach. Theology and philosophy judge correctly because they employ study and the investigation of reason; but the Gift of Wisdom has a right judgment because it depends, not on analysis or argumentation, but on a supernatural knowledge had through faith (or vision in case of the blessed) and a supernatural experience of God through charity. Wisdom may express itself, indeed, in the concepts and language of philosophy or theology, but it is not through scientific processes that it knows and judges.

(f) The Gift of Wisdom is infused into the soul along with sanctifying grace; for, like the other Gifts of the Holy Ghost, it is intended to supplement through the action of the Holy Spirit the control exercised by grace, which is imperfect on account of the limitations of the virtues. The Gift of Wisdom, therefore, is an ordinary and normal fact in the spiritual life, and must not be confused with rare and extraordinary phenomena—with the "word of wisdom" (I Cor., xii. 8), which was granted to the Apostles and at times to other preachers of the faith, nor with the clear contemplation of God bestowed in the state of innocence, nor with the infused knowledge or light of glory enjoyed by Christ and some of the Saints while on earth. Thus, while all who are in the state of grace possess the Gift of Wisdom, comparatively only a few have received the "word of wisdom"—that is, the ability to instruct others in the higher mysteries of faith and to explain to them with ease and in suitable language the meaning of these mysteries and their relation to supreme causes. Both these graces are supernatural, but, while the Gift of Wisdom is needed by each individual for his own sanctification, the word of wisdom is needed only in certain cases for the sanctification of others.

1611. From the foregoing definition it is seen that Wisdom belongs both to the will and to the intellect.

(a) In its cause, Wisdom belongs to the will. The cause of right judgment by means of divine things is either the suitability of the intellect, which knows well how to judge, or the suitability of the will, which is inclined towards divine things. Thus, he who is well versed in moral science will give a correct decision about a case of chastity as it falls under the inquiry of reason, and he who is chaste will judge correctly about the same case, even without moral science, but from the sympathy he has for the virtue. The intellectual virtue of Wisdom, then, judges aright because the intellect is sound in its procedures; but the Gift of Wisdom is right in its judgments, because the will has been united to God through charity, so that there has resulted in one a suitability for judging about the things of God: "Give me one who loves, and he will understand what I say" (Augustine,*Tract. xxvi. in Joan.*).

(b) In its essence, Wisdom belongs to the intellect, for it consists in judgment, and this is an act that is exercised, not by the affections, but by the reason. Through love the soul becomes one spirit with God (I Cor., vi. 17), and the will experiences the sweetness of this union (Ps. xxxiii. 9); the intellect then judges concerning the divine which has been the object of its mystical communion. The Gift of Wisdom, built as it is on faith and charity, differs utterly from private interpretation of revelation (which is subversive of faith) and from the Modernistic experience of the divine (which is explained as a natural intuition had by a special religious sense of a reality that is divine and yet only subjective and unknowable).

1612. From the definition and explanation of the Gift of Wisdom it also follows that this Gift is practical as well as speculative.

(a) Primarily, Wisdom is speculative, for one must consider divine things in themselves before one applies them to other things; and, moreover, the object of Wisdom is God, who is the first truth in the order of knowledge or speculation. It is by Wisdom, then, as well as by the other intellectual Gifts or extraordinary graces, that the act of supernatural contemplation is exercised; but Wisdom, more perfect than the other Gifts, ascends at once to things that are heavenly, divine and eternal, and thinks of God as transcending in perfection every known or knowable degree of created excellence, and as being most true, most beautiful, most lovable (Eph., iii. 17-19).

(b) Secondarily, Wisdom is practical, for God whom it contemplates is the supreme rule of action, as well as the first truth. Thus does the higher Gift of Wisdom unite in itself what are found separate in lower virtues—the speculative quality of the virtue of Wisdom and the practical quality of Prudence (see 1620).

1613. The practical uses of the Gift of Wisdom are indicated in Coloss., iii. 16-17, iv. 6: "Let the word of Christ dwell in you abundantly, in all Wisdom, teaching and admonishing one another in psalms, hymns and spiritual canticles, singing in grace in your hearts to God. All whatsoever you do in word or in work, do all in the name of the Lord Jesus Christ. . . . Walk with Wisdom towards them that are without, redeeming the time. Let your speech be always with grace, seasoned with salt."

(a) The contemplation of divine things is useful for instruction in the truths of faith and the duties of religion ("teaching and admonishing one another"); for the mind becomes in a way divine, like the things on which it dwells, filled with knowledge of God and of Christ and of the means of holiness.

(b) Wisdom helps one to fulfill the duty of praying to God with reverence and interior devotion ("singing in your hearts to God"); for Wisdom makes one perceive and feel the sweetness and attraction of the things of God.

(c) It directs one in both words and works ("do all in the name of Christ"); for the intellect which judges things in the light of eternity and with the fervor of divine charity will not mislead in matters of salvation.

(d) It enables one to profit by opportunities of edification ("redeeming the time"); for the example of a life directed by tender love of God and by kindness and courtesy to all is a recommendation of virtue and religion in the sight of the world.

1614. Wisdom is a Gift of the Holy Ghost, and is numbered with the other six communications of the Spirit: "And the Spirit of the Lord shall rest upon him, the Spirit of Wisdom, etc." (Is., xi. 2).

(a) Likeness to the Other Gifts.—The Gifts of the Holy Ghost are energies diffused in the powers of the soul as instruments of the supernatural governance of the indwelling Spirit, just as the moral virtues are the instruments of the natural governance of reason. The infused virtues (e.g., faith or charity), unlike the acquired virtues (e.g., temperance or fortitude), do not suffice for the government of the soul; for, while these latter are according to nature, the former surpass nature, and are received by it imperfectly. Hence the need of the Gifts, which on earth supplement the infused virtues, strengthening them against contrary vices, developing secondary acts of the virtues which the virtues only initiate, and in heaven perfecting the blessed in good.

(b) Unlikeness to the Other Gifts.—Wisdom, which is enumerated by Isaias in the first place, is also given the highest rank among the Gifts by theologians, on account of its greater elevation, more universal scope, and the directive power it exercises. Fittingly, then, is Wisdom assigned as the Gift that serves Charity, the queen of the virtues: Charity loves God above all things; Wisdom dwells with delight upon the object of this love (Wis., viii. 16), looks upon life with the eyes of love, and in directing its human actions communicates to them something of the savor and sweetness of divine charity.

1615. The Persons Who Possess Wisdom.—The Gift of Wisdom, as said above (see 1610), is given with sanctifying grace, and hence only those and all those who are in God's friendship have this supernatural endowment.

(a) Only those in the state of grace have divine Wisdom, for without love of God it is impossible to have that right judgment of things that is consequent on the relish for and connaturality with divine things. Hence, it is said: "Wisdom will not enter into a malicious soul, nor dwell in a body subject to sins" (Wis., i. 4).

(b) All those who are in the state of grace have the Gift of Wisdom, for man is so weak and the supernatural virtues are so far above him that, even when he has received these virtues, he is unable to make proper use of them or to preserve them in time of temptation, unless he has received the supplementary forces that will enable him to obey more easily and promptly the voice and impulse of the Holy Ghost. Thus,

Charity destines man to beatitude, but, unless he has Wisdom to value this virtue and privilege, to spurn the false wisdom of the world, to think on the love of God with delight and to make it the norm of his judgments and decisions, he will not progress in Charity, nor retain it, nor arrive at the beatitude to which it destines him.

1616. Though all who are in the state of grace possess all the Gifts of the Holy Ghost, these Gifts are not had in the same way by all their possessors. Thus, the following points should be noted with reference to the Gift of Wisdom:

(a) The Gifts, like the infused virtues, are possessed habitually by baptized children and insane persons, and actually by adults. Just as infants have the possession but not the use of certain natural gifts (such as reason and responsibility), so likewise supernatural life and powers are granted them through baptismal regeneration, but the exercise of this life and of these powers is prevented by their inability to realize what they possess and to make use of it. The lack of bodily development, which impedes the use of natural reason, also impedes the use of supernatural Wisdom.

(b) The Gift of Wisdom is had in itself by all who are in the state of grace; but in its extension, which is the "word of Wisdom," it is possessed only by highly gifted souls who have a special mission from God (see above, 1610 sqq.). With sanctifying grace, each one receives the supernatural Gift of judging rightly about heavenly things and of regulating his conduct by them in so far as is necessary for the attainment of salvation; otherwise, we should have to say that grace is inferior to nature, and does not provide what is necessary for its end. But the ability to explain heavenly things so as to draw others to the truth, and to apply heavenly doctrines to the guidance of others so as to lead them to good, is one of the gifts freely given, which the Spirit divides according as He wills (I Cor., xii. 11): "To one by the Spirit is given the word of Wisdom, to another the word of Knowledge, etc." (ibid, 8).

1617. The Gift of Wisdom in itself (i.e., as intended directly for the benefit of the recipient and not for the benefit of others) is also had in varying degrees. (a) Thus, different persons do not possess this Gift in equal measure; for to some is granted the contemplation of loftier mysteries not granted to others, and suprahuman Wisdom plays a greater part in the direction of some lives than in that of others. (b) The same persons do not possess Wisdom in an equal degree at all times. Thus, in Baptism all the Seven Gifts are received, but in Confirmation they are in some way perfected, either in themselves by a greater refinement or sensibility to the action of the Holy Spirit, or as regards their possession by their subject through a firmer hold of them.

1618. The Exercise of the Gift of Wisdom.—(a) The external magisterium (i.e., revelation and the teaching Church) conveys the truths of faith to the mind of the believer. (b) The internal Teacher, the Holy Ghost, illuminates the soul with Wisdom, so that it ponders on the first principles of faith and makes the love of them control its judgments, Words, and actions: "You have the unction from the Holy One and know all things" (I John, ii. 20), that is, all that is needed for salvation.

1619. The Beatitude and the Fruits that Correspond to Wisdom.—The Gifts of the Holy Ghost, by supplying for what is imperfect in the habits of virtue (e.g., by protecting faith against dullness of perception, hope against presumption, charity against distaste for divine things), give to these virtues a perfectionment like to that which they will have in the state of beatitude, and to their exercise a corresponding enjoyment. Hence, to the Gifts, which are most excellent habits, correspond those most perfect or most delightful acts of virtue known as Beatitudes and Fruits (see 159 sqq.).

(a) There appears a special correspondence of the seventh beatitude ("Blessed are the peacemakers, for they shall be called the sons of God," Matt., v. 9) with Wisdom, both as regards their merit, and as regards their reward. The work of Wisdom is to reduce all things to unity, to see life and the world as a whole, to look upon creatures as parts of one great divine plan. Similarly, the work of the peacemakers is to put an end to dissension and division and to reconcile the warring powers of the soul, or to introduce harmony between those that are at enmity: "The Wisdom that is from above is peaceable" (James, iii. 17). Again, the reward promised the peacemakers is that they shall be called the sons of God, and of Wisdom it may be said that it makes one the image of the Son of God, who is Eternal Wisdom.

(b) The Fruits of the Holy Ghost that are assigned to Wisdom are, with regard to God: charity, or a tender love of God ("The charity of God is poured out in our hearts," Rom., v. 5.), joy, or delight at union with God ("Rejoice in the Lord always," Phillip., iv. 4), peace, or security in the enjoyment of God ("There is much peace to them that love Thy law," Ps. cxviii. 165). The Fruits that have reference to the love of neighbor are: goodness, or an internal benevolence characterized by sweetness ("The fruit of the light is in all goodness," Eph., v. 9), and kindness, or a beneficence accompanied by cheerfulness ("The Lord loves the cheerful giver," II Cor., ix. 7).

1620. St. James (iii. 17, 18) describes the direction which Wisdom gives to human actions (see 1612, 1613) and the fruit of peace to which it conducts them, as follows: "The Wisdom that is from above, first indeed is chaste, then peaceable; modest, easy to be persuaded; consenting to the good, full of mercy and good fruits, without judging, without dissimulation. And the fruit of justice is sown in peace to them that make peace."

(a) Thus, first, Wisdom directs one to be free from sin ("chaste"), for the fear of the Lord is the beginning of Wisdom (Ps. cx. 110).

(b) Next, Wisdom directs one to work for peace within one's own soul, by following moderation where one can decide for oneself ("modest"), by seeking advice where one is in doubt ("easy to be persuaded").

(c) Further, Wisdom directs one to be peaceful towards others, to be well disposed towards their good or benefit ("consenting to the good"), compassionate and helpful in their distress ("full of mercy and good fruits"), not partial or hypocritical in criticizing their defects ("without judging, without dissimulation").

(d) Finally, Wisdom, having sown in peace, reaps the peace of righteousness. False wisdom leads to wrangling and disorder, true Wisdom to concord and harmony.

1621. The Sins Opposed to Wisdom.—Just as blindness and dullness—that is, the want of all or of sufficient perceptiveness in spiritual things—are opposed to the Gift of Understanding (see 912), so stupidity and foolishness—that is, the want of all or of sufficient good judgment about spiritual things—are opposed to the Gift of Wisdom.

1622. Foolishness is defined as "a slowness and darkness of mind that is due to some moral defect, and that makes it difficult for one to judge rightly about the Last End of things and the Chief Good."

(a) Foolishness is slow and darksome, and thus the contrary of Wisdom, which is alert and discerning.

(b) It is a defect of judgment, and so differs from the sins of blindness and dullness of heart.

(c) It is an error of judgment about the chief concern of life and the things of greatest value, and thus it is different from the innocent simplicity of many good persons, whose judgment is not sound in affairs of this world.

(d) It is brought on by moral fault, and is therefore not to be identified with invincible ignorance, which is a physical imperfection caused by nature, as in the weak-minded and the insane.

1623. Just as true Wisdom seems foolishness to the world, so does true foolishness seem wisdom to the world (I Cor., iii. 18 sqq.). There is a counterfeit wisdom, which places its last end in some created good, and which is therefore foolishness before God. St. James (iii. 15) describes false wisdom as "earthly, sensual, devilish"; and these words express very well three chief classes of worldly wisdom. (a) Some of the worldly-wise aim above all things at amassing and increasing wealth or other external possessions (earthly wisdom). (b) Others seek chiefly pleasure, health, comfort, or other bodily goods (animal wisdom). (c) Others imitating Lucifer, who is king over all the sons of pride (Job, xli. 25), devote their whole lives solely to the pursuit of inordinate excellence of some kind—that is, of selfish domination or honors or glory, etc. (devilish wisdom).

1624. The foolishness we are now considering is sinful, for it is a voluntary choice of evil, a violation of commandments, and the ruination of man. In scripture the term "fool" is applied to the wicked, the impious, the objects of divine anger (Ps. xiii. 1), and hence it was that our Lord declared severe penalty against those who call another a fool (Matt., v. 22).

(a) Foolishness is a voluntary choice of evil, for it consists in a turning away from spiritual things or an entire absorption in the things of this world, with the result that one becomes unfitted to judge aright concerning the values of human existence: "The animal man does not perceive the things of the Spirit of God" (I Cor., ii. 14). But the fact that his taste is perverted, and that he has no relish for the spiritual, is due to his own deliberate rejection of good and the cultivation of evil.

(b) Foolishness is a violation of commandments about the knowledge and employment of truth (see 914 sqq.): "See how you walk, not as unwise, but as wise" (Eph., v. 15, 16).

(c) Foolishness leads to perdition, for, being defective in its judgment, it barters away the future for present satisfaction and sells its birthright for a mess of pottage: "The prosperity of fools destroys them" (Prov., i. 32); "Thou fool, this night shall thy soul be required of thee" (Luke, xii. 20).

1625. The causes of the sin of foolishness, as was said above (see 1623), are the wrong and sinful views taken of life, which make men judge all things by the standards of gain or pleasure or power, rather than by the standard of the First Cause, in comparison with whom all these lower goods are but trivial. But, among all the vices that lead mankind astray from Wisdom, the preeminence is held by lust, for its attraction is greater and its hold on the soul more complete. As chastity especially disposes for heavenly contemplation and Wisdom (see 912) by the refinement and elevation and spirituality it gives the mind, so does sensuality especially indispose for these goods by the coarseness and degradation and materialism that follow in its wake.

Made in the USA
Columbia, SC
08 April 2024

34111050R00367